"E. J. W. GIBB MEMORIAL"
SERIES

NEW SERIES, IV. 4

THE MATHNAWÍ
OF
JALÁLU'DDÍN RÚMÍ

EDITED FROM THE OLDEST MANUSCRIPTS
AVAILABLE: WITH CRITICAL NOTES,
TRANSLATION, & COMMENTARY

BY

REYNOLD A. NICHOLSON
LITT.D., LL.D., F.B.A.

*Sir Thomas Adams's Professor of Arabic, Fellow of
Trinity College, and sometime Lecturer in Persian
in the University of Cambridge*

VOLUME IV
CONTAINING THE TRANSLATION
OF THE THIRD & FOURTH BOOKS

PUBLISHED AND DISTRIBUTED BY
THE TRUSTEES OF
THE "E. J. W. GIBB MEMORIAL"

ISBN 0 906094 09 7

*Printed and bound in Great Britain by Biddles Ltd,
www.biddles.co.uk*

INTRODUCTION

WHILE the First and Second Books of the *Mathnawí* were already accessible to European readers before the appearance of the present translation, the four remaining Books, comprising more than two-thirds of the poem, have hitherto been known very imperfectly. These contain about 17,500 verses, of which some 2000 were translated by Whinfield in his abridged version (Trübner's Oriental Series, 1880; 2nd edition, 1898); and so far as I am aware, this is the only contribution that has yet been made by a Western scholar towards the study of Books III–VI. Good as his renderings are from a general point of view, I cannot say that I owe much to them, since they are seldom precise enough to afford help in dealing with obscure and doubtful passages. Regarding the character and purpose of my translation I have nothing to add to what was said in the Introduction to the previous volume. Although, by itself, it may serve as a guide to the meaning of the text, its main function is to provide a sound basis for the commentary without which it cannot be fully understood. Growing familiarity with the author's thought and style has removed some difficulties and lightened others; but there are still many to be cleared up.

For reasons which are set forth in the Introduction to vol. III, I consider the Qóniya MS. (G), dated 677 A.H., to be the most authoritative text of the *Mathnawí*. The text of the present edition from Book III, *v.* 2836, to the end of Book IV is founded on that ancient and admirable MS., and in the Appendices to vol. III I have recorded those readings of G which differ from the text of my edition in the First and Second Books and in the first half of the Third Book. The present volume, therefore, contains an Appendix showing what changes the adoption of these readings would involve in the English version of the corresponding portions of the poem. As it will be some time before the Commentary on the First and Second Books can appear, a few suggestions for improving the translation of these Books are now brought together in a separate list.

REYNOLD A. NICHOLSON

CAMBRIDGE

April 1930

CORRECTIONS IN THE TRANSLATION OF THE FIRST AND SECOND BOOKS

BOOK I

v. 1477. *Read* cleaves the mountain by means of sea (water-channel) and mine.

v. 1605. *For* O bold seeker *read* O seeker of the (Divine) allowance (bounty). The correct reading is طالب جِری .

v. 2132. *Read* (yet) they are under the protection of the clear-sighted people. خلق should be written with the *iḍáfat*.

v. 2315, *Heading*. Read "*Don't talk in excess of (beyond) thy merit.*"

v. 3617. *Read in the second hemistich* The might and majesty and (power of inflicting) probation, which belong to the Unseen, are (then) gone.

BOOK II

v. 165. *See* Appendix.

v. 332. *Read* (Yet) how shouldst thou flee from Paradise to Hell...? قرار is a mistake for فرار .

v. 536. *Read* sharers in this ditty.

v. 537. *Read* (They continued) beating their feet (dancing) to this ditty till dawn.

TABLE OF CONTENTS

BOOK III

BOOK III

IN THE NAME OF GOD THE COMPASSIONATE, THE MERCIFUL.

The sciences of (Divine) Wisdom are God's armies, where-with He strengthens the spirits of the initiates, and purifies their knowledge from the defilement of ignorance, their justice from the defilement of iniquity, their generosity from the defilement of ostentation, and their forbearance from the defilement of foolishness; and brings near to them whatever was far from them in respect of the understanding of the state hereafter; and makes easy to them whatever was hard to them in respect of obedience (to Him) and zealous endeavour (to serve Him). And they (these sciences) are amongst the evidences and proofs of the prophets, giving information concerning the mysteries and sove-reignty of God, (the knowledge whereof is) bestowed on the gnostics exclusively, and how He causes the revolution of the Luminous Sphere appertaining to the *Raḥmán* and the Pearl, (the Sphere) which rules over the vaporous globular sphere, even as the intellect rules over the bodies (created) of dust and (over) their external and internal senses; for the revolution of that spiritual Sphere rules over the vaporous sphere and the gleaming meteors and the radiant lamps (of heaven) and the fostering winds and the outspread earths and the flowing waters. May God benefit His servants thereby (by these sciences) and increase their understanding! Now every reader understands according to the measure of his intelligence, and the devotee practises devotion according to the measure of his power to exert himself (therein), and the mufti decides questions of law according to the amount of judgement he possesses, and the alms-giver gives alms in pro-portion to his ability, and the donor is generous in proportion to his means, and the recipient of generosity obtains (only) so much of his bounty as he (the donor) approves. But (neverthe-less) he who searches for water in the desert will not be prevented from seeking it by his knowledge of what is (contained) in the seas, and he will be earnest in seeking the Water of this (spiritual) life ere he is cut off from it by preoccupation with the means of subsistence and hindered by illness and want, and ere (other) objects come between him and that (goal) to which he is hasten-ing, since none who prefers vain desire or is inclined to ease or turns back from his search or has fears for himself or feels anxiety about his means of livelihood will ever attain unto Knowledge, unless he take refuge with God and prefer his spiritual affairs to his temporal and take from the treasure of Wisdom the great riches, which neither lose their value nor are inherited like riches (of this world), and the majestic lights and noble jewels and precious estates (of Wisdom), giving thanks for

His bounty, glorifying His dispensation, magnifying His allotment; and unless he seek refuge with God from the vileness of (worldly) interests and from an ignorance (so blind) that he makes much of the little which he sees in himself and makes little of the much and great (which he finds) in others, and admires himself on account of that (self-conceit) for which God hath not given him permission. But it behoves one who hath knowledge and is seeking (God) that he should learn whatever he does not know, and teach (others) what he knows already, and deal gently with those of weak intelligence, and neither be made conceited by the stupidity of the stupid nor harshly rebuke him that is dull of understanding. *Such were ye aforetime, but God hath been gracious unto you.* Transcendent is God and exalted above the sayings of the blasphemers, and the belief of those who attribute partners (to Him), and the imputation of defect (to Him) by those deficient (in knowledge), and the comparison (of Him) by the comparers, and the evil conceptions of the thinkers, and the descriptions (of Him) by those who vainly imagine. And to Him be the praise and the glory for the composition of the Divine, Lordly Book of the *Mathnawí*, since He is the Helper to success and the Giver of bounty, and to Him belongs the (power of) conferring abundant benefits and favours, especially upon His servants, the gnostics, in despite of a party who desire to extinguish the Lights of God with their mouths—but God will bring His Light to completion, even if the unbelievers are loth. *Verily, We have sent down the Warning (the Qur'án) and verily We will guard it. And whoever shall alter it after he hath heard it, surely the guilt thereof is upon those who alter it: verily, God is Hearing and Knowing. And praise be to God, the Lord of all created beings!*

In the Name of God the Merciful, the Compassionate.

O Light of the Truth, Ḥusámu'ddín, bring (into verse and writing) this Third Book, for "three times" has become a *sunna*[1].
ˈOpen the treasury of mysteries; in respect of the Third Book leave excuses alone.

Thy power flows from the power of God, not from the veins which throb because of (bodily) heat.

This lamp, the sun, which is bright—it is not (made bright) by means of wick and cotton and oil.

The vault of heaven, which is so enduring, is not supported 5 by any tent-rope or pillar.

The power of Gabriel was not from the kitchen; it was from beholding the Creator of existence.

Likewise, know this power of the *Abdál*[2] of God to be (derived) from God, not from viands and from trays (of food).

Their bodies too have been moulded of the Light, so that they have transcended the Spirit and the Angel.

Inasmuch as thou art endowed with the qualities of the Almighty, pass beyond the fire of the maladies (of the sensual self), like Khalíl[3].

To thee also the fire will become *coolness and safety*, O thou to 10 whose complexion (constitution) the elements are slaves.

The elements are the substance of every complexion, but this complexion of thine is superior to every grade.

This complexion of thine is of the simple (uncompounded) world; it has now gathered up (amassed and absorbed) the attributes of Unity.

Oh, alas, the area of the people's understandings is exceeding narrow: the people have no throat[4].

O Light of the Truth[5], through the keenness of thy perception thy sweetmeat bestows a throat (even) on (one dull as) stone.

Mount Sinai in the (Divine) epiphany gained a throat, so that 15 it quaffed the wine; but it could not bear the wine.

Thereby the mountain was shattered and cloven asunder: have ye seen a mountain amble like a camel?

Bestowal of mouthfuls comes (to pass) from every clustered fruit-tree (well-to-do person), (but) bestowal of a throat is the work of God alone.

He bestows a throat on the body and on the spirit; He bestows a separate throat for every part of you.

---

[1] A practice sanctioned by the example of the Prophet.
[2] The perfect saints.
[3] "The Friend (of God)," *i.e.* Abraham.
[4] *I.e.* capacity for the apprehension of spiritual truths.
[5] Ḥusámu'ddín.

This He bestows at the time when you become Majestical and become void of vanity and deceit,

20   So that you will not tell the King's secret to any one nor pour out sugar before flies.

The secrets of the (Divine) Majesty are drunk in by the ear of that one who, like the lily, hath a hundred tongues and is dumb.

The grace of God bestows a throat on the earth, to the end that it may drink water and make a hundred herbs to grow.

Again, He bestows on the creature of earth (the animal) a throat and lip, in order that it may eat its (the earth's) herbage in desire.

When the animal has eaten its herbage, it becomes fat: the animal becomes a mouthful for Man and goes (disappears).

25   In turn it becomes earth and becomes a devourer of Man, when the spirit and the sight are separated from Man.

I beheld the atoms (of created existence) with their mouths all open: if I should tell of their food, it (the tale) would become long.

Provisions have (their) provision from His bounty; His universal grace is the nourisher of them that nourish.

He bestoweth gifts (of sustenance) on the gifts (which sustain life), for how should wheat spring forth without (receiving) any sustenance?

There is no end to the explanation of this matter. I have told a portion: you may know the (remaining) portions (by analogy).

30   Know that all the world is eating and eaten; know that those who have everlasting life (in God) are fortunate and accepted.

This world and its inhabitants are (in the end) dispersed; that (other) world and its travellers are continuing (for ever).

This world and its lovers are cut off; the people of that (other) world are eternalised and united.

The (truly) noble, then, is he that gives to himself the Water of Life that remains unto everlasting.

The noble one is (the very essence of) *the good works which endure*: he has been freed from a hundred banes and perils and fears.

35   If they (the noble) are thousands (externally), there is no more than one (in reality): 'tis not like the fancies of him that thinks of number.

(Both) the eater and the eaten have a throat and windpipe: (both) the victor and the vanquished have understanding and mental perception.

He (God) bestowed a throat on the rod of justice[1], (so that) it devoured all those many rods and ropes;

And in it was no increase from all that eating, because its eating and its form were not animal.

---

[1] The rod of Moses, which swallowed the rods of the sorcerers.

To Faith also He gave a throat like (that of) the rod, so that it devoured every vain fancy that was born.

Hence the spiritual and intelligible things, like the concrete 40 (sensible) things, have throats, and the giver of food to the throat of the spiritual and intelligible things is also (none but) God.

Therefore from the Moon to the Fish there is nothing in creation that hath not a throat in respect of its drawing sustenance (from God).

(When) the spirit's throat is emptied of thought for the body, then its apportioned sustenance becomes Majestical.

Know that the necessary condition (for gaining this sustenance) is the transformation of the (sensual) nature, for the death of evil men is (arises) from (their) evil nature.

When it has become natural to a human being to eat clay, he grows pale and ill-complexioned and sickly and miserable;

(But) when his ugly nature has been transformed, the ugliness 45 departs from his face, and he shines like a candle.

Where is a nurse for the suckling babe?—that with kindness she may sweeten the inner part of its mouth,

And, though she bar its way to her teat, may open up for it the way to a hundred gardens (of delight)?—

Because the teat has become to that feeble (infant) a barrier (separating it) from thousands of pleasures and dishes (of food) and loaves (of bread).

Our life, then, depends on weaning. Endeavour (to wean yourself) little by little. The discourse is (now) complete.

When man was an embryo his nourishment was blood: in like 50 fashion the true believer draws purity from filth.

Through (his) being weaned from blood, his nourishment became milk; and through (his) being weaned from milk, he became a taker of (solid) food.

And through (his) being weaned from food he becomes (a sage) like Luqmán; he becomes a seeker (hunter) of the hidden game.

If any one were to say to the embryo in the womb, "Outside is a world exceedingly well-ordered,

A pleasant earth, broad and long, wherein are a hundred delights and so many things to eat,

Mountains and seas and plains, fragrant orchards, gardens 55 and sown fields,

A sky very lofty and full of light, sun and moonbeams and a hundred stars.

From the south-wind and from the north-wind and from the west-wind the gardens have (the appearance of) wedding-feasts and banquets.

Its marvels come not into (are beyond) description: why art thou in tribulation in this darkness?

(Why) dost thou drink blood on the gibbet of this narrow place (the womb) in the midst of confinement and filth and pain?"—

60 It (the embryo), in virtue of its present state, would be incredulous, and would turn away from this message and would disbelieve it,

Saying, "This is absurd and is a deceit and delusion," because the judgement of the blind has no imagination.

Inasmuch as its (the embryo's) perception has not seen anything of the kind, its incredulous perception would not listen (to the truth);

Just as in this world the *Abdál* speak of that (other) world to the common folk,

Saying, "This world is an exceeding dark and narrow pit; outside is a world without scent or colour":

65 Naught (of their words) entered into the ear of a single one of them, for this (sensual) desire is a barrier huge and stout.

Desire closes the ear (and hinders it) from hearing; self-interest closes the eye (and hinders it) from beholding,

Even as, in the case of the embryo, desire for the blood which is its nourishment in the low abodes

Debarred it from (hearkening to) the news of this world: it knows no breakfast but blood.

Story of those who ate the young elephant from greed and because they neglected the advice of the sincere counsellor.

Hast thou heard that in India a sage espied a party of friends?

70 Left hungry, lacking provisions, and naked, they were coming from travel on a far road.

His wisdom's love was stirred (within him), and he gave them a fair greeting and blossomed like a rose-bush.

"I know," he said, "that anguish has gathered upon you from this Karbalá (of suffering)[1] in consequence of hunger and emptiness;

But, for God's sake, for God's sake, O illustrious company, let not your food be the young of the elephant!

The elephant is in this direction that ye are now going; do not tear in pieces the elephant's offspring, but hearken (to me).

75 The young elephants are on your road: to hunt them down is what your hearts desire exceedingly.

They are very weak and tender and very fat, but their mother is searching (after them and) lying in wait.

She will roam a hundred leagues' distance in quest of her children, moaning and making lament.

---

[1] Karbalá, a little town near Kúfa, was the scene of one of the most tragic events in Islamic history, the martyrdom of Husayn, who fell in battle together with many of his family and kinsmen in A.D. 680.

Fire and smoke issue from her trunk: beware of (hurting) those pitied (cherished) children of hers!"

O son, the saints are God's children: (both) in (their) absence and presence (He is) well aware (of what befalls them).

Do not deem absence (from Him) to be the result of imperfec- 80 tion on their part, for He takes vengeance for the sake of their spirits (which are one with Him).

He said, "These saints are My children in exile, sundered from (My) dominion and glory;

(They are) despised and orphaned for the sake of probation, but secretly I am their friend and intimate.

All of them are supported by My protections: you may say they are in sooth parts of Me.

Take heed! Take heed! These are My dervishes; they are a hundred thousand thousand and (yet) they are one body."

Else, how should a Moses have overthrown Pharaoh by means 85 of one goodly rod?

Else, how should Noah have submerged East and West in his Flood by means of one evil curse?

One prayer of the generous Lot would not have rased (to the ground) all their (his people's) city (and left them) in despair.

Their city, resembling Paradise, became a lake of black water: go, behold the sign!

This sign and this information (admonition) lies in the direction of Syria: you will see it as you pass on the way to Jerusalem.

Hundreds of thousands of prophets who worshipped God— 90 truly there have been chastisements (inflicted by them) in every generation.

If I should tell on and if this narration should increase (in length), not only (men's) hearts but the (very) mountains would bleed[1].

The mountains bleed and again become solid, (but) you do not see them bleed: you are blind and reprobate.

A marvellous blind man, (who is) far-sighted and keen-eyed, but sees naught of the camel except the hair!

Man, from the parsimony of greed, inspects hair by hair: like a bear, he keeps dancing to no purpose.

Dance (only) where you break (mortify) yourself and (when 95 you) tear away the cotton from the sore of lust.

(Holy) men dance and wheel on the (spiritual) battle-field: they dance in their own blood.

When they are freed from the hand (dominion) of self, they clap a hand; when they escape from their own imperfection, they make a dance.

---

[1] Literally, "What is the liver indeed? for the mountains would become blood."

From within them musicians strike the tambourine; at their ecstasy the seas burst into foam.

You see it not, but for their ears the leaves too on the boughs are clapping hands.

100 You do not see the clapping of the leaves: one must have the spiritual ear, not this ear of the body.

Close the ear of the head to jesting and lying, that you may see the resplendent city of the soul.

The ear of Mohammed draws out the hidden meaning in the words (of the religious hypocrites), for God saith of him in the Qur'án, "*He is an ear.*"

This Prophet is entirely ear and eye; we are refreshed by him: he is (as) the suckler and we (as) the (infant) boy

This discourse hath no end. Go back to those who had to do with the elephant, and start at the beginning.

The remainder of the Story of those who molested the young elephants.

105 "The elephant takes a sniff at every mouth and keeps poking round the belly of every man,

To see where she will find the roasted flesh of her young, so that she may manifest her vengeance and strength."

You eat the flesh of God's servants: you backbite them, you will suffer retribution.

Beware, for he that smells your mouths is the Creator: how shall any one save his life except him that is true (to God)?

Woe to the scoffer whose smell shall be tested in the grave by[1] Munkar or Nakír!

110 There is no possibility of withdrawing the mouth from those mighty ones, nor of sweetening the mouth with medicinal ointments.

(In the grave) there is no water and oil to cover the face[2], there is no way of evasion (open) to intelligence and sagacity.

How many a time will the blows of their maces beat upon the head and rump of every vain gabbler!

Look at the effect of the mace of 'Azrá'íl, (even) if you do not see the wood and iron in (their material) forms.

Sometimes too they appear in (material) form: the patient (himself) is aware thereof.

115 The patient says, "O my friends, what is this sword over my head?"

(They reply), "We do not see it; this must be fancy." What fancy is this? (Nay), for it is (the hour of) departure (to the other world).

---

[1] Literally, "whose smeller in the grave shall be."
[2] *I.e.* no means of dissimulation.

What fancy is this, from terror of which this inverted sphere (the sky) has now become (as insubstantial as) a phantom?

To the sick man the maces and swords became perceptible (visible), and his head dropped down[1].

He sees that that (vision) is for his sake: the eye of foe and friend (alike) is barred from it.

Worldly greed vanished, his eye became keen: his eye became illumined at the moment of bloodshed (death). 120

That eye of his, from the result of his pride and his anger, became (like) the cock that crows unseasonably[2].

It is necessary to cut off the head of the bird that rings the bell (crows) at the wrong time.

At every moment thy particular spirit[3] is struggling with death: in thy spirit's death-struggle look to thy faith!

Thy life is like a purse of gold: day and night are like him who counts the gold coins (the money-changer).

He (Time) counts and gives the gold without stopping, 125 until it (the purse) is emptied and there comes the eclipse (death).

If you take away from a mountain and do not put (anything) in the place (of what you have taken), the mountain will be demolished[4] by that giving.

Therefore, for every breath (that you give out), put an equivalent in its place, so that by (acting in accordance with the text) *and fall to worship and draw nigh* you may gain your object.

Do not strive so much to complete (your worldly) affairs: do not strive in any affair that is not religious.

(Otherwise) at the end you will depart incomplete, your (spiritual) affairs marred and your bread unbaked.

And the beautifying of your grave and sepulchre is not (done) 130 by means of stone and wood and plaster;

Nay, but by digging for yourself a grave in (spiritual) purity and burying (your) egoism in His egoism,

And by becoming His dust and buried in love of Him, so that your breath may gain replenishments from His breath.

A tomb with domes and turrets—that is not good (approved) on the part of the followers of Reality.

Look now at a living person attired in satin: does the satin help[5] his understanding at all?

His soul is in hateful torment, the scorpion of grief is in his 135 grief-laden heart.

Outside, on his exterior, broideries and decorations; but within he is sorely lamenting from (bitter) thoughts,

[1] Literally, "was turned upside down."
[2] Literally, "the untimely bird." The dying man sees the truth too late.
[3] *I.e.* "thy spirit which is part of the Universal Spirit."
[4] Literally, "will slip away from its foot."
[5] Literally, "take the hand of."

While you may see another in an old patched frock, his thoughts (sweet) as the sugar-cane and his words (like) sugar.

Returning to the Story of the elephant.

Said the sincere adviser, "Hearken to this counsel of mine, so that your hearts and souls may not be afflicted.

Be content with herbage and leaves, do not go in chase of the young elephants.

140   I have put off from my neck (I have discharged) the debt of admonition: how should the end (final result) of admonition be aught but felicity?

I came to deliver the message, that I may save you from (fruitless) repentance.

Beware! Let not greed waylay you, let not greed for victual tear you up by the roots!"

This he said, and gave a farewell and departed; their famine and hunger waxed great on the way.

Suddenly, in the direction of a highroad, they espied a fat young elephant, newly born.

145   They fell upon it like furious wolves, ate it clean up, and washed their hands.

One of the fellow-travellers did not eat (of it) and exhorted (the others to abstain), for the sayings of that dervish were remembered by him.

Those words hindered him from (eating) its roasted flesh: old intelligence bestows on thee a new fortune.

Then they all fell down and slept, but the hungry one (was awake) like the shepherd in the flock.

He saw a frightful elephant approaching: first she came and ran towards him who was keeping guard.

150   She smelt his mouth thrice: no disagreeable smell came from it.

She paced round him several times and went off: the huge queen-elephant did him no hurt.

She smelt the lips of every sleeper, and the smell (of her young one's flesh) was coming to her from each of those slumbering men.

He (each man) had eaten of the roasted flesh of the young elephant: the (mother) elephant quickly tore him to pieces and killed him.

At once she set about rending the people of that company one by one, and she had no awe of (doing) it.

155   She tossed each one in the air recklessly, so that he dashed on the earth and was cloven asunder.

O drinker of the people's blood, begone from the way, lest their blood wage war against thee.

Know for sure that their property is (as) their blood, because property comes into one's hand (is acquired) by strength (of body).

The mother of those young elephants[1] will exact vengeance: (her) retribution will slay him that eats the young elephant.

O eater of bribes[2], thou eatest the young elephant: from thee too the Master of the elephant will wring the breath[3].

The smell put to shame the deviser of fraud: the elephant 160 knows the smell of her child.

He that perceives the smell of God from (distant) Yemen, how should not he perceive the smell of falsehood from me?

Inasmuch as Muṣṭafá (Mohammed) smelt (this) from far away, how should not he smell the odour from our mouths?

He does smell it, but he conceals (the fact) from us: the good and bad smells go up to Heaven.

Thou art sleeping, and (meanwhile) the smell of that unlawful deed (of thine) is beating on the azure sky.

It accompanies thy foul breaths, it ascends to the smellers 165 (examiners) in the celestial sphere.

The smell of pride and the smell of greed and the smell of concupiscence will become, in speaking, like (the smell of) onions[4].

If thou take oath, saying, "When have I eaten them? I have abstained from onions and garlic,"

The breath of thy oath will inform (against thee) and will strike upon the noses of those who sit beside thee.

Many prayers are rejected because of the smell thereof: the corrupt heart shows in the tongue.

The answer to such a prayer is " *Get ye gone* ": the requital for 170 every knave is the cudgel of repulse.

(But) if thy words be wrong and thy meaning right, that wrongness of expression is acceptable to God.

Explaining that in the sight of the Beloved a fault committed by lovers is better than the correctness of strangers.

The veracious Bilál in (uttering) the call to prayer used, from ardent feeling, to pronounce *ḥayya* as *hayya*,

So that they (some people) said, "O Messenger (of God), this fault is not right (permissible) now when 'tis the beginning of the edifice (of Islam).

O Prophet and Messenger of the Creator, get a muezzin who speaks more correctly.

---

[1] *I.e.* the righteous and innocent, who are "mothered" by the prophets and saints.
[2] *I.e.* extortionate oppressor.
[3] *I.e.* will bring thee to utter perdition.
[4] *I.e.* these qualities will appear in thy speech.

175   At the commencement of religion and piety, it is a disgrace to mispronounce *ḥayy ʿala 'l-faláḥ*[1]."

The Prophet's wrath boiled up, and he gave one or two indications of the hidden favours (which God had bestowed upon Bilál),

Saying, "O base men, in God's sight the (mispronounced) *ḥayy* of Bilál is better than a hundred *ḥá*'s and *khá*'s and words and phrases.

Do not stir me to anger, lest I divulge your secret—(both) your end and your beginning."

If thou hast not a sweet breath in prayer, go and beg a prayer from the pure (in heart).

How God most High commanded Moses, on whom be peace, saying, "Call unto Me with a mouth with which thou hast not sinned."

180   He (God) said, "O Moses, beseech Me for protection with a mouth thou hast not sinned withal."

Moses said, "I have not such a mouth." God said, "Call unto Me by the mouth of others."

When didst thou sin by the mouth of others? Invoke (God) by the mouth of others, crying, "O God!"

Act in such wise that (their) mouths may pray for thee in the nights and days.

Ask pardon by a mouth with which thou hast committed no sin—and that will be the mouth of others—

185   Or (else) make thine own mouth pure, make thy spirit alert and nimble.

Praise of God is pure: when purity has come, defilement packs and goes out.

Contraries flee from contraries: night flees when the light (of dawn) shines forth.

When the pure (holy) Name comes into the mouth, neither impurity remains nor (any) sorrows.

Showing that the supplicant's invocation of God is essentially the same thing as God's response to him[2].

One night a certain man was crying "Allah!" till his lips were growing sweet with praise of Him.

190   The Devil said, "Prithee, O garrulous one, where is the (response) 'Here am I' to all this 'Allah'?

Not a single response is coming from the Throne: how long will you cry 'Allah' with grim face?"

He became broken-hearted and laid down his head (to sleep): in a dream he saw Khaḍir amidst the verdure.

---

[1] *I.e.* "Hasten to welfare." These words form part of the call to prayer.
[2] Literally, "God's saying *Labbayka*' ('Here am I')."

He (Khaḍir) said, "Hark, you have held back from praising God: how is it that you repent of having called unto Him?"

He said, "No 'Here am I' is coming to me in response, hence I fear that I may be (a reprobate who is) driven away from the Door."

He (Khaḍir) said, "(God saith), That 'Allah' of thine is My 195 'Here am I,' and that supplication and grief and ardour of thine is My messenger (to thee).

Thy shifts and attempts to find a means (of gaining access to Me) were (in reality) My drawing (thee towards Me), and released thy feet (from the bonds of worldliness).

Thy fear and love are the noose to catch My favour: beneath every 'O Lord' (of thine) is many a 'Here am I' (from Me)."

Far from this prayer is the soul of the fool, because to him it is not permitted to cry "O Lord."

On his mouth and heart are lock and bolt, to the end that he may not moan unto God in the hour of bale.

He (God) gave to Pharaoh hundredfold possessions and riches, 200 so that he claimed (Divine) might and majesty.

In his whole life that man of evil nature felt no (spiritual) headache, lest he should moan unto God.

God gave him all the empire of this world, (but) He did not give him grief and pain and sorrows.

Grief is better than the empire of the world, so that you may call unto God in secret.

The call of the griefless is from a frozen heart[1], the call of the grieving one is from rapture:

('Tis) to withdraw the voice under the lips, to bear in mind 205 (one's) origin and beginning;

('Tis) the voice become pure and sad, (crying) "O God!" and "O Thou whose help is besought!" and "O Helper!"

(Even) the moan of a dog for His sake is not void of (Divine) attraction, because every one who desires (Him) is a brigand's captive[2]—

As (for example) the dog of the Cave[3], which was freed from (eating) carrion and sat at the table of the (spiritual) emperors:

Until the Resurrection, before the Cave it is drinking in gnostic wise without (any) pot the water of (Divine) mercy.

Oh, there is many a one in a dog's skin, who hath no name 210 (and fame), yet is not without that cup (of Divine knowledge) in secret.

Give thy life for this cup, O son: how may victory be (won) without (spiritual) warfare and patience?

[1] Literally, "congelation."
[2] *I.e.* "every seeker of God falls a prey to tribulation, with which God afflicts him in order that it may be the means of drawing him towards God."
[3] See *Qur'án*, xviii, 17.

To show patience for the sake of this is no hardship: show patience, for patience is the key to joy.

From this ambush none escaped without some patience and prudence: to prudence, indeed, patience is the foot and hand.

Exercise prudence in eating (and drinking), for this (food and drink) is poisonous herbage: to exercise prudence is the strength and light of the prophets.

215 He that jumps at every breath of wind is (like) straw, (but) how should the mountain attach any weight to the wind?

On every side a ghoul is calling you—"Hark, O brother, (if) you wish (to find) the way, come (hither).

I will show (you) the way, I will be your kind fellow-traveller, I am the guide (for you) on this intricate path."

She (the ghoul) is not the guide, and she does not know the way. O Joseph, do not go towards that wolfish one!

Prudence is this, that you be not beguiled by the fat things and sweets and snares of the World[1];

220 For she hath neither fat nor sweet: she chants spells of magic and breathes (them) into your ear,

Saying, "Come in as my guest, O light (of my eyes): the house is yours, and you are mine."

Prudence is this, that you say (to her), "I have indigestion" or "I am ill, I am a sick man in this charnel-house";

Or "My head aches: take away my headache," or "the son of my maternal uncle has invited me"—

For she will give you one (draught of) honey (mixed) with (venomous) stings, so that her honey will plant in you (many) sores.

225 Whether she give you fifty or sixty (pieces of) gold, she gives you, O fish, (nothing but) flesh on a hook.

If she give, when does that deceitful one really give (aught)? The words of the swindler are (like) rotten walnuts.

Their rattling robs you of understanding and brain and does not reckon myriads of understandings (even) as one[2].

(In travelling) your bag and your purse are your friend, (do not care for anything else): if you are Rámín, seek none but your Wísa.

'Tis your essential self that is your Wísa and beloved, and all these external things are banes to you.

230 Prudence is this, that when they (worldlings) invite you, you should not say, "They are enamoured and fond of me."

Know that their invitation is (like) the bird's whistle which the fowler gives (while) concealed in (his) place of ambush:

He has put forward a dead bird, (pretending) that this (bird) is making this plaintive noise and cry.

---

[1] Literally, "this caravanseray."
[2] *I.e.* regards them as naught and easily overcomes them.

The birds think he is one of their kind: they gather round, and he rends their skins—

Except, no doubt, the bird on which God has bestowed prudence, so that it may not be fooled by that bait and enticement[1].

Imprudence is assuredly (attended by) repentance. Hear the following story in explanation of this. 235

How the countryman deceived the townsman and invited him
with humble entreaties and great importunity.

In the past, O brother, there was a townsman (who was) intimate with a countryman.

Whenever the countryman came to town, he would pitch his tent in the street of the townsman.

He would be his guest for two or three months, he would be in his shop and at his table,

And the townsman would provide, free of cost, everything that he wanted during that time.

(Once) he turned to the townsman and said, "Sire, are you never coming to the country for a holiday[2]? 240

Bring all your children, (I beg you) in God's name, for this is the time of the rose-garden and the springtide;

Or come in summer, in the fruit-season, that I may brace my belt to do you service.

Bring your retinue and your children and kinsfolk, and stay in our village three or four months,

For in spring the countryside is pleasant; there are sown fields and lovely anemones."

The townsman was (always) putting him off with promises[3], until eight years had elapsed since the (first) promise (was given). 245

Every year he (the countryman) would say, "When will you set out on the journey?—for the month of December is (already) come,"

And he (the townsman) would make an excuse, saying, "This year we have a guest who has come from such and such a district;

(But) next year I will run (down) to that part (of the country), if I can escape from the pressing affairs (which keep me at home)."

He (the countryman) said, "My family are (anxiously) expecting your children, O benefactor."

Every year he was coming back, like the stork, to reside in the townsman's pavilion, 250

[1] Literally, "feigned affection."
[2] Literally, "seeking recreation."
[3] Literally, "was always giving him promises as a means of putting off the present occasion."

And every year the Khwája would expend his gold and wealth upon him and open his wings (wide)[1].

On the last occasion, that paladin set dishes (of food) before him at morn and eve for three months.

From shame he again said to the Khwája, "How long (nothing but) promises? How long will you deceive me?"

The Khwája said, "My body and soul are eager for the meeting, but every change depends on the decree of Him (God).

255   Man is like a ship or sail: (he must wait) to see when the Driver of the wind shall send the (favourable) breeze."

Once more he (the countryman) adjured him, crying, "O generous man, take your children and come and behold the pleasures (of the country)."

He took his hand three times in covenant, saying, "In God's name, come quickly, make the utmost effort!"

After ten years—and every year the same sugared entreaties and promises—

The Khwája's children said, "O father, the moon and the clouds and the shadows too have their journeys.

260   You have laid obligations on him, you have taken great pains on his account,

And he wishes to repay some part of that obligation when you become his guest.

He gave us many injunctions in secret: 'Bring him to the country,' said he, 'coaxing (him to come).'"

He (the townsman) said, "This is true, but, O Síbawayh[2], be on thy guard against the malice of him to whom thou hast shown kindness.

Love is the seed (that bears fruit at the moment) of the last breath: I fear that it may be corrupted by estrangement."

265   There is a friendship like a cutting sword, (destructive) as December in the gardens and cornfields;

There is a friendship like the season of spring, whence (come) restorations and produce incalculable.

Prudence is this, that you think evil, so that you may flee and become quit of evil.

The Prophet has said, "Prudence is (consists in) thinking evil": know that for every footstep there is a snare, O fool!

The surface of the plateau is level and broad, (but at) every step there is a snare: do not advance boldly.

270   The mountain-goat runs on, saying, "Where is the snare?" As it speeds onward, the snare lights on its throat.

O thou who saidst "Where?" look and see! Thou sawest the plain, (but) thou didst not see the ambush.

---

[1] *I.e.* "would be open-handed in his munificence."
[2] Name of a celebrated grammarian. Here the meaning is, "O sagacious one."

Without ambush and snare and hunter, O cunning one, how should there be a sheep's tail (laid in a trap) amidst the cornfield?

They that came along boldly on the earth—see their bones and skulls!

When you go to the graveyard, O you with whom God is pleased, ask their bones concerning that which is past,

That you may see clearly how those blind intoxicated men 275 went down into the pit of delusion.

If you have eyes, do not walk blindly; and if you have not eyes, take a staff in your hand.

When you have not the staff of prudence and judgement, make the (seer's) eye your leader;

And if there is no staff of prudence and judgement, do not stand on every road without a guide.

Step in the same fashion as a blind man steps, in order that your foot may escape from the pit and the dog.

He (the blind man) plants his foot tremblingly and with fear 280 and precaution, so that he may not fall into derangement[1].

O you who have jumped away from some smoke and fallen into a fire, you who have sought a mouthful (of food) and become a mouthful for a snake,

(*Story of the people of Sabá and how prosperity made them froward.*)

You have not read the story of the people of Sabá, or you have read it and seen (heard) naught but the echo.

The mountain itself (which produces the echo) is not aware of the echo: the mind of the mountain hath no way (of access) to the meaning.

Without ear and mind, it goes on making a noise; when you are silent, it also becomes silent.

God bestowed on the people of Sabá much ease—myriads of 285 castles and palaces and orchards.

(But) those bad-natured ones rendered no thanks for that (bounty): in fidelity they were less than dogs.

When to a dog there comes from the door a piece of bread, he will gird up his loins at the door.

He will become the watcher and guardian of the door, even though violence and hard treatment befall him.

Still will he stay and abide at that door: he will deem it ingratitude to prefer another.

And (again), if a strange dog come by day or night (to a quarter 290 of the town), the dogs there will at once teach him a lesson,

Saying, "Begone to the place that is thy first lodging: obligation for that kindness is the heart's pledge (which it must redeem)."

---

[1] *I.e.* "may not be upset."

They will bite him, saying, "Begone to thy place, do not any more leave (unpaid) the obligation for that kindness."

From the door of the spirit and spiritual men how long didst thou drink the water of life, and thine eyes were opened!

Much food from the door of the spiritual, (in the form) of (mystical) intoxication and ecstasy and selflessness, didst thou cast upon thy soul.

295 Afterwards, through greed, thou didst abandon that door, and (now) thou art going round about every shop, like a bear.

For the sake of worthless *tharíd*[1] thou art running to the doors of those (worldly) patrons whose pots are (full of) fat.

Know that here (where the saints abide) the (meaning of) "fat" is that the soul becomes fat (flourishing), and (know that) here the plight of the desperate is made good.

How the smitten would assemble every morning at the door of the (monastic) cell of Jesus, on whom be peace, craving to be healed through his prayer.

The table of the spiritual is (like) the cell of Jesus: O afflicted one, beware, beware! Do not forsake this door!

From all sides the people would gather—blind and lame and palsied and clothed in rags—

300 At the door of the cell of Jesus in the morning, that he by his breath might deliver them from tribulation.

As soon as he finished his litanies, that man of goodly religion (Jesus) would go forth at morningtide,

And would see troops of afflicted feeble folk seated at the door in hope and expectancy.

(Then) he would say, "O ye that are smitten, the wants of all you here present have been granted by God.

Hark, set off and go without pain or trouble towards the forgiveness and kindness of God."

305 All, like tethered camels whose knees you unbind with foresight,

At his prayer would begin to run on their feet, hastening gladly and joyously to their homes.

(So too) thou hast experienced many maladies in thyself, and hast gained health from these kings of religion (the saints).

How oft hath thy limping been turned into a smooth (easy) gait, how oft hath thy soul been made void of grief and pain!

O heedless one, tie a string to thy foot, that thou mayst not become lost to (unconscious of) thyself even, O sluggard!

310 Thy ingratitude and forgetfulness did not call to mind thy (former) drinking of honey.

---

[1] Broken bread soaked in gravy.

Necessarily, that way (by which spiritual blessings were conveyed) became barred to thee, since the hearts of the "men of heart" were made sore by thee.

Quickly overtake them and ask pardon of God; weep lamentably like a cloud,

In order that their rose-garden may open its blossoms to thee, and that the ripe fruits may burst and reveal themselves[1].

Pace round that same door: do not be less than a dog, if thou hast become (associated as) a fellow-servant with the dog of the Cave,

Because even dogs admonish dogs, saying, "Fix thy heart on 315 thy first home,

Hold fast to the first door where thou didst eat bones, and fulfil thy obligation: do not leave that (debt unpaid)."

They keep biting him (the strange dog), that from a sense of duty he may go thither and be prospered by his first abode.

They bite him, saying, "O naughty dog, begone! Do not become an enemy to thy benefactor.

Be attached, like the door-ring, to that same door; keep watch and be nimble and ready to spring.

Do not be the type of our breaking faith, do not recklessly 320 make (our) disloyalty notorious.

Since fidelity is the badge by which the dogs are known, begone and do not bring opprobrium and ill-fame upon the dogs."

Inasmuch as unfaithfulness has (always) been a disgrace (even) to dogs, how shouldst thou deem it right to show unfaithfulness?

The high God hath boasted of faithfulness: He hath said, *"Who but I am most faithful in keeping a promise?"*

Know that faithfulness (to others when it is accompanied) with rejection of God is unfaithfulness: no one hath precedence over (hath a prior claim to) God's rights.

Thy mother's right (only) arose after that Bounteous One had 325 made her indebted (to Him) for thy embryo.

He bestowed on thee a form within her body, He gave ease to her during pregnancy and accustomed her (to the burden).

She deemed thee as a part joined (to herself); His providence separated (from her) that which was joined.

God hath prepared thousands of artifices and contrivances, so that thy mother hath thrown (her) love upon thee.

Therefore God's right is prior to (that of) the mother: whoever does not recognise that right is an ass.

(If thou deny it), do not even admit that He created mother, 330 teat, and milk, and united her with the father!

O Lord, O Thou whose beneficence is eternal, Thine is both that which I know and that which I know not.

---

[1] Literally, "burst back upon themselves."

Thou didst command, saying, "Remember God, because My right shall never grow old.

Remember the kindness which I did unto you that morn by protecting (you) in the ship (ark) of Noah.

At that time I gave to the stock[1] of your fathers security from the Flood and from its waves.

335   Water, like fire in (its deadly) nature, had covered the earth: its waves were sweeping away the highest peaks of the mountains.

I protected you, I did not spurn you, in the bodies of the ancestors of the ancestors of your ancestors.

Now that you have come to the head[2], how should I smite the sole of your foot[3]? How should I let My workshop go to waste?

How are you becoming devoted to the unfaithful and going in that direction from ill thoughts (of Me)?

I am clear of negligence and infidelities, (yet) you come to Me and think evil.

340   Think this evil thought against the place where you cringe[4] before one like yourself.

You got many powerful friends and companions: if I ask you, 'Where (is so-and-so)?' you will say, 'He is gone.'

Your good friend is gone up to the highest Heaven, your wicked friend is gone to the bottom of the earth.

You are left in the middle (between them) so helpless (as you are), like a fire (left behind) from a caravan."

O valiant friend, lay hold of the skirt of Him who is exempt from "above" and "below."

345   Neither doth He ascend to Heaven, like Jesus, nor go (down) into the earth, like Qárún (Korah).

He is with you in space and in the spaceless (world) when you leave house and shop behind.

He brings forth purity from defilements, He takes your acts of wrong as faithful performance (of duty).

When you commit wrong, He sends chastisement, to the end that you may go back from imperfection towards perfection.

When you have neglected a part of your orisons in the Way, there comes over you a painful and hot feeling of contraction.

350   That is the corrective act (of God), meaning, "Do not make any change in the ancient covenant

Before (the day when) this contraction shall become a chain, (and when) this which (now) grips the heart shall become a fetter gripping the foot."

---

[1] Literally, "cocoon."
[2] *I.e.* risen to the dignity of Man.
[3] *I.e.* reject you with ignominy.
[4] Literally, "become double."

Your mental pain shall become perceptible to the senses and manifest. See (therefore) that you do not hold this indication as naught.

The (spiritual) contractions (which occur) in (the case of) sins affect (only) the heart; after death (these) contractions become (actual) chains.

"Whosoever here (in this world) shall turn his back upon Our commemoration, We shall give him a straitened life (hereafter) and reward him with blindness[1]."

When a thief is carrying off people's property, contraction and 355 straitness of heart prick his heart (conscience),

(And) he says, "I wonder what this contraction is": (say), "The contraction (distress) of the injured person who wept at thy wickedness."

When he pays no regard to this contraction, the wind of perseverance (in evil) blows (fans) its (the evil's) fire.

The contraction that grips the heart turns into the grip of the policeman: inevitably those ideas become sensible (materialised) and display themselves.

The pangs have become prison and the cross (crucifixion): the pang is (as) the root, and the root produces boughs.

The root was hidden, it is (now) revealed. Consider (your) 360 inward contraction and expansion as a root.

When it is a bad root, smite it quickly, so that an ugly thorn may not grow in the garden.

You have felt the contraction: seek a remedy for it, because all heads (excrescences)[2] grow from the bottom (root).

You have felt the expansion: water your expansion, and when the fruit appears, give it to your friends.

The remainder of the Story of the people of Sabá.

Sabá were folk given over to dalliance and foolish; 'twas their practice to show ingratitude to the generous.

By way of illustration, it would be ingratitude to dispute with 365 your benefactor,

Saying, "I do not want this kindness, I am annoyed by it: why art thou troubling (about it)?

Do (me) a favour, take away this kindness; I do not desire an eye: blind me at once!"

Hence the people of Sabá said, "(O Lord), put a far distance between us: our blemish is better for us, take away our adornment.

We do not desire these palaces and orchards, nor fair women nor that safety and ease (which we now enjoy).

---

[1] Qur'án, xx, 123, altered for metrical reasons.
[2] I.e. branches, leaves and fruit.

370   Towns near to each other are bad; the desert, where the wild
beasts are, is good."

Man craves winter in summer, and when winter comes, he
likes it not,

For he is never content with any state (of things), neither with
poverty nor with a life of plenty.

May Man be killed! How ungrateful he is! Whenever he ob-
tains guidance, he spurns it.

The carnal soul is of this sort, hence it ought to be killed:
that Exalted One hath said, "*Kill yourselves.*"

375   It is a triagonal thorn: however you may place it, it will pierce,
and how will you escape from its stab?

Set the thorn on fire with renunciation of sensual passion, and
cling to the righteous friend.

When the people of Sabá carried (their ingratitude) beyond
bounds, saying, "In our opinion, pestilence is better than the
zephyr,"

Their counsellors began to admonish (them) and restrain
(them) from impiety and ingratitude;

(But) they sought to take the lives of their counsellors, and
sowed the seed of impiety and unthankfulness.

380   When the (Divine) decree comes to pass, this (whole) world
becomes cramped (so that there is no escape); by the (Divine)
decree sweetmeat becomes anguish to the mouth.

He (the Prophet) said, "When the Decree comes, the (widest)
expanse is narrow; when the Decree comes, the eyes are veiled."

The eye is bandaged at the time of the Decree, so that the eye
does not see the eye's collyrium[1].

When the cunning of that Horseman has raised the dust, the
dust keeps thee off from calling for aid.

Go towards the Horseman, go not towards the dust; else the
cunning of the Rider will beat upon thee.

385   God said, "He whom this wolf devoured, he saw the wolf's
dust: how did not he make piteous moan?"

Did not he know the wolf's dust? (Then), with such know-
ledge, why did he graze?

Sheep know the smell of the harmful wolf and creep away in
every direction.

The brain of animals knows the smell of the lion and bids
farewell to grazing.

Thou hast smelt the lion of (God's) wrath. Turn back! Con-
sort with prayer and dread!

390   That multitude (of Sabá) did not turn back from the wolf's
dust, and after the dust the wolf of tribulation came on in his
might.

---

[1] *I.e.* the eye-salve.

In wrath he tore to pieces those sheep which shut their eyes
to the shepherd, Wisdom.

How oft did the shepherd call them! and they came not: they
were throwing the dust of resentment in the eyes of the shep-
herd,

Saying, "Begone: we ourselves are better shepherds than thou.
How should we become¦ (thy) followers? We are chieftains,
every one (of us).

We are food for the wolf, and we are not for the Friend; we
are fuel for the Fire, and we are not for dishonour[1]."

A heathen pride was in their brains: the raven croaked disaster 395
over the traces of their habitation.

They were digging a pit for the oppressed: they (themselves)
fell into the pit, crying "Alas!"

They tore the coats of the Josephs (the prophets and saints),
and that which they gave they got, piece by piece.

Who is that Joseph? Thy God-seeking heart, bound as a
captive in thy abode.

Thou hast bound a Gabriel on a pillar, thou hast wounded his
wings and plumes in a hundred places.

Thou settest before him a roasted calf, thou fetchest (ground) 400
straw and bringest him to the straw-barn,

Saying, "Eat; this is a dainty meal for us," (although) for him
there is no food but meeting God face to face.

On account of this torment and tribulation that afflicted
(heart) is complaining of thee to God,

Crying, "O God, deliver (me) from this old wolf!" He (God)
saith to it, "Lo, the hour is (wellnigh) come: have patience.

I will demand justice for thee from every heedless one: who
gives justice but God, the Dealer of justice?"

It (the heart) says, "My patience is lost in separation from 405
Thy face, O Lord.

I am (like) Aḥmad (Mohammed) left forsaken in the hands of
the Jews, I am (like) Ṣáliḥ fallen into prison (amongst the people)
of Thamúd.

O Thou that bestowest felicity on the souls of the prophets,
either slay me or call me back (to Thee) or come (Thyself).

(Even) the infidels cannot endure to be separated from Thee:
he (every infidel) is saying, '_O would that I had been dust!_'

This is the state of him (the infidel) who in sooth belongs to
that side (is beyond the pale): how (then) should one that belongs
to Thee be (patient) without Thee?"

God saith, "Yea, O pure (heart); but hearken (unto Me) and 410
have patience, for patience is better.

The dawn is near. Hush, do not wail! I am striving for thee,
do not thou strive."

---

[1] _I.e._ "we would rather suffer damnation than dishonour."

The rest of the Story of the Khwája's going to the
village on the invitation of the countryman.

It (this digression) has passed beyond bounds: return, O
valiant friend. The countryman, mark you, took the Khwája to
his house.

Put aside the story of the people of Sabá: tell how the Khwája
came to the village.

The countryman used blandishments in ingratiating himself,
until he made the Khwája's prudence crazy.

415 He (the Khwája) was distracted by message upon message,
till the clear water of his prudence became turbid.

On the same side his children in approval (of the country-
man's invitation) were joyously striking up "*Let us frolic and
play*,"

Like Joseph, whom by the wondrous (act of Divine) pre-
destination (the words) "*Let us frolic and play*" carried off from
his father's shadow (protection).

That is not (joyful) play; nay, 'tis play with one's life[1], 'tis
cunning and deceit and contrivance of fraud.

Whatsoever would fling you asunder from the Friend, do not
listen to it, for it holds loss, loss.

420 (Even) if the gain be a hundred hundredfold, do not accept it:
do not, for the sake of the gold, break with the Treasurer, O
dervish!

Hear how many a rebuke, hot and cold (kindly and severe),
God addressed to the Companions of the Prophet,

Because, in a year of distress (famine), at the sound of the
drum[2] they (quitted) without tarrying (and) made void the
Friday congregation,

"Lest" (so they said) "others should buy cheap and get the
advantage over us in respect of those imported goods."

The Prophet was left alone in prayer with two or three poor
men firm (in their faith) and full of supplication.

425 He (God) said, "How did the drum and the pastime and a
trading affair sunder you from a man of God?

Ye have dispersed (and run) madly towards the wheat, and
left a Prophet standing (in prayer).

On account of the wheat ye sowed the seed of vanity and for-
sook that Messenger of God.

Companionship with him is better than pastime and riches:
(look and) see whom thou hast forsaken, rub an eye!

Verily, to your greed did not this become certain, that I am
the Provider and the best of them that provide?"

---

[1] *I.e.* a deadly game.
[2] Announcing the approach of a caravan with merchandise.

He that giveth sustenance from Himself unto the wheat, how 430
should He let thy acts of trust (in Him) be wasted?

For the sake of wheat thou hast become parted from Him who
hath sent the wheat from Heaven.

How the falcon invited the ducks to come
from the water to the plain.

Says the falcon to the duck, "Arise from the water, that thou
mayst see the plains diffusing sweetness,"

(But) the wise duck says to him, "Away, O falcon! The water
is our stronghold and safety and joy."

The Devil is like the falcon. O ducks, make haste (to guard
yourselves)! Beware, do not come out of your stronghold, the
water.

Say to the falcon, "Begone, begone! Turn back and keep thy 435
hand off our heads, O kind friend[1]!

We are quit of thy invitation: (keep) the invitation for thyself:
we will not listen to these words of thine, O infidel!

The stronghold (the water) is (enough) for us: let the sugar
and sugar-fields be thine! I do not desire thy gift: take it for
thyself!

Whilst there is life (in the body), food will not fail; when there
is an army, banners will not fail."

The prudent Khwája offered many an excuse and made many
a pretext to the (countryman who resembled the) obstinate
Devil.

"At this moment," said he, "I have serious matters (in hand); 440
if I come (to visit you), they will not be set in order.

The King has charged me with a delicate affair, and because of
(anxiously) expecting me he has not slept during the night.

I dare not neglect the King's command, I cannot fall into
disgrace[2] with the King.

Every morning and evening a special officer arrives and re-
quests of me (desires me to provide) a means of escape (from the
difficulty).

Do you deem it right that I should go into the country, with
the result that the King would knit his brows (in wrath)?

How should I heal (assuage) his anger after that? Surely, by 445
this (offence) I should bury myself alive."

He related a hundred pretexts of this sort, (but his) expedients
did not coincide with God's decree.

If (all) the atoms of the world contrive expedients, they are
naught, naught, against the ordinance of Heaven.

---

[1] Literally, "footman," "helper." The word is used ironically here.
[2] Literally, "become pale-faced."

How shall this earth flee from Heaven, how shall it conceal itself from it?

Whatsoever may come from Heaven to the earth, it (the earth) has no refuge or device or hiding-place.

450 Is fire from the sun raining upon it, it has laid its face (low) before his fire;

And if the rain is making a flood upon it and devastating the cities upon it,

It (the earth) has become resigned to it (Heaven), like Job, saying, "I am captive: bring (on me) whatever thou wilt."

O thou who art a part of this earth, do not lift up thy head (in rebellion); when thou seest the decree of God, do not withdraw (from it disobediently).

Since thou hast heard "*We created thee of dust*," (know that) He (God) hath required thee to be (humble and submissive as) dust: do not avert thy face (from Him).

455 (God saith), "Mark how I have sown a seed in the earth: thou art dust of the earth, and I have raised it aloft.

Do thou once more adopt the practice of earthiness (self-abasement), that I may make thee prince over all princes."

Water goes from above to below; then from below it goes up above.

The wheat went beneath the earth from above; afterwards it became ears of corn and sprang up quickly.

The seed of every fruit entered into the earth; afterwards it raised up heads (shoots) from the buried (root).

460 The source of (all) blessings descended from Heaven to the earth and became the nutriment of the pure (vital) spirit.

Forasmuch as it came down from Heaven on account of humility, it became part of the living and valiant man.

Hence that inanimate matter (rain and sunlight) was turned into human qualities and soared joyously above the empyrean,

Saying, "We came at first from the living world, and have (now) gone back from below to above."

All particles (of phenomenal being), (whether) in movement (or) at rest, are speakers (and declare): "*Verily, to Him we are returning*."

465 The praises and glorifications of the hidden particles have filled Heaven with an uproar[1].

When the Decree (of God) set out to (use) enchantments[2], the countryman checkmated a townsman.

Notwithstanding thousands of (good) resolutions, the Khwája was checkmated, and from that journey (which he undertook) he fell into the midst of calamities[3].

---

[1] Literally, "have thrown an uproar into Heaven."
[2] *I.e.* to delude and mislead.
[3] Literally, "into the place where contaminations appear and occur.

His reliance was upon his own firmness, (but) though he was (as) a mountain, a half-flood[1] swept him away.

When the Decree puts forth its head from Heaven, all the intelligent become blind and deaf;

Fishes are cast out of the sea; the snare catches miserably the 470 flying bird.

Even genie and demon go into the bottle; nay, a Hárút goes into (the pit of) Babylon.

(All are lost) except that one who has taken refuge with the Decree: his blood no (astrological) quadrature (ever) shed[2].

Except that you take refuge with the Decree, no contrivance will give you release from it.

The Story of the people of Zarwán and how they contrived that they should pick the fruit in their orchards without being troubled by the poor.

You have read the story of the people of Zarwán: then why have you persisted in seeking expedients?

Several (noxious) men who stung like scorpions were con- 475 triving that they might cut off part of the daily bread of some poor folk.

During the night, the whole night, they were devising a plot; many a 'Amr and Bakr had put their faces together.

Those wicked men were speaking their inmost thoughts in secret, lest God should discover it.

Did the clay devise (evil) against the Plasterer? Is the hand doing any work that is hidden from the heart?

He (God) hath said, "Doth not He who created (thee) know thy desire, (doth not He know) whether in thy secret conversation there is sincerity or cajolery?"

How should a traveller who has set out at morn be unheeded 480 by One who sees plainly where shall be his lodging to-morrow?

Wheresoever he has descended or mounted, He hath taken charge of it and *reckoned (it) up by number.*

Now purge your ear of forgetfulness and listen to the separation (forlorn plight) of the sorrowful one.

Know that when you set your ear to his tale, that is the alms which you give to the sad;

(For) you will hear the sorrows of the heart-sick—the starvation of the noble spirit by the water and clay (of the body).

(Though it is) one filled with knowledge, it hath a house filled 485 with smoke: open a window for it by listening.

---

[1] *I.e.* a small flood.
[2] The term *tarbí'* (quadrature) denotes the quartile aspect of any two planets, *i.e.* when they are 90 degrees distant from each other.

When your ear becomes a way of breath (relief) for it, the bitter smoke will decrease (and disappear) from its house.

Show sympathy with us, O well-watered (prosperous) one, if you are faring towards the most high Lord.

This vacillation is a prison and gaol that will not let the soul go in any direction.

This (motive) draws (you) in one direction, and that (motive) in another, each (motive) saying, "I am the right way."

490 This vacillation is a precipice on the Way to God: oh, blest is he whose feet are loosed (from its bonds).

He fares on the right way without vacillation: (if) you do not know the way, seek (to find) where his footprints are.

Cleave to the footprints of the deer and advance safely, that from the deer's footprints you may attain to the musk-gland.

By means of this wayfaring you will ascend to the most luminous zenith, O brother, if you will walk on the fire (of tribulation)

(There is) no fear of sea or waves or foam, since you have heard the (Divine) allocution, "*Be not afraid*."

495 Know that it is (a fulfilment of) *Be not afraid*, when God hath given you the fear (which causes you to refrain from sin): He will send the bread, since He hath sent the tray to you[1].

The fear (danger) is for that one who has no fear (of God); the anguish (is) for that one who does not frequent this place (where God is feared).

The Khwája's departure to the country.

The Khwája got to work and made preparations (for the journey): the bird, his resolve (to set out), sped rapidly towards the country.

His kinsfolk and children made ready for the journey and threw the baggage upon the ox of departure,

Rejoicing and hastening towards the country, saying, "We have eaten some fruit (in anticipation): give (us) the glad news of (arrival in) the country!

500 The place for which we are bound is a sweet pasturage, and our friend there is kind and charming.

He has invited us with thousands of wishes, he has planted for us the shoot of kindness.

From him we shall bring back to town the store of the country-side (to sustain us) during the long winter.

Nay, he will give up the orchard for our sake, he will make a place for us in the middle of his soul.

Hasten, friends, that ye may get gain!" (But) Reason from within was saying (to them), "*Do not rejoice!*"

---

[1] *I.e.* the tray (fear of God) is accompanied by the bread (security).

Be gainers by the gain of God: *lo, my Lord loveth not them* 505
that rejoice (overmuch).

Rejoice (but) moderately *on account of what He causeth to*
come to you: everything that comes and is a source of pre-
occupation diverts you (from Him).

Rejoice in Him, do not rejoice in aught except Him: He is
(as) the spring, and (all) other things (as) the month of December.

Everything other than He is the (means of) leading you
gradually to perdition, (even) though it is your throne and
kingdom and your crown.

Rejoice in sorrow, for sorrow is the snare of (means of attain-
ing to) union (with God): in this Way the ascent is downwards[1].

Sorrow is a treasure, and your pain is as the mine, but how 510
should this (saying) catch hold of (make an impression on)
children?

When children hear the name of "play," they all run (after it)
with the speed of a wild ass.

O blind asses, in this direction there are snares; in this direc-
tion there are bloodsheds (concealed) in ambush.

The arrows are flying, (but) the bow is hidden: from the
Unseen World come upon youth a hundred arrows of hoary eld.

You must set foot on the plain of the heart (spirit), because in
the plain of (the body's) clay there is no opening (for spiritual
progress).

The heart is the abode of security, O friends; (it has) foun- 515
tains and rose-gardens within rose-gardens.

Turn towards the heart and journey on, O night-travellers:
therein are trees and (many) a flowing spring.

Do not go to the country: the country makes a fool of a man,
it makes the intellect void of light and splendour.

O chosen one, hear the Prophet's saying: "To dwell in the
country is the grave of the intellect."

If any one stay in the country a single day and evening, his
intellect will not be fully restored for a month.

For a (whole) month foolishness will abide with him: what 520
but these things should he reap from the parched herbage of the
country?

And he that stays a month in the country, ignorance and
blindness will be his (lot) for a long time.

What is "the country"? The Shaykh that has not been united
(with God), but has become addicted to[2] conventionality and
argument.

Compared with the town, (which is) Universal Reason, these
senses (of ours) are like asses (going round and round) in an ass-
mill with their eyes bandaged.

---

[1] *I.e.* through lowliness and self-abasement.
[2] Literally, "has put his hand to."

Leave this (inner meaning) and take the outward form of the tale: let the pearlseed alone and take the cornseed.

525 If there is no way to the pearl, come, take the wheat; if there is no way for you in that (direction), push on in this direction.

Take its outward (form)! Though the outward (form) fly crookedly (not straight), the outward (form) at last will lead (you) to the inward (meaning).

In sooth, the first (stage) of every human being is the form; after that (comes) the spirit, which is beauty of disposition.

How is the first (stage) of every fruit anything but the form? After that (comes) the delicious taste which is its real meaning.

First they make or buy a tent; afterwards they bring the Turcoman (their beloved) as a guest.

530 Deem your form to be the tent, your real essence the Turcoman; regard your essence as the sailor, your form as the ship.

For God's sake, quit this (topic) for a moment, so that the Khwája's ass may shake its bell (proceed on its journey).

How the Khwája and his family went to the country.

The Khwája and his children prepared an outfit and galloped on their beasts towards the country.

Merrily they rode afield; they chanted, "Travel, that ye may gain advantage";

For by travelling the moon becomes (splendid, like) Kay Khusraw: how should it become an emperor (*khusraw*) without travelling?

535 Through travel the pawn becomes a noble queen, and through travel Joseph gained a hundred objects of desire.

By day they scorched their faces in the sun, by night they were learning the way from the stars.

The bad road to them seemed good: from (their) delight in the country the road seemed like Paradise.

From sweet-lipped ones (even) bitterness becomes sweet; from the rose-garden (even) thorns become charming.

Colocynth turns into dates (when it comes) from the beloved; the (narrow) house is made (like) spacious fields by the housemate.

540 Oh, (there is) many a dainty youth that suffers thorns (of anguish) in the hope of (winning) a rose-cheeked moon-like (sweetheart).

Oh, (there is) many a porter, his back torn with wounds for the sake of the moon-faced one to whom he has lost his heart.

The ironsmith has blackened his beauty, that (when) night comes he may kiss the face of (a beloved like) the moon.

The merchant (sits), racked, on a bench (in his shop) till nightfall, because (some one tall and slender as) a cypress has taken root in his heart.

A trader is faring over sea and land: he runs (makes those swift journeys) for love of one who sits at home.

Whoever has a passion for that which is dead, 'tis in hope of 545 (gaining) one who has the features of the living.

The carpenter turns his face (attention) to wood, in the hope of rendering service to a fair one whose face is like the moon.

Do thou exert thyself in hope of the Living One who does not become lifeless after a day or two!

Do not from meanness choose a mean person as thy friend: that friendship in him is borrowed (unessential).

If thy friends other than God possess constancy (permanence), where is thy friendship with thy mother and father?

If any one but God is worthy to be relied upon, what has be- 550 come of thy friendship with thy nurse and tutor[1]?

Thy friendship with the milk and the teat did not endure, thy shyness of (going to) school did not endure.

That (friendship) was a radiance (cast) upon their wall: that sign (of the Sun) went back towards the Sun.

On whatsoever thing that radiance may fall, thou becomest in love with that (thing), O brave man.

On whatsoever existent thing thy love (is bestowed), that (thing) is gilded with Divine qualities.

When the goldenness has gone to its original source and 555 (only) the copper remains, (thy) nature is surfeited and proceeds to divorce (discard) it.

Withdraw thy foot from that which is gilded by His qualities, do not from ignorance call the base alloy beautiful;

For in base coin the beauty is borrowed: beneath the comeliness is the substance uncomely.

The gold is going from the face of the false coin into the mine (whence it came): do thou too go towards the Mine to which it is going.

The light is going from the wall up to the sun: do thou go to that Sun which ever goes (moves) in proportion (with eternal right and justice).

Henceforth take thou the water (that comes) from Heaven, 560 forasmuch as thou hast not found faithfulness in the aqueduct.

The lure to catch the wolf is (the sheep's tail; it is) not the place (shop) where the sheep's tail came from: how should that fierce wolf know the place of provenance?

---

[1] *Lálá*, the slave entrusted with the education of young boys, παιδαγωγός.

They (the Khwája and his family) imagined (that there would
be) gold tied in knots[1], (so) the deluded (party) were making
haste to (reach) the countryside.

Thus were they going along, laughing and dancing and cara-
coling towards the water-wheel[2].

Whenever they saw a bird flying in the direction of the country,
(their) patience rent its garments;

565   (And) they would kiss joyfully the face of any one who came
from the country, from his (the countryman's) neighbourhood,

Saying, "You have seen the face of our friend, therefore to
the (beloved) Soul you are (as) the soul, and to us (as) the eye."

How Majnún petted the dog that lived in Layla's abode.

(They behaved) like Majnún, who was (seen) petting a dog
and kissing it and melting (with fondness) before it:

He was pacing round it, stooping humbly in circumambula-
tion; he was also giving it pure sugar-julep (to drink).

An idle talker said, "O half-baked Majnún, what hypocrisy is
this that thou art always displaying?

570   A dog's muzzle is ever eating filth; a dog scrapes its séant
with its lips."

He recounted the dog's faults at some length: no one who
perceives faults (*'aybdán*) has got (even) a scent (inkling) of him
that knows the things unseen (*ghaybdán*)[3].

Majnún said, "Thou art entirely (external) form and body:
come within, and view it (the dog) through my eyes;

For this (dog) is a talisman sealed by (the hand of) the Lord:
this (dog) is the guardian of the abode of Laylá.

Look at its high aspiration and its heart and soul and know-
ledge; (consider) where it chose (to live) and made its dwelling-
place.

575   It is the dog of blessed countenance, (the dog) of my Cave[4];
nay, it is the sharer of my grief and woe.

The dog that stays in her abode, how should I give a single
hair of it to the lions?

Oh, since to her dogs the lions are (devoted) slaves, there is
no possibility of speaking (further). Silence, and farewell!"

If ye pass beyond form, O friends, 'tis Paradise and rose-
gardens within rose-gardens.

When thou hast broken and destroyed thine own form, thou
hast learned to break the form of everything.

580   After that, thou wilt break every form: like Ḥaydar ('Alí), thou
wilt uproot the gate of Khaybar.

---

[1] *I.e.* made ready for them and securely packed.
[2] *I.e.* the secondary cause of their anticipated wealth. Cf. v. 560.
[3] *I.e.* either the holy man or God himself.
[4] Referring to the dog of the Seven Sleepers. Cf. v. 208 *supra*.

That simple Khwája was duped by form, for he was going to the country on (the strength of) infirm words (vain promises).

(He was going) joyously towards the snare of that flattery, as a bird towards the bait of tribulation.

The bird deemed the bait a mark of kindness (on the part of the fowler), (although) that gift is (really) the extreme of cupidity and is not munificence;

(So) in desire for the bait the little birds are merrily flying and running towards that imposture.

If I acquaint thee (fully) with the joy of the Khwája, I fear, 585 O wayfarer, lest I make thee late.

I will abridge. When the village came in sight, it was not in sooth that village (which he was seeking), (so) he chose another road.

For about a month they were hurrying from village to village, because they did not well know the way to the (countryman's) village.

If anybody goes on the way without a leader, every two days' journey becomes one of a hundred years.

Whoever speeds towards the Ka'ba without a guide becomes contemptible, like these bewildered men.

Whoever takes up a trade (or profession) without (having) a 590 teacher becomes a laughing-stock in town and country.

Except it be (a) singular (case), (in the whole world) between East and West does a descendant of Adam put forth his head (come to birth) without parents?

He gains wealth who earns something; 'tis an extraordinary event when one hits upon a (buried) treasure.

Where is a Muṣṭafá (Mohammed) whose body is spirit, so that the Merciful (God) should teach (him) the *Qur'án*[1]?

For all those who are attached to the body He (God), in profusion of bounty, raised (the banner of) "*He taught by the pen*" as the means (of acquiring knowledge)[2].

O son, every greedy person is deprived (of spiritual blessings): 595 do not thou run like the greedy, (go) more slowly.

On that journey they (the townsman's party) suffered pains and anguish like the torment of a land-bird in fresh water.

They became sick of the village and the country and of the sugared expressions of such an uninstructed boor.

---

[1] Literally, "so that he should be (the object of the text) *The Merciful taught (him) the Qur'án*."

[2] *I.e.* God proclaimed in the *Qur'án* that He has made the pen the means of acquiring knowledge.

How the Khwája and his kinsfolk arrived at the village, and how the countryman pretended not to see or recognise them.

When, after a month, they arrived in that quarter, themselves without provisions and their beasts without fodder,

See how the countryman, from evil intent, still inflicts (on them) calamities small and great,

600 And keeps his face hidden from them by day, lest they should open their mouths in the direction of his orchard.

'Tis better that a face like that, which is wholly (composed of) hypocrisy and malice, should be hidden from Moslems.

There are faces on which demons are settled like gnats, as (though they were) guardsmen.

When you behold his (such a one's) face, they (the demons) fall upon you: either do not behold that face, (or) when you have beheld (it), do not laugh pleasantly.

Concerning such a wicked, sinful face God hath said, " *Verily, We will drag (him) by the forelock.*"

605 When they (the townsman's party) had made enquiry and found his (the countryman's) house, they hurried like kinsfolk to the door.

(Thereupon) the people in his house bolted the door. At this perverseness, the Khwája became mad-like,

But indeed it was no time for asperity: when you have fallen into the pit, what is the use of being enraged?

Five days they remained at his door: (they passed) the night in the cold, the day itself in the blaze of the sun.

Their remaining (there) was not from· heedlessness or asininity; nay, it was from necessity and want of an ass[1].

610 From necessity, the good are (often) bound to the vile: from sore hunger the lion will eat a putrid carcase.

He (the townsman) would see him (the countryman) and salute him, saying, "I am so-and-so, this is my name."

"Maybe," he said; "how should I know who thou art, whether thou art a dirty fellow or an honest gentleman[2]?"

"This moment," said he, "resembles the Resurrection, since a brother has come *to flee from his brother.*"

He would explain to him (the countryman), saying, "I am he from whose table thou didst eat viands manifold[3].

615 On such and such a day I bought that merchandise for thee: every secret that goes beyond the two (who share it) is published (to all).

---

[1] *I.e.* because they had no means of moving on.
[2] Literally, "associated with honesty."
[3] Literally, "twofold."

The people heard the secret of our affection; (as a rule) when the gullet has received bounty, the face hath (signs of) bashfulness[1]."

He (the countryman) would say to him, "Why dost thou talk nonsense? I know neither thee nor thy name nor thy dwelling-place."

On the fifth night there began such a (storm of) cloud and rain that the sky might (well) be astonished at its raining.

When the knife reached the bone[2], the Khwája knocked at the door, crying, "Call the master!"

When (at last), in response to a hundred urgent entreaties, he 620 came to the door, he said, "Why, what is it, my dear sir[3]?"

He replied, "I abandon those claims (to thy gratitude), I renounce that (recompense) which I was fancying.

I have suffered five years' pain: five days my miserable soul (hath been) amidst this heat and blaze."

One injustice from kindred and friends and family is in heaviness as three hundred thousand,

Because he (the sufferer) did not set his mind on (anticipate) his (the friend's) cruelty and injustice: his soul was accustomed to kindness and faithfulness from him.

Whatsoever is tribulation and sore grief to men, know for sure 625 that this is in consequence of its being contrary to habit.

He (the townsman) said (further), "O thou the sun of whose love is in decline, if thou hast shed my blood, I acquit thee.

On this night of rain give us a nook (to shelter in), so that at the Resurrection thou mayst obtain a viaticum (reward for the good work)."

"There is a nook," he replied, "belonging to the keeper of the vineyard: he keeps watch there against the wolf,

(With) bow and arrow in his hand on account of the wolf, so that he may shoot if the fierce wolf should come.

If thou wilt do that service, the place is thine; and if not, have 630 the kindness to seek another place."

He said, "I will do a hundred services, (only) give thou the place, and put that bow and arrow in my hand.

I will not sleep, I will guard the vines; if the wolf raise his head, I will shoot the arrow at him.

For God's sake do not leave me to-night, O double-hearted (hypocrite), (with) the rain-water overhead and the mud underneath!"

A nook was cleared, and he with his family went thither: ('twas) a narrow place and without room to turn.

Mounted upon one another, like locusts, (and crowded) from 635 terror of the flood into the corner of the cavern,

---

[1] *I.e.* "it is usual to show respect and gratitude to one's benefactor."
[2] *I.e.* in the extremity of his distress.
[3] Literally, "O soul of thy father."

During the night, the whole night, they all (were) crying, "O God, this serves us right, serves us right, serves us right."

This is what is deserved by him that consorted with the vile, or showed worthiness for the sake of the unworthy.

This is what is deserved by him that in vain desire gives up paying homage to the dust of the noble.

That you lick the dust and the wall of the pure (elect) is better (for you) than the vulgar and their vines and rose-gardens.

640 That you become a slave to a man of enlightened heart is better (for you) than that you should walk upon the crown of the head of kings[1].

From the kings of earth you will get nothing but the (empty) noise of a drum, O courier of (many) roads.

Even the townsmen are brigands in comparison with the Spirit. Who is the countryman? The fool that is without spiritual gifts.

This is what is deserved by him who, (when) the cry of a ghoul came to him, without rational foresight chose to move (towards the ghoul).

When repentance has gone from the (core of the) heart to the pericardium[2] after this it is of no use to acknowledge (one's sin).

645 (With) the bow and arrow in his hand, he (was) seeking the wolf all night to and fro.

The wolf, in sooth, was given power over him, like sparks of fire: (he was) seeking the wolf (outside), and (was) unaware of the wolf (within himself).

Every gnat, every flea, had become as a wolf and inflicted a wound upon them in that ruined place.

There was no opportunity even of driving away those gnats, because of (their) dread of an attack by the contumacious wolf,

Lest the wolf should[3] inflict some damage, (and then) the countryman would tear out the Khwája's beard.

650 In this wise (they were) gnashing their teeth till midnight: their souls were coming (up) from the navel to the lip.

Suddenly the figure of a deserted (solitary) wolf raised its head (appeared) from the top of a hillock.

The Khwája loosed the arrow from the thumbstall and shot at the animal, so that it fell to the ground.

In falling, wind escaped from the animal: the countryman uttered a wail and beat his hands,

(Crying), "O ungenerous (wretch), it is my ass-colt!" "Nay," said he, "this is the devilish wolf[4].

---

[1] *I.e.* "than that you should be a favourite of kings."
[2] *I.e.* "when the heart is filled with repentance."
[3] Reading نبايد.   [4] Literally, "the wolf like Ahriman."

The features of wolfishness are apparent in it; its form makes 655
(one) acquainted with its wolfishness."

"Nay," he said, "I know the wind that escaped from its arse
as well as (I know) water from wine.

Thou hast killed my ass-colt in the meadows—mayst thou
never be released from anguish!"

"Make a better investigation," he replied; "it is night, and
at night material objects are screened from the beholder.

Night causes many a thing to appear wrong and changed
(from its proper aspect): not every one has the (power of) seeing
correctly by night.

(Now there is) both night and clouds and heavy rain withal: 660
these three darknesses produce great error."

He said, "To me 'tis as (manifest as) bright day: I know (it),
it is the wind of my ass-colt.

Amongst twenty winds I know that wind as the traveller
(knows) his provisions for the journey."

The Khwája sprang up, and losing patience[1] he seized the
countryman by his collar,

Crying, "O fool and cutpurse, thou hast shown hypocrisy:
thou hast eaten both beng and opium together.

Amidst three darknesses thou knowest the wind of the ass: 665
how dost not thou know *me*, O giddy-head?

He that knows a colt at midnight, how should he not know
his own ten years' comrade?"

Thou art feigning to be distraught (with love of God) and a
gnostic: thou art throwing dust in the eyes of generosity,

Saying, "I have no consciousness even of myself: in my heart
there is no room for aught but God.

I have no recollection of what I ate yesterday: this heart takes
joy in nothing except bewilderment.

I am sane and maddened by God: remember (this), and 670
(since I am) in such a state of selflessness, hold me excusable.

He that eats carrion, that is to say, (drinks) date-wine—the
(religious) Law enrols him amongst[2] those who are excused.

The drunkard and eater of beng has not (the right of) divorce
or barter; he is even as a child: he is a person absolved and
emancipated.

The intoxication that arises from the scent of the unique
King—a hundred vats of wine never wrought *that* (intoxication)
in head and brain.

To him (the God-intoxicated man), then, how should the
obligation (to keep the Law) be applicable? The horse is fallen
(out of account) and has become unable to move[3].

---

[1] Literally, "he became impatient."
[2] Literally, "drew him to the side of."
[3] Literally, "has become without hand or foot."

675 Who in the world would lay a load upon the ass-colt? Who would give lessons in Persian to Bú Murra[1]?

When lameness comes, the load is taken off: God hath said, *It is no sin in the blind.*

I have become blind in regard to myself, seeing by (the grace of) God: therefore I am absolved from the small (obligation) and from the great."

Thou braggest of thy dervishhood and selflessness, (thou utterest) the wailful cries of those intoxicated with God,

Saying, "I know not earth from heaven." The (Divine) jealousy hath tried thee, tried thee (and found thee wanting).

680 Thus hath the wind of thy ass-colt put thee to shame, thus hath it affirmed the existence of thy self-negation[2].

In this wise doth God expose hypocrisy, in this wise doth He catch the quarry that has started away.

There are hundreds of thousands of trials, O father, for any one who says, "I am the captain of the Gate."

If the vulgar do not know him by (putting him to) the trial, (yet) the adepts of the Way will demand from him the token (of his veracity).

When a churl pretends to be a tailor, the king will throw down a piece of satin in front of him,

685 Saying, "Cut this into a wide undervest (*baghaltáq*)": from (as the result of) the trial there appear two horns on him[3].

Were there not a testing of every vicious person, every effeminate would be a Rustam in the fray.

Even suppose that the effeminate has put on a coat of mail: as soon as he feels the blow, he will become as a captive.

How will he that is intoxicated with God be restored to his senses by (the soft breath of) the west-wind[4]? The God-intoxicated man will not come to himself at the blast of the trumpet (of Resurrection).

The wine of God is true, not false: thou hast drunk buttermilk, thou hast drunk buttermilk, buttermilk, buttermilk!

690 Thou hast made thyself out to be a Junayd or a Báyazíd, (saying), "Begone, for I do not know a hatchet from a key."

How by means of hypocrisy, O contriver of fraud, wilt thou conceal depravity of nature and (spiritual) sloth and greed and concupiscence?

Thou makest thyself a Mansúr-i Halláj and settest fire to the cotton of thy friends,

---

[1] Abú Murra is the *kunya* (name of honour) of Iblís, who represents the supreme type of unteachable folly.
[2] These words are ironical. The speaker means that such an affirmation is equivalent to a denial.
[3] *I.e.* he is put to shame.
[4] *I.e.* if he were truly "intoxicated" he would not come to his senses on such a slight provocation.

Saying, "I do not know 'Umar from Bú Lahab, (but) I know
the wind of my ass-colt at midnight."

Oh, the ass that would believe this from an ass like thee, and
would make himself blind and deaf for thy sake!

Do not count thyself one of the travellers on the Way; thou 695
art a comrade of them that defile the Way: do not eat dung (do
not talk rubbish)!

Fly back from hypocrisy, hasten towards Reason: how shall
the wing of the phenomenal (unreal) soar to Heaven?

Thou hast feigned to be a lover of God, (but in truth) thou
hast played the game of love with a black devil.

At the Resurrection lover and beloved shall be tied in couples
and quickly brought forward (to judgement).

Why hast thou made thyself crazy and senseless? Where is
the blood of the vine[1]? Thou hast drunk *our* blood,

(Saying), "Begone, I do not know thee: spring away from me. 700
I am a gnostic who is beside himself and (I am) the Buhlúl[2] of
the village."

Thou art conceiving a false opinion of thy nearness to God,
thinking that the Tray-maker is not far from the tray;

(And) thou dost not see this, that the nearness of the
saints (to God) hath a hundred miracles and pomps and
powers.

By David iron is made (soft as) a piece of wax; in thy hand
wax is (hard) as iron.

Nearness (to God) in respect of (His) creating and sustaining
(us) is common to all, (but only) these noble ones[3] possess the
nearness (consisting) of the inspiration of Love.

Nearness is of various kinds, O father: the sun strikes (both) 705
on the mountains and on the gold (in the mine);

But between the sun and the gold there is a nearness (affinity)
of which the *bíd*-tree hath no knowledge.

(Both) the dry and fresh bough are near to the sun: how should
the sun be screened off from either?

But where[4] is the nearness of the sappy bough, from which
you eat ripe fruit?

From nearness to the sun let the dry bough get (if it can) any-
thing besides withering sooner!

O man without wisdom, do not be an inebriate of the sort that 710
(when) he comes (back) to his wits he feels sorry;

Nay, be one of those inebriates on account of whom, whilst
they are drinking the wine (of Divine Love), mature (strong)
intellects suffer regret[5].

---

[1] *I.e.* "thou art not drunken with (spiritual) wine."
[2] Buhlúl, one of the so-called "rational madmen," was a celebrated saint.
[3] The prophets and saints.   [4] *I.e.* "how much greater."
[5] *I.e.* they regret that they are not similarly "intoxicated."

O thou who, like a cat, hast caught (nothing better than) an old mouse, if thou art pot-valiant[1] with that wine (of Love), catch the Lion!

O thou who hast drunk of the phantom cup of Naught do not reel like them that are intoxicated with the (Divine) realities.

Thou art falling to this side and that, like the drunken: O thou (who art) on this side, there is no passage for thee on that side.

715　If thou (ever) find the way to that side, thenceforth toss thy head now to this side, now to that!

Thou art all on this side, (therefore) do not idly boast of that side: since thou hast not (died) the death (to self), do not agonise thyself in vain.

He with the soul of Khadir, (he) that does not shrink from death—if he know not the created (world), 'tis fitting.

Thou sweetenest thy palate with the savour of false imagination; thou blowest into the bag of selfhood and fillest it:

Then, at one prick of a needle thou art emptied of wind— may no intelligent man's body be fat (swollen) like this!

720　Thou makest pots of snow in winter: when they see the water how shall they maintain that (former) constancy?

How the jackal fell into the dyeing-vat and was dyed with many colours and pretended amongst the jackals that he was a peacock.

A certain jackal went into the dyeing-vat, stayed in the vat for a while,

And then arose, his skin having become particoloured, saying, 'I have become the Peacock of 'Illiyyín[2].''

His coloured fur had gained a charming brilliance, and the sun shone upon those colours.

He beheld himself green and red and roan and yellow, (so) he presented himself (gleefully) to the jackals.

725　They all said, "O little jackal, what is the matter, that thou hast in thy head manifold exultation?

Because of exultation thou hast turned aside from us (with disdain): whence hast thou brought this arrogance?"

One of the jackals went to him and said, "O so-and-so, hast thou acted deceitfully or hast thou (really) become one of those whose hearts rejoice (in God)[3]?

Thou hast acted deceitfully to the end that thou mayest jump on to the pulpit and by thy palaver give this folk (the feeling of) regret[4].

---

[1] See note on Book II, verse 343.
[2] A place in the Seventh Heaven.
[3] *I.e.* "art thou a hypocrite seeking to pose as a saint?"
[4] *I.e.* cause them to envy thy felicity.

Thou hast striven much, (but) thou hast not felt any (spiritual) ardour; hence from deceit thou hast exhibited a piece of impudence."

(Spiritual) ardour belongs to the saints and prophets; on the 730 other hand, impudence is the refuge of every impostor;

For they draw the people's attention to themselves, saying, "We are happy (with God)," though within (at heart) they are exceedingly unhappy.

How a braggart greased his lips and moustache every morning with the skin of a fat sheep's tail and came amongst his companions, saying, "I have eaten such and such (viands)."

A person, who (on account of his poverty) was lightly esteemed, used to grease his moustaches every morning

And go amongst the munificent (the rich), saying, "I have eaten some well-greased food at the party."

He would gaily put his hand on his moustache as a sign, meaning, "Look at my moustache!

For this is the witness to the truth of my words, and this is 735 the token of my eating greasy and delicious food."

His belly would say in soundless (mute) response, "May God destroy the plots of the liars!

Thy boasting hath set me on fire: may that greasy moustache of thine be torn out!

Were it not for thy foul boasting, O beggar, some generous man would have taken[1] pity on me;

And if thou hadst shown the ailment and hadst not played false, some physician would have prepared a remedy for it."

God hath said, "Do not move ear or tail crookedly: *their* 740 *veracity shall profit the veracious.*"

Ne recurvatus in antro dormiveris, O tu qui passus es nocturnam pollutionem[2]: reveal that which you have, and *act straight*;

Or if you tell not your fault, at least refrain from (idle) talk: do not kill yourself by ostentation and trickery.

If you have got any money, do not open your mouth: there are touchstones on the Way,

And for the touchstones too there are tests concerning their own (inward) states.

God hath said, "From birth unto death *they are tried every* 745 *year twice.*"

There is test upon test, O father: beware, do not (be ready to) buy yourself at the smallest test[3].

[1] Literally, "would have let fall."
[2] *I.e.* "do not attempt to hide thy fault."
[3] *I.e.* "do not be self-satisfied and conceited after you have undergone a slight probation."

How Balʿam the son of Báʿúr was (felt himself) secure, because the Lord had made (many) tests (of him) and he had come through them honourably[1].

Balʿam the son of Báʿúr and the accursed Iblís were disgraced at the ultimate test.

He (the boastful hypocrite), by his pretension, desires to be (reputed) rich, (but) his belly is execrating his moustache,

Crying, "Display that which he is hiding! He has consumed me (with anguish): O God, expose him!"

750 All the members of his body are his adversaries, for he prates of spring (while) they are in December.

Vain talk repels acts of kindness and tears off the bough of pity from the trunk of the tree.

Bring forward (practise) honesty, or else be silent, and then behold pity and enjoy it.

That belly became the adversary of his moustache and secretly had recourse to[2] prayer,

Crying, "O God, expose this idle brag of the base, in order that the pity of the noble may be moved towards me."

755 The belly's prayer was answered: the ardency of need put out a flag[3].

God hath said, "Though thou be a profligate and idolater, I will answer when thou callest Me."

Do thou cleave fast unto prayer and ever cry out: in the end it will deliver thee from the hands of the ghoul.

When the belly committed itself to God, the cat came and carried off the skin of that sheep's tail.

They ran after the cat, (but) she fled. The child (of the braggart), from fear of his scolding, changed[4] colour (turned pale).

760 The little child came into (the midst of) the company and took away the prestige of the boastful man.

It said, "The sheep's tail with which every morning you greased your lips and moustaches—

The cat came and suddenly snatched it away: I ran hard, but the effort was of no use."

Those who were present laughed from astonishment, and their feelings of pity began to be moved again.

They invited him (to eat) and kept him full-fed, they sowed the seed of pity in his soil.

765 When he had tasted honesty from the noble, he without arrogance (humbly) became devoted to honesty.

---

[1] Literally, "with a white face."
[2] Literally, "took hold of."
[3] *I.e.* "the fervour of the prayer produced a manifest effect."
[4] Literally, "shed."

How the jackal which had fallen into the dyer's vat pretended to be a peacock.

(In like fashion) that particoloured jackal came secretly and tapped on the lobe of the rebuker's ear.

"Prithee look at me and at my colour: truly the idolater possesses no idol like me.

Like the flower-garden I have become many-hued and lovely: bow in homage to me, do not withdraw from me (in aversion).

Behold my glory and splendour and sheen and radiance and colour! Call me the Pride of the World and the Pillar of the Religion!

I have become the theatre of the Divine Grace, I have become 770 the tablet on which the Divine Majesty is unfolded.

O jackals, take heed, do not call me a jackal: how should a jackal have so much beauty?"

Those jackals came thither *en masse*, like moths around the candle.

"Say then, what shall we call thee, O creature of (pure) substance?" He replied, "A peacock (brilliant) as Jupiter."

Then they said to him, "The spiritual peacocks have displays (with the Beloved) in the Rose-garden:

Dost thou display thyself like that?" "No," said he: "not 775 having gone into the desert, how should I tread[1] (the valley of) Miná?"

"Dost thou utter the cry of peacocks?" "Nay," said he. "Then, Master Bu 'l-'Alá[2], thou art not a peacock.

The peacock's garment of honour comes from Heaven: how wilt thou attain thereto by means of colours and pretences?"

Comparison of Pharaoh and his pretence of divinity to the jackal which pretended to be a peacock.

Thou art even as Pharaoh, who bejewelled his beard and in his asinine folly soared higher than Jesus.

He too was born of the generation of the she-jackal and fell into a vat of riches and power.

Every one who beheld his power and riches bowed down to 780 him in worship: he swallowed the worship of the idle mockers (worldlings).

That beggar in tattered cloak became miserably drunken with the people's worship and feelings of amazement.

Riches are a snake, for therein are poisons; and popular favour and worship is a dragon.

Ah, do not assume a virtue (which thou dost not possess), O Pharaoh: thou art a jackal, do not in any wise behave as a peacock.

---

[1] Reading ڪبود.   [2] A name signifying "Father of sublimity."

If thou appear in the direction of the peacocks, thou art incapable of (their) display and thou wilt be put to shame.

785 Moses and Aaron were as peacocks: they flapped the wings of display upon thy head and face.

Thy foulness and disgrace were exposed, thou didst fall headlong from thy height.

When thou sawest the touchstone, thou becamest black, like adulterated coin: the leonine figure vanished, and the dog was revealed.

O foul mangy dog, through greed and exuberant insolence do not clothe thyself in the lion's skin.

The roar of the lion will demand from thee the test (of thy sincerity). The figure of a lion, and then the dispositions of dogs!

Explanation of (the text), And thou wilt surely know them in the perversion of their speech.

790 God said to the Prophet in the course (of the *Qur'án*), "One sign of the hypocritical is easier (to perceive than other signs):

Though the hypocrite be big, handsome, and terrible, thou wilt recognise him in his perverse enunciation and speech."

When you are buying earthenware pots, you make a trial, O purchaser.

You give the pot a tap with your hand: why? In order that you may know the cracked one by the sound (which it makes).

The voice of the cracked one is different; the voice is a *cháwúsh* (beadle): it goes in front of it (the pot).

795 The voice comes in order to make it known: it determines (the character of) it, as the verb (determines the form of) the *maṣdar* (verbal noun)[1].

When the subject of (Divine) probation cropped up[2], the story of Hárút at once came into my memory.

The Story of Hárút and Márút and their boldness in encountering the probation of God most High.

Before this (occasion)[3], we had told a little of it: what, indeed, should we tell? (We can tell only) one (item) of its thousands.

I wished to speak of the (spiritual) truths (contained) in it, (but) till now they have remained (untold) on account of hindrances[4].

(Now) once again a little of its much shall be told—the description (as it were) of a single limb of the elephant.

---

[1] The verb, which in Arabic determines the form of the *maṣdar*, is compared to the voice which indicates the qualities of the person or thing whence it proceeds.
[2] Literally, "showed a face." [3] See Book I, v. 3321 ff.
[4] *I.e.* because the discourse led me away in other directions.

Listen to (the tale of) Hárút and Márút, O thou[1] to whose 800
face we are (devoted) slaves and servants.

They (Hárút and Márút) were intoxicated with the spectacle
of God and with the marvels of the King's gradual temptation
(of them).

Such intoxication arises (even) from God's gradual temptation,
so that (you may judge) what intoxications are wrought by the
ascension to God.

The bait in His snare produced intoxication like this: what
things, (then), can the table of His bounty reveal!

They were drunken and freed from the noose: they were
uttering rapturous cries in the fashion of lovers;

(But) in their road there was one ambush and trial: its mighty 805
wind would sweep the mountain away like straw.

The (Divine) trial was turning them upside down, (but)
how should one that is drunken have consciousness of these
things?

To him pit and open field are one, to him dungeon and pit are
a pleasant path to tread.

The mountain-goat runs up that high mountain for the sake
of (getting) some harmless food[2].

Whilst he browses, suddenly he sees another trick played by
the ordinance of Heaven.

He casts his gaze upon another mountain: on that other moun- 810
tain he espies a she-goat.

Straightway his eye is darkened: he leaps madly from this
mountain to that.

To him it seems as near (and easy) as to run round the sink
(in the court) of a house.

Those thousands of ells (are made to) appear to him (as) two
ells, in order that from mad infatuation the impulse to leap may
come to him.

As soon as he leaps, he falls midway between the two pitiless
mountains.

He had fled to the mountain (to escape) from the hunters: his 815
very refuge shed his blood.

The hunters are seated between the two mountains in ex-
pectation of this awesome decree (of God).

The capture of this (mountain-)goat is, for the most part,
(accomplished) in this manner; else (it would be difficult, for)
he is agile and nimble and quick to see the enemy.

Though Rustam have (a huge) head and moustache, lust will
certainly be the snare to catch his feet.

Be cut off, like me, from the intoxication of lust: look at the
intoxication of lust in the camel!

---

[1] Husámu'ddín.   [2] *I.e.* in order to feed unmolested.

820 Know, again, that this intoxication of lust in the (terrestrial) world is (to be) deemed of small account beside the intoxication of the angels.

The intoxication of that one (the angel) breaks (reduces to insignificance) the intoxication of this one (the human being): how should he (the angel) show any propensity to lust?

Until you have drunk sweet water, briny water is sweet, sweet as the light in the eye;

(But) a single drop of the wines of Heaven causes the soul to be rapt away from the wine and cupbearers (of this world)—

So that (you may imagine) what intoxications befall the angels and the spirits purified by the Divine glory,

825 Who have set their hearts on that wine at one smell (of it), and have broken the jar of this world's wine;—

Except, maybe, them that are in despair and far (from God), (outcasts) like infidels hidden (buried) in graves,

(Them that) have lost all hope of both worlds and have sown thorns without end.

Therefore they (Hárút and Márút), because of their feelings of intoxication, said, "Alas, we would rain upon the earth, like clouds;

We would spread in this place of injustice (a carpet of) justice and equity and devotions and faithfulness."

830 This they said, and the Divine decree was saying (to them), "Stop! before your feet there is many an unseen pitfall."

Beware, do not run boldly into the desert of woe! Beware, do not push on blindly into the Karbalá (of tribulation)[1],

For because of the hair and bones of the perished the travellers' feet find no way.

The whole way is (covered with) bones and hair and sinews: many is the thing that the sword of Vengeance hath made nothing.

God hath said that (His) servants (who are) attended by (His) help walk on the earth quietly and meekly.

835 How should a bare-footed man go into the thorn-thicket save with halting and reflection and cautiously?

The Decree was saying this (to them), but their ears were closed in the (muffling) veil of their hotheadedness.

(All) eyes and ears have been closed, except for them that have escaped from themselves.

Who but Grace shall open the eyes? Who but Love shall allay the (Divine) Wrath?

Truly, may no one in the world have toil without (God's) prospering (it)! And God best knoweth the right course.

---

[1] See note on v. 73, *supra*.

The Story of Pharaoh's dream of the coming of Moses, on whom be peace, and how he took thought to relieve himself (of the threatened danger).

Inasmuch as Pharaoh's toil was unblest (by God), whatsoever 840 he would stitch, that (stitching) was (in effect an act of) ripping asunder.

He had a thousand astrologers at his beck, and also a countless multitude of dream-interpreters and magicians.

There was shown to him in a dream the coming of Moses, who would destroy Pharaoh and his kingdom.

He said to the interpreters and astrologers, "How may (the fulfilment of) the ill-boding phantasm and dream be warded off?"

They all said to him, "We will contrive something, we will waylay the birth (of Moses), like brigands."

(They waited) till the night arrived on which the begetting 845 (of Moses) took place; those Pharaoh's men deemed it advisable,

Early on that day, to bring forth the King's banquet and throne towards the *maydán* (public arena outside of the city),

(Proclaiming), "Welcome, O all ye Israelites! The King calls you from that place (where ye are),

That he may show unto you his face unveiled, and do kindness unto you for the sake of the (Divine) recompense";

For to those captives there was naught but farness (from Pharaoh's presence): the sight of Pharaoh was not permitted (to them).

If they fell in with him on the road, they would lie (flat) on 850 their faces on account of the law.

The law was this: no captive in or out of season shall behold the countenance of that Prince,

And whenever on the road he hears the shout of the (royal) beadles, he shall turn his face towards a wall, that he may not see;

And if he see his face, he shall be guilty of a crime, and the worst punishment shall befall him[1].

They (the Israelites) had a greed for the inaccessible countenance, since Man is greedy for that which has been forbidden.

How they summoned the Israelites to the maydán, as a device to prevent the begetting of Moses, on whom be peace.

"O captives, go ye to the *maydán*, for there is hope (for you) 855 of seeing (Pharaoh) and (experiencing) munificence from the King of kings."

When the Israelites heard the glad news, they were thirsting and longing exceedingly for that (spectacle).

[1] Literally, "that which is worse (worst) shall come upon his head.'

They swallowed the trick and hastened in that direction and made themselves ready for the (promised) unveiling.

Story.

('Twas) even as (when) here the crafty Moghul said, "I am seeking a certain one of the Egyptians.

Bring the Egyptians together on this side, in order that he who is wanted may come to hand."

860 Whenever any one came, he said, "'Tis not this one: oh, come in, sir, and sit in that corner,"

Till in this fashion they all were assembled, and they (the Moghuls) beheaded them by means of this trick.

(Through) the ill-starredness (which they incurred in consequence) of the fact that they would not obey God's summoner (and turn submissively) towards the call to prayer,

The invitation of the deceiver inveigled them. O righteous man, beware of the deceit of the Devil!

Hearken to the cry of the poor and needy, lest thine ear receive (with approval) the cry of a cunning rogue.

865 (Even) if the beggars (dervishes) are covetous and depraved, (yet) seek the man of heart (the spiritual man) amongst the gluttons.

At the bottom of the sea there are pearls (mingled) with pebbles: glories are (to be found) amidst shames.

The Israelites, then, bestirred themselves mightily, running betimes towards the *maydán*.

When he (Pharaoh) by cunning had brought them into the *maydán*, he displayed his face to them, looking very fresh (cheerful and gay).

He showed fondness and gave presents: that Emperor bestowed both gifts and promises.

870 After that, he said: "For your lives' sake, do ye all sleep in the *maydán* to-night!"

They answered him, saying, "We will do service (to thee): if thou desire, we will dwell here a month."

How Pharaoh returned from the maydán to the city, glad at having parted the Israelites from their wives on the night of the conception (of Moses).

At nightfall the King came back (to the city), rejoicing and saying (to himself), "The conception is to-night, and they are far from their wives."

'Imrán, his treasurer, also came to the city in attendance upon him as his companion.

He said, "O 'Imrán, do thou sleep at this door. Beware! go not to thy wife or seek to lie with her."

He replied, "I will sleep at this portal of thine; I will think of 875
naught but thy pleasure."

'Imrán, too, was one of the Israelites, but he was (dear as)
heart and soul to Pharaoh.

How should he (Pharaoh) have thought that he ('Imrán)
would disobey (Pharaoh's orders) and do that which (was) the
dread of Pharaoh's soul?

*How 'Imrán lay with the mother of Moses and how the mother of
Moses, on him be peace became pregnant.*

The King departed, and he ('Imrán) slept at the door; at mid-
night his wife came to see him.

The wife fell upon him and kissed his lips: she roused him
from his slumber in the night.

He awoke and saw that his wife was fair and that she rained 880
kisses from her lips upon his.

'Imrán said, "How didst thou come at this time?" She said,
"From desire (of thee) and from the Divine ordinance."

The man drew her lovingly into his arms; at that moment he
did not rise to (did not engage in) battle with himself.

Concubuit cum ea et depositum (semen) tradidit; then he
said, "O wife, this is not a small matter.

A steel struck upon the stone, and a fire was born—a fire that
shall take vengeance on the King and his empire.

I am as the cloud, thou the earth, and Moses the plant. God 885
is (as) the king on the chessboard, and we are checkmated,
checkmated[1].

Deem (both) checkmate and victory (to proceed) from the
King[2], O spouse: do not deem them to be from us, do not jeer
at us.

That of which this Pharaoh is afraid came into being at the
moment when I lay with thee.

*How after having lain with her 'Imrán charged his wife to
pretend that she had not visited him.*

Do not reveal aught of these things, do not breathe a word,
lest there come upon me and thee a hundred sorrows.

In the end the effects of this will be made manifest, forasmuch
as the signs have (already) appeared, O beloved."

Forthwith from the direction of the *maydán* loud cries were 890
(heard) coming from the people, and the air was filled (with
noise).

Thereupon the King, in terror, sprang forth bare-footed (from
his chamber), saying, "Hark, what are these tumults?

[1] *I.e.* "God is omnipotent, and we are helpless."   [2] God.

What is the noise and uproar from the direction of the *maydán*, in fear whereof genie and demon are fleeing in dismay?"

'Imrán said, "May our King live (long)! The people of Israel are rejoicing on account of thee.

Because of the bounty of the King they are making merry and dancing and clapping their hands."

895 He (Pharaoh) said, "Maybe it is this, but it makes me very suspicious and anxious.

How Pharaoh was frightened by the noise.

This sound hath marred my soul and aged me with bitter pain and grief."

The King was pacing to and fro, all night he was even as a woman in the hour of childbirth.

Every moment he would say, "O 'Imrán, these clamours have upset me mightily."

Poor 'Imrán had not the courage to relate his intercourse with his wife,

900 How the wife of 'Imrán had stolen to his side, so that the star of Moses appeared.

Whenever any prophet enters into the womb, his star becomes conspicuous in the sky.

The appearance of the star of Moses, on whom be peace, in the sky and the outcry of the astrologers in the maydán.

His star appeared in the sky, to the confusion of Pharaoh and his plots and devices.

Day broke: he (Pharaoh) said to him ('Imrán), "O 'Imrán, go, inform thyself concerning that uproar and noise."

'Imrán rode to the *maydán* and said, "What uproar was this? The King of kings has not slept."

905 Every astrologer, with head bare and garment rent, kissed the earth (before him), like mourners.

Their voices were choked with lamentation, like mourners, and their guise (dishevelled).

They had plucked out their beards and hair; their faces were torn; they had cast earth on their heads, and their eyes were filled with blood.

He ('Imrán) said, "Is it well (with you)? What is this perturbation and emotion? Does the unlucky year give an evil sign?"

They offered excuses and said, "O Amír, the hand of His predestination hath made us captive.

910 We have done all this, and (now) Fortune is darkened: the King's enemy has come into being and has prevailed.

During the night the star of that boy became clearly visible, to our confusion, on the front of heaven.

The star of that prophet shot up in the sky: we, from weeping, began to shed stars (glistening tears)."

'Imrán, with a right glad heart and from hypocrisy, was beating his hands on his head and crying, "Alas, all is lost[1]."

'Imrán feigned to be wrathful and grim, he went (amongst them) senseless and witless, like madmen.

He feigned to be ignorant and pushed forward and addressed 915 to the company (of astrologers) words exceeding rough.

He made himself out to be bitterly annoyed and grieved, he played (with) reversed dice.

He said to them, "Ye have deceived my King, ye have not refrained from treachery and covetousness.

Ye roused the King (to go) towards the *maydán*, ye let our King's honour go to waste.

Ye put your hands on your breasts in warrant, saying, 'We will set the King free from cares.'"

The King too heard (how the astrologers excused themselves) 920 and said, "O traitors, I will hang you up without quarter.

I exposed myself to derision, I squandered riches on my enemies,

To the end that to-night all the Israelites might remain far away from meeting with their wives.

Wealth and honour are gone, and all is done in vain: is this (true) friendship and (are these) the deeds of the noble?

For years ye have been taking stipends and robes of honour and devouring kingdoms as ye pleased[2].

Was this (the only result of) your judgement and wisdom and 925 astrology? Ye are lickspittles and deceivers and ill-omened.

I will rend you to pieces and set you ablaze, I will tear off your noses and ears and lips.

I will make you fuel for the fire, I will make your past pleasure unsweet to you."

They prostrated themselves and said, "O Khedive, if (this) one time the Devil has prevailed against us,

(Yet) for years we have warded off afflictions: the imagination is dumbfounded by that which we have done.

(Now) it (the prevention of this calamity) has eluded us, and 930 his conception has occurred: semen ejus exsiliit et in uterum irrepsit;

But (we crave) pardon for this, (and) we shall watch the day of birth, O King and Sovereign.

We shall observe (by the stars) the day of his nativity, that this event may not escape and evade us.

---

[1] Literally, "Alas, the (grief of) parting!"
[2] Literally, "(permission having been) freely granted."

If we do not keep watch for this, kill us, O thou to whose judgement (our) thoughts and intelligence are slaves."

For nine months he was counting day after day, lest the arrow of the Decree that transfixes its enemy should fly (from the bow).

935   Any one who makes a night-attack upon (lies in wait to oppose) Doom falls headlong and drinks of his own blood.

When the earth shows enmity to the sky, it becomes salty (barren) and presents a spectacle of death[1].

(When) the picture (creature) struggles hand to hand with the Painter (Creator), it (only) tears out its own moustaches and beard.

How Pharaoh summoned the women who had new-born children to the maydán, (doing this) also for the sake of his plot (against Moses).

After nine months the King brought out his throne to the *maydán* and made a strict proclamation.

" O women, go with your babes to the *maydán*; go forth, all ye of Israel.

940   Just as last year robes of honour were bestowed on the men, and every one of them bore away gold,

Hark, O women, this year it is your fortune, so that each one (of you) may obtain the thing she desires.

He will give the women robes of honour and donations; on the children too he will put mitres of gold.

Take heed! Every one of you that has borne a child during this month shall receive treasures from the mighty King."

The women went forth with their babes: they came joyfully to the King's tent.

945   Every woman that had newly given birth went forth from the city to the *maydán*, unsuspicious of guile and vengeance.

When all the women were gathered around him, they (the King's officers) took away from the mothers whatever was male,

And cut off its head, saying, "This is a precaution, that the (King's) enemy may not grow up and that disorder may not increase."

How Moses was born and how the officers came to 'Imrán's house and how it was divinely revealed to the mother of Moses that she should cast Moses into the fire.

'Imrán's wife herself, who had brought Moses (with her), kept aloof[2] from that turmoil and fume.

That villain (Pharaoh) sent the midwives into the houses for the purpose of spying.

---

[1] Literally, "lifts up its head (rises into view) from a state of death."
[2] Literally, "gathered in (withdrew) her skirt."

They gave information of her, saying, "Here is a child: she 950 (his mother) did not come to the *maydán*: (make inquiry), for she is under suspicion and doubt.

In this street there is a comely woman: she has a child, but she is an artful one."

Then the officers came: she, by the command of God, cast the child into the stove.

From that omniscient One revelation came to the woman that this boy is of the stock of the Friend (of God)[1],

(And that) through the protection of (the Divine word), "*O fire, be cool*," the fire will not be hot and untamed.

In consequence of the revelation the woman cast him amidst 955 the sparks: the fire produced no effect on the body of Moses.

Then the officers went away without having attained their object, (but) again the informers, who were aware of it[2],

Raised an altercation with the officers before Pharaoh for the sake of (earning) some petty coins,

Saying, "O officers, go back thither, and look very carefully in the upper rooms."

How it was divinely revealed to the mother of Moses that she should throw Moses into the water.

Once more the revelation came: "Throw him into the water; keep thy face in hope and do not tear thy hair.

Throw him into the Nile and put trust (in Me): I will bring 960 thee to him happily[3]."

This discourse hath no end. All his (Pharaoh's) plots (only) entangled his (own) legs and feet.

He was killing hundreds of thousands of children outside, (whilst) Moses (remained) indoors in the upper part of the house.

Wherever were embryos (new-born children), in his frenzy that far-seeing blind man was killing them by cunning devices.

The craft of the iniquitous Pharaoh was a dragon: it had devoured the craft of the kings of the world;

But one that was a greater Pharaoh than it came into sight and 965 swallowed both him and his craft.

It (Pharaoh's craft) was a dragon: the rod (of Moses) became a dragon, and this devoured that by the aid of God.

Hand is above hand: how far is this (series)? Up to God, for *unto Him is the end.*

For that (Omnipotence) is a sea without bottom or shore: beside it all the seas together are (but) as a torrent.

---

[1] Abraham.
[2] *I.e.* "who knew that Moses was there."
[3] Literally, "with (thy) face white."

If (human) devices and expedients are a dragon, (yet) beside
(*there is no god*) *except Allah* they all are naught.

970   Now that my exposition has reached this point, it lays down
its head and expires; and God best knoweth the right course.

That which was in Pharaoh, the same is in thee, but thy
dragon is confined in the pit[1].

Alas, all this (concerning Pharaoh) is what passes in thee:
thou wouldst fain fasten it on Pharaoh.

If they say it of thee, there arises in thee a feeling of estrange-
ment[2]; and (if they tell it) of another, it seems to thee a fable.

What ruin is wrought in thee by the accursed sensual soul!
This familiar casts thee exceeding far (from God).

975   Thy fire hath not Pharaoh's fuel; otherwise, it is one that
throws out flames like Pharaoh.

Story of the snake-catcher who thought the frozen serpent was dead and wound it in ropes and brought it to Baghdád.

Listen to a tale of the chronicler, in order that you may get an
inkling of this veiled mystery.

A snake-catcher went to the mountains to catch a snake by
his incantations.

Whether one be slow or speedy (in movement), he that is a
seeker will be a finder.

Always apply yourself with both hands (with all your might)
to seeking, for search is an excellent guide on the way.

980   (Though you be) lame and limping and bent in figure and
unmannerly, ever creep towards Him and be in quest of Him.

Now by speech and now by silence and now by smelling,
catch in every quarter the scent of the King.

Jacob said to his sons, "Make search for Joseph beyond (all)
bounds.

In this search earnestly direct your every sense towards every
side, like one that is ready."

He (Jacob) said, "*Do not despair of God's breath (mercy)*";
go thou (also) to and fro as one that has lost his son.

985   Inquire by means of the sense of the mouth[3], and lay your
ears on the four roads of that (which ye seek)[4].

Whenever a sweet scent comes, smell in that direction, for ye
are acquainted with that direction.

Whenever thou art aware of a kindness from any one, 'tis
possible thou mayst find the way to the source of the kindness.

---

[1] *I.e.* "thy passions are held in restraint by lack of the means to indulge
them."

[2] *I.e.* "thou art bitterly offended."

[3] *I.e.* by means of speech.

[4] *I.e.* "listen attentively, so that you may hear whatever information comes
from any quarter."

All these lovely things are from a deep Sea: leave the part and keep thine eye (fixed) upon the Whole.

The wars of mankind are for the sake of Beauty; the garniture of ungarnishedness is the sign of the Ṭúbá tree.

The angers of mankind are for the sake of Peace; restlessness 990 is ever the snare for Rest.

Every blow is for the sake of fondness; every complaint makes (thee) aware of gratitude (due for benefits received).

Smell (all the way) from the part to the Whole, O noble one; smell (all the way) from opposite to opposite, O wise one.

Assuredly wars bring peace; the snake-catcher sought the snake for the purpose of friendship.

Man seeks a snake for the purpose of friendship and cares for one that is without care (for him)[1].

He (the snake-catcher) was searching round about the moun- 995 tains for a big snake in the days of snow.

He espied there a huge dead dragon, at the aspect whereof his heart was filled with fear.

(Whilst) the snake-catcher was looking for snakes in the hard winter, he espied a dead dragon.

The snake-catcher catches snakes in order to amaze the people—behold the foolishness of the people!

Man is a mountain: how should he be led into temptation? How should a mountain become amazed at a snake?

Wretched Man does not know himself: he has come from a 1000 high estate and fallen into lowlihood.

Man has sold himself cheaply: he was satin, he has sewn himself on (become attached) to a tattered cloak.

Hundreds of thousands of snakes and mountains are amazed at him: why (then) has he become amazed and fond of a snake?

The snake-catcher took up that snake and came to Baghdád for the sake of (exciting) astonishment.

In quest of a paltry fee he carried along a dragon like the pillar of a house,

Saying, "I have brought a dead dragon: I have suffered 1005 agonies[2] in hunting it."

He thought it was dead, but it was living, and he did not see it very well[3].

It was frozen by frosts and snow: it was alive, but it presented the appearance of the dead.

The world is frozen: its name is *jamád* (inanimate): *jámid* is (means) "frozen," O master.

Wait till the sun of the Resurrection shall become manifest, that thou mayst see the movement of the world's body.

---

[1] *I.e.* he attaches himself to the carnal soul, and feels affection towards the world and its vanities.

[2] Literally, "I have consumed livers."   [3] *I.e.* his view was superficial.

1010 When here (in this world) the rod of Moses became a snake, information was given to the intellect concerning motionless (inanimate) beings.

Since He (God) made thy piece of earth a man, thou shouldst recognise (the real nature of) the entire sum of the particles of earth:

(That) from this standpoint they are dead and from that standpoint they are living; (that they are) silent here and speaking yonder.

When He sends them from that quarter towards us, the rod becomes a dragon in relation to us.

The mountains too make a song like that of David, and the substance of iron is (as) wax in the hand.

1015 The wind becomes a bearer for Solomon, the sea becomes capable of understanding words in regard to Moses[1].

The moon becomes able to see the sign in obedience to Aḥmad (Mohammed)[2], the fire becomes wild-roses for Abraham[3].

The earth swallows Qárún (Korah) like a snake; the Moaning Pillar[4] comes into (the way of) righteousness.

The stone salaams to Aḥmad (Mohammed); the mountain sends a message to Yaḥyá (John the Baptist)[5].

(They all say), "We have hearing and sight and are happy, (although) with you, the uninitiated, we are mute."

1020 Forasmuch as ye are going towards (are inclined to) inanimateness (worldliness), how shall ye become familiar with the spiritual life of inanimate beings?

Go (forth) from inanimateness into the world of spirits, hearken to the loud noise of the particles of the world.

The glorification of God by inanimate beings will become evident to thee; the doubts suggested by (false) interpretations will not carry thee away (from the truth).

Since thy soul hath not the lamps (the lights necessary) for seeing, thou hast made interpretations,

Saying, "How should visible glorification (of God) be the meaning intended? The claim to see (that glorification) is an erroneous fancy.

1025 Nay, the sight of that (inanimate object) causes him that sees it to glorify God at the time when he regards its significance.

Therefore, inasmuch as it reminds you of glorification[6], that indication (which it gives to you) is even as (equivalent to its) uttering (the words of glorification)."

---

[1] Qur'án, xxvi, 63–66.
[2] Alluding to the splitting of the moon, a miracle said to have been performed by Mohammed.
[3] The fire into which Abraham was cast by order of Nimrod.
[4] Book I, vv. 2113 ff.
[5] When Yaḥyá was fleeing from the Jews, a mountain offered to conceal him in its interior.   [6] I.e. "leads you to glorify God."

This is the interpretation of the Mu'tazilites and of those who do not possess the light of immediate (mystical) intuition.

When a man has not escaped from sense-perception, he will be a stranger to the ideas of the unseen world.

This discourse hath no end. The snake-catcher, with a hundred pains, was bringing the snake along,

Till (at last) the would-be showman[1] arrived at Baghdád, 1030 that he might set up a public show at the cross-roads.

The man set up a show on the bank of the Tigris, and a hubbub arose in the city of Baghdád—

"A snake-catcher has brought a dragon: he has captured a marvellous rare beast."

Myriads of simpletons[2] assembled, who had become a prey to him as he (to it) in his folly.

They were waiting (to see the dragon), and he too was waiting for the scattered people to assemble.

The greater the crowd, the better goes the begging and con- 1035 tributing (of money).

Myriads of idle babblers assembled, forming a ring, sole against sole[3].

Man took no heed of woman: on account of the throng they were mingled together like nobles and common folk at the Resurrection.

When he (the snake-catcher) began to move the cloth (which covered the dragon), the people in the crowd strained their throats (necks),

And (saw that) the dragon, which had been frozen by intense cold, was underneath a hundred kinds of coarse woollen cloths and coverlets.

He had bound it with thick ropes: that careful keeper had 1040 taken great precaution for it.

During the delay (interval) of expectation and coming to-gether, the sun of 'Iráq shone upon the snake.

The sun of the hot country warmed it; the cold humours went out of its limbs.

It had been dead, and it revived: from astonishment (at feel-ing the sun's heat) the dragon began to uncoil itself[4].

By the stirring of that dead serpent the people's amazement was multiplied a hundred thousandfold.

With amazement they started shrieking and fled *en masse* from 1045 its motion.

It set about bursting the bonds, and at that loud outcry (of the people) the bonds on every side went crack, crack.

---

[1] Literally, "he who sought (to attract) a crowd."
[2] Literally, "those whose beards are immature."
[3] *I.e.* standing closely packed together on tiptoe.
[4] Literally, "to move upon itself."

It burst the bonds and glided out from beneath—a hideous dragon roaring like a lion.

Many people were killed in the rout: a hundred heaps were made of the fallen slain.

The snake-catcher became paralysed with fear on the spot, crying, "What have I brought from the mountains and the desert?"

1050 The blind sheep awakened the wolf: unwittingly it went towards its 'Azrá'íl (Angel of death).

The dragon made one mouthful of that dolt: blood-drinking (bloodshed) is easy for Hajjáj[1].

It wound and fastened itself on a pillar and crunched the bones of the devoured man.

The dragon is thy sensual soul: how is it dead? It is (only) frozen by grief and lack of means.

If it obtain the means of Pharaoh, by whose command the water of the river (Nile) would flow,

1055 Then it will begin to act like Pharaoh and will waylay a hundred (such as) Moses and Aaron.

That dragon, under stress of poverty, is a little worm, (but) a gnat is made a falcon by power and riches.

Keep the dragon in the snow of separation (from its desires); beware, do not carry it into the sun of 'Iráq.

So long as that dragon of thine remains frozen, (well and good); thou art a mouthful for it, when it gains release.

Mortify it and become safe from (spiritual) death; have no mercy: it is not one of them that deserve favours;

1060 For (when) the heat of the sun of lust strikes upon it, that vile bat of thine flaps its wings.

Lead it manfully to the (spiritual) warfare and battle: God will reward thee with access (to Him).

When that man brought the dragon into the hot air, and the insolent brute became well (again),

Inevitably it wrought those mischiefs, my dear friend, (and others) too, twenty times as many as we have told.

Dost thou hope, without using violence, to keep it bound in quiet and faithfulness?

1065 How should this wish be fulfilled for any worthless one? It needs a Moses to kill the dragon.

By his dragon[2] hundreds of thousands of people were killed in the rout, as he had designed[3].

---

[1] The tyrannical governor of 'Iráq, who died in A.D. 714.
[2] *I.e.* by his rod which became a dragon.
[3] Literally, "from his design."

How Pharaoh threatened Moses, on whom be peace.

Pharaoh said to him, "Why didst thou, O Kalím[1], kill the people and cause fear to fall (on them)?

The people were put to flight and rout by thee; in the rout the folk were killed through slipping (and being crushed to death).

Necessarily, the folk have come to regard thee as their enemy; (both) men and women have conceived hatred of thee in their breasts.

Thou wert calling the people to (follow) thee, (but) it has 1070 turned out contrariwise: the folk cannot but resist thee.

I too, though I am creeping (shrinking) back from thy malice, am concocting a plan[2] to requite thee.

Put away from thine heart the thought[3] that thou wilt deceive me or that thou wilt get any follower but thy shadow.

Be not deluded by that which thou hast contrived: thou hast (only) cast terror into the hearts of the people.

Thou mayst bring (forward) a hundred such (devices), and thou wilt be exposed in the same way; thou wilt become despicable and the laughing-stock of the mob.

Many have been impostors like thee, (but) in our Egypt they 1075 have been brought to disgrace in the end."

The answer of Moses to Pharaoh concerning the threats which he made against him.

He (Moses) said, "I admit nothing as co-partner with the command of God: if His command shall shed my blood, there is no fear (on my part).

I am content, I am thankful, O adversary: here (I am) disgraced, but with God (I am) honoured.

In the sight of the people (I am) contemptible and wretched and a laughing-stock: in God's sight (I am) loved and sought and approved.

I say this (merely as a matter) of words[4]; otherwise (in fact), to-morrow (on the Day of Judgement) God will make *thee* one of the black-faced.

Glory belongs to Him and to His servants (alone): recite 1080 (from the *Qur'án*) the sign thereof (made manifest) through Adam and Iblís.

The explanation of (the attributes of) God, like God (Himself), hath no limit. Take heed, close thy mouth and turn over a (new) leaf."

---

[1] See note on Book II, v. 360.
[2] Literally, "am cooking a pot."
[3] Literally, "remove thy heart from this."
[4] *I.e.* the truth is just the reverse of what the people say.

The reply of Pharaoh to Moses, on whom be peace.

Pharaoh said to him, "The leaf is under my authority; the book and register of authority is mine at this moment.

The people of the world have chosen[1] me: art thou wiser than all, O fellow?

O Moses, thou hast vaunted[2] thyself. Hark, begone! Have less regard for thyself, be not self-deluded.

1085   I will assemble the magicians of the world, that I may exhibit thy foolishness to the city.

(But) this will not be done in a day or two: give me time (and wait) till the forty days (which end in the month) of Tamúz."

The answer of Moses, on whom be peace, to Pharaoh.

Moses said, "This is not permitted to me: I am the slave (of God): the giving of time to thee is not commanded.

If thou art powerful and I in sooth have no ally, (yet) I am subject to His command: I have nothing to do with that.

I will combat thee with all my might so long as I live; what have I to do with helping (God)? I am a slave.

1090   I will fight till the decision of God comes to pass: He (alone) separates every adversary from an adversary."

The reply of Pharaoh to Moses, and the coming of a Divine revelation to Moses, on whom be peace.

He (Pharaoh) said, "Nay, nay, thou must appoint a certain respite: do not give cajoleries, do not talk vain things[3]."

At once the high God made a revelation to him, saying, "Give him an ample respite: be not afraid of that.

Willingly give him these forty days, that he may bethink him of divers plots.

Let him endeavour, for I am not asleep; bid him advance quickly, (for) I have barred the way in front (of him).

1095   I will confound all their devices, and I will reduce to little that which they increase.

Let them fetch water, and I will make (it) fire; let them get honey and sweets and I will make (it) bitter.

Let them join in a bond of love, and I will destroy it; I will do that which they conceive not.

Have thou no fear, and give him a lengthy respite; bid him bring together his host and prepare a hundred devices."

---

[1] Literally, "purchased."
[2] Literally, "purchased."
[3] Literally, "do not measure wind."

How Moses, on whom be peace, gave Pharaoh a respite, that he might assemble the magicians from the cities.

He (Moses) said, "The (Divine) command hath come. Go, the respite is (granted) to thee. I depart to my dwelling-place: thou art delivered from me."

He was going (on his way), and at his heels (went) the dragon 1100 wise and loving, like the hunter's dog.

Like the hunter's dog, wagging its tail: it made the stones (crumble as) sand beneath its hoof.

With its breath it drew in stone and iron (to its jaws) and visibly chewed the iron into small fragments.

In the air it was making itself (rise) above the zodiac, so that Greeks and Georgians would flee from it in panic.

From its palate it cast out foam, like a camel: whomsoever a drop hit, he was smitten with tubercular leprosy.

The gnashing of its teeth would break the heart; the souls of 1105 black lions would be distraught (with terror)[1].

When that chosen one (Moses) reached his kinsfolk, he took hold of the corner of its mouth, and it became again a staff.

He leaned upon it, saying, "O wonder! to me ('tis clear as) the sun, to my enemy ('tis dark as) night.

O wonder! How doth this host not see a whole world filled with the sun at morningtide?

Eyes open, and ears open, and this sun! I am amazed at God's eye-bandaging.

I am amazed at them, and they too at me: (we are) from one 1110 springtime, (but) they are thorns and I am jasmine.

I bore to them many a cup of pure wine: its juice turned to stone before this company.

I twined a handful of roses and carried it to them: every rose became as a thorn, and the honey turned to poison.

That (pure wine) is the portion allotted to the selfless: since they are with themselves (not freed from self), how should it be shown (to them)?

With us, one must needs be a waking sleeper, that in the state of wakefulness he may dream dreams."

Thought of created things is an enemy to this sweet (waking) 1115 sleep: until his (any one's) thought is asleep, his throat is shut[2].

A (mystical) bewilderment is needed to sweep (such) thought away: bewilderment devours (all) thought and recollection.

The more perfect he is in (worldly) science, the more backward he is in reality and the more forward in appearance.

He (God) hath said, "(*Verily, to Him we are*) *returning*"; and the return is in the same wise as a herd turns back and goes home.

---

[1] Literally, "would pass beyond control."
[2] *I.e.* he cannot receive spiritual ideas.

When the herd has turned back from (after) going down to water, the goat that was the leader (now) falls behind (becomes the hindmost),

1120   And the lame hindmost goat is now in front: the return caused the faces to laugh of them that were frowning (before).

How did this party (the prophets and saints) become lame and give up glory and purchase ignominy in vain?

This party go on the pilgrimage (to Reality) with broken legs, (because) there is a secret way from straitness to ease.

This company washed their hearts (clean) of (the exoteric) kinds of knowledge, because this knowledge does not know this Way.

(In order to tread this Way) one needs a knowledge whereof the root is Yonder, inasmuch as every branch is a guide to its root.

1125   How should every wing fly across the breadth of the Sea? (Only) the esoteric knowledge will bear (thee) to the Presence (of God).

Why, then, should you teach a man the knowledge of which it behoves him to purify his breast?

Therefore do not seek to be in front: be lame on this side, and be the leader at the moment of return.

O clever one, be thou (according to the Prophet's saying, "*We are) the hindmost and the foremost*": the fresh fruit is prior to the tree.

Although the fruit comes last into being, it is the first, because it was the object.

1130   Say, like the angels, "*We have no knowledge*," to the end that "*Thou hast taught us*" may take thy hand (come to thy aid).

If in this school thou dost not know the alphabet, (yet) thou art filled, like Aḥmad (Mohammed), with the light of Reason.

If thou art not famous in the world, (yet) thou art not deficient[1]: God knoweth best concerning His servants.

A treasure of gold is (hidden), for safety's sake, in a desolate spot that is not well-known.

How should they deposit the treasure in a well-known place? On this account it is said[2], "Joy is (hidden) beneath sorrow."

1135   Here the mind may bring (suggest) many difficulties, but a good beast will break the tether.

His (God's) love is a fire that consumes difficulties: the daylight sweeps away every phantom.

O thou with whom He is pleased, seek the answer from the same quarter from which this question came to thee.

The cornerless corner of the heart is a King's highway: the radiance that is neither of the east nor of the west is (derived) from a Moon.

---

[1] *I.e.* "thou art none the worse for that."
[2] Literally, "it (the proverb) came."

Why on this side and on that, like a beggar, O mountain of
Reality, art thou seeking the echo?

Seek (the answer) from the same quarter to which, in the hour 1140
of pain, thou bendest low[1], crying repeatedly, "O my Lord!"

In the hour of pain and death thou turnest in that direction:
how, when thy pain is gone, art thou ignorant?

At the time of tribulation thou hast called unto God, (but)
when the tribulation is gone, thou sayest, "Where is the
way?"

This is because (thou dost not know God): every one that
knows God without uncertainty is constantly engaged in that
(commemoration of Him),

While he that is veiled in intellect and uncertainty is some-
times covered (inaccessible to spiritual emotion) and sometimes
with his collar torn (in a state of rapture).

The particular (discursive) intellect is sometimes dominant, 1145
sometimes overthrown; the Universal Intellect is secure from
the mischances of Time.

Sell intellect and talent and buy bewilderment (in God): be-
take thyself to lowliness, O son, not to Bukhárá!

Why have I steeped myself in the discourse, so that from
story-telling I have become a story?

I become naught and (unsubstantial as) a fable in making
moan (to God), in order that I may gain influence over (the hearts
of) them that prostrate themselves in prayer[2].

This (story of Moses and Pharaoh) is not a story in the eyes of
the man of experience: it is a description of an actual (spiritual)
state, and it is (equivalent to) the presence of the Friend of the
Cave[3].

That (phrase) "*stories of the ancients*," which the disobedient 1150
(infidels) applied to the words of the *Qur'án*, was a mark of
(their) hypocrisy.

The man transcending space, in whom is the Light of God—
whence (what concern of his) is the past, the future, or the
present?

His being past or future is (only) in relation to thee: both are
one thing, and thou thinkest they are two.

One individual is to him father and to us son: the roof is be-
low Zayd and above 'Amr.

The relation of "below" and "above" arises from those two
persons: as regards itself, the roof is one thing only.

These expressions are not (exactly) similar to that (doctrine 1155
of spiritual timelessness): they are a comparison: the old words
fall short of the new meaning.

---

[1] Literally, "thou becomest double."   [2] Cf. *Qur'án*, XXVI, 219.
[3] "The Friend of the Cave" is a title given to Abú Bakr; here it denotes
the Shaykh or Spiritual Director.

Since there is no river-marge, close thy lips, O waterskin:
this Sea of candy hath (ever) been without marge or shore.

How Pharaoh sent (messengers) to the cities
in search of the magicians.

When Moses had returned (home) and he (Pharaoh) re-
mained (with his own people), he called his advisers and
counsellors to his presence.

They deemed it right that the King and Ruler of Egypt
should assemble them (the magicians) from all parts of Egypt.

Thereupon he sent many men in every direction to collect the
sorcerers.

1160   In whatsoever region there was a renowned magician, he set
flying towards him ten active couriers.

There were two youths, famous magicians: their magic pene-
trated into the heart of the moon.

They milked the moon publicly and openly; in their journeys
they went mounted on a wine-jar.

They caused the moonshine to appear like a piece of linen:
they measured and sold it speedily,

And took the silver away: the purchaser, on becoming aware
(of the fraud), would smite his hand upon his cheeks in grief.

1165   They were the inventors of a hundred thousand such (tricks)
in sorcery, and were not (following others) like the rhyme-
letter.

When the King's message reached them, (to this effect): "The
king is now desiring help from you,

Because two dervishes[1] have come and marched in force
against the King and his palace.

They have naught with them except one rod, which becomes
a dragon at his (Moses') command.

The King and the whole army are helpless: all have been
brought to lamentation by these two persons.

1170   A remedy must be sought in magic, that maybe thou wilt save
(their) lives from these two enchanters—"

When he (the messenger) gave the message to those two
magicians, a (great) fear and love descended on the hearts of
them both.

When the vein of homogeneity began to throb[2], they laid their
heads upon their knees in astonishment.

Inasmuch as the knee[3] is the Súfí's school, the two knees are
sorcerers for solving a difficulty.

---

[1] Moses and Aaron.
[2] *I.e.* when their spiritual affinity to Moses made itself felt.
[3] Referring to the attitude of Súfís whilst engaged in holy meditation.

*How those two magicians summoned their father from the grave
and questioned their father's spirit concerning the real nature of
Moses, on whom be peace.*

Afterwards they said, "Come, O mother, where is our father's
grave? Do thou show us the way."

She took them and showed the way to his grave: then they 1175
kept a three days' fast for the sake of the King.

After that they said, "O father, the King in consternation
hath sent us a message

(To say) that two men have brought him to sore straits and
have destroyed his prestige with the army.

There is not with them any weapons or soldiers; nothing but
a rod, and in the rod is a calamity and bane.

Thou art gone into the world of the righteous, though to out-
ward seeming thou liest in a tomb.

If that is magic, inform us; and if it be divine, O spirit of our 1180
father,

(In that case) also inform us, so that we may bow down (be-
fore them) and bring ourselves in touch with an elixir[1].

We are despairing, and a hope has come; we are banished, and
Mercy has drawn us (towards favour)."

How the dead magician answered his sons.

He cried, "O my dearest sons[2], it rests (with God)[3] to de-
clare this (matter) plainly.

It is not permitted to me to speak openly and freely, yet the
mystery is not far from mine eye.

But I will show unto you a sign, that this hidden thing may 1185
be made manifest to you.

O light of mine eyes, when ye go thither, become acquainted
with the place where he sleeps,

And at the time when that Sage is asleep, make for the rod,
abandon fear.

If thou shalt steal it and art able (to do so), he is a magician:
the means of dealing with a magician is present with thee;

But if thou canst not (steal it), beware and beware! That
(man) is of God: he is the messenger of the Glorious (God) and
is (divinely) guided.

Though Pharaoh occupy the world, east and west, he will fall 1190
headlong: God and then war[4]!

---

[1] *I.e.* "that by associating with them we may transmute our copper into
gold (become spiritually pure)."
[2] Literally, "my soul and sons."
[3] Literally, "it is pledged," *i.e.* kept back till the appointed time.
[4] *I.e.* "to fight against God is an absurdity."

I give (thee) this true sign, O soul of thy father: inscribe it (in thy heart): God best knoweth the right course.

O soul of thy father, when a magician sleeps, there is none to direct his magic and craft.

When the shepherd has gone to sleep, the wolf becomes unafraid: when he sleeps, his exertion ceases;

But the animal whose shepherd is God—how hath the wolf hope or way (of getting) there?

1195 The sorcery which God practises is real and true: 'tis wrong to call that real thing sorcery.

O soul of thy father, this is the decisive sign: even if he (a prophet) die, God exalteth him."

Comparison of the sublime Qur'án to the rod of Moses, and the death of Muṣṭafá (Mohammed), on whom be peace, to the sleep of Moses, and those who seek to alter the Qur'án to the two young magicians who attempted to carry off the rod of Moses when they found him asleep.

The lovingkindnesses of God made a promise to Muṣṭafá (Mohammed), saying, "If thou shalt die, (yet) this Lesson (the Qur'án) shall not die.

I am exalting thy Book and Miracle, I am defending the Qur'án from those who would make it more or less.

I am exalting thee in both worlds, I am driving away the scoffers from thy Tidings.

1200 None shall be able to make additions or omissions therein. Do not thou seek another protector better than Me.

Day by day I will increase thy splendour, I will strike thy name on gold and on silver.

For thy sake I will prepare pulpit and prayer-niche: in (My) love (for thee) thy vengeance hath become My vengeance.

They (thy followers), from fear, are uttering thy name covertly and hiding when they perform their prayers;

From terror and dread of the accursed infidels thy Religion is being hidden underground;

1205 (But) I will fill the world, from end to end, with minarets; I will make blind the eyes of the recalcitrant.

Thy servants will occupy cities and (seize) power: thy Religion will extend from the Fish to the Moon.

We shall keep it living until the Resurrection: be not thou afraid of the annulment of the Religion, O Muṣṭafá.

O My Messenger, thou art not a sorcerer: thou art truthful, thou wearest the mantle of Moses.

To thee the *Qur'án* is even as the rod (of Moses): it swallows up (all) infidelities, like a dragon.

If thou sleepest beneath a sod, (yet) deem as his rod that which 1210 thou hast spoken (My Word).

Assailants have no power over his rod. Do thou (then) sleep, O King, a blessed sleep!

(Whilst) thy body is asleep (in the tomb), thy Light in Heaven hath strung a bow for thy war (against the infidels).

The philosopher and that which his mouth doeth—the bow of thy Light is piercing him (and it) with arrows."

Thus He did, and (even) more than He said: he (the Prophet) slept (the sleep of death), but his fortune and prosperity slumbered not.

"O soul of thy father[1], when a magician goes to sleep, *his* work 1215 becomes tarnished and dim[2]."

Both (the magician's sons) kissed his grave and went away to Egypt for the purpose of this mighty struggle.

When they came to Egypt for the sake of that enterprise, they sought after Moses and his house.

It chanced that on the day of their arrival Moses was asleep under a palm-tree,

So the folk gave them a clue to him, saying, "Go, seek yonder in the direction of the palm-grove."

When he (the magician's son) came (thither), he espied 1220 amongst the date-trees a sleeper who was the wakefullest man in the world.

For pleasure's sake he had shut the two eyes of his head, (but) all Heaven and Earth were under his gaze.

Oh, (there is) many a one whose eye is awake and whose heart is asleep: what, in truth, should be seen by the eyes of creatures of water and clay?

(But) he that keeps his heart awake—though the eye of his head may sleep, it (his heart) will open a hundred eyes.

If you are not one of (illumined) heart, be awake (keep vigil), be a seeker of the (illumined) heart, and be (always) in strife (with your fleshly soul);

But if your heart hath been awakened, sleep sound: thy 1225 (spiritual) eye is not absent from the seven (heavens) and the six (directions).

The Prophet said, "Mine eye slumbers, but when doth my heart slumber in drowsiness?"

The King is awake: suppose the guardsman is asleep, (what does it matter?). May (my) soul be sacrificed to the sleepers whose hearts are seeing!

The description of the heart's wakefulness, O spiritual man, would not be contained in thousands of rhymed couplets.

---

[1] Here the spirit of the dead magician addresses his sons.
[2] Literally, "becomes without splendour and brilliance," unlike the work of a prophet.

When they (the magicians) saw that he was sleeping out-stretched, they made preparations for stealing the rod.

1230   The magicians quickly approached the rod, saying, "We must go behind him and then snatch it (from him)."

When they prepared (to approach) a little nearer, the rod began to shake.

The rod quivered upon itself in such wise (that) both (magicians) on the spot became petrified by the shock (of terror).

After that, it turned into a dragon and made a rush (at them): both fled, and pale of countenance

Began to fall on their faces from affright, tumbling panic-stricken down every slope.

1235   Then to them it became certain that he (Moses) was from Heaven, since they were seeing the limit of (the power of) magicians.

Afterwards diarrhoea and fever appeared in them, and their case reached the last gasp and the death-agony.

Then at once they sent a man to Moses to excuse that (which they had done),

Saying, "We have put (thee) to the test, and how should (the thought of) testing thee occur to us unless there be envy (as a motive)?

We are sinners against the King (God): do thou crave pardon for us, O thou that art the elect of the elect of the Court of God."

1240   He pardoned (them), and at once they became well; they were striking their heads upon the earth (prostrating themselves) in the presence of Moses.

Moses said, "I pardon (you), O nobles: your bodies and souls have become unlawful to (immune from) Hell.

Verily ('tis as though) I did not see you; O (my) two friends, make yourselves strangers to (refrain from) exculpation.

Come, even as ye are, alien in appearance (but) familiar (in reality), to combat for the King (God)."

Then they kissed the earth and departed: they were waiting in expectation of the time and opportunity.

How the magicians from the cities assembled before Pharaoh and received robes of honour and laid their hands upon their breasts, (pledging themselves) to subdue his enemy (Moses), and saying, "Write this down against us."

1245   Those magicians came unto Pharaoh, and he gave them robes of honour exceedingly precious.

He made promises to them, and also gave them in advance slaves and horses and money and goods and provisions.

After that, he was saying, "Hark, O ye that are foremost (in your art), if ye prove superior in the trial,

I will scatter over you so many gifts that the veil of bounty and munificence will be rent[1]."

Then they said to him, "Through thy fortune, O King, we shall prevail, and his cause shall be ruined.

We are heroes[2] and champions in this art: no one in the world 1250 can resist us."

The mention of Moses has become a chain (obstruction) to the thoughts (of my readers), (for they think) that these are stories (of that) which happened long ago.

The mention of Moses serves for a mask, but the Light of Moses is thy actual concern, O good man.

Moses and Pharaoh are in thy being: thou must seek these two adversaries in thyself.

The (process of) generation from Moses is (continuing) till the Resurrection: the Light is not different, (though) the lamp has become different.

This earthenware lamp and this wick are different, but its 1255 light is not different: it is from Yonder.

If thou keep looking at the glass (lantern), thou wilt be lost, because from the glass arise the numbers of (the plurality inherent in) dualism;

But if thou keep thy gaze (fixed) upon the Light, thou wilt be delivered from dualism and the numbers (plurality) of the finite body.

From the place (object) of view, O (thou who art the) kernel of Existence, there arises the difference between the true believer and the Zoroastrian and the Jew.

The disagreement as to the description and shape of the elephant.

The elephant was in a dark house: some Hindús had brought it for exhibition.

In order to see it, many people were going, every one, into 1260 that darkness.

As seeing it with the eye was impossible, (each one) was feeling it in the dark with the palm of his hand.

The hand of one fell on its trunk: he said, "This creature is like a water-pipe."

The hand of another touched its ear: to him it appeared to be like a fan.

Since another handled its leg, he said, "I found the elephant's shape to be like a pillar."

---

[1] *I.e.* "all other munificence will be put to shame."
[2] Literally, "cleavers of the (hostile) ranks."

1265   Another laid his hand on its back: he said, "Truly, this elephant was like a throne."

Similarly, whenever any one heard (a description of the elephant), he understood (it only in respect of) the part that he had touched.

On account of the (diverse) place (object) of view, their statements differed: one man entitled it "*dál*," another "*alif*[1]."

If there had been a candle in each one's hand, the difference would have gone out of their words.

The eye of sense-perception is only like the palm of the hand: the palm hath not power to reach the whole of him (the elephant).

1270   The eye of the Sea[2] is one thing, and the foam[3] another: leave the foam and look with the eye of the Sea.

Day and night (there is) the movement of foam-flecks from the Sea: thou beholdest the foam, but not the Sea. Marvellous!

We are dashing against each other, like boats: our eyes are darkened, though we are in the clear water.

O thou that hast gone to sleep in the body's boat, thou hast seen the water, (but) look on the Water of the water.

The water hath a Water that is driving it; the spirit hath a Spirit that is calling it.

1275   Where were Moses and Jesus when the (Divine) Sun was giving water to the sown field of existent things?

Where were Adam and Eve at the time when God fitted this string to the bow?

This (manner of) speech, too, is imperfect and maimed; the speech that is not imperfect is Yonder.

If he (the saint) speak from that (source), thy foot will stumble; and if he speak naught of that, oh, alas for thee!

And if he speak in the likeness of a (material) form[4], thou wilt stick to that form, O youth.

1280   Thou art foot-bound on the earth, like grass: thou noddest thy head at a (breath of) wind, (though thou art) without certainty[5].

But thou hast no (spiritual) foot that thou shouldest make a departure or perchance drag thy foot out of this mud.

How shouldst thou drag thy foot away? Thy life is from this mud: 'tis mighty hard for this life of thine to go (on the Way to God).

(But) when thou receivest life from God, O dependent one[6], then thou wilt become independent of the mud and wilt go (aloft).

---

[1] *I.e.* crooked like the letter د or straight like the letter ا.
[2] *I.e.* the eye of Reality.   [3] *I.e.* phenomena.
[4] *I.e.* figuratively.
[5] *I.e.* "thou noddest in assent to every word, although thou hast no comprehension of the real meaning."   [6] Literally, "rhyme-letter."

When the sucking (babe) is separated from its nurse, it be-
comes an eater of morsels and abandons her.

Thou, like seeds, art in bondage to the milk of earth: seek to 1285
wean thyself by (partaking of) the spiritual food[1].

Drink the word of Wisdom, for it hath become a hidden
(veiled) light, O thou who art unable to receive the unveiled
Light,

To the end that thou mayst become able, O Soul, to receive
the Light, and that thou mayst behold without veils that which
(now) is hidden,

And traverse the sky like a star; nay, (that thou mayst) journey
unconditioned, without (any) sky.

('Twas) thus thou camest into being from non-existence.
Say now, how didst thou come? Thou camest drunken (un-
conscious).

The ways of thy coming are not remembered by thee, but we 1290
will recite to thee a hint (thereof).

Let thy mind go, and then be mindful! Close thine ear, and
then listen!

Nay, I will not tell (it), because thou still art unripe: thou art
in (thy) springtime, thou hast not seen (the month of) Tamúz.

This world is even as the tree, O noble ones: we are like the
half-ripened fruit upon it.

The unripe (fruits) cling fast to the bough, because during
(their) immaturity they are not meet for the palace.

When they have ripened and have become sweet—after that, 1295
biting their lips[2], they take (but) a feeble hold of the boughs.

When the mouth has been sweetened by that felicity, the
kingdom of the world becomes cold (unpleasing) to Man.

To take a tight hold and to attach one's self strongly (to the
world) is (a sign of) unripeness: so long as thou art an embryo,
thy occupation is blood-drinking.

Another thing remains (to be said), but the Holy Spirit will
tell thee the tale of it, without me.

Nay, thou wilt tell it even to thine own ear—neither I nor
another than I (will tell it thee), O thou that art even I—

Just as, when thou fallest asleep, thou goest from the presence 1300
of thyself into the presence of thyself:

Thou hearest from thyself, and deemest that such or such a
one has secretly told thee in the dream that (which thou hast
heard).

Thou art not a single "thou," O good comrade; nay, thou art
the sky and the deep sea.

Thy mighty "Thou," which is nine hundredfold, is the ocean
and the drowning-place of a hundred "thou's."

[1] Literally, "the food of hearts."
[2] *I.e.* "in remorse for having clung so tightly to the tree."

Indeed, what occasion (is there) for the terms[1] wakefulness and sleep? Do not speak, for God knoweth best what is right.

1305   Do not speak, so that thou mayst hear from the Speakers that which came not into utterance or into explanation.

Do not speak, so that thou mayst hear from the Sun that which came not into book or into allocution.

Do not speak, so that the Spirit may speak for thee: in the ark of Noah leave off swimming!

(Be not) like Canaan, who was swimming and saying, "I do not want the ark of Noah, (who is) my enemy."

(Noah said), "Hey, come and sit in thy father's ark, that thou mayst not be drowned in the Flood, O despicable one!"

1310   He answered, "Nay, I have learned to swim: I have lighted a candle other than thy candle."

(Noah said), "Beware! Do it not, for these are the waves of the Flood of tribulation; to-day hand and foot and swimming are naught.

'Tis the wind of vengeance and the woe that extinguishes the candle (of contrivance). No candle but God's is enduring. Be silent!"

He said, "Nay, I will go up that high mountain: that mountain will protect me from every hurt."

(Noah said), "Beware! Do it not, for at this time the mountain is (but) a straw. He giveth safety to none except His beloved."

1315   He answered, "When have I listened to thy advice, that thou shouldst hope (as thou didst) that I am of this family[2]?

Thy words were never pleasing to me: I am quit of thee in both worlds."

(Noah said), "Beware, _bábá_[3], do it not, for (this) is not the day for disdain. God hath no kinship or partner.

Until now thou hast shown (disdain), and at this moment there is disdain (on the part of God): whose disdain is of any effect in this Court[4]?

From eternity He is (the One that) _begetteth not, nor is He begotten:_ He hath neither father nor son nor uncle.

1320   How will He suffer the disdain of sons? How will He hearken to the disdain of fathers?

(God saith), 'I am not begotten: O old man, do not be proud. I am not a begetter: O youth, do not strut.

I am not a husband, I am not connected with lust: here, O lady, leave off being disdainful.'

Excepting humility and slavishness and utter helplessness, naught hath consideration in this Presence."

---

[1] Literally, "the limitation of (denoted by the terms) wakefulness and sleep," _i.e._ these terms are only analogical.

[2] See _Qur'án_, XI, 47–48.

[3] Here and in v. 1327 Noah addresses his son as _bábá_ (father).

[4] _I.e._ "in the presence of God."

He (Canaan) said, "Father, for years thou hast said this; (now) thou art saying (it) again: thou art deranged with folly.

How many of these things hast thou said to every one, so that 1325 oftentimes thou hast heard a cold (rough) answer!

This cold breath (tiresome discourse) of thine did not enter my ear, (nor will it), especially now when I have become wise and strong."

He (Noah) said, "*Bábá*, what harm will it do if thou listen once to the advice of thy father?"

On this wise was he (Noah) speaking kindly counsel, and on that wise was he (Canaan) uttering harsh refusal.

Neither did the father become weary of admonishing Canaan, nor did a single breath (word) enter the ear of that graceless man.

They were (engaged) in this talk when a fierce billow dashed 1330 upon Canaan's head, and he was shivered to fragments.

Noah said, "O long-suffering King, my ass is dead, and Thy Flood hath carried away the load.

Many times Thou didst promise me, saying, 'Thy family shall be saved from the Deluge.'

I (in) simple (faith) fixed my heart on hope of Thee: why, then, has the Flood swept my garment away from me?"

He (God) said, "He was not of thy family and kinsfolk: didst not thou thyself see (that) thou art white, he blue?"

When the worm (of decay) has fallen upon thy tooth, it is not 1335 a tooth (any more): tear it out, O master.

In order that the rest of thy body may not be made miserable by it, become quit of it, although it was (once) thine.

He (Noah) said, "I am quit of aught other than Thy Essence; he that has died in Thee is not other (than Thou).

Thou knowest how I am to Thee: I am (to Thee) as the orchard to the rain, and twenty times as much[1]—

Living by Thee, rejoicing because of Thee, a pauper receiving sustenance without any medium or intervention;

Not united, not separated, O Perfection; nay, devoid of 1340 quality or description or causation.

We are the fishes, and Thou the Sea of Life: we live by Thy favour, O Thou whose attributes are excellent.

Thou art not contained in the bosom of any thought, nor art Thou joined with the effect, as a cause.

Before this Flood and after it, Thou hast been the object of my address in (every) colloquy.

I was speaking with Thee, not with them, O Thou that art the Giver of speech (both) newly and of old.

Is it not the case that the lover, day and night, converses now 1345 with the ruins (of the beloved's abode), now with the traces (of her habitation)?

---

[1] Literally, "I am twenty times as much as the orchard to the rain."

To outward seeming, he has turned his face towards the ruins,
(but) to whom is he (really) saying that song of praise, to whom?

Thanks (be to Thee)! Now Thou hast let loose the Flood and
removed the ruins which stood between (me and Thee)[1].

(I thank Thee) because they were vile and evil ruins, uttering
neither a cry nor an echo.

I desire such ruins to speak with as answer back, like the
mountain, by an echo,

1350   So that I may hear Thy name redoubled, (for) I am in love
with Thy soul-soothing name.

That is why every prophet holds the mountains dear: ('tis)
that he may hear Thy name redoubled.

That low mountain, resembling stony ground, is suitable for
a mouse, not for us, as a resting-place[2].

(When) I speak, it does not join with me: the breath of my
speech remains without (any) echo[3].

'Tis better that thou level it with the earth; it is not in accord
with thy breath (voice): thou shouldst join it with thy foot[4]."

1355   He (God) said, "O Noah, if thou desire, I will assemble them
all and raise them from (their graves in) the earth.

I will not break thy heart for the sake of a Canaan, but I am
acquainting (thee) with (their real) states."

He (Noah) said, "Nay, nay, I am content that Thou shouldst
drown me too, if it behove Thee (to do so).

Keep drowning me every instant, I am pleased: Thy ordi-
nance is my (very) soul, I bear it (with me) as my soul[5].

I do not look at any one (but Thee), and even if I do look at
(any one), he is (only) a pretext, and Thou art the (real) object
of my regard.

1360   I am in love with Thy making (both) in (the hour of) thanks-
giving and (in the hour of) patience[6]; how should I be in love,
like the infidel, with that which Thou hast made?"

He that loves God's making is glorious; he that loves what
He hath made is an unbeliever.

*Reconciliation of these two Traditions: "To be satisfied with
infidelity is an act of infidelity," and "If any one is not satisfied
with My ordainment, let him seek a lord other than Me."*

Yesterday an inquirer put a question to me, because he was
fond of disputation.

He said, "This Prophet uttered the deep saying, 'To be
satisfied with infidelity is an act of infidelity'; his words are
(conclusive like) a seal.

---

[1] Literally, "the intermediate link (consisting) of the ruins."
[2] Literally, "at the time when the camels kneel for unloading."
[3] Or possibly, "it remains without (any) echo at the moment of my speaking."
[4] *I.e.* trample it underfoot.   [5] *I.e.* "I cherish it as my life."
[6] *I.e.* "whether I enjoy Thy favour or endure Thy affliction."

Again, he said that the Moslem must be satisfied (acquiesce) in every ordainment, must be satisfied.

Is not infidelity and hypocrisy the ordainment of God? If 1365 I become satisfied with this (infidelity), 'twill be opposition (disobedience to God),

And if I am not satisfied, that too will be detrimental: between (these two alternatives), then, what means (of escape) is there for me?"

I said to him, "This infidelity is the thing ordained, it is not the ordainment; this infidelity is truly the effects of the ordainment.

Therefore know (distinguish), sire, the ordainment from the thing ordained, so that thy difficulty may be removed at once.

I acquiesce in infidelity in that respect that it is the ordainment (of God), not in this respect that it is our contentiousness and wickedness.

In respect of the ordainment, infidelity indeed is not in- 1370 fidelity. Do not call God 'infidel,' do not stand here[1].

Infidelity is ignorance, and the ordainment of infidelity is knowledge: how, pray, should *ḥilm* (forbearance) and *khilm* (anger) both be one (and the same)?

The ugliness of the script is not the ugliness of the artist; nay, 'tis an exhibition of the ugly by him.

The power (skill) of the artist is that he can make both the ugly and the beautiful."

If I develop the investigation of this (subject) methodically, so that question and answer become lengthy,

The savour of Love's mystery will go from me, the form of 1375 piety will be deformed[2].

A parable illustrating the fact that (mystical) bewilderment prevents investigation and consideration.

A certain man, whose hair was of two colours[3], came in haste to a highly esteemed barber[4].

He said, "Remove the hoariness from my beard, for I have chosen a new bride, O young man."

He cut off his beard and laid the whole of it before him, and said, "Do thou pick out (the white hairs), for it happens that I have some important business[5]."

That "pick (them) out" is dialectic[6], for religious emotion has no care for these things (hair-splitting disputes).

---

[1] *I.e.* "do not persist in this false notion."
[2] Literally, "the form of (devout) service will become another form."
[3] *I.e.* black and white.   [4] Literally, "mirror-holder."
[5] Literally, "an important affair has happened to me."
[6] Literally, "is this question and that answer," *i.e.* the method of the scholastic theologians.

1380   A certain man slapped Zayd on the neck; he (Zayd) at once rushed at him with warlike purpose[1].

The assailant said, "I will ask thee a question, so answer me (first) and then strike me.

I struck the nape of thy neck, and there was the sound of a slap: at this point I have a question (to ask thee) in concord:

Was this sound caused by my hand or by the nape of thy neck, O pride of the noble?"

He (Zayd) said, "On account of the pain I have no leisure to stop (occupy myself) in this reflection and consideration.

1385   Do thou, who art without pain, ponder on this; he that feels the pain has no such thought. Take heed!"

Story.

Amongst the Companions (of the Prophet) there was scarcely any one that knew the *Qur'án* by heart, though their souls had a great desire (to commit it to memory),

Because, inasmuch as its kernel had filled (them) and had reached maturity, the rinds became very thin and burst.

Similarly, the shells of the walnut and the pistachio-nut and the almond—when the kernel has filled them, the rind decreases.

(When) the kernel, knowledge, increases, its rind decreases (and vanishes), because the lover is consumed by his beloved.

1390   Since the quality of being sought is the opposite of seeking, the Revelation and the flashing of the (Divine) Light consume the prophet with burning.

When the Attributes of the Eternal have shone forth, then the mantle of temporality is burned.

Every one that knew a quarter of the *Qur'án* by heart was hearing from the Companions (the words), "Great is he amongst us."

To combine the (outward) form with such a deep (inner) meaning is not possible, except on the part of a mighty (spiritual) king.

In such (mystical) intoxication (as his) the observance of due respect (to the letter of the *Qur'án*) will not be there at all; or if it be, 'tis a wonder.

1395   To observe humility in (the state of spiritual) independence is to combine two opposites, like "round" and "long."

Truly the staff is loved by the blind; the (inwardly) blind man himself is a coffer (full) of the *Qur'án*.

He (a certain one) said, "In sooth the blind are coffers full of the words of the *Qur'án* and commemoration (of God) and warning."

---

[1] Literally, "for war."

Again, a coffer full of the *Qur'án* is better than he that is (like) an empty coffer in the hand.

Yet again, the coffer that is empty of (any) load is better than the coffer that is full of mice and snakes.

The sum (of the matter is this): when a man has attained to 1400 union, the go-between becomes worthless to him.

Since you have reached the object of your search, O elegant one, the search for knowledge has now become evil.

Since you have mounted to the roofs of Heaven, it would be futile to seek a ladder.

After (having attained to) felicity, the way (that leads) to felicity is worthless except for the sake of helping and teaching others.

The shining mirror, which has become clear and perfect— 'twould be folly to apply a burnisher (to it).

Seated happily beside the Sultan (and) in favour (with him) 1405 —'twould be disgraceful to seek letter and messenger.

Story of a lover's being engrossed in reading and perusing a love-letter in the presence of his beloved, and how the beloved was displeased thereat. It is shameful to seek the proof in the presence of that which is proved, and blameworthy to occupy one's self with knowledge after having attained to that which is known.

A certain man, (when) his beloved let (him) sit beside her, produced a letter and read it to her.

In the letter were verses and praise and laud, lamentation and wretchedness and many humble entreaties.

The beloved said, "If this is for my sake, (to read) this at the time of (our) meeting is to waste one's life.

I am here beside thee, and thou reading a letter! This, at any rate, is not the mark of (true) lovers."

He replied, "Thou art present here, but I am not gaining my 1410 pleasure well (completely).

That which I felt last year on account of thee is non-existent at this moment, though I am experiencing union (with thee).

I have drunk cool water from this fountain, I have refreshed eye and heart with its water.

I am (still) seeing the fountain, but the water is not there: maybe some brigand has waylaid (and cut off) my water."

She said, "Then I am not thy beloved: I am in Bulghár[1], and the object of thy desire is in Qutú[2].

Thou art in love with me and (also) with a state of feeling; the 1415 state of feeling is not in thy hand (in thy possession), O youth.

[1] A town on the Volga, in the province of Kazan.
[2] Perhaps identical with Qúchú, the capital of the Uighúr Turks of Turfán. See M. Nazim, *The Life and Times of Sultan Maḥmúd of Ghazna*, p. 56, note 5.

Therefore I am not the whole of that which is sought by thee;
I am (only) part of the object of thy quest at the present time.

I am (only) the house of thy beloved, not the beloved (herself): (true) love is for the cash, not for the coffer (that contains it)."

The (real) beloved is that one who is single, who is thy beginning and end.

When thou findest him, thou wilt not remain in expectation (of aught else): he is both the manifest and also the mystery.

1420   He is the lord of states of feeling, not dependent on any state: month and year are slaves of that Moon.

When he bids the "state," it does his behest; when he wills, he makes bodies (become) spirit.

One that is stopped (on the way) is not (at) the (journey's) end; he will be seated, waiting and seeking the "state."

His (the perfect saint's) hand is the elixir that transmutes the "state": (if) he move his hand, the copper becomes intoxicated with him.

If he will, even death becomes sweet; thorns and stings become narcissus and wild-rose.

1425   He that is dependent on the "state" is (still) a human being: at one moment he is (made) greater by the "state," at another moment he is in decrease.

In similitude the Súfí is "the son of the time[1]," but the pure one (sáfí) is unconcerned with "time" and "state."

"States" are dependent on his decision and judgement; (they are) vivified by his Messiah-like breath.

"Thou art in love with thy 'state,' thou art not in love with me; thou art attached to me in the hope of (experiencing) the 'state.'"

He that at one moment is deficient and at another moment perfect is not He that was worshipped by Khalíl (Abraham): he is one that sinks;

1430   And he that is liable to sink and is now that and (now) this is not the (true) beloved: "*I love not them that sink.*"

He that is now pleasing and now unpleasing, at one time water and at one moment fire,

May be the mansion of the Moon, but he is not the Moon; he may be the picture of the Adored One[2], but he is not conscious.

The Súfí that seeks purity is 'the son of the time': he has clasped the 'time' tightly as (though it were) his father.

The pure one (sáfí) is plunged in the Light of the Glorious (God); he is not the son of any one, (he is) free from 'times' and 'states'—

---

[1] "Time" (*waqt*), in its technical sense, denotes the spiritual mood or emotion that is predominant at the moment.
[2] Literally, "the idol."

Plunged in the Light which is unbegotten: (the description) 1435
He neither begetteth nor is He begotten belongs to God (alone).

Go, seek a love likĕ this, if thou art (spiritually) alive; otherwise, thou art a slave to the changing "time."

Do not regard thy ugly or beauteous form; regard Love and the object of thy search.

Do not regard the fact that thou art despicable or infirm; look upon thy aspiration, O noble one.

In whatsoever state thou be, keep searching; O thou with dry lip, always be seeking the water,

For that dry lip of thine gives evidence that at last it will reach 1440 the spring-head.

Dryness of lip is a message from the water (to say) that this agitation (anxious search) will certainly bring thee to the water[1],

For this seeking is a blessed motion; this search is a killer of obstacles on the Way to God.

This search is the key to the things sought by thee; this (search) is thy army and the victory of thy banners.

This search is like chanticleer crowing and proclaiming that the dawn is at hand.

Although thou hast no equipment, do thou be ever seeking: 1445 equipment is not necessary on the Way of the Lord.

Whomsoever thou seest engaged in search, O son, become his friend and cast thy head before him[2],

For through being the neighbour of the seekers thou (thyself) wilt become a seeker, and from the shadows (protection) of the conquerors thou (thyself) wilt become a conqueror.

If an ant has sought (to attain) the rank of Solomon, do not look languidly (contemptuously) on its quest.

Everything that thou hast of wealth and (skill in) a handicraft (or profession)—was it not at first a quest and a thought?

Story of the person who in the time of David, on whom be peace, used to pray night and day, crying, " Give me a lawful livelihood without trouble (on my part)."

In the time of the prophet David a certain man, beside every 1450 sage and before every simpleton,

Used always to utter this prayer: "O God, bestow on me riches without trouble!

Since Thou hast created me a lazybones, a receiver of blows, a slow mover, a sluggard,

One cannot place on sore-backed luckless asses the load carried by horses and mules.

---

[1] Or "bring thee to us (to me)."   [2] *I.e.* devote thyself to him.

Inasmuch as Thou, O perfect One, hast created me lazy, do Thou accordingly give me the daily bread by the way of laziness.

1455   I am lazy and sleeping in the shade in (the world of) existence: I sleep in the shade of this Bounty and Munificence.

Surely for them that are lazy and sleeping in the shade Thou hast prescribed a livelihood in another fashion.

Every one that has a foot (power to move) seeks a livelihood: do Thou show some pity[1] towards every one that has no foot.

Send the daily bread to that sorrowful one: waft the rain-clouds towards every land.

Since the land has no foot, Thy munificence drives the clouds doubly towards it.

1460   Since the babe has no foot (means of seeking nutriment), its mother comes and pours the ration (of milk) upon it[2].

I crave a daily portion (that is bestowed) suddenly without fatigue (on my part), for I have naught of endeavour except the seeking[3]."

Thus was he praying for a long time, (all) day until night and all night until morning.

The people were laughing at his words, at the folly of his hope, and at his contention,

Saying, "Marvellous! What is he saying—this idiot[4]? Or has some one given him beng (that is the cause) of senselessness?

1465   The way of (getting) daily bread is work and trouble and fatigue; He (God) hath given every one a handicraft and (the capacity for) seeking (a livelihood):

'Seek ye your daily portions in the means thereof: enter your dwellings by their doors.'

At present the King and ruler and messenger of God is the prophet David, one endowed with many accomplishments.

Notwithstanding such glory and pride as is in him, forasmuch as the favours of the Friend have chosen him out—

His miracles are countless and innumerable, the waves of his bounty are tide upon tide[5]:

1470   When has any one, even from Adam till now, had a (melodious) voice like an organ,

Which at every preaching causes (people) to die? His beautiful voice made two hundred human beings non-existent.

At that time the lion and the deer unite (in turning) towards his exhortation, the one oblivious of the other;

The mountains and the birds are accompanying his breath (voice), both are his confidants in the hour of his calling (unto God);

---

[1] Literally, "heart-burning."
[2] *I.e.* into its mouth.
[3] *I.e.* "except the supplications and entreaties which I address to Thee."
[4] Literally, "man with a weak beard."
[5] Literally, "supply upon supply."

These and a hundred times as many miracles are (vouch-
safed) to him; the light of his countenance is (both) transcendent
and immanent[1]—

Notwithstanding all (this) majesty, God must have made his 1475
livelihood to be bound up with seeking and endeavour.

Without weaving coats of mail[2] and (without) some trouble (on
his part), his livelihood is not coming (to him), notwithstanding
all his victoriousness.

(Yet) a God-forsaken abandoned one like this, a low scoundrel[3]
and outcast from Heaven,

A backslider of this sort, desires, without trading, at once to
fill his skirt (pocket) with gain!

Such a crazy fellow has come forward, saying, 'I will climb
up to the sky without a ladder.'"

This one would say to him derisively, "Go and receive (it), 1480
for your daily portion has arrived and the messenger has come
with the good news";

And that one would laugh, (saying), "Give us too (a share) of
what you get as a gift, O headman of the village."

(But) he was not diminishing his prayers and wheedling en-
treaties because of this abuse and ridicule from the people,

So that he became well-known and celebrated in the town as
one who seeks (to obtain) cheese from an empty wallet.

That beggar became a proverb for foolishness, (but) he would
not desist[4] from this petitioning.

How a cow ran into the house of him that was praying importunately.
The Prophet, may God bless him and grant him peace, has said,
"God loves them that are importunate in prayer," because the
actual asking (of anything) from God most High and the im-
portunity (itself) is better for the petitioner than the thing which
he is asking of Him.

Until suddenly one day, (when) he was uttering this prayer 1485
with moaning and sighs at morningtide,

Suddenly a cow ran into his house; she butted with her horns
and broke the bolt and key.

The cow boldly jumped into the house; the man sprang for-
ward and bound her legs.

Then he at once cut the throat of the cow without pause,
without consideration, and without mercy.

After he had cut off her head, he went to the butcher, in
order that he might quickly rip off her hide forthwith.

---

[1] Literally, "without and within (spatial) relations."
[2] See *Qur'án*, XXI, 80.
[3] Literally, "one whose house is ruined." But probably the correct
reading is خانه‌کنده, "one whose house is stinking."
[4] Literally, "become separate."

The Poet's excusing himself and asking help.

1490   O Thou that makest demands within (me), like the embryo—
since Thou art making a demand, make easy

The fulfilment of this (task), show the way, give aidance, or
(else) relinquish the demand and do not lay (the burden) upon
me!

Since Thou art demanding gold from an insolvent, give him
gold in secret, O rich King!

Without Thee, how should poesy and rhyme dare to come
into sight at eve or morn?

Poesy and homonymy and rhymes, O Knowing One, are the
slaves of Thy Command from fear and dread,

1495   Inasmuch as Thou hast made everything a glorifier (of Thee)
—the undiscerning entity and the discerning (alike).

Each glorifies (Thee) in a different fashion, and that one is
unaware of the state of this one.

Man disbelieves in the glorification uttered by inanimate
things, but those inanimate things are masters in (performing)
worship.

Nay, the two-and-seventy sects, every one, are unaware of
(the real state of) each other and in a (great) doubt.

Since two speakers have no knowledge of each other's state,
how will (it) be (with) wall and door[1]?

1500   Since I am heedless of the glorification uttered by one who
speaks, how should my heart know the glorification performed
by that which is mute?

The Sunní is unaware of the Jabrí's (mode of) glorification[2];
the Jabrí is unaffected by the Sunní's (mode of) glorification.

The Sunní has a particular (mode of) glorification; the Jabrí
has the opposite thereof in (taking) refuge (with God).

This one (the Jabrí) says, "He (the Sunní) is astray and lost,"
(being) unaware of his (real) state and of the (Divine) command,
"Arise (and preach)!"

And that one (the Sunní) says, "What awareness has this one
(the Jabrí)?" God, by fore-ordainment, hath cast them into
strife.

1505   He maketh manifest the real nature of each, He displays the
congener by (contrast with) the uncongenial.

Every one knows (can distinguish) mercy from vengeance,
whether he be wise or ignorant or vile,

But a mercy that has become hidden in vengeance, or a
vengeance that has sunk into the heart of mercy,

---

[1] *I.e.* "how should a human being be acquainted with the manner in which
inanimate objects glorify God?"

[2] "Jabrí" is one who holds the doctrine of *jabr* (necessitarianism).

No one knows except the divine (deified) man in whose heart is a spiritual touchstone.

The rest hold (only) an opinion of these two (qualities)[1]: they fly to their nest with a single wing.

Explaining that Knowledge has two wings, and Opinion (only) one:
"Opinion is defective and curtailed in flight"; and a comparison
illustrating opinion and certainty in knowledge.

Knowledge has two wings, Opinion one wing: Opinion is 1510 defective and curtailed in flight.

The one-winged bird soon falls headlong; then again it flies up some two paces or (a little) more.

The bird, Opinion, falling and rising, goes on with one wing in hope of (reaching) the nest.

(But) when he has been delivered from Opinion, Knowledge shows its face to him: that one-winged bird becomes two-winged and spreads his wings.

After that, he walks erect and straight, not falling flat on his face or ailing.

He flies aloft with two wings, like Gabriel, without opinion 1515 and without peradventure and without disputation.

If all the world should say to him, "You are on the Way of God and (are following) the right religion,"

He will not be made hotter[2] by their words: his lonely soul will not mate with them;

And if they all should say to him, "You are astray: you think (you are) a mountain, and (in reality) you are a blade of straw,"

He will not fall into opinion (doubt) because of their taunts, he will not be grieved by their departure (estrangement from him).

Nay, if seas and mountains should come to speech and should 1520 say to him, "You are wedded to perdition,"

Not the least jot will he fall into phantasy or sickness on account of the taunts of the scoffers.

Parable of a man's being made (spiritually) ill by vain conceit of
the veneration in which he is held by the people and of the suppli-
cation addressed to him by those seeking his favour; and the
(following) story of the Teacher.

The boys in a certain school suffered at the hands of their master from weariness and toil.

They consulted about (the means of) stopping (his) work, so that the teacher should be reduced to the necessity (of letting them go),

---

[1] *I.e.* the mercy latent in vengeance and the vengeance latent in mercy.
[2] *I.e.* more fervent in his faith.

(Saying), "Since no illness befalls him, which would cause him to take[1] absence for several days,

1525   So that we might escape from (this) imprisonment and confinement and work, (what can we do?). He is fixed (here), like a solid rock."

One, the cleverest (of them all), planned that he should say, "Master, how are you (so) pale?

May it be well (with you)![2] Your colour is changed[3]: this is the effect either of (bad) air or of a fever."

(He continued), "At this he (the master) will begin to fancy a little (that he is ill): do you too, brother, help (me) in like manner.

When you come in through the door of the school, say (to him), 'Master, is your state (of health) good?'

1530   (Then) that fancy of his will increase a little, for by a fancy a sensible man is driven mad.

After us let[4] the third (boy) and the fourth and the fifth show sympathy and sorrow likewise,

So that, when with one consent thirty boys successively tell this story, it may find lodgement (in his mind)."

Each (of the boys) said to him (the ringleader), "Bravo, O sagacious one! May your fortune rest on the favour (of God)!"

They agreed, in firm covenant, that no fellow should alter the words;

1535   And afterwards he administered an oath to them all, lest any tell-tale should reveal the plot[5].

The counsel of that boy prevailed over all (the others), his intellect was going in front of the (whole) flock.

There is the same difference in human intellect as (there is) amongst loved ones in (their outward) forms.

From this point of view, Aḥmad (Mohammed) said in talk, "The excellence of men is hidden in the tongue."

People's intellects differ in their original nature, (though) according to the Mu'tazilites they are (originally) equal and the difference in intellects arises from the acquisition of knowledge.

You must hear (and believe) in accordance with the Sunnís (that) the difference in (people's) intellects was original,

1540   In contradiction to the doctrine of the Mu'tazilites, who hold that (all) intellects were originally equal,

(And who maintain that) experience and teaching makes them more or less, so that it makes one person more knowing than another.

---

[1] Literally, "so that he would take."
[2] Meaning, "What is the matter? I hope you are well."
[3] Literally, "is not *in statu.*"
[4] Reading نمایند.   [5] Literally, "tell what had passed."

This is false, because the counsel of a boy who has not experience in any course of action—

From that small child sprang up a thought (which) the old man[1] with a hundred experiences did not smell out (detect and apprehend) at all.

Truly, the superiority that is from (any one's) nature is even better than the superiority that is (the result of) endeavour and reflection.

Tell (me), is the gift of God better, or (is it better) that a lame person should (learn to) walk smoothly (without stumbling)? 1545

How the boys made the teacher imagine (that he was ill).

Day broke, and those boys, (intent) on this thought, came from their homes to the shop (school).

They all stood outside, waiting for that resolute fellow to go in first,

Because he was the source of this plan: the head is always an Imám (leader and guide) to the foot.

O imitator (follower of convention and tradition), do not thou seek precedence over one who is a source of the heavenly light.

He (the boy) came in and said to the master "Salaam! I hope you are well. Your face is yellow in colour." 1550

The master said, "I have no ailment. Go and sit down and don't talk nonsense, hey!"

He denied (it), but the dust of evil imagination suddenly struck a little (made a slight impression) upon his heart.

Another (boy) came in and said the like: by this (second suggestion) that imagination was a little increased.

(They continued) in like manner, until his imagination gained strength and he was left marvelling exceedingly as to his state (of health).

How Pharaoh was made (spiritually) ill by vain imagination arising from the people's reverence (for him).

The people's prostrating themselves—women, children, and men—smote the heart of Pharaoh and made him ill. 1555

Every one's calling him lord and king made him so tattered (infamous) from a vain imagination,

That he dared to pretend to divinity: he became a dragon and would never be sated.

Imagination and opinion are the bane of the particular (discursive) reason, because its dwelling-place is in the darkness.

---

[1] *I.e.* the teacher.

If there be a path half an ell wide on the ground, a man will
walk safely without imagining;

1560   (But) if you walk on the top of a high wall, you will stagger[1]
even if its width be two ells;

Nay, through (the force of) imagination and from trembling of
heart, you will be (on the point of) falling. Consider well and
understand the fear that is due to imagination.

How the teacher was made ill by imagination.

The master became unnerved by imagination and dread; he
sprang up and began to drag his cloak along[2],

Angry with his wife and saying, "Her love is weak: I am in
this state (of health), and she did not ask and inquire.

She did not even inform me about my colour: she intends to
be freed from my disgrace[3].

1565   She has become intoxicated with her beauty and the display
(of her charms) and is unaware that I have fallen from the roof,
like a bowl[4]."

He came (home) and fiercely opened the door—the boys
(were following) at the master's heels.

His wife said, "Is it well (with thee)? How hast thou come
(so) soon? May no evil happen to thy goodly person!"

He said, "Are you blind? Look at my colour and appearance:
(even) strangers are lamenting my affliction,

(While) you, at home, from hatred and hypocrisy do not see
the state of anguish I am in."

1570   His wife said, "O sir, there is nothing wrong with thee: 'tis
(only) thy vain unreal imagination and opinion."

He said to her, "O strumpet, are you still obstinately dis-
puting (with me)? Don't you see this change (in my appearance)
and (this) tremor?

If you have become blind and deaf, what fault of mine is it?
I am in this (state of) pain and grief and woe."

She said, "O sir, I will bring the mirror, in order that thou
mayst know that I am innocent."

"Begone," said he; "may neither you nor your mirror be
saved! You are always (engaged) in hatred and malice and
sin.

1575   Lay my bed at once, that I may lie down, for my head is
sore."

The wife lingered; the man shouted at her, saying, "O hateful
one, (be) quicker! This (behaviour) is worthy of you."

---

[1] Literally, "become crooked."
[2] *I.e.* "to walk (home) slowly and with difficulty."
[3] *I.e.* "she thinks it a disgrace to be my wife and wishes to get rid of me."
[4] *I.e.* "that I am manifestly broken down."

How the master went to bed and moaned,
imagining himself to be ill.

The old woman brought the bed-clothes and spread them.
She said, "There is no possibility (of speaking), and my heart
is filled with burning (grief).

If I speak, he will hold me suspect; and if I say nothing, this
affair will become serious."

A man who has not suffered any pain is made ill by a bad
omen.

It is obligatory to accept the saying of the Prophet, "If ye 1580
pretend to be sick beside me, ye will become (actually) sick."

"If I tell him (that he is not ill), he will cast up (conceive) a
vain fancy (and will think to himself), 'My wife has an (evil)
design, for she is making arrangements to be alone.

She is getting me out of the house, she is plotting and
cajoling for the purpose of some wickedness.'"

She prepared his bed, and the master fell down (upon it):
sighs and moans were arising from him.

The boys sat there, reciting their lesson with a hundred
sorrows in secret,

Thinking, "We have done all this and (still) we are prisoners: 1585
it was a bad building (a badly devised plan), and we are bad
builders."

How for the second time the boys made the master imagine (that he
was ill), saying that their recitation of the Qur'án would increase
his headache.

The clever boy said, "O good fellows, recite the lesson and
make your voices loud."

When they were reciting (loudly), he said, "Boys, the noise
we are making will do the master harm.

The master's headache will be increased by the noise: is it
worth while that he should suffer pain for the sake of (a few)
pence?"

The master said, "He is speaking the truth: depart. My head-
ache is worse: go out (of the house)!"

How the boys escaped from school by this trick.

They bowed and said, "O honoured sir, may illness and 1590
danger be far from you!"

Then they bounded off to their homes, like birds in desire of
grain.

Their mothers became angry with them and said, "A school-
day and you at play!¹"

¹ Literally, "coupled with play."

They offered excuses (every one of them), saying, "Stop, mother! This sin does not proceed from us and is not caused by our fault.

By the destiny of Heaven our master has become ill and sick and afflicted."

1595   The mothers said, "It is a trick and a lie: ye bring forward a hundred lies because of your greed for buttermilk[1].

In the morning we will come to (visit) the master, that we may see (what is at) the bottom of this trick of yours."

"Go in God's name," said the boys; "inform yourselves as to our lying or telling the truth."

How the mothers of the boys went to visit the sick master.

At morning those mothers came; (they found) the master in bed like one who is gravely ill,

Perspiring on account of the great number of coverlets, his head bandaged and his face enveloped in the quilt.

1600   He was moaning softly: they too all began to cry "*Lá ḥawl.*"

They said, "Master, we hope all will be well. This headache—by thy soul, we were not aware of it."

He replied, "I also was not aware of it; the whoresons (the scoundrelly boys) made me aware (of it), mark you.

I did not notice (it), through being busy with discourse (teaching), (but) within (me) there was such a severe malady."

When a man is busy in earnest, he is blind to the sight of (unconscious of) his pain.

1605   It has become an oft-told tale concerning the women of Joseph's Egypt that consciousness departed from them on account of their pre-occupation (with the beauty of Joseph).

(Hence) they cut their fore-arms to pieces: (in such a case) the spirit is distraught, so that it looks neither behind nor before.

Oh, many a brave man in battle whose hand or foot is cut by blows (of the sword),

And he bears that same hand into the combat, thinking that it remains firm (intact).

(Afterwards) indeed he will see that his hand has been injured (and that) much blood has gone from him unawares.

Explaining that the body is as a garment to the spirit, and that this (bodily) hand is the sleeve of the spirit's hand, and that this (bodily) foot is the shoe of the spirit's foot.

1610   (I mention this insensibility to pain) that you may know that the body is like a garment. Go, seek the wearer of the garment, do not lick (kiss) a garment.

---

[1] "Buttermilk" is often used in Persian to signify "deceit." Here it seems to mean "play and amusement."

To the spirit the knowledge of the Unity (of God) is sweeter (than care for the body): it hath a hand and foot different from those which are visible.

You may behold in dream the (spiritual) hand and foot and their connexion (with the spiritual body): deem that (vision) a reality, deem it not to be in vain.

You are such that without the (material) body you have a (spiritual) body: do not, then, dread the going forth of the soul from the body.

Story of the dervish who had secluded himself in the mountains, with an account of the sweetness of severance (from the world) and seclusion and of entering upon this path, for (God hath said), "I am the companion of them that commemorate Me and the friend of them that take Me as their friend.
If thou art with all, thou art without all when thou art without Me;
And if thou art without all, thou art with all when thou art with Me."

There was a dervish dwelling in a mountainous place: solitude was his bedfellow and boon-companion.

Since the refreshing breeze[1] (of favour) was coming for him 1615 from the Creator, he was weary of the breaths of man and woman.

Just as staying at home is easy to us, so travelling is easy to another class of people.

In the same way as thou art in love with dominion, that worthy man is in love with the ironsmith's handicraft.

Every one has been made for some particular work, and the desire for that (work) has been put into his heart.

How should hand and foot be set in motion without desire? How should sticks and straws go (from their place) without any water or wind?

If thou see (that) thy desire (is) towards Heaven, unfold the 1620 wings of empire, like the *Humá*[2];

But if thou see (that) thy desire (is) towards the earth, keep lamenting, cease not at all from moaning.

The wise, indeed, make lamentations at first; the foolish beat their heads at the last.

From the beginning of the affair discern the end (thereof), so that thou mayst not be repenting on the Day of Judgement.

How a goldsmith discerned the end of the affair and spoke in accordance with the end to one who wished to borrow his scales.

A certain man came to a goldsmith, saying, "Give me the scales, that I may weigh some gold."

[1] Literally, "the north-wind."
[2] The lammergeier (great bearded vulture). According to popular belief, the falling of its shadow on any one was a sign that he would become king.

1625 The master (goldsmith) said, "Go, I have no sieve." "Give me the scales," he replied, "and don't stop to jest like this."

He said, "I have no broom in the shop." "Enough, enough!" cried the other; "leave these jokes.

Give (me) the scales which I am asking for; don't make yourself out to be deaf, don't jump in every direction[1]."

He (the goldsmith) said, "I heard what you said, I am not deaf; you must not think that I am nonsensical.

I heard this (request), but you are a shaky old man: your hand is trembling and your body is not erect;

1630 And moreover that gold of yours consists of little tiny filings: your hand trembles, so the fragments of gold will drop (from it);

Then you will say, 'Sir, fetch a broom, that I may look in the dust for my gold.'

When you sweep (with the broom), you will gather dust (along with the gold); you will say to me, 'I want the sieve, O gallant man.'

I from the beginning discerned the end complete. Go from here to some other place, and farewell!"

The rest of the Story of the ascetic of the mountain who had made a vow that he would not pluck any mountain fruit from the trees or shake the trees or tell any one to shake them, either plainly or in veiled terms, and that he would only eat what the wind might cause to fall from the trees.

On that mountain were trees and fruits; there were many mountain-pears—(they were) numberless.

1635 The dervish said, "O Lord, I make a covenant with Thee (that) I will not pluck any of these during the time (of my life).

I will not pluck from the raised-up (lofty) trees (aught) but the fruit that the wind has caused to fall."

For a while he kept his vow faithfully: (he kept it) till the tribulations of Destiny came on.

On this account He (God) hath commanded, saying, "Make the exception: attach (the words) 'if God will' to your promise.

Every instant I give to the heart a different desire, every moment I lay upon the heart a different brand.

1640 At every dawn I have a new employment: nothing turns aside from that (course) which I have willed."

It has come down in the Traditions (of the Prophet) that the heart is like a feather in a desert, the captive of a violent blast.

The wind drives the feather recklessly in every direction, now left, now right, with a hundred diversities.

In another Tradition (the Prophet said), "Deem this heart to be as water boiling in a cauldron from (the heat of) fire."

---

[1] *I.e.* "don't talk at random."

At every time the heart has a different resolution: that (resolution) is not (derived) from it, but from a certain place.

Why, then, will you trust in the heart's resolution and make a covenant, that in the end you should be shamed? 1645

This too is from the effect of the (Divine) ordinance and decree, (that) you see the pit and cannot take precaution.

'Tis no wonder, indeed, for the flying bird not to see the snare (and so) fall into destruction;

The wonder is that it should see both the snare and the net-pin and fall (into the snare) willy-nilly.

(With) eye open and ear open and the snare in front, it is flying towards a snare with its own wings.

A comparison (showing that) the bonds and snares of Destiny, though outwardly invisible, are manifest in their effects.

You may see a nobleman's son in a tattered cloak, bare-headed, fallen into affliction. 1650

(He is) consumed with passion for some ne'er-do-well, (he has) sold his furniture and properties.

His household (is) gone, (he has) become ill-famed and despised; he walks along like (one in) misfortune, to the joy of his foes.

(If) he sees an ascetic, he will say, "O venerable sir, bestow on me a benediction[1] for God's sake,

For I have fallen into this ugly misfortune and have let wealth and gold and happiness go from my hand.

(Give me) a benediction, so that maybe I shall be delivered from this (woe) and maybe escape from this dark clay." 1655

He is begging this prayer of high and low, crying, "Release and release and release!"

His hand is free and his foot free, and there is no chain, no custodian (standing) over him, no iron (gyve).

From what chain art thou seeking release, and from what imprisonment art thou seeking to escape?

(From) the hidden chain of fore-ordainment and destiny, which none but the elect spirit may behold.

Though it is not visible, it is (there) in ambush; it is worse than prison and chains of iron, 1660

Because that (iron chain) the ironsmith may break, and the excavator may even dig up the bricks (foundations) of the prison;

(But), O wonder, this heavy hidden chain the ironsmiths are powerless to shatter.

Vision of that chain (of Destiny) belongs to Aḥmad (Mohammed): (he saw it) on the throat bound with *a cord of palm-fibres*[2].

---

[1] Literally, "exert some spiritual influence (on me)."
[2] *Qur'án*, CXI, 5.

He saw a load of firewood on the back of Abú Lahab's wife and said, *the carrier of faggots (for Hell-fire)*[1].

1665 The cord and the firewood no eye beheld but his, for to him every unseen thing becomes visible.

All the rest interpret it (falsely), for this (vision) arises from senselessness (spiritual rapture), and they are sensible—

But from the effect of that (chain) his (the sufferer's) back has been bent double, and he is moaning before you,

(And crying), "A prayer! a benediction! that I may be delivered and that I may escape from this hidden chain."

He who sees these signs clearly, how should not he know the damned from the blest?

1670 He knows, and by command of the Almighty he conceals (it), for it would not be lawful to divulge the secret of God.

This discourse hath no end. That dervish, through hunger, became feeble and his body a prisoner.

How the dervish who had made the vow was reduced (by hunger) to plucking the pears from the tree, and how God's chastisement came (upon him) without delay.

For five days the wind did not cause a single pear to drop, and on account of the fire (pangs) of hunger his patience was fleeing (deserting him).

He espied several pears on a bough, (but) once more he acted with patience and restrained himself.

The wind came and lowered the end of the bough and caused his carnal nature to prevail for the eating of that (fruit).

1675 Hunger and weakness and the strength of Destiny's pull made the ascetic unfaithful to his vow.

When he had plucked fruit from the pear-tree, he became frail (false) in his vow and promise.

At the same instant God's chastisement arrived: it opened his eye and pulled his ear.

How the Shaykh[2] *was suspected of being in company with thieves and had his hand cut off.*

In that place there were twenty thieves and more, dividing the things they had stolen.

The prefect had been apprised by an informer: the prefect's men quickly fell upon them.

1680 He (the officer in charge) cut off on the spot the left feet and right hands of them all, and a great hubbub arose.

The ascetic's hand too was cut off by mistake; he (the officer) was about to make his foot also fall (to the ground),

---

[1] *Qur'án*, CXI, 4.   [2] *I.e.* the dervish who had broken his vow.

(When), just in time, a very elect cavalier came up and shouted at the officer, "Look out, O dog!

This is such-and-such a Shaykh and *Abdál* (exalted saint) of God: why have you severed his hand?"

The officer rent his garment and went speedily to the prefect and gave him the information at once.

The prefect came bare-footed, begging pardon. "I did not 1685 know," he said; "God will bear me witness.

Pray now absolve me from this foul deed, O generous man and chief of the (destined) inhabitants of Paradise!"

He (the Shaykh) said, "I know the cause of this (wound inflicted by the) knife: I recognise my sin.

I violated the sanctity of His oaths: therefore His judgement (sentence) took my right hand away.

I broke my covenant and knew 'twas evil (to break it), so that (in consequence of my breaking it) that ill-omened audacity reached (recoiled upon) my hand.

May my hand and my foot and brain and skin be offered in 1690 sacrifice, O governor, to the decree of the Beloved!

'Twas my (destined) lot. I absolve thee from this. Thou didst not know: thou hast no guilt (to answer for).

And He that knew, He is the One whose command is (everywhere) carried into execution: where is the power of struggling with God?"

Oh, many the bird flying in search of grain whose gullet was cut by its gullet (greediness)!

Oh, many the bird that, through its belly (appetite) and pangs of hunger, was made captive in a cage on the edge of a terrace!

Oh, many the fish that, because of its gullet's greed, was 1695 caught by a hook in water hard to reach!

Oh, many the chaste (woman) in a curtained bower that was brought to open shame by the misfortune of lust and gluttony[1]!

Oh, many the learned and honest judge that was disgraced[2] by greed and bribery!

Nay, in the case of Hárút and Márút that wine (of lust) debarred them from ascending to Heaven.

On this account Báyazíd took precaution: he observed in himself remissness in (the performance of) the ritual prayer.

(When) that possessor of the marrow[3] (of spiritual knowledge) 1700 meditated concerning the cause, he perceived that the cause was (too) much water-drinking.

He said, "For a year I will not drink water." He acted accordingly, and God bestowed on him the power (to abstain).

---

[1] Literally, "infelicitate cunni et gulae."
[2] Literally, "made pallid."
[3] Literally, "the crumb (soft part) of bread."

This was his least penance for the Religion's sake: he became
a (spiritual) sultan and the Pole of the Gnostics.

Since the ascetic's hand had been cut off by reason of his
gullet (appetite), he closed the door of complaint[1].

His name amongst the people came to be Shaykh Aqta'[2]: the
calamities (which he suffered because) of his gullet made him
well-known by this (name).

The miraculous gifts of Shaykh Aqta', and how he used
to weave palm-leaf baskets with both hands.

1705   A visitor found him in his hut, (and saw) that he was weaving
a basket with both hands.

He (the Shaykh) said to him, "O enemy of thine own life,
thou hast come putting thy head into my hut.

Why hast thou made such hot haste[3]?" He replied, "From
excess of love and longing."

Then he (the Shaykh) smiled and said, "Now come in, but
keep this (thing) secret, O noble sir.

Till I die, do not tell this to any one, neither to a comrade nor
to a beloved nor to a worthless fellow."

1710   Afterwards other folk, (looking) through his window, became
acquainted with his weaving.

He said, "O Creator, Thou knowest the wisdom (the purpose
in this). I conceal (my secret), Thou hast revealed it."

The Divine inspiration came to him: "There were a number
of people who were beginning to disbelieve in thee in (conse-
quence of) this affliction,

Saying, 'Perchance he was a hypocrite in the Way (of God),
so that God made him infamous among humankind.'

I do not wish that that party should become infidels and in
thinking evil (of thee) fall into perdition;

1715   (Hence) We divulged this miracle—(namely), that We give
thee a hand in thy working-time—

To the end that these wretched evil-thinking men may not be
turned back from the Lord of Heaven.

Erstwhile, indeed, without these miracles I was giving thee
consolation from My Person;

This miracle I have given thee for their sake, and on that
account have I bestowed on thee this (spiritual) lamp.

Thou art past being afraid of bodily death and dismember-
ment of the limbs.

1720   Vain imagination concerning the dismemberment of head and
foot has gone from thee: there has come to thee, for a defence
against imagination, a shield exceeding strong."

---

[1] *I.e.* he refrained from making complaint (to God).
[2] *Aqta'* means "a person whose hand has been cut off."
[3] Literally, "such haste in seeking to be beforehand (with me)," *i.e.* to
enter my hut before I had granted permission.

*The reason why the magicians of Pharaoh had courage
to suffer the amputation of their hands and feet.*

Is it not (the fact) that the accursed Pharaoh threatened (the magicians with) punishment on the earth,

Saying, " I will cut off your hands and feet on opposite sides, then I will hang you up: I will not hold you exempt (from punishment) "?

He thought that they were (still) in the same imagination and terror and distraction and doubt,

So that they would be trembling and terrified and affrighted by the vain imaginings and threats of the carnal soul.

He did not know that they had been delivered and were seated 1725 at the window of the light of the heart;

(And that) they had recognised (the difference of) their (bodily) shadows from their (real) selves, and were brisk and alert and happy and exulting;

(And that), if the mortar of the Sky (Fortune) should pound them small a hundred times in this miry place (the material world),

(Yet), since they had seen the origin of this (corporeal) composition, they were not afraid of the derivatives (which belong to the domain) of imagination.

This world is a dream—do not rest in (false) opinion; if in dream a hand go (be lost), 'tis no harm.

If in dream a pruning-fork has cut off your head, not only is 1730 your head (still) in its place but your life is (still) prolonged.

If in dream you see yourself (cut) in two halves, you are sound in body when you rise, not sick.

The sum (of the matter is this): in dreams it is no harm for the body to be maimed or to be torn into two hundred pieces.

The Prophet said of this world, which is substantial in appearance, that it is the sleeper's dream.

You have accepted this (statement) conventionally, (but) the travellers (on the mystic Way) have beheld this (truth) clairvoyantly, without (relation from) the Prophet.

You are asleep in the daytime: do not say that this is not 1735 sleep. The shadow (reflexion) is derivative, the origin (of it) is naught but the moonlight.

Know, O comrade[1], that your sleep and waking (your life in this world) is as though a sleeper should dream that he has gone to sleep.

He thinks, "Now I am asleep," (and is) unaware that he is (really) in the second sleep.

If the potter break a pot, he himself will restore it (to a perfect state) when he wishes.

[1] Literally, "O aider."

The blind man at every step is afraid of (falling into) the pit:
he walks on the road with a thousand fears;

1740   (But) the seeing man has seen the width of the road, so he
knows (all about) the hole and the pit;

His legs and knees do not tremble at any time: how should he
look sour because of any affliction?

"Arise, O Pharaoh (and do thy worst)! for we are not such
(so deluded) as to stop at every cry and (every) ghoul.

Rend our (bodily) mantle! There is One who will sew (it
again); and if not, truly the more naked we are, the better for us.

Without raiment we would fain clasp this Beauteous One to
our bosoms, O enemy good-for-naught!

1745   There is nothing sweeter than to be stripped of the body and
the (bodily) temperament, O stupid uninspired Pharaoh!"

*How the mule complained to the camel, saying, "I am often
falling on my face, while thou fallest but seldom."*

Said the mule to the camel, "O good friend, in hill and dale
and in the obscure (difficult) track

Thou dost not tumble on thy head but goest happily along,
while I am tumbling on my head, like one who has lost his way.

At every moment I am falling on my face, whether (it be) in a
dry place or a wet.

Declare to me what is the cause of this, that I may know how
I must live."

1750   He (the camel) said, "My eye is clearer than thine; further-
more, it is also looking from on high:

When I come up to the top of a high hill, I regard attentively
the end of the pass;

Then too God reveals to my eye all the lowness and loftiness
of the way,

(So that) I take every step with (clear) sight and am delivered
from stumbling and falling,

(Whereas) thou dost not see two or three steps in front of
thee: thou seest the bait, but thou dost not see the pain of the
snare.

1755   *Are the blind and the seeing equal* before you (according to
your opinion) in their abiding and their alighting and their
journeying?"

When God gives a spirit to the embryo in the womb, He im-
plants in its (the spirit's) temperament (the desire of) drawing
particles together.

By means of food it draws the particles together and weaves
the warp and woof of its body:

Till (the age of) forty years, God will have made it desirous
of drawing particles together in (the process of) growth.

The incomparable King taught the spirit to draw particles to-
gether: how should He (himself) not know how to draw particles
together?

The assembler of (all) these motes was the (Divine) Sun: He 1760
knows how to seize thy (bodily) particles (and draw them
together again) without nutrition.

At the moment when thou emergest from sleep, He quickly
recalls the departed consciousness and sensation.

To the end that thou mayst know that those (faculties) have
not become absent from Him, they come back (to thee) when
He commands them to return[1].

*How by permission of God the particles of the ass of 'Uzayr
were assembled after putrefaction and recompounded before the
eyes of 'Uzayr.*

"Hey, 'Uzayr, look upon thine ass which hath rotted and
crumbled beside thee.

We will collect its parts in thy presence—its head and tail and
ears and legs."

There is no (visible) hand, and (yet) He is putting the parts 1765
together and giving a unitedness to the (scattered) pieces.

Consider the art of a Tailor who sews old rags (together)
without a needle:

No thread or needle at the time of sewing; He sews in such
wise that no seam is visible.

"Open thine eyes and behold the resurrection plainly, that
there may not remain in thee doubt concerning the Day of
Judgement,

And that thou mayst behold My unitive power entire, so that
at the time of death thou wilt not tremble with anxiety,

Even as at the time of sleep thou art secure from (hast no fear 1770
of) the passing of all the bodily senses:

At the time of sleep thou dost not tremble for thy senses,
though they become scattered and ruined."

How a certain Shaykh showed no grief at the death of his sons.

Formerly there was a Shaykh, a (spiritual) Director, a heavenly
Candle on the face of the earth,

One like a prophet amongst religious communities, an opener
of the door of the garden of Paradise.

The Prophet said that a Shaykh who has gone forward (to
perfection) is like a prophet amidst his people.

One morning his family said to him, "Tell us, O man of good 1775
disposition, how art thou (so) hard-hearted?

[1] Literally, "commands, saying, 'Return!'"

We with backs (bent) double are mourning for the death and loss of thy sons:

Why art not thou weeping and lamenting? Or hast thou no pity in thy heart?

Since thou hast no pity within, what hope for us is there now from thee?

We are in hope of thee, O guide, that thou wilt not leave us to perish.

1780   When the throne is set up on the Day of Resurrection, 'tis thou that art our intercessor on that grievous day.

On such a merciless day and night we are hopeful of thy kindness.

Our hands will cling to thy skirt[1] at that moment when security remains not to any sinner."

The Prophet has said, "On the Day of Resurrection how should I leave the sinners to shed tears?

I will intercede with (all) my soul for the disobedient, that I may deliver them from the heavy torment.

1785   I will deliver by my efforts the disobedient and those who have committed capital sins from (suffering) punishment for breaking their covenant.

The righteous of my community are, in sooth, free from (have no need of) my intercessions on the Day of Woe;

Nay, they have (the right to make) intercessions, and their words go (forth) like an effective decree.

No burdened one shall bear another's burden, (but) I am not burdened: God hath exalted me."

O youth, the Shaykh is he that is without a burden and is like a bow in the hand (a mere instrument) in receiving (the command of) God.

1790   Who is a "Shaykh"? An old man (*pír*), that is (to say), white-haired. Do thou apprehend the meaning of this "(white) hair," O hopeless one.

The black hair is his self-existence: (he is not "old") till not a single hair of his self-existence remains.

When his self-existence has ceased, he is "old" (*pír*), whether he be black-haired or grizzled.

That "black hair" is the attribute of (sensual) men; that "hair" is not the hair of the beard or the hair of the head.

Jesus in the cradle raises a cry, saying, "Without having become a youth, I am a Shaykh and a Pír."

1795   If he (the Súfí) has been delivered from (only) a part of the attributes of (sensual) men, he is not a Shaykh; he is grey (middle-aged), O son.

---

[1] Literally, "'tis our hand and thy skirt."

When there is not on him a single black hair (of the self-existence) which is our attribute, (then) he is a Shaykh and accepted of God;

(But) if, when his hair is white, he is (still) with himself (self-existent), he is not a Pír and is not the elect of God;

And if a single hair-tip of his (sensual) attributes is surviving, he is not of heaven: he belongs to the (material) world.

How the Shaykh excused himself for not weeping on the death of his sons.

The Shaykh said to her (his wife), "Do not think, O gracious one, that I have not pity and affection and a compassionate heart.

I have pity for all the unbelievers, though the souls of them all are ungrateful. 1800

I have pity and forgiveness for dogs, saying (to myself), 'Why do they suffer chastisement from the stones (which are cast at them)?'

I utter a prayer for the dog that bites, crying, 'O God, deliver him from this (evil) disposition!

Keep also these dogs in that (good) thought, so that they may not be stoned by the people.'"

He (God) brought the saints on to the earth, in order that He might make them *a mercy to (all) created beings.*

He (the saint) calls the people to the Portal of Grace[1]; he calls unto God, saying, "Give (them) release in full!" 1805

He earnestly strives to admonish them in regard to this, and when it does not succeed, he says, "O God, do not shut the door!"

To the vulgar belongs (only) the particular mercy; the universal mercy belongs to the hero (the perfect saint).

His particular (individual) mercy has been united with the universal: the mercy of the Sea is the guide on (all) the ways.

O (thou who hast the) particular mercy, become joined to the universal: deem the universal mercy the true guide, and go (forward).

So long as he is (only) a part, he does not know the way to the Sea: he makes out every pool to be like unto the Sea. 1810

Inasmuch as he does not know the way to the Sea, how should he act as a guide? How should he lead the people towards the Sea?

(When) he becomes united with the Sea, then he guides to the Sea, like a torrent or river.

And if (before this) he call (the people to God), it is in a conventional fashion; it is not from vision and inspiration or any (Divine) aid.

[1] Literally, "the private door or court."

She (the Shaykh's wife) said, "Then, since thou hast pity on all, and art like the shepherd (going watchfully) around this flock,

1815 How mournest thou not for thine own sons, when Death, the Bleeder, has pierced them with his lancet?

Since the evidence of pity is tears in the eyes, why are thine eyes without moisture and tearless?"

He turned towards his wife and said to her, "Old woman, verily the season of December is not like Tamúz (July)[1].

Whether they are dead or living, when are they absent and hid from the eye of the heart?

Inasmuch as I see them distinct before me, for what reason should I rend my face as thou doest?

1820 Although they are outside of Time's revolution, they are with me and playing around me.

Weeping is caused by severance or by parting; I am united with my dear ones and embracing them.

(Other) people see them (their dear ones) in sleep; I see them plainly in (my) waking state.

I hide myself for a moment from this world, I shake the leaves of sense-perception from the tree (of my bodily existence)."

Sense-perception is captive to the intellect, O reader; know also that the intellect is captive to the spirit.

1825 The spirit sets free the chained hand of the intellect and brings its embarrassed affairs into harmony.

The (bodily) senses and (sensual) thoughts are like weeds on the clear water—covering the surface of the water.

The hand of the intellect sweeps those weeds aside; (then) the water is revealed to the intellect.

The weeds lay very thick on the stream, like bubbles; when the weeds went aside, the water was revealed.

Unless God loose the hand of the intellect, the weeds on our water are increased by sensual desire.

1830 Every moment they cover the water (more and more): that desire is laughing, and thy intellect is weeping;

(But) when piety has chained the hands of desire, God looses the hands of the intellect.

So, when the intellect becomes thy captain and master, the dominant senses become subject to thee.

He (who is ruled by the intellect), without being asleep (himself), puts his senses to sleep, so that the unseen things may emerge from (the world of) the Soul.

Even in his waking state he dreams dreams and opens withal the gates of Heaven.

---

[1] *I.e.* "the cause of my shedding no tears is not coldness of heart; my tears are not frozen, but they are utterly dried up in the fiery heat of Divine Love."

*Story of the blind old man's reading the Qur'án in front (of him)
and regaining his sight when he read.*

Once upon a time a dervish Shaykh saw a *Qur'án* in the 1835
house of a blind old man.

He became his guest in (the month) Tamúz: the two ascetics
were together for several days.

He said (to himself), "Oh, I wonder what the Book is (here)
for, as this righteous dervish is blind."

(Whilst he was occupied) in this reflection, his perplexity in-
creased: (he said to himself), "No one lives here except him.

He is alone, (and yet) he has hung a Book (on the wall). I am
not (so) unmannerly or muddled (in my wits)

As to ask (him the reason). Nay, hush! I will be patient, in 1840
order that by patience I may gain my object."

He showed patience and was in a quandary for some time,
(till at last) it (the secret) was disclosed, for patience is the key
to joy (relief).

*How Luqmán, when he saw David, on whom be peace, making
(iron) rings, refrained from questioning him, with the intention
that this act of self-control should be the cause of relief (from
perplexity).*

Luqmán went to David, the pure of heart, and observed that
he was making rings of iron,

(And) that the exalted King was casting all the steel rings into
each other.

He had not seen the armourer's[1] handicraft (before), (so) he
remained in astonishment and his curiosity increased—

"What can this be? I will ask him what he is making with 1845
the interfolded rings."

Again he said to himself, "Patience is better: patience is the
quickest guide to the object of one's quest."

When you ask no question, the sooner will it (the secret) be
disclosed to you: the bird, patience, flies faster than all (others);

And if you ask, the more slowly will your object be gained:
what is easy will be made difficult by your impatience.

When Luqmán kept silence, straightway that (work of making
rings) was finished by David's craftsmanship.

Then he fashioned a coat of mail and put it on in the presence 1850
of the noble and patient Luqmán.

"This," he said, "is an excellent garment, O young man, for
warding off blows on the battle-field and in war."

---

[1] Literally, "maker of coats of mail."

Luqmán said, "Patience too is of good effect[1], for it is the protection and defence against pain everywhere."

He (God) hath joined ṣabr (patience) with ḥaqq (the real and permanent): O reader, recite attentively the end of (the Súra) Wa'l-'aṣr[2].

God created hundreds of thousands of elixirs, (but) Man hath not seen an elixir like patience.

The remainder of the story of the blind man and his reading the Qur'án.

1855   The guest showed patience, and of a sudden the difficult case was unveiled to him all at once.

At midnight he heard the sound of (recitation of) the Qur'án; he sprang up from sleep and beheld a marvel—

That the blind man was reading correctly from the Qur'án. He became impatient and sought from him (an explanation of) that matter.

"Oh, wonderful!" he cried. "Thou with sightless eyes, how art thou reading, (how art thou) seeing the lines?

Thou hast touched[3] that which thou art reading: thou hast laid thy hand upon the words of that (passage).

1860   Thy finger, in motion, makes it evident that thou hast thine eye resting on the words[4]."

He replied, "O thou who hast been separated from the body's ignorance, dost thou feel this wonder at the work of God?

I begged of God, crying, 'O Thou whose help is sought, I am (as) covetous of reading the Book as (I am) of life.

I do not know it by heart: at the time of reading it, bestow on my two eyes an untroubled[5] light.

Give me back my eyes at that moment, so that I may take the Book and read it plain.'

1865   From the Divine Presence came the cry (in response): 'O man of (devotional) work, O thou that hast hope of Me in every grief,

Thou hast the good thought (of Me) and the fair hope that at each moment bids thee mount higher.

Whensoever thou intendest to read (the Qur'án) or wantest the lection from (different) copies[6],

At that moment I will restore thine eye, in order that thou mayst read, O venerable being[7].'

Even so He did, and whenever I open the Book to read,

1870   That all-knowing One who never becomes forgetful of His work, that honoured Sovereign and Maker,

---

[1] Literally, "of good breath."   [2] Súra CIII, 3.
[3] Literally, "hast fallen on."
[4] Literally, "hast thine eye on the words (which serve) as a resting-place (for it)."   [5] Literally, "unknotted."
[6] I.e. in order to ascertain what variations in the form of the Text are adopted by the chief authorities.   [7] Literally, "substance."

That incomparable King at once gives my sight back to me,
like a lamp that makes an end of[1] the (darkness of) night."

On this account the saint has no objection (to raise against the
Divine ordainment): whatsoever He (God) takes away, He
sends compensation.

If He burn your vineyard, He will give you grapes; in the
midst of mourning He will give you festivity.

To the handless paralytic He gives a hand, to the (person
who is a) mine of grief He gives the (joyous) heart of an in-
toxicated one.

(The feeling denoted by the words) "We will not submit" 1875
and (the desire to raise) objection have gone from us (saints),
since there is coming a great recompense for what has been lost.

Inasmuch as heat comes to me without fire, I am content if
He extinguish my fire.

Inasmuch as He gives light without any lamp—if your lamp
is gone, why are you lamenting?

*Description of some saints who are content with the (Divine)
ordainments and do not pray and beseech (God) to change this
decree.*

Now listen to a story of those travellers on the Way who have
no objection in the world.

Those of the saints who make invocation are in sooth different
(from these travellers): sometimes they sew and sometimes they
tear.

I know another class of saints whose mouths are closed to 1880
invocation.

Because of the content (quietism) that is subservient to
(possessed by) those noble ones, it has become unlawful for
them to seek to avert Destiny.

In (submitting to) Destiny they experience a peculiar delight:
it would be (an act of) infidelity for them to crave release.

He (God) hath revealed to their hearts such a good opinion
(of Him) that they do not put on the blue garb (of mourning)
on account of any sorrow.

How Buhlúl questioned a certain dervish.

Buhlúl said to a certain dervish, "How art thou, O dervish?
Inform me."

He said, "How should that one be, according to whose desire 1885
the work of the world goes on?—

According to whose desire the torrents and rivers flow, and
the stars move in such wise as he wills;

[1] Literally, "rolls up."

And Life and Death are his officers, going to and fro[1] according to his desire.

He sends (what entails) condolence wheresoever he will; he bestows (what entails) felicitation wheresoever he will.

The travellers on the Way (go) according to his pleasure; they that have lost the Way (are fallen) in his snare.

1890   No tooth flashes with laughter in the world without the approval and command of that imperial personage[2]."

He (Buhlúl) said, "O King, thou hast spoken truly: 'tis even so: this is manifest in thy (spiritual) radiance and (glorious) aspect.

Thou art this and a hundred times as much, O veracious one; but expound this (mystery) and explain it very well,

In such fashion that (both) the virtuous (wise) and the man given to vanity (folly) may assent when it comes to their ears.

Expound it in thy discourse in such a way that the understanding of the vulgar may profit thereby."

1895   The perfect speaker is like one who distributes trays of viands, and whose table is filled with every sort of food,

So that no guest remains without provisions, (but) each one gets his (proper) nourishment separately:

(Such a speaker is) like the *Qur'án* which is sevenfold in meaning, and in which there is food for the elect and for the vulgar.

He (the dervish) said, "This at least is evident to the vulgar, that the world is subject to the command of God.

No leaf drops from a tree without the predestination and ordainment of that Ruler of Fortune.

1900   No morsel goes from the mouth towards the gullet till God says to that morsel, '*Enter!*'

The inclination and desire which is Man's nose-rein—its movement is subject to the command of that Self-sufficient One.

In (all) the earths and heavens not an atom moves a wing, not a straw turns,

Save by His eternal and effectual command. To expound (this) is impossible, and presumption is not good.

Who may number all the leaves of the trees? How may the Infinite become amenable to speech?

1905   Hear this much, (however): since all action (in the universe) only comes to pass by the command of the Maker,

When the predestination of God becomes the pleasure of His servant, he (the servant) becomes a willing slave to His decree,

Not (because of) tasking himself, and not on account of the (future) reward and recompense; nay, his nature has become so goodly.

---

[1] Literally, "(from) street to street."
[2] Literally, "that one whose edict is carried into execution."

He does not desire his life for himself nor to the end that he may enjoy the life that is found sweet (by others).

Wheresoever the Eternal Command takes its course, living and dying are one to him.

He lives for God's sake, not for riches; he dies for God's sake, 1910 not from fear and pain.

His faith is (held) for the sake of (doing) His will, not for the sake of Paradise and its trees and streams.

His abandonment of infidelity is also for God's sake, not for fear lest he go into the Fire.

That disposition of his is like this originally: it is not (acquired by) discipline or by his effort and endeavour.

He laughs at the moment when he sees (the Divine) pleasure: to him Destiny is even as sugared sweetmeat."

The servant (of God) whose disposition and character is (like) 1915 this—does not the world move according to his command and behest?

Then why should he make entreaty and cry in prayer, "O God, avert this destiny"?

For God's sake his (own) death and the death of his children is to him like sweetmeat in the gullet.

To that loyal one the death-agony of his children is like honey-cakes to a destitute old man.

Why, then, should he invoke (God), unless perchance he see the pleasure of the (Divine) Judge in (such) invocation?

That righteous servant does not make that intercession and 1920 invocation from his own mercifulness.

He has burned up (consumed away) his own mercifulness at the moment when he has lighted the lamp of love of God.

Love is the Hell-fire of his attributes, and it has burnt up the attributes of self, hair by hair.

When did any night-traveller understand this distinction[1] except Daqúqí? (He understood it), so that he sped into this (spiritual) empire.

The story of Daqúqí and his miraculous gifts.

That Daqúqí had a fair front; he was a (spiritual) lord who loved (God) and possessed miraculous gifts.

He walked on earth as the moon in heaven: by him the spirits 1925 of the night-travellers became illumined.

He would not make his abode in any one place, he would not spend two days in a village.

He said, "If I stay two days in one house, love of that dwelling-place is kindled in me.

---

[1] I.e. the distinction between selfish and selfless prayer.

I am afraid of being beguiled by the dwelling-place: migrate, O my soul, and travel to independence.

I will not accustom my heart's nature to locality, (and I do this) in order that it may be pure in the (hour of) trial."

1930   During the day he was (engaged) in travel, during the night in ritual prayer: his eye (was) open on the King, and he (himself was) like the falcon.

(He was) severed from the creatures (of God), (but) not on account of ill-nature; isolated from man and woman, (but) not because of dualism[1].

A compassionate man to the creatures and beneficial (to them) as water; a goodly intercessor, and his prayers were answered.

(He was) kind to the good and the bad, and a sure refuge (for them); (he was) better than a mother, dearer than a father.

The Prophet said, "O sirs, to you I am compassionate and kind as a father,

1935   Because ye all are parts of me." Why (then) will ye tear the part away from the whole?

(When) the part is severed from the whole, it becomes useless; (when) the limb is severed from the body, it becomes carrion.

Till it is joined once more to the whole, it is dead: it has no consciousness of life;

And if it move, yet it has no support: the newly severed limb also moves.

If the part be severed and fall asunder from this (spiritual) whole, this is not the (kind of) whole that is liable to defect.

1940   .Separation from it and conjunction with it are not (really) predicable; the defective thing has been mentioned (only) for the sake of comparison.

Return to the story of Daqúqí.

He (the Prophet) once compared 'Alí to a lion, (but) the lion is not like him, though he (the Prophet) used (this expression).

From comparison (*mithál*) and likeness (*mithl*) and the difference between those (terms) push on, O youth, towards the story of Daqúqí:

That one who in giving legal judgements was the Imám of the people and in piety bore away the ball[2] from the angels;

That one who checkmated (eclipsed) the moon in wayfaring, while the Religion (itself) was jealous of his religiousness.

---

[1] *I.e.* not because he regarded God's creatures as other than God.
[2] We should say "bell" or "palm." The metaphor is derived from the game of polo.

Notwithstanding such piety and devotions and (nights passed 1945 in) performance of the ritual prayer, he was always seeking the elect (the saints) of God.

In travel his chief object was that he might come in touch for a moment with an elect servant (of God).

Whilst he was going along the road, he would be saying, "O God, make me a companion of the elect.

O Lord, to those (saints) whom my heart knows I am a slave and one who has girt his loins and is ready to do (them) good service;

And (as for) those whom I know not, do Thou, O God of the soul, make them kindly disposed to me who am debarred (from knowing them)."

The Lord would say to him, "O most noble prince, what 1950 passion is this and what unquenchable thirst is this?

Thou hast My love: why art thou seeking other (than Mine)? When God is with thee, how dost thou seek man?"

He would answer, "O Lord, O Knower of the secret, Thou hast opened in my heart the way of supplication.

If I am seated in the midst of the Sea, yet have I set my desire on the water in the jug.

I am like David: I have ninety ewes, and yet desire for my rival's ewe hath arisen in me.

Greed for Thy love is glorious and grand; greed for (the love 1955 of) any besides Thee is shameful and corrupt."

The lust and greed of the manly is advancement (in the spiritual Way), while that of the effeminate is disgrace and irreligion.

The greed of (true) men is by the forward way, (but) greed in the effeminate goes backward.

The one greed belongs to the perfection of manliness, while the other greed is (a cause of) opprobrium and disgust.

Ah, there is a very occult mystery here in (the fact) that Moses sets out to run towards a Khiẓr.

By God, do not tarry in anything (any spiritual position) that 1960 thou hast gained, (but crave more) like one suffering from dropsy who is never sated with water.

This (Divine) court is the Infinite Plane. Leave the seat of honour behind: the Way is thy seat of honour[1].

The mystery of Moses seeking Khiẓr, notwithstanding his perfection as a prophet and as one nigh unto God.

Learn from him with whom God spake, O noble sir! See what Kalím (Moses) says in his longing!

---

[1] *I.e.* the highest degree is not attainment, but infinite aspiration after having attained.

"Notwithstanding such a dignity and such a prophetic office (as I possess), I am a seeker of Khizr, (I am) quit of self-regard."

(They said), "O Moses, thou hast forsaken thy people; thou hast wandered distraught in search of a blessed man.

1965   Thou art an emperor delivered from fear and hope: how long wilt thou wander? How long wilt thou seek? To what bound?

(He that is) thine is with thee, and thou art conscious of this. O (thou who art exalted as the) sky, how long wilt thou traverse the (low) earth?"

Moses said, "Do not make this reproach (against me), do not waylay the Sun[1] and the Moon[2].

I will fare as far as *the meeting-place of the two seas*, that (afterwards) I may be accompanied by the Sovereign of the time.

I will make Khizr a means to (the achievement of) my purpose: (either) that, *or I will go onward* and journey by night *a long while*.

1970   I will fly with wings and pinions for years: what are years? For thousands of years."

(He said) "I will fare," meaning, "Is it not worth that (toilsome journey)? Do not deem the passion for the Beloved to be less than the passion for bread (worldly goods)."

This discourse hath no end, O uncle. (Now) tell the story of Daqúqí.

Resuming the story of Daqúqí.

That Daqúqí, God have mercy on him, said: "I travelled a long time between His two horizons[3].

Years and months I went on my journey for love of the Moon, unconscious of the way, lost in God."

1975   (Some one asked him), "(Why) dost thou go bare-foot over thorns and stones?" He said, "I am bewildered and beside myself and crazed."

Do not regard these feet (that walk) on the earth, for assuredly the lover (of God) walks on his heart;

(And) the heart that is intoxicated with the Sweetheart[4], what should it know of road and stage or of short (distance) and long?

That "long" and "short" are attributes of the body: the faring of spirits is another (kind of) faring.

You have journeyed from the seed to rationality: 'twas not by (taking) a step or (travelling from stage to) stage or moving from one place to another.

1980   The journey of the spirit is unconditioned in respect of Time and Space: our body learned from the spirit how to journey.

---

[1] Khizr.   [2] Moses.
[3] *I.e.* (in the literal sense), East and West.
[4] Literally, "He who cherishes the heart."

Now it[1] has relinquished the bodily manner of journeying: it moves unconditioned, (though) masked in the form of conditionedness.

He (Daqúqí) said, "One day I was going along like him that yearns, that I might behold in man the radiance of the Beloved,

That I might behold an ocean in a drop of water, a sun enclosed in a mote.

When I came on foot[2] to a certain shore, the day had turned late, and 'twas eventide.

The apparition of what seemed like seven candles in the direction of the shore.

Of a sudden I beheld from afar seven candles and hastened 1985 along the shore towards them.

The light of the flame of each candle thereof ascended beauteously to the loft of the sky.

I became amazed, (so that) even amazement (itself) became amazed: the waves of bewilderment passed over the head of my understanding.

(I thought), 'What kind of candles are these (that) He hath lighted, so that the eyes of His creatures are screened from them[3]?'

The people had gone to seek a lamp in the presence of that (sevenfold) candle which was surpassing the moon (in splendour).

Wonderful! There was a bandage over their eyes: they were 1990 bound by (the Divine destiny implied in the text) *He guideth aright those whom He will.*

How the seven candles became what seemed like one candle.

Then I saw the seven (candles) become one, its light cleaving the bosom (rim) of the sky.

Then again that one became seven once more: my intoxication and bewilderment waxed mighty.

(There were) such connexions between the candles as may not come (may not be uttered) on my tongue and (in) my speech.

That which one look perceives, 'tis impossible during years to show it forth by the tongue.

That which intellectual apprehension sees in one moment, 'tis 1995 impossible during years to hear it by the ear.

Since it hath no end, go (back) to thyself[4], for (as the Prophet aid), 'I cannot reckon (worthy) any praise of Thee.'

---

[1] *I.e.* the body of the saint.
[2] Literally, "by footsteps."
[3] Literally, "sewn (and debarred) from (seeing) them."
[4] Daqúqí tells himself to return to his narrative.

I advanced farther, running (and marvelling) what thing those candles are (which are one) of the signs of the Divine Majesty.

(Thus) I was going, beside myself and dumbfounded and deranged, till I fell down from making haste and speed.

In this (state), senseless and witless, I lay fallen awhile upon the dust of the earth.

2000   Then I came back to my senses and rose up: you would say that in my faring I had neither head nor foot.

How those candles appeared to the eye as seven men.

The seven candles appeared to the eye as seven men: their light was mounting to the azure vault.

Beside those lights the daylight was (murky as) dregs: by their intensity they were obliterating (all other) lights.

How those candles now became seven trees.

Then each man assumed the shape of a tree: my eye was happy in their greenery.

On account of the denseness of the leaves no boughs were visible; the leaves too had become scant (had almost vanished) on account of the plenteous fruit.

2005   Every tree had thrown its boughs above the *Sidra*[1]: what of the *Sidra?* They had reached beyond the Void.

The root of each (tree) had gone (down) into the bottom of the earth: assuredly it was lower than the Ox and the Fish[2].

Their roots were more smiling of face than the boughs: the intellect (was turned) upside down (confused and bewildered) by their shapes.

From the fruit that was bursting forcibly flashes of light would spurt forth, like juice.

How those trees were invisible to the people.

More wondrous (than all else) was this, that hundreds of thousands of people were passing through the desert and plain beside them,

2010   Hazarding their lives (ready to sacrifice everything) in desire for shade, and making a parasol out of a woollen garment,

And not seeing the shade of those (trees) at all. A hundred spittings on (such) distorted eyes!

The wrath of God had sealed their eyes, so that he (such a one) should not see the moon, (but) should see (only) Suhá[3].

---

[1] The Lote-tree above the highest Paradise.
[2] By which the terrestrial globe is upheld.
[3] A small star.

He sees a mote, (but) not the sun; yet he is not despairing of the grace and lovingkindness of God.

The caravans are without food, and (yet) these fruits are dropping ripe (beside them): O God, what magic is this?

With parched throats the people, having fallen pell-mell to 2015 plunder, were gathering the rotten apples,

(While) every leaf and bud of those boughs said continually, '*Oh, would that my people knew!*'

From the direction of every tree was coming the cry, 'Come towards us, O ye folk of evil fortune,'

(While) from (the Divine) jealousy there was coming to the trees the cry, 'We have bandaged their eyes; *nay, there is no refuge.*'

If any one had said to them 'Go in this direction, that ye may seek happiness from these trees,'

They all would have said, 'By Divine destiny this poor in- 2020 toxicated wretch has become mad:

Through long melancholy and through austerities the brain of this poor wretch has turned putrid, like an onion.'

He would have remained in astonishment, saying, 'O Lord, what is the matter? What is this veil (blindness) and mis- guidance that is upon the people?'

The people of every sort, (though endowed) with manifold discernment and understanding, do not move a foot in that direction.

By one consent the intelligent and acute amongst them have become incredulous of such a garden as this and undutiful.

Or have I become mad and crazy? Has the Devil cast some- 2025 thing (of delusion) upon my head?

At every moment I rub my eyes, (considering) whether I am dreaming and beholding a phantom in (the world of) time.

How can it be a dream? I go up the trees, I eat their fruit: how should I not believe?

(But) again, when I look at the incredulous ones who turn aside from this orchard,

Devoting their lives with the utmost indigence and penury because of their desire for half an unripe grape;

(When I see) these destitute folk uttering grievous lamenta- 2030 tion in their longing and greed for a single leaf,

(And when I see) these hundred thousands on thousands of people fleeing from this tree and these fruits—

Once more I say, 'Marvellous! Am I beside myself? Have I laid hold of a bough of phantasy?'"

Repeat (the text) *until when the Messengers (of God) despaired* down to (the words) *they thought they had been belied (kudhibú)*[1].

---

[1] *I.e.* disappointed of the fulfilment of the promise which God had made to them.

Recite (the verse) with this reading (*kudhibú*), for the omission of the *tashdíd* in *kudhibú* signifies[1] that he (the Messenger) deems himself debarred (from receiving the promised aid from God).

2035   The souls of the prophets fell into misgiving through the concurrence of disbelief (on the part) of the wicked;

(But) Our aid came to them after (their) doubting. Take leave of them (the misguided people) and climb the tree of the spirit.

Eat (of the fruit of this tree) and give it to every one that hath an allotted portion (thereof): at each moment and each instant there are lessons in (spiritual) magic (for him).

"The people are saying, 'Oh, how wonderful! What is this cry?—since the wilderness is devoid of trees and fruit.

We have been fooled by the words of the madmen (who tell us) that beside us there are gardens and trays (of fruit).

2040   We rub our eyes, (but) no garden is here; 'tis either a desert or a difficult road.

Oh, how wonderful! This tale (related by the prophets and saints) is so long: how should it be vain? And if it really is (as they say), where (is that which they tell of)?'

I, like them, am saying, 'Oh, how wonderful! Why has the action of the Lord put such a seal (upon their eyes)?'"

By these contentions (on the part of the unbelievers) Mohammed was astonished; Abú Lahab also remained in astonishment (at him).

Between this astonishment and that astonishment there is a profound difference. (Let us see) what the Almighty King will do (to the infidels in the end).

2045   O Daqúqí, advance more quickly (in thy quest for Unity). Hark, be silent! Inasmuch as there is a dearth of ears, how long wilt thou speak, how long?

How the seven trees became one.

He (Daqúqí) said, "I, the fortunate one, pushed forward; again all the seven (trees) became one tree.

At every moment they were becoming seven and (also) a single one: (you may imagine) what I was becoming like, through bewilderment.

After that, I beheld the trees (engaged) in the ritual prayer, drawn up in line and (properly) arranged like the congregation (of Moslems):

One tree (was) in front like the Imám, the others (were) standing behind it.

2050   That standing and kneeling and bowing low on the part of the trees seemed to me very marvellous.

Then I called to mind the word of God: He said, concerning *the stalkless plants and the trees, 'they bow down.'*

_____
[1] Literally, "is this."

Those trees had neither knee nor waist: what (a marvel) is such a regulation (regular performance) of the ritual prayer (in their case)!

The Divine inspiration came (upon me), saying, 'O illustrious one, art thou still wondering at Our action?'

How the seven trees became seven men.

After a long while those (trees) became seven men, all seated (in contemplation) for the sake of God who is single.

I keep rubbing my eyes (and wondering) who are those seven 2055 heroes[1] and what they have of this world.

When by (traversing) the road I came near (to them), I saluted them alertly.

The company (the seven men) answered that salutation, saying, 'O Daqúqí, glory and crown of the noble!'

'Why,' said I (to myself), 'how did they recognise me? They never set eyes on me before this (moment).'

At once they knew of my unspoken thought, and looked covertly[2] at one another,

And smilingly answered, 'O honoured one, is this hidden 2060 from thee even now?

How should the mystery of left and right be hidden from the heart that is in (the state of) bewilderment with God?'

I said (to myself), 'If[3] they are open to (in communication with) the (spiritual) realities, (yet) how are they acquainted with names (consisting) of letters attached to the form (of words)?'

He (one of the seven men) said, 'If a name vanish from (the consciousness of) a saint, know that that is (the result arising) from (his) absorption (in God), not from ignorance.'

Afterwards they said, 'We desire to follow thy leadership (in prayer), O holy friend.'

'Yes,' said I, 'but (wait) awhile—for I have certain difficulties 2065 (derived) from the revolution of Time—

In order that they may be solved by means of holy companionships; for through companionship a grape grows from the earth.

A kernelly seed graciously consorted in solitary intercourse with the dark earth;

It effaced itself entirely in the earth, so that no colour or scent or red or yellow (hue) remained to it.

After that effacement its constriction ceased: it opened its wings and expanded and sped on its way[4].

Inasmuch as it became selfless in the presence of its origin, 2070 the form departed (from it) and its real essence was displayed.'

---

[1] Literally, "lions."   [2] Literally, "from below."   [3] Reading ﺭﮔ for ﺯﮔ.
[4] Literally, "drove (forward) the animal on which it rode."

They nodded so (as though saying), 'Hark, 'tis for thee to command,' and from their nodding so a flame arose in my heart.

When for a while I had taken part with that elect company in contemplation (of God) and had been separated from myself,

At that very hour my spirit was freed from hours (of Time); (I say 'freed') because hours make the young old."

All changes have arisen from the hours: he that is freed from the hours is freed from change.

2075 When for an hour you escape from the hours, relation[1] abides not: you become familiar with that which is without relation[1].

The hours are not acquainted with hourlessness (timelessness), because for him (who is conscious of time) there is no way thither except bewilderment.

In this world of search and seeking every set of people have been tied in the stable peculiar to them,

And over each stable a trainer has been appointed; save by (his) permission no recalcitrant comes (into another place).

If, from vain desire, he should break away from the stable and intrude into the stable of others,

2080 At once the nimble and goodly stablemen seize the corner of his halter and drag (him back).

O cunning one, if you behold not your keepers, behold your choice (and perceive that it is) involuntary.

You are making a choice, and your hands and feet are loosed: why (then) are you imprisoned, why?

You have betaken yourself to denying (the action of) the keeper: you have called it 'threats of the fleshly soul.'

How Daqúqí went forward to act as Imám.

This discourse hath no end. "Run quickly! Hark, the (time for) prayer is come. Go forward, O Daqúqí!

2085 O unique one, come, perform the twofold (genuflexion)[2], that Time may be adorned by thee.

O clear-sighted Imám, in the ritual prayer a clear eye is requisite in the leader[3]."

According to the religious Law it is objectionable, O worthy (reader), to put forward a blind man in the office of Imám.

Though he know the *Qur'án* by heart and be quick and learned in divinity, the clear-sighted man is superior, even if he be a fool.

The blind man has no (means of) abstention from filth: the eye is the source of abstention and precaution.

2090 He does not see the dirt in passing by. May no true believer have blind eyes!

---

[1] Literally, "how."   [2] The morning-prayer.

[3] The translation follows the text, but the correct reading is چشم روشن بايد ايدر. See Appendix.

The man outwardly blind is in outward (material) filthiness;
the man inwardly blind is in inward (spiritual) filthiness.

This outward filthiness may be removed by some water; that
inward filthiness (gradually) increases.

It cannot be washed away save by water of the eye (tears),
when (once) the inward filthinesses have become manifest.

Since God has called the infidel "filth," that filthiness is not
on his outward part.

The infidel's outward part is not defiled by this (outward 2095
filth); that filthiness is in (his) disposition and religion.

The smell of this (outward filth comes (extends to a distance
of) twenty paces; but the smell of that (inward) filth (reaches)
from Rayy to Damascus;

Nay, its smell goes up to the heavens and mounts to the brain
of the houris and Riẓwán[1].

What I am saying is according to the measure of your under-
standing: I die in grief for (the absence of) a sound under-
standing.

The understanding is (like) the water, and the bodily ex-
istence (is like) the jug: when the jug is cracked, the water spills
from it.

This jug has five deep holes: neither water will stay in it nor 2100
even snow.

You have heard, too, the command (of God), "Close ye your
eyes tightly[2]"; (yet) you have not walked aright[3].

Your speech bears away your understanding by (way of) the
mouth; your ear is like sand: it drinks (sucks up) your under-
standing.

Similarly, your other holes (avenues of sense-perception) are
drawing (off) the hidden water of your understanding.

If you expel the water from the sea without (admitting) com-
pensation, you will make the sea a desert.

'Tis late; otherwise, I would declare the (true) state of the 2105
case (as to) the entrance of compensations and substitutes,

(And tell) whence come to the sea those compensations and
substitutes after (such) expenditures.

Hundreds of thousands of animals drink of it; from outside
also the clouds take it (its water) away;

(But) again the sea draws (into itself) those compensations—
whence (they come) is known to the righteous.

We began the stories in haste; in this Book (the *Mathnawí*)
they are left without (being brought to) the (final) issue[4].

---

[1] The Keeper of Paradise.   [2] Cf. *Qur'án*, XXIV, 30.
[3] Literally, "you have not planted your hoof rightly."
[4] *I.e.* their spiritual meanings and implications are not fully explained.
I have translated مَخْلَص. If مُخْلَص be retained, the literal translation is
"they are left without the choicest part," *i.e.* the moral.

2110   O Light of God, noble Ḥusámu'ddín, a king whose like the
sky and the elements have never brought to birth,
Seldom hast thou come into (the world of) soul and heart, O
thou at whose advent heart and soul are abashed.
How oft have I praised the people of the past! Of necessity,
thou wert (the object of) my quest in (praising) them.
Verily the invocation knows its own house: attach the praise
to the name of whomsoever you will.
God hath set down these tales and parables for the purpose of
concealing (the true nature of) the praise from the unworthy.
2115   Even if such praise is abashed before thee, yet God accepts
the (utmost) exertion of one that has little (to give).
God accepts a crust (of bread) and absolves (the giver), for
from the eyes of a blind man two drops (of light) are enough.
Birds and fishes know the (real meaning of) the ambiguous
style[1] in which I have praised compendiously this person of
goodly name,
To the end that the sighs of the envious may not blow upon
him, and that he (the envier) may not bite the (false) idea of him
(Ḥusámu'ddín) with the teeth (of malice).
Where should the envious man find even the idea of him?
When did a parrot rest in the abode of a mouse?
2120   That idea of him (Ḥusámu'ddín) arises (in the mind of the
envious man) from cunning practice[2] (on his part): it is the hair
of his eyebrow, not the new moon[3].
I sing thy praise outside of the five (senses) and the seven
(heavens). Now write "Daqúqí went forward."

How Daqúqí went forward to lead that company (in prayer).

In the salutations and benedictions addressed to the righteous
(saints) praise of all the prophets is blended.
The praises are all commingled (and united): the jugs are
poured into one basin.
Inasmuch as the object of praise Himself is not more than
One, from this point of view (all) religions are but one religion.
2125   Know that every praise goes (belongs) to the Light of God
and is (only) lent to (created) forms and persons.
How should folk praise (any one) except Him who (alone) has
the right (to be praised)?—but they go astray on (the ground of)
a vain fancy.
The Light of God in relation to phenomena is as a light
shining upon a wall—the wall is a link (focus) for these splen-
dours:

---

[1] *Íhám* is a rhetorical figure which consists in using words that suggest a
meaning not directly intended by the writer.
[2] Reading احتيال.   [3] See Book II, v. 112 foll.

Necessarily, when the reflexion moved towards its source, he who had gone astray lost the moon and ceased from praise;

Or (again) a reflexion of the moon appeared from a well, and he (the misguided one) put his head into the well and was praising that same (reflexion):

In truth he is a praiser of the moon, although his ignorance 2130 has turned its face towards its (the moon's) reflexion.

His praise belongs to the moon, not to that reflexion, (but) that (praise) becomes infidelity when the matter is misapprehended;

For that bold man was led astray by (his) perdition: the moon was above, while he fancied it was below.

The people are distracted by these idols (objects of desire), and (afterwards) they repent of the lust which they have indulged,

Because he (such a one) has indulged his lust with a phantom and has remained farther away from the Reality (than he was before).

Your desire for a phantom is like a wing, so that by means of 2135 that wing he (the seeker) may ascend to the Reality.

When you have indulged a lust, your wing drops off; you become lame, and that phantom flees from you.

Preserve the wing and do not indulge such lust, to the end that the wing of desire may bear you to Paradise.

The people fancy they are enjoying themselves: they are (really) tearing out their wings for the sake of a phantom.

I have become a debtor for (I owe) the explanation of this topic. Give me time, I am destitute; on that account I keep silence.

How the company followed the leadership of Daqúqí.

Daqúqí advanced to perform the prayer: the company were 2140 (as) the satin robe and he (as) the embroidered border.

Those (spiritual) kings followed his leadership, (standing) in a row behind that renowned exemplar.

When they pronounced[1] the *takbírs*[2], they went forth from this world, like a sacrifice.

O Imám, the (real) meaning of the *takbír* is this: "We have become a sacrifice, O God, before Thee."

At the moment of slaughtering (the victim) you say *Alláh akbar*: even so (do) in slaughtering the fleshly soul which ought to be killed.

[1] Literally, "became joined with," "entered upon."
[2] *Takbír* is the act of reciting the words "*Alláh akbar*," "God is most great," which are repeated several times at the beginning and in the course of the ritual prayer.

2145   The body is like Ismá'íl (Ishmael)[1], and the spirit like
Abraham: the spirit has pronounced the *takbír* over[2] the noble
body.

By lusts and desires the body was (merely) killed, (but) by
(the words) *bismilláh* (uttered) in the ritual prayer it was
sacrificed.

Whilst performing the prayer (they were) drawn up in ranks
before God, as at the Resurrection, and engaged in self-examina-
tion and orisons,

Standing in God's presence and shedding tears, like one who
rises erect on (the Day of) rising from the dead.

(On that Day) God will say, "What hast thou produced for
Me during this term of respite which I gave thee?

2150   In what (work) hast thou brought thy life to its end? In what
hast thou consumed thy food and strength?

Where hast thou dimmed the lustre of thine eye? Where hast
thou dissipated[3] thy five senses?

Thou hast expended eyes and ears and intellect and the pure
celestial substances[4]: what hast thou purchased from the earth?

I gave thee hands and feet as spade and mattock (for tilling
the soil of good works). When did those become (existent) of
themselves?"

Even so hundreds of thousands of such sorrowful messages
come from the Lord.

2155   At the time of standing (in prayer)[5] these words return (from
God to the worshipper), and from shame he is bent double in
the genuflexion.

From shame the power of standing remains not, and from
abashment he recites a litany of glorification while his knees are
bowed.

Then comes the (Divine) command, "Lift up thy head from
the genuflexion and tell over (what thou hast to say in) answer
to God."

The shamefaced one lifts up his head from the genuflexion;
then that man whose works are unripe (imperfect) falls on his
face.

Again the (Divine) command comes to him, "Lift up thy
head from the prostration and give an account of thy deeds."

2160   Once more the shamefaced one lifts up his head, and falls
again on his face, (flat) as a snake.

Again He says, "Lift up thy head and relate (thy deeds), for
I will inquire of thee (concerning them), hair by hair."

---

[1] Whom Abraham was ordered to sacrifice. See *Qur'án*, xxxvii, 99 foll.
[2] *I.e.* "has performed the funeral prayer over."
[3] Literally, "strained off," "poured away."
[4] *I.e.* the Divine nature reflected in Man.
[5] This passage describes the real essence of the ritual prayer, which shall
be made manifest at the Resurrection. Cf. verse 2174 *infra*.

He hath no power to stand on foot, since the words of awe
addressed to him have smitten his soul;

So he sits down because of that heavy burden. (Then) the Lord
says to him, "Speak plainly!

I gave thee bounty: tell (Me), what were thy thanks? I gave
thee capital: come, show (Me) the interest."

(Then) he (the worshipper) turns his face to the right hand in 2165
the salutation[1]—towards the spirits of the prophets and those
of the noble (saints),

Meaning to say, "O kings, (vouchsafe) intercession, for this
vile one's feet and mantle are stuck fast in the mire."

*Explaining that the salutation (in prayer) towards the right hand
at the Resurrection indicates (the worshipper's) dread of being
examined by God and (his) seeking help and intercession from the
prophets.*

The prophets say, "The day for remedy is past; the remedy
and the strong implement (for tilling the soil of good works)
were *there*[2].

Thou art an untimely bird[3]. Begone, O miserable one, take
leave of us, do not wade in our blood[4]."

(Then) he turns his face to the left hand towards his family
and kinsfolk: they say to him, "Be silent!

Hark, answer for thyself to the Creator. Who are we? Sire, 2170
keep thy hands off us[5]!"

No succour comes either from this side or from that: the
soul of this desperate man is (torn into) a hundred pieces.

The wretched personage loses hope of all; then he lifts up
both hands in supplication,

Crying, "O God, I have lost hope of all: Thou art the First
and the Last and the ultimate Bourn."

Behold in the ritual prayer these goodly indications, in order
that you may know these will certainly come to pass.

From the ritual prayer, which is (as) the egg, hatch the chick[6]; 2175
do not peck[7] like a bird without reverence or propriety.

*How during the ritual prayer Daqúqí heard cries of distress
from a ship that was about to sink.*

Daqúqí made ready to act as Imám: he began to perform the
ritual prayer on the shore,

---

[1] The blessing, "Peace be on you, and the mercy of God!" with which the
prayer-service ends.
[2] *I.e.* in the earthly life.
[3] Like the cock that crows before dawn.
[4] *I.e.* "do not endeavour to make our hearts bleed for thee."
[5] *I.e.* "refrain from calling upon us for help."
[6] *I.e.* the corresponding spiritual feelings and qualities.
[7] Literally, "do not move your head rapidly."

While that company stood up behind him. Look you, a goodly company, and an elect Imám!

Of a sudden his eye turned towards the sea, because he heard (cries of) "Help! Help!" (coming) from the direction of the sea.

He saw amidst the waves a ship in (the hour of its) fate, and in tribulation and an evil plight.

2180   (There were) both night and clouds and huge waves: these three darknesses, and (also) fear of (being drowned in) the whirlpool.

A fierce wind, like 'Azrá'íl[1], arose; the waves tossed on left and right.

The people in the ship were faint with terror: cries of woe had arisen,

And in lamentation they were beating their heads with their hands: infidel and deist—they all had become sincere (in devotion to God),

Making heartfelt[2] promises and vows to God with a hundred humble entreaties in that hour.

2185   Bare-headed in the prostrate attitude (of Divine worship) were those whose faces, because of (their) perversity, had never seen the *qibla* at all[3].

They (formerly) said, "This worship of God is useless"; (but) in that hour (of despair) they saw a hundred lives (precious advantages) therein.

They had entirely abandoned hope of all—of friends and maternal and paternal uncles and father and mother.

At that moment ascetic and reprobate (alike) had become God-fearing as a wicked man at the time of the death-agony.

Neither on the left nor on the right was there any help for them: when (all) expedients are dead, (then) is the time to invoke God.

2190   They were (engaged) in invocation and lament and moaning: a black smoke went up from them to heaven.

Then the Devil cried in enmity, "Avaunt! Avaunt! O dog-worshippers[4], (ye shall be afflicted with) two maladies.

Death and woe (to you)! O unbelievers and hypocrites, this will befall (you) in the end,

(That) after deliverance ye will rejoice[5] to become peculiar devils for the sake of (gratifying) your lust,

And will not remember that in the day of peril God took your hands (to save you) from His decree."

2195   This cry was coming from the Devil; but these words are unheard except by a good ear.

---

[1] The Angel of death.   [2] Literally, "with (all their) soul."
[3] *I.e.* they had never turned their faces towards Mecca, as Moslems do when performing the ritual prayers.
[4] *I.e.* devotees of the carnal soul.
[5] Literally, "Your eyes will be wet (refreshed)."

Muṣṭafá (Mohammed), the Pole and the Emperor and the Sea of Purity, has told us truly,

That what the ignorant will see in the end the wise see from the first step.

If matters are hidden and secret at the beginning, the wise man sees at first, while that obstinate one (sees) at last.

The beginning thereof is concealed, and both the wise man and the ignorant will see the end in (the moment of its) manifestation;

(But) if you, O contumacious one, do not see the hidden event 2200 (before it comes to pass)—when did the torrent sweep away your prudence?

What is prudence? To think ill. In this world he (the prudent man) at every moment will (expect to) see a sudden calamity.

The ideas of the prudent man.

'Tis as when a lion has suddenly come up and seized a man and dragged him into the jungle.

At (the moment of) that carrying off, what will he think of? Consider (this), and think of the same thing, O thou who art learned in the (Mohammedan) Religion.

The lion, Destiny, is dragging into the jungles (of death) our souls which are preoccupied with (worldly) business and trades.

That (case) is like (the fact) that the people (of this world) 2205 have fear of poverty, plunged (as they are) up to their throats in the briny water.

If they should fear the Creator of poverty, treasures would be opened to them on the earth.

Through fear of affliction they all are in the very essence of affliction: in their quest for (material) existence they have fallen into non-existence[1].

Daqúqí's entreaty and intercession for the deliverance of the ship.

When Daqúqí beheld that turmoil[2], his pity was stirred and his tears flowed fast[3].

He said, "O Lord, do not look at their deeds! Take their hands (to succour them), O auspicious King!

Bring them back well and safe to the shore, O Thou whose 2210 hand (power) reaches (both) sea and land!

O Gracious One, O Merciful and Everlasting One, pass over this wickedness committed by devisers of evil!

O Thou who hast given, free of cost, a hundred eyes and ears, and, without bribe, hast dispensed intellect and understanding;

---

[1] *I.e.* privation of real existence.   [2] Literally, "Resurrection."
[3] Literally, "ran."

Who hast bestowed the gift before the merit (was existent), having suffered from us the whole (sum) of ingratitude and transgression:

O Almighty One, Thou art able to pardon our great sins in privacy[1].

2215 We have burnt ourselves from concupiscence and greed, and even this invocation we have learned from Thee.

(We beseech Thee) in reverence for Thy having taught (us) to invoke (Thee) and for having lighted the lamp (of invocation) amidst darkness like this."

Thus was the invocation running on his tongue[2] at that time, like (the words of) faithful mothers.

The tears were flowing from his eyes, and that invocation was going up to Heaven from him (while he was) beside himself (unconscious).

That unconscious invocation is, in truth, different: that invocation is not from him (the speaker), it is spoken by the (Divine) Judge.

2220 God is making that invocation, since he (the speaker) is naughted (*faná*): the invocation and the answer (to it) are (both) from God.

There is not present (at that time) the medium, namely, the created person: body and spirit (alike) are unaware of making that supplication.

The (chosen) servants of God are merciful and long-suffering: they possess the disposition of God in regard to putting things right.

They are kind and bribeless ones, helpers in the hard plight and the heavy (grievous) day.

Hark, seek this (saintly) company, O afflicted one! Hark, hold them (as) a prize[3] before the (coming of) affliction.

2225 Through the breath (prayer) of that (spiritual) hero the ship was saved, while the people in the ship thought (they were saved) by their own efforts,

(Supposing) that maybe in (the hour of) dread their arm had skilfully shot an arrow at the target.

Foxes, in the chase, are saved by their legs, but the foxes inconsiderately deem that (safety to proceed) from their tails.

(Hence) they play fondly with their tails, thinking, "These save our lives in the ambuscade (of calamity)."

O fox, preserve your legs from (being broken by) brickbats; when you have no legs, what use is your tail, O bold-eyed one?

2230 We are like foxes, and the noble (saints) are (as) our legs: they save us from a hundred kinds of vengeance.

---

[1] *I.e.* without making them known.
[2] Literally, "his utterance."
[3] *I.e.* seize the opportunity of consorting with them.

Our subtle contrivance is as our tails: we play fondly with our tails, left and right.

We wag our tails in argumentation and cunning, in order that Zayd and Bakr[1] may remain amazed at us.

We have sought to excite the amazement of the people; we have eagerly grasped at Divinity[2],

That by means of guile we may gain possession of (the people's) hearts; we do not see that we are in a ditch.

You are in the ditch and in the pit, O scoundrel: keep your 2235 hands off the moustache of others[3]!

When you arrive at a fair and beauteous garden, after that lay hold of the people's skirts and lead them.

O you who dwell in the prison of the four (elements) and the five (senses) and the six (directions), lead others also to (such) a goodly place[4]!

O you who, like an ass-servant, are the comrade of the ass's rump, you have found a (fine) spot to kiss: take us (to it)!

Since (true) servitude to the Beloved has not been granted you[5], whence has arisen in you the wish for sovereignty?

In your desire that they should say to you "Bravo!" you have 2240 tied a bowstring on the neck of your soul.

O fox, abandon this tail, (which is) contrivance, and devote your heart to the lords of the heart (the saints).

(Whilst you are) under the protection of the lion, roast-meat will not fail; O fox, do not hasten towards the carcase.

O heart, thou wilt be regarded (with favour) by God at the moment when, like a part, thou goest towards thy Whole.

God saith, "Our regard is (bestowed) on the heart; it is not (bestowed) on the external form, which is (only) water and earth."

You say, "I too have a heart"; (but) the heart is above the 2245 empyrean, it is not below.

Certainly in the dark earth also there is water, but 'tis not proper for you to wash your hands with that water,

Because, though it is water, it is overcome by the earth. Do not, then, say of your heart, "This too is a heart."

The heart that is higher than the heavens is the heart of the saint or the prophet.

That (heart) has become cleansed of earth and purified; it has come to (full) growth and has been made complete.

It has taken leave of earth and has come to the Sea; it has 2250 escaped from the prison of earth and has become of the Sea.

---

[1] Equivalent to "Tom, Dick, and Harry."
[2] *I.e.* "we have emulated Pharaoh in our desire for worldly pomp and power."
[3] *I.e.* "first correct your own faults."
[4] This and the next verse are ironical.
[5] Literally, "has not given its hand (yielded itself) to you."

(But) our water has remained imprisoned in earth. Hark, O Sea of Mercy, draw us out of the clay!

The Sea says, "I draw thee into myself, but thou art vainly pretending to be the sweet water.

Thy vain pretence is keeping thee deprived of fortune: abandon that (idle) fancy and enter into me."

The water in the earth (of the body) desires to go into the Sea, (but) the earth has seized the water's foot and is dragging (it back).

2255   If it release its foot from the hand of the earth, the earth will be left dry, and it (the water) becomes absolutely free.

What is that drawing back of the water by the earth? (It is) your drawing (towards you) the dessert and unmixed wine (of sensuality).

Even so every lust in the world, whether it be (for) riches or power or bread—

Each of these things produces an intoxication (ardent desire) in you, and when you gain it not, it inflicts a headache upon you.

This headache of grief has become a proof that your intoxication was caused by that missed object (of desire).

2260   Do not partake of these (objects) but according to the measure of (your) necessity, lest they grow predominant and become rulers over you.

You scornfully refused (help), saying, "I am the owner of a (purified) heart: I have no need of any one else, I am united (with God)."

That is as though the water in the earth should scornfully refuse, saying, "I am the water, and why should I seek aid?"

You fancied this polluted (heart) was the (pure) heart; consequently you averted your heart from those possessed of (purified) hearts.

Do you indeed think it possible that this heart which is in love with milk and honey should be that (pure) heart?

2265   The deliciousness of milk and honey is the reflexion of the (pure) heart: from that heart the sweetness of every sweet thing is derived.

Hence the heart is the substance, and the world is the accident: how should the heart's shadow (reflexion) be the object of the heart's desire?

Is that (pure heart) the heart that is enamoured of riches and power, or is submissive to this black earth and water (the body),

Or to vain fancies which it worships in the darkness for the sake of fame?

The heart is naught but the Sea of Light: is the heart the place for vision of God—and then blind?

The heart is not (contained) in hundreds of thousands (of 2270 persons) noble or common; it is in a single one: which is he? Which?

Leave (what is only) a fragment of the heart and seek the (perfect) heart, in order that by means of it that fragment may become as a mountain.

The (perfect) heart is encompassing (the whole of) this realm of existence and scattering gold in beneficence and bounty.

It chooses to lavish blessings derived from the Blessedness of God upon the people of the world.

Whosoever's skirt is right and ready, the largesse of the heart comes to that person.

Your skirt (to catch that largesse) is supplication and presence 2275 (with God): beware, do not put in your skirt the stone of iniquity,

In order that your skirt may not be torn by those stones and that you may distinguish the sterling coin (of truth) from the colours (of falsehood).

You have filled your skirt with stones (of iniquity) from this world, and also with stones of silver and gold, as children (do).

Inasmuch as from that fancy of silver and gold there was no (real) gold, the skirt of your sincerity was rent and your sorrow increased.

How should the (coloured) stone appear to the children as stone, till Reason lays hold of their skirts?

The Elder (*Pír*) is Reason, not that white hair (of eld): hair 2280 is not contained in (has nothing to do with) this fortune and hope (which is bestowed by Reason).

How the company (of the Seven) took offence at Daqúqí's invocation and intercession, and flew away and disappeared in the Veil of the Unseen World; and how Daqúqí was bewildered (and did not know) whether they had gone into the air or on the earth.

"When the ship was saved and (the voyagers) attained to their desire, simultaneously the (ritual) prayer of that company was finished[1].

They began to murmur to one another[2], saying, 'O father, which of us is this (interfering) busybody?'

Each one spoke in secret to the other, (whilst they were) concealed (from view) behind Daqúqí's back,

And each one said, 'I did not make this invocation just now, either externally or internally.'

He (one of the company) said, 'It would seem that this Imám 2285 of ours, (moved) by grief, has meddlesomely offered an orison.'

Said the other, 'O thou who art familiar with (intuitive) certainty, so it appears to me too.

[1] Here Daqúqí resumes his narrative.
[2] Literally, "a murmuring with one another fell upon them.'

He has been meddlesome: (prompted) by distress he has interfered with Him who chooseth (as He pleaseth), the Absolute One.'

When I looked behind (me) to see what those noble ones were saying,

I did not see one of them in their place: they had all gone from their place.

2290   (They were) neither on the left nor on the right nor above nor below: my keen eye was unable to find the company (anywhere).

You might say that they were pearls (which) had become water: there was neither footprint nor any dust (to show where they had gone) in the desert.

At that moment they all (had) entered into the tents of God: into what garden had the troop (of them) gone?

I remained in amazement as to how God caused this company to be concealed from mine eye."

In such wise did they vanish from his eye, like the plunge of fishes into the water of a stream.

2295   During (many) years he continued to grieve for (the loss of) them; during (many) lifetimes he shed tears in longing for them.

You may say, "How should a man of God bring into view the thought of (take any thought of) human beings beside God?"

You are in a hole[1] here, O so-and-so, because you have regarded them as flesh, not as spirit.

You have come to ruin[2], O foolish man, because like the vulgar you regarded these (persons) as human beings.

You have regarded (them) in the same way as the accursed Iblís (regarded Adam): he said, "I am of fire, (while) Adam is of earth."

2300   Bandage your Satanic eye for one moment: how long, pray, will you regard the (external) form? How long, how long?

O Daqúqí with (thy) streaming eyes[3], come, do not abandon hope: seek them!

Come, seek (them), for search is the pillar (foundation) of fortune: every success consists in (depends on) fixing the heart (upon the object of desire).

Unconcerned with all the business of the world, keep saying with (all) thy soul kú, kú[4], like the dove.

Consider this well, O thou who art veiled (by worldliness), that God hath tied "invocation" to "I will answer[5]."

2305   Whosoever's heart is purged of infirmity, his invocation will go unto the Lord of glory.

---

[1] Literally, "the ass is lying down," i.e. "you cannot make any progress in this matter."
[2] Literally, "the affair is ruined."
[3] Literally, "with two eyes like a stream."
[4] I.e. "where? where?"
[5] Qur'án, XL, 62.

Explaining further the story of him who in the time of David, on whom be peace, sought to receive (from God) lawful means of livelihood without working or taking trouble, and how his prayer was answered favourably.

The story has come into my mind how that poor man used to moan and lament day and night,

And beg of God à lawful means of livelihood without pursuit and trouble and work and movement (from one place to another).

We have formerly related a part of what happened to him[1], but hindrance intervened and became fivefold.

(Now) too we shall tell (the rest of) it. Whither will it (the story) flee, since wisdom has poured (on us) from the clouds of God's bounty?

The owner of the cow espied him and said "Hey, O you to 2310 whose unrighteousness my cow has fallen a prey[2],

Hey, tell (me) why did you kill my cow? Fool! Cutpurse! Deal fairly (with me)[3]."

He said, "I was begging God for daily bread and preparing a *qibla* (for myself) of supplication[4].

That ancient prayer of mine was answered (by God). She (the cow) was my portion of daily bread: I killed her. Behold the answer (to your question)!"

He (the owner of the cow) came angrily and seized his collar; having lost patience, he struck him in the face with his fist several times.

How both the adversaries went to the prophet David, on whom be peace.

He led him to the prophet David, saying, "Come, O you 2315 crazy fool and criminal!

Drop (this) silly argument, O impostor; let (some) intelligence into your body and come to your senses!

What is this that you are saying? What is the prayer (you speak of)? Do not laugh at my head and beard and your own (too), O scoundrel!"

He (the poor man) said, "I have offered (many) prayers to God, I have borne much toil and pain[5] in this supplication.

I possess the certainty (that) the prayer has been answered. Dash your head against the stones, O foul-spoken one!"

---

[1] See p. 83.
[2] Literally, "has become pawned."
[3] Literally, "enter into equity," *i.e.* "be fair and answer my question."
[4] *I.e.* "I was concentrating all my thoughts upon supplication."
[5] Literally, "I have drunk much blood."

2320 He cried, "Hey, gather round, O Moslems! Behold the drivel and raving of this imbecile!

O Moslems, for God's sake, how should prayer make my property belong to him?

If it were so, by means of a single prayer of this kind the whole world would carry off (one another's) possessions by force.

If it were so, the blind beggars would have become grandees and princes;

(For) they are (engaged) day and night in invocation and praise (of God), uttering entreaties and crying, 'O God, do Thou give unto us!

2325 Unless Thou give, assuredly no one will give (us anything): O Opener, do Thou open the lock of this (bounty)!'

Supplication and prayer is the means whereby the blind earn their livelihood, (yet) they get no gift but a crust of bread."

The people said, "This Moslem speaks the truth, and this prayer-monger is one who seeks to act unjustly.

How should this prayer be a means of acquiring property? When forsooth did the religious Law enter this on the roll[1]?

A thing becomes your property by sale and donation or by bequest and gift or by some means of this kind.

2330 In what book is this new statute (to be found)? Give back the cow or go to prison!"

He (the poor man) was turning his face to Heaven (and saying), "None knoweth my (spiritual) experience save Thee.

Thou didst put that prayer into my heart, Thou didst raise a hundred hopes in my heart.

Not idly was I uttering that prayer: like Joseph, I had dreamed dreams."

Joseph saw (in dream) the sun and the stars bowing low before him, like servants.

2335 He relied upon the true dream: in the dungeon and prison he sought nothing but that.

Because of his reliance upon that, he cared naught for servitude and reproach, whether more or less.

He had a (great) reliance upon his dream which was shining in front of him like a candle.

When they cast Joseph into the well, there came to his ear a cry from God—

"O paladin, one day thou wilt become king, so that thou mayst rub this wrong upon their faces[2]."

2340 He who utters this cry is not visible, but the heart (of Joseph) recognised the Speaker from the effect (of the words).

---

[1] Literally, "string this on the thread," *i.e.* include prayer amongst the means of acquiring property.
[2] *I.e.* requite them for this injustice.

From that (Divine) allocution a (great) strength and peace and support fell into the midst of his soul.

Through that Majestical cry the well became to him a rose-garden and banquet, as the fire to Abraham.

By means of that strength he cheerfully endured every affliction that came to him afterwards—

Even as the delicious savour of the cry *Am not I (your Lord)?* subsists in the heart of every true believer till the Resurrection,

So that they do not rebel against tribulation or shrink from 2345 (obeying) the commands and prohibitions of God.

The rose-conserve (of spiritual delight) digests the morsel, that is, the (Divine) decree, which bestows bitterness;

(But) he that does not rely upon the rose-conserve vomits the morsel in disgust.

Any one who has dreamed of the Day of *Alast*[1] is drunken in the path of devotional works, drunken:

Like a drunken (frenzied) camel, he is bearing this (heavy) sack without flagging and without questioning and without fatigue;

The froth round his muzzle, namely, his confession of faith, 2350 has become a witness to his (inward) intoxication and heart-burning.

Through the strength (bestowed on him) the camel becomes like a fierce lion; beneath the heavy burden he eats little (food).

In (his) longing for the she-camel a hundred starvations (lie lightly) on him; the mountain seems to him (as) a strand of hair.

(But) he who has not dreamed such a dream in *Alast* does not become a servant and seeker (of God) in this world;

Or if he does become (such), (he is) always changing and shifting[2] in vacillation: he gives thanks (to God) for one moment and utters complaints for a year.

He steps forward and backwards in the Way of the Religion 2355 with a hundred vacillations and without (any) certainty.

I am owing (you) the exposition of this. Lo, (you have received) the pledge[3]; and if you are in haste, hear (the complete exposition) from (the Súra beginning with the words) *Have not We opened...*[4]?

Since the explanation of this subject has no end, proceed[5] to (speak of) the litigant (who claimed redress on account) of the cow.

He (the man who had killed the cow) said, "That impostor has called me blind because of (my having committed) this crime: O God, 'tis a very Satanic inference (of his).

---

[1] The Covenant made between God and the spirits of the elect in the state of pre-existence.
[2] Literally, "(he is) in a hundred minds."
[3] *I.e.* the partial exposition which I have given already.
[4] *Qur'án,* XCIV, 1.   [5] Literally, "drive the ass."

When have I been praying in the fashion of the blind? When have I begged of any one except the Creator?

2360   The blind man in his ignorance hath hope of (Thy) creatures; (but) I (have hope) of Thee (alone), by whom every difficult thing is (made) easy.

That blind fellow[1] has reckoned me amongst the blind: he has not seen my soul's humble supplication and my entire devotion (to Thee).

This blindness of mine is the blindness of love: it is (a case of) 'Love makes one blind and deaf,' O Ḥasan[2].

I am blind to aught other than God, I am (made) seeing by Him: this is what Love demands. Say, (is it not so?).

Do not Thou (O God), who art seeing, deem me to be one of the blind: I am revolving round Thy grace, O Axis (of all).

2365   Just as Thou didst show a dream to the veracious Joseph, and it became a support to him,

To me too Thy grace showed a dream: that endless prayer of mine was not an idle play.

(Thy) creatures do not understand my hidden thoughts and they regard my words as drivel.

They have the right (to do so), for who knows the mystery of the Unseen save the Knower of secrets and the Coverer of faults?"

His adversary said to him, "Turn your face to me! Tell the truth! Why have you turned your face towards Heaven, uncle?

2370   You are employing fraud, you are casting error (suggesting falsehood): you are prating of love and nearness (to God).

Inasmuch as you are spiritually dead, with what face have you turned[3] your face towards the heavens?"

On this account an uproar arose in the city, (while) that Moslem laid his face (flat) on the ground,

Crying, "O God, do not put this servant (of Thine) to shame: if I am wicked, yet do not divulge my secret.

Thou knowest (the truth), and the long nights (know it) during which I was calling unto Thee with a hundred supplications.

2375   Albeit this (supplication) has no worth in the sight of the people, in Thy sight it is like a shining lamp."

How David, on whom be peace, heard what both the litigants had to say, and interrogated the defendant.

When the prophet David came forth, he said, "Hey, what is (all) this about? What is it?"

---

[1] The owner of the cow.
[2] This and the following verse are addressed to the owner of the cow or to one of the bystanders.
[3] *I.e.* "how have you dared to turn?"

The plaintiff said, "O prophet of God, (give me) justice!
My cow strayed into his house.

He killed my cow. Ask him why he killed my cow, and (bid
him) explain what happened."

David said to him (the poor man), "Speak, O noble one!
How did you destroy the property of this honourable person?

Take care! Do not talk incoherently, (but) bring forward 2380
(your) plea, in order that this claim and cause may be (settled
and) laid aside."

He said, "O David, for seven years I was (engaged) day and
night in invocation and entreaty.

This (is what) I was seeking from God: 'O God, (I said),
I want a means of livelihood (that will be) lawful and without
trouble (on my part).'

(Both) men and women are acquainted with my lamentation;
the children (can) describe this happening.

Ask whomsoever thou wilt for information about this, so that
he may tell (thee) without torture and without (suffering)
harm.

Inquire of the people both openly and secretly what this 2385
beggar with the tattered cloak used to say.

After all this invocation and outcry, suddenly I saw a cow in
my house.

My eye became dim, not on account of the food, (but) for joy
that the supplication had been accepted.

I killed her that I might give (alms) in thankfulness that He
who knoweth things unseen had hearkened to my prayer."

How David, on whom be peace, gave judgement against the slayer of the cow.

David said, "Wipe out these words and declare (set forth) a
legal plea in this dispute.

Do you deem it allowable that, without any (such) plea, I 2390
should establish a wrong ordinance in the city?

Who gave you this (cow)? Did you buy or inherit her? How
will you take the crop? Are you the farmer?

Know, uncle, that the acquisition (of property) is like agri-
culture: unless you sow (the land), the produce does not belong
to you;

For you reap what you sow: that is yours. Otherwise, this
act of injustice is proved against you.

Go, pay the Moslem's money, and don't speak falsely. Go, try
to borrow (the money), and pay (it to him), and don't seek (to
do) wrong."

"O King," he replied, "thou art saying to me the same thing 2395
as the oppressors say."

How that person earnestly appealed (to God) against
the judgement of David, on whom be peace.

He prostrated himself and said, "O Thou who knowest (my
inward) ardour, cast that flame into the heart of David!

Put in his heart that which Thou hast secretly let fall into
mine, O my Benefactor!"

He said this and began to weep with loud cries of lamentation,
so that David's heart was moved exceedingly[1].

"Hark," said he, "O demander of (redress on account of) the
cow, give me a respite to-day and do not search into these
matters of dispute,

2400   So that I may go to a solitary place and ask the Knower of
mysteries about these matters, (whilst I am engaged) in prayer.

During prayer I am accustomed to turn thus (to God): (that
is) the meaning of (the words of the Tradition), 'the delight[2]
I feel in the ritual prayer[3].'

The window of my soul is opened, and from the purity (of
the Unseen World) the Book of God comes (to me) without
intermediary.

The Book and the rain (of Divine grace) and the Light are
falling through my window into my house from my (real and
original) source."

The house that is without a window is Hell: to make a win-
dow, O servant (of God), is the foundation of the (true) Religion.

2405   Do not ply the axe on every thicket: oh, come and ply the
axe in excavating a window.

Or dost not thou know that the light of the sun is the re-
flexion of the Sun beyond the veil?

Thou knowest that the animals too have seen the light of this
(external sun): what, then, is (the illumination signified in the
text) "*I bestowed honour* on My Adam?"

"I am plunged in the Light, like the sun; I cannot dis-
tinguish myself from the Light[4].

My going to prayer and to that solitude is for the purpose of
teaching the people the Way.

2410   I put (things) crooked[5] in order that this world may become
straight": this is (the meaning of) "War is deceit," O paladin.

There is not permission (for me to say more); otherwise, he
(David) would have poured out (the whole matter)[6] and would
have raised dust from the sea[7] of the mystery.

---

[1] Literally, "went forth from its place."
[2] Literally, "the coolness of my eye."
[3] The Prophet is said to have mentioned this as one of the three things he
loved best in the world.
[4] The speaker is David.
[5] *I.e.* "I do not show things as they are in reality." The mystical doctrine
of the Divine Unity must not be divulged.
[6] *I.e.* "I, speaking by the mouth of David, would have revealed all."
[7] *I.e.* "he would have cloven a dry path through the sea."

David went on speaking in this tenor, (so that) the under-
standing of the people was on the point of being burned up.

Then some one pulled his collar from behind, saying, "I have
not any doubt as to His unity."

(Thereupon) he came to himself, cut short his discourse,
closed his lips, and set out for the place where he was alone.

How David went into seclusion in order that
the truth might be made manifest.

He shut the door, and then went quickly to the prayer-niche 2415
and (betook himself to) the invocation that is answered (by God).

God revealed the entire matter to him[1]: he became aware of
him that was (really) deserving of punishment.

Next day all the litigants came and formed ranks before
David.

Thus the questions (left) in dispute came up again: the plain-
tiff at once uttered violent reproaches.

How David gave judgement against the owner of the cow, bidding
him withdraw from the case concerning the cow; and how the
owner of the cow reproached David, on whom be peace.

David said to him, "Be silent! Go, abandon (your claim),
and acquit this Moslem of (responsibility for) your cow.

Inasmuch as God has thrown a veil over you (concealed 2420
your guilt), O youth, depart and keep silence and acknowledge
the obligation of (giving thanks to God for His) concealment."

He cried, "Oh, woe is me! What judgement is this, what
justice? Wilt thou establish a new law on my account?

The fame of thy justice has gone so far that earth and heaven
have become fragrant (with the scent thereof).

This wrong has never been done (even) to blind dogs; rock
and mountain are burst asunder of a sudden by this iniquity."

In such fashion was he uttering reproaches publicly, crying,
"Hark ye, 'tis the time of injustice, hark ye!"

How David pronounced sentence against the owner of the cow,
saying, "Give him (the defendant) the whole of your property."

After that, David said to him, "O contumacious man, give 2425
the whole of your wealth to him immediately;

Otherwise, your plight will become grievous. I tell you (this)
in order that your crime may not be made manifest through
him."

[1] Literally, "God showed unto him that which He showed unto him in
its entirety."

He put dust on his head and tore his raiment, crying, "At every instant thou art adding an injury."

Once more he went on in this (strain of) reproach; then David called him to his presence,

And said, "Since 'twas not your fortune (to be saved), O you whose fortune is blind, little by little your wickedness has come to light.

2430   Cacavisti, then (you advance to) the high seat and the place of honour. Oh, may sticks and straw be withheld from such an ass as you are!

Begone! Your children and your wife have (now) become his slaves. Say no more!"

He (the plaintiff) was dashing stones against his breast with both hands and running up and down in his folly.

The people too began to blame (David), for they were unaware of the hidden (circumstances) of his (the plaintiff's) action.

How should one that is subject, like a straw, to (the wind of) sensuality know the oppressor from the oppressed?

2435   He that cuts off the head of his wicked self—he (alone) finds the way to (discriminating) the oppressor from the oppressed.

Otherwise, that oppressor, which is the fleshly soul within (us), (being moved) by frenzy, is the adversary of the oppressed.

A dog always attacks the poor; so far as it can, it inflicts wounds upon the poor.

Know that lions feel shame, (but) not dogs, because he (the lion) does not prey on his neighbours.

The mob, which slays the oppressed and worships the oppressor—their dog (carnal soul)[1] sprang forth from ambush (and rushed) towards David.

2440   That party (of the people) turned their faces to David, saying, "O chosen prophet, who hast compassion on us,

This is unworthy of thee, for this is a manifest injustice: thou hast abased an innocent man for naught."

How David, on whom be peace, resolved to summon the people to a certain plain, in order that he might disclose the mystery and make an end of all arguments.

He said, "O friends, the time has come that his hidden secret should be displayed.

Arise, all (of you), that we may go forth, so that we may become acquainted with that hidden secret.

In such and such a plain there is a huge tree, its boughs dense and numerous and curved.

---

[1] Reading سكشان. The text reading means "in dog fashion."

Its tent and tent-pegs are very firm; from its roots the smell 2445 of blood is coming to me.

Murder has been done at the bottom of that goodly tree: this man of sinister fortune has killed his master.

The clemency of God has concealed that (crime) till now, (but) at last (it has come to light) through the ingratitude of that scoundrel,

Who never a single day looked upon his master's family, not (even) at Nawrúz and (other) seasons of festival,

And never searched after the destitute (children, to relieve their want) with a single morsel of food, or bethought him of the former obligations (which he had received),

(And so continued), till for the sake of a cow this accursed 2450 wretch is now felling his (master's) son[1] to the earth.

He, of himself, has lifted the veil from his crime; else God would have concealed his sin."

In this cycle of woe[2] the infidel and the profligate rend their veils of their own accord.

Wrong is covered (from sight) in the inmost thoughts of the soul: the wrong-doer exposes it to men,

Saying, "Behold me! I have horns! Behold the cow of Hell[3] in full view!"

How hands and feet and tongue give evidence concerning the secret of the wicked, even in this world.

Even here, then, your hands and feet, in (doing) harm, bear 2455 witness to your conscience.

Since your (evil) conscience becomes (as) an overseer to you and says, "Speak! Do not keep back your belief,"

And, especially at times of anger and quarrelling, makes manifest your secret thought, hair by hair;

Since wrong and injustice become your overseer and say, "Display me, O hands and feet,"

And since the (evil conscience which bears) witness to the secret thought seizes the reins—in particular at times of emotion and anger and revenge—

That One, then, who appoints this (conscience) as overseer, 2460 that it may unfurl the banner of the secret on the field—

(Surely), then, He can also create, on the Day of Judgement, other overseers for the purpose of unfolding (the secret thoughts).

O thou who hast entered most recklessly[4] upon (a course of) injustice and malice, thy true nature is evident: this (advertisement of it) is not needed.

[1] This should be "grandson." Cf. *v.* 2474.
[2] *I.e.* the world.
[3] The hellish carnal soul.
[4] Literally, "with ten hands."

It is not necessary to become celebrated for (doing) harm:
they (who possess discernment) are acquainted with thy fiery
(hellish) conscience.

Thy fleshly soul every moment emits a hundred sparks,
saying, "Behold me! I am of the people of the Fire.

2465   I am a part of the Fire: I go to my whole; I am not (composed
of) light, so that I should go to the Lord"—

Even as this unjust and ungrateful man wrought so much con-
fusion (made such a great disturbance) for the sake of a cow.

He carried off from him (the defendant) a hundred cows and
a hundred camels[1]: this (wickedness) is the fleshly soul: O father,
cut yourself asunder from it.

Besides, never once did he make humble supplication to God:
never once did a cry of "O Lord!" come from him in sorrow—

"O God, content my adversary: if I have inflicted loss upon
him (yet) do Thou bestow profit (upon me)[2]!

2470   If I killed him by mistake, the (payment of the) blood-price
falls on my kin: Thou hast been my spirit's kin from (the Day
of) *Alast.*"

He (God) does not give (worthless) stones in return for the
pearls of contrition[3]; (nay), this, O noble spirit, is the justice of
the fleshly soul.

How the people went forth to that tree.

When they went forth to that tree, he (David) said, "Tie his
hands fast behind him,

In order that I may bring to light his sin and crime, and may
plant the banner of justice on the field.

O dog," said he, "you have killed this man's grandfather.
You are a slave: by this means you have become a lord.

2475   You killed your master and carried off his property: God hath
made manifest what happened to him.

Your wife was his handmaid; she has acted unjustly towards
this same master.

Whatever (children) she bore to him, female or male—all of
them from beginning to end are the property of the (master's)
heir.

You are a slave: your gains and goods are his property. You
demanded the Law: take the Law and go: 'tis well.

You killed your master miserably by violence, (whilst) your
master was crying for mercy on this very spot.

2480   In your haste you hid the knife under the soil, because of the
terrible apparition which you beheld.

---

[1] *I.e.* the property of the defendant's grandfather.
[2] *I.e.* by causing me to repent.
[3] Literally, "in return for (your) asking forgiveness, which is (as) pearls."

Lo, his head together with the knife is under the soil! Dig
ye back the soil, thus!

On the knife, too, the name of this dog is written, (who)
dealt with his master so deceitfully and injuriously."

They did even so (as he ordered), and when they cleft (the
earth) they found in the soil the knife and the head.

Thereupon tumultuous lamentation arose amongst the people:
every one severed the girdle (of unbelief) from his waist.

After that, he (David) said to him (the murderer), "Come, 2485
O demander of justice, (and) with that black face (of yours)
receive the justice due to you!"

*How David, on whom be peace, ordered that retaliation
should be taken on the murderer after his conviction.*

He ordered retaliation (by killing him) with that same knife:
how should contrivance deliver him from the knowledge of
God?

Although God's clemency bestows (many) kindnesses, yet
when he (the sinner) has gone beyond bounds, He exposes
(him).

Blood sleepeth not: the desire to investigate and lay bare
(discover the solution of) a difficulty falls into every heart.

The craving prompted by the ordainment of the Lord of the
Judgement[1] springs up in the conscience of all and sundry[2]—

(So that they ask), "How was it with such-and-such? What 2490
happened to him? What became of him?"—just as the sown
seed shoots up from the loam.

Those inquiries, the pricking of (conscience in men's) hearts
and the investigation and discussion, are the stirring of the
(murdered man's) blood.

When the mystery of his (the murderer's) case had been
divulged, David's miracles became doubly manifest[3].

All the people came bare-headed and cast their heads in
prostration on the earth,

(Saying), "We all have been (as those who are) blind from
birth, (though) we have seen from thee marvels of a hundred
kinds.

The stone came to speech with thee overtly, and said, 'Take 2495
me for Saul's expedition (against Goliath)';

Thou camest with three pebbles and a sling and didst rout
a hundred thousand men:

---

[1] Cf. مالك يومِ الدّين, *Qur'án* 1, 3.
[2] Literally, "rears its head from the conscience of that (person) and this."
[3] Literally, "became manifest and doubled."

Thy pebbles broke into a hundred thousand pieces, and each one drank the blood of an enemy.

Iron became as wax in thy hand when the (craft of) fashioning coats of mail was made known to thee.

The mountains became thy thankful accompanists: they chant the psalms with thee, as one who teaches the recitation of the Qur'án.

2500 Hundreds of thousands of spiritual eyes were opened and through thy breath were made ready for (contemplation of) the Unseen;

And that (miracle) is stronger than all those (others), for this one is lasting: thou bestowest the life that is enduring for ever."

This indeed is the soul of all miracles, that it (the miracle) should bestow everlasting life on the (spiritually) dead.

The wicked man was killed and a whole world (of people) were quickened with life: every one became anew a (devoted) servant to God.

Explaining that Man's fleshly soul is in the position of the murderer who had become a claimant on account of the cow, and that the slayer of the cow is the intellect, and that David is God or the Shaykh who is God's vicar, by means of whose strength and support it is possible to kill the wicked (murderer) and be enriched with (spiritual) daily bread that is not earned by labour and for which there is no reckoning.

Kill your fleshly soul and make the world (spiritually) alive; it (your fleshly soul) has killed its master: make it (your) slave.

2505 Hark! your fleshly soul is (as) the claimant (of compensation) for the cow: it has made itself a master and chief.

The slayer of the cow is your intellect (rational soul): go, do not be offended with the slayer of the cow, (which is) your body.

The intellect is a captive and craves of God daily bread (won) without toil, and bounty (placed before it) on a tray.

Upon what does its daily bread (won) without toil depend? Upon its killing the cow which is the origin of (all) evil.

The fleshly soul says, "How shouldst thou kill my 'cow'?"— because the "cow" of the fleshly soul is the (outward) form of the body.

2510 The intellect, (typified by) the master's son, is left destitute, (while) the fleshly soul, (typified by) the murderer, has become a master and leader.

Do you know what is the daily bread (won) without toil? It is the food of spirits and the daily bread of the prophet.

But it depends upon sacrificing the cow: know (that) the (spiritual) treasure (is found) in (sacrifice of) the cow, O you who dig in (holes and) corners!

Yesternight I ate something; otherwise, I would have given the reins entirely into the hand of your understanding[1].

(The words), "yesternight I ate something," are an idle tale: whatsoever comes (to pass) is from the secret chamber (of Divine Destiny).

Wherefore have we fixed our eyes on (secondary) causes, if 2515 we have learned from those with beauteous eyes[2] how to glance amorously?

Over the (secondary) causes there are other (primary) causes: do not look at the (secondary) cause; let thy gaze fall on that (primary cause).

The prophets came in order to cut (the cords of secondary) causes: they flung their miracles at Saturn (in the Seventh Heaven).

Without cause (means) they clove the sea asunder; without sowing they found heaps of corn.

Sand, too, was turned into flour by their work; goat's hair became silk as it was pulled (from the hide).

The whole of the *Qur'án* consists in (is concerned with) the 2520 cutting off of (secondary) causes: (its theme is) the glory of the poor (prophet or saint) and the destruction of (those like) Abú Lahab.

A swift drops two or three pebbles and shatters the mighty host of Abyssinia:

The pebble of a bird that flies aloft lays low the elephant, riddled with holes (wounds).

(God said), "Inflict (a blow with) the tail of the killed cow upon the murdered man, in order that at the same moment he may come to life (again) in the winding-sheet,

(And that) he whose throat was cut may spring up from his place and seek (vengeance for) his blood from the shedder of his blood[3]."

In like manner, from the beginning of the *Qur'án* to the end, 2525 'tis (wholly concerned with) the abandonment of (secondary) causes and means. And (now) farewell (to this subject).

The explanation (of the mystery) thereof is not (given) by the meddlesome intellect: do service (to God), in order that it may become clear to you.

The philosopher is in bondage to things perceived by the intellect; (but) the pure (saint) is he that rides as a prince on the Intellect of intellect[4].

The Intellect of intellect is your kernel, (while) your intellect is (only) the husk: the belly of animals is ever seeking husks.

[1] *I.e.* "I would have given you a complete explanation of this matter."
[2] *I.e.* the prophets.
[3] *Qur'án*, II, 67–8.
[4] *I.e.* Universal Intellect.

He that seeks the kernel has a hundred loathings for the husk: to the goodly (saints) the kernel (alone) is lawful, lawful.

2530   When the intellect, (which is) the husk, offers a hundred evidences, how should the Universal Intellect take a step without having (intuitive) certainty?

The intellect makes books entirely black (with writing); the Intellect of intellect keeps the horizons (the whole universe) filled (with light) from the Moon (of Reality).

It is free from blackness and whiteness: the light of its moon rises (and shines) upon heart and soul.

If this black and white[1] has gotten (any) power (value), 'tis from the Night of Power[2] that shone forth like a star.

The value of scrip and purse is (derived) from the gold: without the gold, scrip and purse are docked[3].

2535   Even as the worth of the body is (derived) from the soul, (so) the worth of the soul is (derived) from the radiance of the Soul of souls.

If the soul were now alive without (that) radiance, would He (God) ever have called the infidels "*dead*"[4]?

Come, speak (O my soul)! for the Logos is digging a channel, to the end that some water may reach a generation after us.

Although (in) every generation there is one who brings the word (of God), yet the sayings of them that have gone before are helpful[5].

Is it not (the case) that the Pentateuch and the Gospel and the Psalms have borne witness to the truth of the *Qur'án*, O thankful one?

2540   Seek a (spiritual) livelihood (won) without toil and without reckoning, so that Gabriel may bring you apples from Paradise;

Nay, (that there may come to you) a livelihood from the Lord of Paradise, without headache (trouble) on the part of the gardener and without the toil of sowing.

Inasmuch as in that (spiritual) bread the benefit of (conferred by) the bread is His (God's) gift, He gives you that benefit (directly), without making the husk a means (of imparting it to you).

The savour is hidden; the outward form of the bread is (visible) like a table-cloth: the bread that is without table-cloth is a portion (reserved) for the saint.

How will you, notwithstanding (all your) endeavour and search, gain the spiritual livelihood except through the justice of the Shaykh who is your David?

---

[1] *I.e.* ink and paper.   [2] See *Qur'án*, XCVII.
[3] *I.e.* deprived of worth.

[4] *Qur'án*, XXXIX, 31, where the word مَيِّتُون is used in the sense of "mortal."
[5] Literally, "a helper."

When the fleshly soul sees your steps (joined) with (those of) 2545 the Shaykh, willy-nilly[1] it becomes submissive to you.

Then (and then only) did the owner of the cow become submissive, when he was made aware of the (inspired) words of David.

The intellect, in chase (of spiritual truth), prevails over your currish fleshly soul (only) at the time when the Shaykh is its helper.

The fleshly soul is a dragon with hundredfold strength and cunning: the face of the Shaykh is the emerald that plucks out its eye[2].

If you wish the owner of the cow[3] to be abased, goad him in that direction[4], as (you would goad) asses, O contumacious man!

When he approaches him (the saint) who is nigh unto God, 2550 his tongue, a hundred ells long, is shortened.

(He hath) a hundred tongues, and each tongue of him (hath) a hundred languages: his fraud and guile come not into (the bounds of) description.

The claimant for the cow, the fleshly soul, is eloquent and brings forward hundreds of thousands of unsound pleas.

He deceives (all in) the city except the king: he cannot waylay the sagacious king.

The fleshly soul hath glorification of God (on its tongue), and the Qur'án in its right hand; (but) in its sleeve (it hath) dagger and sword.

Do not believe its Qur'án and hypocritical ostentation, do not 2555 make yourself its confidant and comrade;

(For) it will take you to the tank to perform the ritual ablution, and will cast you to the bottom thereof.

The intellect is luminous and a seeker of good: how (then) does the dark fleshly soul prevail over it?

(It prevails) because it is at home, (while) your intellect is a stranger: the dog at his own door is (like) a terrible lion.

Wait till the lions[5] go (back) to the jungle[6], and these blind dogs[7] will believe (in them) there.

The common folk of the city do not know the deceit of the 2560 fleshly soul and of the body: it (the fleshly soul) is not subdued save by (Divine) inspiration in the heart.

Every one that is its congener becomes its friend, except, to be sure, the David who is your Shaykh;

---

[1] Literally, "from the roots of the teeth." The phrase can also mean " with all one's heart."
[2] The emerald was supposed to have the power of blinding snakes.
[3] I.e. the fleshly soul.
[4] I.e. towards the Shaykh.
[5] The illumined spirits and intellects.
[6] The spiritual world hereafter.
[7] The carnal souls.

For he has been transmuted, and whomsoever God hath seated in the abode of the heart, he (that person) is no more the body's congener.

All the (other) people are (rendered) infirm by (that which lies in) ambush (within them): 'tis certain that infirmity associates with infirmity.

Every worthless fellow pretends to be (a) David; every one who lacks discernment lays hold of him (attaches himself to him):

2565 He hears the bird's note from a fowler and, (like a) foolish bird, he keeps going in that direction.

He does not distinguish fact from fiction: he is misguided. Come, flee from him, even if he is spiritual (in appearance).

What has grown (genuinely) and what has been tied on (artificially) is (all) one to him: though he may claim (to possess) intuitive certainty, he is (really) in a (great) doubt.

If such a one is absolutely keen-witted, (still), when he has not this (power of) discernment, he is a fool.

Hark, flee from him as the deer from the lion: do not hasten boldly towards him, O wise man!

How Jesus, on whom be peace, fled to the top of
a mountain (to escape) from the fools.

2570 Jesus, son of Mary, was fleeing to a mountain: you would say that a lion wished to shed his blood.

A certain man ran after him and said, "(Is it) well (with thee)? There is no one in pursuit of thee: why dost thou flee, like a bird?"

(But) he (Jesus) still kept running with haste[1] so (quickly) that on account of his haste he did not answer him.

He pushed on in pursuit of Jesus for the distance of one or two fields, and then invoked Jesus with the utmost earnestness,

Saying, "For the sake of pleasing God, stop one moment, for I have a difficulty concerning thy flight.

2575 From whom art thou fleeing in this direction, O noble one? There is no lion pursuing thee, no enemy, and there is no fear or danger."

He said, "I am fleeing from the fool. Begone! I am saving myself. Do not debar me!"

"Why," said he, "art not thou the Messiah by whom the blind and the deaf are restored (to sight and hearing)?"

He said, "Yea." Said the other, "Art not thou the King in whom the spells of the Unseen World have their abode[2]?—

---

[1] Literally, "coupled with haste.'
[2] Literally, "who art the abode for the spells."

(So that) when thou chantest those spells over a dead man, he springs up (rejoicing) like a lion that has caught his prey."

He said, "Yea, I am he." Said the other, "Dost not thou 2580 make (living) birds out of clay, O beauteous one?"

He said, "Yea." Said the other, "Then, O pure Spirit, thou doest whatsoever thou wilt: of whom hast thou fear?

With such (miraculous) evidence, who is there in the world that would not be one of the slaves (devoted) to thee?"

Jesus said, "By the holy Essence of God, the Maker of the body and the Creator of the soul in eternity[1];

By the sanctity of the pure Essence and Attributes of Him, for whose sake the collar of Heaven is rent[2],

(I swear) that the spells and the Most Great Name which I 2585 pronounced over the deaf and the blind were good (in their effects).

I pronounced (them) over the stony mountain: it was cloven and tore upon itself its mantle down to the navel.

I pronounced (them) over the corpse: it came to life. I pronounced (them) over nonentity: it became entity.

I pronounced them lovingly over the heart of the fool hundreds of thousands of times, and 'twas no cure (for his folly).

He became hard rock and changed not from that disposition; he became sand from which no produce grows."

Said the other, "What is the reason that the Name of God 2590 availed there[3], (while) it had no advantage (good effect) here[4]?

That (physical infirmity) is disease too, and this (folly) is a disease: why did it (the Name of God) not become a cure for this, since it cured that?"

He (Jesus) said, "The disease of folly is (the result of) the wrath of God; (physical) disease and blindness are not (the result of Divine) wrath: they are (a means of) probation."

Probation is a disease that brings (Divine) mercy (in its train); folly is a disease that brings (Divine) rejection.

That which is branded on him (the fool) He (God) hath sealed: no hand can apply a remedy to it.

Flee from the foolish, seeing that (even) Jesus fled (from them): 2595 how much blood has been shed by companionship with fools!

The air steals away (absorbs) water little by little: so too does the fool steal away religion from you.

He steals away your heat and gives you cold, like one who puts a stone under your rump.

The flight of Jesus was not caused by fear, (for) he is safe (from the mischief done by fools): it was for the purpose of teaching (others).

[1] Literally, "in priority."
[2] *I.e.* "on whose account Heaven is enraptured."
[3] *I.e.* "in those cases which have been mentioned."
[4] *I.e.* "in the case of the fool."

Though intense frost fill the world from end to end, what harm (would it do) to the radiant sun?

The story of the people of Sabá and their folly, and how the admonition of the prophets produces no effect upon the foolish.

2600 I am reminded of the story of the people of Sabá—how their (balmy) zephyr (*ṣabá*) was turned into pestilence (*wabá*) by the words of the foolish.

That (kingdom of) Sabá resembles the great big city (which) you may hear of from children in (their) tales.

The children relate tales, (but) in their tales there is enfolded many a mystery and (moral) lesson.

(Though) in (their) tales they say (many) ridiculous things, (yet) in all ruined places do thou ever seek the treasure.

(Once) there was a city very huge and great[1], but its size was the size of a saucer, no more (than that).

2605 (It was) very huge and very broad and very long, ever so big, as big as an onion[2].

The people of ten cities were assembled within it, but the whole (amounted to) three fellows with unwashed (dirty) faces.

Within it there were numberless people and folk, but the whole of them (amounted to) three beggarly fools.

The soul that has not made haste towards the Beloved—(even) if it is thousands, (yet) it is (only) half a body.

One (of the three) was very far-sighted and blind-eyed—blind to Solomon and seeing the leg of the ant;

2610 And the second was very sharp of hearing and extremely deaf—a treasure in which there is not a barleycorn's weight of gold;

And the other (the third) was naked and bare, pudendo patefacto, but the skirts of his raiment were long.

The blind man said, "Look, an army is approaching: I see what people they are and how many."

The deaf man said, "Yes; I heard their voices (and know) what they are saying openly and secretly."

The naked man said, "I am afraid they will cut off (something) from the length of my skirt."

2615 The blind man said, "Look, they have come near! Arise and let us flee before (we suffer) blows and chains."

"Yes," says the deaf man, "the noise is getting nearer. Come on, my friends!"

The naked man said, "Alas, from covetousness they will cut off my skirt, and I am unprotected."

[1] This is the children's tale.
[2] Literally, "extremely big, big—the size of an onion."

They (the three) left the city and came forth and in their flight entered a village.

In that village they found a fat fowl, but not a mite of flesh on it: ('twas) abject—

A dried-up dead fowl, and its bones through being pecked at 2620 by[1] crows had become bare like threads.

They were eating thereof as a lion (eats) of his prey: each of them (became) surfeited, like an elephant, with eating it.

All the three ate thereof and grew exceedingly fat: they became like three very great and big elephants,

In such wise that each young man, because of fatness, was too stout to be contained[2] in the world.

Notwithstanding such bigness and seven stout limbs[3], they sprang forth through a chink in the door and departed.

The way of creaturely death is an invisible way: it comes not 2625 into sight: 'tis a marvellous place of exit.

Lo, the caravans are following one after another through this chink which is hidden (from view) in the door.

If you look on the door for that chink, you will not find it: (it is) extremely unapparent, though (there are) so many processions[4] through it.

Explaining (what is signified by) the far-sighted blind man, the deaf man who is sharp of hearing, and the naked man with the long skirts.

Know that Hope is the deaf man who has (often) heard of our dying, (but) has not heard of his own death or regarded his own decease.

The blind man is Greed: he sees other people's faults, hair by hair, and tells them from street to street,

(But) his blind eyes do not perceive one mote of his own 2630 faults, albeit he is a fault-finder.

The naked man is afraid that his skirt will be cut off: how should they (any one) cut off the skirt of a naked man?

The worldly man is destitute and terrified: he possesses nothing, (yet) he has dread of thieves.

Bare he came and naked he goes, and (all the while) his heart is bleeding with anxiety on account of the thief.

At the hour of death when a hundred lamentations are (being made) beside him, his spirit begins to laugh at its own fear.

At that moment the rich man knows that he has no gold; the 2635 keen-witted man, too, knows that he is devoid of talent.

---

[1] Literally, "from the blows of."
[2] Literally, "from stoutness would not be contained." [3] *I.e.* "stout body."
[4] Literally, "the conducting of the bride to her husband."

('Tis) like (as when) a child's lap (is) filled with potsherds, for he (the child) is trembling for them, like the owner of riches.

If you take a piece away, he begins to weep; and if you give the piece back to him, he begins to laugh.

Since the child is not endued with knowledge[1], his weeping and laughter have no importance.

Inasmuch as the magnate regarded that which is (only) a loan as (his) property, he was quivering (with anxiety) for that false wealth.

2640 He dreams that he has wealth and is afraid of the thief who may carry off his sack (of gold).

When Death pulls his ear and makes him[2] start up from slumber, then he falls to mocking at his fears.

Even such (is) the trembling of these learned scholars who have the intelligence and knowledge of this world.

On account of these accomplished (and) intelligent men, God said in the *Qur'án*, *They do not know*.

Each (of them) is afraid of some one's stealing (his time): he fancies that he possesses a great deal of knowledge.

2645 He says, "They are wasting my time," (but) in truth he has no time that is profitable.

He says, "The people have taken me away from my work," (but) his soul is plunged in idleness up to the throat.

(Like) the naked man (he) is frightened and says, "I am trailing a (long) skirt: how shall I save my skirt from their clutches?"

He knows a hundred thousand superfluous matters[3] connected with the (various) sciences, (but) that unjust man does not know his own soul.

He knows the special properties of every substance, (but) in elucidating his own substance (essence) he is (as ignorant) as an ass,

2650 Saying, "I know (what is) permissible and unpermissible[4]." Thou knowest not whether thou thyself art permissible or (unpermissible as) an old woman[5].

Thou knowest this licit (thing) and that illicit (thing), but art thou licit or illicit? Consider well!

Thou knowest what is the value of every article of merchandise; (if) thou knowest not the value of thyself, 'tis folly.

Thou hast become acquainted with the fortunate and inauspicious stars; thou dost not look to see whether thou art fortunate or unwashed (spiritually foul and ill-favoured).

---

[1] Literally, "has not knowledge as a garment."
[2] Literally, "when the ear-puller makes him."
[3] Reading فضل.　　　[4] *I.e.* the science of jurisprudence.
[5] "The religion of old women" is synonymous with ignorance and superstition.

This, this, is the soul of all the sciences—that thou shouldst know who thou shalt be on the Day of Judgement.

Thou art acquainted with the fundamentals (*uṣúl*) of the 2655 (Mohammedan) Religion, but look upon thine own fundamental (*aṣl*) and see whether it is good.

Thine own fundamentals are better for thee than the two fundamentals[1] (of the Mohammedan Religion), so that thou mayst know thine own fundamental (essential nature), O great man.

Description of the luxuriance of the city of the Sabaeans and their ingratitude.

Their fundamental (nature) was bad: those inhabitants of Sabá were recoiling from the means (which lead) to meeting (with God);

(Yet) He gave them so many estates and orchards and meadowlands, on the left hand and the right, for (their) leisure (pastime and diversion).

Inasmuch as the fruit was falling (to the ground) from abundance, there was no room for any one to pass on the road[2],

(For) the scattered largesse of fruit would block the way: the 2660 wayfarer (would be) in amazement at the plenty of the fruit.

In their groves, through the dropping of the fruit, a basket on the head would be filled involuntarily.

The breeze would scatter the fruit, not (the hand of) any one: by that fruit a multitude of skirts would be filled.

Huge clusters, having come low down, would strike against the head and face of the wayfarer.

On account of the plenty of gold a bath-stoker might have tied a golden belt on his waist.

The dogs would trample buns underfoot; the desert wolf 2665 would have indigestion from the (rich) food.

Town and village had become safe from robbers and wolves; the goat was not afraid even of the fierce wolf.

If I explain (all) the blessings bestowed upon the people (of Sabá), which were increasing day by day,

It will hinder (me) from (speaking of) important matters. The prophets brought (to the Sabaeans) the (Divine) command, namely, "*Do thou, therefore, be righteous.*"

How the prophets came from God to admonish the people of Sabá.

Thirteen prophets came thither: all (of them) were ready to guide those who had lost the way,

---

[1] Jurisprudence (*fiqh*) and scholastic theology (*kalám*).
[2] Literally, "the thoroughfare was becoming (too) narrow to traverse."

2670   Saying, "Come, the benefit has increased: where is the thanksgiving? If the steed of thanksgiving lie down, set (it) in motion.

In (the view of) reason it is necessary to give thanks to the Benefactor; otherwise, the door of everlasting wrath will be opened.

Hark, behold the lovingkindness (of God)! And in sooth would any one (but God) do this—namely, be content with a single thanksgiving for such benefits?

He bestows a head and asks as thanksgiving (only) one act of bowing; He bestows feet and asks as thanksgiving (only) one act of sitting (in piety and devotion)."

The people said, "The ghoul has carried off our thanksgiving: we have become weary of giving thanks and receiving benefits.

2675   We have become so disgusted with the bounty that neither piety nor sin pleases us.

We do not desire benefits and orchards: we do not desire means (of enjoyment) and leisure."

The prophets said, "In your hearts is a malady whence there is (produced) a canker in the acknowledgment of obligations,

And whereby the benefit is wholly turned into disease: how should food become (a source of) strength in the sick?

How many a sweet thing came to thee, O persistent (in sin), and they all grew unsweet, and their pure (quality) became turbid!

2680   Thou didst become a foe to these sweetnesses: on whatsoever thing thou didst lay thy hand, it became unsweet.

Whosoever became (in reality) thy familiar and friend became despicable and vile in thy sight;

And every one, too, that (in reality) would be alien to thee is, in thy opinion, very grand and venerable.

This (false opinion) also is from the effect produced by that sickness: its poison pervades all associated (with it).

It behoves (thee) quickly to remove that malady, for with that (disease) sugar will seem filth;

2685   Every sweet thing that comes to thee grows unsweet: if the Water of Life arrive, it turns into fire.

That (morbid) quality is the elixir of death and woe: thereby thy (spiritual) life is at last turned into death.

There was many a food by which thy heart (spirit) was revived: when it entered thy body, it became stinking.

There is many a dear one that was hunted (by thee) with blandishments: when he became thy prey, he became cheap in thine eyes.

When from sincerity the friendship of intellect with intellect arises, every moment the devotion is increased;

(But) know for sure, the friendship of the carnal soul with 2690
any base carnal soul is momently diminished,

Because his carnal soul hovers round disease and soon corrupts the (friendly) acquaintance.

If thou dost not wish thy friend to be averse (to thee) on the morrow[1], take (choose) friendship with the intelligent and with the intellect.

Inasmuch as thou art sick from the simoom of the carnal soul, whatever thou mayst take thou art the instrument for (infecting it with) disease.

If thou take a jewel, it becomes a (common) stone; and if thou take kindness of heart, it becomes a hatred[2];

And if thou take a fine original[3] saying, after thy apprehension 2695 (of it) it has become tasteless and gross—

'I have heard this many a time; it has become old: tell something else besides this, O trusty friend[4].'

Suppose that something else fresh and new has been said, again to-morrow thou art surfeited with it and averse.

Remove the disease: when the disease is eradicated, every old tale will become new to thee,

So that the old (tale) will bring forth new leaves: the old (tale) will cause a hundred clusters to blossom from the ditch.

We are the (spiritual) physicians, the disciples of God: the 2700 Red Sea beheld us *and was cloven*[5].

Those natural physicians are different, for they look into the heart by means of a pulse.

We look well into the heart without intermediary, for through clairvoyance we are in a high belvedere.

Those (others) are physicians of food and fruit: by them the animal soul is (made) strong.

We are physicians of deeds and words: the ray of the light of (Divine) Majesty is our inspirer,

(So that we know) that a deed like this will be beneficial to 2705 thee, while a deed like that will cut (thee) off from the Way;

And that words like these will lead thee on (to grace), while words like those will bring anguish to thee.

To those (other) physicians a (sample of) urine is evidence, whereas this evidence of ours is the inspiration of the Almighty.

We do not desire a fee from any one: our fee comes from a Holy Place.

Hark, come hither for the incurable disease! We, one by one, are a medicine for the (spiritually) sick."

---

[1] On the Day of Judgement.
[2] Literally, "a war."
[3] Literally, "virgin."
[4] Literally, "O (my) support."
[5] *Qur'án*, XXVI, 63.

How the people (of Sabá) demanded miracles from the prophets.

2710   The people said, "O ye company of impostors, where is the evidence of (your) knowledge of medicine and (your) usefulness?

Since ye are in bondage, like us, to this same sleep and food (and) are pasturing in the country—

Since ye are entrapped by this water and earth, how are ye hunters of the Símurgh (which is) the heart?

Love of power and dominion induces (a man) to reckon himself amongst the prophets.

We will not put in our ears such vain boasts and lies and (thereby) fall into deception[1]."

2715   The prophets said, "This (disbelief) arises from that malady: the original blindness[2] (of your hearts) is the screen (which hinders you) from seeing (the truth).

Ye have heard our call, and (yet) ye do not see this jewel in our hands.

This jewel is a test for the people: we turn it about round (their) eyes.

Whosoever says, 'Where is the evidence?' his words are an evidence that he does not see the jewel and is in thrall to blindness."

(Suppose that) a sun has come to speech (and says), "Arise! for the day has risen; jump up, do not dispute!"

2720   (And suppose that) you say, "O sun, where is the evidence?"— it will say to you, "O blind one, beg of God (that He give you) an eye."

If any one seek a lamp in bright daylight, the very fact of seeking (it) announces his blindness.

And if you do not see (the daylight) but have formed an opinion that 'tis the dawn and that you are in a veil,

Do not proclaim your blindness by (saying) these words; keep silence and be in expectation of the (Divine) grace.

To say in the midst of day "Where is the day?" is to expose yourself, O day-seeker.

2725   Patience and silence attract the (Divine) mercy, whereas to seek this sign (evidence) is a sign of infirmity.

Accept (the Divine command), "*Be ye silent*," in order that the recompense of "*Be ye silent*" may come to your soul from the Beloved.

If you do not desire (to suffer a) relapse in the presence of this Physician, dash to the ground your gold (*zar*) and your head (*sar*), O man of understanding.

[1] Literally, "buttermilk."
[2] Literally, "the original stock of blindness."

Sell your superfluous speech and buy sacrifice of life and sacrifice of position and sacrifice of gold,

That the grace of Him (*Hú*) may utter praise of you, so that Heaven will be envious of your high estate.

When ye have regard for the hearts (feelings and wishes) of 2730 the physicians, ye will see yourselves and will become ashamed of yourselves.

'Tis not in the power of created beings to remove this blindness, but the honouring of the physicians (by you) is from Divine guidance.

Become devoted to these physicians with (all your) soul, that ye may be filled with musk and ambergris.

How the people suspected the prophets.

The people said, "All this is fraud and deceit: how should God make a vicar of Zayd and Bakr[1]?

Every king's messenger must be of his (the king's) kind: where are water and clay in comparison with the Creator of the heavens?

Have we eaten ass's brains that we, like you, should deem a 2735 gnat to be the confidant of the *humá*[2]?

Where is a gnat in comparison with the *humá*? Where is earth in comparison with God? What relation to the mote has the sun in the sky?

What resemblance is this, and what connexion is this, that it should enter into any mind and brain?

Story of the hares who sent a hare as ambassador to the elephant, bidding him say, ' I come to thee as the ambassador of the Moon in heaven to bid thee beware of (drinking from) this water-spring,' as is told in full in the Book of Kalíla (and Dimna).

This (claim made by you) resembles the saying of a certain hare—'I am the ambassador of the Moon and companion to the Moon.'

For all the beasts of chase were in woe on account of a herd of elephants (dwelling) beside that limpid spring;

All were deprived (of water) and (were kept) far from the 2740 spring by dread: since (their) strength was inferior, they made a plot.

From the mountain-top the old hare cried towards the elephants on the first night of the new-moon—

'Come on the fourteenth, O king elephant, that thou mayst find within the spring the proof of this (assertion).

[1] See p. 125, note 1.   [2] See p. 91, note 2.

O king elephant, I am the ambassador in thy presence. Stop! Ambassadors are not subjected to imprisonment and violence and wrath.

The Moon says, "O elephants, depart! The spring is mine, turn aside from it;

2745   And if (ye depart) not, I will make you blind. I have declared the wrong (which ye are doing) and have thrown off my neck (all responsibility for what will happen if ye trespass farther).

Take leave of this spring and depart, that ye may be safe from the blows of the Moon's sword[1].'

Lo, the token (of my veracity) is that the Moon (reflected) in the spring will be disturbed by the water-craving elephant.

Come and be present on the such-and-such a night, O king elephant, in order that within the spring thou mayst find the proof of this (assertion).'

When seven and eight (fifteen nights) of the month had passed, the king elephant came to drink from the spring.

2750   When on that night the elephant put his trunk in the water, the water was disturbed, and the Moon showed disturbance.

The elephant believed that speech of his (the hare's), when the Moon in the spring showed disturbance.

O company (of prophets), we are not (to be reckoned) among those stupid elephants who are terrified by the disturbance of the Moon."

The prophets said, "Ah, (our) spiritual admonition has (only) made your (carnal) bondage more grievous, O ye fools!

How the prophets answered their sneers and uttered parables unto them.

Oh, alas that in (the case of) your disease the remedy has become for you the poison of soul-wringing (Divine) vengeance.

2755   This lamp (of spiritual admonition) has increased the darkness of that (diseased) eye, since God has set (over it) the veil of wrath.

What dominion shall we crave from you? for our dominion is greater than the sky."

What glory should the sea of pearls acquire from the ship—especially a ship that has been filled with dung?

Oh, alas for that eye blind and blear[2]! Therein a sun seemed as (insignificant as) a mote.

In an Adam who was without like or equal the eye of Iblís discerned naught but a piece of clay.

---

[1] تیغ مه, "the Moon's sword," can also mean "moonbeams."
[2] Literally, "blue."

The devilish eye showed (saw) his (Adam's) spring as winter: 2760 it moved in the direction where its (original) home was[1].

Oh, many a fortune that comes now and then to the unfortunate one, and he turns away (from it)!

Oh, many a beloved who comes unbeknown to an ill-starred one, and he knows not how to make love[2]!

This that misleads the eye is our (original) damnation, and this that turns the heart (from seeing the truth) is (our) evil destiny.

Since to you the idol of stone has become an object of adoration, the curse (of God) and blindness have o'ershadowed you.

When your stone is a fitting partner for God, how are not 2765 intellect and spirit fitting confidants of God?

The dead gnat[3] has become the consort of the *humá*: how (then) is the living one[4] not fit to be the confidant of the King?

Or, maybe, ('tis because) the dead one is fashioned by you, (whereas) the living gnat is fashioned by God.

Ye are in love with yourselves and the thing manufactured by yourselves: to serpents' tails the serpent's head is a law.

In that tail there is no fortune or happiness; in that head there is no pleasure or delight.

That serpent's tail is circling around the head: both those 2770 friends are fit and suited (to each other).

So says the Sage of Ghazna[5] in the *Iláhí-náma*, if thou wilt hearken well—

"Do not behave as a (presumptuous) meddler in the decree of (Divine) fore-ordainment: the ass's shape is suited to the ass's ear."

Limbs and bodies are congruous; qualities are congruous with souls.

Unquestionably the quality of every soul has congruity with the soul; for God fashions it (accordingly).

Inasmuch as He hath joined the quality to the soul, know that 2775 it (the quality) is congruous, like eyes and face.

The (good and evil) qualities are congruous in the good and evil (souls): congruous are the letters that God hath written.

The eye and the heart are between two fingers like a pen in the hand of the writer, O Ḥusayn.

(These) are the fingers of Grace and Wrath, and between them the pen, the heart, is in a state of distress or ease (caused) by these fingers.

O pen, if thou art one that (duly) magnifies (God), consider whose two fingers thou art between.

---

[1] *I.e.* it turned towards its own original nature and character.
[2] Literally, "to make love-play, to dally with love."
[3] The idol.
[4] The prophet.   [5] Saná'í.

2780   All thy volition and movement are (controlled) by this finger:
thy head (point) is on the crossways of the assembly-place[1].

These letters (symbolising) thy (diverse) states are of His
inditing: thy forming a purpose and changing it is just from
His forming a purpose and changing it.

There is no way but supplication and self-abasement: not
every pen is conscious of this subjection to (Divine) control.

The pen knows this (control), but (only) according to its
(fore-ordained) measure: it manifests its measure (of knowledge)
in good and evil (actions).

(As regards) that (apologue) which they attached to the hare
and the elephant, so that they confused (the dispensation of)
eternity with (mere) tricks,

[*Explaining that it is not seemly for every one to adduce
parables, especially concerning Divine actions.*]

2785   How is it seemly for you to make these similitudes and cast
them at (apply them to) that holy Court?

That use of similitudes belongs to the Lord, for He is the
(sole) authority for the knowledge of the hidden and the
manifest.

What dost thou know of the hidden nature of anything, that
thou, baldpate, shouldst use a lock of hair or a cheek as simili-
tudes?

A Moses deemed that (wood) a rod, but it was not (a rod): it
was a dragon: its hidden nature was opening its lips (revealing
itself).

Inasmuch as such a (spiritual) king knows not the hidden
nature of wood, how shouldst thou know the hidden nature of
this snare and bait[2]?

2790   Since the eye of Moses was at fault in the similitude, how
should a meddling mouse find an entrance (to perception of the
truth)?

He (God) will make that comparison of thine a dragon, that
in answer it may tear thee to pieces[3].

The accursed Iblís used this (kind of) comparison[4], so that
he fell under God's curse till the Day of Judgement.

Qárún (Korah) from contumacy used this (kind of) com-
parison, so that he sank down into the earth with his throne and
diadem.

---

[1] *I.e.* "thou must follow either the road of Divine Mercy or the road of
Divine Wrath to meet thy ultimate destiny in 'the assembly-place' on the
Day of Judgement."
[2] Literally, "this snare and grains," *i.e.* the temptation of Divine fore-
ordainment.
[3] On the Day of Judgement.
[4] Iblís refused to worship Adam on the ground that fire is superior to clay.

Know that this comparison of thine is like crows and owls
by which[1] a hundred households are laid low.

How the people of Noah uttered similitudes derisively at the time of his building the Ark.

Noah built an Ark in the desert: a hundred speakers of parables 2795
ran up to ridicule (him).

"He is making a ship (Ark) in the desert where no well of
water exists: what an ignorant fool he is!"

One was saying, "O ship, run!" while another said, "Make
wings for it too!"

He (Noah) said, "This is by the command of God: this will
not be defeated by jeers."

Story of the thief who was asked, "What are you doing at the bottom of this wall at midnight?" and replied, "I am beating a drum."

Hear this parable—how a wicked thief was cutting a hole at
the bottom of a wall.

Some one half-awake, who was ill, heard the soft tapping of 2800
his (pick),

And went on the roof and hung his head down and said to him,
"What are you about, O father?

All is well, I hope. What are you doing (here) at midnight?
Who are you?" He said, "A drummer, O honourable sir."

"What are you about?" He said, "I am beating the drum."

He (the sick man) said, "Where is the noise of the drum, O
artful one[2]?"

He said, "You will hear this noise to-morrow, (namely) cries
of 'Oh, alas!' and 'Oh, woe is me!'"

That (story of the hare and the elephant) is a lie and false and 2805
made up; moreover, thou hast not perceived the secret (the
esoteric meaning) of that falsehood.

The answer to the parable which the unbelievers related concerning the hare's being sent as ambassador with a message to the elephant from the Moon in heaven.

Know that the hidden nature of that hare is the insolent Devil
who came as an ambassador to thy soul,

In order that he might deprive thy foolish soul of the Water
of Life whence Khizr drank.

---

[1] I.e. through the ill-fortune which they bring.
[2] Literally, "O father of ways (ingenious expedients)." It is a remarkable
coincidence that the Hindí word سابَل or سَبَل denotes an iron pick used by
housebreakers, so that اى بو سَبَل would mean "O burglar!"

Thou hast perverted its (the parable's) meaning, thou hast uttered blasphemy: prepare thyself for the sting (of Divine chastisement).

Thou hast spoken of the moon's being disturbed in the limpid water, whereby the jackal (hare) frightened the elephants;

2810 Thou relatest the story of the hare and the elephant and the water, and the elephant's fear of the moon when it was disturbed:

O ye half-baked blind men, pray, how does this bear any resemblance to the Moon to whom (both) lords and commons are subject?

What is the moon and what is the sun and what is the sky? What are intelligences and souls and angels?

"The Sun of the sun of the sun": what is this I am saying (of God)? Surely I am asleep.

The wrath of the (spiritual) kings has overthrown hundreds of thousands of cities, O ye wicked who have lost the way.

2815 At their beck the mountain splits on itself into a hundred fissures; a sun goes round (the sky) like an ass-mill.

The wrath of (holy) men makes the clouds dry; the wrath of (saintly) hearts has laid worlds waste.

Look, O ye unembalmed dead, upon the place where the city of Lot suffered punishment!

What is the elephant even? for three flying birds crushed the bones of those wretched elephants[1].

The *ababíl* is the weakest of birds, and (yet) it rent the elephant irreparably[2].

2820 Who is there that has not heard of the Flood of Noah, or of the battle of Pharaoh's host with the Spirit[3]?

The Spirit routed them and cast them pell-mell into the water: the water was shattering them to atoms.

Who is there that has not heard what happened to Thamúd and how the *ṣarṣar* wind swept the 'Ádites away?

Open thine eyes for once (and look) upon such elephants (mighty prophets), who were killers of elephants (tyrants) in war.

Such elephants and unjust kings as those are always in excommunication under the wrath of the (prophet's) heart.

2825 Unto everlasting they go from a darkness to a darkness, and there is no succour, no mercy.

Perchance ye have not heard the name of good and evil. All have seen, and ye are seeing not.

Ye feign not to see the visible, but death will open your eyes well.

---

[1] *Qur'án*, cv.
[2] Literally, "and it does not admit of repair."
[3] *I.e.* the Divine inspiration of Moses.

Suppose the world is full of sun and light: when thou goest into a darkness like the grave,

Thou becomest without (any) share in that great light; thou art window-shut to the bounteous moon.

Thou hast gone from the belvedere into the pit: how are the 2830 spacious worlds to blame[1] (for their being invisible to thee)?

The soul that has remained in the quality of wolfishness, how should it behold the face of Joseph? Say!

The music of David reached (affected) rock and mountain, (but) the ears of those stony-hearted ones heard it not.

Blessing ever be on reason and justice!—and God best knoweth the right way.

Believe noble Messengers, O Sabá! Believe a spirit made captive by Him who captured it.

Believe them—they are rising suns—and they will preserve 2835 thee from the ignominies of al-Qári'a[2].

Believe them—they are shining full-moons—ere they confront thee with al-Sáhira[3].

Believe them—they are the lamps of darkness; honour them— they are the keys of hope.

Believe those who hope not for your bounty; do not go astray, do not turn others away (from the Truth).

Let us speak Persian: come, abandon Arabic. Be the Hindú (slave) of that Turcoman (the Divine Beloved), O (man of) water and clay.

Hark, listen to the testimonies of the (spiritual) kings; the 2840 heavens have believed (them): believe ye!

The meaning of prudence, and a parable of the prudent man.

Either consider what happened to the former (peoples), or fly with a (great) prudence towards the latter end.

What is prudence? Precaution in (the case of) two (alternative) plans: of the two you will take that one which is far from craziness.

One person may say, "On this road there is no water for seven days, and there is foot-scorching sand."

Another may say, "This is false: push on, for you will find a running fountain every night."

It is prudence that you take water (with you), so that you may 2845 be saved from dread and may be on the right (side).

If there be water (on the road), spill this (water which you have taken with you); and if there be none, alas for the obstinate man!

---

[1] Literally, "what sin have the spacious worlds?"
[2] The Day of Judgement.
[3] *Qur'án*, LXXIX, 14. The word is variously explained. According to some, it is a name of Hell; others say that it is "the face of the earth" from which the bodies of the dead arise at the Resurrection.

O children of the Vicegerent (Adam), deal justly: act with prudence for the sake of the Day of Tryst (Judgement).

That enemy who took vengeance upon your father and dragged him from 'Illiyyín[1] to prison,

And checkmated that king of the spiritual chessboard and made him, (cast out) from Paradise, a thrall to calamities—

2850   How often in combat did he seize him by sleight, that he might wrestle with him and throw him (to the ground) in disgrace[2]!

Thus hath he done to that paladin (Adam): do not regard him with contempt, O ye others!

That envious one nimbly snatched away our mother's and father's crown and ornament.

There he made them naked and wretched and despicable: (many) years did Adam weep bitterly,

So that (sweet) herbs grew from the tears of his eyes: (he wept, wondering) why he was inscribed in the scroll of *lá* (negation)[3].

2855   Judge thou of his (the Devil's) impudent cheatery from the fact that on account of him such a prince (as Adam) rends his beard (in sorrow).

Beware, O clay-worshippers, of his malice: smite the sword of *lá hawl*[4] on his head!

For he sees you from ambush, so that ye see him not. Take care!

The fowler scatters grain incessantly: the grain is visible, but the deceit is hidden.

Wherever you see the grain, beware, lest the trap confine your wings and pinions,

2860   Because the bird that takes leave of (relinquishes) the grain (bait), eats grain from the spacious field (of Reality) that is without imposture.

With that (grain) it is contented, and escapes the trap: no trap confines its wings and pinions.

The banefulness of the action of the bird that abandons prudence from (motives of) greed and vain desire.

Again, a bird settles on a wall and fastens its eyes upon the grain in a trap.

Now it looks towards the open country, (while) now its greed leads it to look at the grain.

---

[1] "The register of the righteous," or a place in the seventh heaven where that record is kept.
[2] Literally, "pale-faced."
[3] *I.e.* the register of those who disobey God.
[4] See Vol. II, p. 232, note 2.

This look struggles with that look and suddenly makes it (the bird) empty of wisdom.

Again, a bird that has abandoned that vacillation turns its 2865 gaze away from that (grain) and fixes it upon the open fields.

Glad (glistening) are its wings and pinions: how goodly it is, since it has become the leader of all the free.

Every one who makes it his model is saved and sits in the abode of security and freedom,

Because his heart has become the king of the prudent, so that the rosery and garden (of Paradise) has become his dwelling-place.

Prudence is pleased with him, and he pleased with Prudence: do likewise, if you would act with foresight and resolution.

Many a time have you fallen into the snare of greed and given 2870 up your throat to be cut;

Again He that graciously disposes (hearts) to repentance hath set you free and accepted your repentance and made you glad.

He hath said, "*If ye return* thus, *We will return* thus: We have wedded the actions to the retribution.

When I bring one mate to Myself, the other mate inevitably comes running (after it).

We have mated this action with the effect: when one mate arrives, another mate arrives."

When a raider carries off the husband from the wife, the wife 2875 comes after him, seeking her husband.

Once more ye have come towards this snare and have thrown dust in the eyes of repentance.

Again that Forgiving One[1] hath loosed that knot for you and hath said, "Beware! Flee! Set not your face in this direction!"

Again, when the mandate of forgetfulness[2] arrived, it drew your soul towards the Fire.

O you moth, do not show any forgetfulness and doubt: look once at your burnt wing!

Since you are saved, the thanksgiving is this, that you should 2880 have no inclination towards that grain,

In order that, when you say thanks, He may bestow on you the daily bread that is without snare and without fear of the enemy.

In thanksgiving for the bounty shown in setting you free, it behoves you to commemorate the bounty of God.

How oft in sorrows and in tribulation have you cried, "O God, deliver me from the snare,

---

[1] Literally, "that one who disposes (hearts) to repentance."

[2] The word پروانه can mean either "mandate" or "moth." In the following verse it is used in the latter sense. Some commentators think it has the meaning "moth" here also; but the translation given above seems to me to be more natural. I cannot believe that the poet would describe even a meta-phorical moth as "arriving" and "drawing souls into perdition."

That I may do suchlike service (to Thee) and practise bene-
ficence and throw dust in the eyes of the Devil!"

*Story of the vow made by the dogs every winter that when next
summer comes they will build a house for the winter.*

2885 In winter the bones of the dog are drawn together: the blows
of the frost make him so small

That he says, "Having such a little body, I must build a
stone house.

When summer comes, I will build with my claws a stone
house against the cold."

(But) when summer comes, his bones expand from the relief
(which he feels), and his skin grows sleek,

And, when he sees himself stout, he says, "In what house
should I find room, O noble sir?"

2890 He grows stout and slinks into a shady place—a lazy, full-fed,
cowardly, self-opinionated (creature)!

His heart (conscience) says to him, "Build a house, O uncle!"
He says, "How shall I find room in the house? Tell (me that)."

In the hour of pain the bones of your greed shrink together
and diminish in compass,

And you say penitently, "I will build a house: it will be a
resting-place (refuge) for me in winter";

(But) when the pain is gone and your greed has grown stout,
the desire for the house departs from you, just as (in the case of)
the dog.

2895 Thanksgiving for the bounty is sweeter than the bounty
(itself): how should he that is addicted to thanksgiving go to-
wards (direct his attention to) the bounty[1]?

Thanksgiving is the soul of the bounty, and the bounty is as
the husk, because thanksgiving brings you to the abode of the
Beloved.

Bounty produces heedlessness, and thanksgiving alertness:
hunt after bounty with the snare of thanksgiving to the King.

The bounty of thanksgiving will make you contented and
princely, so that you will bestow a hundred bounties on the
poor.

You will eat your fill of the viands and dessert of God, so that
hunger and begging will depart from you.

*How the unbelievers stopped the prophets, on whom be peace, from
giving admonition and brought forward Necessitarian arguments.*

2900 The people (of Sabá) said, "O admonishers, what ye have
said is enough, if there be any one in this village[2].

---

[1] *I.e.* he turns towards the Benefactor instead of occupying himself with
the benefit.   [2] *I.e.* "if any one will listen to you."

God hath set a lock upon our hearts; none can prevail against the Creator.

That Artist made the picture of us to be this: this will not be altered by talking.

A hundred years you may tell the pebble to become a ruby, a hundred years you may tell the old to become new;

You may tell earth to assume the qualities of water, you may tell water to become honey or milk—

('Tis all in vain): He is the Creator of the heavens and the 2905 heavenly ones, the Creator of water and earth and earthly beings.

To heaven He gave its circling motion and its purity; to (the mixed) water and earth its dark appearance and its (power of) growth.

How can heaven choose turbidity? How can (the mixed) earth and water buy purity?

To every one He hath allotted a certain course: how should a mountain by any effort become as a straw?[1]"

The answer of the prophets, on whom be peace, to the Necessitarians.

The prophets said, "Yes: He hath created some qualities from which it is impossible to withdraw one's self,

And He hath (also) created qualities (which are only) acci- 2910 dental, so that a hated person becomes acceptable.

If you bid a stone become gold, 'tis futile; (but) if you bid copper become gold, the way (of transmuting it) exists.

If you bid sand become clay, it is incapable (of doing so); (but) if you bid earth become clay, that is possible.

He hath given (ordained to us) maladies for which there is no remedy, such as lameness, flatness of the nose, and blindness;

He hath given maladies for which there is a remedy, such as facial paralysis and headache.

These medicines He hath made for the sake of (restoring) 2915 harmony: these maladies and medicines are not in vain.

Nay, most maladies have a cure: when you seek in earnest, it will come to hand."

How the infidels repeated the Necessitarian arguments.

The people said, "O company (of prophets), this malady of ours is not one of those that admit of cure.

For years ye uttered spells and admonitions of this kind, and by them our bondage[2] was made sorer every moment.

If this disease were susceptible of cure, some particle of it would at last have been removed.

---

[1] Or, "how should one like a straw...become a mountain?"

[2] *I.e.* the bolts and locks which prevent your warnings from reaching our hearts.

2920   When hepatitis occurs, water does not enter the liver: if he (the patient) should drink up the (whole) sea, it (the water) would go somewhere else;

Consequently the hands and feet become swollen: that water-drinking does not defeat the thirst."

How the prophets, on whom be peace, answered them again.

The prophets said, "Despair is wicked: the grace and the mercies of the Creator are infinite.

'Tis not proper to despair of such a Benefactor: cling to the saddle-strap of this Mercy.

Oh, many a plight became hard in the beginning, (but) afterwards it was relieved, and the hardship passed away.

2925   After despair there are many hopes; after darkness there are many suns.

I grant indeed that ye have become stony and have put locks upon your ears and hearts;

(But) we have naught to do with any acceptance (on your part): our business is to resign ourselves (to God) and fulfil His command.

He hath commanded us (to perform) this service: we have not this office of proclaimer (prophetship) from ourselves.

We possess life (only) for the purpose of (executing) the command of God: if He bid us (sow) in a tract of sand, we sow.

2930   The prophet's soul hath no friend except God: he hath naught to do with the acceptance or rejection of (his message by) the people.

The reward for delivering His messages comes from Him (God): we have become hateful and wear the aspect of enemies (to the people) for the Beloved's sake.

At this (Divine) Portal[1] we are not weary, so that we should halt everywhere because of the distance of the way.

Oppressed in heart and weary is that one (alone) who is in prison through being parted from the Friend.

The Heart-ravisher and Desired One is present with us: amidst the largesse of His mercy our souls are giving thanks.

2935   In our hearts is an anemone-field and rose-garden: there is no way (of entrance) for old age and decay;

We are ever fresh and young and gracious, unfaded and sweet and laughing and debonair.

To us a hundred years are the same as a single hour, for long and short (time) is a thing disjoined from us.

That length and shortness is in bodies (alone): where is that long and short in the soul?

---

[1] *I.e.* "since we dwell with God."

The three hundred and nine years of the Men of the Cave[1]
seemed to them one day (that passed) without grief and woe;

And (only) then did it seem to them one day even, when 2940
their spirits came back from non-existence into their bodies.

When there is no day and night and month and year, how
should there be satiety and old age and weariness?

Since there is (for us) selflessness in the rose-garden of non-
existence, there is (for us) intoxication caused by the goblet of
Divine grace.

Any one that has not drunk (thereof is in the same case as
those to whom the saying, 'Whoso) has not tasted does not
know' (is applicable): how should the dung-beetle conceive the
(fragrant) breaths of the rose?

It[2] is not conceivable: if it were conceivable, it would become
non-existent, like (all) objects of conception.

How should Hell conceive Paradise? Does a beauteous face 2945
shine (forth) at all from an ugly pig?

Hark, do not cut your own throat! Take heed, O despicable
one, (when) such a morsel as this has reached your mouth.

We have brought the hard ways to an end; we have made the
way easy for our own people."

*How the people (of Sabá) repeated their resistance to the (prophets')
hope (of converting them and set themselves) against the prophets,
on whom be peace.*

The people (of Sabá) said, "If ye bring good luck to your-
selves, ye are ill-starred for us and are opposed (to us) and
rejected (by us).

Our souls were free from cares: ye have cast us into grief and
trouble.

Through your evil presage the delightful[3] concord and agree- 2950
ment that existed (amongst us) has been turned into a hundred
separations.

(Formerly) we were parrots eating sugar for dessert; (now)
through you we have become birds that meditate on death.

Wheresoever is a grief-spreading tale, wheresoever is an
odious rumour,

Wheresoever in the world is an evil presage, wheresoever is a
monstrous transformation, a terrible punishment, an infliction
of chastisement[4]—

(All those things) are (contained) in the parable of your story
and in your evil presage: ye have an appetite for rousing
grief."

---

[1] The Seven Sleepers.
[2] *I.e.* the intoxication of Divine grace.
[3] Literally, "the delight of."

[4] Properly "a place where chastisement is inflicted," but مأخَذ seems to
be used here in the same sense as مؤَاخَذه.

How the prophets, on whom be peace, answered them once more.

2955   The prophets said, "The foul and evil presage has its support from within your souls.

If you are asleep in a perilous place, and a dragon is approaching you from a spot close at hand[1],

And a kindly person has made you aware (of it), saying, 'Jump up quickly, or else the dragon will devour you'—

If you say, 'Why are you uttering an evil presage?' (he will reply), 'What (evil) presage? Jump up and see in the light of day.

I myself will deliver you from the midst of the evil presage and will take you home.'

2960   He (such a person) is one that acquaints (you) with things hidden, like the prophet who has seen what the people of this world have not seen.

If a physician say to you, 'Do not eat unripe grapes, for such an illness (as is caused by them) will produce (grave) trouble and mischief,'

And if you say, 'Why are you uttering an evil presage?'— then you are making out your sincere adviser to be culpable.

And if an astrologer say to you, 'By no means set about[2] such an affair to-day,'

Though you see the falsehood of the astrologer a hundred times, (yet if) it (the prediction) come true once or twice, you are eager to trust him[3].

2965   These stars of ours are never at variance (with the truth): how does their truth remain concealed[4] from you?

The physician and the astrologer inform (you) from (their own) opinion, and verily we (inform you) from clairvoyance:

We behold the smoke and fire rushing from afar towards the unbelievers.

You are saying, 'Be silent (and refrain) from these words, for the words of evil presage are hurtful to us.'"

O you who hearken not unto the admonition of the admonishers, the evil presage is with you wherever you go.

2970   A viper is walking on your back: he (the admonisher) sees it from a roof and makes (you) aware;

You say to him, "Hush! do not vex me": he says, "Be happy! Truly, the words have gone (have been spoken)[5]."

When the viper darts its mouth at your neck, all your desire for happiness is made bitter.

---

[1] Literally, "from the direction of your head." Cf. باش اوجى in Turkish.
[2] Literally, "put into preparation."
[3] Literally, "you buy (him)."
[4] Literally, "in the sheath."
[5] *I.e.* "I will say no more."

Then you say to him, "O so-and-so, was this all (the warning you gave me)? Why didn't you tear your collar in outcry,

Or why weren't you throwing a stone at me from above, in order that that grave calamity and misfortune might be shown to me (plainly)?"

He says, "(I refrained) because you were annoyed"; you say 2975 (ironically), "You have made me very happy!"

He says, "I bestowed counsel generously, that I might deliver you from this sterile (unprofitable) bondage.

From vileness you acknowledged no obligation for that (generosity): you made (it) a source of injury and insolence."

This is the nature of base villains: he (such a one) does evil to thee when thou doest good (to him).

As for the fleshly soul, bend it double (mortify it) by means of this renunciation[1], for it is vile, and kindness suiteth it not.

If thou show beneficence to a noble man, 'tis fitting: he will 2980 give seven hundred (benefits) in exchange for every one (conferred upon him);

(But be merciless to the ignoble): when thou treatest a villain with violence and cruelty, he becomes a very faithful servant to thee.

The infidels in (their) prosperity sow (the seed of) cruelty; again (afterwards) in Hell their cry is "O Lord, (deliver us)!"

The wisdom of (God's) having created Hell in the world hereafter and the prison of (tribulation in) the present world to the end that they may be places of worship for the arrogant (evil-doers): "Come ye willingly or unwillingly[2]."

For in (suffering) cruelty the vile are purified; when they receive kindness, they themselves become cruel.

Therefore Hell is the mosque where they perform their devotions: a trap is the (only) fetter for a wild bird.

Prison is the cloister of the thief and villain, that there he may 2985 be constantly mindful of God.

Inasmuch as Divine worship was the object (in the creation) of mankind, Hell-fire was made the place of worship for the rebellious.

Man hath the power (of action) in everything, but this service (of God) has (ever) been the (final) object of him.

"*I did not create the Jinn and mankind (save that they might serve Me)*." Recite this (text). The (final) object of the world is naught but Divine worship:

Though the (final) object of a book is the science (which it contains), (yet) if you make it a pillow (to rest on), it will become (serve as) that too;

---

[1] *I.e.* by withholding from it its good, namely, the indulgence of its appetites.   [2] *Qur'án*, XLI, 10.

2990   But this (function of being a) pillow was not its (final) object:
it (the final object) was learning and knowledge and right
guidance and profit.

If you have made the sword a tent-pin, you have preferred
defeat to victory.

Although the (final) object of Man is knowledge (of God) and
to be rightly directed (in religion), (yet) every man hath a par-
ticular place of worship.

The place where (the means whereby) the noble man wor-
ships is your treating him with kindness; the place where (the
means whereby) the vile man worships is your making him sick
(your maltreating him).

Smite the vile, that they may bow their heads; give to the
noble, that they may yield (good) fruit.

2995   Necessarily God hath created a mosque for each of the twain[1]
—Hell for those, and increase (of bounty)[2] for these.

Moses built the Báb-i Saghír (the Small Gate) at Jerusalem,
in order that the people tormented (by evil passions) might
lower their heads,

Because they were insolent and arrogant. Hell is (like) that
Báb-i Saghír and (place of) humiliation.

*Explaining how God most High has made the bodily form of kings
a means of subduing the insolent (sinners) who are not subject to
God, just as Moses, on whom be peace, built the Báb-i Saghír in
the wall of Jerusalem in order that the insolent (and wicked) men
among the Israelites might bow low when they entered in,
(according to the text), "Enter the gate, prostrating yourselves,
and say 'hittat^{un}[3].'"*

Likewise God hath built a Báb-i Saghír from the flesh and
bones of kings. Take heed!

The people of this world make prostration before them, since
they are opposed to prostration before the Divine Majesty.

3000   He (God) hath made a little dunghill their *mihráb* (place
of worship): the name of that *mihráb* is "prince" and
"paladin."

Ye (worldlings) are not fit for this holy Presence: holy men
are (like) the sugar-cane; ye are (like) the empty reed.

These vile wretches grovel before those curs[4]; (but) it is a
disgrace to the lion[5] that they should be complaisant to him.

The cat is the (dreaded) overseer of every mouse-natured one:
who is the mouse that it should be afraid of the lions?

---

[1] Literally, "both the mosques."
[2] *I.e.* Paradise. Cf. *Qur'án*, L, 34.
[3] *I.e.* "pray God to let you put down your burden of sin."
[4] *I.e.* the princes of this world.
[5] *I.e.* the prophet or saint.

Their fear is (only) of the curs of God: how should they have fear of the Sun of God[1]?

The litany of those great (venerable) ones is "my Lord the 3005 most High"; "my lord the most low" is suitable to these fools.

How should the mouse fear the lions of the (spiritual) battle-field? Nay, (they that fear the lions are) those who have the speed and the musk-bag of the deer[2].

O licker of pots, go to him that licks basins and write him down as thy lord and benefactor!

Enough! If I give a far-reaching exposition, the (worldly) prince will be angered; and besides he knows that it (his case) is (such as has been described).

The upshot is this:—"O noble man, do evil to the vile, that the villain may lay his neck (before thee)."

When he (the noble man) deals kindly with the villain, his 3010 (fleshly) soul, the wicked soul shows ingratitude, like the vile.

'Twas on this account that the afflicted are thankful, (while) the fortunate are rebellious and deceitful.

The bey with his gold-embroidered coat is rebellious; the distressed wearer of a coarse woollen cloak ('abá) is thankful.

How should thankfulness grow from possessions and riches? Thankfulness grows from tribulation and sickness.

Story of the Ṣúfí's being enamoured of the empty food-wallet.

One day a Ṣúfí espied a food-wallet (hanging) on a nail: he began to whirl and rend his garments,

Crying, "Lo, the food of the foodless! Lo, the remedy for 3015 famines and pangs (of hunger)!"

When his smoke and tumult (his ecstasy) waxed great, every one that was a Ṣúfí joined him (imitated his behaviour).

They were shouting and shrieking: several were becoming intoxicated and beside themselves.

An idle busybody said to the Ṣúfí, "What is the matter? (Only) a food-wallet hung (on a nail), and it is empty of bread!"

He (the Ṣúfí) said, "Begone, begone! Thou art a (mere) form without spirit: do thou seek existence (not non-existence), for thou art no lover."

The lover's food is love of the bread, without (the existence of) 3020 the bread: no one that is sincere (in his love) is in thrall to existence.

Lovers have naught to do with existence: lovers have the interest without (having) the capital.

They have no wings, and (yet) they fly round the world; they have no hands, and (yet) they carry off the ball from the polo-field.

[1] I.e. the divinely illumined man.
[2] I.e. eminent holy men are revered only by those who are endowed with spiritual apprehension and mystical knowledge.

That dervish who scented (perceived) Reality used to weave baskets though his hand had been cut off[1].

Lovers have pitched their tents in non-existence[2]: they are of one colour (quality) and one essence, like non-existence.

3025 How should the sucking babe know the taste of viands? To the Jinní scent is meat and drink.

How shall a human being scent (perceive) his (the Jinní's) scent, inasmuch as his (the man's) nature is contrary to his (the Jinní's) nature?

That scent-inhaling Jinní gains from the scent (a great delight): thou wilt not gain that (delight) from a hundred maunds of sweet dainties.

To the Copt the water of the Nile is blood; to the goodly Israelite it is water[3].

By the Israelites the sea is (made) a highway; by the ruffian Pharaoh it is (made) a drowning-place.

How Jacob, on whom be peace, was privileged to taste the cup of God from the face of Joseph, and inhale the scent of God from the scent of Joseph; and the exclusion of his (Joseph's) brethren and others from both these (privileges).

3030 That which Jacob experienced from (beholding) the face of Joseph was peculiar to him: when did that (delight) come to his (Joseph's) brethren?

This one (Jacob), from love of him (Joseph), puts himself in the pit, while that one (Joseph's brother) digs a pit for him (Joseph) in hatred.

In the sight of this one (Joseph's brother) his (Joseph's) food-wallet is empty of bread; in the sight of Jacob it is full, for he is desiring eagerly.

None with face unwashed beholds the faces of the houris: he (the Prophet) said, "There is no ritual prayer without the ablution."

Love is the meat and drink of souls; hunger, from this point of view, is the food of souls.

3035 Jacob had hunger for Joseph; (hence) the smell of the bread was reaching him from afar.

He that took the shirt (of Joseph) was hastening (on his way) and was not perceiving the scent of Joseph's shirt,

While he that was a hundred leagues (distant) from that quarter was smelling the perfume, since he was Jacob.

Oh, there is many a learned man that hath no profit of (his) knowledge: that person is one who commits knowledge to memory, not one who loves (it).

---

[1] See p. 96, *supra.*
[2] *I.e.* in the world of Reality, which has no sensible existence.
[3] See Book IV, v. 3431 foll.

From him the hearer (but not the learned man himself) per-
ceives the scent (of knowledge), though the hearer be of the
common sort,

Because the shirt in his (the learned man's) hand is a borrowed 3040
thing, like a slave-girl in the hands of a slave-dealer.

The slave-girl is useless to the slave-dealer: she is in his
hands (only) for the sake of the purchaser.

The dispensation of God is a bestowal of the allotted portion:
no one's (portion) has access (can find its way) to another.

A good fancy becomes that (blessed) man's garden (of Para-
dise); an ugly fancy waylays this (unblest) man (and brings
him to perdition).

That Lord who hath made from one fancy the garden (of
Paradise), and from one fancy Hell and the place of melting
(torment)—

Then who (but He) should know the way to His roseries? 3045
Then who (but He) should know the way to His furnaces?

The sentry of the heart, while on his round, does not see from
what corner of the soul the fancy comes.

If he saw its rising-place, he would contrive to bar[1] the way to
every unlovely fancy;

(But) how should the foot of the scout reach that spot?—for
it is the watch-tower and mountain-fortress of Non-existence[2].

Blindly lay hold of the skirt of His grace: this is the blind
man's seisin (act of taking legal possession), O king.

His skirt is His command and behest: fortunate is he to 3050
whom piety is (as) his soul.

The (blessed) one is in (the midst of) meadows and water-
brooks, while the other (unblest) one beside him is in torment.

He (the latter) remains in wonderment, saying, "Wherefore
is this man's delight?" and the other remains in wonderment,
saying, "In whose prison is this man?

Hark, why art thou parched?—for here are fountains. Hark,
why art thou pale?—for here are a hundred remedies.

Hark, neighbour, come into the garden!" He (the unblest
man) says, "O (dear) soul, I cannot come."

*Story of the Amír and his slave who was very fond of the ritual
prayer and had a great joy in the ritual prayer and in com-
muning with God.*

At dawn the Amír wanted (to go to) the hot bath: he shouted, 3055
"Ho, Sunqur, rouse yourself[3]!

Get from Altún the basin and the napkin and the clay, that
we may go to the hot bath, O indispensable one."

---

[1] Literally, "by contrivance he would bar."
[2] *I.e.* the world of Reality which is inaccessible to human thought.
[3] Literally, "lift up your head."

Sunqur at that (very) moment took up the basin and a fine napkin and set out with him—the two together[1].

There was a mosque on the road, and the call to prayer came publicly into Sunqur's ear.

Sunqur was very fond of the ritual prayer: he said, "O my Amír, O kind master[2],

3060   Stay patiently for a while on this bench, that I may perform the obligatory prayers and may recite (the Súra beginning with the words) *lam yakun*[3]."

When the Imám and the people had come forth and finished the prayers and litanies,

Sunqur remained there till near the forenoon: the Amír awaited him for some time;

(Then) he said, "O Sunqur, why don't you come out?" He replied, "This artful One will not let me (out)[4].

Have patience! Behold, I come, O light (of my eyes)! I am not heedless, for thou art in my ear."

3065   Seven times in succession did he show patience and (then) shout—till at last the man was reduced to despair by his (Sunqur's) trifling.

His (Sunqur's) reply was (always) this—"He will not let me come out yet, O revered (master)."

He (the master) said, "Why, there is no one left in the mosque. Who is detaining you there? Who has made you sit (fast)?"

He (Sunqur) said, "He who has chained thee outside (of the mosque) has chained me too inside (of it).

He who will not let thee come in will not let me come out.

3070   He who will not let thee set foot in this direction has chained the foot of this slave (so that it cannot move) in this (opposite) direction."

The sea does not let the fish out; the sea does not let the creatures of earth in.

Water is the original home of the fish, and the (gross) animal is of the earth: here device and contrivance are of no avail.

Strong is the lock (of Divine destiny), and the (only) opener is God: cling to resignation and acquiescence (in God's will).

Though the atoms, one by one, should become keys, (yet) this opening is not (effected) save by the Divine Majesty.

3075   When you forget your own contrivance, you will gain that young (happy) fortune from your spiritual Guide.

When you are forgetful of self, you are remembered (by God): (when) you have become a slave (to Him), then you are set free.

---

[1] Literally, "two by two."

[2] Literally, "O thou who treatest thy slave with kindness."

[3] *Qur'án*, XCVIII.

[4] Or, reading ای ذو فنون, "He (God) will not let me out, O accomplished (master)."

How the prophets lost hope of being accepted and approved by the unbelievers, as God hath said: "Until, when the (Divine) Messengers despaired...."

The prophets said to their hearts (to themselves), "How long shall we continue giving exhortation and counsel to this one and that one?

How long shall we misguidedly beat a piece of cold iron? Hark, till when (how long shall we continue) to breathe into a cage[1]?"

The motion (action) of created beings is (caused) by Divine destiny and appointment: the sharpness of the teeth is (caused) by the burning (hunger-pangs) of the stomach.

The First Soul pushed (produced an effect) upon the second 3080 soul[2]: a fish stinks from the head, not from the tail.

But, whilst recognising (this), still[3] speed on[4] like an arrow: since God hath said, "*Deliver (the Divine message),*" there is no escape (from doing so).

You do not know which of these two[5] you are: strive (then) so long (as is necessary) that you may discern what you are.

When you put a cargo on board a ship, you are making that venture on trust,

(For) you do not know which of the two you are—whether you are (destined to be) drowned on the voyage or saved (from death).

If you say, "Until I know which I am, I will not hasten on to 3085 (embark on) the ship and the ocean;

On this voyage I am (to be) saved or drowned: reveal (to me) to which party I belong.

I will not start upon this voyage with doubt and in idle hope, like the others"—

(Then) no traffic will be done by you, because the secret of these two aspects (possibilities) is in the Unseen.

The merchant of timid disposition and frail[6] spirit neither gains nor loses in his quest;

Nay, he suffers loss, for he is deprived (of fortune) and 3090 despicable: (only) he that is an eater of flames (ardent in search) will find the light.

Inasmuch as all affairs turn upon hope, the affair of religion is most worthy (to inspire hope), for by this means you may win salvation.

---

[1] *I.e.* "to waste our breath."

[2] *I.e.* the Universal Soul determines the character and fate of particular souls.

[3] Literally, "recognise (this) and still."

[4] Literally, "drive the ass (forward)."

[5] *I.e.* the two categories mentioned in vv. 3071-2.

[6] Literally, "(like) glass."

Here it is not permitted to knock at the door (with impor-
tunity); naught but hope (is permissible): God best knoweth the
right course.

Explaining how the faith of the conventional (worldly)
man consists in fear and hope.

The motive in every trade is hope and chance, even though
their necks are (worn thin), like a spindle, from (incessant)
toil.

When he (the trader) goes in the morning to his shop, he is
running (thither) in the hope and chance of (earning) a liveli-
hood.

3095   (If) you have not the chance of (earning) a livelihood, why do
you go (to your shop)? There is the fear (danger) of dis-
appointment: how (then) are you strong (confident)?

In (the case of) earning food, how has the fear of eternal
(eternally predestined) disappointment not made you feeble in
your search?

You will say, "Though the fear of disappointment is before
(me), this fear is greater (when I am) in idleness.

(When I am) at work my hope is greater: (when I am) in
idleness I have more risk."

Then, O evil-thinking man, why is this fear of loss holding
you back[1] in the matter of religion?

3100   Or have not you seen in what a gainful trade the people of
this bazaar of ours, the prophets and the saints, are (engaged),

And what mines (of treasure) have appeared to them from
this going to the (spiritual) shop, and how they have gotten gain
in this market?

To that one[2] the fire became submissive, like an anklet; to
that one[3] the sea became submissive and carried him on its
shoulders[4];

To that one[5] the iron became submissive and wax-like; to that
one[6] the wind became a slave and subject.

Setting forth how the Prophet, on whom be peace, said, " Verily,
God most High hath friends who are concealed."

Another party go (to and fro) exceedingly hidden: how should
they become well-known to the people of externals?

3105   They possess all this (spiritual dominion), and (yet) no one's
eye falls upon their sovereignty for one moment.

Both their miracles and they (themselves) are in the (Divine)
sanctuary: even the *Abdál* do not hear their names.

[1] Literally, "taking hold of your skirt."
[2] Abraham.   [3] Moses.
[4] Literally, "and became a carrier."
[5] David.   [6] Solomon.

Or art thou ignorant of the bounties of God who is calling thee to come yonder?

The whole world of six directions is (filled with) His bounty: wheresoever thou lookest, it is making Him (His bounty) known[1].

When a generous man bids thee come into the fire, come in quickly and do not say, "It will burn me."

The story of Anas, may God be pleased with him: how he cast a napkin into a fiery oven, and it was not burnt.

It has come (down to us) concerning Anas son of Málik that a 3110 certain person became his guest.

He (that person) related that after the meal Anas saw the table-napkin (was) yellow in hue,

Dirty and stained; and said, "O maid-servant, throw it into the oven at once."

Thereupon the intelligent (maid) threw it into the oven, which was full of fire.

All the guests were astounded thereat: they were in expectation of (seeing) the smoke of the (burning) napkin.

After a short time she took it out of the oven, clean and white 3115 and purged of[2] that filth.

The party (of guests) said, "O venerable Companion (of the Prophet), how didn't it burn, and how too did it become cleansed?"

He replied, "Because Muṣṭafá (Mohammed) often rubbed his hands and lips on this napkin."

O heart afraid of the fire and torment (of Hell), draw nigh unto such a hand and lip as that!

Since it (the Prophet's blessing) bestowed such honour upon a lifeless object, what things will it reveal to the soul of the lover!

Inasmuch as he (the Prophet) made the clods of the Ka'ba 3120 the *qibla* (towards which the Moslems turn), do thou, O soul, be (as) the dust of[3] holy men in (thy) war (against the flesh).

Afterwards they said to the maid-servant, "Wilt not thou tell (us) thine own feelings about all this?

Why didst thou (so) quickly cast it (into the oven) at his behest? I suppose he was acquainted with[4] the secrets[5],

(But) why didst thou, mistress, throw such a precious napkin into the fire?"

She answered, "I have confidence in the generous: I do not despair of their bounty.

---

[1] Literally, "there is the making known of Him." Another reading is اَعْلَامِ اوسْت, *i.e.* "there are the evidences of Him."

[2] Literally, "far from."

[3] *I.e.* "humbly devoted to."

[4] Literally, "has tracked (and discovered)."

[5] *I.e.* the miraculous qualities of the napkin.

3125   What of a piece of cloth? If he bid me (myself) go without regret into the very essence of the fire,

I, from perfect confidence (in him), will fall (throw myself) in: I have great hope of them that are devoted to God.

I will throw myself in, not (only) this napkin, because of my confidence in every generous one who knows the mystery."

O brother, apply thyself to this elixir: the faith of a man must not be less than the faith of a woman.

The heart of the man that is less than a woman is the heart that is less (in worth) than the belly.

Story of the Prophet's, on whom be peace, coming to the aid of a caravan of Arabs who had been brought to sore straits by thirst and lack of water and had set their minds on death: (both) the camels and the people (of the caravan) had let their tongues drop out (of their mouths from exhaustion).

3130   In that wadi (was) a company of Arabs: their water-skins had become dry from lack of rain:

A caravan amidst the desert in sore distress—they had rehearsed their own death.

Suddenly he who succours both worlds, Muṣṭafá (Mohammed), appeared on the way, for help's sake.

He saw there an exceeding great caravan on the scalding sand and (engaged in) a hard and terrible journey;

The tongues of their camels hanging out, the people strown everywhere on the sand.

3135   He took pity and said, "Hark, go at once, some of your comrades, and run to yonder sandhills,

For a negro on camelback will (presently) bring a water-skin, (which) he is conveying with all speed to his master.

Bring to me that negro camel-driver along with the camel by force, if need be[1]."

Those seekers approached the sandhills: after a short while they saw 'twas even so:

A negro slave was going with a camel, the water-skin filled with water, like one bearing a gift.

3140   Then they said to him, "The Pride of mankind, the Best of created beings, invites thee (to come) in this direction."

He said, "I do not know him: who is he?" He (the spokesman) said, "He is that moon-faced sweet-natured one."

They described to him the diverse qualities which exist (in the Prophet): he said, "Belike he is that poet (wizard)

Who subdued a multitude by magic: I will not come half a span towards him."

---

[1] Literally, "with bitter command."

Dragging him along, they brought him thither: he raised an outcry in revilement and heat (of anger).

When they dragged him before that venerable one, he 3145 (the Prophet) said, "Drink ye the water and carry it away withal."

He satisfied the thirst of them all from that water-skin: the camels and every person drank of that water.

From his (the negro's) water-skin he filled large and small water-skins: from jealousy of him the clouds in the sky were distraught.

Has any one seen (such a wonder as) this, that the burning glow of so many Hells (of thirst) should be cooled by a single water-skin?

Has any one seen (such a wonder as) this, that all these water-skins were filled from a single water-skin without trouble?

The water-skin itself was a veil, and (in reality) at his (the 3150 Prophet's) command the waves of (Divine) bounty were coming (to them) from the Sea of origin.

"Water by boiling is converted into air, and that air by cold is turned into water."

Nay, (it is not so); without cause and beyond these maxims of (natural) philosophy the (Divine) act of bringing into existence produced the water from non-existence.

Inasmuch as you have observed (secondary) causes from your childhood, through ignorance you have stuck to the (secondary) cause.

(Being occupied) with causes you are forgetful of the Causer: hence you are inclining towards these veils.

When (all secondary) causes are gone, you will beat your 3155 head and cry many a time, "O our Lord! O our Lord!"

The Lord will say, "Betake thyself to the (secondary) cause! How hast thou remembered My work? Oh, wonderful!"

He (the believer in secondary causes) says, "Henceforth I will behold Thee entirely: I will not look towards the cause and that deception (by which I was led astray)."

He (God) will reply to him, "Thy case is (described in the text), '(If) they were sent back (to the world), they would surely return (to what they were forbidden to do),' O thou who art weak in thy repentance and covenant;

But I will not regard that, I will show mercy: My mercy is abounding, I will be intent on mercy.

I will not regard thy bad promise, I from lovingkindness will 3160 bestow the gift at this (very) moment, since thou art calling unto Me."

The (people of the) caravan were amazed at his (the Prophet's) deed. (They cried), "O Muḥammad, O thou that hast the nature of the Sea, what is this?

Thou hast made a small water-skin a veil (a means of disguise): thou hast drowned (abundantly satisfied the thirst of) both Arabs and Kurds."

How he (the Prophet) miraculously filled the slave's water-skin with water from the Unseen World and made the face of that negro slave white by permission of God most High.

"O slave, now behold thy water-skin full (of water), that thou mayst not say (anything) good or bad in complaint."

The negro was astounded at his (the Prophet's) evidentiary miracle: his faith was dawning from (the world of) non-spatiality.

3165　He saw that a fountain had begun to pour from the air (of yonder world) and that his water-skin had become a veil to the emanation of that (fountain).

The veils also were rent by that (illumined) sight (of his), so that he distinctly beheld the fountain of the Unseen.

Thereupon the slave's eyes were filled[1] with tears: he forgot his master and his dwelling-place.

Strength failed him[2] to go on his way: God cast a mighty commotion into his soul.

Then again he (the Prophet) drew him back for (his) good, saying, "Come to thyself; return, O thou who wilt gain advantage (by doing so).

3170　'Tis not the time for bewilderment: bewilderment is in front of thee; just now advance on thy way briskly and speedily."

He (the slave) laid the hands of Muṣṭafá (Mohammed) on his face and gave (them) many loving kisses.

Then Muṣṭafá rubbed his blessed hand on his (the slave's) face and made it fortunate.

That Abyssinian negro became white as the full moon, and his night turned into bright day.

He became a Joseph in beauty and in coquetry: he (the Prophet) said to him, "Now go home[3] and relate what has befallen thee."

3175　He was going along, without head or foot, intoxicated (with ecstasy): in going he knew not foot from hand.

Then from the neighbourhood of the caravan he came hastening with two full water-skins to his master.

How the master saw his slave white and did not recognise him and said, "Thou hast killed my slave: the murder hath found thee out, and God hath thrown thee into my hands."

The master espied him from afar and remained bewildered: from amazement he called (to his presence) the people of the village.

---

[1] Literally, "the slave filled his eyes."
[2] Literally, "his hand and foot were left helpless."
[3] Literally, "to the village."

"This," said he, "is my water-skin and my camel: where, then, is my swart-browed slave gone?

This man coming from afar is (like) a full-moon: the light from his countenance strikes upon (and prevails against) the daylight.

Where is my slave? Perchance he has lost his way, or a wolf 3180 has overtaken him and he has been killed."

When he came before him, he (the master) said, "Who art thou? Art thou a native of Yemen or a Turcoman?

Tell (me), what hast thou done to my slave? Speak the truth! If thou hast killed him, declare it! Do not seek evasion."

He replied, "If I have killed him, how have I come to thee? How have I come with my own feet into this blood[1]?"

(He asked again), "Where is my slave?" He (the slave) said, "Lo, I am (he): the hand of God's grace hath made me resplendent."

"Eh, what art thou saying? Where is my slave? Hark, thou 3185 wilt not escape from me except by (telling) the truth."

He (the slave) said, "I will relate all thy secret dealings with that slave, one by one;

I will relate what has passed (between us) from the time when thou didst purchase me until now,

That thou mayst know I am the same in (my spiritual) existence, though a (bright) dawn has opened forth from my night-hued (body).

The colour is changed; but the pure spirit is free from colour and from the (four) elements and the dust."

They that know the body (alone) soon lose us[2]; (but) they that 3190 quaff the (spiritual) water abandon the (bodily) water-skin and jar.

They that know the spirit are free from numbers (plurality): they are sunk in the Sea that is without quality or quantity.

Become spirit and know spirit by means of spirit: become the friend of vision (clairvoyant), not the child of ratiocination.

Forasmuch as the Angel is one in origin with Intelligence, (and) they have (only) become two (different) forms for the sake of (the Divine) Wisdom—

The Angel assumed wings and pinions like a bird, while this Intelligence left wings (behind) and assumed (immaterial) splendour—

Necessarily both became co-adjutors: both the beauteous ones 3195 became a support to one another.

The Angel as well as the Intelligence is a finder of God: each of the twain is a helper and worshipper of Adam.

The Flesh (nafs) and the Devil have (also) been (essentially) one from the first, and have been an enemy and envier of Adam.

---

[1] I.e. "how have I, of my own accord, given myself up to be slain?"
[2] I.e. they are unable to recognise us when our bodies change and decay.

He that regarded Adam as a body fled (from him in disdain),
while he that regarded (him as) the trusty Light bowed (in
worship).

Those two (the Angel and the Intelligence) were (made)
clairvoyant by this (Adam), while the eye of these two (the
Flesh and the Devil) saw nothing but clay.

3200　This discourse is now left (floundering) like an ass on the ice,
since it is not fitting to recite the Gospel to Jews.

How can one speak of 'Umar to Shí'ites? How can one play
a lute before the deaf?

But if there is any one (hidden) in a nook in the village, the
hue and cry that I have raised is enough.

To him that is worthy to (hear) the exposition, stones and
brickbats become an articulate and well-grounded exponent.

*Explaining that whatsoever God most High bestowed and created—
the heavens and the earths and the substances and the accidents—
He created all (this) at the demand of need, and that one must
make one's self in need of a thing, so that He may bestow it; for
" . . . Or He who answers the sorely distressed when he calls
unto Him?" Sore distress is the evidence of worthiness (to receive
the Divine bounty).*

'Twas Mary's want and pain that made such a babe (as Jesus)
begin to speak (in the cradle).

3205　Part of her spoke on her behalf without her: every part of thee
hath speech in secret.

Thy hands and feet become witnesses (against thee), O slave:
how long wilt thou set hand and foot (strenuously apply thyself)
to denial?

And if thou art not worthy of (hearing) the exposition and the
speech, the rational soul of the speaker saw thee (to be unworthy)
and went to sleep (refrained from action).

Whatsoever grew has grown for the sake of the needy, in
order that a seeker may find the thing he sought.

If God most High has created the heavens, He has created
them for the purpose of removing needs.

3210　Wherever a pain is, the cure goes thither; wherever a poverty
is, the provision goes thither.

Wherever a difficult question is, the answer goes thither;
wherever a ship is, the water goes thither.

Do not seek the water, (but) get thirst, so that the water may
gush forth from above and below.

Until the tender-throated babe is born, how should the milk
for it begin to flow from the (mother's) breast?

Go, run on these hills and dales, to the end that thou mayst
become thirsty and a prey[1] to heat;

_____

[1] Literally, "a pawn."

After that, from the noise of the hornet of the air (the thunder- 3215
cloud) thou wilt hear the noise of the water of the stream, O
king.

Thy need is not less than (that of) dry plants: thou takest
water and art drawing it towards them;

Thou takest the water by the ear and drawest it towards the
dry crops that they may obtain refreshment.

For the spiritual crops, whose essences are concealed, the
cloud of (Divine) mercy is full of the water of Kawthar.

In order that (the words) *their Lord gave them to drink* may be
addressed (to thee), be thirsty! God best knoweth the right
course.

*How the unbelieving woman came to Muṣṭafá (Mohammed), on
whom be peace, with a sucking babe, and how it spoke, like Jesus,
of the miracles of the Prophet, God bless and save him!*

A woman of the same village, one of the unbelievers, ran to 3220
the Prophet for the sake of testing (him).

She came in to the Prophet, (her face covered) with the veil:
the woman had a two months old infant in her lap.

The child said, "God give peace unto thee, O Messenger of
Allah! We have come to thee."

Its mother said to it angrily, "Hey, be silent! Who put this
testimony into thine ear?

Who taught thee this, O little child, so that thy tongue became
fluent in infancy?"

It replied, "God taught (me), then Gabriel: I am Gabriel's 3225
accompanist in (this) declaration."

She said, "Where (is Gabriel)?" It replied, "Above thy
head: dost not thou see? Turn thine eye aloft.

Gabriel is standing above thee: to me he has become a guide in
a hundred diverse ways."

She said, "Dost thou see (him)?" "Yes," it replied; "(I see
him) shining above thee like a perfect full-moon.

He is teaching me the qualities of the Prophet and delivering
me by means of that sublimity from this degradation."

Then said the Prophet to it (the infant), "O sucking child, 3230
what is thy name? Say (it) forth and comply (with my request)."

"'Abdu 'l-'Azíz[1]," said the child, "is my name with God;
(but) 'Abd-i 'Uzzá[2] with this handful of reprobates.

I am clear and free and quit of 'Uzzá, (I swear it) by the truth
of Him who gave thee this prophethood."

The two months old child, (illumined) like the full-moon,
pronounced the discourse of an adult, as those who occupy the
seat of honour.

---

[1] *I.e.* "slave of the Almighty."
[2] *I.e.* "slave of 'Uzzá," a goddess worshipped by the heathen Arabs.

Then at that instant arrived balm from Paradise, so that the brain of child and mother drew in the scent.

3235   Both (of them) were saying, "For fear of falling (from that high estate), 'tis best to surrender one's soul to the scent of this balm."

As for that one whom God endows with knowledge, things inanimate and growing (living) utter a hundred expressions of belief in him.

As for that one whom God protects, birds and fish become his guardians.

How an eagle seized the boot of the Prophet, on whom be peace, and carried it into the air and turned it upside down, and how a black serpent dropped down from the boot.

They were thus engaged, when Muṣṭafá (Mohammed) heard from aloft the call to the ritual prayer.

He asked for water and renewed the ablution: he washed his hands and face with that cold water.

3240   He washed both his feet and gave attention to (was about to take) his boot: a boot-snatcher carried off the boot.

That man of sweet address moved his hand towards the boot: an eagle snatched the boot from his hand,

And bore it away into the air, (swift) as the wind; then she turned it upside down, and a serpent dropped from it.

From the boot dropped a black serpent: on account of that (Divine) care (for the Prophet) the eagle became his benevolent friend.

Then the eagle brought back the boot and said, "Come, take it and go to prayers.

3245   I did this presumptuous act from necessity: I am abashed[1] by (my feeling of) reverence (for thee).

Woe to him that steps (behaves) presumptuously without necessity (and only) because vain desire authorises him[2]!"

Then the Prophet thanked her (the eagle) and said, "I deemed this (act of thine) rudeness, but it really was kindness.

Thou didst carry off the boot, and I was perturbed: thou took'st away my grief, and I was aggrieved.

Although God hath shown to me every unseen thing, at that moment my heart was occupied with myself."

3250   She (the eagle) said, "Far be it from thee that forgetfulness grew up in thee: my seeing that invisible thing is (from) thy reflexion.

(If) I, in the air, see the serpent in the boot, 'tis not of myself, 'tis thy reflexion, O Muṣṭafá."

[1] Literally, "I have a sense of being *shikasta-shákh* (broken-horned or broken-armed)."

[2] Literally, "gives a legal decision in his favour."

The reflexion of the man of light is wholly resplendent; the reflexion of the man of darkness is wholly (like) a bath-stove (ash-heap).

The reflexion of the servant of God is wholly luminous; the reflexion of the stranger (to God) is wholly blindness.

Know every one's reflexion: see (it plainly), O my soul. (Then) ever sit beside the congener whom thou desirest.

The right way of taking a lesson from this story and knowing with certainty that "verily, together with hardship there is ease."

That tale is a lesson to thee, O my soul, to the end that thou 3255 mayst acquiesce in the decree of God;

So that thou wilt be quick to understand and wilt have good thoughts (of God) when thou seest a calamity (befall thee) of a sudden.

(While) others turn pale from dread of it, thou (wilt be) laughing in the hour of gain or loss, like the rose.

Because the rose, though thou tear it petal by petal, does not leave off laughing[1] and does not become bent (with grief).

"Why," it says, "should I fall into grief on account of a thorn? Indeed I have brought laughter (into my possession) by means of the thorn."

Whatsoever by (Divine) destiny becomes lost to thee, know 3260 for sure that it has redeemed thee from affliction.

(Some one asked), "What is Ṣúfism?" He (the Shaykh) said, "To feel joy in the heart at the coming of sorrow."

Regard His chastisement as the eagle which carried off the boot from that man of excellent disposition[2],

That she might save his foot from the serpent's bite. Oh, happy is the understanding that is undimmed[3].

He (God) hath said, "*Grieve not for that which escapeth you,*" if the wolf come and destroy your sheep,

For that (God-sent) affliction keeps off great afflictions, and 3265 that loss prevents huge losses.

How a certain man demanded of Moses (that he should teach him) the language of the beasts and birds.

A young man said to Moses, "Teach me the language of the animals,

That perchance from the voice of animals and wild beasts I may get a lesson concerning my religion.

Since the languages of the sons of Adam are entirely for the sake of (acquiring) water and bread and renown,

---

[1] *I.e.* remains fresh and blooming.
[2] The Prophet.
[3] Literally, "without dust."

It may be that the animals have a different care, (namely), that of taking thought for the hour of passing away (from this world)."

3270 "Begone," said Moses; "abandon this vain desire, for this (desire) holds (involves) much danger before and behind.

Seek the lesson and the (spiritual) wakefulness (which you want) from God, not from books and speech and words and lips."

The man became more eager in consequence of the refusal which he (Moses) made to him: a man always becomes more eager from being refused (what he craves).

He said, "O Moses, since thy light has shone forth, whatever was a thing has gained (its) thinginess[1] from thee.

'Tis not worthy of thy bounty, O generous one, to disappoint me of this object of desire.

3275 At this time thou art the vicegerent of God: it will be despair (for me) if thou prevent me."

Moses said, "O Lord, surely the stoned (accursed) Devil has subdued this simple man.

If I teach him, it will be harmful to him; and if I do not teach him, he will become faint-hearted[2]."

He (God) said, "Teach him, O Moses, for We in our loving-kindness never have rejected (any one's) prayer."

He (Moses) said, "O Lord, he will feel repentance and gnaw his hands and rend his garments.

3280 Power is not suitable to every one: weakness is the best stock-in-trade for the devout."

For this reason poverty is everlasting glory, since the hand that cannot reach (to objects of desire) is left with fear of God (and nothing else).

Riches and the rich are spurned (by God) because acts of self-denial are relinquished by power.

Weakness and poverty are security for a man against the tribulation of the covetous and anxious (fleshly) soul.

That anxiety arises from the wanton desires[3] to which that (man who falls a) prey to the ghoul has become habituated.

3285 The eater of clay has a desire for clay: rose-flavoured sugar is indigestible for that wretched man.

How Revelation came from God most High to Moses that he should teach him the thing demanded by him, or part of it.

God said, "Do thou grant his need: let him have a free hand to choose (good or evil)[4]."

Choice (free-will) is the salt of devotion; otherwise (there would be no merit): this celestial sphere revolves involuntarily;

---

[1] *I.e.* its proper value and rank in the order of things.
[2] Literally, "his heart will become bad."
[3] Literally, "desires for excess and vanity."
[4] Literally, "release his hand for choosing."

(Hence) its revolution has neither reward nor punishment, for free-will is (accounted) a merit at the time of the Reckoning.

All created beings indeed are glorifiers (of God), (but) that compulsory glorification is not wage-earning.

"Put a sword in his hand, pull him away from weakness (in- 3290 capacity to choose), so that he may become (either) a holy warrior or a brigand,

Because *We have honoured* Man[1] by (the gift of) free-will: half (of him) is honey-bee, half is snake."

The true believers are a store of honey, like the bee; the infidels, in sooth, are a store of poison, like the snake,

Because the true believer ate choice herbs, so that, like a bee, his spittle became (a means of giving) life;

(While), again, the infidel drank sherbet of filthy water: accordingly from his nourishment poison appeared in him.

Those inspired by God are the fountain of life; those allured 3295 by the enticements of sensuality are the poison of death.

In the world this praise and "well done!" and "bravo!" are (bestowed) in virtue of free-will and watchful attention[2].

All profligates, when they are in prison, become devout and ascetic and invokers of God.

When the power (to act freely) is gone, the work becomes unsaleable (worthless). Take heed lest Doom seize the capital (which thou hast).

The power (of free action) is thy profit-earning capital. Hark, watch over the moment of power and observe (it well)!

Man rides on the steed of "*We have honoured (the sons of* 3300 *Adam)*": the reins of free-will are in the hand of his intelligence.

Once more did Moses admonish him kindly, saying, "The thing thou desirest will make thy face pale.

Abandon this vain passion and be afraid of God: the Devil has schooled thee for the purpose of deception."

How that seeker was content to be taught the language of domestic fowls and dogs, and how Moses, on whom be peace, complied with his request.

He said, "At any rate (teach me) the language of the dog which is at the door and the language of the domestic fowl which has wings."

"Hark," said Moses, "thou knowest (best)! Go, it (the fulfilment of thy wish) has arrived: the language of both of these will be revealed to thee."

At daybreak, in order to make trial, he stood waiting on the 3305 threshold.

---

[1] Literally, "because Man became (the object of the Divine words) *We have honoured*" (*Qur'án*, XVII, 72).
[2] Literally, "vigilant maintenance of attention." Cf. *v.* 3299.

The maid-servant shook the table-cloth, and a piece of bread, the remnants of last night's meal, fell out.

A cock snatched it up as (though it were) the stake (in a race). The dog said, "You have done injustice to me. Begone!

You can eat a grain of corn, while I am unable to eat grains in my abode.

You can eat corn and barley and the rest of the grains, while I cannot, O jubilant one.

3310 This crust of bread, the bread which is our portion—you are taking away from the dogs such a (small)[1] quantity (of food) as this!"

The cock's answer to the dog.

Then the cock said to him, "Be silent, do not grieve, for God will give you something else instead of this.

The horse of this Khwája is about to die: to-morrow eat your fill and be not sorrowful.

The horse's death will be a feast-day for the dogs: there will be abundant provender without toil or earning."

When the man heard (this speech), he sold the horse. That cock of his was disgraced[2] in the eyes of the dog.

3315 Next day the cock carried off the bread in the same fashion (as before), and the dog opened his lips at him,

Saying, "O beguiling cock, how long (will you tell) these lies? You are unrighteous and false and without lustre.

Where is the horse that you said would die? You are (like) a blind man who tells of the stars and you are deprived of truth."

That knowing cock said to him, "His horse died in another place.

He sold the horse and escaped from loss: he cast the loss upon others;

3320 But to-morrow his mule will die: that will be good fortune for the dogs, (so say) no more."

The covetous man immediately sold the mule and at that instant obtained deliverance from grief and loss.

On the third day the dog said to the cock, "O prince of liars with your drums and kettledrums!"

He (the cock) said, "He sold the mule in haste, (but)," said he, "to-morrow his slave will be stricken down,

'And when his slave dies, the next of kin will scatter pieces of bread upon the dogs and beggars."

3325 He (the master) heard this and sold his slave: he was saved from loss and his face was lit up[3] (with joy).

---

[1] *I.e.* "you are not only a thief, but a mean thief."
[2] Literally, "became pale-faced."
[3] Literally, "he lit up his face."

He was giving thanks and making merry, saying, "I have been saved from three calamities in the world.

Since I learned the language of the fowl and the dog I have pierced the eye of evil destiny."

Next day the disappointed dog said, "O drivelling cock, where are the sundries[1] (you promised me)?

[How the cock became abashed before the dog on account of being false in those three promises.]

How long, pray, how long (will) your falsehood and deceit (continue)? Truly, nothing but falsehood flies out of your nest."

He said, "Far be it from me and from my kind that we should 3330 become afflicted with falsehood.

We cocks are veracious like the muezzin: we are observers of the sun as well as seekers of the (right) time.

We are watchers of the sun inwardly, though you may turn a basin upside down over us."

The watchers of the Sun (of Reality) are the saints: in the flesh (they are) acquainted with the Divine mysteries.

"God gave our family as a gift to Man to call (him) to the ritual prayer (and) in preparation (for that purpose).

If a mistake be committed by us in (giving) the call to prayer 3335 at the wrong time, it will become the cause of our being killed.

To say at the wrong time 'Come to welfare[2]' will make our blood of no account and licit (liable to be shed with impunity)."

'Tis only the (spiritual) cock, the Soul of (Divine) inspiration, that is protected (by God from sin) and purged of error.

His (the master's) slave died in the house of the purchaser: that was the purchaser's loss entirely.

He saved his money[3], but he shed his own blood. Understand (this) well!

One loss would have prevented (many) losses: our bodies and 3340 money are the ransom for our souls.

In the presence of kings, in (the hour of their) dispensing punishment, you offer money and purchase your head (life):

How (then) have you become, in (the case of Divine) destiny, (like) a churl—withholding your money from the (Supreme) Judge?

How the cock foretold the death of the Khwája.

"But to-morrow he will certainly die: his heir, in mourning (for him), will slaughter a cow.

The owner of the house will die (and) depart (from this world): lo, to-morrow a great deal of food will reach you.

---

[1] Literally, "the odd and even."
[2] These words form part of the *adhán* (call to prayer).
[3] Literally, "caused his property to escape (from loss)."

3345   High and low will get pieces of bread and dainty morsels and viands in the midst of the street.

(The flesh of) the sacrificed cow and thin loaves of bread will be scattered quickly over the dogs and the beggars."

The death of the horse and mule and the death of the slave were bringing round the doom of this foolish deluded man.

He fled (escaped) from the loss of wealth and from grief thereat: he increased his wealth and shed his own blood.

These austerities of dervishes—what are they for? (The reason is) that that tribulation (imposed) on the body is (in effect) the everlasting life of spirits.

3350   Unless a (mystic) traveller gains the everlasting life of his (spiritual) self, how should he make his body a sick and perishing (thing)?

How should he move his hand to (acts of) altruism and (devotional) work unless he sees (the salvation of) his soul in exchange for what is given (by him)?

That one who gives without expectation of (any) gains—that one is God, is God,

Or the friend of God (the saint), who has assumed the nature of God and has become luminous and has received the Absolute Radiance;

For He is rich, while all except Him are poor: how should a poor man say "Take" without compensation?

3355   Till a child sees that the apple is there, it will not give up from its hand the stinking onion.

All these market-folk, for the sake of this (worldly) object, are seated on the benches (in the shops) in the hope of (receiving) compensation:

They offer a hundred fine articles of merchandise, and within their hearts they are intent on compensations.

O man of the (true) Religion, you will not hear a single salaam (blessing) whereof the end will not pluck your sleeve (and demand something of you).

I have never heard a disinterested salaam from high or low, O brother—and (I give) the salaam (to thee)[1]—

3360   Except the salaam of God. Come, seek that (salaam) from house to house, from place to place, and from street to street!

From the mouth of the man who has a good scent (for spiritual things) I heard both the message and the salaam of God;

And in the hope of that (salaam) I am listening with my heart to the salaams of (all) the rest (as though they were) sweeter than life.

His (the saint's) salaam has become the salaam of God because he has set fire to the household of self.

_____

[1] *I.e.* "peace be with thee."

He has died to self and become living through the Lord: hence the mysteries of God are on his lips.

The death of the body in self-discipline is life: the sufferings 3365 of this body are (the cause of) everlastingness to the spirit.

That wicked man had lent ear: he was hearing from his cock the news (of his death).

How that person ran to Moses for protection when he heard from the cock the announcement of his death.

When he heard these things, he started running in hot haste: he went to the door of Moses, with whom God conversed.

He was rubbing his face in the dust from fear, saying, "Save me from this (doom), O Kalím!"

He (Moses) said, "Go, sell thyself and escape! Since thou hast become expert (in avoiding loss), jump out of the pit (of death)!

Throw the loss upon true believers! Make thy purses and 3370 scrips double (in size)!

I beheld in the brick this destiny which to thee became visible (only) in the mirror.

The intelligent man sees with his heart the end (final result) at the first (in the beginning); he that is lacking in knowledge sees it (only) at the end."

Once more he (the doomed man) made lamentation, saying, "O thou who hast goodly qualities, do not beat me on the head, do not rub into my face (the sin I have committed).

That (sin) issued from me because I was unworthy: do thou give good recompense to my unworthy (action)."

He (Moses) said, "An arrow sped from the (archer's) thumb- 3375 stall, my lad: 'tis not the rule that it should come back to the source (the place whence it started);

But I will crave of (God's) good dispensation that thou mayst take the Faith away with thee at that time (of departing from the world).

When thou hast taken the Faith away (with thee), thou art living: when thou goest with the Faith, thou art enduring (for ever)."

At the same instant the Khwája became indisposed[1], so that he felt qualms[2], and they brought the basin.

'Tis the qualms of death, not indigestion: how should vomiting avail thee, O foolish ill-fortuned man?

Four persons carried him to his house: he was rubbing (one) 3380 leg on the back of (the other) leg[3].

---

[1] Literally, "the Khwája's state changed (for the worse)."
[2] Literally, "his heart was disturbed."
[3] *I.e.* he lay in the posture of a dying man. Cf. *Qur'án*, LXXV, 29.

(If) you hearken not to the counsel of (a) Moses and show dis-
respect, you dash yourself against a sword of steel.

The sword feels no shame (to restrain it) from (taking) your
life: this is your own (fault)[1], O brother, your own (fault).

How Moses prayed for that person, that he might depart from the world (die) in the Faith.

At dawn Moses began (his) orison, saying, "O God, do not
take the Faith from him, do not carry it away!

Act in royal fashion, forgive him, for he has erred and behaved
with impudence and transgressed exceedingly.

3385   I said to him, 'This knowledge is not meet for thee,' (but) he
deemed my words a thwarting (of his desire) and vain."

That one lays hands on the dragon (and that one alone) whose
hand makes the rod a dragon.

To learn the secret of the Unseen is fitting for him (alone) who
can seal his lips (and refrain) from speech.

None but the water-fowl is proper for the sea. Understand
(this)—and God best knoweth the right course.

"He (the obstinate man) went into the sea, and he was not a
water-fowl: he sank. Take his hand (succour him), O Loving
One!"

How God most High answered favourably the prayer of Moses, on whom be peace.

3390   He (God) said, "Yes, I bestow the Faith upon him, and if thou
wish I will bring him to life at this moment;

Nay, I will at this moment bring to life all the dead in the
earth for thy sake."

Moses said, "This is the world of dying: raise (them to) that
(other) world, for that place is resplendent.

Inasmuch as this abode of mortality is not the world of (real)
Being, the return to a borrowed (impermanent) thing is not
much gain.

Strew a gift of mercy upon them even now in the secret
chamber of *assembled in Our presence*."

3395   (I have related this story) that you may know that loss of the
body and of wealth is gain to the spirit and delivers it from bane.

Therefore be a purchaser of (ascetic) discipline with (all) your
soul: you will save your soul when you have given up your body
to service (of God).

And if the discipline come to you without free choice (on your
part), bow your head (in resignation) and give thanks, O suc-
cessful one.

---

[1] Literally, "this (is the penalty which) belongs to you," *i.e.* "it serves
you right."

Since God has given you that discipline, render thanks: you
have not done (it); He has drawn you (to it) by the command,
"Be!"

*Story of the woman whose children never lived (long), and how,
when she made lamentation (to God), the answer came—" That
is instead of thy (unpractised) ascetic discipline and is for thee in
lieu of the self-mortification of those who mortify themselves."*

That woman used to bear a son every year, (but) he never
lived more than six months;

Either (in) three months or four months he would perish. The 3400
woman made lamentation, crying, "Alas, O God,

For nine months I have the burden (of pregnancy), and for
three months I have joy: my happiness is fleeter[1] than the rain-
bow."

That woman, because of the terrifying anguish (which she
suffered), used to make this plaintive outcry[2] before the men of
God.

In this wise twenty children (of hers) went into the grave: a
fire (of destruction) fell swiftly upon their lives,

Till, one night, there was shown to her (the vision of) a garden
everlasting, verdant, delectable, and ungrudged.

I have called the Unconditioned Bounty a garden, since it is 3405
the source of (all) bounties and the assembly of (all) gardens;

Otherwise, (it is that which) no eye hath beheld: what place
is there for (how is it proper to speak of) a garden? (Yet the
term "garden" may be applied to it): God hath called the Light
of the Unseen "a lamp."

'Tis not a comparison, 'tis a parable thereof, (which is used)
in order that he who is bewildered may get a scent (of the
reality).

In short, the woman saw that (Bounty) and became in-
toxicated: at that revelation the weak (creature) fell into an
ecstasy[3].

She saw her name written on a palace: she who was of goodly
belief knew that it (the palace) belonged to her.

After that, they said (to her), "This Bounty is for him who has 3410
risen up with constant sincerity[4] in self-devotion.

Thou must needs have done much service (to God), in order
that thou might'st partake of this repast[5];

(Hence), as thou wert remiss in taking refuge (with God), God
gave thee those afflictions instead."

---

[1] Literally, "departing more quickly."
[2] Literally, "outcry (consisting) of this complaint."
[3] Literally, "went out of hand."
[4] Literally, "has not risen up except sincerely."
[5] Literally, "morning-meal."

"O Lord," cried she, "give me such-like (afflictions) for a hundred years and more! Do Thou shed my blood!"

When she advanced into that garden, she saw there all her children.

3415 She said, "They were lost to me, (but) they were not lost to Thee." Without (possessing) the two eyes of the Unseen, no one becomes the Man (pupil of the eye)[1].

You did not let blood (by cupping), and (therefore) the superfluous blood ran from your nose, to the end that your life might be saved from fever.

The core of every fruit is better than its rind: deem the body to be the rind, and its friend (the spirit) to be the core.

After all, Man has a goodly core: seek it for one moment, if you are of (if you belong to those inspired by) that (Divine) breath.

How Ḥamza, may God be well-pleased with him, came to battle without a coat of mail.

Whenever at the end (of his life) Ḥamza went into the ranks (on the battle-field), he would enter the fray (like one) intoxicated, without a coat of mail.

3420 Advancing with open breast and naked body, he would throw himself into the sword-bearing ranks.

The people asked him, saying, "O uncle of the Prophet, O Lion that breakest the ranks (of the foemen), O prince of the champions[2],

Hast not thou read in the Message of God (the Qur'án) 'Do not cast yourselves with your own hands into destruction'?

Then why art thou casting thyself thus into destruction on the field of battle?

When thou wert young and robust and strongly-knit[3], thou didst not go into the battle-line without a coat of mail.

3425 Now that thou hast become old and infirm and bent, thou art knocking at the curtains (doors) of recklessness,

And with sword and spear, like one who recks of naught, thou art grappling and struggling and making trial (of thyself).

The sword hath no respect for the old: how should sword and arrow possess discernment?"

In this manner were the ignorant sympathisers giving him counsel zealously.

---

[1] I.e. no one attains to the degree of the Perfect Man (the eye of the world) without possessing the oculi cordis which enable him to contemplate the spiritual universe.
[2] Literally, "stallions."
[3] Literally, "strung tight."

The reply of Ḥamza to the people.

Ḥamza said, "When I was young, I used to regard farewell to this world as death.

How should any one go to death eagerly? How should he 3430 come naked (unarmed) to meet the dragon?

But now, through the Light of Mohammed, I am not subject to this city (the world) that is passing away.

Beyond (the realm of) the senses, I behold the camp of the (Divine) King thronged with the army of the Light of God,

Tent on tent and tent-rope on tent-rope. Thanks be to Him who awakened me from slumber!"

That one in whose eyes death is destruction—he takes hold of (clings to) the (Divine) command, "*Do not cast (yourselves into destruction)*";

And that one to whom death is the opening of the gate—for 3435 him in the (Divine) Allocution (the *Qur'án*) there is (the command), "*Vie ye with each other in hastening.*"

Beware, O ye who regard death! Surpass one another (in dread of death)! Quick, O ye who regard the Resurrection! *Vie ye with each other in hastening!*

Welcome, O ye who regard the (Divine) grace! Rejoice! Woe (to you), O ye who regard the (Divine) wrath! Be sorrowful!

Whosoever deems it (death) to be (lovely as) Joseph gives up his soul in ransom for it; whosoever deems it to be (like) the wolf turns back from (the path of) right guidance.

Every one's death is of the same quality as himself, my lad: to the enemy (of God) an enemy, and to the friend (of God) a friend.

In the eyes of the Turcoman the mirror hath a fair colour; 3440 similarly in the eyes of the Ethiopian the mirror is (dark as) an Ethiopian.

Your fear of death in fleeing (from it) is (really) your fear of yourself[1]. Take heed, O (dear) soul!

'Tis your (own) ugly face, not the visage of Death: your spirit is like the tree, and death (is like) the leaf.

It has grown from you, whether it is good or evil: every hidden thought of yours, foul or fair, is (born) from yourself.

If you are wounded by a thorn, you yourself have sown; and if you are (clad) in satin and silk, you yourself have spun.

Know that the act is not of the same complexion as the re- 3445 quital: the service is nowise of the same complexion as the payment given (in return for it).

The labourers' wage does not resemble the work, inasmuch as the latter is the accident, while the former is the substance and permanent.

---

[1] Literally, "that which you fear from death in flight—you are (really) fearing that from yourself."

The former is wholly hardship and effort and sweat, while the latter is wholly silver and gold and trays (of food).

If suspicion fall upon you from some quarter, (the reason is that) the person whom you wronged has invoked (God) against you in an affliction (which you have brought upon him).

You say, "I am free (from guilt): I have not laid suspicion on any one."

3450 (No; but) you have committed another form of sin; you sowed the seed: how should the seed resemble the fruit?

He (the celibate) committed adultery, and the penalty was a hundred blows with the stick. "When," says he, "did I strike any one with wood?"

Was not this infliction the penalty for that adultery? How should the stick resemble adultery (committed) in secret?

How should the serpent resemble the rod, O Kalím (Moses)? How should the pain resemble the remedy, O doctor?

When you, instead of (casting down) the rod, semen ejecisti (in uterum), that (semen) became (eventually) a fine (human) figure.

3455 That semen of yours became a friend (to you) or (like) a (noxious) serpent: why (then) is this astonishment at the rod (of Moses) on your part?

Does the semen at all resemble that child? Does the sugar-cane at all resemble the candy?

When a man has sown a prostration (in prayer) or a genu-flexion, in yonder world his prostration becomes Paradise.

When praise of God has flown from his mouth, *the Lord of the daybreak* fashions it into a bird of Paradise.

Your praise and glorification does not resemble the bird, though the bird's semen is (naught but) wind and air[1].

3460 When altruism and almsgiving have grown up (proceeded) from your hand, (the act of) this (generous) hand becomes on yonder side (in the world hereafter) date-palms and (fresh) herbage.

The water (semen), (namely) your renunciation, became a river of water in Paradise; your love and affection (for God) is a river of milk in Paradise.

Delight in devotion became a river of honey; behold your (spiritual) intoxication and longing as a river of wine.

These causes did not resemble those effects: none knows how He (God) installed it (the effect) in the place of that (cause).

Since these causes were (obedient) to your command, the four rivers (of Paradise) likewise showed obedience to you.

3465 You make them flow in whatever direction you wish: (even) as that quality (of disposition) was (in this world), such do you make it (the effect) to be (in the next world),

---

[1] *I.e.* "though the bird was produced from the breath of your praise." There is an allusion to the belief that birds are impregnated by means of air.

As (for example) your semen, which is at your command—
the progeny thereof are ready to (obey) your command.

Your young son runs (obediently) at your command, saying,
"I am the part of thee which thou didst deposit (in my mother's
womb)."

That (praiseworthy) quality was (obedient) to your command
in this world: likewise (in the next world) those rivers flow at
your command.

Those trees (of Paradise) are obedient to you, because those
trees are (made) fruitful by your (good) qualities.

Since these qualities are (obedient) to your command here, so 3470
your recompense is at your command there.

When blows proceeded from your hand against the victim of in-
justice, they became a tree (in Hell): the Zaqqúm grew from them.

When in anger you threw fire into (people's) hearts, you be-
came the source of Hell-fire.

Since here (in this world) your fire was burning mankind,
that which was born of it was kindling men (in Hell).

Your fire (of anger) makes an attack on the people (here): the
fire that sprang from it rushes against the people (there).

Your words resembling snakes and scorpions have become 3475
snakes and scorpions and are seizing your tail (assailing you
from behind).

You kept the friends (of God) waiting: (hence) you will be
kept waiting at the Resurrection[1].

Your promise, "To-morrow" and "the day after to-morrow,"
has become your waiting on the Day of Congregation: alas for you!

You will remain waiting on that long Day, (engaged) in
rendering an account (of your actions) and (standing) in the
soul-consuming sun,

Because you were wont to keep Heaven waiting and sow the
seed of "I will go on the Way to-morrow."

Your anger is the seed of Hell-fire: take heed, extinguish this 3480
Hell of yours, for this is a trap.

The extinction of this fire is not (to be effected) save by the
Light: "thy light hath put out our fire[2], we are the grateful[3]."

If you are devoid of the Light and do an act of clemency,
'tis evil: your fire (of anger) is (still) alive and is (still) lurking in
the embers.

Beware! That (clemency) is (mere) ostentation and masking
(the truth): nothing will extinguish the fire (of anger) except
the Light of Religion.

[1] Literally, "the wait at the Resurrection has become your (destined)
associate."

[2] According to a Tradition, on the Day of Judgement Hell will say to the
true believer, whilst he is crossing the Bridge Ṣirát, "Cross (in safety), for
thy light hath put out my fire."   [3] Read الشُّكُور, plural of شاكِر.

Do not be secure till you behold the Light of Religion, for the hidden fire will one day become manifest.

3485   Deem the Light to be a water, and cleave to the water withal: when you have the water, be not afraid of the fire.

The water will extinguish the fire, because the fire by its nature burns up its (the water's) progeny and children.

Go, for a while, to those water-birds, that they may lead you to the Water of Life.

The land-bird and the water-bird have the same body (outward appearance), but they are (really) opposites: they are (like) water and oil.

Each (of them) is devoted to its own origin; have a care (in discriminating between them): they resemble each other (externally),

3490   Just as both (Satanic) suggestion and Divine inspiration[1] are intelligible[2], and yet there is a (great) difference (between them).

Both (these) brokers in the market of Conscience extol their wares, O prince.

If you are a spiritual money-changer, one who recognises thought, distinguish the real nature of the two thoughts which resemble slave-dealers (commending the slaves they hope to sell);

And if from (your own) opinion you do not know (the true nature of) these two thoughts, say, "No deception!" and be not in a hurry and do not push forward.

The means of preventing one's self from being swindled in sale and purchase.

A certain friend said to the Prophet, "I am always being swindled[3] in commerce.

3495   The deceit of every one who sells or buys is like magic and leads me off the track."

He (the Prophet) said, "When thou art afraid of being duped in a commercial transaction, stipulate (that thou shalt have) for thyself three days (in which) to choose[4],

For deliberation is assuredly from the Merciful (God); thy haste is from the accursed Devil."

When you throw a morsel of bread to a dog, he (first) smells, then he eats, O careful one.

He smells with the nose, we too (who are endowed) with wisdom smell it (the object submitted to us) with the purified intelligence.

---

[1] Literally, "the inspiration of *Am not I (your Lord)?*"
[2] *I.e.* things of the intelligible world.
[3] Literally, "I am coupled with being swindled."
[4] Literally, "the option, for three days, (of accepting or rejecting the proposed bargain)."

This earth and the (heavenly) spheres were brought into 3500
existence by God with deliberation (extending) to six days;

Otherwise, He was able—"*Be, and it is*"—to bring forth a
hundred earths and heavens (from non-existence).

Little by little till forty years (of age) that Potentate makes the
human being a complete man,

Although He was able in a single moment to set flying (raise
up) fifty persons from non-existence.

Jesus by means of one prayer was able to make the dead spring
up (to life) without delay:

Is the Creator of Jesus unable, without delay, to bring (full- 3505
grown) men in manifold succession[1] (into existence)?

This deliberation is for the purpose of teaching you that you
must seek (God) slowly without (any) break.

A little rivulet which is moving continually does not become
defiled or grow fetid.

From this deliberation are born felicity and joy: this delibera-
tion is the egg, fortune is like the birds (hatched from the egg).

How should the bird resemble the egg, O obstinate one,
though it is produced from the egg?

Wait till your limbs, like eggs, hatch birds ultimately (at the 3510
Resurrection)!

Though the serpent's egg resembles the sparrow's egg in (out-
ward) likeness, the distance (between them) is far.

Again, though the seed of the quince resembles the seed of the
apple, recognise the differences, O honoured (sir).

Leaves are of the same colour to look at, (but) fruits, every one,
are of a diverse sort.

The leaves, (namely) the bodies, are similar, but every soul
lives with a (different) produce (which it yields).

In the bazaar the people go (about their business) all alike, 3515
(but) one is in glee and another sorrowful.

Even so in death: we go all alike, (but) half of us are losers[2]
and (the other) half are (fortunate as) emperors.

How Bilál, may God be well-pleased with him, died rejoicing.

When Bilál from weakness became (thin) as the new-moon,
the hue of death fell upon Bilál's face.

His wife saw him (in this state) and cried, "Oh, sorrow!"
Then Bilál said to her, "Nay, nay! (Say, 'Oh, joy!'

Until now I have been in sorrow from living: how shouldst
thou know how delightful death is, and what it is (in reality)?"

He was saying this, and at the very moment of saying it his 3520
countenance was blooming with narcissi, rose-leaves, and red
anemones.

---

[1] Literally, "fold by fold."   [2] Literally, "in loss."

The glow of his face and his eye full of radiance were giving testimony to (the truth of) his words.

Every black-hearted one was regarding him as black (and despising him); (but) why is the man (pupil) of the eye black?

The man (spiritually) blind is black-faced, (but) the Man of the (inward) eye (the Seer) is the mirror for the Moon[1].

Who in the world, indeed, sees the man of your (inward) eye except the Man of piercing sight[2]?

3525   Since none but the Man of the eye beheld it, who, then, but he attained to (knowledge of) its (essential) colour?

Therefore all except him (the Seer) are imitators (without immediate knowledge) in regard to the attributes of the sublime man of the eye.

His (Bilál's) wife said to him, "(This is) the parting, O man of goodly qualities." "Nay, nay," said he, "'tis the union, the union (with God)."

The wife said, "To-night thou wilt go to a strange country, thou wilt become absent from thy family and kindred."

"Nay, nay," he replied; "contrariwise, to-night in sooth from a strange country my spirit is coming home."

3530   She said, "Where shall we behold thy face?" He answered, "In God's chosen circle."

His chosen circle adjoins you, if you look upward, not downward.

In that circle the Light from the Lord of created beings is gleaming like the bezel in the circle (of the seal-ring).

"Alas," she said, "this house has been ruined." "Look on the moon," said he, "do not look on the cloud.

He has ruined it in order that He may make it more flourishing: my kinsfolk were numerous and the house was (too) small.

The (Divine) wisdom in ruining the body by death.

3535   Formerly, like Adam, I was imprisoned in grief; now East and West are filled with my spirit's progeny.

I was a beggar in this dungeon-like house; (now) I have become a king: a palace is needed for a king."

Truly, palaces are the place for (spiritual) kings to take their pleasure in; for him that is (spiritually) dead a grave is a sufficient house and dwelling.

To the prophets this world seemed narrow: like kings, they went into (the world of) spacelessness.

To the (spiritually) dead this world appears splendid: its external (aspect) is large, but in reality it is narrow[3].

3540   If it were not narrow, for what reason is this lamentation? Why has every one become (more) doubled (bowed with affliction) the more he lived in it?

---

[1] I.e. God.   [2] Literally, "the Man who increases (his) sight."
[3] Literally, "narrow-breasted."

When during the time of sleep the spirit is freed (from this world), behold how it rejoices in that place (to which it goes)!

The wicked man is (then) delivered from the wickedness of his nature, the prisoner escapes from thoughts of confinement.

This very wide earth and heaven becomes exceedingly narrow at the time of lying down (to sleep).

It (the world) is an eye-bandage (a spell that blinds the eye)[1]: (it is) wide (in appearance), and (in reality) mighty narrow: its laughter is weeping, its glory is entirely shame.

Comparison of this world, which is wide in appearance and narrow in reality, (to a bath-room), and comparison (of the next world) to sleep, which is the (means of) release from this narrowness.

(This world is) like a bath-room which is very hot, (so that) 3545 you are distressed and your soul is melted (with anguish).

Although the bath-room is broad and long, your soul is distressed and fatigued by the heat.

Your heart does not expand (you feel no relief) till you come out: what advantage, then, is the spaciousness of the room to you?

Or (it is) as though you should put on tight shoes, O misguided one, and go into a wide desert.

The spaciousness of the desert becomes narrow (distressing); that desert and plain becomes a prison to you.

Whoever sees you from afar says, "He blooms like a fresh 3550 anemone (he is cheerful and happy) in that desert";

He does not know that you, like the wicked, are outwardly in the rose-garden, (while) your soul is in lamentation.

Your sleep is to put those shoes off, for (then) your soul is free from the body for a while.

To the saints, O reader, sleep is a kingdom, as (it was to) the Men of the Cave in this world.

They (sleep and) dream, and no (physical) sleep is there; they go into non-existence, and no (material) door (is there).

"(The body is) a narrow house, and the soul within is 3555 cramped: He (God) ruined it in order that He might make a royal palace[2].

I am cramped like the embryo in the womb: I have become nine months old: this migration has become urgent.

Unless the throes of childbirth overtake my mother, (what should I do?): in this prison I am amidst the fire.

My mother, namely, my nature (natural body), in consequence of its death-throes, is giving birth[3] (to the spirit), to the end that the lamb (the spirit) may be released from the ewe,

---

[1] Reading چشم‌بند. The reading given in the text means: "it (the world) is the body's prison," or "the body is a prison."
[2] Bilál is speaking.   [3] Literally, "is making a way (of exit)."

So that the lamb may graze in the green fields. Come, open
thy womb, for this lamb has grown big."

3560　If the pain of childbirth is grievous to the pregnant (woman),
it is, for the embryo, the breaking of (its) prison.

The pregnant woman weeps at childbirth, saying, "Where is
the refuge?"—but the embryo laughs, saying, "Deliverance has
appeared."

Whatever mothers (bodies) there are under the sky—mineral,
animal, or vegetable—

They are heedless, every one, of another's pain, except those
persons that are discerning and perfect.

How should the man with a bushy beard[1] know of his own
house that which the man with a few hairs on his chin[2] knows
of (other) people's houses?

3565　What the man of heart (the clairvoyant mystic) knows of your
condition you do not know of your own condition, O uncle.

*Setting forth that whatever is (denoted by the terms) heedlessness
and anxiety and indolence and darkness is all (derived) from
the body, which belongs to the earth and the lower world.*

Heedlessness was (derived) from the body: when the body
has become spirit, it inevitably beholds the mysteries (of the
Unseen).

When the earth is removed from the celestial atmosphere,
there is neither night nor shade nor sunset[3].

Wherever shade and night or shadowy place exist, 'tis (caused)
by the earth, not by the heavens and the moon.

Likewise, 'tis from the faggots that the smoke always arises,
not from the resplendent fires.

3570　The imagination falls into error and mistake; the intellect is
(engaged) only in acts of true perception.

Every state of heaviness (sloth) and indolence, indeed, is (de-
rived) from the body; the spirit, from its lightness (subtlety), is
all on the wing[4].

The face is red from the predominance of blood; the face is
yellow from the movement (action) of the yellow bile.

The face is white from the power of the phlegm; 'tis from the
black bile that the face is swarthy.

In reality He (God) is the creator of effects, but followers of
the husk (formalists) see nothing but the (secondary) cause.

3575　The kernel (intellect) that is not separated from the husks has
no means (of escape) from doctor and disease[5];

---

[1] *I.e.* the stupid man.　　　　　　　　[2] *I.e.* the intelligent man.

[3] Reading, with G, باشد نه دَلَك. The text-reading means "for me and
thee."　　　　　　　　　　　　　[4] Literally, "(engaged) in flying."

[5] *I.e.* it needs a doctor to cure its disease.

(But) when a son of man is born twice, he plants his foot upon the head[1] of (all) causes:

The First Cause is not his religion; the particular (secondary) cause has no enmity against him (does him no harm).

He flies, like the sun, in the (spiritual) horizon with the bride, sincerity; and (material) form (is) as a veil (for him).

Nay, beyond horizons and skies he is without locality, like spirits and intelligences.

Nay, our intellects are the shadows (reflexions) of him: they 3580 fall, like shadows, at his feet.

Whenever the *mujtahid* (legist) knows a Statute, in that case he will not think of (employing) analogy;

(But) in a case where he does not find a Statute, there he will produce an example from analogy.

Comparison between Statute and analogy.

Know for sure that Statute is the Revelation of the Holy Spirit and that the analogy made by the individual intellect is under (subordinate to) this.

The intellect is endued with apprehension and enlightenment by the Spirit: how should the Spirit become subject to its supervision?

But the Spirit makes an impression on the intellect, and in 3585 consequence of that impression the intellect exercises a certain governance.

If the Spirit has declared a belief in you[2], as (in) Noah, where is the Sea and the Ship (Ark) and the Flood of Noah[3]?

The intellect deems the impression to be the Spirit, but the light of the sun is very far from (being) the orb of the sun.

Hence a pilgrim (on the Mystic Way) is content with a loaf of bread (*qurṣī*)[4], in order that by its light he may be thrown (directed) towards the (Divine) Orb (*Qurṣ*),

Because this light which is below is not lasting: it is sinking (every) day and night,

While he that has his abode and dwelling-place in the (Divine) 3590 Orb is plunged in that Light continually.

Neither does cloud waylay him nor setting (of the sun): he is delivered from heart-wringing[5] separation.

Such a person's origin was from the heavens, or if he was of the earth, he has been transmuted,

Because a creature of earth cannot endure that its (the Sun's) beams should strike upon it everlastingly.

---

[1] Literally, "the line which parts the hair on the crown of the head."
[2] *I.e.* "has chosen you as a *ṣiddīq* (a true witness to God)."
[3] *I.e.* "where are your proofs?"
[4] *I.e.* a type and symbol.   [5] Literally, "breast-beating."

If the radiance of the sun strike upon the earth continually, it will be burned in such wise that no fruits will come from it.

3595 The business of the fish is always in the water: how has a snake the power of accompanying it (the fish) on its way?

But in the mountain[1] are artful snakes (who) perform the actions of fish in this Sea.

Though their cunning make the people mad[2], still their aversion to the Sea exposes them (as hypocrites);

And in this Sea are artful fish, (who) by magic turn snakes into fishes—

The fish of the deepest depth of the Sea of (Divine) Majesty: the Sea has taught them lawful magic;

3600 Therefore through their illumination the (thing that was) absurd became a fact: the ill-starred one went thither and became auspicious.

Though I should speak on this topic till the Resurrection, a hundred Resurrections would pass, and this (discourse would still be) incomplete.

The rules to be observed by listeners and disciples at the emanation of wisdom from the tongue of the Shaykh.

To the weary this is (only) repetition, (but) in my eyes it is the bringing of repeated life.

The candle goes upward (burns higher) from repeated flashes (of flame); earth becomes gold in consequence of repeated heat.

If there are thousands of (eager) seekers (of knowledge) and a single weary (disgusted) one, the Messenger will refrain from delivering his message.

3605 These mystery-telling Messengers of the hidden Mind require a hearer who has the nature of Isráfíl.

They have a haughtiness and pride like (that of) kings: they require service from the people of the world.

Until you perform the observances due to them, how will you gain profit from their message?

How will they deliver that deposit to you till you are bowed double before them?

How is every (kind of) observance acceptable to them?—for they have come from the Sublime Palace.

3610 They are not beggars, that they should be grateful to you, O impostor, for every service.

But, O (thou who art the) inmost consciousness (of God), notwithstanding (their) lack of desire (to hear thy message), scatter the (Divine) Sultan's charity: do not withhold it!

O heavenly Messenger, do not regard the disgusted ones and let thy horse bound onward!

---

[1] The world.   [2] *I.e.* infatuate them and rob them of their wits.

Blest is the Turcoman who lays contention aside and whose horse gallops into the moat of fire—

(Who) makes his horse so hot (in the race) that it seeks to mount to the zenith of the sky;

(Who) has shut his eyes to other (than God) and to jealousy[1]; 3615 (who), like fire, has consumed (both) dry and wet.

If repentance find fault with him, he first sets fire to repentance[2].

Verily, repentance does not spring forth from non-existence (does not show itself at all), when it sees the ardour of him whose presence brings fortune.

How every animal knows the smell of its enemy and takes precaution. The folly and perdition of him that is the enemy of that One against whom precaution is impossible, and flight is impossible, and resistance is impossible.

The horse, though it is an animal, knows the roar and smell of the lion except in rare instances;

Nay, every animal indeed knows its own enemy by sign and mark.

The little bat durst not fly in the daytime: it came out at 3620 night, like thieves, and pastured (got food for itself).

The bat (bat-like man) was more damned than all (others), because he was the enemy of the manifest Sun[3].

He cannot be wounded in battle with him (the Sun)[4], nor can he drive him (the Sun) away by cursing.

The Sun who turns his back on account of the rage and violence of the bat—

'Tis the extreme of kindness and perfection on his part; otherwise, how should the bat prevent him (from exacting vengeance)?

(If) you take (any one as) an enemy, take within your limit 3625 (capacity), so that it may be possible for you to make (him your) prisoner.

When (one like) a drop of water contends with the Ocean, he is a fool: he is tearing out his own beard.

His cunning does not pass beyond his moustache: how should it penetrate the vaulted chamber of the Moon?

This (preceding discourse) was a rebuke (addressed) to the enemy of the Sun[3], O enemy of the Sun of the Sun[5].

O enemy of the Sun at whose glory His sun and stars tremble,

You are not His enemy, you are the adversary of yourself: 3630 what does the Fire care that you have become firewood?

---

[1] *I.e.* he is so absorbed in God that he has no thought of jealously guarding the Divine mysteries from those who are unfit to receive them.
[2] *I.e.* if doubt and weakness attack him, he consumes them with the fire of love before they can prevail. [3] The prophet or saint.
[4] *I.e.* he cannot face him in open fight. [5] God.

Oh, marvellous! Shall He suffer defect through your burning, or shall He become full of sorrow for the pain of your burning?

His mercy is not the mercy of Adam, for sorrow is mingled with the mercy of Adam.

The mercy of the creature is anxious; the mercy of God is exempt from sorrow and anxiety.

Know that the mercy of the Unconditioned (God) is like this, O father; naught but the effect thereof comes into the imagination (is conceivable to us).

The difference between knowing a thing by comparison and convention and knowing the quiddity of that thing.

3635   The effects and fruit of His mercy are manifest, but how should any one except Him know its quiddity?

None knows the quiddities of the attributes of (Divine) Perfection except through (their) effects and by means of comparison.

The child does not know the quiddity of concubitus, except that you say, "It is like sweetmeat to thee."

How should the quiddity of the pleasure of sexual intercourse be like the quiddities of sweetmeat, O master[1]?

But, since you are childish, that intelligent man offered you the analogy respecting the sweetness (of it),

3640   In order that the child might know it by comparison, though he does not know the quiddity or essence of the matter.

Therefore, if you say "I know," 'tis not far (from the truth); and if you say, "I do not know," 'tis not a lie and a falsehood.

If some one say (to you), "Do you know Noah, the Messenger of God and the Light of the spirit?"—

And if you reply, "How should not I know (him)? for that (spiritual) Moon is more celebrated than the sun and moon:

The little children at school and all the Imáms in the mosques

3645   Recite his name distinctly in the *Qur'án* and tell plainly his story (as it has come down) from the past"—

You, veracious man, know him by way of description, though the quiddity of Noah has not been revealed (to you).

And if you reply, "How should I know Noah? (Only) one like him can know him, O youth.

I am a lame ant. How should I know the elephant? How should a gnat know Isráfíl?"—

This saying (answer) is also true in regard to the fact that you do not know him in his quiddity, O so-and-so.

3650   To be unable to perceive the quiddity, uncle, is the condition of common men: do not say it absolutely,

---

[1] Literally, "O obeyed one."

Inasmuch as quiddities and their inmost secret are clearly visible to the eyes of the Perfect.

Where in existence is (anything) more remote from understanding and mental perception than the consciousness and essence of God?

Since that does not remain hidden from (His) familiars, what is the essence and attribute that should remain concealed?

The intellect of the scholastic theologian says, "This is far (from reasonable) and deeply involved (in error)[1]: do not listen to an absurdity without some explanation."

The Quṭb (the Head of the Saints) replies, "To thee, O in- 3655 firm one, that which is above thy (spiritual) state seems absurd."

The visions which are now revealed to you, is it not the case that at first they seemed absurd to you?

Inasmuch as the (Divine) Bounty has released you from ten prisons, do not make the (wide) desert an oppressive prison to yourself.

How the negation and affirmation of one (and the same) thing may be combined and reconciled from the standpoint of relativity and difference of aspect.

It is possible to deny and affirm the same thing: when the point of view is different, the relation is twofold.

(The text) *thou didst not throw when thou threwest* is relative: it is negation and affirmation: both are authorised.

Thou threwest that (gravel), since it was on thy hand; thou 3660 didst not throw, for God manifested (His) power.

The strength of one born of Adam has a limit: how should a handful of earth become (the cause of) the rout of an army?

"(O Mohammed), the handful is thy handful, and the throwing is from Me": on account of these two relations (both) the denial and the affirmation of it (the throwing) are right.

The prophets are known by their enemies, just as their (the enemies') children are not doubtful (to their parents).

The unbelievers know them (the prophets) as (they know) their children by a hundred indications and a hundred signs,

But, from jealousy and envy, they conceal (their knowledge) 3665 and attach themselves to (become addicted to saying) "I do not know."

Then, since He (God) hath said, "*He (the unbeliever) knows,*" how hath He said in another place?—"None knoweth them except Me, so leave off (seeking to know them);

Verily, they are hidden beneath My tents." None knows them by (immediate) experience except God.

---

[1] Literally, "a (deep) ditch."

Regard also as (explicable) by means of relation this (subject) which was opened (above), (namely) that you know and do not know Noah.

The question of the faná and baqá of the dervish[1].

The speaker said, "There is no dervish in the world; and if there be a dervish, that dervish is (really) non-existent."

3670   He exists in respect of the survival of his essence, (but) his attributes have become non-existent in the attributes of Him (God).

Like the flame of a candle in the presence of the sun, he is (really) non-existent, (though he is) existent in (formal) calculation.

Its (the flame's) essence is existent, so that, if you put cotton upon it, it (the cotton) will be consumed by the sparks;

(But) it is (really) non-existent: it gives you no light: the sun will have naughted it.

When you have thrown an ounce of vinegar into two hundred maunds of sugar, and it has become dissolved therein,

3675   The flavour of the vinegar, when you taste (the sugar), is non-existent, (though) the ounce exists (as a) surplus when you weigh.

In the presence of a lion a deer becomes senseless: her existence becomes a (mere) veil for his existence.

These analogies drawn by imperfect men concerning the action of the Lord are (like) the emotion of love, (they are) not from irreverence.

The lover's pulse bounds up without reverence, he lays himself on the scale of the King's balance[2].

None is more irreverent than he in the world (outwardly); none is more reverent than he in secret (inwardly).

3680   Know, O chosen one, that these two opposites also, "reverent" and "irreverent," are reconciled by means of relation.

He (the lover) is irreverent when you regard the outward aspect, for his claim of love is (involves) equality (with the Beloved);

(But) when you regard the inward aspect, where is the claim? He and (his) claim are naughted in the presence of that Sultan.

Máta Zayd^un (Zayd died): if Zayd is the agent (grammatical subject), (yet) he is not the agent, for he is defunct.

He is the agent (only) in respect of the grammatical expression; otherwise, he is the one acted upon (the object of the action), and Death is his slayer.

3685   What agent (is he), since he has been so overpowered and all the qualities of an agent have been removed from him?

---

[1] Faná, "passing away from self-existence"; baqá, "subsistence in God."
[2] I.e. "levels himself with the King."

Story of the Ṣadr-i Jahán's Wakíl (minister), who fell under suspicion and fled from Bukhárá in fear of his life; then love drew him back irresistibly[1], for the matter of life is of small account to lovers.

In Bukhárá the servant of the Ṣadr-i Jahán incurred suspicion and hid from his Ṣadr (prince).

During ten years he roamed distractedly[2], now in Khurásán, now in the mountain-land, now in the desert.

After ten years, through longing he became unable to endure the days of separation (from his beloved).

He said, "Henceforth I cannot bear to be parted (from him) any more: how can patience allay (the lover's) state of abandonment?"

From separation these soils are nitrous (barren), and water 3690 becomes yellow and stinking and dark;

The life-increasing wind (air) becomes unhealthy and pestilential; a fire turns to ashes and dust.

The orchard which resembled Paradise becomes the abode of disease, (with) its leaves yellow and dropping in decay.

The penetrating intellect, through separation from its friends, (becomes) like an archer whose bow is broken.

From separation Hell has become so burning; from separation the old man has become so trembling.

If I should speak of separation, (which is) like sparks of fire, 3695 till the Resurrection, 'twould be (only) one (part) out of a hundred thousand.

Therefore do not breathe (a word) in description of its burning: say only "Lord, save (me)! Lord, save (me)!"

Everything by which you are rejoiced in the world—think at that time of the parting from it.

Many a one has been gladdened by what made you glad: at last it escaped from him and became even as wind.

It will escape from you also: set not your heart upon it. Do you yourself escape from it before it escapes (from you).

The appearance of the Holy Spirit (Gabriel) in the shape of a man to Mary when she was undressed and washing herself, and how she took refuge with God.

Before the slipping away of your possessions, say to the form 3700 (of created things), like Mary, "(I take) refuge from thee with the Merciful (God)."

Mary in her chamber saw a form that gave increase of life— a life-increasing, heart-ravishing one.

That trusted Spirit rose up before her from the face of the earth, like the moon and the sun.

[1] Literally, "drawing his face (along)."
[2] Literally, "his head reeling."

Beauty unveiled rose up from the earth (in) such (splendour) as the sun rises from the East.

A trembling came over Mary's limbs, for she was undressed and was afraid of evil.

3705   ('Twas) such a form that if Joseph had beheld it plainly, he would have cut his hand in amazement, like the (Egyptian) women.

It blossomed from the earth like a rose before her—like a phantasy which lifts its head from the heart.

Mary became selfless (beside herself), and in her selflessness she said, "I will leap into the Divine protection,"

Because that pure-bosomed one had made a habit of betaking herself[1] in flight to the Unseen.

Since she deemed the world a kingdom without permanence, she prudently made a fortress of that (Divine) Presence,

3710   In order that in the hour of death she should have a stronghold which the Enemy would find no way to attack.

She saw no better fortress than the protection of God: she chose her abiding-place near to that castle.

When she beheld those amorous reason-destroying glances whereby hearts were ever being pierced (as) by arrows[2]—

King and army are enthralled by Him[3], the sovereigns of wit (intelligence) are made witless by Him;

Hundreds of thousands of kings are held in servitude by Him; hundreds of thousands of full-moons He hath given over to (love's) wasting fever;

3715   Zuhra hath not the courage to breathe (a word); Universal Reason, when it sees Him, humbles itself.

What shall I say? for He has sealed my lips: His furnace has consumed the place (channel) of my breath.

"I am the smoke of that fire, I am the evidence for it"—far from that King be their false interpretation[4]!

Verily, there is no evidence for a sun except the light of the lofty sun.

Who (what) is the shadow that it should be an evidence for Him? 'Tis enough for it that it should be abased before Him.

3720   This majesty (which I have attributed to Him) in (the matter of) evidence[5] declares the truth: all perceptions are behind (Him), He is outstripping (them).

All perceptions are (mounted) on lame asses; He is mounted on the wind that flies like an arrow.

---

[1] Literally, "carrying her baggage."
[2] This sentence is left unfinished, but the conclusion can easily be supplied from the following verses.
[3] The Holy Divine Spirit manifested in Gabriel.
[4] Literally, "Far be it from that King! False is their interpretation."
[5] *I.e.* His transcendence of all external evidence.

If He flee, none (of them) finds the dust of[1] the King; and if they flee, He bars the way in front (of them).

All the perceptions are unquiet: it is the time for battle[2], not the time for the (festal) cup.

One perceptive faculty is flying like a falcon, while another, (swift) as an arrow, is tearing its place of passage;

And another is like a ship with sails, and another is turning 3725 back every moment.

When an object of chase appears to them from afar, all those birds (the perceptions) increase (the speed of) their onset.

When it vanishes from sight, they become lost: like owls, they go to every wilderness,

Waiting, with one eye closed and one eye open, that the delectable prey may appear.

When it tarries long, they say (from weariness), "We wonder whether it was a (real) prey or a phantom."

The right course is that, for a short while, they should gather 3730 some strength and vigour by (taking) a rest.

If there were no night, on account of cupidity all people would consume themselves by the agitation (of pursuit).

From desire and greed of amassing gain, every one would give his body to be consumed.

Night appears, like a treasure of mercy, that they may be delivered from their greed for a short while.

When a feeling of (spiritual) contraction comes over you, O traveller, 'tis (for) your good: do not become afire (with grief) in your heart,

For in that (contrary state of) expansion and delight you are 3735 spending: the expenditure (of enthusiasm) requires an income of (painful) preparation (to balance it).

If it were always the season of summer, the blazing heat of the sun would penetrate the garden

And burn up from root and bottom the soil whence its plants grow, so that the old (withered) ones would never again become fresh.

If December is sour-faced, (yet) it is kind; summer is laughing, but (none the less) it is burning (destroying).

When (spiritual) contraction comes, behold expansion therein: be fresh (cheerful) and do not let wrinkles fall on your brow.

Children are laughing, and sages are sour: sorrow appertains 3740 to the liver, and joy arises from the lungs.

The eye of the child, like (that of) the ass, is (fixed) on the stall; the eye of the wise man is (engaged) in reckoning the end.

---

[1] *I.e.* overtakes.
[2] *I.e.* "for strenuously pursuing the spiritual quest."

He (the child) sees the rich fodder in the stall, while this (wise man) sees his ultimate end to be death by (the hand of) the Butcher.

That fodder is bitter (in the end), for this Butcher gave it: He set up a pair of scales for our flesh.

Go, eat the fodder of wisdom which God hath given (us) disinterestedly from pure bounty.

3745 O slave (to your lusts), you have understood bread, not wisdom, (to be meant) in that (text) which God hath spoken unto you—*Eat ye of His provision.*

God's provision in the (present) stage (of your existence) is wisdom that will not choke you at the last (in the world hereafter).

(If) you have closed this (bodily) mouth, another mouth is opened, which becomes an eater of the morsels of (spiritual) mysteries.

If you cut off your body from the Devil's milk, by (thus) weaning it you will enjoy much felicity.

I have given a half-raw (imperfect) explanation of it, (like) the Turcomans' ill-boiled meat: hear (it) in full from the Sage of Ghazna[1].

3750 In the *Iláhí-náma* that Sage of the Unseen and Glory of them that know (God) explains this (matter).

(He says), "Eat (feel) sorrow, and do not eat the bread of those who increase (your) sorrow (hereafter), for the wise man eats sorrow, the child (eats) sugar (rejoices)."

The sugar of joy (hereafter) is the fruit of the garden of sorrow (here): this (sensual) joy is the wound and that (spiritual) sorrow is the plaster.

When you see (spiritual) sorrow, embrace it with passionate love: look on Damascus from the top of Rubwa[2].

The wise man is seeing the wine in the grape, the lover (of God) is seeing the thing (entity) in the non-existent.

3755 The day before yesterday the porters were quarrelling (and crying), "Don't you lift (it), let me lift his load (and carry it off) like a lion!"

Since they were seeing profit in that toil, each one was snatching the load from the other.

What comparison is there between God's reward and the reward given by that worthless creature? The former gives you a treasure as your reward, and the latter a groat.

(God gives you) a golden treasure that remains with you when you lie (buried) under the sand and is not left as a heritage.

It runs before your hearse and becomes your companion in the tomb and in the state where all is strange.

---

[1] Saná'í.

[2] A proverb meaning here, "View things from the standpoint of reality."

For the sake of your death-day be dead (to self), now, so that 3760 you may be (united) with everlasting Love, O fellow-servant.

Through the curtain of the struggle (against self) renunciation sees the face like a pomegranate-flower and the two tresses of the Desired One.

Sorrow is as a mirror before the struggler, for in this contrary there appears the face of the (other) contrary.

After the (one) contrary, (which is) pain, the other contrary, that is, gladness and triumph, shows its face.

Observe these two qualities (contraction and expansion) in the fingers of your hand: assuredly after the closing of the fist comes the opening.

If the fingers be always closed or entirely (invariably) open, 3765 he (their owner) is like an afflicted person.

His work and action[1] is regulated by these two qualities: these two conditions are (as) important for him as the bird's wings (to the bird).

When Mary was all at once dismayed, like those fishes on land,

[*How the Holy Spirit said to Mary, "I am sent to thee by God: be not agitated and do not hide from me, for this is the (Divine) command."*]

The Exemplar of (Divine) Bounty cried out to her, "I am the trusted (messenger) of the Lord: be not afraid of me.

Do not turn thy head away from the exalted (favourites) of (Divine) Majesty, do not withdraw thyself from such goodly confidants."

He was saying this, and (meanwhile) from his lips a wick 3770 (ray) of pure light was going up to Simák (Arcturus) step by step (uninterruptedly).

"Thou art fleeing from my existence into non-existence (the Unseen World): in non-existence I am a King and standard-bearer.

Verily, my home and dwelling-place is in non-existence: solely my (outward) form is before the Lady (Mary).

O Mary, look (well), for I am a difficult form (to apprehend): I am both a new-moon and a phantasy in the heart.

When a phantasy comes into thy heart and settles (there), it is (still) with thee wheresoever thou fleest—

Except an unsubstantial and vain phantasy which is one that 3775 sinks (and disappears) like the false dawn.

I am of the light of the Lord, like the true dawn, for no night prowls around my day.

---

[1] Literally, "acquisition." God creates all human actions; man only appropriates them.

Hark, do not cry *Lá hawl*[1] against me, O daughter of 'Imrán[2], for I have descended hither from *Lá hawl*.

Lá hawl was my origin and sustenance—the light of that *Lá hawl* which was prior to the spoken word.

Thou art taking refuge from me with God: I am in eternity the image of (Him who is) the (only) refuge.

3780   I am the refuge that was oft (the source of) thy deliverance. Thou takest refuge (from me), and I myself am that refuge.

There is no bane worse than ignorance: thou art with thy Friend and dost not know how to make love.

Thou art deeming thy Friend a stranger: upon a joy thou hast bestowed the name of a grief."

Such a date-palm, which is our Friend's favour—since we are robbers, His date-palm is our gallows.

Such a musky (fragrant) object, which is the tress of our Prince—since we are demented, this (tress) is our chain.

3785   Such a (Divine) grace is flowing like a Nile—since we are Pharaohs, it is becoming like blood.

The blood is saying, "I am water. Beware, do not spill (me)! I am (really) Joseph, (but) you make me the wolf[3], O contentious man."

Don't you see that a long-suffering friend becomes like a snake when you have grown hostile to him?

His flesh and fat (real nature) is unchanged: ('tis) only in appearance (that) he has become so evil.

How that Wakíl, (moved) by love, made up his mind to return to Bukhárá recklessly.

Leave the candle of Mary lighted, for that ardent (lover) is going to Bukhárá,

3790   Mightily impatient and in the blazing furnace (of love). Go, make a transition to the (story of the) Ṣadr-i Jahán.

This "Bukhárá" is the source of knowledge; therefore every one who has that (knowledge) is a native of "Bukhárá."

In the presence of a Shaykh you are in "Bukhárá": see that you do not look on "Bukhárá" as lowly.

Save with lowliness (shown by you), its difficult ebb and flow[4] will not give (you) entrance into the "Bukhárá" of his heart.

Oh, happy he whose carnal soul is abased! Alas for that one whose recalcitrance destroys (him)!

---

[1] "There is no power (except in God)."

[2] The *Qur'án* confuses Mary or Miriam, the daughter of 'Imrán and sister of Moses, with Mary, the mother of Jesus.

[3] Literally, "on account of you I am the wolf." Joseph's brethren pretended that a wolf had devoured him.

[4] The heart of the Shaykh is compared to a sea which demands the most cautious navigation.

Separation from the Ṣadr-i Jahán had shattered (the Wakíl's) 3795 foundations to pieces in his soul.

He said, "I will rise up and go back thither: if I have become an infidel, I will believe once more.

I will go back thither and fall before him—before its (Bukhárá's) kindly-thinking Ṣadr (Prince).

I will say, 'I throw myself before thee: revive (me) or cut off my head, like a sheep!

'Tis better to be slain and dead before thee, O Moon, than to be the king of the living in another place.

I have put it to the test more than a thousand times: I do not 3800 deem my life sweet without thee.

Sing to me, O object of my desire, the melody of resurrection! Kneel, O my she-camel! The joy is complete.

O earth, swallow my tears—surely they are enough. Drink, O my soul, a draught that is now pure!

Thou hast returned to us, O my festival! Welcome! How goodly is the refreshment thou hast brought, O Zephyr!'"

He said, "Farewell, my friends: I have set out towards the Ṣadr who commands and is obeyed.

Moment by moment I am being roasted in the flames (of 3805 separation from him): I will go thither, come what may!

Although he is making his heart like a hard rock (against me), my soul is bound for Bukhárá.

It is the abode of my Friend and the city of my King: in the lover's eyes this is (the meaning of) love of one's native land."

How a loved one asked her lover who had travelled in foreign countries, "Which city didst thou find the fairest and most thronged and the most magnificent and rich and charming?"

A loved one said to her lover, "O youth, thou hast seen many cities abroad.

Which of them, then, is the fairest?" He replied, "The city where my sweetheart is."

Wherever the carpet is (spread) for our King, (there) is the 3810 (spacious) plain, though it (that place) be (as narrow as) the eye of a needle.

Wherever a Joseph (beautiful) as the moon may be, 'tis Paradise, even though it be the bottom of a well.

How his friends hindered him from returning to Bukhárá and threatened him, and how he said, "I don't care."

A candid adviser said to him, "O imprudent man, think of the end (consequence), if thou hast (any) skill.

Consider reasonably the future and the past: do not let thyself be burnt like a moth.

How art thou going to Bukhárá? Thou art mad, thou art (only) fit for chains and the prison-house.

3815 He (the Ṣadr-i Jahán) is champing iron in his wrath against thee; he is seeking thee with twenty eyes.

He is sharpening the knife for thee: he is (like) the starving dog, and thou (like) the bag of flour.

After thou hast escaped and God has given thee the (open) road, thou art going (back) to prison: what is the matter with thee?

Had there been ten sorts of custodians over thee, intelligence would have been needed in order that thou might'st become quit of them.

Since no one is a custodian over thee, wherefore have the future and the past become sealed to thee?"

3820 Secret love had made him (the Wakíl) captive: the warner (his critic) was not seeing that custodian.

Every custodian's custodian is hidden; else, wherefore is he (the wicked custodian) in thrall to (his) currish nature?

The anger of Love, the King, settled upon his soul and chained him to the (base) office of a myrmidon and to ignominy[1].

It (anger) is striking him and saying, "Hark, strike him (thy captive)!" Woe is me on account of those hidden myrmidons[2].

Whomsoever you see going in a (path of) detriment, he, though (apparently) alone, is going along with a (hidden) myrmidon.

3825 If he were aware of him, he would cry out in distress and go into the presence of the King of kings,

And scatter earth on his head before the King, that he might find security from the frightful Devil.

(But) you, O less than an ant, deemed yourself a prince: hence, blind (as you are), you did not see that custodian.

You were deluded by these false wings and plumes—the wings and plumes that lead to woe.

(If) he keep his wings light (unencumbered), he journeys upward; when he becomes defiled with earth, he makes heavinesses (which weigh him down).

How the lover, impelled by love, said " I don't care"
to the person who counselled and scolded him.

3830 He said, "O counsellor, be silent! How long, how long (wilt thou chide)? Do not give advice, for the bonds (on me) are very grievous.

My bonds are more grievous than thy advice: thy doctor (who taught thee) was not acquainted with love.

---

[1] Literally, "blackness of face."
[2] *I.e.* "what excites my indignation is not the wicked man himself, but the passions by which he is ruled."

In that quarter where love was increasing (my) pain, Bú Ḥanífa and Sháfi'í gave no instruction.

Do not thou threaten me with being killed, for I thirst lamentably for mine own blood."

For lovers, there is a dying at every moment: verily, the dying of lovers is not of one sort.

He (the lover) hath two hundred souls (lives) from the Soul 3835 of Guidance, and those two hundred he is sacrificing at every instant.

For each soul (life) he receives ten as its price: read from the Qur'án "ten like unto them."

If that One of friendly countenance shed my blood, dancing (in triumph) I will strew (lavish) my soul (life) upon Him.

I have tried it: my death is (consists) in life: when I escape from this life, 'tis to endure for ever.

"Kill me, kill me, O trusty friends! Lo, in my being killed is life on life[1]."

O Thou that makest the cheek radiant, O Spirit of ever- 3840 lastingness, draw my spirit to Thyself and generously bestow on me the meeting (with Thee).

I have a Beloved whose love roasts the bowels (of my heart): if He wished to walk upon mine eye, He would walk (upon it, and be welcome).

Speak Persian[2], though Arabic is sweeter: Love indeed hath a hundred other tongues (besides these two).

When the scent of that Charmer of hearts begins to fly (abroad), all those tongues become dumbfounded.

I will cease (from speech): the Sweetheart has begun to speak, be (all) ear—and God best knoweth the right course.

Since the lover has repented, now beware (of misappre- 3845 hension)[3], for he will lecture, like the adepts (in mystical love), on the gallows.

Although this lover is going to Bukhárá, he is not going to (attend) lectures or to (learn from) a teacher.

For lovers, the (only) lecturer is the beauty of the Beloved, their (only) book and lecture and lesson is His face.

They are silent (outwardly), but the shrill noise of their repetition is going up to the throne and high-seat of their Friend.

Their (only) lesson is enthusiasm and the whirling dance and quaking agitation; not the Ziyádát[4] and the chapter on "the chain[5]."

---

[1] This is a quotation. The author of the verse is the famous Ḥalláj.
[2] The three preceding verses are in Arabic.
[3] I.e. "do not imagine that he has repented of loving."
[4] Title of a well-known manual of jurisprudence.
[5] "The chain" and "the circle," like "the question of the purse" below, refer to nice points of law.

3850   The "chain" of these people (the lovers of God) is the musk-dropping curls (of the Beloved); they have the question of "the circle," but it is the "circle" of the Friend.

If any one ask you about the question of "the purse," tell (him) that God's treasure is not contained in purses.

If talk of *khul'*[1] and *mubárá*[2] is going on (among them), do not disapprove: (inwardly) mention is being made of "Bukhárá."

The mention (recollection) of any thing produces a particular (spiritual) effect, inasmuch as every quality has a quiddity.

In Bukhárá you attain to (perfection in) the sciences: when you turn to lowliness (*ba-khwárí*), you are freed from them.

3855   That man of Bukhárá had not the vexation of knowledge: he was fixing his eyes on the sun of vision.

No one who in solitude has found the way to vision will seek power by means of the (diverse) kinds of knowledge.

When he has become a boon-companion to the beauty of the Soul, he will have a disgust of traditional learning and knowledge.

Vision is superior to knowledge: hence the present world prevails (over the next world) in the view of the vulgar,

Because they regard this world as ready money, while they deem what concerns that (other) world to be (like) a debt.

How that loving servant turned his face towards Bukhárá.

3860   With throbbing heart the lover, who shed tears mingled with blood, set out for Bukhárá in hot haste.

The sands of Ámún seemed to him like silk, the river Oxus seemed to him like a pond[3].

To him that wilderness was like a rose-garden: he was falling on his back from laughter, like the (full-blown) rose.

The (material) candy is in Samarcand; but his lip got it from "Bukhárá," and that (spiritual) candy became his creed.

"O Bukhárá, thou hast increased understanding (in others) but thou hast robbed me of understanding and religion.

3865   I am seeking the Full Moon: hence I am (thin) as the new moon. I am seeking the Ṣadr (Prince) in this 'shoe-row' (vestibule)[4]."

When he descried that "Bukhárá" looming black (in the distance)[5], a whiteness (a mystic illumination) appeared in the blackness of his grief.

---

[1] Divorce of a wife at her own request.
[2] Dissolution of marriage by mutual consent.
[3] This verse is imitated from a well-known poem by Rúdakí.
[4] *I.e.* "in this low world."
[5] Literally, "the blackness of that Bukhárá."

He fell (and lay) awhile senseless and outstretched: his reason flew into the garden of the mystery.

They were sprinkling rose-water on his head and face; they were unaware of the rose-water of his love.

He had beheld a hidden rose-garden: the raiding foray of Love had cut him off from himself.

Thou, frozen (in spirit), art not worthy of this (inspiring) 3870 breath (of love): though thou art a reed (cane), thou art not associated with sugar.

The baggage of intellect is with thee, and thou art (still) possessed of thy wits, for thou art unaware of *armies which ye did not see.*

How the reckless lover entered Bukhárá, and how his friends deterred him from showing himself.

Joyously he entered Bukhárá near his beloved and (him who was) the abode of (his) security,

Like the man intoxicated (with love) who (in imagination) flies to heaven: the Moon embraces him and says, "Embrace (me)!"

Every one that saw him in Bukhárá said (to him), "Arise (and go) before showing thyself! Do not sit (still)! Flee!

For that Prince is seeking thee in anger, that he may wreak a 3875 ten years' vengeance on thy life.

By God, by God, do not plunge in thine own blood, do not rely on thy artful words and wiles.

Thou wert the Ṣadr-i Jahán's constable and a noble; thou wert the trusted (agent) and master-engineer (in his affairs).

(Then) thou didst act treacherously and flee from punishment: thou hadst escaped: how hast thou let thyself be caught again?

With a hundred devices thou didst flee from tribulation: has folly brought thee hither or (thy) fate?[1]

O thou whose intellect jeers at Mercury (the celestial Scribe), 3880 Destiny makes a fool of intellect and the intelligent.

Luckless is the hare that seeks (to encounter) the lion: where is thy cleverness and intelligence and quick-wittedness?

The wiles of Destiny are a hundred times as many (as thine): he (the Prophet) has said, 'When Destiny comes, the wide field is straitened.'

There are a hundred ways and places of refuge on left and right, (but) they are barred by Destiny, for it is a dragon."

---

[1] Literally, "the appointed term (of thy life)."

*How the lover answered those who scolded
and threatened him.*

He said, " I am dropsical: the water draws me, though I know
that the water too will kill me.

3885 None afflicted with dropsy will flee from the water, even if it
checkmate and ruin him two hundred times.

If my hands and belly become swollen, (yet) the passionate
desire for the water will not abate (and depart) from me.

At the time when they ask me of my inward state, I say,
'Would that the Sea were flowing within me!'

Let the water-skin, my belly, be burst by the waves of the
water: if I die, my death is acceptable.

Wherever I see the water of a stream, jealousy comes over me
(and I wish) that I might be in its place.

3890 (With) hands (swollen) like a tambourine and belly like a
drum, I am beating the drum of (I am proclaiming) my love
for the water, as the rose (does)[1].

If that Trusty Spirit[2] spill my blood, I will drink draught on
draught of blood, like the earth.

I am a blood-drinker, like the earth and like the embryo:
(ever) since I became a lover I am (engaged) in this trade.

During the night I boil on the fire, like a kettle; (all) day till
nightfall I drink blood, like the sand.

I repent that I set contrivance afoot (in order to escape) and
fled from that which his anger desired.

3895 Let him drive on (let him not restrain) his anger against my
intoxicated soul: he is the Feast of the Sacrifice, and the lover is
the buffalo (for slaughter).

Whether the buffalo sleep or whether it eat something, he
nurtures (fattens) it for the Feast and the slaughter.

Deem me to be (as) the cow of Moses that gave life (to the
murdered man): each limb of me is the (means of) raising from
the dead every one that is (spiritually) free.

The cow of Moses was one offered in sacrifice: her smallest
limb brought a murdered man to life.

At its touch the murdered man sprang up from his place—at
the words spoken (by God), *Strike him with part of her*[3].

3900 O my noble (friends), slaughter this cow (the fleshly soul), if
ye desire to raise to life the spirits (possessed) of insight.

I died to the inorganic state and became endowed with
growth, and (then) I died to (vegetable) growth and attained to
the animal.

I died from animality and became Adam (man): why, then,
should I fear? When have I become less by dying?

---

[1] Because the rose derives its beauty from the water which nourishes it.
[2] *I.e.* my Beloved who resembles Gabriel. Cf. *Qur'án*, XXVI, 193.
[3] *Qur'án*, II, 68.

At the next remove I shall die to man, that I may soar and
lift up my head amongst the angels;

And I must escape[1] even from (the state of) the angel: *every-
thing is perishing except His Face.*

Once more I shall be sacrificed and die to the angel: I shall 3905
become that which enters not into the imagination.

Then I shall become non-existence: non-existence saith to
me, (in tones loud) as an organ, *Verily, unto Him shall we
return.*

Know death to be (the thing signified by) what the (Moham-
medan) community are agreed upon, namely, that the Water of
Life is hidden in the (Land of) Darkness.

Grow from this river-bank, like the water-lily, greedy and
craving for death as the sufferer from dropsy.

The water is death to him, and (yet) he is seeking the water
and drinking it—and God best knoweth the right course.

Oh, the cold lover, clad in the felt (garment) of shame, who 3910
from fear of (losing) his life is fleeing from the Beloved!

O thou disgrace (even) to women, behold hundreds of
thousands of souls clapping their hands (and rushing) towards
the sword of His love!

Thou hast seen the river: spill thy jug in the river: how should
the water take flight from the river?

When the water in the jug goes into the river-water, it dis-
appears in it, and it becomes the river.

His (the lover's) attributes have passed away, and his essence
remains: after this, he does not dwindle or become ill-favoured.

I have hanged myself on His palm-tree in excuse for having 3915
fled from Him."

How that lover reached his Beloved when he washed
his hands of (gave up) his life.

Prostrating himself on face and head, like a ball, he went with
wet eyes towards the Ṣadr (Prince).

All the people were waiting, their heads in the air, (to see)
whether he would burn or hang him.

"Now" (they said) "he will show to this simpleton that which
Time (Fortune) shows to the unfortunate.

Like the moth, he (the lover) deemed the (fiery) sparks to be
the light: foolishly he fell in and was cut off from (deprived of)
life."

But the candle of Love is not like that (external) candle: it is 3920
radiance in radiance in radiance.

It is the reverse of the fiery candles: it seems to be fire, while
(in reality) it is all sweetness.

[1] Literally, "leap out of the river."

*Description of the lover-killing mosque and of the death-
seeking reckless lover who became a guest there.*

Lend ear to a story, O well-conducted man! There was a
mosque on the outskirts of the city of Rayy.

No one ever slept the night there but on the same night (he
died) from terror (and) his children became orphans.

Many the naked (destitute) stranger that went into it (at
nightfall) and went at dawn, like the stars, into the grave.

3925 Make thyself very attentive to this (tale)! The dawn is come,
cut short thy slumber!

Every one used to say that in it there were fierce Jinnís who
killed the guests with blunt swords[1].

Another would say, "It is the magic and talisman, for this
enchantment[2] is the foe and enemy of life."

Another would say, "Put an inscription (notice) conspicuously
on its door—'O guest, do not stay here.

Do not sleep the night here, if you want to live; otherwise,
death will unmask an ambush for you in this place.'"

3930 And another would say, "Bolt (the door) at night, (and when)
a heedless person comes, do not admit him."

How the guest came into the mosque.

(So it continued) till a guest arrived at nightfall who had heard
that marvellous rumour.

He was testing (it) in order to put (it) to the proof, for he was
very valiant and surfeited with life.

He said (to himself), "I take little account of a (sheep's) head
and belly[3]: suppose that one grain is gone from the spirit's
treasure, (what does it matter?)[4]

Let the bodily form go: who am I (in reality)? Is not the
(bodily) figure of small account when I am enduring for ever?

3935 Since by the grace of God the (Divine) spirit was breathed
into me[5], I am the breath of God (which is) kept apart from the
windpipe of the body,

To the end that the sound of His breathing should not fall in
this direction, and that that (spiritual) pearl should escape from
the narrow (bodily) shell.

Since God said, '*Desire death*, O ye that are *sincere*,' I am
sincere: I will lavish my soul upon this (I will sacrifice my life
for this object)."

---

[1] *I.e.* barbarously.

[2] For this meaning of رَصَد cf. Dozy, *Supplément.*   [3] *I.e.* the body.

[4] *I.e.* such a trifle as the death of the body inflicts no loss upon the spirit.

[5] Literally, "I was (the object of the verse of the *Qur'án* in which God
says) '*I breathed*'."

How the people of the mosque blamed the lover-guest for
(his intention of) sleeping the night there and threatened him.

The people said to him, "Beware! Do not sleep here, lest the
Taker of the soul[1] pound thee like the dregs of sesame-grain,

For thou art a stranger and ignorant of the fact that any one
who sleeps in this place perishes.

This is not an (accidental) occurrence: we and all those 3940
possessed of intelligence have ofttimes witnessed this.

To whomsoever that mosque gave lodging for a single night,
poisonous death came to him at midnight.

We have seen this not (only) once but a hundred times[2]: we
have not heard it at second-hand[3] from any one.

The Prophet said, 'The (Mohammedan) religion is (consists
in) sincerity (*naṣīḥat*)': that *naṣīḥat* etymologically is the
opposite of *ghulúl* (unfaithfulness).

This *naṣīḥat* is 'to be true in friendship': in an act of *ghulúl*
you are treacherous and currish[4].

We are showing this sincerity towards thee, without treachery, 3945
from (motives of) love: do not turn away from reason and justice!"

The lover's reply to those who chid him.

He said, "O sincere advisers, I have become unrepentantly
weary of the world of life.

I am an idle vagabond, seeking blows and desiring blows: do
not seek rectitude from the vagabond on the road.

(I am) not the vagabond who in sooth is a seeker of provender:
I am the reckless vagabond (who is) the seeker of death.

(I am) not the vagabond who gets small money into his palm,
(but) the nimble vagabond who would cross this bridge (to the
world hereafter)—

Not the one who cleaves to every shop; nay, but (the one who) 3950
springs away from (phenomenal) existence and strikes upon a
mine (of reality).

Death and migration from this (earthly) abode has become as
sweet to me as leaving the cage and flying (is sweet) to the
(captive) bird—

The cage that is in the very midst of the garden, (so that) the
bird beholds the rose-beds and the trees,

(While) outside, round the cage, a multitude of birds is
sweetly chanting tales of liberty:

At (the sight of) that verdant place neither (desire for) food
remains to the bird in the cage, nor patience and rest,

---

[1] The Angel of Death.
[2] Literally, "from one to a hundred."
[3] Literally, "with blind conformity."
[4] Literally, "having the skin of a dog."

3955 (But) it puts out its head through every hole, that perchance
it may tear off this fetter from its leg.

Since its heart and soul are (already) outside like this, how
will it be when you open the cage?"

Not such is the bird caged amidst anxieties—cats round
about it in a ring:

How, in this dread and sorrow, should it have the desire to
go out of the cage?

It wishes that, (to save it) from this unwelcome plucking (of
its feathers), there might be a hundred cages round about this
cage (in which it is confined).

*The love of (a) Galen is for this present life, for only here does his
art avail; he has not practised any art that avails in yonder
market*[1]: *there he sees himself to be the same as the vulgar.*

3960 That[2] is even as wise Galen said on account of (his) passion
for this world and because of what he desired (in it)—

"I am content that (only) half of my vital spirit should re-
main, so that I may see the world through the arse of a mule."

He sees around him cats in troops: his bird has despaired of
flying;

Or he has deemed all except this world to be non-existence
and has not perceived in non-existence a hidden resurrection.

Like the embryo which (the Divine) Bounty is drawing forth:
it is fleeing back towards the belly.

3965 (The Divine) Grace is turning its (the embryo's) face towards
the place of exit, (while) it (the embryo) is making its abode in
the mother's loins,

Saying, "Oh, I wonder, if I fall outside of this city and
(abode of) pleasure[3], shall I see with my eye this dwelling-
place;

Or would there be in that noisome city[4] a door, so that I might
gaze into the womb,

Or would there be for me a path, (narrow) as the eye of a
needle, so that the womb might become visible to me from
outside?"

That embryo, too, is unaware of a world (outside): it is one
unfamiliar (therewith), like Galen.

3970 It does not know that the humours which exist (in the womb)
are supplied (to it) from the external world,

Even as the four elements in this world obtain a hundred
supplies (means of support) from the City beyond space.

---

¹ *I.e.* in the next world.
² *I.e.* the wish of the bird described in the preceding verse.
³ *I.e.* the womb.   ⁴ *I.e.* the world.

If it has found water and seeds in its cage, those have ap-
peared (there) from a Garden and Expanse.

The spirits of the prophets behold the Garden from this cage
at the time of their being transported and freed (from the
body);

Hence they are free of Galen and the world: they are shining
like the moon in the skies.

And if this saying (as related) from Galen is a fiction, then my 3975
answer is not for Galen,

(But) this is the answer to the person who said it, for the
luminous heart has not been his mate.

The bird, his spirit, became a mouse seeking a hole, when it
heard from the cats (the cry), "Halt ye!"

On that account his spirit, mouse-like, deemed its home and
abode to be in this world-hole.

In this hole, too, it began to build and acquired a knowledge
suitable to the hole;

It chose the trades advantageous to it, which would be of use 3980
in this hole.

Inasmuch as it turned its heart away from (relinquished the
desire for) going forth, the way of deliverance from the body was
barred.

If the spider had the nature of the 'Anqá, how should it have
reared a tent (made) of some gossamer?

The cat has put its claws into the cage: the name of its claws
is pain and delirium and gripes.

The cat is Death, and its claws are disease: it is striking at the
bird and its plumage.

He (the sick man) darts (like the bird) from corner to corner 3985
towards the remedy. Death is like the cadi, and the disease is
the witness.

This witness comes (to you), like the cadi's footman (officer),
who summons you to the place of judgement.

You, in flight (from your doom), beg him (to grant you) a
respite: if he consent, it is granted; otherwise, he says, "Arise
(and go with me)."

The seeking of a respite consists in remedies and cures, that
you may patch (thereby) the tattered cloak, the body.

At last, one morning, he comes angrily, saying, "How long
will the respite be? Now, prithee, be ashamed!"

O envious man, ask your pardon of the King ere such a day 3990
as that arrives.

And he who rides his horse into the darkness and altogether
removes his heart from the Light

Is fleeing from the witness and his purpose; for that witness
is calling him to judgement.

How the people of the mosque blamed the guest once more
for (his intention of) sleeping in the mosque by night.

The people said to him, "Do not act with foolhardiness;
depart, lest thy (bodily) vesture and thy soul become in pawn
(to Death)."

From afar it seems easy, (but) look well! for in the end the
passage is grievous.

3995 Many a man hanged himself and broke (his neck) and at the
moment of agony sought something for his hand to cling to.

Before the battle, the fancy of good or evil is slight (makes no
deep impression) in a man's heart;

(But) when he enters into the fray, then to that person the
matter becomes woeful.

Since you are not a lion, beware, do not step forward, for
that Doom is a wolf, and your soul is the sheep;

But if you are one of the *Abdál* (saints) and your sheep has
become a lion, come on securely, for your death has been over-
thrown.

4000 Who is the *Abdál*? He that becomes transmuted, he whose
wine is turned into vinegar by Divine transmutation.

But you are drunken, pot-valiant[1], and from (mere) opinion
think yourself to be a lion. Beware, do not advance!

God hath said of the unrighteous Hypocrites, "*Their valour
amongst themselves is a great valour.*

Amongst one another they are manly, (but) in a warlike
expedition they are as the women of the house."

The Prophet, the commander-in-chief of the things unseen,
said, "There is no bravery, O youth, before the battles."

4005 The drunken make a froth when there is talk of war, (but)
when war is raging they are as unskilled (useless) as froth.

At the time when war is spoken of, his (such a one's) scimitar
is long (drawn and extended); at the time of combat his sword
is (sheathed) like an onion.

At the time of premeditation his heart is eager for wounds;
then (in action) his bag is emptied (of air) by a single needle.

I marvel at the seeker of purity who at the time of polishing
shrinks from being handled roughly.

Love is like the lawsuit; to suffer harsh treatment is (like) the
evidence: when you have no evidence, the lawsuit is lost.

4010 Do not be aggrieved when this Judge demands your evidence:
kiss the snake in order that you may gain the treasure.

That harshness is not towards you, O son; nay, towards the
evil qualities within you.

The blows of the stick with which a man beats a rug he inflicts,
not on the rug, but on the dust (in the rug).

---

[1] Literally, "lion-catching."

If that vindictive fellow lashes the horse, he directs the blows, not at the horse, but at its stumbling,

In order that it may be delivered from (the vice of) stumbling and may move well: you imprison must (in the vat) in order that it may become wine.

He (some one) said, "Thou hast struck that little orphan so 4015 many blows: how wert not thou afraid of the Divine wrath?"

He (the striker) said, "O (dear) soul and friend, when did I strike him? I struck at the devil that is in him."

If your mother say to you, "Mayst thou die!" she wishes the death of that (evil) nature (of yours) and the death of iniquity.

The folk who fled from correction dishonoured[1] their (own) manhood and (true) men.

The railers drove them back from the war, so that they remained so infamous and effeminate.

Do not thou hearken to the boasting and roaring of the 4020 driveller: do not go into the battle-line with such fellows.

Since *they would have added to you (naught but) corruption*, God said, "Turn the leaf (avert yourself) from pusillanimous comrades,

For if they go along with you, the warriors will become pithless, like straw.

They put themselves in line with you (on the field of battle); then they flee and break the heart of the line.

Therefore, better a little army without these persons than (that) it should be mustered (reinforced) with the Hypocrites."

A few well-sifted almonds are better than a great many (sweet 4025 ones) mixed with bitter.

The bitter and the sweet are one thing (alike) in respect of rattling (against each other, when poured out); the defect arises from their not being the same at heart.

The infidel is of timorous heart, for, (judging) from opinion, he lives in doubt as to the state of that (the other) world.

He is going along the road, (but) he does not know any stage: one blind in heart steps timidly.

When the traveller does not know the way, how does he go? He goes with (many) hesitations, while his heart is full of blood (anguish).

If any one says (to him), "Hey! this is not the way[2]," he will 4030 halt there and stand still in affright.

But if his (the traveller's) wise heart knows the way, how should every hey and ho go into his ear?

Therefore do not journey with these camel-hearted (craven) ones, for in the hour of distress and danger they are the ones who sink;

---

[1] Literally, "spilt the water of."
[2] Literally, "the way is not in this direction."

Then they flee and leave thee alone, though in boasting they
are (powerful as) the magic of Babylon.

Beware! Do not thou request sybarites to fight; do not re-
quest peacocks to engage in the hunt and the chase.

4035   The carnal nature is a peacock: it tempts thee and talks idly,
that it may remove thee from thy (spiritual) post.

*How Satan said to the Quraysh, "Go to war with Aḥmad (Mo-
hammed), for I will aid you and call my tribe to help"; and how,
when the two battle-lines confronted each other, he fled.*

As (for example) Satan became the hundred-and-first[1] in the
army (of the Quraysh) and spake beguiling words[2], saying,
"*Verily, I am a protector for you.*"

When the Quraysh had assembled at his bidding, and the two
armies confronted each other,

Satan espied a host of angels on a road beside the ranks of the
Faithful.

(He espied) those *troops that ye saw not*, drawn up in ranks;
and from terror his soul became (like) a fire-temple.

4040   Turning on his heel[3], he began to retreat, saying, "I behold a
marvellous host"—

That is, "*I fear God:* I have no help from Him. Get ye gone!
Verily, I see what ye see not."

Ḥárith said, "Hey, O thou that hast the form of Suráqa, why
wert not thou saying such-like words yesterday?"

He replied, "At this moment I see destruction (before me)."
He (Ḥárith) said, "Thou seest the most puny of the Arabs.

Thou art seeing naught but this; but, O thou disgrace, that
was the time of talk, and this is the time of battle.

4045   Yesterday thou wert saying, 'I pledge myself that victory and
Divine aid will always be yours.'

Yesterday thou wert the surety for the army, O accursed one,
and now thou art cowardly, good-for-nothing, and vile,

So that (after) we swallowed those (deceitful) words of thine
and came (to battle), thou hast gone to the bath-stove and we
have become the fuel."

When Ḥárith said this to Suráqa, that accursed one was en-
raged at his reproaches.

He angrily withdrew his hand from his (Ḥárith's) hand, since
his heart was pained by his words[4].

4050   Satan smote his (Ḥárith's) breast and fled: by means of this
plot he shed the blood of those wretched men.

After he had ruined so great a multitude, he then said, "*Lo,
I am quit of you.*"

---

[1] *I.e.* leader and chief.
[2] Literally, "chanted spells."
[3] Literally, "having drawn his foot backward."
[4] Literally, "since heartache came to him from his words."

He smote him on the breast and overthrew him; then he turned to flee, since terror urged him on.

The fleshly soul and the Devil both have (ever) been one person (essentially); (but) they have manifested themselves in two forms,

Like the angel and the intellect, which were (really) one, (but) became two forms for the sake of His (God's) wise purposes.

You have such an enemy as this in your inward part: he is the 4055 preventer of the intellect, and the adversary of the spirit and of religion.

At one moment he dashes forward like the Libyan lizard; then (again) in flight he darts away into a hole.

Just now he has (many) holes in the (human) heart, and from every hole he is putting out his head.

The name that denotes the Devil's becoming hidden from (men's) souls and going into that hole is *khunús* (slinking back),

For his *khunús* is like the *khunús* of the hedgehog: like the head of the hedgehog, he pops in and out[1];

For God hath called the Devil *Khannás* (the slinker), because 4060 he resembles the head of the little hedgehog.

The head of the hedgehog is continually being hidden because of its fear of the cruel hunter,

Until, when it has found an opportunity, it puts out its head: by such a stratagem the snake becomes its prey.

If the fleshly soul had not waylaid you from within, how would the brigands have any power to lay a hand upon you?

On account of the exigent myrmidon, who is Lust, the heart is captive to greed and cupidity and bane.

On account of that inward myrmidon you have become 4065 thievish and depraved, so that the way is (open) for the (external) myrmidons to coerce you.

Hearken to this good counsel in the Traditions (of the Prophet)—"Your worst enemy is between your two sides."

Do not listen to the pompous talk of this enemy[2], (but) flee, for she is like Iblís in obstinately wrangling and quarrelling.

For the sake of this world and for contention's sake she has made the everlasting torment (seem) easy (of small account) to you.

What wonder, if she makes death (seem) easy? By her magic she does a hundred times as much (as this).

Magic makes a straw a mountain by artifice; (or) again, it 4070 weaves a mountain like a straw.

It makes ugly things beautiful by means of sleight; it makes beautiful things ugly by means of (false) opinion.

The work of magic is this, that it breathes (incantations) and at every breath (moment) transforms realities.

[1] Literally, "he has incoming and outgoing."
[2] The fleshly soul.

At one time it shows a man in the guise of an ass, (at another time) it makes an ass (look like) a man and a notable.

Such a magician is within you and latent: truly, there is a concealed magic in temptation (exerted by the fleshly soul);

4075 (But) in the world in which are these magic arts, there are magicians who defeat sorcery.

In the plain where this fresh (virulent) poison grew, there has also grown the antidote, O son.

The antidote says to you, "Seek from me a shield, for I am nearer than the poison to thee.

Her (the fleshly soul's) words are magic and thy ruin; my words are (lawful) magic and the counter-charm to her magic."

How the fault-finders repeated their advice to the guest of the guest-killing mosque.

The Prophet said, "Verily, there is a magic in eloquence"; and that goodly hero spake the truth.

4080 "Hey, do not commit a foolhardy act, (but) depart, O generous man, and do not make the mosque and us suspected on this account;

For an enemy will speak from enmity; and to-morrow the villain will rouse a fire (of suspicion) against us[1],

Saying, 'Some wicked man strangled him, (knowing that) on the pretext of the mosque he was safe (from suspicion),

So that he might impute the murder to the mosque[2] and, since the mosque has a bad name, might escape.'

Do not lay any suspicion upon us, O man of valiant spirit, for we are not secure from the craft of (our) enemies.

4085 Come now, depart! Do not be foolhardy, do not cherish vain desire, for it is impossible to measure (the planet) Saturn by the ell.

Many like thee have prated of (their) luck, (and in the end) they have torn out their beards, one by one, piecemeal.

Hey, begone! Cut short this palaver! Do not cast thyself and us into woe!"

How the guest answered them and adduced the parable of the guardian of the cornfield who, by making a noise with the tomtom, sought to drive away from the cornfield a camel on whose back they were beating the big kettle-drum of (Sultan) Maḥmúd.

He said, "O friends, I am not one of the devils, that (the strength of) my sinews should fail at a single lá hawl[3].

---

[1] Literally, "will cast some fire at us."
[2] Literally, "lay the pretended cause of the murder on the mosque."
[3] *I.e.* on hearing the invocation, "There is no power (*lá hawl*) or strength but in God Almighty."

A boy, who was the guardian of a cornfield, used to beat a tomtom in order to keep off the birds,

So that the birds, at (the sound of) the tomtom, were scared 4090 away from the field, and the field became safe[1] from evil birds.

When the Sultan, the noble King Maḥmúd, pitched a great tent in that neighbourhood as he passed on the way

With an army like the stars of heaven (in number), numerous and victorious, one that pierces the ranks (of the enemy) and takes possession of empire—

There was a camel that carried the kettle-drum: 'twas a Bactrian (camel), going in front (of the army) like a cock:

Day and night he (the driver) used loudly to beat the big kettle-drum and the (ordinary) drum on its back in returning (from an expedition) and in setting out.

That camel entered the cornfield, and the boy beat his tom- 4095 tom to protect the corn.

An intelligent man said to him, 'Don't beat the tomtom, for he (the camel) is well-seasoned[2] by the drum; he is accustomed to it.

What is thy little tomtom, child, to him, since he carries the Sultan's drum twenty times the size?'

I am a lover, one who has been sacrificed to Naught[3]: my soul is the band-stand for the drum of tribulation.

Verily, these threats (of yours) are (as) a little tomtom beside that which these eyes (of mine) have seen.

O comrades, I am not one of those (without experience), that 4100 because of idle fancies I should halt on the Way.

I am unafraid (of death), like the Ismá'ílís; nay, like Ismá'íl (Ishmael) I am free from (care for my) head.

I am done with pomp and ostentation. '*Say, come ye*': He (the Beloved) said to my soul, 'Come.'"

The Prophet has said that one who feels sure of the recompense will give generously beforehand.

Whoever sees a hundred compensations for the gift will at once give away the gift with this object (in view).

All have become tied (to their business) in the bazaar (this 4105 world), to the end that when (the chance of) gain occurs they may give their money.

With gold in their money-bags, they are seated expectantly (in the hope) that the gain may come and that he who persists (in waiting) may begin to squander (his gold).

When he sees a piece of merchandise exceeding (his own) in profit, his fondness for his own goods becomes chilled;

---

[1] Literally, "without fear."
[2] Literally, "cooked," *i.e.* matured and fully experienced.
[3] *I.e.* "I have died to self."

(For hitherto) he has remained enamoured of[1] those, because he perceived no profit and advantage superior to his own goods.

Similarly, (in the case of) knowledge and accomplishments and trades: (a man is engrossed with them) since he has not seen (anything) superior to them in excellence.

4110   Whilst nothing is better than life, life is precious; when a better appears, the name of life becomes a slippery (futile) thing.

The lifeless doll is as (dear as) life to the child until he has grown up to manhood[2].

This imagination and fancy are (like) the doll: so long as you are (spiritually) a child, you have need of them;

(But) when the spirit has escaped from childishness, it is in union (with God): it is done with sense-perception and imagination and fancy.

There is no confidant (familiar with this mystery), that I should speak without insincerity (reserve). I will keep silence, and God best knoweth the (true) accord[3].

4115   The goods (of this world) and the body are snow melting away to naught; (yet) God is their purchaser, for *God hath purchased*.

The snows seem to you better than the price[4], because you are in doubt: you have no certainty (no sure faith),

And in you, O contemptible man, there is this marvellous opinion that does not fly to the garden of certainty.

O son, every opinion is thirsting for certainty and emulously flapping its wings (in quest thereof).

When it attains to knowledge, then the wing becomes a foot[5], and its knowledge begins to scent certainty,

4120   For in the tested Way knowledge is inferior to certainty, but above opinion.

Know that knowledge is a seeker of certainty, and certainty is a seeker of vision and intuition.

Seek this (difference between knowledge and intuitive certainty) now, in (the Súra which begins with) *Alhákum*, after (the word) *kallá* and after (the words) *lau ta'lamún*[6].

Knowledge leads to vision, O knowing one: if it (knowledge) became (intuitive) certainty, they would see Hell.

Vision is immediately born of certainty, just as fancy is born of opinion.

---

[1] Literally, "warm for."
[2] Literally, "until in growing up he has become able to beget children."
[3] *I.e.* the real union which exists between God and me.
[4] *I.e.* "you prefer the things of this world to the (spiritual) Paradise, which God gives you in exchange for them."
[5] *I.e.* the aspiration becomes a basis for further progress.
[6] *Qur'án*, CII, 1–5.

See in *Alhákum* the explanation of this, (namely), that *the* 4125 *knowledge of certainty* becomes *the intuition of certainty*.

"I am higher than opinion and certainty, and my head is not to be turned aside by blame.

Since my mouth ate of His sweetmeat, I have become clear-eyed and a seer of Him.

I step boldly when I go (to my spiritual) home: I do not let my feet tremble, I do not walk like the blind.

That which God said to the rose, and caused it to laugh (in full-blown beauty), He said to my heart, and made it a hundred times more (beautiful).

(He bestowed on my heart) that which touched the cypress 4130 and made its stature straight, and that of which the narcissus and wild-rose partook;

That which made sweet the soul and heart of the sugar-cane, and that from which the creature of earth[1] gained the form of Chigil[2];

That which made the eyebrow so ravishing and made the face rose-coloured and (like) the pomegranate-flower;

(That which) gave a hundred enchantments to the tongue, and that which gave the (pure) gold of Ja'far to the mine.

When the door of the Armoury was opened, the amorous glances became archers,

And shot arrows at my heart and frenzied me and made me in 4135 love with thanksgiving and sugar-chewing.

I am the lover of that One to whom every 'that' belongs: of (even) a single pearl of His the bodyguard is Intellect and Spirit.

I do not boast, or if I boast, ('tis only in appearance, for) like water, I have no trouble in quenching fire[3].

How should I steal when He is the keeper of the treasury? How should not I be hard-faced (bold and resolute)? He is my support.

Every one whose back is warmed by the Sun will be hard-faced: he will have neither dread nor shame.

His face has become foe-burning and veil-rending, like the 4140 face of the peerless Sun.

Every prophet was hard-faced in this world, and beat single-handed against the army of the kings,

And did not avert his face from any fear or pain, (but) single and alone dashed against a (whole) world.

The rock is hard-faced and bold-eyed: it is not afraid of the world that is full of brickbats;

---

[1] Man.

[2] *I.e.* comeliness. Chigil was a town in Turkistán, famed for the beauty of its inhabitants.

[3] *I.e.* "it is not an idle boast when I say that I have no fear of death."

For those brickbats were made solid by the brick-maker, (while) the rock was hardened by Divine art.

4145   If the sheep are beyond count, (yet) how should the butcher be afraid of their numerousness?

'Each of you is a shepherd[1]': the prophet is as the shepherd. The people are like the flock; he is the overseer.

The shepherd is not afraid of the sheep in (his) contention (with them), but is their protector from hot and cold (from all calamities).

If he cry out in wrath against the flock, know 'tis from the love which he hath for them all.

(My) new Fortune[2] says (whispers) into my ear every moment, 'I will make thee sorrowful, (but) be not sorrowful (on that account).

4150   I will make thee sorrowful and weeping, to the end that I may hide thee from the eyes of the wicked.

I will cause thy temper to be soured with sorrows, in order that the evil eye may be averted from thy face.

Thou art not (really) a hunter and seeker of Me; (nay), thou art My slave and prostrate before My providence.

Thou art thinking of devices whereby thou mayst attain unto Me: (both) in quitting and in seeking Me thou art helpless.

Thy anguish is seeking a means for (attaining unto) Me: I was hearkening yestereve to thy heavy sighs.

4155   I am even able, without this waiting, to give (thee) access and show unto thee the way of passage,

That thou mayst be delivered from this whirlpool of Time and mayst set thy foot upon the treasure of union with Me;

But the sweetness and delights of the resting-place are in proportion to the pain of the journey.

(Only) then wilt thou enjoy thy (native) town and thy kinsfolk when thou sufferest pains and tribulations from exile.'"

Comparison of the true believer's fleeing (from tribulation) and his impatience in affliction to the agitation and restlessness of chickpeas and other pot-herbs when boiling in the pot, and to their running upwards in order to jump out.

Look at a chickpea in the pot, how it leaps up when it is subjected to the fire.

4160   At the time of its being boiled, the chickpea comes up continually to the top of the pot and raises a hundred cries,

Saying, "Why are you setting the fire on me? Since you bought (and approved) me, how are you turning me upside down?"

---

[1] The Prophet said, "Each of you is a shepherd and will be asked concerning his flock."   [2] *I.e.* the Beloved.

The housewife goes on hitting it with the ladle. "No!" says she: "boil nicely and don't jump away from one who makes the fire.

I do not boil you because you are hateful to me: nay, 'tis that you may get taste and savour,

So that you may become nutriment and mingle with the (vital) spirit: this affliction of yours is not on account of (your) being despised.

You, when green and fresh, were drinking water in the garden: 4165 that water-drinking was for the sake of this fire."

His (God's) mercy is prior to His wrath, to the end that by (God's) mercy he (the afflicted person) may suffer affliction.

His (God's) mercy (eternally) preceded His wrath in order that the stock-in-trade, (which is) existence, should come to hand (be acquired);

For, without pleasure, flesh and skin do not grow; and unless they grow, what shall the love of the Friend consume[1]?

If, because of that requirement, acts of wrath come to pass, to the end that you may give up that stock-in-trade,

(Yet) again (afterwards) the Grace (of God) will come in 4170 order to excuse it (the act of wrath), saying, "(Now) thou hast washed thyself (clean) and hast leaped forth from the river (of tribulation)."

She (the housewife) says, "O chickpea, thou didst feed in the springtime: (now) Pain has become thy guest: entertain him well,

That the guest may return (home), giving thanks (for his entertainment), and may relate thy generosity in the presence of the King,

So that the Bestower of favour may come to thee instead of the favour, and that all favours may envy thee.

I am Khalíl (Abraham), and thou art my son: lay thy head before the knife: *lo, I see (in a dream) that I shall sacrifice thee*[2].

Lay thy head before (my) wrath, with heart unmoved, that 4175 I may cut thy throat, like (that of) Ismá'íl (Ishmael).

I will cut off thy head, but this head is the head that is immune from being cut off and (from) dying;

Yet thy giving thyself up is the object of (God's) eternal purpose: O Moslem, thou must seek to give thyself up.

Continue, O chickpea, to boil in tribulation, that neither existence nor self may remain to thee.

If thou hast (formerly) laughed in that (earthly) garden, (yet) thou art the rose of the garden of the spirit and the (spiritual) eye.

---

[1] *I.e.* how can Divine Love manifest itself except through the mortification of the carnal nature?

[2] *Qur'án*, XXXVII, 101, slightly altered.

4180 If thou hast been parted from the garden of water and earth, (yet) thou hast become food in the mouth and hast entered into the living.

Become nutriment and strength and thoughts! (Formerly) thou wert milk (sap): (now) be a lion in the jungles!

By God, thou grewest from His (God's) attributes in the beginning: go back nimbly and fleetly into His attributes.

Thou camest from the cloud and the sun and the sky; then didst thou become (diverse) attributes and ascend to heaven.

Thou camest in the form of rain and heat: thou wilt go into the goodly (Divine) attributes.

4185 Thou wert a part of the sun and the cloud and the stars: thou becamest soul and action and speech and thoughts."

The existence of the animal arose from the death of the plant: (hence the command) "slay me, O trusty friends" is right.

Since there is such a victory for us after the checkmate (of death), (the words) "verily, in my being slain there is a life" are true.

Action and speech and sincerity became the food of the angel, so that by means of this ladder he mounted to heaven,

Just as (when) that morsel became the food of Man, it mounted from (the state of) inanimateness and became possessed of soul.

4190 As regards this topic, a wide (far-reaching) explanation will be given in another place.

"The caravan (of spirits) is incessantly arriving from heaven, that they may traffic (on the earth) and go back again.

Go, then, sweetly and gladly with free-will, not with bitterness and loathing, like a thief.

I am speaking bitter words to thee, in order that I may wash thee (clean) of bitternesses.

The frozen grape is thawed[1] by cold water and lays aside its coldness and congealment.

4195 When, from (having endured) bitterness (self-mortification), thy heart is filled with blood (like the grape), then thou wilt escape from all bitternesses.

A comparison showing how the true believer becomes patient when he understands the inward meaning and the beneficial nature of tribulation.

(If) a dog is not (kept) for hunting, he has no collar: the raw and unboiled is naught but the insipid."

The chickpea said, "Since it is so, O lady, I will gladly boil: give me help in verity!

---

[1] Literally, "is freed," *i.e.* its juice is made to flow.

In this boiling thou art, as it were, my architect: smite me
with the skimming-spoon, for thou smitest very delightfully.

I am as the elephant: beat and brand my head, that I may not
dream of Hindustán and (its) gardens;

So that I may yield myself (submit) to the boiling, to the end 4200
that I may find a way to that embrace (of the Beloved);

Because Man, in (the state of) independence, grows insolent
and becomes hostile, like the dreaming elephant.

When the elephant dreams of Hindustán, he does not hearken
to the driver and displays viciousness."

*(Showing) how the housewife made apologies to the chickpea, and
(explaining) the wise purpose in her keeping the chickpea on
the boil.*

The dame says to it, "Formerly I, like thee, was a part of the
earth.

After I had drunk a (cup of) fiery self-mortification, then I
became an acceptable and worthy one.

For a long while, I boiled in (the world of) Time; for another 4205
long while, in the pot of the body.

By reason of these two boilings I became (a source of) strength
to the senses: I became (animal) spirit: then I became thy teacher.

(Whilst I was) in the inanimate state I used to say (to myself),
'Thou art running (to and fro in agitation) to the end that thou
mayst become (endued with) knowledge and spiritual qualities.'

Since I have become (animal) spirit, now (let me) boil once
more and pass beyond animality."

Beseech God continually that you may not stumble over these
deep sayings and that you may arrive at the (journey's) end,

For many have been led astray by the *Qur'án*: by (clinging to) 4210
that rope a multitude have fallen into the well.

There is no fault in the rope, O perverse man, inasmuch as
you had no desire for (reaching) the top.

*The remainder of the story of the guest of that guest-killing
mosque, and his firmness and sincerity.*

That high-aspiring[1] stranger to the town said, "I will sleep
in this mosque at night.

O mosque, if thou become my Karbalá[2], thou wilt be the
Ka'ba that fulfils my need.

Hark, give me leave, O chosen house, that I may perform a
rope-dance, like Mansúr (Halláj)[3]!

[1] Literally, "seeking the top."
[2] See p. 8, note 1.
[3] *I.e.* "let me enter thee and put my life to the hazard (devote myself to
death), like Halláj." There is a play on the double meaning of *dár* (house and
gallows).

4215   If in counselling (me) ye have become (as) Gabriel, (yet)
Khalíl (Abraham) will not crave succour in the fire[1].

Begone, O (thou who art like) Gabriel, for, having been kindled
(with the flame of love), I, like aloes-wood and ambergris, am
better (when) burnt.

O Gabriel, although thou art helping and guarding (me) like
a brother,

(Yet), O brother, I am eager for the fire: I am not that
(animal) spirit, that I should become more and (then) less."

The animal spirit is increased by fodder: it (the animal spirit)
was a fire and was consumed like firewood.

4220   Had it not become firewood, it would have been fruitful: it
would have prospered unto everlasting and would have caused
prosperity.

Know that this fire is a burning wind: it is a ray of fire, not
the essence thereof.

Assuredly the essence of fire is in the aether: on the earth
there is (only) its ray and shadow (reflexion).

Of necessity, the ray, on account of quivering, does not
endure: it is speedily returning to its source.

Your stature is normally invariable, (but) your shadow is now
short, now long.

4225   Inasmuch as no one finds permanence in the ray, (all) the
reflexions return to (their) origins.

Hark, close thy mouth: Mischief has opened its lips. Dry up!
God best knoweth the right way.

Account of the conception of evil fancies by those deficient in understanding.

Ere this tale reaches the conclusion, there comes from the
envious a vapour of stench.

I am not pained by it, but this kick may break the nerve of a
simple-hearted man's mind.

Well did the Sage of Ghazna set forth the (following) spiritual
parable for the sake of those who are veiled (from perception of
the truth),

4230   (Saying) that if one see in the *Qur'án* naught but words, this
is not surprising on the part of them that have lost the (right)
way,

Since the eye of the blind is sensible of naught but heat from
the beams of the luminous sun.

Suddenly a great booby popped his head out of an ass-stable,
like a railing woman,

---

[1] The guest reminds his critics that Abraham, on the point of being cast
into the fire by Nimrod, refused to invoke the help of Gabriel or any one
except God.

(Saying) that this discourse, namely, the *Mathnawí*, is low; (that) it is the story of the Prophet and (consists of) imitation;

(That) there is no mention of (theosophical) investigation and the sublime mysteries towards which the saints make their steeds gallop;

(That) from the stations of asceticism to the passing away 4235 (from self-existence), step by step up to union with God,

(It contains not) the explanation and definition of every station and stage, so that by means of the wings thereof a man of heart (a mystic) should soar.

When the Book of God (the *Qur'án*) came (down), the unbelievers railed likewise at it too,

Saying, "It is (mere) legends and paltry tales; there is no profound inquiry and lofty speculation;

The little children understand it; 'tis naught but things approved and disapproved—

The account of Joseph, the account of his curly locks, the 4240 account of Jacob and Zalíkhá and her passion.

It is plain, and every one finds the way (to its meaning): where is the exposition in which the intellect becomes lost?"

He (God) said, "If this seems easy to thee, say (compose) one Súra (in the style that is) so 'easy' as this (*Qur'án*).

Let the Jinn and mankind and the skilled among you produce a single verse of this 'easy' (style)."

Commentary on the Tradition of Muṣṭafá (Mohammed), on whom be peace, that the Qur'án hath an exterior (sense) and an interior (sense), and that its interior (sense) hath an interior (sense), (and so on) to seven interior (senses).

Know that the words of the *Qur'án* have an exterior (sense), and under the exterior (sense) an interior (sense), exceedingly overpowering;

And beneath that inward (sense) a third interior (sense), 4245 wherein all intellects become lost.

The fourth interior (sense) of the *Qur'án* none hath perceived at all, except God the peerless and incomparable.

In the *Qur'án* do not thou, O son, regard (only) the exterior: the Devil regards Adam as naught but clay.

The exterior (sense) of the *Qur'án* is like a man's person, for his features are visible, while his spirit is hidden.

A man's paternal and maternal uncles (may see him) for a hundred years, and of his (inward) state not see (so much as) the tip of a hair.

It is explained that the going of the prophets and the saints, on whom be peace, to mountains and caves, is not for the purpose of hiding themselves and on account of their fear of being disturbed by the people, but for the purpose of guiding the people in the right way and inciting them to abandon this world as much as is possible.

4250 As for their saying that the saints are (dwelling) in the mountains in order that they may be hidden from the eyes of men,

In the sight of the people they are higher than a hundred mountains and plant their footsteps on the Seventh Heaven.

Why, then, should he who is beyond a hundred seas and mountains become hidden and seek (refuge in) the mountains?

He has no need to flee to the mountains, he in pursuit of whom the colt, Heaven, has dropped a hundred horse-shoes.

The celestial sphere revolved (so long) and never saw the dust of the spirit[1]; (hence) Heaven donned the garb of mourning.

4255 If, outwardly, the peri is hidden, (yet) Man is a hundred times more hidden than the peris.

In the view of the intelligent, Man is indeed a hundred times more hidden than the peri who is concealed.

Since, in the view of the intelligent, Man is hidden, how (hidden) must be the Adam who is pure (chosen of God) in the unseen world!

Comparison of the form of the saints and the form of the speech of the saints to the form of the rod of Moses and to the form of the incantation of Jesus, peace be on them both!

Man is like the rod of Moses; Man is like the incantation of Jesus.

For the sake of justice and for the sake of decorum, the true believer's heart is in the hand of God, between (His) two fingers.

4260 Its (the rod's) exterior (form) is a piece of wood, but (all created) existence is one mouthful to it when it opens its throat.

In the incantation of Jesus do not regard (merely) the letter and the sound: regard the fact that Death turned and fled from it.

In his incantation do not regard the petty words: consider that the dead sprang up and sat down.

In (the case of) that rod, do not regard the easy getting (of it): regard the fact that it cleft the green sea.

You have seen from afar the black canopy: take a step forward and behold the army!

---

[1] *I.e.* "never saw a trace of the spirit."

From afar you see nothing but the dust: advance a little and 4265
see the man in the dust.

His dust makes eyes bright; his manliness uproots mountains.

When Moses came up from the remotest part of the desert,
at his advent Mount Sinai began to dance.

*Commentary on (the text), O ye mountains, repeat (the praise
    of God) in accord with him, and the birds (likewise).*

The face of David shone with His glory: the mountains sang
plaintively after him.

The mountain became an accompanist to David: both the
minstrels (were) drunken in love for a King.

Came the (Divine) command, "*O ye mountains, repeat (the* 4270
praise of God)": both joined their voices and kept the tune
together.

He (God) said, "O David, thou hast suffered separation: for
My sake thou hast parted from thine intimates."

O lonely stranger who hast become friendless, from whose
heart the fire of longing hath flamed up,

Thou desirest minstrels and singers and boon-companions:
the Eternal One brings the mountains unto thee.

He makes (them) minstrels and singers and pipers: He makes
the mountain blow in measure before thee,

To the end that thou mayst know that, since the mountain is 4275
permitted to sing, the saint (likewise) hath plaintive songs
(uttered) without lips or teeth.

The melody of the particles of that pure-bodied one is reach-
ing his sensuous ear every moment.

His companions hear it not, (but) he hears (it): oh, happy is
the soul that believes in his hidden mystery.

He (the saint) beholds a hundred discourses in himself, while
his companion has gotten no scent (perception thereof).

Within thy heart a hundred questions and a hundred answers
are coming from (the realm of) non-spatiality to thy dwelling-
place.

Thou hearest (them); the ears (of another) do not hear (them), 4280
(even) if he bring his ear nigh to thee.

O deaf man, I grant that truly thou hearest them not; (but)
since thou hast seen their (external) emblem[1], how wilt not thou
believe?

*Reply to him who rails at the Mathnawí on account of
    his being deficient in understanding.*

O railing cur, you are bow-wowing and practising evasion
for the purpose of railing at the *Qur'án.*

_____
[1] *I.e.* spiritual words spoken or written.

This is not such a lion that you will save your life from it or carry off your faith (secure) from the claws of its vengeance.

The *Qur'án* is proclaiming till the Resurrection—"O people devoted to ignorance,

4285   Who were deeming me to be an idle tale and were sowing the seed of raillery and infidelity,

(Now) ye yourselves have seen (the truth of) what ye were scoffing at, (namely), that ye were perishable and an idle tale.

I am the Word of God and subsistent through the (Divine) Essence; I am the Food of the soul of the soul, and (I am) the Jacinth of purity.

I am the Sunlight that hath fallen upon you, but I have not become separate from the Sun.

Lo, I am the Fountain of the Water of Life, that I may deliver the lovers (of God) from death.

4290   If your greed had not raised such a stench, God would have poured a draught (of that Water) on your graves."

Nay; I will accept the rede and counsel of the Sage (of Ghazna): I will not let my heart be sickened (wounded) by every taunt.

Parable of the foal's refusing to drink the water because of the bawling of the grooms.

As he has said in his discourse, the foal and its mother were drinking the water.

Those persons (the grooms) were bawling incessantly at the horses, "Come on! Hey, drink!"

(The noise of) that bawling reached the foal: it was lifting its head and refusing to drink.

4295   Its mother asked, "O foal, why art thou always refusing to drink this water?"

The foal said, "These people are bawling: I am afraid of the occurrence of their shouts.

Therefore my heart is trembling and jumping: dread of the occurrence of the outcry is coming on me."

The mother said, "Ever since the world existed, there have been busybodies of this sort on the earth."

Hark, do your own business, O worthy man: soon will they tear their beards (in sorrow).

4300   The time is restricted, and the abundant water is flowing away: (drink) ere, through being parted (from it), you fall to pieces.

There is a famous conduit, full of the Water of Life: draw the Water, in order that verdure may grow up from you.

We are drinking the water of Khiẓr from the river of the speech of the saints: come, O heedless thirsty man!

If you do not see the water, artfully after the fashion of the blind bring the jug to the river, and dip it in the river.

Forasmuch as you have heard that there is water in this river-bed, (go and try): the blind man must practise conformity.

Carry down to the river the water-skin that has thoughts of 4305 the water, so that you may find your water-skin heavy.

When you have found it heavy, you will be led to infer (the truth): at that moment your heart is delivered from dry conformity.

If the blind man does not see the river-water ocularly, yet he knows, when he finds the jug heavy,

That some water has gone from the river into the jug; for this (jug) was light, and (now) it has become heavy and swollen with water;

"Because," (he will say), "every wind used to sweep me away, (but now) the wind does not sweep me away: my weight has increased."

The foolish are swept away by every gust of desire, because 4310 they have no weight (ballast) of (intellectual) faculties.

The wicked man is an anchorless ship, for he finds no precaution (means of defence) against the perverse (contrary) wind.

To the intelligent man the anchor of intelligence is security: beg (such) an anchor from the intelligent.

Since he (the Sage) has borne away the succours (supplies) of intelligence from the pearl-treasury of that Sea of Bounty,

By such succours (replenishments) the heart is filled with knowledge: it (that knowledge) shoots from the heart, and the eye too becomes illuminated,

Because the light from the heart has settled upon this eye so 4315 that your eye, having become the heart, is (physically) inactive.

When the heart too has come into contact with the intellectual Lights, it bestows a portion thereof on the eyes also.

Know, then, that the blessed Water from Heaven is the inspiration of (men's) hearts and the true explanation (of every mystery).

Let us also, like that foal, drink the water of the stream; let us pay no regard to the evil suggestions of the railer.

(If) you are a follower of the prophets, tread the Way: deem all the railing of (human) creatures to be a (vain and empty) wind.

When have the Masters who have traversed the Way lent ear 4320 to the clamour of curs?

The remainder of the story of the guest in the guest-killing mosque.

Relate what appeared in the mosque to that self-sacrificing valiant man, and what he did.

He slept in the mosque, (but) where (how) in sooth had he sleep? How should a submerged man sleep in the river?

Always, for the lovers (of God) beneath the flood of a (great) passion, there is (only) the sleep of birds and fishes.

At midnight came an awful voice, "I come, I come upon thee, O thou that seekest advantage."

4325   Five times came such a terrible voice, and his heart was being rent piecemeal.

Commentary on the verse (*of the Qur'án*): "And raise the battle-cry against them with thy horsemen and men on foot."

When you earnestly resolve to be religious, the Devil in your nature cries out at you,

"Go not in that direction! Bethink you, O misguided one; for you will become captive to distress and poverty.

You will become destitute, you will be cut off from friends, you will be despised, you will feel sorry."

From fear of the outcry of that accursed Devil you flee away from certain truth into error,

4330   Saying, "Ho, to-morrow is mine and after to-morrow: I will run in the Way of religion, I have (plenty of) time."

Then again you see Death killing your neighbours on left and right, so that the cry (of lamentation) is raised.

Now, in fear of (your) life, you resolve to be religious: for a while, you make yourself a (true) man;

So you put on the armour of knowledge and wisdom, saying, "I will not shrink from any danger."

Again he (the Devil) deceitfully cries out at you—"Be afraid and turn away from the sword of poverty!"

4335   Once more you flee from the Way of Light and cast off that armour of knowledge and virtue.

(For many) years, you are a slave to him because of a cry: you have laid down the blanket (have lain down to rest) in such darkness as this!

Dread of the cry of the devils has bound the people and taken hold of their throats,

Till their souls have become as hopeless of the Light as the spirits of the infidels who dwell in the tombs.

Such is the terror of the cry of that accursed one: how (great) must be the dread of the Divine cry!

4340   Dread of the falcon is (falling) upon the noble partridge: the fly hath no portion of that dread,

Because the falcon is not a hunter of flies: only spiders catch flies.

The spider, (which is) the Devil, hath dominion over flies like you, not over the partridge and the eagle.

The cry of the devils is the drover of the damned; the cry of the Lord is the guardian of the (blessed) saints,

To the end that, by reason of these two cries (being) far distant (from each other), not a drop of the sweet sea may mingle with the briny sea.

How the talismanic cry came at midnight to (the ears of) the guest in the mosque.

Now hear the tale of the terrible cry, by which that good- 4345 fortuned man was not dismayed[1].

He said, "How should I fear? for this is the drum of the Festival. Let the drum fear, since blows belong to it.

O empty drums without hearts, your share in the festival of the spirit is (naught but) blows of the (drum-)stick.

The Resurrection is the Festival, and the irreligious are the drum: we, like the festive folk, are laughing as the rose."

Now hear how, when this drum boomed, he (the guest) cooks the pot containing the broth of felicity.

When that man of insight heard the drum, he said, "How 4350 should my heart be afraid of the drum of the Festival?"

He said to himself, "Beware, do not let thy heart tremble, for (only) the souls of the faint-hearted who lack faith have died at this (noise of the drum).

The time has come for me, like Ḥaydar ('Alí), to seize a kingdom, or to quit the body."

He sprang up and shouted, "O prince, lo, here am I: if thou art a man, come on!"

At his voice that talisman instantly was shattered: the gold poured down, diverse sorts, in every direction.

So much gold poured down that the youth feared lest, from 4355 its abundance, it might block the doorway.

Afterwards that ready lion (valiant man) rose up, and till dawn he was carrying out the gold

And burying it and coming (back) to it once more with sack and bag.

That self-devoting one laid by (great) stores thereof, to the confusion of (in despite of) the timidity of the backsliders.

(The thought that) this (is) external (material) gold has occurred to the mind of every blind, God-forsaken [2] gold-worshipper.

(Similarly) children break potsherds, give the name of gold 4360 (to the fragments), and put them in their skirts.

When in that game you mention the name of gold, (the idea of) that (potsherd) crosses the child's mind.

---

[1] Literally, "did not go from (his) place."
[2] Literally, "far (from God)."

Nay, ('tis) the gold stamped with the Divine stamp, (the gold) which does not become obsolete, (but) is everlasting;

The gold from which this (worldly) gold gained lustre and derived sheen and splendour and brilliance;

The gold whereby the heart is made rich: it surpasses the moon in brightness.

4365 That mosque was the candle, and he (the guest) was the moth: that man of moth-like nature gambled himself away (sacrificed himself).

It burnt his wings, but it complied with him (granted his desire): his throwing (himself into the flame) was very blessed.

That man of happy fortune was like Moses who beheld a fire in the direction of the tree[1].

Since the (Divine) favours were plenteously bestowed on him, he (only) fancied it was fire, and really it was the Light.

O son, when you see a man of God, you suppose (that you see) in him the fire of human nature.

4370 You are coming (to that conclusion) from yourself, and that (human nature) is in you (not in him): the fire and thorns of vain opinion are in this quarter.

He is the tree of Moses and filled with radiance: come, now, call him the Light, do not call him fire.

Did not the weaning from this world seem (as) a fire? The pilgrims went (on their way), and that (weaning) was really the Light.

Know, then, that the Candle of Religion is always mounting (shining more and more): this is not like the candle of flames.

This (flaming candle) seems to be Light, (but) it burns its friend, while that (Candle of Religion) is fire in appearance, but is (delicious as) roses to (its) visitors.

4375 The former is like a complaisant (friend), but it is a burner, while that (other) is an illuminator of the heart at the moment of union.

To those present (with God) the appearance of the spark of pure and worthy Light is luminous, while to those far (from God) it is like fire.

The meeting of the lover with the Ṣadr-i Jahán.

The man of Bukhárá also cast himself upon the candle: because of his passion that suffering had become easy to him.

His burning sighs went up to heaven: kindness (for him) came into the heart of the Ṣadr-i Jahán,

(Who) said, (communing) with himself at dawn, "O (Thou who art) One, how fareth that distraught wanderer of Ours?

[1] *Qur'án*, XXVIII, 29.

He committed a sin, and We saw (it), but he was not well 4380
acquainted with Our mercy.

The sinner's heart becomes afraid of Us, but in his fear there
are a hundred hopes.

I frighten the impudent man who has lost the (right) way:
why should I frighten him who is afraid?

Fire is used for the cold pot, not for that (pot) which is
boiling over.

I frighten the unafraid by (My) knowledge; I take away the
fear of the afraid by (My) clemency.

I am a patcher: I put the patch in (its proper) place; I give 4385
drink to every one in due measure."

A man's inmost consciousness is like the root of a tree; hence
his leaves grow from the hard wood.

The leaves grow according to the root, in the tree and in souls
and in minds.

From the trees of faithfulness there are wings (that soar) to
heaven[1]: *its root is fast (in the earth), and its branch is in
the sky.*

Since through love grew the wing (that soars) to heaven, how
should it not grow in the heart of the Ṣadr-i Jahán?

Forgiveness of the sin was surging in his heart, forasmuch as 4390
there is a window from each heart to (every other) heart;

For assuredly there is a window from heart to heart: they are
not separate and far (from each other), like two bodies.

The earthenware (basins) of two lamps are not joined, but
their light is mingled in (its) passage.

No lover, in sooth, is seeking union without his loved one
seeking him;

But the love of lovers makes the body (thin as) a bowstring,
(while) the love of loved ones makes it comely and fat.

When the lightning of love for the beloved has shot into *this* 4395
heart, know that there is love in *that* heart.

When love for God has been doubled in thy heart, without
any doubt God hath love for thee.

No sound of clapping comes forth from one hand of thine
without the other hand.

The thirsty man is moaning, "O delicious water!" The
water moans too, saying, "Where is the water-drinker?"

This thirst in our souls is the attraction exerted by the Water:
we are Its, and It is ours.

The Wisdom of God in destiny and in decree made us lovers 4400
of one another.

Because of that fore-ordainment all the particles of the world
are paired as mates and are in love with their own mate.

---

[1] The two oldest MSS read پرها (wings); the rest have برها (fruits).

Every particle of the universe is desiring its mate, just like amber and the blade of straw.

Heaven says to the earth, "Welcome! To thee I am (in the same relation) as the iron and the magnet."

In (the view of) the intellect, heaven is man and the earth woman: whatever that (heaven) casts forth this (earth) fosters.

4405   When it (the earth) hath no heat remaining, it (heaven) sends it; when no freshness and moisture remains, it bestows it.

The terrene sign (of the zodiac) is (supplying) replenishment to the dust of the earth; the aqueous sign produces freshness therein;

The aerial sign wafts the clouds towards it, that they may sweep away the pestilential vapours;

The fiery sign is the source of the sun's heat, (which is) like a frying-pan (made) red-hot, back and front, by fire.

Heaven is turning giddily in (the world of) Time, like men (prowling) around (in search of) gain for the wife's sake;

4410   And this earth practises housewiferies: it attends to births and to suckling that (which it bears).

Therefore regard earth and heaven as endowed with intelligence, since they do the work of intelligent beings.

Unless these two sweethearts are tasting (delight) from one another, then why are they creeping together like mates?

Without the earth how should roses and *arghawán*-flowers grow? What, then, would be born of the water and heat of heaven?

The desire (implanted) in the female for the male is to the end that they may perfect each other's work.

4415   God put desire in man and woman in order that the world should be preserved by this union.

He also implants the desire of every part for another part: from the union of both an act of generation results.

Likewise night and day are in mutual embrace: (they are) different in appearance, but (are really) in agreement.

Day and night, outwardly, are two contraries and enemies, but they both attend on one truth—

Each desiring the other, like kinsfolk, for the sake of perfecting their action and work.

4420   (Both serve one purpose) because, without night, the nature (of man) would receive no income: what, then, should the days expend[1]?

---

[1] *I.e.* night provides the energy which is expended by day.

*How each element attracts its congener that has been imprisoned in
the human constitution by the non-homogeneous (elements).*

Earth says to the earth of the body, "Return! Take leave of
the spirit, come to me like the dust.

Thou art my congener, thou art more suited (to be) with me:
'tis better that thou shouldst escape from that body and that
moisture."

It answers, "Yes; but I am fettered, although like thee I am
weary of separation."

The waters seek the moisture of the body, saying, "O mois-
ture, come back to us from exile."

The aether is calling the heat of the body, saying, "Thou art 4425
of fire: take the way to thy origin."

There are two-and-seventy diseases in the body, (caused) by
the elements pulling without cord.

Disease comes to shatter the body, so that the elements may
abandon each other.

These elements are four birds with their legs tied (together):
death and sickness and disease loose their legs.

When it (death) has released their legs from one another,
assuredly every bird-element flies away.

The pull between these originals and derivatives continually 4430
implants some pain in our bodies,

In order that it may rend these coalitions asunder (and that)
each part, like a bird[1], may fly to its home;

(But) Divine Providence hinders them from this hastening
and keeps them together in health till the appointed term,

And says, "O parts, the term is not certainly known (to you):
'tis useless for you to take wing before the term."

Inasmuch as every part (of the body) seeks support[2], what
must be the state of the soul, a stranger, in separation (from its
home)?

*How likewise the soul is drawn to the world of spirits, and how it
craves and desires its home, and becomes severed from the bodily
parts which are a fetter on the leg of the spiritual falcon.*

It (the soul) says, "O my base earthly parts, my exile is more 4435
bitter (than yours): I am celestial."

The desire of the body for green herbs and running water is
because its origin is from those;

The desire of the soul is for Life and for the Living One, be-
cause its origin is the Infinite Soul.

The desire of the soul is for wisdom and the sciences; the
desire of the body is for orchards and meadows and vines.

---

[1] Literally, "the bird, (which is) each part."
[2] *I.e.* seeks to rejoin its whole.

The desire of the soul is for ascent and exaltedness; the desire of the body is for gain and the means of procuring fodder.

4440   That exaltedness too hath desire and love towards the soul: from this (fact) understand (the meaning of) *He loves them* and *they love (Him).*

If I explain this, 'twill be endless: the *Mathnawí* will amount to eighty volumes.

The gist is that whenever any one seeks, the soul of the object sought by him is desiring him.

(Whether it be) man, animal, plant, or mineral, every object of desire is in love with everything that is without (has not attained to) the object of desire.

Those who are without their object of desire attach themselves to an object of desire, and those desired ones draw them (on);

4445   But the desire of the lovers makes them lean, (while) the desire of the loved ones makes them fair and beauteous.

The love of the loved ones illumines the cheeks; the love of the lover consumes his soul.

The amber loves (the straw) with the appearance of wanting naught, (while) the straw is making efforts (to advance) on that long road.

Leave this (topic). The love of that thirsty-mouthed man shone (was reflected) in the breast of the Ṣadr-i Jahán.

The smoke of the love and pain of the fire-temple (his burning heart) entered his lord (and) turned into compassion.

4450   But on account of (his) glory and pride and magnificence he was ashamed to inquire for him:

His mercy had begun to yearn after that lowly man, (but) his majesty hindered (him) from (showing) this kindness.

The intellect is bewildered, wondering whether this one (the Ṣadr-i Jahán) attracted him (the lover), or whether the attraction came from that quarter (from the lover) to this side.

Abandon presumption, for thou art ignorant of this. Close thy lips: God best knoweth the secret.

Henceforth I will bury this topic. That Drawer is drawing me (in another direction): what can I do?

4455   Who is he that is drawing thee, O solicitous one? He who doth not allow thee to utter this word.

Thou makest a hundred resolutions to journey (to a certain spot): He draweth thee to some other place.

He turns the (horse's) bridle in every direction in order that the untrained horse may gain knowledge of the rider.

The clever horse is well-paced because it knows that the rider is (mounted) on it.

He fixed thy heart on a hundred passionate desires, disappointed thee, and then broke thy heart.

Inasmuch as He broke the wings of that first intention (of 4460 thine), how was not the existence of the Wing-breaker perfectly established (in thy mind)?

Since His ordainment snapped the cord of thy contrivance, how was not God's ordainment perfectly established (clearly proven) to thee?

(Showing that) the annulment and destruction of (human) resolutions (is) in order to let man know that He (God) is the Lord and the Almighty; and His occasional non-annulment of his (man's) resolution and His carrying it into effect (is) in order that hope may urge him to form a resolution, so that He again may destroy it, to the end that warning may follow on warning.

In the course of events your resolutions and purposes now and then come right (are fulfilled),

In order that, through hope of that (fulfilment), your heart may form an intention, and that He may once more destroy your intention.

For if He were to keep you wholly unsuccessful, your heart would despair: how would it sow (the seed of) expectation?

And unless it sowed (the seed of) expectation, how from its 4465 barrenness would its subjection (to the Divine will) become apparent to it?

By their failures (to achieve success) the lovers are made aware of their Lord.

Unsuccess is the guide to Paradise: hearken, O man of goodly nature, to (the tradition), "Paradise is encompassed (with pains)."

(Granted) that all that you desire is broken-legged (unsuccessful), then there is One whose pleasure is fulfilled.

Therefore the sincere (believers) have become broken (abased) before Him; but where indeed is (their abasement in comparison with) the abasement of those who love (Him)?

The intelligent are abased before Him from necessity; the 4470 lovers are abased with hundredfold free-will.

The intelligent are bond-slaves to Him; the lovers are like sugar and candy to Him[1].

"*Come against your will*" is the toggle for the intelligent; "*come willingly*" is the spring-time of them that have lost their hearts.

How the Prophet, on whom be peace, looked at the captives ana smiled and said, "I marvel at folk who are dragged to Paradise in chains and shackles."

The Prophet saw a troop of captives being taken along, and they were in loud lamentation.

---

[1] *I.e.* they show sweetness and delight in resigning themselves to His will.

That wary Lion saw them in chains: (he saw them) looking askance at him,

4475 So that each (of them) was gnashing his teeth and chewing his lips in anger against the veracious Prophet;

(But) notwithstanding that anger, they dare not utter a word, because they are in the ten-maund[1] chain of violence.

Their custodian is marching them along to the city: he is taking them by force from the land of the infidels.

(They say to each other), "He (the Prophet) will not accept any ransom or any gold: no intercession is coming from any prince.

He is called a mercy to the world, and he is cutting the throats and gullets of a (whole) world (of people)."

4480 With a thousand (feelings of) disbelief they marched along, railing under their breath at the actions of the (spiritual) king,

(Saying), "We remedied (our former troubles), but in this case there is no remedy: truly this man's heart is not inferior (in hardness) to a rock.

We, thousands of men brave as lions, (fighting) with two or three feeble and half-dead naked fellows,

Are left helpless like this: is it on account of (our) wrong-doing or (unlucky) stars, or is it sorcery?

His fortune tore up our fortune; our throne was overturned by his throne.

4485 If his cause became mighty (was made to prevail) by sorcery, we too practised sorcery: how did not it succeed?

[*Commentary on the verse (of the Qur'án),* "If ye ask for a decision, the decision has indeed come to you. *O railers, ye were saying,* 'Give the decision and victory to us or to Mohammed, whichever is in the right'; *and ye were saying this in order that it might be supposed that ye were seeking the right disinterestedly. Now We have given the victory to Mohammed, to the end that ye may see the champion of the right.*"]

We besought the idols and God, saying, 'Destroy us if we are untrue.

Whichever is right and true, between us and him, give the victory to that one and desire him to be victorious.'

Ofttimes we made this invocation and (bowed down in) prayer before Lát and 'Uzzá and Manát,

Saying, 'If he is in the right, make him manifest[2]; if he is not in the right, make him subject to us.'

4490 When we recognised (what had come to pass), he was the one to whom victory was given: we all were darkness, he was the light.

_____
[1] About twenty pounds in weight.   [2] *I.e.* show him to be in the right.

This is our answer (from God)—'(Concerning) that which ye desired (to know), it has become evident that ye are the un-true.'"

Then, again, they were blindfolding (hiding) this thought from their reflective faculty and banishing it from their memory,

Saying, "This thought too has arisen from our ill-luck, (namely, the thought) that his being in the right should be perfectly established (proven beyond doubt) in our minds.

What, indeed, does it matter if he has prevailed (against us) several times? Time (Fortune) brings every one to predominance (now and then).

We also were made successful by the Days (Fortune), and at 4495 times became victorious over him."

(But) again they were saying (to themselves), "Although he was defeated, it was not disgraceful and vile like our defeat,"

Because in (the hour of) defeat (his) good fortune gave him underhand a hundred secret joys;

For he did not at all resemble one defeated, as he felt no sorrow or distress thereat,

Since to be vanquished is the mark of the true believers; yet in the true believer's defeat there is goodness.

If you crush some musk or ambergris, you will fill a (whole) 4500 world with (a scent like) the exhalation of sweet herbs;

And if you suddenly crush the dung of an ass, the houses will be filled to the top with stench.

At the moment of the (Prophet's) ignominious return from Ḥudaybiya, the empire of *Lo, We have opened (to thee the way to a conspicuous) victory* proclaimed itself[1].

The hidden reason why God most High gave the title of "victory" to the return of the Prophet, on whom be peace, from Ḥudaybiya without having gained his purpose: as (God said), "Lo, We have opened (to thee the way to) victory"; for it was a locking in appearance (only), and in reality an opening, just as the crushing of musk is apparently a crushing, but really the confirmation of its muskiness and the exhibition of its virtues in their perfection.

From the (Divine) empire came to him the message, "Go, be not saddened by the withholding of this victory,

For in this present abasement of thee there are victories: lo, such and such a fortress, such and such a town, are (given) to thee."

Consider, after all, when he retreated in haste, what (great 4505 things) he did[2] against Qurayẓa and Naḍír.

[1] Literally, "beat the drum."
[2] Literally, "what proceeded from him."

The fortresses, also, round those two settlements submitted (to him), and (many) advantages (in the shape) of spoils (came into his hands).

And if that be not so[1], consider that this class (of persons)[2] are sorrowful and woeful and distraught and enamoured (of God).

They eat the poison of abasement, like sugar; they feed, like camels, on the thistle of sorrows.

(This they do) for the sake of the sorrow itself, not for the sake of relief (from sorrow): in their eyes this lowliness is as a ladder.

4510   So glad are they at the bottom of the pit that they are afraid of the throne and the tiara.

Every place where the Beloved himself is their companion is above the sky, not below the earth.

Commentary on the Tradition that Muṣṭafá (Mohammed), on whom be peace, said, "Do not declare me to be more excellent than Yúnus ibn Mattá."

The Prophet said, "No preference is (to be given) to my ascension as being superior to the ascension of Yúnus (Jonah).

Mine was up to heaven, and his was down below (in the belly of the Fish), because nighness unto God is beyond calculation."

To be nigh (unto God) is not to go up or down: to be nigh unto God is to escape from the prison of existence.

4515   What room hath non-existence for "up" and "down"? Non-existence hath no "soon" or "far" or "late."

The laboratory and treasure of God is in non-existence. Thou art deluded by existence: how shouldst thou know what non-existence is?

The sum of the matter (is that) this defeat of theirs[3], O sire, does not resemble our[4] defeat at all.

They rejoice in being abased and destroyed, just as we (rejoice) in the hour of success and honour.

The provision of unprovidedness is all (that has been assigned to the Prophet as) his fief: poverty and lowliness are his pride and glory.

4520   One (of the captives) said, "If that adversary (of ours) is such (as you describe), how did he laugh when he saw us bound (in chains)?

Since (as you assert) he has been transmuted, and (since) his joy is not caused by this (worldly) prison and this freedom of his (from worldly embarrassments),

---

[1] *I.e.* even if there be no victory in defeat.
[2] The prophets and saints.
[3] The true believers.   [4] The infidels.

How, then, did he rejoice at the subjection of (his) enemies?
How was he puffed up by this victory and conquest?

His soul rejoiced because he easily gained the (Divine) help
and the upper hand and the victory over fierce lions (like us).

Hence we knew that he is not free (from the bondage of the
flesh), and that only on account of this world is he happy and
glad at heart.

Else, how should he laugh (at us)? for the otherworldly are 4525
compassionate and kind to the evil and the good (alike)."

Thus did those captives mutter to each other under their
breath in discussing that (question),

(Saying, "Beware) lest the custodian hear (us) and spring
upon us and personally carry our words to the ear of that
(spiritual) Sultan."

How the Prophet, on whom be peace, became aware of their chiding him for his exultation.

Though the custodian did not hear those words, they entered
into the ear that was (hearing) from the presence (of God).

The scent of Joseph's spirit was not perceived by its keeper,
but Jacob inhaled it.

The devils on the high front of Heaven do not hear the secret 4530
of the mystery-knowing Tablet;

(But when) Mohammed went to sleep and reclined (on his
bed), the secret came (to him) and circled round him.

He whose allotted portion is open (for him to take) eats the
sweetmeat, not he whose fingers are long.

The gleaming star became a watchman and drove the devils
away, saying, "Abandon theft and receive the secret from
Aḥmad (Mohammed)."

O thou whose eyes from early (in the day) are (turned) towards
(thy) shop, hark, go to the mosque and seek the portion allotted
by God.

The Prophet, then, apprehended their words and said, "That 4535
laughter of mine was not from hostility.

They (the captives) are dead and rotted by decay: in my
judgement it is not the part of a (true) man to kill the dead.

Who are they indeed? for the moon is split when I plant my
foot on the battle-field.

At the time when ye were free and powerful, I was seeing you
bound (in chains), like this.

O thou that pridest thyself on thy possessions and household,
in the view of the intelligent thou art (as) the camel on the
water-spout[1].

---

[1] *I.e.* on the brink of destruction.

4540   (Ever) since the bowl, (which is) the bodily form, fell from
the roof[1], there has rolled before my (inward) eye (the reality
denoted by the words) 'Everything that is (destined) to come
shall come.'

I look on the unripe grape, and I see the wine clearly; I look
on nonentity, and I see the entity clearly.

I look on the inmost consciousness, and I see a universe
hidden, (with) Adam and Eve not (yet) arisen from the world.

You I have seen, fettered and overthrown and abject, at the
time (when mankind were assembled in the shape) of ants (on
the Day) of *Alast*[2].

That which I had (already) known was not increased by the
coming into existence of the pillarless heaven.

4545   I have ever seen you (fallen) headlong, ere I grew from the
water and the clay.

I did not see (anything) new, that I should rejoice thereat:
I used to see this (same thing) during your former prosperity.

Bound in (the chains of) invisible Wrath—and then what
(a fearful) Wrath!—ye were eating sugar wherein poison was
contained.

If thy enemy delight in eating such a poisonous sugar, what
envy of him would come to thee?

Ye were eating that poison with glee, (while) Death had
secretly laid hold of both your ears.

4550   I did not make war for the sake of gaining victory and con-
quering the world,

For this world is a carcase and carrion and vile: how should
I be covetous of such carrion as this?

I am not a dog that I should tear off the top-knot of the dead;
I am (like) Jesus: I come to make him (the dead) living.

I was cleaving the battle-ranks for the purpose that I might
deliver you from destruction.

I do not cut men's throats in order that power and glory and
followers may be mine,

4555   (But) I cut some throats in order that a (whole) world (of
people) may obtain deliverance from those throats,

For ye in your ignorance make a habit of rushing thus, like
moths, at the fire,

(While) I, (furiously) as a drunken man, drive you away with
both hands (to save you) from falling into the fire.

That which ye deemed victories for yourselves—(thereby) ye
were sowing the seed of your damnation.

Ye were calling one another most earnestly (to fight against
me), (and by doing so) ye were riding your horses towards the
dragon.

---

[1] *I.e.* ever since the illusion of my bodily existence was shattered.
[2] See *Qur'án*, VII, 171.

Ye were overpowering (me), whilst in the very act of over- 4560
powering ye yourselves were being overpowered by the lion
(which is) Time."

Showing that the rebellious sinner in the very act of overpowering
is overpowered, and in the very moment of victory is made
captive.

The robber overpowered (murdered) the merchant and
carried off the gold: he was just engaged in that (business),
(when) the magistrate arrived.

If at that time he had fled from the merchant, how should the
magistrate have set the police on him?

The robber's overpowering (the merchant) was (in reality)
his being overpowered (and punished), because his act of
violence took away his head (life).

(His) prevailing over the merchant becomes a trap for him,
in order that the magistrate may arrive and take retaliation (on
the murderer).

O thou that hast become mighty over the people and art 4565
steeped in warfare and victory,

That One (God) hath purposely caused them to be routed,
that all the while drawing thee on He may (at last) bring thee
into the net.

Beware, draw rein! Do not push on in pursuit of this fugitive,
lest thou have thy nostrils pierced with a nose-ring.

When by this device He hath drawn thee into the trap, after
that thou wilt see the onset (of the people) pressing in crowds
(upon thee).

When did the intellect (ever) rejoice in this victory, inasmuch
as in this victory it saw ruin?

The intellect is keen-eyed, possessed of foresight[1], for God 4570
hath powdered it with His own collyrium.

The Prophet said that the folk of (destined for) Paradise are
feeble (worsted) in quarrels, because of (their noble) accom-
plishments—

Because of the perfection of their prudence and thinking ill
(of themselves), not from deficiency (of intellect) and cowardice
and weakness of (religious) faith.

In giving the advantage (to their enemies) they have hearkened
in secret to the wisdom of (the text), *Had not there been true-*
believing men....

To keep their hands off the accursed infidels became a duty
for the sake of delivering the true believers.

Read the story of the covenant of Ḥudaybiya: (*it was*) *He* 4575
(*who*) *restrained your hands* (*from them*): from that (saying) per-
ceive (what is the meaning of) the whole (story).

[1] Literally, "a seer of what is in front (of it)."

Even in victory he (the Prophet) deemed himself subdued by the snare of Divine Majesty.

" 'Tis not because I suddenly marched against you before dawn (and took you captive) that I laugh at your chains;

I laugh because I am dragging you in chains and shackles to the cypress-garden and the roses (of Paradise).

O wonder, that we are bringing you in bonds from the merciless fire to the place abounding in verdure;

4580 With heavy chains I am dragging you from the direction of Hell to the everlasting Paradise."

Every blind follower in this Way, be he good or evil, He (God) is dragging, bound like that, into His Presence.

All go along this Way in the chains of fear and tribulation, except the saints.

They are dragged along this Way reluctantly, except those persons who are acquainted with the mysteries of the (Divine) action.

Endeavour that thy (inward) light become radiant, so that thy travelling (in the path of devotion) and service (to God) may be made easy.

4585 You take children to school by force, because they are blind to the benefits (of knowledge);

(But) when he (the child) becomes aware (of the benefits), he runs to school: his soul expands (with joy) at going.

A child goes to school in sore distress because he has seen nothing of the wages for his work;

When he puts in his purse a single *dáng* earned by his handiwork, then he goes without sleep at night, like the thief.

Endeavour that the wages for obedience (to God) may arrive: then you will envy the obedient.

4590 (The command) *come against your will* is for him that has become a blind follower (of religion); *come willingly* is for him that is moulded of sincerity.

The former loves God for the sake of some (secondary) cause, while the other hath indeed a pure disinterested love.

The former loves the Nurse, but for the sake of the milk, while the other has given his heart for the sake of this Veiled One.

The child (the blind follower) hath no knowledge of Her beauty: he hath no desire of Her in his heart except for milk,

While the other is, truly, the lover of the Nurse: he is disinterested, single-minded in (passionate) love.

4595 Hence he that loves God because of hope and fear reads studiously the book of blind conformity,

While he that loves God for God's sake—where is he? for he is apart from (all) self-interests and (secondary) causes.

Whether he be like this or like that, inasmuch as he is a seeker (of God), God's attraction is drawing him towards God.

Whether he love God for something other than He, that he may continually partake of His good,

Or whether he love God for His very Self, for naught besides Him, in fear of separation from Him—

The quests and seekings of both (these lovers) are from that 4600 Source: this captivation of the heart is from that Heart-ravisher.

How the Beloved attracts the lover in such wise that the lover neither knows it nor hopes for it, nor does it occur to his mind, nor does any trace of that attraction appear in the lover except the fear that is mingled with despair, though he still perseveres in the quest.

We came to this point (in the tale), that if the attraction of that lover had not been hidden in the Ṣadr-i Jahán,

How would he (the lover) have been impatient of separation, and how would he have come running back to his home?

The desire of loved ones is hidden and veiled; the desire of the lover is (accompanied) with a hundred drums and trumpets.

Here is (the place for) a story (worthy) of consideration, but the man of Bukhárá has become desperate from waiting expectantly;

(So) we omit it, for he is (engaged) in search and seeking, that 4605 before death he may see the face of his beloved,

To the end that he may escape from death and gain deliverance, because the sight of the beloved is the Water of Life.

Any one the sight of whom does not repel death is not the beloved, for he hath neither fruit nor leaf.

The (essential) matter, O intoxicated longing lover, is that matter in which death, if it befall thee, is sweet.

O youth, the token of sincerity of faith is that (matter) in which death comes sweet to thee.

If thy faith, O (dear) soul, is not like this, it is not perfect: go, 4610 seek to make (thy) religion perfect.

Whosoever in (this) matter of thine has become death-loving (and desires thy death) without dislike (without being hateful) to thy heart, he is (thy) beloved.

When dislike is gone, verily 'tis not death: 'tis (only) the semblance of death, and (in reality) 'tis a migration.

When dislike is gone, dying becomes advantageous; hence it comes true that death is repelled.

The beloved is God and the person to whom He hath said, "Thou art Mine and I am thine."

4615 Now listen, for the lover is coming whom Love bound *with a cord of palm-fibre.*

When he beheld the countenance of the Ṣadr-i Jahán, you might say the bird, his spirit, flew out of his body.

His body fell like dry wood: his vital spirit became cold from the crown of his head[1] to his toes.

Whatsoever they applied of incense and rose-water, he neither stirred nor spoke[2].

When the King saw his saffron-coloured (pallid) face, he dismounted from his steed (and came) towards him.

4620 He said, "The lover hotly seeks the beloved: when the beloved comes, the lover is gone."

Thou art a lover of God, and God is such that when He comes there is not a single hair of thee (remaining).

At that look (of His) a hundred like thee vanish away: methinks, sire, thou art in love with self-naughting.

Thou art a shadow and in love with the sun: the sun comes, the shadow is naughted speedily.

How, in the presence of Solomon, on whom be peace, the gnat appealed for justice against the Wind.

The gnat came from the garden and the grass, and the gnat began to demand justice from Solomon,

4625 Saying, "O Solomon, thou dealest out justice to the devils and the children of men and the Jinn.

Bird and fish are under the protection of thy justice: who is the lost one whom thy bounty hath not sought out?

Give justice to us, for we are very miserable: we are deprived of the orchard and the rose-garden.

The difficulties of every weakling are solved by thee: the gnat in sooth is the (proverbial) similitude for weakness.

We are celebrated for weakness and frailty[3]: thou art celebrated for kindness and care of the lowly.

4630 O thou who hast reached the limit in (traversing) the stages of Power, (while) we have reached the limit in failure and aberration,

Do justice, relieve us from this sorrow, take our hand (to help us), O thou whose hand is the hand of God."

Then Solomon said, "O seeker of equity, tell (me), against whom art thou demanding justice and equity?

Who is the oppressor that in (his) insolence[4] has done thee injury and scratched thy face?

---

[1] Reading فَرْق with *sukún.*
[2] Literally, "came to speech."
[3] Literally, "broken-wingedness."
[4] Literally, "wind and moustache," "bluster."

Oh, wonderful! Where, in Our epoch, is the oppressor that is not in Our prison and chains?

When We were born, on that day Injustice died: who, then, 4635 hath produced (committed) in Our epoch an act of injustice?

When the light dawned, the darkness vanished: darkness is the origin and support of injustice.

Look, (some of) the devils are doing work and service; the others are bound in shackles and bonds.

The origin of the injustice of the oppressors was from the devil: the devil is in bondage: how did violence appear?

(The Divine Will uttered in) 'Be, and it was' hath bestowed the kingdom on Us, that the people may not cry out in lament to Heaven;

That burning sighs[1] may not soar upward; that the sky and 4640 the stars[2] may not be shaken;

That the empyrean may not tremble at the orphan's wail; that no (living) soul may be marred by violence.

We established a law (of justice) throughout the kingdoms (of the earth), to the end that no (cry of) 'O Lord!' should go up to the skies.

O oppressed one, do not look to Heaven, for thou hast a heavenly king in the temporal world."

The gnat said, "My appeal is against the hand (might) of the Wind, for he opened the two hands of oppression against us.

Through his oppression we are in sore straits: with closed 4645 lips we are drinking blood (suffering torment) from him."

How Solomon, on whom be peace, commanded the plaintiff gnat to bring its adversary to the court of judgement.

Then Solomon said, "O thou with the pretty voice, it behoves thee to hearken with (all thy) soul to the command of God.

God hath said to me, 'Beware, O Judge! Do not hear one litigant without the other litigant.

Until both litigants come into the presence, the truth does not come to light before the judge.

If the (one) litigant alone raise a hundred clamours, beware, beware! Do not accept his word without (hearing) his adversary.'

I dare not avert my face from the (Divine) command. Go, 4650 bring thy adversary before me."

It (the gnat) said, "Thy words are an argument (conclusive) and sound. My adversary is the Wind, and he is in thy jurisdiction."

The King shouted, "O East-wind, the gnat complains of thy injustice: come!

---

[1] Literally, "smokes."
[2] Literally, "Suhá," the name of a small star.

Hark, come face to face with thy adversary and reply to thy adversary and rebut thy opponent."

When the Wind heard (the summons), he came very rapidly: the gnat at once took to flight.

4655 Then Solomon said, "O gnat, where (art thou going)? Stop, that I may pass judgement on (you) both."

It (the gnat) answered, "O King, my death is from his being: verily, this day of mine is black from his smoke.

Since he has come, where shall I find rest? for he wrings the (vital) breath out of my body."

Even such is the seeker of the Court of God: when God comes, the seeker is naughted.

Although that union (with God) is immortality on immortality, yet at first that immortality (baqá) consists in dying to self (faná).

4660 The reflexions that are seeking the Light are naughted when His Light appears.

How should the reason remain when He bids it go?[1] *Everything is perishing except His Face.*

Before His Face the existent and the non-existent perish: existence in non-existence is in sooth a marvellous thing!

In this place of presence (all) minds are lost beyond control; when the pen reaches this point, it breaks.

How the Beloved caressed the senseless lover, that he might return to his senses.

The Ṣadr-i Jahán, from kindness, was drawing him little by little from senselessness into (the capacity for) clear expression.

4665 The Prince cried into his ear, "O beggar, I bring gold to scatter o'er thee: spread out thy skirt.

Thy spirit, which was quivering (with distress) in separation from me—since I have come to protect it, how has it fled?

O thou who hast suffered heat and cold in separation from me, come to thyself from selflessness and return!"

The domestic fowl, in the manner of a host, foolishly brings a camel to her house.

When the camel set foot in the hen's house, the house was destroyed and the roof fell in.

4670 The hen's house is our (weak) intelligence and understanding: the good intelligence is a seeker of God's she-camel.

When the she-camel put her head into its water and clay, neither its clay remained there (in existence) nor its soul and heart.

Pre-eminence in love made Man overweening: because of this desire for excess he is *very unjust* and *very ignorant.*

---

[1] Literally, "when He gives (it its) head, *i.e.* dismisses (it)."

He is ignorant, and in this difficult chase the hare is clasping a lion in his arms.

How would he clasp the lion in his arms, if he knew and saw the lion?

He is unjust to himself and to his own soul: behold an in- 4675 justice that bears away the ball (the palm) from (all) justices!

His ignorance is the teacher to (all) knowledges, his injustice has become the right way for (all) justices.

He (the Ṣadr-i Jahán) took his (the lover's) hand, saying, "This man whose breath has departed will (only) then come (to life) when I give him (spiritual) breath.

When this man whose body is dead shall become living through Me, (then) it will be My spirit that turns its face towards Me.

By means of this spirit I make him possessed of high estate: (only) the spirit that I give sees (experiences) My bounty.

The unfamiliar (unprivileged) spirit does not see the face of 4680 the Beloved: (none sees it) except that spirit whose origin is from His dwelling-place.

Butcher-like, I breathe upon this dear friend, in order that his goodly inward part may leave the skin."

He said, "O spirit that hast fled from tribulation, We have opened the door to union with Us: welcome!

O thou whose selflessness and intoxication is (caused by) Our Self, O thou whose being is incessantly (derived) from Our Being,

Now, without lip, I tell thee the old mysteries anew: hearken!

(I tell thee silently) because those (bodily) lips are fleeing from 4685 (are unable to apprehend) this Breath (Word): it is breathed forth on the lip (bank) of the hidden River.

At this moment open the ear of earlessness for the sake of (hearing) the mystery of *God doeth what He willeth*."

When he began to hear the call to union, little by little the dead man began to stir.

He (the lover of God) is not less than the earth which at the zephyr's blandishments puts on (a garment of) green and lifts up its head from death;

He is not less than the seminal water from which at the (Divine) bidding there are born Josephs with faces like the sun;

He is not less than a wind (from which) at the command 4690 "Be!" peacocks and sweet-voiced birds came to being in the (bird's) womb;[1]

He is not less than the mountain of rock which by parturition brought forth the she-camel that brought forth a she-camel[2].

---

[1] The semen of birds was believed to consist of air.
[2] The prophet Ṣáliḥ, who was sent to the people of Thamúd, miraculously caused a she-camel big with young to come forth from a rock.

Leave all this behind. Did not the substance of non-existence bring forth, and will it not bring forth continually, a (whole) universe?

He (the man of Bukhárá) sprang up and quivered and whirled once or twice (in dance) joyously, joyously; (then) fell to worship.

How the senseless lover came to himself and turned his
face in praise and thanksgiving to the Beloved.

He said, "O 'Anqá of God, (thou who art) the place of the spirit's circling flight, (I give) thanks that thou hast come back from yonder mountain of Qáf.

4695   O Siráfíl (Seraphiel) of Love's resurrection-place, O Love of love and O Heart's-desire of love,

I desire, as the first gift of honour thou wilt give me, that thou lay thine ear on my window.

Albeit through (thy) purity thou knowest my feelings, lend ear to my words, O cherisher of thy slave.

Hundreds of thousands of times, O unique Prince, did my wits fly away in longing for thy ear—

That hearing of thine and that listening of thine, and those life-quickening smiles of thine;

4700   That hearkening unto my lesser and greater (matters), (and unto) the beguilements of my evil-thinking (suspicious) soul.

Then my false coins, which are well-known to thee, thou didst accept as (though they were) genuine money,

For the sake of the boldness (importunity) of one (who was) impudent and deluded, O thou beside whose clemency (all) clemencies are (but) a mote!

Firstly, hear that when I abandoned[1] (thy) net the first and the last (this world and the next) shot away (disappeared) from before me;

Secondly, hear, O loving Prince, that I sought long, (but) there was no second to thee;

4705   Thirdly, since I have gone away from thee, 'tis as though I have said, '*the third of three*'[2];

Fourthly, forasmuch as my cornfield is burnt up[3], I do not know the fifth (finger) from the fourth[4].

Wherever thou findest blood on the sods, (if) thou investigate, it will certainly (prove to) be (blood) from mine eye.

My words are (as) the thunder, and this noise and moaning demands of the cloud that it should rain upon the earth.

---

[1] Literally, "remained apart from."
[2] *I.e.* "I have been guilty of polytheism, like the Christians who hold the doctrine of the Trinity (*Qur'án*, v. 77)."   [3] *I.e.* "I have lost my wits."
[4] Or, "I do not know Khámisa (Quinta) from Rábi'a (Quarta)."

Between words and tears I continue (in doubt) whether I should weep or speak: how shall I do?

If I speak, the weeping will be lost; and if I weep, how shall 4710 I render thanks and praise?

Heart's blood is falling from mine eye, O King: see what has befallen me from mine eye!"

The emaciated man said this and began to weep (so violently) that both base and noble wept for him.

So many ecstatic cries came up from his heart (that) the people of Bukhárá made a ring around him.

(He was) speaking crazily, weeping crazily, laughing crazily: men and women, small and great, were bewildered.

The (whole) city, too, shed tears in conformity with him: 4715 men and women were gathered together as (at) the Resurrection.

At that moment the heaven was saying to the earth, "If thou hast never seen the Resurrection, behold it (now)!"

The intellect (was) bewildered, saying, "What is love and what is ecstasy? (I know not) whether separation from Him or union with Him is the more marvellous."

The sky read the letter (announcement) of Resurrection (and was so distraught that) it rent its garment up to the Milky Way.

Love hath estrangement with (is a stranger to) the two worlds: in it are two-and-seventy madnesses.

It is exceedingly hidden, and (only) its bewilderment is 4720 manifest: the soul of the spiritual sultans is pining for it.

Its religion is other than (that of) the two-and-seventy sects: beside it the throne of kings is (but) a splint-bandage.

At the time of the *samá'* Love's minstrel strikes up this (strain): "Servitude is chains and lordship headache."

Then what is Love? The Sea of Not-being: there the foot of the intellect is shattered[1].

Servitude and sovereignty are known: loverhood is concealed by these two veils.

Would that Being had a tongue, that it might remove the 4725 veils from existent beings!

O breath of (phenomenal) existence, whatsoever words thou mayest utter, know that thereby thou hast bound another veil upon it (the mystery).

That utterance and (that) state (of existence) are the bane of (spiritual) perception: to wash away blood with blood is absurd, absurd.

Since I am familiar with His frenzied ones, day and night I am breathing forth (the secrets of Love) in the cage (of phenomenal existence).

---

[1] *I.e.* the intellect is unable to swim in that Sea.

Thou art mightily drunken and senseless and distraught:
yesternight on which side hast thou slept, O (my) soul?

4730   Beware, beware! Take heed lest thou utter a breath! First
spring up and seek a trusted friend.

Thou art a lover and intoxicated, and thy tongue (is) loosed!
—God! God! thou art (like) the camel on the water-spout[1]!

When the tongue tells of His mystery and coquetry, Heaven
chants (the prayer), "O Thou that art goodly in covering!"

What covering (can there be)? The fire is in the wool and
cotton: whilst thou art covering it up, it is (all the) more
manifest.

When I endeavour to hide His (Love's) secret, He lifts up
His head, like a banner, saying, "Look, here am I!"

4735   In despite of me He seizes both my ears, saying, "O scatter-
brain, how wilt thou cover it? Cover it (if thou canst)!"

I say to Him, "Begone! Though thou hast bubbled up (hast
become fervid), (yet) thou art (both) manifest and concealed,
like the soul."

He says, "This body of mine is imprisoned in the jar, (but)
like wine I am clapping hands (making a merry noise) at the
banquet."

I say to Him, "Go ere thou art put in pawn (confinement),
lest the bane of intoxication befall (thee)."

He says, "I befriend the day with (my) delicious cup until
the evening-prayer.

4740   When evening comes and steals my cup, I will say to it, 'Give
(it) back, for my evening hath not come.'"

Hence the Arabs applied the name *mudám*[2] to wine, because
the wine-drinker is never sated.

Love makes the wine of realisation to bubble: He is the cup-
bearer to the *siddíq* (true lover) in secret.

When you seek (the reality) with good help (from God), the
water (essence) of the spirit is the wine, and the body is the
flagon.

When He increases the wine of His help, the potency of the
wine bursts the flagon.

4745   The water (the spirit) becomes the Cup-bearer, and the water
(is) also the drunken man. Tell not how! And God best
knoweth the right.

'Tis the radiance of the Cup-bearer that entered into the
must: the must bubbled up and began to dance and waxed strong.

On this matter, ask the heedless (sceptic), "When did you
(ever) see must like this?"

To every one who hath knowledge it is (self-evident) without
reflection, that together with the person disturbed there is a
Disturber.

---

[1] See p. 253, n. 1.   [2] *Mudám* signifies "continual."

*Story of the lover who had been long separated (from
his beloved) and had suffered much tribulation.*

A certain youth was madly enamoured of a woman: the
fortune of union was not granted to him.

Love tortured him exceedingly on the earth: why, in sooth, 4750
does Love bear hatred (to the lover) from the first?

Why is Love murderous from the first, so that he who is an
outsider runs away?

Whenever he sent a messenger to the woman, the messenger
because of jealousy would become a highwayman (barring the
way against him);

And if his secretary wrote (a letter to be sent) to the woman,
his delegate (messenger) would read the letter (to her) with
tashif[1];

And if in good faith he made the zephyr his envoy, that
zephyr would be darkened by a (cloud of) dust.

If he sewed the letter on the wing of a bird, the bird's wing 4755
would be burnt by the ardour of the letter.

The (Divine) jealousy barred (all) the ways of device and
broke the banner of the army of cogitation.

At first, expectation was the comforting friend of (his)
sorrow; at last, there broke him—who? Even (the same)
expectation.

Sometimes he would say, "This is an irremediable affliction";
sometimes he would say, "No, it is the life of my spirit."

Sometimes (self-)existence would lift up a head from him
(appear in him); sometimes he would eat of the fruit of non-
existence.

When this (bodily) nature became cold (irksome and useless) 4760
to him, the fountain of union (with the beloved) would boil
hotly.

When he put up with (contented himself with) the un-
providedness of exile, the provision of unprovidedness hastened
towards him.

The wheat-ears of his thought were purged of chaff: he be-
came, like the moon, a guide to the night-travellers.

Oh, there is many a parrot that speaks though it is mute; oh,
there is many a sweet-spirited one whose face is sour.

Go to the graveyard, sit awhile in silence, and behold those
eloquent silent ones;

But, if you see that their dust is of one colour, (yet) their 4765
active (spiritual) state is not uniform.

The fat and flesh of living persons is uniform, (yet) one is sad,
another glad.

---

[1] *I.e.* incorrectly. *Tashīf* is the perversion of a word's meaning by alteration
of its diacritical points, *e.g.* by changing بوسه into توشه.

Until you hear their words, what should you know (of their feelings), inasmuch as their (inward) state is hidden from you?

You may hear words—(cries of) *háy, húy*; (but) how will you perceive the (inward) state that hath a hundred folds?

Our (human) figure is uniform, (yet) endued with contrary qualities: likewise their dust is uniform, (yet) their spirits are diverse.

4770 Similarly, voices are uniform (as such), (but) one is sorrowful, and another full of charms.

On the battle-field you may hear the cry of horses; in strolling round (a garden) you may hear the cry of birds.

One (voice proceeds) from hate, and another from harmony; one from pain, and another from joy.

Whoever is remote from (ignorant of) their (inward) state, to him the voices are uniform.

One tree is moved by blows of the axe, another tree by the breeze of dawn.

4775 Much error befell me from (I was greatly deceived by) the worthless pot, because the pot was boiling (while) covered by the lid.

The fervour and savour of every one says to you, "Come"— the fervour of sincerity and the fervour of imposture and hypocrisy.

If you have not the scent (discernment derived) from the soul that recognises the face (reality), go, get for yourself a (spiritual) brain (sense) that recognises the scent.

The brain (sense) that haunts yon Rose-garden—'tis it that makes bright the eyes of (all) Jacobs.

Come now, relate what happened to that heart-sick (youth), for we have left the man of Bukhárá far behind, O son.

How the lover found his beloved; and a discourse showing that the seeker is a finder, for he who shall do as much good as the weight of an ant shall see it (in the end).

4780 (It happened) that for seven years that youth was (engaged) in search and seeking: from (cherishing) the phantasy of union he became like a phantom.

(If) the shadow (protection) of God be over the head of the servant (of God), the seeker at last will be a finder.

The Prophet said that when you knock at a door, at last a head will come forth from that door.

When you sit (wait) on the road of a certain person, at last you will see also the face of a certain person.

When, every day, you keep digging the earth from a pit, at last you will arrive at the pure water.

(Even) if you may not believe (it), all know this, (that) one 4785 day you will reap whatsoever you are sowing.

You struck the stone (flint) against the iron (steel): the fire did not flash out! This may not be; or if it be (so), 'tis rare.

He to whom felicity and salvation are not apportioned (by God)—his mind regards naught but the rarities.

(He says) that such and such a one sowed seed and had no crop, while that (other) one bore away an oyster-shell (from the sea), and the shell had no pearl (within it).

(He says that in the cases of) Bal'am son of Bá'úr and the accursed Iblís, their acts of worship and their religion availed them not.

The hundreds of thousands of prophets and travellers on 4790 the Way do not come into the mind of that evil-thinking man.

He takes these two (examples) which produce (spiritual) darkness: how should (his) ill fate put aught but this in his heart?

Oh, there is many a one that eats bread with a glad heart, and it becomes the death of him: it sticks in his gullet.

Go, then, O ill-fated man, do not eat bread at all, lest thou fall like him into bale and woe!

Hundreds of thousands of folk are eating loaves of bread and gaining strength and nourishing the (vital) spirit.

How hast thou fallen into that rare (calamity), unless thou art 4795 deprived (of blessedness) and art born a fool?

He (the ill-fated man) has forsaken this world full of sunshine and moonlight and has plunged his head into the pit,

Saying, "If it is true, then where is the radiance?" Lift up thy head from the pit and look, O miserable wretch!

The whole world, east and west, obtained that light, (but) whilst thou art in the pit it will not shine upon thee.

Leave the pit, go to the palace and the vineyards; do not wrangle here, know that quarrelling is unlucky.

Beware! Do not say, "Mark you, such and such a one sowed 4800 seed, and in such and such a year the locusts devoured what he had sown.

Why, then, should I sow? for there is danger in this respect. Why should I scatter this corn(-seed) from my hand?"

And (meanwhile) he who did not neglect to sow and labour fills his barn (with grain), to your confusion.

Since he (the lover) was patiently knocking at a door, at last one day he obtained a meeting in private.

From fear of the night-patrol he sprang by night into the orchard: (there) he found his beloved, (radiant) as candle and lamp.

4805 At that moment he said to the Maker of the means (by which
he had attained to his desire), "O God, have mercy on the
night-patrol!

Unbeknown (to me), Thou hast created the means: from the
gate of Hell Thou hast brought me to Paradise.

Thou hast made this affair (dread of the night-patrol) a
means, to the end that I may not hold (even) a single thorn in
contempt."

In (consequence of) the fracture of a leg God bestows a
wing; likewise from the depths of the pit He opens a door (of
escape).

(God saith), "Do not consider whether thou art on a tree or
in a pit: consider Me, for I am the Key of the Way."

4810 If you wish (to read) the rest of this tale, seek (it), O my
brother, in the Fourth Book.

BOOK IV

IN THE NAME OF GOD THE COMPASSIONATE, THE MERCIFUL.

The Fourth Journey to the best of abodes and the greatest of advantages: by its perusal the hearts of gnostics will be rejoiced as the meadows rejoice in the downpour[1] of the clouds and as the eyes delight in the pleasantness of sleep. Therein is cheer for spirits and healing for bodies; and it is like what the sincere (in devotion to God) crave and love, and like what the travellers (on the Way to God) seek and wish for—a refreshment to eyes, and a joy to souls; the sweetest of fruits for them that cull, and the most sublime of things desired and coveted; bringing the sick man to his physician and guiding the lover to his beloved. And, to God be the praise, it is the grandest of gifts and the most precious of prizes; the renewer of the covenant of friendship (with God) and the easer of the difficulty of those in trouble. The study of it will increase the sorrow of them that are estranged (from God) and the joy and thankfulness of them that are blest. Its bosom holds a cargo of fineries such as are not carried on the bosoms of young ladies, to be a compensation to followers of the theory and practice (of Ṣúfism); for it is like a full-moon that hath risen and a fortune that hath returned, exceeding the hope of the hopeful and providing forage for the doers of (good) works. It raises expectation after depression and expands hope after contraction—like a sun that shone forth radiantly amidst clouds dispersed. It is a light to our friends and a treasure for our (spiritual) descendants.

And we ask God to help us to give Him thanks, for indeed thanksgiving is a means of binding fast that which is already in hand and of capturing more besides, albeit naught comes to pass but what He purposes.

"And one of the things that stirred me to love-desire was that I was sleeping, diverted (from my grief) by the sweet exhalations of the cool air,

Till a grey dove in the boughs of a thicket called (to me), trilling beautifully with long-drawn sobs.

And if, before her sobbing, I had sobbed from passion for Su‘dá, I should have healed my soul (of its pain) ere repenting (of my tardiness);

But she sobbed before me, and ('twas) her sobbing (that) roused me to sob, and I said, 'The pre-eminence belongs to him that leads the way[2].'"

May God have mercy on those who lead the way and those

---

[1] Instead of صَوْب all my MSS. read صَوْت, noise, *i.e.* thunder-claps.

[2] These verses by the Umayyad poet, ‘Adí b. al-Riqá‘, are celebrated. Ḥarírí quotes the third and fourth in the preface to his *Maqámát*.

who come behind and those who fulfil (their vows) and those who seek to fulfil (the same), (and may He bless them) with His grace and bounty and with His large benefits and favours! For He is the best object of petition and the noblest object of hope; *and God is the best protector and the most merciful of them that show mercy*, and the best of friends and the best of heirs and the best replacer (of what has been consumed) and provider for the devotees who sow and till (the soil of good works).

And God bless Mohammed and all the Prophets and Messengers! Amen, O Lord of created beings!

IN THE NAME OF GOD THE MERCIFUL AND COMPASSIONATE.

O Ẓiyá'u 'l-Ḥaqq (Radiance of God), Ḥusámu'ddín, thou art he through whose light the *Mathnawí* hath surpassed the moon (in splendour).

O thou in whom hopes are placed, thy lofty aspiration is drawing this (poem) God knows whither.

Thou hast bound the neck of this *Mathnawí*: thou art drawing it in the direction known to thee.

The *Mathnawí* is running on, the drawer is unseen—unseen by the ignorant one who hath no insight.

Inasmuch as thou hast been the origin of the *Mathnawí*, if it 5 become increased (in size), ('tis) thou (who) hast caused it to increase.

Since thou wishest it so, God wishes it so: God grants the desire of the devout.

In the past thou hast been (as) "he belongs to God," so that (now) "God belongs (to him)" hath come in recompense.

On thy account the *Mathnawí* had thousands of thanksgivings (to render): it lifted up its hands in prayer and thanksgiving.

God saw thanksgiving to thee on its lips and in its hands: (therefore) He showed grace and bestowed favour and increase;

For to him that gives thanks increase is promised, just as 10 nighness (unto God) is the reward for prostration (in the ritual prayer).

Our God hath said, "*And prostrate thyself and come nigh (unto Me)*": the prostration of our bodies is become the nighness of the spirit (unto God).

If increase is accruing (to the *Mathnawí*), it is for this reason, it is not for the sake of vainglory and (empty) noise.

We are glad with thee as the vineyard (is glad) in the summer heat: thou hast the authority: come, draw (it on), that we may always be drawing (it on after thee).

Draw happily this caravan (onward) to the Pilgrimage, O Commander of "Patience is the key to joy."

The (formal) Pilgrimage consists in visiting the House (of 15 God), (but only) the Pilgrimage to the Lord of the House is worthy of a (true) man.

I called thee Ẓiyá (Radiance) Ḥusámu'ddín (Sword of the Religion) because thou art the Sun, and these two (words) are epithets descriptive (of the sun);

For, mark you, this sword and this radiance are one: the sun's sword (beam) is certainly of the radiance.

Núr (light) belongs to the moon, and this *ẓiyá* (radiance) belongs to the sun: read this in the *Qur'án*.

The *Qur'án* has called the sun *ẓiyá*, O father, and it has called the moon *núr*[1]. Consider this!

20 Since the sun is more exalted even than the moon, know, then, that *ẓiyá* is superior to *núr* in dignity.

Many a one did not see the way in the moonlight, (but) it became visible as soon as the sun rose.

The sun displayed (all) objects of exchange perfectly: of necessity, markets were (held) in the daytime,

In order that the false coin and the good money[2] might come into view, and that he (the merchant) might be far (immune) from swindling and trickery.

(The sun rose) until its light came to perfection on the earth, *a universal mercy*[3] to the traders;

25 But to the false coiner it is hateful and grievous, because by it his money and wares are made unsaleable.

Hence the false coin is the mortal foe of the money-changer: who is the enemy of the dervish but the dog?

The prophets contend with their enemies; then the angels utter cries of "Save (them), O Lord,"

Saying, "Keep this Lamp, which is light-disseminating, far from the puffs and breaths of thieves."

Only the thief and the coiner are adversaries of the light: succour (us) from these twain, O Succourer!

30 Shed light upon the Fourth Book, for the sun rose from the Fourth Heaven.

Come, give light, like the sun, from the Fourth (Book), so that it may shine upon (all) countries and inhabited lands.

Whoever reads it (as) an idle tale, he is (as) an idle tale; and he who regards it as money in his own hands (real truth to be applied to himself) is like a man (of God).

It is the water of the Nile, which seemed blood to the Egyptian, (but) to the people of Moses was not blood, but water.

At this moment the enemy of these words (the *Mathnawí*) is pictured in (thy) sight (falling) headlong into Hell-fire[4].

35 O Ẓiyá'u 'l-Ḥaqq (Radiance of God), thou hast seen his (evil) state: God hath shown unto thee the answer to his (evil) actions.

Thine eye which beholds the invisible is a master(-seer) like the Invisible: may this vision and gift not vanish from this world!

If thou wilt here complete this story, which is the current coin of (directly applicable to) our present state, 'tis fitting.

Leave the unworthy folk for the sake of the worthy: bring the tale to the end and conduct it to the issue.

If this story was not finished there (in the Third Book), 'tis (now) the Fourth Volume: set it out in order.

---

[1] *Qur'án*, x, 5.   [2] Reading نَقْد with *iḍáfat*.   [3] *Qur'án*, xxi, 107.

[4] Cf. *Nafaḥátu 'l-Uns* (ed. Nassau Lees), p. 541, l. 19 foll.

*Conclusion of the story of the lover who fled from the night-patrol
into an orchard unknown to him, and for joy at finding his beloved
in the orchard called down blessings on the night-patrol and said,
"It may be that ye loathe a thing although it is better for you."*

We were at the point (of the story) where that person (fled) 40
in terror from the night-patrol (and) galloped into the orchard.

In the orchard was the beauteous one for love of whom this
(youth) had been in tribulation eight years.

He had no possibility of seeing (even) her shadow: he was
(only) hearing the description of her, as (of) the 'Anqá,

Except (for) one meeting which happened to him by (Divine)
destiny at the first and enravished his heart.

After that, however much effort he made, in sooth that cruel
one would give him no opportunity.

Neither entreaty nor wealth availed him: that (fresh) sapling 45
was fully satisfied and without desire.

(In the case of) the lover of any craft or object of pursuit, God
has touched[1] his lip (with honey or the like) at the beginning of
the affair;

(But) when at that contact they have entered upon the quest,
He lays a snare before their feet every day.

When He has plunged him (the lover) into search for the
matter (which he has at heart), after that He shuts the door,
saying, "Bring the dowry."

Still they cling to that (sweet) scent (hope) and go (on their
quest): at every moment they become hopeful and despairing.

Every one (of them) hath hope of (winning) the fruit whereto 50
a door was opened to him on a certain day;

Then it was shut (upon them) again; (but) that devotee to the
door, (continuing) in the same hope, has become fire-footed[2].

When the youth joyously entered that orchard, verily on a
sudden his foot sank in (struck upon) the (buried) treasure.

God had made the night-patrol the means, so that in fear of
him he (the lover) should run into the orchard by night

And should see the beloved one searching with a lantern for
a ring in the rivulet of the orchard.

Therefore at that moment, from the delight (which he ex- 55
perienced), he conjoined praise of God with prayers for the
night-patrol,

Saying, "I caused loss to the night-patrol by fleeing (from
him): scatter o'er him twenty times as much silver and gold.

Set him free from policing: make him glad even as I am
glad.

---

[1] Literally, "besmeared."
[2] *I.e.* moving restlessly and swiftly like fire.

Keep him blest in this world and in that world, deliver him from policing and currishness—

Though it is the nature of that policeman, O God, that he always desires the people to be afflicted."

60 If news come that the king has imposed a fine upon the Moslems, he (the policeman) waxes big and exultant;

And if news come that the king has shown mercy and has generously taken off[1] that (penalty) from the Moslems,

A mournfulness falls upon his soul thereat: the policeman hath a hundred such depravities.

He (the lover) was bringing the policeman into the prayer (of benediction), because such solace had come to him from the policeman.

He (the policeman) was poison to all (others), but to him (he was) the antidote: the policeman was the means of uniting that longing lover (with the object of his desire).

65 Hence there is no absolute evil in the world: evil is relative. Know this (truth) also.

In (the realm of) Time there is no poison or sugar that is not a foot (support) to one and a fetter (injury) to another—

To one a foot, to another a fetter; to one a poison and to another (sweet and wholesome) like sugar.

Snake-poison is life to the snake, (but) it is death in relation to man.

The sea is as a garden to the water-creatures; to the creatures of earth it is death and a (painful) brand.

70 Reckon up likewise, O man of experience, (instances of) this relativity from a single individual to a thousand.

Zayd, in regard to that (particular) one, may be a devil, (but) in regard to another person he may be a (beneficent) sultan.

That one will say that Zayd is an exalted *ṣiddíq* (saint), and this one will say that Zayd is an infidel who ought to be killed.

Zayd is one person—to that one (he is as) a shield, (while) to this other one (he is) wholly pain and loss.

If you wish that to you he should be (as) sugar, then look on him with the eye of lovers.

75 Do not look on that Beauteous One with your own eye: behold the Sought with the eye of seekers.

Shut your own eye to that Sweet-eyed One: borrow an eye from His lovers.

Nay, borrow eye and sight from Him, and then look on His face with His eye,

So that you may be secure from satiety and weariness: on this account the Almighty said, "God shall belong to him:

I shall be his eye and hand and heart," to the end that His fortunate one should escape from adversities.

---

[1] Literally, "let fall."

Whatsoever is loathed is a lover and friend when it becomes 80
thy guide towards thy beloved.

*Story of the preacher who at the beginning of every exhortation used
to pray for the unjust and hard-hearted and irreligious.*

A certain preacher, whenever he mounted the pulpit, would
begin to pray for the highway robbers (who plunder and maltreat
the righteous).

He would lift up his hand, (crying), "O Lord, let mercy fall
upon evil men and corrupters and insolent transgressors,

Upon all who make a mock of the good people, upon all
whose hearts are unbelieving and those who dwell in the
Christian monastery."

He would not pray for the pure; he would pray for none but
the wicked.

They said to him, "This is unknown (extraordinary): 'tis no 85
generosity to pray for the people of unrighteousness."

He replied, "I have seen (experienced) goodness from these
folk: for this reason I have chosen to pray for them.

They wrought so much wickedness and injustice and op-
pression that they cast (drove) me forth from evil into good.

Whenever I turned my face towards this world, I suffered
blows and beating from them,

And took refuge from the blows Yonder: the wolves were
always bringing me back into the (right) Way.

Inasmuch as they contrived the means of my (spiritual) 90
welfare, it behoves me to pray for them, O intelligent one."

The servant (of God) complains to God of pain and smart:
he makes a hundred complaints of his pain.

God says, "After all, grief and pain have made thee humbly
entreating and righteous.

Make this complaint of the bounty that befalls thee and re-
moves thee far from My door and makes thee an outcast."

In reality every foe (of yours) is your medicine: he is an elixir
and beneficial and one that seeks to win your heart[1];

For you flee away from him into solitude and would fain im- 95
plore help of God's grace.

Your friends are really enemies, for they make you far from
the (Divine) Presence and occupied (with them).

There is an animal whose name is *ushghur* (porcupine): it is
(made) stout and big by blows of the stick[2].

The more you cudgel it, the more it thrives: it grows fat on
blows of the stick.

---

[1] *I.e.* he is really acting as your true friend and well-wisher.

Referring to the porcupine's habit of exserting its quills when attacked.

Assuredly the true believer's soul is a porcupine, for it is (made) stout and fat by the blows of tribulation.

100 For this reason the tribulation and abasement (laid) upon the prophets is greater than (that laid upon) all the (other) creatures in the world,

So that their souls became stouter than (all other) souls; for no other class of people suffered that affliction.

The hide is afflicted by the medicine (tan-liquor), (but) it becomes sweet like Ṭá'if leather;

And if he (the tanner) did not rub the bitter and acrid (liquor) into it, it would become fetid, unpleasant, and foul-smelling.

Know that Man is an untanned hide, made noisome and gross by humours.

105 Give (him)[1] bitter and acrid (discipline) and much rubbing (tribulation), that he may become pure and lovely and exceedingly strong;

But if you cannot (mortify yourself), be content, O cunning one, if God give you tribulation without choice (on your part),

For affliction (sent) by the Friend is (the means of) your being purified: His knowledge is above your contrivance.

The affliction becomes sweet (to the sufferer) when he sees happiness: the medicine becomes sweet (to the sick man) when he regards health.

He sees victory for himself in the very essence of checkmate; therefore he says, "Kill me, O trusty ones[2]!"

110 This policeman became a (source of) profit in respect of another, but he became reprobate in respect of himself.

The mercy appertaining to the Faith was cut off from him; the hate inherent in the Devil enfolded him.

He became a factory of anger and hatred: know that hate is the root of error and infidelity.

How they asked Jesus, on whom be peace, saying, "O Spirit of God, what is the hardest thing to bear of all the hard things in existence?"

A sober-minded man said to Jesus, "What is the hardest to bear of all things in existence?"

He replied, "O (my dear) soul, the hardest is God's anger, on account of which Hell is trembling as we (are)."

115 He said, "What is the security against this anger of God?" Jesus said, "To abandon thine own anger at once."

Therefore, as the policeman became this anger's mine (source), his ugly anger surpassed even (that of) a wild beast.

---

[1] *I.e.* the carnal nature.
[2] The first hemistich of an Arabic verse by Ḥusayn b. Manṣúr al-Ḥallá

What hope is there for him of (Divine) mercy, unless perchance that graceless man should turn back from that (vile) quality?

Although the world cannot do without them, this statement is a (means of) casting (those who hear it) into error.

The world cannot do without urine either, but that urine is not *clear running water*[1].

The lover's attempted perfidy, and how the beloved scolded him.

When that simpleton found her alone, at once he attempted to 120 embrace and kiss her.

The beauty with awesome mien raised her voice against him, saying, "Do not behave impudently, be mindful of good manners!"

He said, "Why, there is privacy, and no people (present): the water at hand, and a thirsty man like me!

None is moving here but the wind. Who is present? Who will hinder (me) from this conquest?"

"O madman," said she, "thou hast been a fool: a fool thou art and hast not hearkened to the wise.

Thou sawest the wind moving: know that a Mover of the 125 wind is here, who drives the wind along."

The fan, namely, the direction of its course by God's action, smote upon this wind and is always keeping it in movement.

The portion of wind (air) that is in our control does not stir till you move the fan.

Without you and without the fan the movement of this portion of wind (air) does not arise, O simpleton.

The movement of the wind of the breath, which is on the lips, follows the course directed by the spirit and the body.

At one time you make the breath to be a eulogy and a 130 (pleasing) message; at another time you make the breath to be a satire and a foul speech.

Understand, then, (from this case) the cases of other winds; for from a part the intellect perceives the whole.

God sometimes makes the wind vernal: in December He divests it of this kindliness.

He makes it a *ṣarṣar* (intensely cold and violent) for the people of 'Ád; again, He makes it perfumed (balmy) for Húd[2].

One wind He makes (deadly as) the poison of the simoom; He (also) makes the advent of the east-wind to be delightful.

He hath founded (stablished) the wind of the breath in you, 135 in order that thereby you may judge analogically of every (other) wind.

---

[1] *Qur'án*, LXVII, 30.
[2] The prophet who was sent to the people of 'Ád:

The breath does not become speech without (assuming the quality of) gentleness or harshness: it is honey for one set of people and poison for another class.

The fan is moving for the benefit of the (favoured) person, and for the subjugation of every fly and gnat.

Why (then) should not the fan of Divine fore-ordainment be fraught with trial and probation (by means of good and evil)?

Inasmuch as the part, namely, the wind of the breath or the fan, is naught but a cause of injury or advantage,

140   How should this north-wind and this east-wind and this west-wind be remote from (showing) favour and conferring bounty?

Look at a handful of wheat from a granary, and apprehend that the whole of it will be just like this (handful).

How should the whole of the wind rush forth from the mansion of the wind in Heaven without (being impelled by) the fan of that Driver of the wind?

Is it not the fact that at winnowing-time the labourers on the threshing-floor beseech God for wind,

In order that the straws may be separated from the wheat, so that it may go into a granary or pits?

145   When the blowing wind is long delayed, you may see them all making humble entreaty to God.

Likewise, in parturition, if the wind of childbirth do not come, there comes (from the mother) a woeful cry for help.

If they (that desire the wind) are not aware that He is its Driver, then what disposes (them) to pray piteously for the wind?

Likewise, those in a ship are desirous of the wind: they all are begging for it from the Lord of Mankind.

Likewise, in (the case of) toothache you beg ardently and earnestly to be defended from the wind.

150   The soldiers beseech God humbly, saying, "Give (us) the wind of victory, O Thou whose every wish is fulfilled!"

Also, in the throes of childbirth, folk beg from every venerated (saint) a piece of paper inscribed with a charm (against evil).

Therefore all have known for certain that the wind is sent by *the Lord of created beings*.

Therefore in the mind of every one possessing knowledge this is certain, that with everything that moves there is a mover.

If you do not see him visibly, apprehend him by means of the manifestation of the effect.

155   The body is moved by the spirit: you do not see the spirit; but from the movement of the body know the spirit (to be its mover).

He (the lover) said, "If I am foolish in manners, I am wise in respect of faithfulness and (eager) pursuit."

She replied, "Truly the manners were these which have been seen; as for the other (things), thou thyself knowest, perverse fellow!

Story of the Ṣúfí who caught his wife with a strange man.

A Ṣúfí came (back) to his house in the daytime: the house had (only) one door, and his wife was with a cobbler.

Uxor copulata erat cum servo (amatore) suo in illo uno cubiculo propter corporis libidinem.

When in the forenoon the Ṣúfí knocked on the door with all 160 his might, both (the lovers) were at a loss (what to do): (there was) neither device nor way (of escape).

It was never known (it was unprecedented) for him to return home from the shop at that time,

But on that day the alarmed man purposely returned to his house at an unseasonable hour, because of a fancy (suspicion).

The wife's confidence was (based) on the fact that he had never come home from his work at this time.

By (Divine) destiny, her reasoning did not come (turn out to be) right: though He (God) is the Coverer (of sins), still He will impose the penalty[1].

When you have done evil, be afraid, do not be secure, since 165 it (the evil) is seed, and God will cause it to grow.

For awhile He covers it up, to the end that sorrow and shame for (having committed) that evil may come to you.

In the time of 'Umar, that Prince of the Faithful gave a thief over to the executioner and officer of police.

The thief cried out, saying, 'O Prince of the land, this is my first offence[2]. Mercy!'

'God forfend,' said 'Umar, 'that God should inflict severe punishment[3] the first time.

He covers up (the sin) many times in order to manifest His 170 grace; then again, He chastises (the sinner) in order to manifest His justice,

To the end that both these attributes may be displayed, and the former be hope-inspiring[4] and the latter deterrent.'

The woman, too, had committed this wickedness many times: it passed lightly (over her) and seemed light to her.

The feeble intelligence (which she had) was unaware that the pitcher does not for ever come (back) whole from the brook.

That (Divine) destiny brought her to such straits as sudden death does (in the case of) the (religious) hypocrite,

---

[1] *I.e.* unless the sinner repents.
[2] Literally, "my offence is (for) the first time."
[3] Literally, "should rain down severity in punishment."
[4] Literally, "announcing glad news."

175   (When there is) neither way (of escape) nor comrade (to help) nor (hope of) quarter, (and when) the Angel (of Death) has put out his hand to (seize) the soul.

(Such is the state of the hypocrite), even as this woman in that chamber of iniquity was paralysed, she and her companion, by the tribulation.

The Ṣúfí said to himself[1], 'O ye two miscreants, I will take vengeance on you, but with patience.

(I will not act in haste) but at this moment I will feign ignorance, that every ear may not hear this bell[2].'

He (God) who manifests the right takes vengeance on you secretly, little by little, like the malady of phthisis.

180   The man suffering from phthisis dwindles incessantly like ice, but at every moment he thinks he is better.

(He is) like the hyena which they (the hunters) are catching, and which is duped by their saying, 'Where is this hyena?'

That woman had no secret room; she had no subterranean cellar or passage, no way to the top (of the house),

No oven where he (her lover) might be concealed, nor any sack that might be a screen for him.

'Twas like the broad plain of Resurrection Day—no hollow or hillock or place of refuge.

185   God hath described this distressful place, (which is) for the scene of the (Last) Congregation, (in the words) *thou wilt not see therein any unevenness.*

How the wife, for the sake of imposition, hid the beloved one under her chádar[3] and offered a false excuse, "for verily, great is the cunning of you (women)."

She quickly threw her *chádar* upon him: she made the man a woman and opened the door.

Beneath the *chádar* the man was exposed to view and clearly seen—very conspicuous, like a camel on a staircase[4].

She said, ''Tis a lady, one of the notables of the town: she has her share of wealth and fortune.

I bolted the door, lest any stranger should come in suddenly unawares.'

190   The Ṣúfí said, 'Oh, what service is there (to be done) for her, that I may perform it without (expecting) any thanks or favour (in return)?'

She (the wife) said, 'Her desire is kinship and alliance (with us): she is an excellent lady, God knows who she is[5].

---

[1] Literally, "to his heart."   [2] *I.e.* that the scandal may not become notorious.
[3] A garment worn by Persian women, which covers the face and envelops the person from head to foot.
[4] This proverbial expression differs in meaning from "a camel on a waterspout". Cf. p. 253, n. 1.
[5] *I.e.* God knows her excellence.

She wished to see our daughter privily; (but) as it happens, the girl is at school;

(So) then she said, Whether she (the daughter) be flour or bran, with (all my) soul and heart I will make her (my son's) bride.

She has a son, who is not in the town: he is handsome and clever, an active lad and one that earns a living.'

The Ṣúfí said, 'We are poor and wretched and inferior (in 195 station); this lady's family are rich and respected.

How should this (girl) be an equal match for them in marriage?—one folding-door of wood and another of ivory!

In wedlock both the partners must be equal, otherwise it will pinch, and (their) happiness will not endure.'

How the wife said that she (the lady) was not bent upon household goods, and that what she wanted was modesty and virtue; and how the Ṣúfí answered her (his wife) cryptically.

She (the wife) said, 'I gave such an excuse, but she said, No, I am not one who seeks (worldly) means.

We are sick and surfeited with possessions and gold; we are not like the common folk in regard to coveting and amassing (wealth).

Our quest is (for) modesty and purity and virtue: truly, 200 welfare in both worlds depends on that.'

The Ṣúfí once more made the excuse of poverty and repeated it, so that it should not be hidden.

The wife replied, 'I too have repeated it and have explained our lack of household goods;

(But) her resolution is firmer than a mountain, for she is not dismayed by a hundred poverties.

She keeps saying, What I want is chastity: the thing sought from you is sincerity and high-mindedness.'

The Ṣúfí said, 'In sooth she has seen and is seeing our 205 household goods and possessions, (both) the overt and the covert—

A narrow house, a dwelling-place for a single person, where a needle would not remain hid.

Moreover, she in (her) guilelessness knows better than we (what is) modesty and purity and renunciation and virtue.

She knows better than we (all) the aspects of modesty, and the rear and front and head and tail of modesty.

Evidently she (our daughter) is without household goods and servant, and she (the lady) herself is well-acquainted with virtue and modesty.

It is not required of a father to dilate on (his daughter's) 210 modesty, when in her it is manifest as a bright day.'

I have told this story[1] with the intent that thou mayst not weave idle talk when the offence is glaring.

O thou who art likewise excessive in thy pretension, to thee (in thy case) there has been this (same hypocritical) exertion and (vain) belief.

Thou hast been unfaithful, like the Ṣúfí's wife: thou hast opened in fraud the snare of cunning,

For thou art ashamed before every dirty[2] braggart, and not before thy God.

The purpose for which God is called Samí' (Hearing) and Baṣír (Seeing).

215 God has called Himself Baṣír (Seeing), in order that His seeing thee may at every moment be a deterrent (against sin).

God has called Himself Samí' (Hearing), in order that thou mayst close thy lips (and refrain) from foul speech.

God has called Himself 'Alím (Knowing), in order that thou mayst fear to meditate[3] a wicked deed.

These are not proper names applicable to God: (proper names are merely designations), for even a negro may have the name Káfúr (Camphor).

The Names (of God) are derivative and (denote) Eternal Attributes: (they are) not unsound like (the doctrine of) the First Cause.

220 Otherwise, it would be ridicule and mockery and deception, (like calling) a deaf person Samí' (Hearer) and blind men Ẓiyá (Radiance);

Or (as though) Ḥayí (Bashful) should be the proper name of an impudent fellow, or Ṣabíḥ (Beautiful) the name of a hideous blackamoor.

You may confer the title of Ḥájjí (Pilgrim) or Ghází (Holy Warrior) on a new-born child for the purpose of (indicating his) lineage;

(But) if these titles are used in praise, they are not correct unless he (the person so described) possess that (particular) quality.

(Otherwise), it would be a ridicule and mockery (so to use them), or madness: God is clear of (untouched by) what the unrighteous say[4].

225 I knew, before (our) meeting, that thou art good-looking but evil-natured;

---

[1] The speaker is the heroine of the First Story in this Book, who, having concluded the Story of the Ṣúfí, now addresses her impudent lover and points out that his behaviour is analogous to that of the Ṣúfí's wife.

[2] Literally, "with unwashed face."

[3] Literally, "in order that, because of (thy) fear, thou mayst not meditate."

[4] Qur'án, XVII, 50.

I knew, before coming face to face (with thee), that by reason of contumacy thou art set fast in damnation.

When my eye is red in ophthalmia, I know it (the redness) is from that disease, (even) if I do not see it (the redness).

Thou deemedst me as a lamb without the shepherd, thou thoughtest that I have none keeping watch (over me).

The cause why lovers have moaned in grief is that they have rubbed their eyes malapropos[1].

They have regarded that Gazelle as being shepherdless, they 230 have regarded that Captive as (one who may be taken) cost-free,

Till (suddenly) an arrow from the glance (of Divine jealousy) comes (descends) upon the heart[2], (as though) to say, 'I am the Keeper: do not look wantonly.'

How am I meaner than a lamb, meaner than a kid, that there should not be a keeper behind me?

I have a Keeper whom it beseems to hold dominion: He knoweth the wind that blows upon me.

Whether that wind was cold or hot, that Knowing One is not unaware, is not absent, O infirm man.

The appetitive soul is deaf and blind to God: I with my heart 235 was seeing thy blindness from afar.

For eight years I did not inquire after thee at all, because I saw thee (to be) full of ignorance, fold on fold.

Why, indeed, should I inquire after one who is in the bath-stove (of lust), and say (to him) 'How art thou?' when he is (plunged) headlong (in sensuality)?"

Comparison of this world to a bath-stove and of piety to the bath.

The lust of this world is like the bath-stove by which the bath, piety, is (made) resplendent;

But the pious man's portion from this stove is (naught but) purity, because he is in the hot-bath and in cleanliness.

The rich resemble those who carry dung for the bath- 240 keeper's fire-making.

God hath implanted cupidity in them, in order that the bath may be hot and well provided.

Abandon this stove and advance into the hot-bath: know that abandonment of the stove is the very essence of that bath.

Any one who is in the stove is as a servant to him that is self-denying and on his guard.

Whosoever has entered the bath, his (characteristic) sign is visible upon his comely face.

The signs of the stokers are conspicuous too—in their dress 245 and in the smoke and dust (which blacken them).

---

[1] *I.e.* they have not purged their inward eye of sensual impressions and therefore have taken a false view.
[2] Literally, "liver."

And if you see not his (the stoker's) face, smell him; smell is (as) a staff for every one that is blind;

And if you have not (the sense of) smell, induce him to speak, and from the new talk learn the old secret.

Then a gold-possessing stoker will say, "I have brought in twenty baskets of filth, (working from dawn) till nightfall."

Your cupidity is like fire in the (material) world: every (flaming) tongue (thereof) has opened a hundred mouths (to swallow filthy lucre).

250   In the sight of Reason, this gold is foul as dung, although, like dung, it is (the cause of) the blazing of the fire.

The sun, which emulates the fire[1], makes the moist filth fit for the fire.

The sun also made the stone gold[2], in order that a hundred sparks might fall into the stove of cupidity.

He who says, "I have collected riches"—what is (the meaning of) it? It means, "I have brought in all this filth."

Albeit this saying is exceedingly disgraceful, there are boasts on this account amongst the stokers.

255   (One of them says), "Thou hast carried (only) six baskets ere nightfall; I have carried twenty baskets without trouble."

He that was born in the stove and never saw purity, the smell of musk produces a painful effect upon him.

Story of the tanner who fainted and sickened on smelling otto and musk in the bazaar of the perfumers.

A certain man fell senseless and curled up[3] as soon as he came into the bazaar of the perfumers.

The scent of the perfume (floating) from the goodly perfumers smote him, so that his head reeled and he fell on the spot.

He fell unconscious, like a carcase, at noontide in the middle of the thoroughfare.

260   Thereupon the people gathered over him, all crying Lá ḥawl[4] and applying remedies.

One was putting his hand on his (the tanner's) heart, while another sprinkled rose-water upon him;

(For) he did not know that from (smelling) rose-water in the meadow (the bazaar) that calamity had overtaken him.

One was massaging his hands and head, and another was bringing moist clay mixed with straw (to serve as a cold plaster);

One compounded incense of aloes-wood and sugar, while another was divesting him of part of his clothes;

---

[1] *I.e.* in giving heat.
[2] Another allusion (cf. Book I, 3779–80) to the belief that the heat of the sun causes gold to grow in the mine.
[3] Literally, "was bent double."
[4] See Book II, translation, p. 230, note 1, and p. 232, note 2.

And another felt his pulse, to see how it was beating; and 265 another was smelling[1] his mouth,

To see whether he had drunk wine or eaten beng or hashish: the people (having exhausted every resource) remained in despair at his insensibility.

So they speedily brought the news to his kinsfolk—"Such and such a person is lying there in a state of collapse;

No one knows how he was stricken with catalepsy, or what it was that led to this public exposure[2]."

That stout tanner had a brother, (who was) cunning and sagacious: he came at once in hot haste.

(With) a small quantity of dog's dung in his sleeve, he cleft 270 (his way through) the crowd and approached (the senseless man) with cries of grief.

"I know," said he, "whence his illness arises: when you know the cause (of a disease), the (means of) curing (it) is manifest.

When the cause is unknown, the remedy for the illness is difficult (to find), and in that (case) there are a hundred grounds to which it may be referred;

(But) when you have ascertained the cause, it becomes easy: knowledge of causes is the means of expelling ignorance."

He said to himself, "The smell of that dog's dung is multiplied[3] in his brain and veins.

Up to the waist in filth, he is absorbed in the tanner's craft 275 till nightfall, seeking his livelihood.

Thus then has the great Jálínús (Galen) said: 'Give the patient that to which he was habituated (before his illness);

For his illness arises from doing the contrary to (his usual) habit: therefore seek the remedy for his illness in that which is habitual (to him).'

He (the tanner), from carrying dung, has become like the dung-beetle: the dung-beetle is made insensible by rose-water.

The remedy for him consists in that same dog's dung to which he is habituated and accustomed."

Recite (the text), *the wicked women for the wicked men*: 280 recognise (both) the front and the back of this saying.

The sincere mentors prepare medicine for him (the wicked man) with ambergris or rose-water to open the door (of Divine Mercy);

(But) sweet words will not do for the wicked: 'tis not fitting and suitable, O ye trusty ones!

When from the perfume of the Revelation they (the wicked infidels) became crooked (disordered in mind) and lost (in error), their lament was, "*We augur evil from you.*

---

[1] Literally, "was taking the smell from."
[2] Literally, "or what happened so that the bowl has fallen from the roof."
[3] Literally, "fold on fold."

This discourse (of yours) is illness and sickness to us: your exhortation is not of good omen to us.

285   If ye once begin to admonish (us) overtly, at that instant we will stone you.

We have waxed fat on frivolity and diversion: we have not steeped ourselves in admonition.

Our food is falsehood and idle boasts and jests: our stomachs are turned by your delivering this message.

Ye are making the illness hundredfold and more: ye are drugging the intelligence with opium."

How the tanner's brother sought to cure him
secretly with the smell of dung.

The youth kept driving the people away from him (the tanner), in order that those persons might not see his treatment (of the sick man).

290   He brought his head (close) to his ear, like one telling a secret; then he put the thing (which he had in his hand) to his (the tanner's) nose;

For he had rubbed the dog's dung on his palm: he had deemed it (to be) the remedy for the polluted brain.

A short while passed: the man began to move: the people said, "This was a wonderful charm;

For this (youth) recited charms and breathed (them) into his ear: he was dead: the charms came to succour him."

The movement of iniquitous folk is to the quarter in which there is fornication and ogling glances and eyebrows.

295   Any one to whom the musk, admonition, is of no use must necessarily make himself familiar with the bad smell.

God has called the polytheists *najas* (uncleanness)[1] for the reason that they were born in dung from of old.

The worm that has been born in dung will nevermore change its evil nature by means of ambergris.

Since the largesse of sprinkled light[2] did not strike upon him (the wicked man), he is wholly body, without heart (spirit), like (empty) husks.

And if God gave him a portion of the sprinkled light, the dung hatched a bird, as is the custom in Egypt—

300   But not the cheap domestic fowl; nay, but the bird of knowledge and wisdom.

"Thou resemblest that (wicked man)[3], for thou art devoid of that light, inasmuch as thou art putting thy nose to filth.

---

[1] *Qur'án*, IX, 28.   [2] Literally, "of the sprinkling of light."
[3] This and the following verses are addressed by the heroine of the First Story in Book IV to her unworthy lover.

Because of being parted (from me) thy cheeks and face have become yellow (pale): thou art (a tree with) yellow leaves and unripened fruit.

The pot was blackened by the fire and became like smoke in colour, (but) the meat, on account of (its) hardness, has remained so raw as this!

Eight years have I boiled thee in separation (from me): thy rawness and hypocrisy have not become less by a single mote.

Thy young grape is indurated; for through sickness[1] the 305 (other) young grapes are now raisins, while thou art (still) immature."

How the lover begged to be excused for his sin, (but) with duplicity and dissimulation; and how the beloved perceived that also.

The lover said, "I made the trial—do not take offence—that I might see whether thou art a hetaera or a modest woman.

I was knowing (it) without the trial, but how should hearing be the same as seeing?

Thou art (like) the sun: thy name is renowned and known to all: what harm is there if I have tested it?

Thou art I: every day I am making trial of myself in profit and loss (good and evil).

The prophets were put to the trial by their enemies, with the 310 result that miracles were displayed by them.

I made trial of my own eye with light, O thou from whose eyes may the evil eye be far!

This world is as the ruin, and thou the treasure (buried there): if I have made investigation concerning thy treasure, be not aggrieved.

I recklessly committed such an indiscretion, that I may always boast (of thy virtue) to (thy) enemies;

So that, when my tongue bestows a name on thee, my eye may give testimonies of this which I have seen.

If I have sought to rob thee of thy honour[2], I come, O Moon 315 (of beauty), with sword and winding-sheet.

Do not cut off my feet and head save with thine own hand, for I belong to this hand, not to another hand.

Thou art talking again of separation: do whatsoever thou wilt, but do not this!"

The way is now made (open for entering) into the realm of Discourse (Exposition); (but) 'tis impossible to speak (on the subject), since there is no time (to do so at present).

We have told the husks (externals), but the kernel (the inner meaning) is buried; if we remain (alive), this will not remain (concealed) as it is now.

---

[1] *I.e.* in consequence of their having been dried and pressed.
[2] Literally, "If I have become a highway robber on the road of respect."

How the beloved rejected the excuses of the lover
and rubbed his duplicity into him¹.

320 The loved one opened her lips to answer him, saying, "On my side it is day, and on thy side it is night.

Why in contention dost thou bring forward dark evasions before those who see (the truth plainly)?

To us, all the deceit and dissimulations that thou hast in thy heart are manifest and clear as day.

If we, in kindness to our servant, cover it up, why dost thou carry shamelessness beyond the limit?

Learn from thy Father; for in (the hour of) sin Adam came down willingly to the vestibule².

325 When he beheld that Knower of secrets, he stood up on his feet to ask forgiveness.

He seated himself on the ashes of contrition: he did not jump from one branch of idle pleading to another³.

He said only, 'O Lord, *verily we have done wrong*,' when he saw the (angelic) life-guards in front and behind.

He saw the life-guards who are invisible, as the spirit is—each one's mace (reaching) to the sky—

Saying, 'Hola! be (as) the ant before Solomon, lest this mace cleave thee asunder.

330 Do not for one moment stand (anywhere) but in the place of truth: a man hath no guardian like the (seeing) eye.

(Even) if the blind man be purified by admonition, he continually becomes polluted again.

O Adam, thou art not blind of vision, but when the Divine destiny comes, the sight becomes blind.'"

Lifetimes are needed—(so) rarely and occasionally (does it happen)—for the seeing man to fall by destiny into the pit.

As regards the blind man, this destiny in sooth is his companion on the way; for 'tis his nature and disposition to fall.

335 He falls into the filth and does not know what the smell is; (he asks himself), "Is this smell from me or from (my) being polluted?"

And likewise, if any one sprinkle some musk over him, he thinks it (comes) from himself and not from the kindness of his friend.

Therefore to you, O man of vision, two clear eyes are (as) a hundred mothers and a hundred fathers;

¹ Literally, "into his face."

² *I.e.* abased himself. پایگاه is here equivalent to صفّ نعال, the place at the lower end of the reception room where visitors take off their shoes.

³ Literally, "from branch to branch, in respect of idle pretence"; *i.e.* he did not *ramify* excuses or develop them systematically.

Especially the eye of the heart (the spiritual eye), which is seventy-fold and of which these two sensible eyes are (only) the gleaners.

Oh, alas, the highwaymen[1] are seated (and lying in wait for me): they have tied a hundred knots beneath my tongue.

How should the smooth-paced horse move well, when his leg 340 is tied? This is a very heavy chain: hold me excused!

These words (of mine) are coming (forth) brokenly, O heart; for these words are pearls, and (the Divine) jealousy is the mill (which breaks them);

(But), though the pearls be broken into small fragments, they become tutty (collyrium) for the sore eye (of the spirit).

O pearl, do not beat thy head (in grief) at thy being broken, for through being broken thou wilt become (radiant) light.

It (the word) has to be uttered thus brokenly and in bandages: God, who is Self-sufficient, will make it whole at last.

If wheat is broken and torn asunder (in the mill), it appears 345 in the (baker's) shop, saying, "Look! a perfect loaf!"

"Thou too, O lover, since thy crime has become manifest, abandon water and oil (specious varnish) and be broken (contrite).

Those who are the elect children of Adam sigh forth (the confession), '*verily we have done wrong.*'

Submit thy petition, do not argue like the accursed hard-faced (impudent) Iblís.

If impudence concealed his fault, go, exert thyself in (show-ing) obstinacy and impudence!

Abú Jahl, like a vindictive Ghuzz Turcoman, demanded a 350 miracle from the Prophet;

But that *Siddíq* of God (Abú Bakr) did not crave a miracle: he said, 'Verily, this face speaks naught but truth.'

How should it beseem one like thee, from egoism, to make trial of a beloved like me?"

How the Jew said to 'Alí, may God honour his person, "If thou hast confidence in God's protection, cast thyself down from the top of this kiosk"; and how the Prince of the Faithful answered him.

One day a contumacious man, who was ignorant of the re-verence due to God, said to Murtazá ('Alí),

On the top of an exceedingly high terrace or pavilion, "Art thou conscious of God's protection, O intelligent man?"

"Yes," he replied; "He is the Protector and the Self-suf- 355 ficient for (preserving) my existence from (the time of) infancy and conception[2]."

---

[1] *I.e.* sceptics and cavillers in whose presence one cannot speak of Divine mysteries.
[2] Literally, "semen."

He (the Jew) said, "Come, cast thyself down from the roof,
put an entire confidence in the protection of God,

So that thy sure faith and thy goodly proven conviction may
become evident to me."

Then the Prince said to him, "Be silent, go, lest for this bold-
ness thy soul be pawned (given over to perdition)."

How is it right for a servant (of God) to venture on[1] an ex-
periment with God by making trial (of Him)?

360 How should a servant (of God) have the stomach[2] vain-
gloriously to put Him to the test, O mad fool?

To God (alone) belongs that (right), who brings forward a
test for His servants at every moment,

In order that He may show us plainly to ourselves (and reveal)
what beliefs we hold in secret.

Did Adam ever say to God, "I made trial of Thee in (com-
mitting) this sin and trespass,

That I might see the utmost limit of Thy clemency, O
King?" Ah, who would be capable of (seeing) this, who[3]?

365 Forasmuch as your understanding is confused, your excuse is
worse than your crime.

How can you make trial of Him who raised aloft the vault of
heaven?

O you that have not known good and evil, (first) make trial
of yourself, and then of others.

When you have made trial of yourself, O such-and-such, you
will be unconcerned with making trial of others.

When you have come to know that you are a grain of sugar,
then you will know that you belong to the sugar-house.

370 Know, then, without making any trial, that (if) you are sugar,
God will not send you to the wrong place.

Without making trial, know this of the King's (God's) know-
ledge: when you are a (spiritual) chief, He will not send you
(down) to the vestibule.

Does any intelligent man let a precious pearl fall into the
midst of a privy full of ordure?

Inasmuch as a sagacious and attentive man will nowise send
wheat to a straw-barn,

If a novice has made trial of the Shaykh who is the (spiritual)
leader and guide, he is an ass.

375 If you make trial of him in the way of religion, *you* will be
tried (by tribulation), O man without faith.

Your audacity and ignorance will become naked and exposed
to view: how should he be made naked by that scrutiny?

If the mote come and weigh the mountain, its scales will be
shattered by the mountain, O youth;

---

[1] Literally, "bring forward."   [2] Literally, "gall-bladder."
[3] Literally, "to whom would there be the capacity for this, to whom?"

For he (the novice) applies the scales of his own judgement and puts the man of God in the scales;

(But) since he (the Shaykh) is not contained by the scales of intellect, consequently he shatters the scales of intellect.

Know that to make trial (of him) is like exercising authority 380 over him: do not seek to exercise authority over such a (spiritual) king.

What authority should the pictures (phenomenal forms) desire to exercise over such an Artist for the purpose of testing Him?

If it (the picture) has known and experienced any trial, is it not the case that the Artist brought that (trial) upon it?

Indeed, this form that He fashioned—what is it worth in comparison with the forms which are in His knowledge?

When the temptation to make this trial has come to you, know that ill fortune has come and smitten your neck.

When you feel such a temptation, at once, at once turn unto 385 God and begin the prostration (in prayer).

Make the place of prostration wet with flowing tears and say, "O God, do Thou deliver me from this doubt!"

At the time when it is your object to make trial (of God), the mosque, namely, your religion, becomes filled with *kharrúb* (carob).

Story of the Farther Mosque[1] and the carob and how, before (the reign of) Solomon, on whom be peace, David, on whom be peace, resolved on building that Mosque.

When David's resolve that he would build the Farther Mosque with stone came to sore straits[2],

God made a Revelation to him, saying, "Proclaim the abandonment of this (enterprise), for (the building of) this place will not be achieved by thy hand.

'Tis not in Our fore-ordainment that thou shouldst raise this 390 Farther Mosque, O chosen one."

He said, "O Knower of the secret, what is my crime, that Thou forbiddest me to construct the Mosque?"

He (God) said, "Without (committing) a crime, thou hast wrought much bloodshed: thou hast taken upon thy neck (art responsible for) the blood of (many) persons who have suffered injustice;

For from (hearing) thy voice a countless multitude gave up the ghost and fell a prey to it (thy voice).

Much blood has gone to the score of (is chargeable to) thy voice, to thy beautiful soul-ravishing song[3]."

---

[1] The Temple of Solomon.
[2] *I.e.* met with grievous difficulties.   [3] Cf. Book iii, vv. 1470-1.

395   He (David) said, "I was overpowered by Thee, drunken with Thee: my hand (power) was tied up by Thy hand.

Was not every one that was overpowered by the King the object of (His) mercy? Was not he (excused on the ground that) 'The overpowered is like the non-existent'?"

He (God) said, "This overpowered man is that non-existent one who is only relatively non-existent. Have sure faith!

Such a non-existent one who hath gone from himself (become selfless) is the best of beings, and the great (one among them).

He hath passèd away (*faná*) in relation to (the passing away of his attributes in) the Divine attributes, (but) in passing away (from selfhood) he really hath the life everlasting (*baqá*).

400   All spirits are under his governance; all bodies too are in his control.

He that is overpowered (overwhelmed) in Our grace is not compelled; nay, he is one who freely chooses devotion (to Us)."

In sooth the end of free-will is that his free-will should be lost here.

The free agent would feel no savour (spiritual delight) if at last he did not become entirely purged of egoism.

If there is delicious food and drink in the world, (yet) his pleasure (in them) is (only) a branch of (derived from) the extinction of (worldly) pleasure.

405   Although he was unaffected by (worldly) pleasures, (yet) he was a man of (spiritual) pleasure and became the recipient of (that) pleasure.

Explanation of "Verily, the Faithful are brothers, *and the* '*ulamá* (*divines*) *are as one soul*"; *in particular, the oneness of David, Solomon, and all the other prophets, on whom be peace: if you disbelieve in one of them,* (*your*) *faith in any prophet will not be perfect; and this is the sign of* (*their*) *oneness, that if you destroy a single one of those thousands of houses, all the rest will be destroyed, and not a single wall will be left standing; for* "We make no distinction between any of them (the prophets)." *Indication is sufficient for him that hath intelligence: this goes even beyond indication.*

(God said to David), "Although it will not be accomplished by thy labour and strength, yet the Mosque will be erected by thy son.

His deed is thy deed, O man of wisdom: know that between the Faithful is an ancient union."

The Faithful are numerous, but the Faith is one: their bodies are numerous, but their soul is one.

Besides the understanding and soul which is in the ox and the ass, Man has another intelligence and soul;

Again, in the owner of that (Divine) breath[1] there is a soul 410
other than the human soul and intelligence.

The animal soul does not possess oneness: seek not thou this
oneness from the airy (vital) spirit.

If this one eat bread, that one is not filled; and if this one
bear a load, that one does not become laden;

Nay, but this one rejoices at the death of that one, and dies
of envy when he sees that one's prosperity.

The souls of wolves and dogs are separate, every one; the
souls of the Lions of God are united.

I have spoken of their souls nominally (formally) in the 415
plural, for that single soul is a hundred in relation to the
body,

Just as the single light of the sun in heaven is a hundred in
relation to the house-courts (on which it shines),

But when you remove the wall, all the lights (falling) on them
are one.

When the (bodily) houses have no foundation remaining, the
Faithful remain one soul.

Differences and difficulties arise from this saying, because this
is not a (complete) similitude: it is (only) a comparison.

Endless are the differences between the corporeal figure of a 420
lion and the figure of a courageous son of man;

But at the moment of (making) the comparison consider, O
thou who hast good insight, their oneness in respect of hazarding
their lives;

For, after all, the courageous man did resemble the lion,
(though) he is not like the lion in all points of the definition.

This abode (the world) does not contain any form (that is)
one (with any other form), so that I might show forth to thee a
(complete) similitude.

Still, I will bring to hand an imperfect comparison, that I may
redeem thy mind from confusion.

At night a lamp is placed in every house, in order that by its 425
light they (the inmates) may be delivered from darkness.

That lamp is (like) this body, its light like the (animal) soul;
it requires a wick and this and that.

That lamp with six wicks, namely, these senses[2], is based
entirely upon sleep and food.

Without food and sleep it would not live half a moment; nor
even with food and sleep does it live either.

Without wick and oil it has no duration, and with wick and
oil it is also faithless (transient),

---

[1] The prophet or saint.
[2] Apparently "the common sense" (*hiss-i mushtarak*), which receives the
perceptions conveyed by the five bodily senses, is itself reckoned here as a sixth
bodily sense.

430   Inasmuch as its light, (being) related to (secondary) causes, is seeking death: how should it live when bright day is the death of it?

Likewise all the human senses are impermanent, because they are naught in the presence of the Day of Resurrection.

The light of the senses and spirits of our fathers is not wholly perishable and naught, like the grass;

But, like the stars and moonbeams, they all vanish in the radiance of the Sun.

'Tis just as the smart and pain of the flea's bite disappears when the snake comes in to you (and bites you).

435   'Tis just as the naked man jumped into the water, that in the water he might escape from the sting of the hornets:

The hornets circle above (him), and when he puts out his head they do not spare him.

The water is recollection (*dhikr*) of God, and the hornet is the remembrance, during this time, of such-and-such a woman or such-and-such a man.

Swallow (hold) your breath in the water of recollection and show fortitude, that you may be freed from the old thought and temptation.

After that, you yourself will assume the nature of that pure water entirely from head to foot.

440   As the noxious hornet flees from the water, so will it be afraid of (approaching) you.

After that, be far from the water, if you wish; for in your inmost soul you are of the same nature as the water, O fellow-servant.

Those persons, then, who have passed from the world are not naught (non-existent), but they are steeped in the (Divine) Attributes.

All their attributes are (absorbed) in the Attributes of God, even as the star is (left) without trace in the presence of the sun.

If you demand a citation from the *Qur'án*, O recalcitrant, recite *all of them shall be brought into Our presence.*

445   (The person denoted by the word) *muḥdarún* (brought into the presence) is not non-existent (*ma'dúm*). Consider (this) well, that you may gain certain knowledge of the everlasting life (*baqá*) of the spirits.

The spirit debarred from everlasting life is exceedingly tormented; the spirit united (with God) in everlasting life is free from (every) barrier.

I have told you the purpose of this lamp of animal sense-perception. Beware of seeking to become one (with it in spirit).

Make your spirit, O such-and-such, to be united speedily with the holy spirits of the Travellers (on the mystic Way).

Your hundred lamps, then, whether they die (are extinguished) or whether they stand (and burn), are separate (from each other) and are not single.

On that account these companions of ours are all at war, (but) 450 no one (ever) heard of war amongst the prophets,

Because the light of the prophets was the Sun, (while) the light of our senses is lamp and candle and smoke.

One (of these lamps) dies, one lasts till daybreak; one is dim, another bright.

The animal soul is (kept) alive by nutriment; however good or bad its state may be, it dies all the same.

If this lamp dies and is extinguished, (yet) how should the neighbour's house become dark?

Inasmuch as without this (lamp) the light in that house is still 455 maintained, hence (it follows that) the lamp of sense-perception is different in every house.

This is a parable of the animal soul, not a parable of the divine soul.

Again, when the moon is born from the Hindú, Night, a light falls upon every window.

Count the light of those hundred houses as one, for the light of this (house) does not remain (in existence) without (the light of) the other[1].

So long as the sun is shining on the horizon, its light is a guest in every house;

Again, when the spiritual Sun sets, the light in all the houses 460 disappears.

This is (only) a parable of the Light, not a (complete) similitude; for you (it is) a true guide, for the enemy (of the Light) a highwayman.

That evil-natured person resembles the spider: he weaves stinking veils (cobwebs).

Of his own gossamer he made a veil over the Light: he made the eye of his apprehension blind.

If one takes hold of a horse's neck, he gains advantage; and if he takes hold of its leg, he receives a kick.

Do not mount the restive horse without a bridle: make 465 Reason and Religion your leader, and farewell.

Do not look scornfully and contemptuously on this quest, for in this Way there is (need of) self-denial and grievous anguish to (men's) souls.

---

[1] *I.e.* when the moon sinks, *all* the houses are left in darkness.

The rest of the Story of the building of the Farther Mosque.

When Solomon began the building—holy like the Ka'ba, august like Miná—

In his building were seen splendour and magnificence: it was not frigid (dull and lifeless) like other buildings.

From the first, every stone in the building—(every stone) that was broken off from the mountain—was saying clearly, "Take me along!"

470 As from the water and earth of the house (bodily tenement) of Adam, (so) did light shine forth from the pieces of mortar.

The stones were coming without carrier, and those doors and walls had become living.

God saith that the wall of Paradise is not lifeless and ugly like (other) walls;

Like the door and wall of the body, it is (endowed) with intelligence: the house (Paradise) is living since it belongs to the King of kings.

Both tree and fruit and limpid water (take part) with the inhabitant of Paradise in conversation and discourse,

475 Because Paradise has not been fashioned out of (the builder's) materials; nay, but it has been fashioned out of (good) deeds and intentions.

This edifice has been (made) of dead water and earth, while that edifice has arisen from living piety.

This (edifice) resembles its foundation (which is) full of defect, and that (edifice resembles) its foundation, which is knowledge and action.

Both throne and palace and crown and robes are (engaged) in question and reply (conversation) with the inhabitant of Paradise.

The carpet (there) is folded without the *farrásh* (carpet-spreader); the house (Paradise) is swept without the broom.

480 Behold the house of the heart: it was disordered by (worldly) cares: without sweeper it was swept (clean) by a (vow of) repentance.

Its throne moved along without carrier; its door-ring and door became (sweet-sounding like) musician and singer.

The life of the everlasting Abode (Paradise) exists in the heart: since it comes not on to my tongue, what is the use (of my attempting to describe it)?

When Solomon went into the Mosque every morning to guide the servants (of God) in the right way,

He would give exhortation, sometimes by speech and melody and harmony, sometimes by act—I mean, a bowing or (service of) prayer.

The exhortation of act draws people more powerfully, for it 485 reaches the soul of every one that hath hearing and (also) the deaf.

In that (kind of exhortation) the conceit of princedom is less (than in the other kind): the impression made by it upon the (prince's) followers is strong.

Story of the beginning of the Caliphate of 'Uthmán, may God be well-pleased with him, and his sermon expounding that the doer who exhorts by deeds is better than the speaker who exhorts by words.

The story (told) of 'Uthmán is that he mounted the pulpit: when he obtained the Caliphate, he made hot haste (to mount it).

('Twas) the pulpit of the Chief (Mohammed), which had three steps: Abú Bakr went and seated himself on the second step.

'Umar, in his reign, (sat) on the third step in order to show reverence for Islam and the (true) Religion.

(When) the reign of 'Uthmán arrived, he, that man of praised 490 (blessed) fortune, went up on to the top of the throne (pulpit) and seated himself.

Then a person given to idle meddling questioned him, saying, "Those two did not sit in the Prophet's place:

How, then, hast thou sought to be higher than they, when thou art inferior to them in rank?"

He replied, "If I tread on the third step, it will be imagined that I resemble 'Umar;

(And if) I seek a seat on the second step, thou wilt say, ' 'Tis (the seat of) Abú Bakr, and (therefore) this one too is like him.'

This top (of the pulpit) is the place of Muṣṭafá (Mohammed): 495 no one will imagine that I am like that (spiritual) King[1]."

Afterwards, (seated) in the preaching-place, that loving man kept silence till near the (time of the) afternoon-prayer.

None dared to say "Come now, preach!" or to go forth from the mosque during that time.

An awe had settled (descended) on high and low (alike): the court and roof (of the mosque) had become filled with the Light of God.

Whoever possessed vision was beholding His Light; the blind man too was being heated by that Sun.

Hence, by reason of the heat, the blind man's eye was per- 500 ceiving that there had arisen a Sun whose strength faileth not.

But this heat (unlike the heat of the terrestrial sun) opens the (inward) eye, that it may see the very substance of everything heard.

[1] Literally, "there is no false notion of my being like that (spiritual) King."

Its heat has (as effect) a grievous agitation and emotion, (but) from that glow there comes to the heart a joyous (sense of) freedom, an expansion.

When the blind man is heated by the Light of Eternity, from gladness he says, "I have become seeing."

Thou art mightily well drunken, but, O Bu 'l-Ḥasan, there is a bit of way (to be traversed ere thou attain) to seeing.

505   This is the blind man's portion from the Sun, (and) a hundred such (portions); and God best knoweth what is right.

And he that hath vision of that Light—how should the explanation of him (his state) be a task (within the capacity) of Bú Síná?

(Even) if it be hundredfold, who (what) is this tongue that it should move with its hand the veil of (mystical) clairvoyance?

Woe to it if it touch the veil! The Divine sword severs its hand.

What of the hand? It (the sword) rends off even its (the tongue's) head—the head that from ignorance puts forth many a head (of pride and self-conceit).

510   I have said this to you, speaking hypothetically; otherwise, indeed, how far is its hand from being able to do that[1]!

Materterae si testiculi essent, ea avunculus esset: this is hypothetical—"if there were."

(If) I say that between the tongue and the eye that is free from doubt there is a hundred thousand years' (journey), 'tis little (in comparison with the reality).

Now come, do not despair! When God wills, light arrives from heaven in a single moment.

At every instant His power causes a hundred influences from the stars to reach the (subterranean) mines.

515   The star (planet) of heaven[2] deletes the darkness; the star of God[3] is fixed in His Attributes.

O thou that seekest help, the celestial sphere, (at a distance) of five hundred years' journey, is in effect nigh unto the earth.

'Tis (a journey of) three thousand five hundred years to Saturn; (yet) his special property acts incessantly (upon the earth).

He (God) rolls it up[4] like a shadow at the return (of the sun): in the sun's presence what is (what avails) the length of the shadow?

And from the pure starlike souls replenishment is ever coming to the stars of heaven.

520   The outward (aspect) of those stars is our ruler, (but) our inward (essence) has become the ruler of the sky.

---

[1] Literally, "where is its hand and where is that?"
[2] The sun and moon.
[3] The spirit of the Perfect Man.
[4] *I.e.* brings the action of Saturn to an end.

Explaining that (while) philosophers say that Man is the microcosm, theosophists say that Man is the macrocosm, the reason being that philosophy is confined to the phenomenal form of Man, whereas theosophy is connected with the essential truth of his true nature.

Therefore in form thou art the microcosm, therefore in reality thou art the macrocosm.

Externally the branch[1] is the origin of the fruit; intrinsically the branch came into existence for the sake of the fruit.

If there had not been desire and hope of the fruit, how should the gardener have planted the root of the tree?

Therefore in reality the tree was born of the fruit, (even) if in appearance it (the fruit) was generated by the tree.

Hence Muṣṭafá (Mohammed) said, "Adam and the (other) 525 prophets are (following) behind me under (my) banner."

For this reason that master of (all) sorts of knowledge has uttered the allegorical saying, "We are the last and the foremost."

(That is to say), "If in appearance I am born of Adam, in reality I am the forefather of (every) forefather,

Since the worship of the angels was (rendered) to him for my sake, and he ascended to the Seventh Heaven on my account.

Therefore in reality the Father (Adam) was born of me, therefore in reality the tree was born of the fruit."

The thought (idea), which is first, comes last into actuality, 530 in particular the thought that is eternal.

To sum up, in a single moment the caravan is going from Heaven and coming here.

This way is not long for this caravan: how should the desert show itself formidable to him who has been granted success (by God)[2]?

The heart (spirit) is faring to the Ka'ba at every moment, and through (Divine) bounty the body assumes the nature of the heart.

This longness and shortness appertains to the body: where God is, what is "long" and "short"?

When God has transmuted the body, He makes its faring to 535 be without league or mile.

There are a hundred hopes at this (present) time. Step (forward), O youth, like a (true) lover and relinquish (idle) disputation.

Albeit thou art closing thine eyelids, thou art asleep in the ship and voyaging (in safety).

[1] Literally, "the outward aspect (which consists) of the branch."
[2] Or, "How should the desert seem formidable in conjunction with success granted (by God)?"

Exposition of the Ḥadíth, " The parable of my community is the parable of the Ship (Ark) of Noah: whoso shall cleave to it is saved, and whoso shall hold back from it is drowned."

On this account the Prophet said, "I am as the Ship (Ark) in the Flood of Time.

I and my Companions are as the Ship of Noah: whoso clings (to us) will gain (spiritual) graces."

540 When you are with the Shaykh you are far removed from wickedness: day and night you are a traveller and in a ship.

You are under the protection of a life-giving spirit: you are asleep in the ship, you are going on the way.

Do not break with the prophet of your days[1]: do not rely on your own skill and footsteps[2].

Lion though you are, you are self-conceited and in error and contemptible when you go on the way without a guide.

Beware! Do not fly but with the wings of the Shaykh, that you may see (receive) the aid of the armies of the Shaykh.

545 At one time the wave of his mercy is your pinion, at another moment the fire of his wrath is your carrier.

Do not reckon his wrath to be the contrary of his mercy: behold the oneness of both (these qualities) in the effect.

At one time he will make you green like the earth, at another time he will make you full of wind, and big.

He gives the quality of inorganic things to the body of the knower (of God), in order that gay roses and eglantines may grow on it;

But he (the Shaykh) alone sees (them), none sees but he: Paradise yields no scent but to the purified brain.

550 Empty your brain of disbelief in the Friend, that it may feel sweet odours from the rose-garden of the Friend;

So that you may feel the scent of Paradise from my Friend, as Mohammed the scent of the Merciful (God) from Yemen.

If you stand in the rank of those who make the (spiritual) ascension, not-being (self-naughtedness) will bear you aloft, like Buráq.

'Tis not like the ascension of a piece of earth (an earthly being) to the moon; nay, but like the ascension of a cane to sugar.

'Tis not like the ascension of a vapour to the sky; nay, but like the ascension of an embryo to rationality.

555 The steed of not-being (self-naughtedness) became a goodly Buráq: it brings you to (real) existence, if you are non-existent (self-naughted).

Its hoof brushes the mountains and seas till it puts the world of sense-perception behind.

---

[1] *I.e.* the Ṣúfí Shaykhs who are the spiritual heirs and representatives of the Prophet.   [2] Reading گامِ خویش.

Set your foot into the ship and keep going quickly, like the soul going towards[1] the soul's Beloved.

(With) no hands and no feet, go to Eternity in the same fashion as that in which the spirits sped from non-existence.

If there had not been somnolence (dullness and inattention) in the hearer's hearing, the veil of logical reasoning would have been torn asunder in the discourse.

O Heaven, shower pearls on his (the Shaykh's)[2] rede! O 560 World, have shame of (be abashed by) his world!

If thou wilt shower (pearls), thy substance will become (increased in splendour) hundredfold: thy inorganic (matter) will become seeing and speaking.

Therefore thou wilt have scattered a largesse for thine own sake, inasmuch as every stock of thine will be centupled.

Story of Bilqís' sending a gift from the city of Sabá to Solomon, on whom be peace.

The gift of Bilqís was forty mules: their whole load consisted of bricks of gold.

When he (the envoy) reached the open plain, belonging to Solomon, he saw that its carpet was (made) entirely of solid gold.

He rode on gold for the distance of forty stages, till gold had 565 no more esteem in his sight.

(Many) times they said, "Let us take the gold back to the treasury: what a (fruitless) quest are we (engaged) in!

A spacious land of which the soil is pure gold—to bring gold thither as a gift is folly."

O thou who hast brought intelligence to God as a gift, there intelligence is less (in value) than the dust of the road.

When the worthlessness of the gift became apparent there (in Solomon's kingdom), shamefacedness was drawing them back (towards Bilqís);

(But) again they said, "Whether it be worthless or valuable, 570 what matter to us? We are slaves (bound) to (obey) the command.

Whether we have to bring gold or earth, the command of the one who gives the command is to be executed.

If they[3] command you to bring it back (to Bilqís), (then) take the gift back according to the command."

When Solomon beheld that (gift), he laughed, saying, "When did I seek *tharíd*[4] from you?

I do not bid you bestow gifts on me; nay, I bid you be worthy of the gifts (which I bestow);

---

[1] Or, reading with G جان و روان, "like the soul and (rational) spirit towards."   [2] Probably Ḥusámu'ddín is meant.
[3] *I.e.* Solomon.   [4] Broken bread moistened with broth.

575   For I have rare gifts (coming) from the Unseen, which human beings durst not even ask for.

Ye worship the star (planet) that makes gold: turn your faces towards Him that makes the star.

Ye worship the sun in heaven, having despised the Spirit (which is) of high price.

The sun, by command of God, is our cook: 'twere folly that we should say it is God.

If thy sun be eclipsed, what wilt thou do? How wilt thou expel that blackness from it?

580   Wilt not thou bring thy headache (trouble and pain) to the court of God, saying, 'Take the blackness away, give back the radiance!'

If they would kill thee at midnight, where is the sun, that thou shouldst wail (in supplication) and beg protection of it?

Calamities, for the most part, happen in the night; and at that time the object of thy worship is absent.

If thou sincerely bow (in prayer) to God, thou wilt be delivered from the stars: thou wilt become intimate (with God).

When thou becomest intimate, I will open my lips (to speak) with thee, that thou may'st behold a Sun at midnight.

585   It hath no Orient but the pure spirit: in (respect of) its rising, there is no difference between day and night.

'Tis day when it (the Sun) rises; when it begins to shine, night is night no more.

(Such) as the mote appears in the presence of the sun, even such is the sun (of this world) in the pure substance (of the Light of God).

The sun that becomes resplendent, and before which the (keenest) sight is blunted and dazzled—

Thou wilt see it as a mote in the light of the Divine Throne, (a mote) beside the illimitable abounding light of the Divine Throne.

590   Thou wilt deem it base and lowly and impermanent, (when) strength has come to thine (inward) eye from the Creator."

(The Divine Light is) the Philosophers' Stone from which a single impression fell on the (primal) vapour, and it (the vapour) became a star;

The unique elixir of which half a gleam struck upon a (region of) darkness and made it the sun;

The marvellous alchemist who by a single operation fastened all these properties on Saturn[1].

Know, O seeker, that the remaining planets and the spiritual substances are (to be judged) according to the same standard.

595   The sensuous eye is subject to the sun: seek and find a divine eye,

[1] *I.e.* caused the properties characteristic of Saturn to inhere in that planet.

In order that the beams of the flaming sun may become sub-
ject (abased) before that vision;
For that vision is luminous, while these (sunbeams) are
igneous: fire is very dark in comparison with light.

The miraculous gifts and illumination of Shaykh 'Abdullah Maghribí, may God sanctify his spirit.

Shaykh 'Abdullah Maghribí said, "During sixty years I never
perceived in night the quality of night.
During sixty years I never experienced any darkness, neither
by day nor by night nor from infirmity."
The Ṣúfís declared his words to be true: "During the night 600
we would follow him
Into deserts filled with thorns and ditches, he going in front
of us like the full-moon.
Without looking behind him, he would say, (though it was)
at night-time, 'Hark! here is a ditch: turn to the left!'
Then, after a little while, he would say, 'Turn to the right,
because a thorn is before your feet.'
Day would break: we would come to kiss his foot, and his foot
would be like the feet of a bride,
No trace of earth or mud on it, none of scratch from thorns 605
or bruise from stones."
God made the Maghribí a Mashriqí: He made the place of
sunset (maghrib) light-producing like the place of sunrise
(mashriq).
The light of this one who belongs to the Sun of suns is riding
(in majesty): by day he is guarding high and low.
How should that glorious light, which brings thousands of
suns into view, not be a guardian?
By his light do thou walk always in safety amidst dragons and
scorpions.
That holy light is going in front of thee and tearing every 610
highwayman to pieces.
Know aright (the meaning of the text) on the Day when He
(God) will not put the Prophet to shame; read (their) light shall
run before them.
Although that (light) will be increased at the Resurrection,
(yet) beg of God (to grant thee) trial (of it) here;
For He bestows spiritual light both on cloud and mist[1], and
God best knoweth how to impart (it).

[1] I.e. the darkness of the sensual nature.

*How Solomon, on whom be peace, bade the envoys of Bilqís return
to her with the gifts which they had brought; and how he called
Bilqís to (accept) the Faith and to abandon sun-worship.*

"O shamefaced envoys, turn back! The gold is yours: bring
unto me the heart, the (pure) heart!

615 Lay this gold of mine on the top of that gold (of yours): date
corporis caecitatem pudendo mulae."

Annulo aureo pudendum mulae idoneum est; the lover's gold
is the pallid yellow countenance;

For that (countenance) is the object of the Lord's regard,
while the mine (of gold) results from the sun's casting looks (of
favour).

How can (that which is) the sunbeams' object of regard be
compared with (that which is) an object of regard to the Lord of
the quintessence[1]?

"Make of your souls a shield against my taking (you) captive[2],
though (in truth) ye are my captives even now."

620 The bird tempted by the bait is (still) on the roof: with wings
outspread, it is (nevertheless) imprisoned in the trap.

Inasmuch as with (all) its soul it has given its heart to (has
become enamoured of) the bait, deem it caught, (though
apparently it is still) uncaught.

Deem the looks which it is directing to the bait to be the
knot that it is tying on its legs.

The bait says, "If thou art stealing thy looks (away from me)[3],
I am stealing from thee patience and constancy.

When those looks have drawn thee after me, then thou wilt
know that I am not inattentive to thee."

*Story of the druggist whose balance-weight was clay for washing
the head; and how a customer, who was a clay-eater, stole some
of that clay covertly and secretly, whilst sugar was being weighed.*

625 A certain clay-eater went to a druggist to buy (a quantity of)
fine hard sugar-loaf.

Now, at the druggist's, (who was) a crafty vigilant[4] man, in
place of the balance-weight there was clay.

He said, "If you want to buy sugar, my balance-weight is
clay[5]."

---

[1] *I.e.* the highest spiritual realities.
[2] *I.e.* protect yourselves against my wrath by surrendering your souls to
God.
[3] *I.e.* feigning not to see me.
[4] Literally, "of two minds": *i.e.* while attending to his business, he
observed what his customer was doing.
[5] *I.e.* "wait till I have rectified the balance."

He (the customer) said, "I am requiring sugar for an urgent affair: let the balance-weight be whatever you wish."

To himself he said, "What does the weight matter to one that eats clay? Clay is better than gold."

As the *dallála* (go-between) who said, "O son, I have found 630 a very beautiful new bride (for you).

(She is) exceedingly pretty, but there is just one thing, that the lady is a confectioner's daughter."

"(All the) better," said he; "if it is indeed so, his daughter will be fatter and sweeter."

"If you have no (proper) weight and your weight is of clay, this is better and better: clay is the fruit (desired) of my heart."

He (the druggist) placed the clay, because of its being ready (to his hand), in one scale of the balance instead of the (proper) weight;

Then, for the other scale, he was breaking with his hand the 635 equivalent amount of sugar[1].

Since he had no pick-axe, he took[2] a long time and made the customer sit waiting.

(Whilst) his face was (turned) towards that (sugar), the clay-eater, unable to restrain himself, began covertly to steal the clay from him,

Terribly frightened lest his (the druggist's) eye should fall upon him of a sudden for the purpose of testing (his honesty).

The druggist saw it, but made himself busy, saying, "Come, steal more, O pale-faced one!

If you will be a thief and take some of my clay, go on (doing 640 so), for you are eating out of your own side.

You are afraid of me, but (only) because you are a (stupid) ass: I am afraid you will eat less (too little).

Though I am occupied, I am not such a fool (as to suffer) that you should get too much of my sugar-cane.

When you see (find) by experience the (amount of) sugar (which you have bought), then you will know who was foolish and careless."

The bird looks pleased at the bait; still, the bait, (though) at a distance (from it), is waylaying it.

If you are deriving some pleasure from the eye's cupidity[3], 645 are not you eating roast-meat from your own side?

This looking from a distance is like arrows and poison: your fond passion is increased (thereby) and your self-restraint diminished.

Worldly riches are a trap for the weak birds; the kingdom of the next world is a trap for the noble birds,

---

[1] Literally, "the sugar in proportion to that (clay)."
[2] Literally, "remained."
[3] Literally, "gullet."

To the end that by means of this kingdom, which is a deep trap, the great birds may be ensnared[1].

"I, Solomon, do not desire your kingdom; nay, but I will deliver you from every destruction;

650 For at this time ye are indeed slaves to the kingdom; the owner of the kingdom is he that escaped from destruction."

Preposterously, O prisoner of this world, thou hast named thyself prince of this world.

O thou slave of this world, thou whose spirit is imprisoned, how long wilt thou call thyself lord of the world?

How Solomon, on whom be peace, showed affection and kindness to the envoys and removed (feelings of) resentment and injury from their hearts and explained to them the reason for declining the gift.

"O envoys, I will send you as envoys (to Bilqís): my refusal (of the gift) is better for you than acceptance.

Relate to Bilqís what marvellous things ye have seen concerning the desert of gold,

655 That she may know we do not covet gold: we have gotten gold from the gold-Creator,

At whose will the whole earth's soil from end to end would become gold and precious pearls."

On that account, O thou who choosest gold, God will make this earth silvern on the Day of Resurrection.

"We have no need of gold, for we are very skilful: we make earthly beings entirely golden.

How shall we beg gold of you? We (can) make you (spiritual) alchemists.

660 Abandon (all) that, (even) if it is the kingdom of Sabá, for beyond (this) water and earth there are many kingdoms."

That which thou hast called a throne is (really) a splint-bandage: thou deemest (it) the seat of honour, but (in truth) thou hast remained at the door.

(If) thou hast not sovereignty over thine own beard, how wilt thou exercise sovereignty over good and evil?

Without thy wish, thy beard grows white: be ashamed of thy beard, O thou whose hopes are perverse.

He (God) is the Possessor of the Kingdom: whosoever lays his head before Him, to him He gives a hundred kingdoms without the terrestrial world;

665 But the (inward) savour of a single prostration before God will be more sweet to thee than two hundred empires:

Then thou wilt cry (in humble entreaty), "I desire not kingdoms: commit unto me the kingdom of that prostration."

---

[1] Literally, "they may bring to capture."

The kings of the world, because of their evil nature, got no scent of the wine of service (to God);

Otherwise, dizzy and dumbfounded like (Ibráhím son of) Adham, without delay they would have dashed their sovereignty to pieces.

But (this they do not inasmuch as), for the maintenance of this world, God set a seal upon their eyes and mouths,

To the end that throne and crown should be sweet to them, 670 "for" (they say) "we will exact tribute from the rulers of the world."

If by way of tribute thou amass gold as (though it were) sand, at last it will be left behind thee as an inheritance.

Sovereignty and gold will not accompany thy spirit on its journey: give thy gold away, get collyrium for thy sight,

In order that thou mayst see that this world is a narrow well, and that, like Joseph, thou mayst grasp that rope,

So that, when thou comest from the well (up) to the roof, the Soul will say, "*Oh, good news* for me! *This is a youth* for me[1]."

In the well (of this world) there are optical inversions, the 675 least (of which is) that stones appear to be gold.

To children at play-time, from infirmity (of mind), those potsherds (with which they play) appear to be gold and riches.

His (God's) knowers have become alchemists, so that mines (of gold) have become worthless in their eyes.

How a dervish saw in dream a company of Shaykhs and begged for a daily portion of lawful food (which he should receive) without being occupied with earning (it) and being (thereby) incapacitated from devotional service; and how they directed him, and how the sour and bitter mountain-fruit became sweet to him through the bounty of those Shaykhs.

A certain dervish said in the night-talk, "I saw in dream those (saints who are) connected with Khiẓr[2].

I said to them, 'Whence shall I (get to) eat a daily portion of lawful food that is not pernicious?'

They took me along towards the mountainous country: they 680 were shaking down the fruit from (the trees in) the forest,

Saying, 'God hath made the fruit (to taste) sweet in thy mouth because of our benedictions.

Come, eat (food that is) clean and lawful, and free of reckoning, without trouble[3] and change of place and (going) up and down.'

Then from that daily provision there appeared in me a (gift of) speech: (the spiritual) savour of my words was transporting (the people's) minds.

---

[1] *Qur'án*, XII, 19.
[2] *I.e.* the saints who possess the mystic knowledge by which Khiẓr is peculiarly distinguished.   [3] Literally, "headache."

I said, 'This is a temptation: O Lord of the world, bestow
(on me) a gift hidden from all (Thy) creatures!'
685   Speech departed from (forsook) me; I gained a joyous heart:
I was bursting with rapture, like the pomegranate;

I said, 'If there be naught in Paradise (for me) but this
delight which I have within my nature,

No other blessing will be desired (by me): I will not be di-
verted from this (delight) by the houris and sugar-cane (of
Paradise).'

Of my (former) earnings one or two small pieces (of money)
had remained with me, sewn in the sleeve of my *jubba*.

*How he formed an intention, saying, 'I will give this money to that
carrier of firewood, since I have obtained daily provision through
the miraculous gifts of the Shaykhs'; and how the carrier of fire-
wood was offended by his secret thought and intention.*

A poor man was carrying firewood: he approached (me),
weary and exhausted, from the forest.
690   So I said (to myself), 'I am independent of (earning) daily
bread: henceforth I have no anxiety for the daily portion.

The loathed fruit has become sweet to me: a special provision
for my body has come to hand.

Since I have been freed from the (cravings of the) gullet,
here are some small pieces of money: I will give him these.

I will give this money to this toil-worn man, that for two or
three brief days he may be made happy by food.'

He himself was knowing my mind, because his (inward)
hearing had illumination from the candle of *Hú* (God).
695   To him the secret of every thought was as a lamp within a
glass.

No mental conception was hidden from him: he was ruler
over the contents of (men's) hearts.

Therefore that wondrous man was muttering to himself under
his breath[1] in answer to my (unspoken) thought,

'Thou thinkest so concerning the (spiritual) kings: how
shouldst thou meet (receive) the daily provision unless they
provide thee (with it)?'

I was not understanding his words, but his rebuke smote my
heart mightily.
700   He approached me with awful mien, like a lion, and laid down
his bundle of firewood.

(Through) the influence[2] of the ecstatic state in which he
laid down the firewood, a trembling fell upon all my seven
limbs.

---

¹ Literally, "lip."   ² Literally, "radiance."

He said, 'O Lord, if Thou hast elect ones whose prayers are blessed and whose feet (comings and goings) are auspicious,

I entreat that Thy grace may become an alchemist (may work a transmutation) and that this bundle of firewood may be turned into gold at this moment.'

Immediately I saw that his firewood was turned into gold, gleaming brightly on the ground, like fire.

Thereat I became beside myself for a long while. When I came to myself (again) out of (that) bewilderment, 705

He said afterwards, 'O God, if those great ones (the saints) are very jealous and are fleeing from celebrity,

At once, without delay, make this (gold) a bundle of firewood again, just as it was (before).'

Immediately those branches of gold turned into firewood: the intellect and the sight were intoxicated (amazed) at his (miraculous) work.

After that, he took up the firewood and went from me in hot haste towards the town.

I wished to follow that (spiritual) king and ask him about (some) difficulties and hear (his answer); 710

(But) the awe (which he inspired) made me (as though I were) bound: the vulgar have no way (admission) to the presence of the elect."

And if the way become (open) to any one, let him offer[1] his head (in utter devotion), for that (admission to their presence) comes from their mercy and their drawing (him towards them).

Therefore, when you gain companionship with the *ṣiddīq* (true saint), deem that Divine favour (conferred on you) to be a precious opportunity.

(Do) not (be) like the fool who wins the favour of the King, and then lightly and easily falls away from the path (of favour).

When more of (the King's) favour is bestowed on him, then he says, "Surely this is the thigh of an ox." 715

This does not consist of the thigh of an ox, O deviser of falsehood: to you it appears to be the thigh of an ox because you are an ass.

This is a royal gift devoid of any corruption: this is pure munificence (springing) from a (great) mercy,

[*How Solomon, on whom be peace, urged the envoys to hasten the emigration of Bilqís (from her kingdom) for the Faith's sake.*]

Even as in (the spiritual) warfare King Solomon drew the cavalry and foot-soldiers of Bilqís (towards him),

Saying, "O honoured men, come quickly, quickly, for the waves have risen from the sea of bounty.

---

[1] Literally, "toss or fling (down)."

720   At every moment the surge of its waves is scattering shore-
wards a hundred pearls without danger (to those who seek them).

We cry (you) welcome, O people of righteousness, for now
Riẓwán[1] hath opened the gate of Paradise."

Then Solomon said, "O couriers, go to Bilqís and believe in
this Religion.

Then bid her come hither with all speed, for *verily God
inviteth to the (abode of) peace*[2]."

Hark, come speedily, O seeker of felicity, for now is (the time
for) manifestations (of spiritual grace) and the opening of the
door.

725   O thou who art not a seeker, come thou also, that thou mayst
gain (the gift of) seeking (felicity) from this faithful Friend.

*The cause of the emigration of (Ibráhím son of) Adham, may God
sanctify his spirit, and his abandoning the kingdom of Khurásán.*

Quickly dash to pieces the kingdom (of this world), like
(Ibráhím son of) Adham, that like him thou mayst gain the
kingdom of everlasting life.

At night that king was asleep on his throne, (while) on the
roof (of the palace) the guards were exercising authority[3].

The king's purpose in (having) the guards was not that he
might thereby keep off robbers and ne'er-do-wells.

He knew that the man who is just is free from (fear of) attack
and secure in his heart.

730   Justice is the guardian of pleasures; not men who beat their
rattles on the roofs at night.

But his object in (listening to) the sound of the rebeck was,
like (that of) ardent lovers (of God), (to bring into his mind) the
phantasy of that (Divine) allocution;

(For) the shrill noise of the clarion and the menace of the
drum somewhat resemble that universal trumpet.

Hence philosophers have said that we received these har-
monies from the revolution of the (celestial) sphere,

(And that) this (melody) which people sing with pandore and
throat is the sound of the revolutions of the sphere;

735   (But) the true believers say that the influences of Paradise
made every unpleasant sound to be beautiful.

We all have been parts of Adam, we have heard those melodies
in Paradise.

Although the water and earth (of our bodies) have caused a
doubt to fall upon us, something of those (melodies) comes
(back) to our memory;

---

[1] The Keeper of Paradise.

[2] *Qur'án*, x, 26. بالسَّلام stands, *metri causâ*, for الَى دارِ ٱلسَّلام.

[3] Literally, "were (engaged) in holding and seizing."

But since it is mingled with the earth of sorrow, how should this treble and bass give (us) the same delight?

When water is mingled with urine and stalings, its temperament is made bitter and acid by the commixture.

There is a small quantity of water in his (a man's) body: 740 suppose it is urine, (yet) it will extinguish a fire.

If the water has been defiled, (still) this natural property of it remains, for by its nature it allays the fire of grief.

Therefore *samá'* (music) is the food of lovers (of God), since therein is the phantasy of composure (tranquillity of mind).

From (hearing) sounds and pipings the mental phantasies gather a (great) strength; nay, they become forms (in the imagination).

The fire of love is made keen (inflamed) by melodies, just as the fire (ardour) of the man who dropped walnuts (into the water).

Story of the thirsty man who dropped walnuts from the top of a walnut-tree into the water-brook that was in the hollow, without reaching the water (himself), in order that he might hear the sound made by the walnuts falling on the water, which thrilled him with joy as (though it were) sweet music.

The water was in a deep place: the thirsty man went up the 745 tree and scattered the walnuts one by one.

The walnuts were falling from the walnut-tree into the water: the sound was coming (to his ears), and he was seeing the bubbles.

A sensible person said to him, "Leave off, O youth: truly the (loss of the) walnuts will bring thirst (regret) to you.

The more the fruit falls into the water—(since) the water is below at a (great) distance from you,

The river-water will have carried it (the fruit) far away before you with effort come down from the top (of the tree)."

He replied, "My purpose in this scattering is not (to obtain 750 possession of) the walnuts: look more keenly, do not stop at this superficial (view).

My purpose is that the sound of the water should come (to my ears); also, that I should see these bubbles on the surface of the water."

What, indeed, is the thirsty man's business in the world? To circle for ever round the base of the tank,

Round the channel and round the Water and the sound of the Water, like a pilgrim circumambulating the Ka'ba of Truth.

Even so, in (composing) this *Mathnawí* thou, O Ẓiyá'u 'l-Ḥaqq (Radiance of God) Ḥusámu'ddín, art my object.

755   The whole *Mathnawí* in its branches and roots is thine: thou
hast accepted (it).

Kings accept (both) good and bad: when they accept (any-
thing), it is reprobate no more.

Since thou hast planted the sapling, give it water. Since thou
hast given it freedom (to grow), untie the knots.

In (all) its expressions my object is (to reveal) thy mystery; in
composing it my object is (to hear) thy voice.

To me thy voice is the voice of God: Heaven forfend that
(I should say) the lover is separate from the Beloved.

760   There is a union beyond description or analogy between the
Lord of Man and the spirit of Man.

But I said *nás* (Man), not *nasnás*[1]; *nás* is none but the spirit
that knows the (Divine) Spirit.

Nás is Man, and where is Manhood? You have never beheld
the head (spiritual principle) of Man: you are a tail.

You have recited (the text) *thou didst not throw when thou
threwest*, but you are a (mere) body: you have remained in
division.

Like Bilqís, O foolish one, abandon the kingdom of your body
for the sake of the prophet Solomon.

765   I am crying "*lá hawl*," not on account of my own words, nay,
but on account of the false suggestions of the person accustomed
to think (evil),

Who is conceiving in his heart a vain fancy about my words,
(a fancy arising) from the false suggestions and incredulities of
(evil) thought.

I am crying "*lá hawl*," that is, "there is no help," because in
your heart there is a contradiction of me.

Since my words have stuck in your throat, I am silent: do you
speak your own (words).

A sweet flute-player was playing the flute: subito e podice
ejus erupit ventus.

770   Fistulam in podice posuit, saying, "If you play better than I,
take it (the flute) and play!"

O Musalmán, (whilst you are still engaged) in the quest, good
manners are indeed nothing but forbearance with every one that
is unmannerly.

When you see any one complaining of such and such a
person's ill-nature and bad temper,

Know that the complainant is bad-tempered, forasmuch as
he speaks ill of that bad-tempered person,

Because he (alone) is good-tempered who is quietly forbearing
towards the bad-tempered and ill-natured.

---

[1] A fabulous monster which is described as "resembling the half of
a human body."

But in (the case of) the Shaykh, the complaint is (made) by the 775 command of God; it is not (made) in consequence of anger and contentiousness and vain desire.

It is not a complaint, it is spiritual correction, like the complaints made by the prophets.

Know that the intolerance of the prophets is by command (of God); otherwise, their clemency is exceedingly tolerant of evil.

They mortified their (carnal) nature in toleration of evil[1]; if there be intolerance (on their part), it is Divine.

O Solomon (of the age), amidst the crows and falcons be thou (a manifestation of) the clemency of God: sort with (adapt thyself to) all the birds.

Oh, two hundred (like) Bilqís are abased before thy clemency, 780 for (thou sayest in the words of the Prophet), "(O God), guide my people, verily they know not."

How Solomon, on whom be peace, sent a threatening message to Bilqís, saying, "Do not think to persist in polytheism and do not make delay."

"Hark, Bilqís, come! Else, it will be bad (for thee): thy army will become thine enemy and will revolt.

Thy chamberlain will destroy thy door: thy soul with (all) its soul will act as an enemy towards thee."

All the atoms of earth and heaven are God's army, (as you will find out) on putting it to the test.

You have seen what the wind did to the people of ʿÁd, you have seen what the water did at the Deluge;

How that vengeful Sea dashed on Pharaoh, and how this 785 Earth behaved to Qárún (Korah);

And what those *bábíl* (swifts) did to the Elephant, and how the gnat devoured the skull of Nimrod;

And how a David hurled with his hand a stone (which) became six hundred pieces and shattered an army.

Stones rained upon the enemies of Lot, so that they were submerged in the black water.

If I relate the help given rationally to the prophets by the inanimate things of the world,

The *Mathnawí* will become of such extent that, if forty 790 camels carry it, they will be unable to bear the full load.

The (infidel's) hand will give testimony against the infidel[2], will become an army of God, and will submit[3] (to the Divine command).

O you that in your actions have studied to oppose God, you are in the midst of His army: be afraid!

---

[1] *I.e.* by suffering ill-treatment from the infidels.
[2] On the Day of Judgement.
[3] Literally, "will lay (down) its head."

Every part of you is an army of God in accord (with Him):
they are obedient to you now, (but) not sincerely[1].

If He say to the eye, "Squeeze (torture) him," eye-ache will
wreak upon you a hundred vengeances;

795 And if He say to the teeth, "Plague (him)," then you will
suffer chastisement from your teeth.

Open the (book of) Medicine and read the chapter on diseases,
that you may see what is done by the army of the body.

Since He is the Soul of the soul of everything, how is it a light
matter to be hostile to the Soul of the soul?

"Let alone the army of demons and genies[2] who, (devoted
to me) from the core of their hearts, cleave the ranks (of my
enemies) for me.

First, O Bilqís, relinquish thy kingdom: when thou gainest
me, all the kingdom is thine.

800 When thou hast come to me, thou thyself wilt know that
without me thou wert (as) a picture in the bath-house."

Even if the picture be the picture of a sultan or a rich man, it
is a (mere) form: it has no savour (consciousness) of its own
spirit.

Its beauty is for others: its eyes and mouth are open in
vain.

O you who have devoted yourself (to contending with others)
in strife, you have not known (discriminated) others from your-
self.

You stop at every form that you come to, saying, "I am this."
By God, you are not that (form).

805 (If) you are left alone by people for a single moment, you re-
main (plunged) up to the throat in grief and anxiety.

How are you this (form)? You are that Unique One, for (in
reality) you are fair and lovely and intoxicated with yourself.

You are your own bird, your own prey, and your own snare;
you are your own seat of honour, your own floor, and your own
roof.

The substance is that which subsists in itself; the accident is
that which has become a derivative of it (of the substance).

If you are born of Adam, sit like him and behold all his
progeny in yourself.

810 What is in the jar that is not (also) in the river? What is in the
house that is not (also) in the city?

This world is the jar, and the heart (spirit) is like the river;
this world is the chamber, and the heart is the wonderful
city.

---

[1] Literally, "from hypocrisy."
[2] *I.e.* "leave them out of account: all God's armies are at my disposal."

How Solomon, on whom be peace, explained (to Bilqís), saying,
"My labour in (bringing about) thy (conversion to the) Faith is
purely for God's sake: I have not one atom of self-interest,
either as regards thy person or thy beauty or thy kingdom. Thou
thyself wilt see (this) when the eye of thy spirit is opened by the
light of God."

"Hark, come, for I am a Messenger (Prophet) sent to call (the people to God): like Death, I am the slayer of lust, I am not given to lust.

And if there be lust (in me), I am the ruler of (my) lust: I am not captive to lust for the face of an idol.

My deepest nature[1] is a breaker of idols, like (Abraham) the Friend of God and all the prophets.

O slave, if I enter the idol-temple, the idol will prostrate 815 itself, not I, in adoration."

(Both) Aḥmad (Mohammed) and Bú Jahl went into the idol-temple; (but) there is a great difference between this going and that going.

This one (Mohammed) enters, the idols lay down their heads before him; that one (Bú Jahl) enters and lays down his head (before the idols), like the peoples (of old).

This world, (which is) associated with lust, is an idol-temple: it is a nest (abode) for the prophets and the infidels (alike),

But lust is the slave of holy men: gold does not burn (in the fire), because it is sterling coin from the mine.

The infidels are alloy, while the holy men are as (pure) gold: 820 both these (classes of) persons are within this crucible.

When the alloy came (into the crucible), it became black at once; (when) the gold came in, its goldenness was made manifest.

The gold gladly cast (itself with) hands and feet into the crucible: its vein (original nature) laughs in the face of the fire.

Our body is our veil in the world: we are like a sea hidden beneath this straw.

O fool, do not regard the king of the (true) Religion as clay; for the accursed Iblís took this view (of Adam).

How is it possible to daub this sun with a handful of earth? 825 Pray, tell me (that)!

Though you pour earth and a hundred ashes over its light, it will come up above them.

Who (what) is straw that it should cover the face of the water? Who (what) is clay that it should cover the sun?

O Bilqís[2] arise royally, like (Ibráhím son of) Adham: raise the smoke from (consume utterly) this kingdom of two or three days' duration.

[1] Literally, "the root of my root."
[2] *I.e.* "O you who resemble Bilqís."

The remainder of the story of Ibráhím son of Adham,
may God sanctify his spirit.

(Reclining) on a throne, that man of good name heard at night
a noise of tramping and shrill cries from the roof.

830 (He heard) loud footsteps on the roof of the palace, and said
to himself, "Who dares to do this?"

He shouted, at the palace-window, "Who is it? This is not
a man, belike it is a genie."

A wondrous folk put their heads down (from the roof), (saying),
"We are going round by night for the purpose of search."

"Eh, what are ye seeking?" "Camels," they replied. He
said, "Take heed! who ever sought camel on a roof?"

Then they said to him, "How art thou seeking to meet with
God on the throne of state?"

835 That was all[1]. None saw him again: he vanished like a genie
from (the sight of) man.

His reality (real self) was hidden, though he was in people's
presence: how should the people see aught but beard and frock
(of the dervish)?

When he became far (disappeared) from his own and the
people's eyes, he became renowned in the world, like the 'Anqá.

Whenever the soul of any (spiritual) bird has come to (Mount)
Qáf, all the world boast and brag on account of it.

When this orient light (from Solomon) reached Sabá, a
tumult arose in Bilqís and her people.

840 All the dead spirits took wing: the dead put forth their heads
from the grave, (which is) the body.

They gave the good news to one another, saying, "Hark! Lo,
a voice is coming from Heaven."

At (the sound of) that voice (men's) religions wax great;
the leaves and boughs of the heart become green.

Like the blast of the trumpet (on Judgement-Day) that
breath from Solomon delivered the dead from the tombs.

May (such) felicity be thine after this (epoch of Solomon)!
This (epoch) is past. God best knoweth the certain truth.

The rest of the story of the people of Sabá, and of the admonition
and guidance given by Solomon, on whom be peace, to the kinsfolk
of Bilqís—to every one (the particular guidance) suitable to his
religious and spiritual difficulties; and how he caught (decoyed)
each sort of conceptional bird with the whistle and bait proper for
that sort of bird.

845 I will tell the story of Sabá in lover's style. When the Zephyr
came towards the tulip-field[2],

[1] Literally, "it was just that (and no more)."
[2] *I.e.* when Solomon's message reached Sabá.

The bodies met (experienced) the day of their union (with the spirits which dwell in them)[1]: the children turned again in the direction of their home.

Amongst the communities the community of secret Love is like a liberality surrounded by the meanness of (spiritual) distemper.

The baseness of spirits is (derived) from their bodies; the nobility of bodies is (derived) from their spirits.

O lovers, the draught (of Love) is given to you. Ye are the everlasting: everlastingness is bestowed on you.

O ye that are forgetful, arise and love! That is the wind of 850 Joseph: smell (its perfume)!

Come, O (master of the) bird-speech of Solomon, sing the song of every bird that comes.

Since God hath sent thee to the birds, He hath instructed thee in the note of every bird.

To the necessitarian bird speak the language of necessitarianism; to the bird whose wings are broken speak of patience (quietism).

Keep the patient bird happy and free from harm; to the bird (resembling the) 'Anqá recite the descriptions of (Mount) Qáf.

Bid the pigeon beware of the falcon; to the falcon speak of 855 forbearance and being on its guard (against acting unjustly).

And as for the bat that is left destitute (of spiritual illumination), make it to consort and to be familiar with the Light.

Cause the warlike partridge to learn peace; to the cocks display the signs of dawn.

Even so proceed from the hoopoe to the eagle, and show the way. And God best knoweth the right course.

How Bilqís was freed from her kingdom and was intoxicated with longing for the Faith, and how at the moment of her (spiritual) emigration the regard of her desire became severed from the whole of her kingdom except from her throne.

When Solomon uttered a single whistling note to the birds of Sabá, he ensnared them all,

Except, maybe, the bird that was without spirit or wings, or 860 was dumb and deaf, like a fish, from the beginning.

Nay, I have spoken wrongly, for if the deaf one lay his head before the inspiration of the Divine Majesty, it will give to him (the power of) hearing.

When Bilqís set out (from Sabá) with heart and soul, she felt remorse too for the bygone time,

---

[1] *I.e.* the people of Sabá rejoiced as on the day when their spirits entered their bodies.

She took leave of her kingdom and riches in the same way as those lovers (of God) take leave of honour and disgrace (reputation).

Those charming pages and handmaidens (of hers seemed) to her eye (loathly) as a rotten onion.

865 For love's sake, orchards and palaces and river-water seemed to her eye (contemptible as) a dunghill.

Love, in the hour of domination and anger, makes the pleasing ones to become hideous to the eye.

Love's jealousy causes every emerald to appear as a leek: this is the (inner) meaning of Lá[1].

O (thou who givest) protection[2], (the meaning of) "There is no god but He" is that the moon should seem to thee a black kettle.

No wealth, no treasury, and no goods or gear were being grudged by her (Bilqís) except her throne.

870 Then Solomon became aware of (this feeling in) her heart, for the way was open from his heart to hers.

He that hears the voice of ants will also hear the cry from the inmost soul of them that are afar.

He that declares the mystery of "an ant said[3]" will also know the mystery of this ancient dome[4].

From afar he (Solomon) discerned that to her (Bilqís) who was following the path of resignation 'twas bitter to part with her throne.

If I explain the reason why she had that love and complaisance to her throne, it (the discourse) will become (too) long.

875 Although this reed-pen is in fact an insensible thing and is not homogeneous with the writer, (yet) it is a familiar friend to him.

Likewise, every tool of a craftsman is, (though) lifeless, the familiar friend of the spirit of Man.

This reason I would have explained precisely, if there were not some moisture (dimness) in the eye of your understanding.

There was no possibility of transporting the throne (from Sabá) because of its hugeness which exceeded (all) bounds.

It was filigree work, and there was danger in taking it to pieces, (since its parts were joined) like the limbs of the body with one another.

880 Therefore Solomon said, "Although in the end the diadem and throne will become chilling (repulsive) to her"—

(For) when the spirit puts forth its head (manifests itself) from the Unity (to which it has attained), in comparison with its splendour the body hath no splendour (at all);

---

[1] "Not," i.e. "there is not any god but Allah."
[2] I.e. "thou who art rich and powerful and able to extend patronage to others."
[3] Qur'án, XXVII, 18.　　　　[4] I.e. the sky or the world.

When the pearl comes up from the depths of the seas, you will look with contempt on the foam and sticks and straws.

(When) the flaming sun lifts up its head, who will make Scorpio's tail his resting-place[1]?—

"Yet, notwithstanding all this, in the actual case (the means of) transporting her throne (hither) must be sought,

In order that she may not feel hurt at the time of meeting 885 (with me), and that her wish may be fulfilled, like (the wishes of) children.

It (the throne) is lightly esteemed by me, but it is exceedingly dear to her: (let it be brought hither), that the devil too may be (present) at the table (banquet) of the houris.

That throne of delight will become a lesson to her soul, like the (coarse) frock and (rustic) shoon in the presence of Ayáz[2],

So that the afflicted one (Bilqís) may know in what (plight) she was (formerly) and from what (low) places to what a (high) place she has arrived."

God is ever keeping the clay and semen and piece of flesh (embryo) before our eyes,

(As though) to say, "O man of evil intention, whence did I 890 bring thee, that thou hast (such) a disgust at it?

Thou wert in love with that (state) in the period thereof: at that time thou wert denying this (present) grace (which I have bestowed on thee)."

Inasmuch as this (present) bounty is the (means of) rebutting the denial which thou didst make in the beginning (when thou wert) amidst the clay,

Thy having been brought to life is the argument against denial (of the Resurrection); (but thou art still denying it): this sick (soul) of thine is made worse by the medicine.

Whence should clay have the (power of) imagining this thing? Whence should semen conceive opposition and denial?

(Nevertheless) since at that moment thou wert devoid of 895 heart and spirit, thou wert (implicitly) denying (the faculty of) reflection and (the possibility of) denial.

Since thy (former) denial arose from the state of lifelessness (irrationality), so by this (present) denial (the certainty of) thy resurrection is established.

Hence the (appropriate) parable of thee is (a case) like (that of) the person who knocks at the door (of a house), and the master replies to him from within, saying, "The master is not (here)."

---

[1] *I.e.* "who will fix his attention, or put reliance, on a malign constellation?" There may be a secondary allusion to the plant known as scorpiurus or scorpion's tail.

[2] The favourite of Sultan Maḥmúd of Ghazna; he used to humble himself by wearing in secret the old shoes and ragged dress which reminded him of his lowly origin.

From this "is not" the person knocking perceives that he is (there), and consequently does not take his hand off the doorring at all.

Therefore the very fact of thy denial is making it clear that He (God) brings about manifold resurrections from lifeless matter.

900   How much (Divine) artifice passed (was expended), O thou denial (incarnate), till the water and clay (of thy original nature) produced denial from (the state signified by the words) *Hal atá*![1]

The water and clay was really saying, "There is no denial" (was really making an affirmation): it was crying, "There is no affirmation" (was uttering a denial), unaware (of the fact that its denial was an implicit affirmation).

I would expound this (topic) in a hundred ways, but the (reader's) mind would stumble at the subtle discourse.

How Solomon, on whom be peace, devised a plan for bringing the throne of Bilqís from Sabá.

A certain 'Ifrít (demon) said, "By (my) art I will bring her throne here before thy departure from this council."

Ásaf[2] said, "By means of the greatest Name (of God) I will bring it here into thy presence in a single moment."

905   Though the 'Ifrít was a master of magic, yet that (miracle) was displayed by the breath (spiritual power) of Ásaf.

The throne of Bilqís came into the presence instantly, but through Ásaf, not through the art of them that have the (malignant) nature of 'Ifríts.

He (Solomon) said, "Praise to God for this and a hundred such (favours) which I have seen (received) from *the Lord of created beings*."

Then Solomon turned his eyes towards the throne. "Yes," he said, "thou art one that catches fools, O tree!"

Oh, many are the fools that lay down their heads before wood and graven stone.

910   (Both) the worshipper and the object of worship are ignorant of the spirit; (but) he (the worshipper) has felt a movement and a slight effect of the spirit.

He has felt, at the moment when he became rapt (in devotion) and bewildered, that the stone spoke and made signs.

When the wretched man bestowed his devotion[3] in the wrong place and deemed the lion of stone to be a (real) lion,

---

[1] *I.e.* "Did not there come (upon Man a period of time when he was not a thing of any account)?" (*Qur'án*, LXXVI, I).
[2] The Vizier of Solomon.
[3] Literally, "played the backgammon of devotion."

The Real Lion, from kindness, showed munificence and at
once threw a bone to the dog,
And said, "Although the dog is not in (due) order, yet as
regards me the bone is a bounty of which all partake."

*Story of Ḥalíma's asking help of the idols when she lost Muṣṭafá
(Mohammed)—on whom be peace—after he was weaned, and
how the idols trembled and prostrated themselves and bore
witness to the grandeur of Mohammed's estate—may God bless
and save him!*

I will tell you the story of Ḥalíma's mystic experience, that 915
her tale may clear away your trouble.
When she parted Muṣṭafá from (her) milk, she took him up
on the palm of her hand as (tenderly as though he were) sweet
basil and roses,
Causing him to avoid every good or evil (hap), that she might
commit that (spiritual) emperor to (the care of) his grandsire.
Since she was bringing the (precious) trust in fear (for its
safety), she went to the Kaʿba and came into the *Ḥaṭím*[1].
From the air she heard a cry—"O *Ḥaṭím*, an exceedingly
mighty Sun hath shone upon thee.
O *Ḥaṭím*, to-day there will suddenly come upon thee a 920
hundred thousand beams from the Sun of munificence.
O *Ḥaṭím*, to-day there will march into thee with pomp[2] a
glorious King, whose harbinger is Fortune.
O *Ḥaṭím*, to-day without doubt thou wilt become anew the
abode of exalted spirits.
The spirits of the holy will come to thee from every quarter
in troops and multitudes, drunken with desire."
Ḥalíma was bewildered by that voice: neither in front nor
behind was any one (to be seen).
(All) the six directions were empty of (any visible) form, and 925
this cry was continuous—may the soul be a ransom for that cry!
She laid Muṣṭafá on the earth, that she might search after
the sweet sound.
Then she cast her eye to and fro, saying, "Where is that king
that tells of mysteries?
For such a loud sound is arriving from left and right. O Lord,
where is he that causes it to arrive?"
When she did not see (any one), she became distraught and
despairing: her body began to tremble like the willow-bough.
She came back towards that righteous child: she did not see 930
Muṣṭafá in his (former) place.

---

[1] The name *Ḥaṭím* is properly given to a semi-circular wall adjoining the
north and west corners of the Kaʿba. Here it denotes the space between the
wall and the Kaʿba.
[2] Literally, "will bring his baggage into thee."

Bewilderment on bewilderment fell upon her heart: from grief her abode became very dark.

She ran to the dwellings (hard by) and raised an outcry, saying, "Who has carried off¹ my single pearl?"

The Meccans said, "We have no knowledge: we knew not that a child was there."

She shed so many tears and made (so) much lamentation that those others began to weep because of her (grief).

935   Beating her breast, she wept so well (mightily) that the stars were made to weep by her weeping.

Story of the old Arab who directed Ḥalíma to seek help from the idols.

An old man with a staff approached her, saying, "Why, what hath befallen thee, O Ḥalíma,

That thou didst let such a fire (of grief) blaze (forth) from thy heart and consume these bowels² (of the bystanders) with mourning?"

She replied, "I am Aḥmad's (Mohammed's) trusted foster-mother³, so I brought him (back) to hand him over to his grandsire.

When I arrived in the *Ḥaṭím*, voices were coming (down) and I was hearing (them) from the air.

940   When I heard from the air those melodious strains, because of that sound I laid down the infant there,

To see whose voice is (the origin of) this cry, for it is a very beautiful cry and very delightful.

I saw no sign of any one around me: the cry was not ceasing for one moment.

When I returned (to my senses) from the bewilderments of my heart, I did not see the child there (where I had left him): alas for my heart!"

He (the old man) said, "O daughter, do not grieve, for I will show unto thee a queen⁴,

945   Who, if she wish, will tell what has happened to the child: she knows the dwelling-place of the child and his setting-out (on the way)."

Then Ḥalíma said, "Oh, my soul be a ransom for thee, O goodly and fair-spoken Shaykh!

Come, show me that queen of clairvoyance who hath knowledge of what has happened to my child."

He brought her to 'Uzzá, saying, "This idol is greatly prized for information concerning the Unseen.

---

¹ Literally, "directed a raid against."   ² Literally, "livers."

³ رضیع has here the meaning of مُرْضِع.

⁴ Here and in *v.* 947 (cf. also *v.* 1044) the Persian has "king."

Through her we have found thousands that were lost, when we hastened towards her in devotion."

The old man prostrated himself before her ('Uzzá) and said 950 at once, "O Sovereign of the Arabs, O sea of munificence!"

(Then) he said, "O 'Uzzá, thou hast done many favours (to us), so that we have been delivered from snares.

On account of thy favour the duty (of worshipping thee) has become obligatory to the Arabs, so that the Arabs have submitted to thee.

In hope of thee this Ḥalíma of (the tribe) Sa'd has come into the shadow of thy willow-bough,

For an infant child of hers is lost: the name of that child is Mohammed."

When he said "Mohammed," all those idols immediately fell 955 headlong and prostrate,

Saying, "Begone, O old man! What is this search after that Mohammed by whom we are deposed?

By him we are overthrown and reduced to a collection of (broken) stones; by him we are made unsaleable and valueless.

Those phantoms which the followers of vain opinion used to see from us at times[1] during the *Fatra*[2]

Will disappear now that his royal court has arrived: the water is come and has torn up (annulled) the ablution with sand[3].

Get thee far off, O old man! Do not kindle mischief! Hark, do 960 not burn us with (the fire of) Aḥmad's (Mohammed's) jealousy!

Get thee far off, for God's sake, O old man, lest thou (too) be burnt by the fire of Fore-ordainment.

What squeezing of the dragon's tail is this? Dost thou know at all what the announcement (of Mohammed's advent) is (in its effects)?

At this news the heart of sea and mine will surge; at this news the seven heavens will tremble."

When the old man heard these words from the stones (idols), the ancient old man let his staff drop (from his hand);

Then, from tremor and fear and dread caused by that pro- 965 clamation (of the idols), the old man was striking his teeth together[4].

Even as a naked man in winter, he was shuddering and saying, "O destruction!"

When she (Ḥalíma) saw the old man in such a state (of terror), in consequence of that marvel[5] the woman lost (the power of) deliberation.

---

[1] *I.e.* the divine powers which, as the idolaters falsely imagined, were sometimes displayed by the idols.

[2] The interval of time between Jesus and Mohammed.

[3] In the absence of water the ritual ablution may be performed with sand.

[4] His teeth were chattering.   [5] Read زآن عجب.

She said, "O old man, though I am in affliction (on account of the loss of Mohammed), I am in manifold bewilderment (not knowing whether I should grieve or rejoice).

At one moment the wind is making a speech to me, at another moment the stones are schooling me.

970   The wind addresses me with articulate words, the stones and mountains give me intelligence of (the real nature of) things.

Once (before) they of the Invisible carried off my child—they of the Invisible, the green-winged ones of Heaven.

Of whom shall I complain? To whom shall I tell this plaint? I am become crazy and in a hundred minds[1].

His (God's) jealousy has closed my lips (so that I am unable) to unfold (the tale of) the mystery: I say (only) this much, that my child is lost.

If I should say anything else now, the people would bind me in chains as though I were mad[2]."

975   The old man said to her, "O Ḥalíma, rejoice; bow down in thanksgiving and do not rend thy face.

Do not grieve: he will not become lost to thee; nay, but the (whole) world will become lost in him.

Before and behind (him) there are always hundreds of thousands of keepers and guardians (watching over him) in jealous emulation.

Didst not thou see how those idols with all their arts[3] fell headlong at the name of thy child?

This is a marvellous epoch on the face of the earth: I have grown old, and I have not seen aught of this kind."

980   Since (even) the stones (idols) bewailed this (prophetic) mission, think what (tribulation) it will set over (bring down upon) sinners!

The stone is guiltless in respect of being an object of worship, (but) you are not under compulsion in worshipping it.

That one[4] that was under compulsion has become so afraid: consider (then) what (terrible) things will be fastened upon the guilty!

How 'Abdu 'l-Muṭṭalib, the grandfather of Muṣṭafá (Mohammed), got news of Ḥalíma's having lost Mohammed, on whom be peace, and searched for him round the city and made lamentation at the door of the Ka'ba and besought God and found him (Mohammed), on whom be peace.

When the grandfather of Muṣṭafá got the news of Ḥalíma and her outcry in public

---

[1] *I.e.* agitated by a multitude of conflicting thoughts and emotions.
[2] Literally, "in the chain of madness."
[3] Literally, "possessed of arts."
[4] *I.e.* the idol.

And of such loud screams and shrieks that the echo of them
was reaching to (the distance of) a mile,

'Abdu 'l-Muṭṭalib at once knew what was the matter: he beat 985
his hands on his breast and wept.

In his grief he came ardently to the door of the Ka'ba, saying,
"O Thou that knowest the secret of night and the mystery of
day,

I see not any accomplishment in myself, that one like me
should be Thy confidant.

I see not any merit in myself, that I should be accepted of this
auspicious door,

Or that my (bowed) head and my prostration (in prayer)
should have any worth, or that because of my tears any fortune
should smile (upon me);

But in the countenance of that unique Pearl (Mohammed) 990
I have beheld the signs of Thy grace, O Bounteous One;

For he doth not resemble us, though he is of us: we all are
(as) the copper, while Aḥmad (Mohammed) is the Elixir.

The wondrous things that I have seen in him I have not seen
in friend or enemy.

None, (even) with a hundred years' endeavour, would (be
ible to) indicate that which Thy bounty has bestowed on him
in childhood.

Since I saw with (intuitive) certainty Thy favours towards
him, (I know that) he is a pearl of Thy sea.

Him I bring (forward) to plead with Thee: tell me his plight, 995
O Thou who knowest (every) plight!"

From within the Ka'ba came at once a cry, "Even now he
will show his face unto thee.

He is blessed by Us with two hundred felicities, he is guarded
by Us with two hundred troops of angels.

We make his outward (appearance) celebrated in the world;
We make his inward (reality) to be hidden from all.

The water and clay was (like) gold of the mine: We are the
goldsmith; for We carve it now into an anklet, now into a seal.

Now We make it the shoulder-belt for a sword, now the chain 1000
on the neck of a lion.

Now We fashion from it the ball (on the top) of a throne, now
the diadem on the heads (of them) that seek empire.

We have great affections towards this earth, because it lies in
the posture of acquiescence.

Now We produce from it a (spiritual) king like this; now We
make it frenzied (with love) in the presence of the king:

On account of him hundreds of thousands of lovers and loved
ones are in lamentation and outcry and search.

This is Our work, to the confusion of that one who hath no 1005
spiritual inclination towards Our work.

We confer this eminence on the earth for the same reason
that We place a portion of food before the destitute,

Because the earth has the external form of dunness, while in-
wardly it has the qualities of luminosity.

Its outward (appearance) has come to be at war with its inward
(reality): its inward is like a jewel and its outward like a (com-
mon) stone.

Its outward says, 'We are this, and no more'; its inward says,
'Look well before and behind!'

1010   Its outward is denying (and says) that the inward is naught;
its inward says, 'We will show (thee the truth): wait (and
see)!'

Its outward and its inward are in strife: necessarily they are
drawing (Divine) aid from this patient endurance.

We make the forms (of existence) from this sour-faced earth:
We make manifest its hidden laughter,

For (though) outwardly the earth is (all) sorrow and tears,
within it there are hundreds of thousands of laughters.

We are the Revealer of the mystery, and Our work is just
this, that We bring forth these hidden things from conceal-
ment.

1015   Although the thief is mute in denial (of his theft), the magis-
trate brings it to light by torture.

These (diverse) earths have stolen (Our) favours, so that
through affliction We may bring them to confess.

Many is the wondrous child that it (the earth) hath had, but
Aḥmad (Mohammed) hath surpassed them all.

Earth and Heaven laugh and rejoice, saying, 'From us two
(who are) joined in wedlock such a king is born!'

Heaven is bursting for joy of him; earth is become like the
lily on account of his purity.

1020   Since thy outward and thy inward, O fair earth, are at war
and (engaged) in struggling (with each other)—

Whoso is at war with himself for God's sake, to the end that
his (inward) reality may become the opponent of (mere) scent
and colour,

(If) his darkness is in combat with his light, the sun of his
spirit will never set.

Whoso shall strive in tribulation for Our sake, Heaven will
put its back under (will support) his feet."

Your outward (form) is wailing because of the darkness; your
inward (spirit) is (like) roses within roses.

1025   It (your outward form) is purposely like Ṣúfís (who are) sour-
faced (sad and mournful) in order that they may not mix with
every one that quenches the (inner) light.

Like the hedgehog, the sour-faced knowers (of God) have
hidden their (spiritual) pleasures in rough prickles (of austerity).

The orchard is hidden, (while) around the orchard those thorns
are plainly seen, saying, "O thievish foe, keep far from this gate!"

O hedgehog, you have made the prickles your guardian and,
like a Ṣúfí, have buried your head in your bosom,

That none of these rose-cheeked thorn-natured ones may
encounter (become acquainted with) a farthing (the least part)
of your pleasure[1].

"Though thy infant (Mohammed) is childish, verily both the 1030
worlds are his parasites (attendants).

We make a (whole) world living through him; We make
Heaven a slave in his service."

'Abdu 'l-Muṭṭalib said, "Where is he now? O Thou that
knowest the secret (of all things), point out the right way!"

*How 'Abdu 'l-Muṭṭalib asked for a clue to the place where
Mohammed was—peace be upon him!—saying, "Where shall
I find him?" and how he was answered from within the Kaʿba
and obtained the clue.*

A voice reached him from within the Kaʿba. It said, "O
seeker, that righteous child

Is in such and such a wadi beneath yonder tree." Then the
good-fortuned old man at once set out.

At his stirrup (were) the princes of Quraysh, for his (Moham- 1035
med's) grandfather was one of the notables of Quraysh.

All his (Mohammed's) ancestors (reaching back) to the loins
of Adam (were) lords in feast and fray and the carnage of battle.

This lineage is (applicable) only to his husk (body), which is
strained pure (in descent) from mighty emperors.

His kernel, in sooth, is remote from lineage, and unsoiled (by
contamination with mankind): none is its congener from the
Fish[2] to Arcturus.

None seeks (to know) the birth and (coming into) existence
of the Light of God[3]: what need of warp and woof hath God's
robe of honour?

The meanest robe of honour that He bestows in recompense 1040
(for good works) excels the embroidered raiment of the sun.

The rest of the story of (the Divine) Mercy's calling Bilqís.

"Arise, O Bilqís! Come and behold the Kingdom! Gather
pearls on the shore of God's Sea!

Thy sisters are dwelling in the glorious Heaven: why dost
thou behave like a sultan on account of (possessing) a carcase?[4]

---

[1] This is a very difficult verse. I take کَمْ شود as equivalent to نشود.
[2] On which the earth was supposed to rest.
[3] *I.e.* the spirit of Mohammed.
[4] According to the *Ḥadíth*, "The world is a carcase, and those who seek
it are curs."

Dost thou know at all what noble gifts that Sultan (God) gave to thy sisters?

How didst thou jubilantly take drummers (into thy service), proclaiming, 'I am queen and mistress of the bath-stove'?"

Parable of Man's being contented with (the goods of) this world, and his greed in seeking (them) and his indifference to the high and blessed estate of the spiritual who are his congeners (and are) crying, "Oh, would that my people might know!"

1045   A dog saw a blind beggar in the street, and was rushing at him and tearing his cloak.

We have (already) related this[1], but it is repeated (here) once again in order to strengthen (the effect of) the story.

The blind man said to it (the dog), "Why, at this moment your friends are hunting and seeking prey on the mountain.

Your kinsfolk are catching onagers in the mountains: you are catching blind men in the streets."

O recalcitrant Shaykh, abandon this imposture: thou art (like) briny water, having gathered some blind men (around thee),

1050   (As though implicitly thou wert) saying, "These are my disciples, and I am (like) briny water: they drink of me and become blind."

Sweeten thy water with the esoteric Sea: do not make the foul water a snare for these blind ones.

Arise, behold the lions of God who catch the onager: how art thou, like a dog, catching the blind with a (display of) hypocrisy?

What onager (do they catch)? They are far from hunting aught but the Beloved. They all are lions and lion-catchers[2] and intoxicated with the Light (of God).

In contemplation of the chase and hunting of the King, they have abandoned the chase and have become dead in bewilderment.

1055   The Friend has taken them, like a dead bird, that (by means of them) He may hunt down their congeners.

The dead bird is compelled (deprived of volition) in respect of being united or separated: you have read (the *Ḥadíth*), "The heart is between two fingers (of the Merciful God)."

Every one that has fallen a prey to His dead bird (will perceive), when he sees (the truth), (that) he has fallen a prey to the King.

Whoever turned his head away from this dead bird never gained the hand of that Hunter.

It (the dead bird) says, "Do not regard my being a carcase: see the King's love (shown) in preserving me.

----

[1] Book ii, *v.* 2354 foll.
[2] *Shírgír*, "lion-catching," also means "pot-valiant."

I am not a carcase: the King hath killed me: my appearance 1060 has become like (that of) the dead.

My former motion was by means of wing and pinion: now my motion proceeds from the hand of the (Divine) Judge.

My perishable motion has gone forth from my skin: now my motion is everlasting, since it proceeds from Him.

If any one move crookedly (misbehave) in the presence of my motion, I will kill him miserably, (even) though he is the Símurgh.

Beware! If thou art (spiritually) alive, do not deem me dead; if thou art a (devoted) slave (of God), regard me (as being) in the hand of the King.

Jesus, by his grace, made the dead to be living: I am in the 1065 hand of the Creator of Jesus.

How should I remain dead in the grasp of God? Likewise, do not hold this to be possible in (the case of) the hand of 'Jesus[1].'

I am 'Jesus'; but every one that hath gained life from (been revived by) my breath will remain unto everlasting.

He (the dead man) was made living by Jesus, but died again. Happy is he that gave up his life to this 'Jesus.'

I am the staff in the hand of my 'Moses': my 'Moses' is hidden, while I am visible in presence.

For the true believers I become a bridge across the sea; for 1070 Pharaoh, again, I become a dragon."

O son, do not regard this staff alone, for the staff would not be like this without the hand of God.

The waves of the Flood too were a staff which, from being aggrieved, devoured the pomp of the votaries of magic.

If I should enumerate the staves of God, I should tear to pieces (expose and confound) the hypocrisy of these followers of Pharaoh;

But leave them to browse on this sweet poisonous grass for a few days.

If there be not the power and dominion of Pharaoh, whence 1075 shall Hell obtain nutriment?

Fatten him, then kill him, O Butcher; for the dogs in Hell are without food.

If there were no adversary and enemy in the world, then the anger in men would die.

That anger is Hell: it needs an adversary that it may live; else Mercy would kill it.

Then clemency would remain without any vengeance or evil: then how would the perfection of Kingship be (manifested)?

Those disbelievers have made a laughing-stock of the parables 1080 and clear exposition of them that glorify (God).

---

[1] Here 'Jesus' stands as a type of the saint who is united with God.

Make (them) a laughing-stock, if thou wishest (O disbeliever):
how long wilt thou live, O carcase, how long?

Rejoice, O lovers (of God), in supplication at this same door,
for it is opened to-day[1].

Every pot-herb, (such as) garlic and caper, has a different
bed in the garden.

Each with its own kind in its own bed drinks moisture (is
watered) for the purpose of becoming mature.

1085   Thou, who art a saffron-bed, be saffron and do not mix with
the others.

Drink the water, O saffron, that thou mayst attain to maturity:
thou art saffron, thou wilt attain to that *halwá* (sweetmeat)[2].

Do not put thy muzzle into the bed of turnips, for it (the
turnip) will not agree with thee in nature and habit.

Thou art planted in one bed, it (the turnip) in another bed,
because God's earth is spacious,

Particularly that earth (the unseen world) where, on account
of its breadth, demon and genie are lost in their journey.

1090   In (seeking to measure) those seas and deserts and mountains
imagination and fancy fail entirely.

In (comparison with) the deserts thereof, this desert (the
material world) is like a single hair in a full sea.

The still water whose course is hidden is fresher and sweeter
than running brooks,

For, like the (vital) spirit and the (rational) soul, it hath
within itself a hidden course and a moving foot.

The auditor is asleep: cut short (conclude) the address:
O preacher, do not draw this picture on water[3].

1095   Arise, O Bilqís[4], for 'tis a keen (busy and lucrative) market:
flee from these vile wretches who ruin (the spiritual) trade[5].

O Bilqís, arise now with free-will, ere Death appear in his
sovereign might[6].

After that, Death will pull thy ear (torment thee) in such wise
that thou wilt come in agony, like a thief to the magistrate.

How long wilt thou be (engaged in) stealing shoes from these
asses? If thou art going to steal, come and steal a ruby!

Thy sisters have gained the kingdom of everlasting life; thou
hast won the kingdom of misery[7].

1100   Oh, happy he that escaped from this kingdom, for Death
makes this kingdom desolate.

---

[1] *I.e.* "venerate the saints, they being the door through which the Divine
grace is conveyed."

[2] *Halwá* was commonly flavoured with saffron.

[3] *I.e.* "do not waste thy eloquence on those who pay no heed."

[4] *I.e.* "O thou of whom Bilqís is a type."

[5] Literally, "who cause flatness (lack of business) to fall (upon the market)."

[6] Literally, "bring (show) taking and holding."

[7] Literally, "blind and blue."

Arise, O Bilqís! Come, behold for once the kingdom of the Sháhs and Sultans of the (true) Religion.

He (such a king) is seated inwardly (in spirit) amidst the rose-garden (of union with God); outwardly (in the body) he is acting as a *hádí*[1] amongst his friends.

The garden is going with him wherever he goes, but it is (always) being concealed from the people.

The fruit is making entreaty, saying, "Eat of me"; the Water of Life is come, saying, "Drink of me."

Make a circuit of heaven without wing and pinion, like the 1105 sun and like the full-moon and like the new moon.

Thou wilt be moving, like the spirit, and (there will be) no foot; thou wilt be eating a hundred dainties, and (there will be) none chewing a morsel.

Neither will the leviathan, Pain, dash against thy ship, nor will ugliness appear in thee from dying.

Thou wilt be sovereign, army, and throne, all together: thou wilt be both the fortunate and Fortune.

(Even) if thou art fortunate and a powerful monarch, (yet) Fortune is other than thou: one day Fortune goes,

And thou art left destitute like beggars. Be thou thine own 1110 fortune, O elect one!

When thou art thine own fortune, O man of Reality, then how wilt thou, who art Fortune, lose thyself?

How wilt thou lose thyself, O man with goodly qualities, when thy Essence has become thy kingdom and riches?

The rest of the story of Solomon, on whom be peace: how he built the Farther Mosque (the Temple of Solomon) by instruction and inspiration from God, (given to him) for wise purposes which He (only) knows; and how angels, demons, genies, and men lent visible aid.

(God said) "O Solomon, build the Farther Mosque: the army of Bilqís has come into (has adopted) the (ritual) prayer."

When he laid the foundation of that Mosque, genies and men came and threw themselves into the work[2],

One party from love, and another company unwillingly, just 1115 as God's servants (do) in the way of obedience (to Him).

The folk (of the world) are (like) demons, and desire is the chain dragging them to shop and crops.

This chain is (the result) of being afraid (of poverty) and crazed (with worldliness): do not regard these folk as unchained.

It drags them to earning and hunting; it drags them to the mine and the seas.

---

[1] *I.e.* exhorting his disciples and speeding them on the Way, like the camel-driver (*hádí*) who incites his camels by singing to them.

[2] Literally, "put their bodies into the work."

It drags them to good and to evil: God hath said, "*On her neck a cord of palm-fibre*[1].

1120 We have put the cord on their necks: We have made the cord (to consist) of their natural dispositions.

There is none ever, (be he) defiled or (be he) recovered (from foul disease), but *his fortune is on his neck*[2]."

Your greed for evil-doing is like fire: the live coal (the evil deed) is (made) pleasing by the fire's pleasing hue.

The blackness of the coal is hidden in the fire: when the fire is gone, the blackness becomes evident.

By your greed the black coal is made live: when the greed is gone, that vicious coal remains.

1125 At that (former) time the coal appeared to be live; that was not (owing to) the goodness of (your) action: it was (owing to) the fire of greed.

Greed had embellished your action: greed departed, and your action was left in squalor[3].

(Only) one who is foolish will think ripe (and sweet) the *ghawla*[4] which the ghouls deck out (describe as being attractive).

When his soul makes trial (of it), its teeth are blunted by the experiment.

From vain desire, the reflexion (distorting influence) of the ghoul, (which is) greed, was causing the trap to appear a (delicious) berry, though in truth it was unripe.

1130 Seek greed (seek to be eager) in the practice of religion and in good works: they are (still) beautiful, (even) when the greed (eagerness) remains not.

Good works are beautiful (in themselves), not through the reflexion of any other thing: if the glow of greed is gone, the glow of good remains;

(But) when the glow of greed is gone from worldly work, of the red-hot coal (only) the black ashes are left.

Folly excites greed (for amusement) in children, so that from gleefulness of heart they ride a cock-horse[5].

When that evil greed of his is gone from the child, he begins to laugh at the other children,

1135 Saying, "What was I doing? What was I seeing in this?" From the reflexion of greed the vinegar appeared to be honey.

That edifice of the prophets was (raised) without greed (self-interest); hence the splendours (of its renown) increased so uninterruptedly.

---

[1] *Qur'án*, CXI, 5, slightly altered.
[2] *Qur'án*, XVII, 14. "Fortune" refers to the scroll in which every one's good and evil actions are recorded.
[3] Literally, "remained blue."
[4] *Ghawla* is not in the dictionaries. According to the Turkish commentator, it is the name of a bitter herb.
[5] Literally, "ride on their skirts."

Oh, many a mosque have the noble (prophets) erected, but "the Farther Mosque" is not its name.

The grandeur which at every moment accrued to the Ka'ba—that (grandeur) was (derived) from the acts done in pure devotion by Abraham.

The excellence of that mosque (which the prophets build) is not from earth and stone, but (because) there is no greed or enmity in its builder.

Their Books are not as the books of others, nor their mosques 1140 nor their means of livelihood nor their houses and homes,

Nor their observance of respect nor their anger nor their chastisement nor their slumber nor their reasoning nor their discourse.

To each one of them belongs a different glory: (in each of them) the bird, their spirit, flies with a different wing.

The heart is trembling at mention of their (high) estate: their actions are the *qibla* (to which we turn for guidance) of our actions.

The eggs laid by their bird (spirit) are golden: at midnight their spirit hath beheld the dawn.

Whatsoever I say with (all) my soul in praise of the company 1145 (of the prophets), I have depreciated (them): I have become a disparager of the company.

O ye noble (seekers of God), build "the Farther Mosque," for Solomon hath returned—and peace (be with you)!

And if the demons and genies refuse this (service)[1], the angels will drag them all into bondage[2].

(If) the demon once make a false step on account of deceit and hypocrisy, the whip comes (down) on his head like lightning.

Become like Solomon, in order that thy demons may hew stone for thy palace.

Be devoid, like Solomon, of thoughts which tempt to evil-doing 1150 and of fraud, that genie and demon may obey thy command.

This heart is thy seal—and take heed lest the seal fall a prey to the demon!

(For) then the demon possessing the seal will always exercise the sway of Solomon over thee: beware (of him), and peace (be with thee)!

O heart, that sway of Solomon is not abrogated: in thy head and inmost consciousness is one that exercises the sway of Solomon.

The demon too exercises the sway of Solomon for a time, but how should every weaver weave satin?

He (the weaver of common cloth) moves his hand like his 1155 (the satin-weaver's) hand, but there is a good difference between the two of them.

---

[1] Literally, "withdraw their heads from this."
[2] Literally, "into the hoop (collar)."

*Story of the poet and how the king gave him a reward and how the
vizier, whose name was Bu 'l-Ḥasan, made it many times
greater.*

A poet brought a poem before the king in hope of (receiving)
robes of honour and bounty and rank.

The king was munificent: he ordered him (to receive) a
thousand (dinars) of red gold and bounties and largesse.

Then the vizier said to him, "This is (too) little: bestow (on
him) a gift of ten thousand (dinars), that he may depart (satisfied).

From a poet like him intellect (displays itself); from thee,
whose hand is like the ocean (in bounty), the (sum of) ten
thousand (dinars) which I mentioned is little."

1160 He argued and reasoned with the king[1] until the tithe on the
threshed grain was made up out of the unthreshed ears of corn
(which remain on the threshing-floor)[2].

He (the king) gave him the ten thousand (dinars) and the
robes of honour suitable to him: his head became a house of
thanksgiving and praise[3].

Then he made inquiry, saying, "Whose work was this? Who
declared my merit to the king?"

So they told him, "(It was) —— al-Dín[4], the vizier, he whose
name is Ḥasan and whose disposition and heart are good
(ḥasan)."

He wrote a long poem in praise of him (the vizier) and re-
turned home.

1165 Without tongue or lip (mutely) that bounty of the king and
those robes of honour bestowed by the king were praising the
king[5].

*How after several years the poet came back in the hope of (re-
ceiving) the same reward, and how the king according to his
custom ordered a thousand dinars to be given to him, and how
the new vizier, who was also named Ḥasan, said to the king,
"This is very much: we have (great) expenses and the treasury
is empty, and I will satisfy him with a tenth of that (sum)."*

After some years the poet, on account of poverty and destitu-
tion, became in need for daily bread and seed-produce (the
means of livelihood).

He said, "At the time of poverty and close-handedness
(want), it is better to seek out one who has been tried.

[1] Literally, "he talked theology and philosophy to the king."
[2] *I.e.* until the matter was threshed out and concluded.
[3] *I.e.* he thanked and praised the king "in his head," *i.e.* silently. The oldest
MS has *sar* (head), not *sir* (inmost soul).
[4] The blank corresponds to *fulán* ("so-and-so").
[5] *I.e.* while the vizier was praised by the poet's words, the king was praised
by his own noble actions.

The court which I have tried in regard to generosity—I will carry the new request to the same quarter."

That (celebrated) Síbawayh said (that) the meaning of (the name) *Alláh* (is that) they (His worshippers) take refuge (*yawlahúna*)[1] with Him in (all) their needs.

He said, "We have repaired for succour (*alihná*) unto Thee 1170 in our needs and have sought them (and) found them with Thee[2]."

In the hour of affliction hundreds of thousands of intelligent persons are all crying (for help) before that unique Judge.

Would any mad fool do this, (namely), continue to beg[3] of a miser incapable (of liberality)?

Unless the intelligent had experienced (God's beneficence) more than a thousand times, how should they have betaken themselves to Him?

Nay, all the fish in the waves (of the sea), all the birds in the lofty regions (of the sky),

The elephant and the wolf and also the hunting lion, the 1175 huge dragon and also the ant and the snake,

Nay, earth and wind (air) and water and every spark (of fire) gain subsistence from Him both in December (winter) and spring.

This heaven is making entreaty unto Him incessantly—"Do not forsake me, O God, for a single moment!

Thy safeguarding and protection (of me) is my pillar (support): all (of me) is enfolded in the might of those two Hands[4]."

And this earth says, "Preserve me, O Thou who hast caused me to ride upon the water."

All have sewn up (filled) their purses from Him and have 1180 learned from Him to give (satisfy) the wants (of others).

Every prophet has received (on behalf of his people) from Him the guarantee (implied in the words) *seek help* of Him *with patience or prayer*[5].

Come, ask of Him, not of any one except Him: seek water in the sea, do not seek it in the dry river-bed.

And if you ask of another, 'tis He that gives; 'tis He that lays generosity on the open hand of his (that other's) inclination.

He who with gold makes one that turns away (from Him in disobedience) a Qárún (Korah), how (much more) will He do (if) you turn your face towards Him in obedience!

The poet, from passionate desire for bounty, set his face a 1185 second time towards that beneficent king.

What is the poet's offering? A new poem: he brings it to the beneficent (patron) and deposits it as his stake.

---

[1] The text has يُؤْلَهُونَ, but I think يَوْلَهُونَ (G) is correct.
[2] *I.e.* we have sought and obtained from Thee the satisfaction of our needs.
[3] Literally, "apply himself to begging."
[4] Cf. *Qur'án*, XXXIX, 67.
[5] The words of *Qur'án*, II, 148 have been slightly altered for metrical reasons.

The beneficent (on their part) have deposited gold and are waiting for the poets with a hundred gifts and liberalities and kindnesses.

In their eyes a poem (*shi'r*) is better than a hundred bales of silk robes (*sha'r*), especially (when it is composed by) a poet who fetches pearls from the depths.

At first a man is greedy for bread, because food and bread are the pillar (support) of life.

1190   On account of greed and expectation he runs every risk[1] in the way of earning his livelihood and seizing property by violence and (employing) a hundred devices.

When, (as happens) rarely, he becomes independent of (earning his) bread, he is in love with fame and the praise of poets,

In order that they may give fruit to (may adorn) his root and branch[2] and may set up a pulpit to declare his excellence,

So that his pomp and magnificence and lavishing of gold may yield a perfume, like (that of) ambergris, in (their) song.

God created us in His image: our qualities are instructed by[3] (are modelled upon) His qualities.

1195   Inasmuch as the Creator desires thanksgiving and glorification, it is also the nature of man to desire praise,

Especially the man of God, who is active in (showing) excellence: he becomes filled with that wind (of praise), like an undamaged leathern bag;

But if he (the recipient of praise) be not worthy, the bag is rent by that wind of falsehood: how should it receive lustre?

I have not invented[4] this parable, O comrade: do not hear it (as though it were) silly, if thou art worthy and restored to thy senses.

The Prophet (Mohammed) said (something like) this, when he heard vituperation (from the infidels who asked), "Why is Ahmad (Mohammed) made fat (happy) by praise?"

1200   The poet went to the king and brought a poem in thanks (and praise) for (his) beneficence, saying that it (beneficence) never died.

The beneficent died, and (their) acts of beneficence remained: oh, blest is he that rode this steed[5]!

The unjust died, and those acts of injustice remained: alas for the soul that practises deceit and fraud!

The Prophet said, "Blest is he who departed from this world and left[6] good deeds behind him."

---

[1] Literally, "he has laid his life on his palm (taken his life in his hand)."
[2] *I.e.* his nature and the virtues belonging to it.
[3] Literally, "take lessons from."
[4] Literally, "I have not told from myself."
[5] *I.e.* "practised beneficence."
[6] Literally, "there remained."

The beneficent man died, but his beneficence died not: with God, religion (piety) and beneficence are not of small account.

Alas for him who died and whose disobedience (to God) died 1205 not: beware of thinking that by death he saved his soul (from punishment).

Dismiss this (topic), for the poet is on the way—in debt and mightily in need of gold.

The poet brought the poem to the king in hope of (receiving) last year's donation and benefit—

A charming poem full of flawless pearls, in hope and expectation of the first (former) munificence.

The Sháh indeed, according to his habit, ordered a thousand (dinars to be paid) to him, since such was the custom of that monarch;

But, on this occasion, the bountiful vizier had departed from 1210 the present life, (mounted) on the Buráq of glory,

And in his place a new vizier had assumed authority[1]; but (he was) very pitiless and mean.

He said, "O king, we have (great) outlays: this donation is not the (fitting) reward for a poet.

With a fortieth part of this (sum), O thou (whose favour is) eagerly sought, I will make the poet man happy and content."

The people said to him, "He carried away a sum of ten thousand (dinars) in ready money from this valiant (king).

After (having eaten) sugar, how should he chew (the empty) 1215 cane? After having been a sultan, how should he practise beggary?"

He (the vizier) replied, "I will squeeze him in torment, that he may be made wretched and worn out by waiting;

Then, if I give him earth from the road, he will snatch it as (though it were) rose-leaves from the garden.

Leave this to me, for I am expert in this, even if the claimant be fiery (hot and fierce).

Though he (be able to) fly from the Pleiades to the earth[2], he will become meek when he sees me."

The king said to him, "Go: 'tis for thee to command; but 1220 make him happy, for he is my eulogist."

He (the vizier) said, "Leave him and two hundred (other) lickers-up of hope to me, and write this (down) against me[3]."

Then the minister threw him into (the pains of) expectation: winter and December passed and spring came.

In expectation of it (the reward) the poet grew old; then he was crushed by this anxiety and making shift to provide (the means of livelihood),

---

[1] Literally, "had become chief."
[2] I.e. "however potent he may be."
[3] I.e. "hold me responsible."

And said (to the vizier), "If there is no gold (for me), please give me abuse[1], so that my soul may be delivered (from expectation) (and that) I may be thy (devoted) slave.

1225 Expectation has killed me: at least bid me go, that this wretched soul may be delivered from bondage."

After that, he (the vizier) gave him the fortieth part of that (gift): the poet remained in heavy thought,

(Thinking), "That (former gift) was so promptly paid[2] and was so much: this one that blossomed late was (only) a handful of thorns."

Then they (the courtiers) said to him, "That generous vizier has departed from this life: may God reward thee!

For those gifts were always multiplied (increased in amount) by him: there was no fault to be found with the donations (then);

1230 (But) now, he is gone and has taken beneficence away (with him): he is not dead[3], (but) beneficence is dead (in this world), yea, verily.

The generous and upright minister is gone from us; the minister who is a flayer of the poor has arrived.

Go, take this (money) and flee from here by night, lest this minister pick a quarrel with thee.

We have obtained this gift from him by a hundred devices, O thou who art ignorant of our exertions."

He turned his face to them and said, "O kindly men, tell (me), whence came this myrmidon (ruffian)?

1235 What is the name of this vizier who tears off the clothes (of the poor)?" The company (of courtiers) said to him, "His name too is Ḥasan."

He (the poet) cried, "O Lord, how are the names of that one and this one the same? Alas, O Lord of the Judgement!

That Ḥasan by name (was such) that by a single pen of his[4] a hundred viziers and ministers are disposed to liberality.

This Ḥasan (is such) that from the ugly beard of this Ḥasan thou canst weave, O (dear) soul, a hundred ropes[5]."

When a king listens to such a minister, he (the minister) disgraces the king and his kingdom unto everlasting.

The resemblance of the bad judgement of this base vizier in corrupting the king's generosity to (that of) the vizier of Pharaoh, namely, Hámán, in corrupting the readiness of Pharaoh to receive (the true Faith).

1240 How many a time did Pharaoh soften and become submissive when he was hearing that Word from Moses!—

---

[1] *I.e.* "dismiss me with obloquy."   [2] Literally, "ready money."
[3] *I.e.* he is living in the spiritual world.
[4] *I.e.* by the example of munificence which he gave in signing orders for donations.   [5] Cf. Book III, *v.* 3564.

That Word (which was such) that from the sweetness of that incomparable Word the rock would have yielded milk.

Whenever he took counsel with Hámán, who was his vizier and whose nature it was to hate,

Then he (Hámán) would say, "Until now thou hast been the Khedive: wilt thou become, through deception, the slave to a wearer of rags?"

Those words would come like a stone shot by a mangonel (ballista) and strike upon his glass house.

All that the *Kalím*[1] of sweet address built up in a hundred days he (Hámán) would destroy in one moment.   1245

Thy intellect is the vizier and is overcome by sensuality: in (the realm of) thy being it is a brigand (that attacks thee) on the Way to God.

(If) a godly monitor give thee good advice, it will artfully put those words (of his) aside,

Saying, "These (words) are not well-founded[2]: take heed, don't be carried away (by them)[3]; they are not (worth) so much: come to thyself (be sensible), don't be crazed."

Alas for the king whose vizier is this (carnal intellect): the place (abode) of them both is vengeful Hell.

Happy is the king whose helper in affairs is a vizier like Áṣaf.   1250

When the just king is associated with him, his (the king's) name is *light upon light*.

A king like Solomon and a vizier like Áṣaf are *light upon light* and ambergris upon *'abír*[4].

(When) the king (is like) Pharaoh and his vizier like Hámán, ill-fortune is inevitable for both.

Then it is (a case of) *darkness, one part over another*: neither intellect nor fortune shall be their friend on the Day of Judgement[5].

I have not seen aught but misery in the vile: if thou hast seen   1255 (aught else), convey (to them) the salaam (of felicitation) from me.

The king is as the spirit, and the vizier as the intellect: the corrupt intellect brings the spirit into movement (towards corruption).

When the angelical intellect became a Hárút, it became the teacher in magic to two hundred devils.

Do not take the particular (individual) intellect as thy vizier: make the Universal Intellect thy vizier, O king.

Do not make sensuality thy vizier, else thy pure spirit will cease from prayer,

---

[1] See Book II (translation), *v.* 360, note.
[2] Literally, "on (the right) place."
[3] Literally, "do not move from (thy) place."
[4] Mixed perfumes.
[5] Literally, "the Day of Review."

1260   For this sensuality is full of greed and sees (only) the immediate present, (whereas) the Intellect takes thought for the Day of Judgement.

The two eyes of the Intellect are (fixed) on the end of things: it endures the pain of the thorn for the sake of that Rose

Which does not fade and drop in autumn—far from it be the wind (breath) of every nose that cannot smell!

How the Demon sat on the place (throne) of Solomon, on whom be peace, and imitated his actions; and concerning the manifest difference between the two Solomons, and how the Demon called himself Solomon son of David.

Even if thou hast intellect, associate and consult with another intellect, O father.

With two intellects thou wilt be delivered from many afflictions: thou wilt plant thy foot on the summit of the heavens.

1265   If the Demon called himself Solomon and won the kingdom and made the empire subject (to him),

(It was because) he had seen (and imitated) the form of Solomon's action; (but) within the form the spirit of demonry was appearing.

The people said, "This Solomon is without excellence: there are (great) differences between (that) Solomon and (this) Solomon."

He (the former) is like wakefulness, this one is like sleep; (there is as much difference) as between that Ḥasan and this Ḥasan[1].

The Demon would reply, "God has bestowed on Ahriman a pleasing form (aspect) in the likeness of me.

1270   God hath given my aspect to the Devil: let him not cast you into his net!

If he appear with the pretence (that he is really I), beware! Do not have regard to his (outward) form."

The Demon was saying this to them from guile, but in good (enlightened) hearts the reverse of this was apparent.

There is no playing tricks with the discerning man, especially (with) him whose discernment and intelligence speak of the Unseen.

No magic and no imposture and fraud will bind a veil upon the owners of (spiritual) empire.

1275   Hence they were saying to themselves in reply (to the Demon), "Thou art going upside down, O thou who art addressed falsely (by the name of Solomon).

Upside down likewise thou wilt go Hellward, the lowest among the low.

---

[1] The two homonymous viziers in the story of the poet, *v.* 1156 foll.

If he (Solomon) has been deposed and reduced to poverty,
(yet) the radiant full-moon is on his forehead.

If thou hast carried off the (royal) signet-ring, (yet) thou art
(as) a Hell frozen like (the region of) piercing cold[1].

On account of (the Demon's) ostentation and vain show and
pomp and grandeur how (should we lay) the head (in obeisance
before him)? for we will not lay (before him) even a hoof.

And if heedlessly we should lay the forehead (on the ground in 1280
homage) to him, a preventing hand will rise up from the earth,

(As though to say), 'Do not lay the head before this headlong-
fallen one; beware, do not bow down to this ill-fated wretch!'"

I would have given a very soul-quickening exposition of this
(story), were it not for the indignation and jealousy of God.

Still, be content and accept this (insufficient) amount, that I
may explain (the whole of) this at another time.

He (the Demon), having called himself by the name of the
prophet Solomon, makes it a mask to deceive every (foolish) boy.

Pass on from the (outward) form and rise beyond the name: 1285
flee from title and from name (and enter) into reality.

Inquire, then, about his (spiritual) degree and his (interior)
actions: in the midst of his degree and actions seek (to discover)
him.

*How Solomon, on whom be peace, entered the Farther Mosque
daily, after its completion, for the purpose of worshipping and
directing the worshippers and devotees; and how medicinal herbs
grew in the Mosque.*

Every morning, when Solomon came and made supplication
in the Farther Mosque,

He saw that a new plant had grown there; then he would say,
"Tell thy name and use.

What medicine art thou? What art thou? What is thy name?
To whom art thou hurtful and for whom is thy usefulness?"

Then every plant would tell its effect and name, saying, 1290
"I am life to that one, and death to this one.

I am poison to this one, and sugar to that one: this is my name
(inscribed) on the Tablet by (the pen of) the Divine decree."

Then (by hearing) from Solomon about those plants the
physicians became learned and wise authorities (on medicine),

So that they compiled medical books and were relieving the
body from pain.

This astronomy and medicine is (knowledge given by)
Divine inspiration to the prophets: where is the way for intellect
and sense (to advance) towards that which is without (spatial)
direction?

---

[1] *I.e.* "thou art devoid of spiritual ardour."

1295 The particular (individual) intellect is not the intellect (capable) of production: it is only the receiver of science and is in need (of teaching).

This intellect is capable of being taught and of apprehending, but (only) the man possessed of Divine inspiration gives it the teaching (which it requires).

Assuredly, in their beginning, all trades (crafts and professions) were (derived) from Divine inspiration, but the intellect added (something) to them.

Consider whether this intellect of ours can learn any trade without a master.

Although it (the intellect) was hair-splitting (subtle and ingenious) in contrivance, no trade was subdued (brought under command) without a master.

1300 If knowledge of a trade were (derived) from this intellect, any trade would be acquired without a master.

How Qábíl (Cain) learned the trade of grave-digging from the crow (raven), before knowledge of grave-digging and graves existed in the world.

When was grave-digging, which was the meanest trade (of all), (acquired) from thought and cunning and meditation?

If Qábíl had possessed this understanding, how should he have placed (the body of) Hábíl (Abel) on his head?—

Saying, "Where shall I hide this murdered one, this man bestained with blood and earth?"

He espied a crow which had taken up a dead crow in its mouth and was approaching (ever) so quickly.

1305 It came down from the air and began skilfully to dig a grave for it (the dead crow) for the purpose of teaching (him).

Then with its talons it raised dust from the ground and speedily put the dead crow in the grave.

It buried it, then it covered it with earth: the crow was endowed with knowledge through the inspiration (given) of God.

Qábíl cried, "Oh, fie on my intellect! for a crow is superior to me in skill."

Concerning the Universal Intellect He (God) hath said, "*The sight did not rove (má zágh)*," (but) the particular intellect is looking in every direction.

1310 The Intellect whose sight does not rove (*'aql-i má zágh*) is the light of the elect; the crow-intellect (*'aql-i zágh*) is the sexton[1] for the (spiritually) dead.

The spirit that flies after crows—the crow carries it towards the graveyard.

_____
[1] Literally, "the grave-master."

Beware! Do not run in pursuit of the crow-like fleshly soul,
for it carries (thee) to the graveyard, not towards the orchard.

If thou go, go in pursuit of the 'Anqá of the heart, towards the
Qáf and Farther Mosque of the heart.

Every moment from thy cogitation a new plant is growing in
thy Farther Mosque.

Do thou, like Solomon, give it its due: investigate it, do not 1315
lay upon it the foot of rejection,

Because the various sorts of plants declare to thee the (inward)
state of this firm-set earth.

Whether in the earth there are sugar-canes or only (common)
reeds, every earth (soil) is interpreted by its plants.

Therefore the heart's soil, whereof thought was (ever) the
plant—(those) thoughts have revealed the heart's secrets.

If I find in the company him that draws the discourse (from
me towards himself), I, like the garden, will grow hundreds of
thousands of roses;

And if at that time I find (there) the scoundrel[1] who kills the 1320
discourse, the deep sayings will flee, like a thief, from my heart.

The movement of every one is towards the Drawer: the true
drawing is not like the false drawing.

Sometimes thou art going astray, sometimes aright: the cord
is not visible, nor He who is drawing thee.

Thou art a blind camel, and thy toggle is in (His) keeping: do
thou regard the act of drawing, do not regard thy toggle.

If the Drawer and the toggle became perceptible (to the
senses), then this world would no longer remain the abode of
heedlessness (delusion).

(If) the infidel saw that he was going after a cur and was being 1325
made subject to the hideous Devil,

How should he go at its heels like a catamite (base syco-
phant)? The infidel too would step back.

If the cow were acquainted with the butchers, how should
she follow them to that (butcher's) shop,

Or eat bran from their hands, or give them milk on account
of (their) coaxing (her)?

And if she ate, how should the fodder be digested by her, if
she were aware of the purpose of the fodder?

Heedlessness (delusion), then, is in sooth the pillar (support) 1330
of this world: what is dawlat (worldly fortune)? for this dawádaw
(running to and fro) is (accompanied) with lat (blows).

The beginning thereof is daw, daw (run, run); in the end (it is)
lat khwar (suffer blows): the death of the ass is not (occurring)
except in this wilderness[2].

---

[1] See Book II (translation), v. 2803, note.
[2] I.e. the foolish worldling dies in his worldliness; if he had been unworldly,
he would have gained everlasting life.

Whenever thou hast earnestly taken a work in hand, its faultiness has become veiled to thee at this moment.

Thou art able to give thyself up to the work, (only) because the Creator veils its faultiness from thee.

Likewise, (with) every thought in which thou art hot (eager), the faultiness of that thought of thine has become hidden from thee.

1335   If its faultiness and disgrace were made visible to thee, thy soul would flee from it (as far as) the distance between east and west.

The state (of mind) in which at last thou repentest of it (of a faulty action)—if this should be thy state (of mind) at first, how wouldst thou run (for the sake of that action)?

Therefore He (God) at first veiled (the real nature of) that from our souls, in order that we might perform that action in accordance with the Divine destiny.

When the Divine destiny brought its ordainment into view, the eye was opened, so that repentance arrived.

This repentance is another (manifestation of the) Divine destiny: abandon this repentance, worship God!

1340   And if thou make (it) a habit and become addicted to repentance, because of this (habitual) repentance thou wilt become more repentant.

One half of thy life will pass in distraction and the other half will pass in repentance.

Take leave of this (anxious) thought and repentance: seek a better (spiritual) state and friend and work.

And if thou hast no better work in hand, then for the omission of what (work) is thy repentance?

If thou knowest the good way, worship (God); and if thou dost not know (it), how dost thou know that this way (in which thou art going) is evil?

1345   Thou dost not know evil till thou knowest good: (only) from (one) contrary is it possible to discern (the other) contrary, O youth.

Since (as thou sayest) thou wert rendered impotent to abandon the thought of this (repentance), at that time thou wert also impotent to commit sin.

Since thou wert impotent (to commit sin), on account of what is thy repentance? Inquire concerning impotence, by whose pull (exertion of power) is it (produced)?

No one has seen impotence in the world without power, nor will it (ever) be (so). Know this (for sure).

Similarly, (with) every desire that thou cherishest, thou art debarred from (perceiving) its faultiness;

1350   And if the viciousness of that desire had been shown, thy soul of its own accord would have recoiled from seeking (to gratify it).

If He (God) had shown unto thee the faultiness of that work,
no one, dragging (thee) along (by force), would have taken thee
in that direction;

And (as regards) that other work from which thou art ex-
ceedingly averse, the reason is that its faultiness has come into
clear view.

O God who knowest the secret and who art gracious in speech,
do not hide from us the faultiness of the evil work;

(And) do not show unto us the faultiness of the good work,
lest we become cold (disgusted) and distracted[1] from journeying
(in the Way).

According to that (aforesaid) habit, the exalted Solomon went 1355
into the Mosque in the brightness (of dawn).

The king was seeking (to observe) the daily rule of seeing the
new plants in the Mosque.

The heart with that pure eye (which it possesses) sees occultly
the (spiritual) herbs that are invisible to the vulgar.

*Story of the Ṣúfí who, head on knee, was engaged in (spiritual)
meditation in the garden: his friends said to him, "Lift up thy
head and enjoy the garden and the sweet herbs and the birds and
the marks of the mercy of God most High."*

In the orchard a certain Ṣúfí laid his face in Ṣúfí fashion upon
his knee for the sake of (mystical) revelation;

Then he sank deep down into himself. An impertinent fellow
was annoyed by his semblance of slumber.

"Why," said he, "dost thou sleep? Nay, look at the vines, 1360
behold these trees and marks (of Divine mercy) and green
plants.

Hearken to the command of God, for He hath said, '*Look
ye*': turn thy face towards these marks of (Divine) mercy."

He replied, "O man of vanity, its marks are (within) the
heart: that (which is) without is only the marks of the marks."

The (real) orchards and verdure are in the very essence of the
soul: the reflexion thereof upon (that which is) without is as
(the reflexion) in running water.

In the water there is (only) the phantom (reflected image) of
the orchard, which quivers on account of the subtle quality of
the water.

The (real) orchards and fruits are within the heart: the re- 1365
flexion of their beauty is (falling) upon this water and earth (the
external world).

If it were not the reflexion of that delectable cypress[2], then
God would not have called it the abode of deception.

---

[1] Literally, "motes in a sunbeam," *i.e.* "dispersed, not concentrated."
[2] The heart of the saint.

This deception is (consists in) that: *i.e.* this phantom (the external world) exists (derives its existence) from the reflexion of the heart and spirit of the (holy) men.

All the deceived ones come to (gaze on) this reflexion in the opinion that this is the place of Paradise.

They are fleeing from the origins of the orchards; they are making merry[1] over a phantom.

1370 When their heedless sleep[2] comes to an end, they see truly— but what use is that sight (to them)?

Then in the graveyard arises uproar and lament: on account of this mistake (they cry) "alas" till the Resurrection.

Oh, happy he that died before death, *i.e.* he got scent of (became acquainted with) the origin of this vineyard.

Story of the growing of the carob in a nook of the Farther Mosque, and how Solomon, on whom be peace, was grieved thereat, when it began to talk with him and told its characteristic property and its name.

Then Solomon saw that a new plant had grown, like an ear of corn, in a nook (of the Mosque).

He saw a very uncommon plant, green and fresh: its greenness took away the light from (dazzled) the sight.

1375 Then that herb at once saluted him: he answered it (returned its salutation) and marvelled at its beauty.

He said, "What is thy name? Say (it) without mouth." It said, "It is 'carob,' O king of the world."

He said, "What special property is (resides) in thee?" It replied, "(Where) I have grown, the place becomes desolate.

I, who am carob (*kharrúb*), am the ruin (*kharáb*) of the abode: I am the destroyer of the building (made) of this water and clay."

Then at that moment Solomon immediately understood that the appointed term (of his life) was come and that the (hour of) departure would (soon) appear.

1380 He said, "So long as I exist, assuredly this Mosque will not be damaged by the banes of the earth.

Whilst I am (here) and my existence continues, how should the Farther Mosque become riven with cracks (fall into decay)?

Know, then, that without doubt the ruin of our mosque does not occur except after our death.

The mosque is the heart to which the body bows down: wherever the mosque is, the bad companion is the carob.

When love for a bad companion has grown in you, beware, flee from him and do not converse (with him).

---

[1] Literally, "they are making those jests (frolics)."
[2] Literally, "sleep of heedlessness."

Tear it up by the root, for if it shoot up its head it will 1385
demolish (both) you and your mosque.

O lover, your carob is falseness: why do you creep, like
children, towards the false?

Know yourself a sinner and call yourself a sinner—do not be
afraid—so that that Master may not steal (secretly take away)
the lesson from you.

When you say, "I am ignorant: give (me) instruction," such
fair-dealing is better than (a false) reputation.

Learn from your father (Adam), O clear-browed man: he said
heretofore, "*O our Lord*" and "*We have done wrong.*"

He made no excuse, nor did he invent falsehood nor lift up 1390
the banner of deceit and evasion.

That Iblís, on the other hand, began to dispute, saying,
"I was red-faced (honourable): Thou hast made me yellow
(disgraced).

The colour is Thy colour: Thou art my dyer, Thou art the
origin of my sin and bane and brand."

Beware! Recite (the text) *because Thou hast seduced me*, in
order that you may not become a necessitarian and may not
weave untruth.

How long will you leap up the tree of necessitarianism and lay
your free-will aside,

Like that Iblís and his progeny, (engaged) in battle and 1395
argument with God?

How should there be compulsion when you are trailing your
skirt (sweeping along) into sin with such complacence?

Does any one under compulsion walk so complacently? Does
any one, having lost his way[1], go dancing (gleefully) like that?

You were fighting like twenty men (to prevail) in the matter
concerning which those others were giving you good advice.

You said, "This is right and this is the only (approved) way:
how should any one but a nobody (worthless person) rail at
me?"

How should one who is compelled speak thus? How should 1400
one who has lost his way wrangle like this?

Whatever your fleshly soul desires, you have free-will (in
regard to that); whatever your reason desires, you plead
necessity (as an excuse for rejecting it).

He that is blessed and familiar (with spiritual mysteries)
knows that intelligence is of Iblís, while love is of Adam.

Intelligence is (like) swimming in the seas: he (the swimmer)
is not saved: he is drowned at the end of the business.

Leave off swimming, let pride and enmity go: this is not a
Jayhún (Oxus) or a (lesser) river, it is an ocean;

---

[1] Literally, "in the plight of one whose way is lost."

1405 And, moreover, (it is) the deep Ocean without refuge: it sweeps away the seven seas like straw.

Love is as a ship for the elect: seldom is calamity (the result); for the most part it is deliverance.

Sell intelligence and buy bewilderment: intelligence is opinion, while bewilderment is (immediate) vision.

Sacrifice your understanding in the presence of Muṣṭafá (Mohammed): say, "*ḥasbiya 'lláh*[1], for God sufficeth me."

Do not draw back your head from the ship (ark), like Kanʿán (Canaan), whom his intelligent soul deluded,

1410 Saying, "I will go up to the top of the lofty mountain: why must I bear gratitude (be under an obligation) to Noah?"

How should you recoil from being grateful to him, O unrighteous one, when even God bears gratitude to him?

How should gratitude to him not be (as an obligation) on our souls, when God gives him words of thankful praise and gratitude?

What do you know (about his exalted state), O sack full of envy? Even God bears gratitude to him.

Would that he (one like Kanʿán) had not learned to swim, so that he might have fixed his hope on Noah and the ark!

1415 Would that, like a child, he had been ignorant of devices, so that, like children, he might have clung to his mother,

Or that he had not been filled with traditional knowledge, (but) had carried away from a saint the knowledge divinely revealed to the heart!

When you bring forward a book (in rivalry) with such a light (of inspiration), your soul, that resembles inspiration (in its nature), reproaches (you).

Know that beside the breath (words) of the Quṭb[2] of the time traditional knowledge is like performing the ritual ablution with sand when there is water (available).

Make yourself foolish (simple) and follow behind (him): only by means of this foolishness will you gain deliverance.

1420 On this account, O father, the Sultan of mankind (Mohammed) hath said, "Most of the people of Paradise are the foolish."

Since intelligence is the exciter of pride and vanity in you, become a fool in order that your heart may remain sound—

Not the fool that is bent double (abases himself) in buffoonery, (but) the fool that is distraught and bewildered (lost) in Him (God).

The foolish are (like) those women (of Egypt) who cut their hands—foolish in respect of their hands, (but) giving (wise) notice to beware of the face (beauty) of Joseph.

---

[1] *I.e.* "God is sufficient for me."
[2] The head of the saintly hierarchy.

Sacrifice your intellect in love for the Friend: anyhow, (all) intellects are from the quarter where He is.

The (spiritually) intelligent[1] have sent their intellects to that 1425 quarter: (only) the dolt has remained in this quarter where the Beloved is not.

If, from bewilderment, this intellect of yours go out of this head, every head (tip) of your hair will become (a new) head and intellect.

In that quarter the trouble of thinking is not (incumbent) on the brain, for (there) the brain and intellect (spontaneously) produce fields and orchards (of spiritual knowledge).

(If you turn) towards the field, you will hear from the field a subtle discourse; (if) you come to the orchard, your palm-tree will become fresh and flourishing.

In this Way abandon ostentation: do not move unless your (spiritual) guide move.

Any one who moves without the head (guide) is a (mere) tail 1430 (base and contemptible): his movement is like the movement of the scorpion.

Going crookedly, night-blind and ugly and venomous—his trade is the wounding of the pure bodies (of the unworldly).

Beat the head of him whose inmost spirit is (like) this, and whose permanent nature and disposition is (like) this.

In sooth 'tis good for him to beat this head (of his), so that his puny soul[2] may be delivered from that ill-starred body.

Take away the weapons from the madman's hand, that Justice and Goodness may be satisfied with you.

Since he has weapons and has no understanding, shackle his 1435 hand; otherwise he will inflict a hundred injuries.

Explaining that the acquisition of knowledge and wealth and rank by men of evil nature is the (means of) exposing him (such a one) to shame and is like a sword that has fallen into the hand of a brigand.

To teach the evil-natured man knowledge and skill is to put a sword in the hand of a brigand.

It is better to put a sword in the hand of an intoxicated negro than that knowledge should come into the possession of a worthless person.

Knowledge and wealth and office and rank and fortune[3] are a mischief in the hands of the evil-natured.

Therefore the Holy War was made obligatory on the true believers for this purpose, (namely) that they might take the spear-point from the hand of the madman.

---

[1] Literally, "the intelligences."
[2] Literally, "small fragment of soul."
[3] Literally, "conjunction (of two auspicious planets)."

1440   His (the evil-natured man's) spirit is (like) the madman, and his body is (like) his (the madman's) sword: take away the sword from that wicked man!

How should a hundred lions inflict the shame which (high) office inflicts upon the ignorant?

His vice is hidden, (but) when he got the instrument (gained power), his snake, (coming out) from its hole, sped along the plain.

The entire plain is filled with snakes and scorpions when the ignorant man becomes king (master) of the bitter (harsh) decree.

The worthless person who acquires wealth and office has become the seeker of his own disgrace.

1445   Either he behaves stingily and gives few presents, or he shows generosity and bestows (them) in the wrong place (unsuitably).

He puts the king in the house (square) of the pawn: the gifts which a fool makes are like this.

When authority falls into the hands of one who has lost the (right) way, he deems it to be a high position (*jáh*), (but in reality) he has fallen into a pit (*cháh*).

He does not know the way, (yet) he acts as guide: his wicked spirit makes a world-conflagration.

When (one who is as) a child in the Way of (spiritual) poverty assumes the part of an Elder (Director of souls), the ghoul of unblessedness seizes those who follow (him).

1450   "Come," says he, "for I will show thee the moon"; (yet) that impure one never saw the moon.

How wilt thou show (the moon) when during (all) thy life thou hast not seen even the reflexion of the moon in the water, O half-baked dunce?

The foolish have become leaders, and from fear (of them) the wise have drawn their heads into the cloak[1].

Commentary on "O thou that wrappest thyself."

For this reason He (God) called the Prophet *muzzammil* (one who wraps himself), saying, "Come forth from the cloak, O thou who art fond of taking flight.

Do not draw thy head into the cloak and do not cover thy face, for the world is a reeling body: thou art the intelligence (rational spirit).

1455   Hark, do not hide on account of the opprobrium of the adversary, since thou hast the resplendent candle of the Revelation.

Hark, *stand up (in prayer) during the night*, for thou art a candle, O prince: at night a candle stands up (and burns).

Without thy radiance, even the bright day is (dark as) night: without thy protection, the lion is captive to the hare.

_____
[1] *I.e.* have concealed themselves.

Be the captain (pilot) of the ship in this sea of (spiritual)
purity, for thou art a second Noah, O Muṣṭafá (elect one).

An expert guide, (endowed) with understanding, is needed
for every road, especially in the road (journey) on the water.

Arise! Look upon the waylaid caravan: everywhere a ghoul 1460
has become captain of the ship.

Thou art the Khiẓr of the time and the Deliverer of every
ship (in distress): do not, like (Jesus) the Spirit of God, practise
solitude.

In the sight of this assembly (of people) thou art as the candle
of heaven: leave off severing thyself (from them) and adopting
seclusion.

'Tis not the time for seclusion: come into the assembly, O
thou who art (as) the *humáy*, while the guidance (of souls) is like
Mount Qáf[1].

The full-moon is moving by night on the upper part of the
sky: it does not cease from its journey because of the outcry of
the dogs.

The scoffers keep making an outcry, like dogs, at thy full- 1465
moon in the direction of thy high place.

These dogs (are) deaf to the (Divine) command, '*Be ye silent*':
from folly (they are) bow-wowing at thy full-moon.

Hark, O (thou who art) the cure for the sick, do not, on account
of anger against the deaf, let go the staff of the blind.

Didst not thou say?—'He that leads a blind man on the
(right) way gains a hundred recompenses and rewards from
God.

Whoever leads a blind man forty steps is pardoned and will
find salvation.'

Do thou, therefore, lead away from this impermanent world 1470
the multitude of the blind, file on file.

This is the business of a guide: thou art the Guide, thou art
the joy for (dispelling) the sorrow of the last (period of) time.

Hark, O Imám of the God-fearing, cause these thinkers of
vain fancies to go (onward) till (they attain unto) certainty.

Whoever hath his heart in pawn (devoted) to plotting against
thee, I will smite his neck: do thou advance joyously.

I will lay (more) blindnesses on the top of his blindness:
he will deem it sugar, and I will (really) give him poison.

(All) intellects have been kindled by My light; (all) plots have 1475
been learned from My plotting.

What indeed is the Turcoman's tent of black felt before the
feet of the male (fierce) elephants of this world?

Before My ṣarṣar wind what in sooth is that lamp of his
(contrivance), O My greatest prophet?

---

[1] *I.e.* "spiritual guidance is thy peculiar sphere, just as Mt Qáf is the home
of the *humáy* (bearded griffon)."

Do thou arise and blow on the terrible trumpet, that thou sands of the dead may spring up from the earth.

Since thou art the upright-rising Isráfíl (Seraphiel) of the time, make a resurrection ere the Resurrection.

1480　O beloved[1], if any one say, 'Where is the Resurrection?' show thyself, saying, 'Behold, I am the Resurrection.

Look, O questioner who art stricken with tribulation, (and see) that from this resurrection a hundred worlds have grown!'

And if he (the scoffer) be not fit for this praise (of Me) and humble supplication, then, O (spiritual) Sultan, the (proper) reply to a fool is silence.

From God's Heaven silence comes in reply when, O (dear) soul, the prayer is unanswered."

Oh, alas, 'tis harvest-time, but by our (ill) fortune the day has become late.

1485　Time is pressing, and the amplitude of this (subject of) discussion (is such that) a perpetual life will be (too) restricted for it.

To dart the lance in these narrow lanes brings to disgrace those who dart the lance.

The time is narrow (limited), and the mind and understanding of the vulgar is narrower a hundredfold than the time, O youth.

Inasmuch as silence is the (proper) reply to the fool, how art thou thus prolonging the discourse?

(Because) He (God), from the perfection of His mercy and the waves of His bounty, bestows rain and moisture on every barren soil.

Showing that (the proverb), "Omission to reply is a reply," confirms the saying that silence is the (proper) reply to the fool. The explanation of both these (sayings) is (contained) in the story which will now be related.

1490　There was a king: he had a slave; he (the slave) was one whose reason was dead and whose lust was alive.

He would neglect the niceties of service to him (the king): he was thinking evil and deeming (it) good.

The monarch said, "Reduce his allowance, and if he wrangle strike his name off the roll."

His reason was deficient, his cupidity excessive: when he saw the allowance reduced he became violent and refractory.

Had there been reason (in him), he would have made a circuit round himself, in order that he might see his offence and become forgiven.

---

[1] Literally, "idol."

When, on account of asininity, a tethered ass becomes violent, 1495 both his (fore-)legs will be shackled in addition[1].

Then the ass will say, "One tether is enough for me"; (but) in sooth do not think (that such is the case), for those two are (result) from the action of that vile creature.

In exposition of the following Ḥadíth of Muṣṭafá (Mohammed), on whom be peace: "Verily, the most High God created the angels and set reason in them, and He created the beasts and set lust in them, and He created the sons of Adam and set in them reason and lust; and he whose reason prevails over his lust is higher than the angels, and he whose lust prevails over his reason is lower than the beasts."

It is related in the *Ḥadíth* that the majestical God created the creatures of the world (in) three kinds.

One class (He made) entirely reason and knowledge and munificence; that is the angel: he knoweth naught but prostration in worship.

In his original nature is no concupiscence and sensuality: he is absolute light, (he is) living through (his) love of God.

Another class is devoid of knowledge, like the animal (which 1500 lives) in fatness from (eating) fodder.

It sees nothing but stable and fodder: it is heedless of (future) misery and glory (felicity).

The third (class) is Adam's descendant and Man: half of him is of the angel and half of him is ass.

The ass-half, indeed, inclines to that which is low; the other half inclines to that which is rational.

Those two classes (the angels and the beasts) are at rest from war and combat, while this Man is (engaged) in torment (painful struggle) with two adversaries.

And, moreover, this (race of) Man, through probation, has 1505 been divided: they (all) are of human shape, but (in truth) they have become three communities (families).

One party have become submerged absolutely and, like Jesus, have attained unto the (nature of the) angel.

The form (of such a one is that of) Adam, but the reality is Gabriel: he has been delivered from anger and sensual passion and (vain) disputation.

He has been delivered from discipline and asceticism and self-mortification: you would say he was not even born of a child of Adam.

The second sort have attained unto (the nature of) asses: they have become pure anger and absolute lust.

The qualities of Gabriel were in them and departed: that 1510 house was (too) narrow, and those qualities (too) grand.

---

[1] Literally, "(a load) on the top."

The person who is deprived of (the vital) spirit becomes dead: when his spirit is deprived of those (angelic qualities), he becomes an ass,

Because the spirit that hath not those (qualities) is vile: this word is true, and the (perfect) Ṣúfí has said (it).

He (the man of animal nature) suffers more anxiety than the beasts, (for) he practises subtle arts in the world.

The cunning and imposture which he knows how to spin— that (cunning) is not produced by any other animal.

1515 To weave gold-embroidered robes, to win pearls from the bottom of the sea,

The fine artifices of geometry or astronomy, and the science of medicine and philosophy—

Which are connected only with this world and have no way (of mounting) up to the Seventh Heaven—

All this is the science of building the (worldly) stable which is the pillar (basis) of the existence of (persons like) the ox and the camel.

For the sake of preserving the animal for a few days, these crazy fools have given to those (arts and sciences) the name of "mysteries."

1520 The knowledge of the Way to God and the knowledge of His dwelling-place—*that* only the owner of the heart knows, or (you may say) his heart (itself).

He (God), then, created in this composite fashion the goodly animal and made him familiar with knowledge.

That (bestial) class (of men) He named "*like the cattle*," for where is the resemblance between waking and sleep?

The animal spirit hath naught but sleep (ignorance): the (bestial) class of men possess inverted sense-perceptions.

(When) waking comes, the animal sleep is no more, and he (the enlightened man) reads the (former) inversion of his senses from the tablet (of his clairvoyant consciousness)—

1525 Like the sense-perceptions of one whom sleep has seized: when he awakes, the inverted quality (of his sense-perceptions whilst he was dreaming) becomes apparent.

Necessarily, he (the bestial man) is the lowest of the low. Take leave of him: *I love not them that sink.*

In exposition of the following Verse: "and as for those in whose hearts is a disease, it (each new Súra of the *Qur'án*) added unto their uncleanness (wicked unbelief)"; *and of His Word:* "thereby He letteth many be led astray, and thereby He letteth many be guided aright."

(The bestial man is the lowest of the low) because he possessed the capacity for transforming himself and striving (to escape) from lowness, but (afterwards) lost it.

Again, since the animal does not possess (that) capacity, its excusability (for remaining) in the bestial state is a thing (most) evident.

When the capacity, which is the guide (to salvation), is gone from him, every nutriment that he eats is the brain of an ass.

If he eats anacardium, it becomes (acts upon him as) opium: 1530 his apoplexy and dementia are increased.

There remains another sort (of men: they are engaged) in warfare: (they are) half animal, half (spiritually) alive and endowed with good guidance.

Day and night in strife and mutual struggle, his (such a one's) last (state) battles with his first.

The battle of the reason against the flesh is like the contention of Majnún with his she-camel: Majnún's inclination is towards the noble woman (Laylá), while the she-camel's inclination is (to go) back towards her foal, as Majnún said (in verse): "My she-camel's love is behind me, while my love is in front of me; and verily I and she are discordant."

Assuredly they (the reason and the flesh) are like Majnún and his she-camel: that one is pulling forward and this one backward in (mutual) enmity.

Majnún's desire is speeding to the presence of that (beloved) Laylá; the she-camel's desire is running back after her foal.

If Majnún forgot himself for one moment, the she-camel 1535 would turn and go back.

Since his body was full of love and passion, he had no resource but to become beside himself.

That which is regardful was (ever) reason: passion for Laylá carried (his) reason away.

But the she-camel was very regardful and alert: whenever she saw her toggle slack

She would at once perceive that he had become heedless and dazed, and would turn her face back to the foal without delay.

When he came to himself again, he would see on the spot[1] 1540 that she had gone back many leagues.

In these conditions Majnún remained going to and fro for years on a three days' journey.

He said, "O camel, since we both are lovers, therefore we two contraries are unsuitable fellow-travellers.

Thy affection and toggle (propensity) are not in accord with me: it behoves (me) to choose parting from thy companionship[2]."

---

[1] I take زجا to be equivalent to مَكَانَهُ; it might also mean "from (recognising) the place."

[2] Literally, "to adopt companionship apart from thee."

These two fellow-travellers (the reason and the flesh) are brigands waylaying each other: lost is the spirit that does not dismount from the body.

1545 The spirit, because of separation from the highest Heaven, is in a (great) want; the body, on account of passion for the thorn-shrub (of sensual pleasure), is like a she-camel.

The spirit unfolds its wings (to fly) upwards; the body has stuck its claws in the earth.

"So long as thou art with me, O thou who art mortally enamoured of thy home[1], then my spirit will remain far from Laylá.

From experiences of this kind my life-time, for many years, has gone (to waste), like (that of) the people of Moses in the desert[2].

This journey to union was (only) a matter of two steps: because of thy noose I have remained sixty years on the way.

1550 The way is near (not far), but I have tarried very late: I have become sick of this riding, sick, sick."

He (Majnún) threw himself headlong from the camel. He said, "I am consumed with grief: how long, how long?"

The wide desert became (too) narrow for him: he flung himself on the stony place.

He flung himself down so violently that the body of that courageous man was cracked.

When he flung himself to the ground thus, at that moment also by (Divine) destiny his leg broke.

1555 He tied up his leg and said, "I will become a ball, I will go rolling along in the curve of His bat."

For this cause the sweet-mouthed Sage[3] utters a curse on the rider who does not dismount from the body.

How should love for the Lord be inferior to love for Laylá? To become a ball for His sake is more worthy.

Become a ball, turn on the side which is sincerity, (and go) rolling, rolling in the curve of the bat of Love,

For henceforth this journey is (accomplished by means of) the pull of God, while that (former) journey on the she-camel is our progression (made by our own efforts).

1560 Such is the extraordinary[4] mode of progression which transcends the utmost exertion of the Jinn and mankind.

Such is the pull—not every common pull—to which Aḥmad (Mohammed) awarded the pre-eminence. And (now) farewell!

---

[1] Literally, "dead for thy home."
[2] Literally, "like the desert and the people of Moses."
[3] The poet Saná'í of Ghazna.
[4] Literally, "excepted from the genus."

How the slave wrote to the King a statement complaining
of the reduction of his allowance.

Cut short the discourse (on these topics) for the sake of (re-turning to the story of) the slave who has written a message to the King[1].

He is sending to the gracious King a statement filled with wrangling and self-conceit and hatred.

The body is (like) a letter: look into it (and see) whether it is worthy of the King; then take it (to Him).

Go into a corner, open the letter, read (it), see whether its 1565 words are suitable to kings.

If it be not suitable, tear it in pieces and write another letter and remedy (the fault).

But do not think it is easy to open the letter which is the body; otherwise every one would plainly see the secret of the heart.

How hard and difficult is it to open the letter! 'Tis a task for men, not for children playing at knuckle-bones[2].

We have all become satisfied with (reading) the table of contents, because we are steeped in cupidity and vain desire.

The table of contents is a snare for the vulgar, that they may 1570 think the text of the scroll is like that (table).

Open the title-page, do not turn your neck aside from these words—and God best knoweth the right course.

That title is like a declaration made by the tongue: examine the text of the scroll, namely, the bosom (your inward self),

(And see) whether it is in agreement with your declaration, in order that your actions may not be hypocritical.

When you are carrying a very heavy sack, you must not fail to look into it[3],

(To see) what of sour and sweet you have in the sack. If it is 1575 worth bringing along, bring it;

Otherwise, empty your sack of the stones (in it), and redeem yourself from this fruitless toil and disgrace.

Put in the sack that (only) which must be brought to righteous sultans and kings.

Story of the divine with a big turban and the man who carried it
off, and how he (the divine) shouted, " Undo it and see what you
are taking: then take it (if you wish)!"

A certain divine had collected some old rags and wound them in his turban,

In order that it might become big and look grand when he came into the assembly in the *Ḥatīm*[4].

---

[1] See *v.* 1490 *supra*.   [2] Literally, "children of the knuckle-bone."
[3] Literally, "no less is necessary than that you should look into it."
[4] See p. 323, n. 1 *supra*.

1580   He had clipped the rags from (various) garments and out-
wardly embellished the turban with them.

The exterior of the turban was like a robe of Paradise, (but)
it was shameful and ugly within, like the hypocrite.

Shreds of *dalq* (dervish-cloak) and cotton and fur were buried
inside that turban.

He had set his face towards the college at dawn[1], that by
means of this false dignity he might gain (material) blessings.

A clothes-robber stood waiting on the dark road to practise
his craft.

1585   He snatched the turban from his head, and then started to
run in order that he might settle the business.

Thereupon the divine shouted at him, saying, "O son, undo
the turban (first), then take it (away with you).

Even as you are flying with four wings (very rapidly), (with
the same speed) undo the gift which you are taking away.

Undo it and rub (feel) with your hand, then take it if you like:
I sanction (that)."

When he who was fleeing undid it, a hundred thousand rags
dropped on the road.

1590   Of that big improper[2] turban of his there remained in his (the
robber's) hand (only) an ell of old cloth.

He dashed the rag on the ground, saying, "O worthless man,
by this fraud you have put me out of business (deprived me of
profit)."

*The World's mute admonition to worldlings, and how it displays
its faithlessness to those who have hope of its keeping faith (with
them).*

He (the divine) said, "I defrauded (you), but (at the same
time) I declared to you the (truth of the) matter by way of
admonition."

Likewise the World, though it blossomed delightfully (made
a fair show), at the same time uttered a (warning) cry and de-
clared its faithlessness.

In this (realm of) existence and corruption, O master,
existence is the fraud and that corruption is the admonition.

1595   Existence says, "Come, I am delectable," and its corruption
says, "Go, I am nothing."

O thou that bitest thy lip (in admiration) at the beauty of
spring, look on the coldness and paleness of autumn.

In the daytime thou didst deem the countenance of the sun
beauteous: remember its death in the moment of setting.

---

[1] Literally, "(at the time of) the morning-drink."
[2] *I.e.* sham, specious.

Thou sawest the full-moon on this lovely firmament[1]: observe also its anguish (caused by the loss of visibility) during the interlunar period.

A boy, on account of his beauty, became the lord of the people: after the morrow he became doting and exposed to the scorn of the people.

If the body of those in the fresh bloom of youth[2] has made 1600 thee a prey, after (it has come to) old age behold a body (bleached) like a cotton plantation.

O thou who hast seen rich viands, arise and see the residue thereof in the latrine.

Say to the filth, "Where is that beauty of thine—the savour and goodliness and (sweet) scent (which thou hadst) in the dish?"

It replies, "That (beauty) was the bait: I was its trap: since thou hast fallen a prey (to it), the bait has become hidden."

Many fingers that in handicraft (skill and dexterity) were the envy of master-craftsmen have at last become trembling.

The soul-like intoxicating narcissus-eye (of the beloved)—see 1605 it dimmed at last and water trickling from it.

The lion (hero) who advances into the ranks of lions (valiant foes)—at last he is conquered by a mouse.

The acute, far-seeing, artful genius—behold it at last imbecile as an old ass.

The curly lock that sheds (a fragrance of) musk and takes away the reason—at last it is like the ugly white tail of a donkey.

Observe its (the World's) existence, (how) at first (it is) pleasing and joyous; and observe its shamefulness and corruption in the end;

For it showed the snare plainly: it plucked out the fool's 1610 moustache in thy presence.

Do not say, then, "The World deceived me by its imposture; otherwise, my reason would have fled from its snare."

Come now, see (how) the golden collar and shoulder-belt have become a shackle and gyve and chain.

Reckon every particle of the World (to be) like this: bring its beginning and its end into consideration.

The more any one regards the end (*ákhir*) the more blessed he is; the more any one regards the stable (*ákhur̤*) the more banned he is.

Regard every one's face as the glorious moon: when the be- 1615 ginning has been seen, see the end (also),

Lest thou become a man blind of one eye, like Iblís: he, like a-person docked (deprived of perfect sight), sees (the one) half and not (the other) half.

---

[1] Literally, "the quadrangular tent (of the sky)."
[2] Literally, "silver-bodied ones."

He saw the clay (*tín*) of Adam but did not see his obedience to God (*dín*): he saw in him this world but did not see that (spirit) which beholds yonder world.

The superiority of men to women, O valorous one, is not on account of strength and money-making and (the possession of) landed estates;

Otherwise the lion and elephant because of (their) strength would be superior to the human being, O blind one[1].

1620   The superiority of men to women, O time-server, is because man is more regardful of the end.

The man who is crooked[2] in respect of seeing the end, he, like a woman, is inferior to those acquainted with the end[3].

From the World are coming two cries in opposition (to each other): (bethink thyself) for which (of them) thou art adapted.

Its one cry is the (means of) quickening the devout with (spiritual) life; and its other cry is the (means of) cajoling the graceless.

(The World says), "I am the thorn-blossom, O sweet cherisher (of love for me): the flower will drop and I shall remain a (mere) thorn-bough."

1625   The cry of its (the World's) blossom is, "Here is the flower-seller![4]" The cry of its thorn is, "Do not strive (to advance) towards me."

(If) thou hast accepted (responded to) this (alluring cry), thou art left (unmoved) by the other, for a lover is deaf to the contrary of the object loved (by him).

The one cry is this, "Here am I, ready"; the other cry is, "Look upon my latter end.

My readiness is like guile and ambush: behold the image of the end in the mirror of the beginning."

When thou hast gone into one of these two sacks, thou hast become contrary and unsuitable to the other.

1630   Oh, happy is he who, from the first, heard that which the intelligences and the (spiritual) ears of (holy) men have heard.

(If) it (the World) has found the house (the heart) empty and taken abode (there), all else appears to him (the owner of the house) perverted or wonderful (extraordinary).

(So with) the new pot that has drawn to itself some urine: water cannot detach that filth (from it).

Everything in the world draws something (to itself): infidelity (draws) the infidel and righteousness him who is guided aright.

---

[1] One of the commentators takes '*amí* as equivalent to '*ammí*, *i.e.* "my uncle."

[2] *I.e.* bent double and groping, so that he cannot see in front of him.

[3] Literally, "to the people of the end."

[4] *I.e.* "come and buy."

There is both the amber and the magnet (lodestone): whether thou art iron or straw thou wilt come to the hook (thou wilt be attracted).

The magnet carries thee off if thou art iron; and if thou art 1635 straw, thou wilt be in contact with the amber.

When any one is not associated with the good, he inevitably becomes a neighbour to[1] the wicked.

Moses is very despicable in the eyes of the Egyptian; Hámán is exceedingly accursed in the eyes of the Israelite.

The spirit of Hámán has drawn the Egyptian (to itself); the spirit of Moses has sought the Israelite.

The belly of the ass draws straw (to itself) at the (moment of) indrawing (deglutition); the belly of Adam (Man) is an attractor of wheat-broth.

If, on account of the darkness (of ignorance), thou dost not 1640 recognise a person (so as to discern his real nature), look at him whom he has made his *imám* (leader);

Explaining that the gnostic hath a nutriment (consisting) of the Light of God, for (the Prophet said), "I pass the night with my Lord: He giveth me meat and drink"; and "Hunger is God's food whereby He revives the bodies of the şiddíqs[2]," that is, "in hunger God's food reaches (them)."

For every foal goes after its dam, so that thereby (the fact of) its being a congener becomes apparent.

The human creature's milk comes from the breast (the upper half); the milk of the ass comes from the under-half.

'Tis the Justice of the Dispenser, 'tis an act of (just) dispensation: the wonder is this, that (in the Divine dispensation) there is neither compulsion nor injustice.

Were there compulsion, how would there be repentance? Were there injustice, how would there be protection?

The day is ended: the lesson will be to-morrow: how should 1645 the day (of this life) contain our mystery?

O thou who hast put firm confidence[3] in the breath (vain words) and flattery of a scoundrel,

Thou hast raised up a tent of bubbles: in the end (thou wilt find that) that tent has exceedingly weak ropes.

Hypocrisy is like lightning, and in its gleam the travellers cannot see the way.

This world and its people are good-for-nothing: both are unanimous in respect of (their) faithlessness.

---

[1] Literally, "beside."
[2] The *şiddíq* is one who is most veracious in bearing personal witness to God.
[3] Literally, "the confidence of one who has firm trust."

1650 The son of the world (the worldling) is faithless like the world: though he turn the face towards thee, that face is (really) the nape (back).

The people of that (other) world, like that world, on account of (their) probity continue for ever in (observance of their) covenant and promise.

When, in sooth, did two prophets oppose each other? When did they wrest (their) evidential miracles (spiritual powers and privileges) from one another?

How should the fruit of that world become stale? Intellectual joy does not turn into sorrows.

The fleshly soul is unplighted (bound by no covenant); for that reason it ought to be killed: it is base, and base is the spot to which its desires are directed.

1655 This assembly (the world) is well-adapted for fleshly souls: the grave and shroud are suitable to the dead.

Although the fleshly soul is sagacious and acute, its *qibla* (objective) is this world, (therefore) regard it as dead.

(But when) the water of God's inspiration has reached this dead (soul), the living (soul) comes into view (rises) from the tomb of a corpse.

Until inspiration comes, do not thou (meanwhile) be duped by that rouge (vanity) of "May his life be long!"

Seek the applause and renown that does not die away, the splendour of the sun that does not sink.

1660 Those abstruse sciences and disputations are (like) the people of Pharaoh: Death is like the water of the Nile.

Although their brilliance and pomp and show and enchantment drag the people along by the scruff of the neck,

Know that all (that) is (like) the enchantments of the magicians; know that Death is (like) the rod (of Moses) which became a dragon.

It made one mouthful of all (their) sorceries. There was a world filled with night: the dawn devoured it.

The light is not made greater and more by that (act of) devouring; nay, it is just the same as it has (always) been before.

1665 It is increased in respect of the effect (which it has produced), but not in respect of its essence: the essence hath (suffers) no increase or diminution.

God was not increased by (His) bringing the world into existence: that which He was not formerly He has not become now;

But the effect (phenomenal being) was increased by (His) bringing created things into existence: there is (a great) difference between these two increases.

The increase of the effect is His manifestation, in order that His attributes and action may be made visible.

The increase of any (so-called) essence is a proof that it (the essence) is originated and subject to causes.

> *Commentary on* "Moses conceived a fear in his heart: We
> said, 'Fear not, verily thou wilt be the superior.'"

Moses said, "Magic too is a bewildering thing: how shall 1670 I act?—for this people have no discernment."

God said, "I will produce discernment, I will make the undiscerning mind able to perceive (the truth).

Howbeit they (the magicians) have raised up foam, like the sea, thou, O Moses, wilt prevail: fear not!"

Magic was glorious in its own time: when the rod became a dragon, those (magic arts) were disgraced.

Every one pretends to excellence and elegance[1]: the stone of Death is the touchstone for (these) elegances.

Magic is gone and the miracle of Moses is past: as regards 1675 both, the bowl has fallen from the roof of (their) being[2].

What has the noise of the bowl of magic left behind but execration? What has the noise of the bowl of religion left behind but sublimity?

Since the touchstone has become hidden from man and woman, O adulterated coin, come now into line (with the genuine coin) and brag!

'Tis the time for thee to brag. Since the touchstone is absent, they will pass thee in honour[3] from hand to hand.

The adulterated coin is ever saying to me arrogantly, "O pure gold, how am I inferior to thee?"

The gold says, "Yes, O fellow-servant; but the touchstone is 1680 coming: be prepared."

The death of the body is a (welcome) gift to the adepts of the mystery: what damage is (done by) the scissors to pure gold?

If the adulterated coin had seen the end in regard to itself, it would have become at first the black (thing) which it became in the end.

Since (in that case) it would have become black at first, in confrontation (with the genuine coin) it would have been far from duplicity and damnation.

It would have sought the elixir of (Divine) grace; its reason would have prevailed over its hypocrisy.

Since it would have become broken-hearted on account of its 1685 (evil) state, it would have seen before it Him who mends them that are broken.

(When) it saw the end and became broken (contrite), it was at once bandaged by the Bone-setter.

---

[1] Literally, "salt."
[2] *I.e.* their true nature is revealed and everywhere proclaimed.
[3] Literally, "because of thy (apparent) honourableness."

The (Divine) grace impelled the pieces of copper towards the elixir; the gilt (coin) remained deprived of (Divine) bounty.

O gilt one, do not make pretensions: recognise that thy purchaser will not (always) remain so blind.

The light of the place of congregation (at the Last Judgement) will cause their (the purchasers') eyes to see and will expose thy blindfolding (of them).

1690 Look at those who have seen the end: they are the amazement of souls and the envy of the eye.

Look at those who have seen (only) the present: their inmost self is corrupt; they are radically decapitated (cut off from the Truth).

To the seer of the present, who is in ignorance and doubt, both the true dawn and the false dawn are one (and the same).

The false dawn has given a hundred thousand caravans to the wind of destruction, O youth.

There is no genuine money that has not a deceptive counterfeit[1]: alas for the soul that does not possess the touchstone and scissors!

Warning the pretender to shun pretension and enjoining him to follow (the true guide).

1695 Bú Musaylim[2] said, "I myself am Aḥmad (Mohammed)[3]: I have cunningly confounded the religion of Aḥmad."

Say to Bú Musaylim, "Do not behave with insolence: be not deluded by the beginning, regard the end.

Do not act thus as a guide from (with the motive of) greed for amassing (wealth and power): follow behind, in order that the Candle (the true guide) may go in front (of thee)."

The Candle, like the moon, shows (clearly) the (traveller's) destination, and whether in this direction there is the grain (of spiritual welfare) or the place for the snare (of perdition).

Whether thou wilt or not, (so long as thou art) with the Lantern the form of falcon and the form of crow become visible (to thee).

1700 Otherwise, (beware, for) these crows have lit (the lantern of) fraud: they have learned the cry of the white falcons.

If a man learn the cry of the hoopoe, (yet) where is the mystery of the hoopoe and the message from Sabá?

Know (distinguish) the natural cry from the artificial one, (know) the crown of kings from the crown (crest) of hoopoes.

These shameless persons have attached to their tongues the speech of dervishes and the deep sayings of gnostics.

---

[1] Literally, "one which injects error."
[2] Musaylima, the false prophet.
[3] *I.e.* the true prophet.

Every destruction of an olden people that there was—(it was) because they deemed sandal-wood to be (common) wood.

They had the discernment that should make that (difference) 1705 evident, but greed and cupidity make (men) blind and deaf.

The blindness of the (physically) blind is not far from (the Divine) mercy; 'tis the blindness of greed that is inexcusable.

Crucifixion (tribulation) inflicted by the King (God) is not far from mercy; the crucifixion (torment) of envy is not forgiven (by God).

O fish, regard the end; do not regard the hook: evil appetite has bandaged (blindfolded) thine eye that sees the end.

See the beginning and the end with both eyes: beware, do not be one-eyed like the accursed Iblís.

The one-eyed man is he who saw only the present—ignorant, 1710 like the beasts, of (what comes) after.

Since the two eyes of an ox are (rated) as one eye (of a man) in (the case of) damages for (their) destruction—for it (the ox) hath no excellence—

Its two eyes are worth (only) a half of its value, inasmuch as thine eye is the support for its two eyes.

But if thou destroy one eye of a son of Adam, by a statute (of the Law) thou must pay half of his value,

Because the human eye works alone by itself without (assistance from) the two eyes of a friend.

Since (the power of) the donkey's eye (to see) the beginning is 1715 not accompanied by (power to see) the end, it (the donkey) is in the same case as the one-eyed man, (even) if it has two eyes.

This topic hath no limit—and that light-minded (foolish) one is writing a letter in hope of loaves.

The rest of the story of the slave's writing a petition for his allowance.

Before (writing) the letter he went to the kitchen-steward and said, "O niggard of the kitchen of the generous king,

'Tis far from him and from his magnanimity that this (small) amount (matter) of my allowance should come into his consideration."

He (the steward) said, "He has ordered (so) for a good object, not on account of stinginess or close-fistedness."

"By God," he replied, "this is a canard[1]: even old gold is 1720 as dust in the king's eyes."

The steward raised up manifold arguments[2]: he rejected them all because of the greed which he had (in him).

---

[1] Literally, "a saying of the lobby," *i.e.* a trumped-up affair, for which the king is not responsible.
[2] Literally, "ten kinds of argument."

When, at the time of the forenoon meal, his (usual) allowance was reduced, he uttered much revilement, (but) it was of no avail.

He said, "Ye are doing these things on purpose." "Nay," said the other, "we obey[1] the (royal) command.

Do not regard this (as proceeding) from the branch (subordinate): regard it (as proceeding) from the root (principal); do not strike at the bow, for the arrow is (really) from the arm.

1725 (The words) *thou didst not throw when thou threwest* are a trial (of men's understandings): do not lay the fault on the Prophet, for that (throwing) is (an act which proceeded) from God.

The water is turbid from the source: O thou who art angry in vain, look farther on, open thine eye once!"

(Moved) by anger and resentment he went into a certain place and wrote an angry letter to the king.

In that letter he lauded the king and threaded the pearl of (descanted eloquently on) the king's munificence and generosity,

Saying, "O thou whose hand exceeds the sea and the clouds in (liberally) fulfilling the want of the suitor,

1730 Because that which the cloud gives, it gives with tears, (while) thy hand incessantly lays the dish (of bounty) with smiles."

Though the outward form of the letter was praise, from (amidst) the praise the scent of anger was showing traces (betraying itself).

All your actions are devoid of light and ugly because you are far, far from the light of your original nature.

The splendour of the actions of the vile becomes unsaleable (fades away), just as fresh fruit soon becomes rotten.

The splendour of the present life soon produces unsaleableness (becomes of no account), inasmuch as it belongs to the world of generation and corruption.

1735 Breasts are not gladdened by an encomium when there are feelings of enmity in the encomiast.

O heart, become purged of enmity and repugnance, and then chant "Glory to God" and be busy (in serving Him).

(To have) "Glory to God" on your tongue and repugnance within is hypocrisy or guile on the tongue's part;

And moreover[2] God hath said, "I do not look to the exterior, I am regarding the interior."

Story of the encomiast who from regard for reputation was thanking the object of his praise, while the scent (signs) of his inward grief and pain and the shabbiness of his outward garb showed that those expressions of gratitude were vain and false.

A certain man came (home) from 'Iráq, (clad) in a tattered cloak: his friends inquired concerning (his) separation (from them).

---

[1] Literally, "we are the slaves of."   [2] Literally, "then."

"Yes," he replied; "there was (the sorrow of) separation, but 1740 the journey was very blessed and fortunate[1] for me,
For the Caliph gave me ten robes of honour—may a hundred praises and laudations (ever) accompany him!"
He was reciting expressions of gratitude and praise till he carried gratitude beyond bound and limit.
Then they said to him, "Thy wretched guise bears witness to thy mendacity.
(Thou art) naked, bare-headed, consumed (with afflictions): thou hast stolen (these) expressions of gratitude or learned (them by rote).
Where are the signs of the gratitude and praise due to thy 1745 prince on thy unplenished head and feet?
If thy tongue is weaving (making up) praise of that king, (yet) thy seven members[2] are complaining (of him).
In the generosity of that king and sultan of munificence was there not (room for) a pair of shoes and trousers for thee?"
He replied, "I gave away what he bestowed: the prince left nothing undone in the way of[3] solicitude.
I received all the presents from the prince and distributed them among the orphans and the poor.
I gave the riches away and received long (everlasting) life in 1750 return, because I was utterly self-sacrificing."
Then they said to him, "Bless thee! the riches are gone: what (then) is this naphtha-smoke within thee?
A hundred loathings like thorns are in thy heart: how should grief be the sign of rejoicing?
Where are the signs of love and charity and being pleased (with God), if what thou hast said of what passed is true?
I grant, forsooth, that the riches are gone: (then) where is (thy) desire (for spiritual riches)? If the torrent has gone by, where is the torrent-bed?
If (as thou pretendest) thine eye was (once) black and soul- 1755 inspiring, and if it is soul-inspiring no longer, (then) why is it blue?
Where are the signs of self-sacrifice, O sour one? The smell of false and empty words is coming (from thee): be silent!"
Charity (for God's sake) hath a hundred signs within (in the heart): the good deed[4] hath a hundred tokens.
If riches be consumed in charity, a hundred lives come into the heart as a substitute.
A sowing of pure seeds in God's earth, and then no income! (That is impossible.)

---

[1] Literally, "bringing good news."
[2] *I.e.* thy body.
[3] Literally, "showed no deficiency of."
[4] Or, "the well-doer."

1760 If the (spiritual) ears of corn grow not from the gardens of *Hú* (God), then tell (me), how should *God's earth* be "spacious[1]"?

Since this earth of mortality is not without produce, how should *God's earth* be (without it)? That (earth of God) is a spacious place.

Verily, the produce of this earth (of God) is infinite: even the least (produce) for a single seed is seven-hundredfold.

You said, "Glory to God!" Where are the signs (in you) of *those who glorify*? Neither in your exterior nor within is there a trace.

(Only) the gnostic's glorification of God is right (perfect), for his feet and hands have borne witness to his glorification.

1765 It hath lifted him up from the dark pit of the body and redeemed him from the bottom of the dungeon of this world.

On his shoulder is the sign of glorification—the silken robe of piety and the light which associates itself (with him).

He is delivered from the transitory world, he is dwelling in the Rose-garden, and (*therein is*) *a running fountain*.

His sitting-place and home and abode is on the throne of the high-aspiring inmost consciousness, and his station

Is *the Seat of sincerity* in which all the *ṣiddíqs*[2] are flourishing and joyous and fresh of countenance.

1770 Their praise (of God), like the garden's praise on account of spring, hath a hundred signs and a hundred pomps.

Fountains and palms and herbs and rose-beds and plots of bright-coloured flowers[3] bear witness to its springtide.

Everywhere thousands of witnesses to the Beloved are (engaged) in bearing testimony, as the pearl (bears testimony) to the oyster-shell.

(But) from your breath (words) comes the smell of a bad conscience, and your (inward) pain is reflected from your head and face, O braggart!

In the battle-field (of this world) there are sagacious ones who know (distinguish) the smell: do not in (your) presumption idly utter (imitate) the ecstatic cries (of the true enthusiasts).

1775 Do not brag of musk, for that smell of onions is revealing the secret (true nature) of your breath (words and professions).

You are saying, "I have eaten rose-sugar," while the smell of garlic is striking (your hearers) and saying (in effect), "Don't talk nonsense."

---

[1] Cf. *Qur'án*, xxxix, 13.
[2] The prophets and saints who bear true witness to God.
[3] Literally, "picture-galleries."

The heart is like unto a great house: the house of the heart hath neighbours concealed (from view):

Through the window-slit and (crevices in) the walls they observe the hidden thoughts—

Through a slit whereof the owner of the house hath no conception and in which he hath no share.

Recite from the *Qur'án* (the verse which declares) that the 1780 Devil and his tribe secretly get scent of (become acquainted with) the (inward) state of humankind[1],

By a way of which humankind are ignorant, because it is not of this sensible (world) or one of these semblances (phenomenal objects).

Do not devise any fraud amongst the assayers: do not address any idle boast to the touchstone, O base spurious coin.

The (spiritual) touchstone hath a way to (know) the genuine and the spurious coin, for God made him the commander of (both) body and heart.

Since the devils, notwithstanding their grossnesses, are acquainted with our inmost soul and thought and belief,

(And) have a passage (means of penetrating) stealthily within, 1785 (so that) we are overthrown by their thievish practices,

(And since) they continually inflict a (great) derangement and damage (upon us), for they are masters of the (interior) tunnel and window-slit—

Why, then, should the illuminated spirits in the world be unaware of our hidden state?

Have the spirits that pitched their tent on Heaven become inferior to the devils in respect of permeation (the power of insinuating themselves into our hearts)?

The devil goes like a thief towards Heaven, and he is pierced with a burning meteor:

He falls down headlong from the sky as the wretched (infidel 1790 falls when smitten) in battle by the blow of the spear-point.

That is caused by the jealousy (indignation) of the delectable spirits (the prophets and saints): (hence) they (the angels) cast them (the devils) headlong from Heaven.

If you are palsied and lame and blind and deaf, (yet) do not hold this (bad) opinion of the great spirits.

Be ashamed and do not utter idle words, do not torment yourself (in vain), for there are many spies (observing you) beyond the (ken of the) body.

[1] *Qur'án*, VII, 26.

*How the divine physicians detect diseases, religious and spiritual,
in the countenance of friend or stranger and in the tones of his
speech and the colour of his eyes, and even without all these
(indications), by the way of the heart; for " verily, they are spies
on the hearts (of men); therefore behave with sincerity when ye
sit with them."*

These physicians of the body have knowledge (of medicine):
they are more acquainted with your malady than you are,

1795   So that they perceive the state (of your health) from the
urine-bottle, though you cannot know your ailment by that
means,

And from your pulse, complexion, and breath alike they
diagnose every kind of disease in you.

How, then, should the divine physicians in the world not
diagnose (disease) in you without word of mouth?

From your pulse and your eyes and your complexion alike they
immediately discern a hundred (spiritual) maladies in you.

In sooth, 'tis (only) these newly-taught physicians that have
need of these (external) signs.

1800   The perfect (the divine physicians) will hear your name from
afar and quickly penetrate[1] into the deepest ground of your being
and existence;

Nay, they will have seen you (many) years before your birth
—you together with all the circumstances (connected with you).

*How Abú Yazíd (Bisṭámí) announced the birth of Abu 'l-Ḥasan
Kharraqání—may God sanctify the spirit of them both—(many)
years before it took place, and gave a detailed description of his
outer and inner characteristics; and how the chronologers wrote
it down for the purpose of observation.*

Have you heard the story of Báyazíd—what he saw before-
hand of the (spiritual) state of Bu 'l-Ḥasan?

One day that sultan of piety was passing with his disciples (on
the way) towards the open country and the plain.

Suddenly there came to him, in the district of Rayy, a sweet
scent from the direction of Kháraqán.

1805   On the spot he uttered the lamentable cry of one who is
yearning, and sniffed the scent from the breeze.

He was inhaling the sweet scent lovingly: his soul was tasting
wine from the breeze.

When "sweat" appears on the outside of a pot that is full of
icy water,

It[2] has been turned into water by the coldness of the air: the
moisture has not escaped from the inside of the pot.

---

[1] Literally, "run."   [2] *I.e.* the air in contact with the pot.

The scent-bearing breeze became water for him; for him too
the water became pure wine.

When the marks of intoxication appeared in him, a disciple 1810
questioned him concerning that breath (Divine afflatus);

Then he asked him, "(What are) these sweet ecstasies which
are beyond the pale of the five (senses) and the six (directions)?

Thy face is becoming now red and now yellow and now
white: what is the (good) hap and the glad tidings?

Thou art inhaling scent, and no flowers are visible: doubtless
it is from the Unseen and from the garden of the Universal.

O thou who art the desire of every one who (wilfully) follows
his own desire (for God), thou to whom there is (coming) at
every moment a message and letter from the Unseen,

Thou to whose (spiritual) organ of smell there is coming at 1815
every moment, as to Jacob, balm from a Joseph,

Spill upon us one drop from that pitcher, give us one word
that smells of that garden.

We are not accustomed, O (thou who art the) beauty of
(spiritual) majesty, that thou shouldst drink alone while our
lips are dry.

O nimble, nimbly-rising traverser of Heaven, spill upon us
one draught of that which thou hast drunk.

There is no other Master of the Revels[1] in the world except
thee: O king, look (with favour) on the boon-companions!

How is it possible to quaff this wine underhand (in secret)? 1820
Certainly wine is the exposer of man.

He may disguise and conceal the scent, (but) how will he hide
his intoxicated eye?

In sooth this is not a scent that thousands of veils will keep
hidden in the world.

The desert and plain are filled with its pungency. What (of
the) plain? for it hath passed even beyond the nine spheres
(of Heaven).

Do not daub the head of the jar with mortar, for indeed this
naked one does not admit of covering.

Show kindness: O thou who knowest and canst tell the mystery, 1825
declare that which thy falcon (thy spirit) has made its prey."

He said, "A marvellous scent is come to me, even as (a scent
came) for the Prophet's sake from Yemen;

For Mohammed said, 'The scent of God is coming to me from
Yemen, (wafted) on the hand of the zephyr.'"

The scent of Rámín is coming from the soul of Wís[2]; the
scent of God, too, is coming from Uways[3].

---

[1] Literally, "president of the assembly (of wine-drinkers)."
[2] The love of Rámín for Wís, the wife of King Múbad of Merv, is the
subject of an early Persian romance.
[3] For Uways al-Qaraní see my translation of Hujwírí's *Kashf al-Mahjúb*,
pp. 83-84.

From Uways and from Qaran a wondrous scent made the Prophet drunken and full of rapture.

1830 Since Uways had passed away from himself, that earthly one (Uways) had become heavenly.

The myrobalan conserved in sugar—its bitter taste is not (retained) any more.

(Similarly) the (spiritual) myrobalan that is freed from egoism hath (only) the appearance of myrobalan, (but) not the flavour.

This topic hath no end. Return (to the story), that (we may see) what that holy man (Báyazíd) said, (moved) by inspiration from the World Unseen.

The words of the Prophet, may God bless and save him, " Verily, I feel the Breath of the Merciful (God) from the direction of Yemen."

He (Báyazíd) said, "The scent of a friend is coming from this quarter, for a (spiritual) monarch is coming into this village.

1835 After such and such a number of years a king will be born (here): he will pitch a tent above the heavens.

His face will be coloured with roses from the rosery of God: he will surpass me in station."

(The disciple asked), "What is his name?" He replied, "His name is Bu 'l-Ḥasan," and described his features—his eyebrows and chin;

He described his height and his complexion and his figure and spoke in detail of his locks of hair and his face.

He also declared his spiritual features—his qualities and the way (he should follow in his religion) and his (spiritual) rank and estate.

1840 The bodily features, like the body (itself), are borrowed (transient): set not your heart on them, for they are lasting (only) one hour.

The features of the natural (animal) spirit also are perishable: seek the features of that spirit which is above the sky.

Its body is on the earth, like a lamp, (but) its light is above the Seventh Roof (of heaven).

Those rays of the sun are in the house, (but) their orb is in the Fourth Dome (of heaven).

The form of the rose is (placed) beneath the nose for idle pleasure's sake, (but) the scent of the rose is on the roof and palace of the brain.

1845 A man asleep sees terror (dreams of something which terrifies him) at Aden[1]: the reflexion thereof appears as sweat on his body.

---

[1] *I.e.* in a place far distant from where he is.

The shirt (of Joseph) was in Egypt in the keeping of one exceedingly careful (of it)[1]: (the land of) Canaan was filled with the (sweet) scent of that shirt.

Thereupon[2] they wrote down the (predicted) date: they adorned the spit with the meat for roasting[3].

When the right time and date arrived, that (spiritual) king was born and played the dice of empire[4].

After those years (had passed), Bu 'l-Ḥasan appeared (in the world) after the death of Báyazíd.

All his dispositions, (whether in the way) of withholding 1850 tenaciously or bestowing liberally, proved to be such as that (spiritual) king (Báyazíd) had foretold.

His (Báyazíd's) guide is "the guarded tablet." From what is it guarded? It is guarded from error.

The inspiration of God is not (like) astrology or geomancy or dreams—and God best knoweth what is right.

The Ṣúfís in explaining (their doctrine) call it (the Divine inspiration) the inspiration of the heart, in order to disguise (its real nature) from the vulgar.

Take it to be the inspiration of the heart, for it (the heart) is the place where He is seen: how should there be error when the heart is aware of Him?

O true believer, thou hast become seeing by the light of God: 1855 thou hast become secure from error and inadvertence.

The reduction of the allowance of God's food for the soul and heart of the Ṣúfí.

How should a Ṣúfí be grieved on account of poverty? The very essence of poverty becomes his nurse and his food,

Because Paradise hath grown from things disliked, and Mercy is the portion of one who is helpless and broken.

He that haughtily breaks the heads (of people), the mercy of God and His creatures cometh not towards him.

This topic hath no end, and that youth (the slave) has been deprived of strength by the reduction of his bread-allowance.

Happy is the Ṣúfí whose daily bread is reduced: his bead be- 1860 comes a pearl, and he becomes the Sea.

Whosoever has become acquainted with that choice (spiritual) allowance, he has become worthy of approach (to the Presence) and of (Him who is) the Source of (every) allowance.

When there is a reduction of that spiritual allowance, his spirit trembles on account of its reduction;

---

[1] Judah, Joseph's brother, to whom Joseph had entrusted his shirt for conveyance to Jacob.
[2] *I.e.* on hearing the prediction.
[3] *I.e.* they prepared to verify the prediction.
[4] *I.e.* displayed his spiritual powers.

(For) then he knows that a fault has been committed (by him) which has ruffled the jasmine-bed of (Divine) approbation,

Just as (happened when) that person (the slave), on account of the deficiency of his crop, wrote a letter to the owner of the harvest.

1865 They brought his letter to the lord of justice: he read the letter and returned no answer.

He said, "He hath no care but for (the loss of) viands: silence, then, is the best answer to a fool.

He hath no care at all for separation (from me) or union (with me): he is confined to the branch (the derivative); he does not seek the root (the fundamental) at all.

He is a fool and (spiritually) dead in egoism, for because of his anxious care for the branch he hath no leisure for the root."

Deem the skies and the earth to be an apple that appeared from the tree of Divine Power.

1870 Thou art as a worm in the midst of the apple and art ignorant of the tree and the gardener.

The other worm[1] too is in the apple, but its spirit is outside, bearing the banner aloft.

Its (the worm's) movement splits the apple asunder: the apple cannot endure that shock.

Its movement has rent (all) veils: its form is (that of) a worm, but its reality is a dragon.

The fire that first darts from (the impact of) the steel puts forth its foot very feebly.

1875 Cotton is its nurse at first, but in the end it carries its flames up to the aether.

At first, man is in bondage to sleep and food; ultimately he is higher than the angels.

Under the protection of cotton and sulphur matches his flame and light rises above Suhá[2].

He illuminates the dark world: he tears the iron fetter (in pieces) with a needle.

Though the fire too is connected with the body, is it not derived from the spirit and the spiritual?

1880 The body hath no share in that glory: the body is as a drop of water in comparison with the sea of the spirit.

The days of the body are increased by the spirit: mark what becomes of the body when the spirit goes (from it).

The range of thy body is an ell or two, no more: thy spirit is a maker of swift flights to heaven.

In the spirit's imagination, O prince, 'tis (but) half a step to Baghdád and Samarcand.

The fat (white) of thine eye is two dirhems in weight: the light of its spirit (reaches) to the lofty region of the sky.

---

[1] *I.e.* the prophet or saint.   [2] Name of a star.

The light sees in dream without this eye: without this light 1885 what would the eye be but ruined?

The spirit is unconcerned with the beard and moustache of the body, but without the spirit the body is a carcase and vile.

Such is the magnificence of the animal spirit: advance farther, behold the human spirit.

Pass beyond Man and (logical) disputation unto the shore of the sea of the spirit of Gabriel.

After that, the spirit of Aḥmad (Mohammed) will bite thy lip (kiss thee lovingly), and Gabriel will creep back in fear of thee,

And will say, "If I come one bow's length towards thee, I 1890 shall be instantly consumed."

How the slave was indignant because no reply to his letter arrived from the king.

Truly this desert hath no head or foot (top or bottom). That youth, (being) without a reply to his letter, is aggrieved

And says, "Oh, 'tis a wonder. How did the king give me no reply? Or (perchance) the carrier of the letter behaved treacherously because of the torment (of envy),

And concealed the letter and did not show it to the king; for he was a hypocrite and (like) a piece of water beneath straw.

I will write another letter by way of test and seek another accomplished messenger."

That heedless man ignorantly puts the blame on the Amír and 1895 the steward and the letter-carrier.

Never does he go round about (inspect) himself and say, "I have acted perversely, like the idolater in (turning away from the true) religion."

How the wind blew perversely against Solomon, on whom be peace, because of his lapse.

The wind moved perversely against Solomon's throne. Then Solomon said, "O wind, do not creep (along) perversely."

The wind too said, "Do not move perversely (act wrongfully), O Solomon; and if thou move perversely, be not angry at my perverseness.

God set up these scales for the purpose that justice might be done to us in eternity.

(If) thou give short measure[1], I will give short measure; so 1900 long as thou art honest with me, I am honest (with thee)."

Likewise, Solomon's tiara swerved to one side and made the bright day (dark) as night to him.

He said, "O tiara, do not become awry on my head: O sun, do not decline from my orient."

---

[1] Literally, "(If) thou make less of the scales."

He was putting the tiara straight with his hand, (but) the tiara always became awry for him again, O youth.

Eight times he straightened it, and (each time) it became awry. He said, "Why, what is the matter, O tiara? Do not sag crookedly."

1905 It replied, "If thou put me straight a hundred times, ('tis useless): I go awry since thou goest awry, O trusted one."

Then Solomon put straight his inward part: he made his heart cold to (caused it to renounce) the lust which it had.

Thereupon his tiara immediately became straight and such as he wished it to be.

Afterwards he was purposely making it awry, (but) the tiara always returned purposely (deliberately), seeking (its correct position on) the crown of his head.

Eight times did that prince make it awry, and (as many times) did it become straight on the crown of his head.

1910 The tiara began to speak, saying, "O king, (now) display pride (proud independence): since thou hast shaken thy wings free from the clay, take flight (soar aloft).

I have no permission to pass beyond this (point) and tear to pieces the veils of the mystery of this (matter).

Lay thy hand on my mouth: shut my mouth (so as to restrain me) from unacceptable speech."

Do not you, then, whatsoever grief befall you, resentfully accuse any one: turn upon yourself.

Do not think evil of another, O you who gratify the desire of your friend: do not do that which that slave was meditating—

1915 Now his quarrel (was) with the messenger and the steward, now his anger (was directed) against the generous emperor.

You are like Pharaoh, who had left Moses (alone) and was taking off the heads of the people's babes:

The enemy (Moses) was in the house of that blind-hearted man, (while) he (outside) was cutting the necks of the children.

You also are bad (malign) to others outside, while you have become complaisant to the grievous self (carnal soul) within.

It is your enemy indeed, (yet) you are giving it candy, while outside you are accusing every one.

1920 You are like Pharaoh, blind and blind-hearted: complaisant to your enemy and treating the guiltless with ignominy.

How long, O (imitator of) Pharaoh, will you slay the innocent and pamper your noxious body?

His understanding was superior to that of (other) kings: God's ordainment had made him without understanding and blind.

God's seal upon the eye and ear of the intelligence makes him (the intelligent man) an animal, (even) if he is a Plato.

God's ordainment comes into view on the tablet (of the heart) in such wise as Báyazíd's prediction of the hidden (future event).

How Shaykh Abu 'l-Ḥasan, may God be well-pleased with him,
heard Báyazíd's announcement of his coming into existence and
of what should happen to him.

It came to pass just as he (Báyazíd) had said. Bu 'l-Ḥasan 1925
heard from the people that (prediction),

(Namely), "Ḥasan will be my disciple and my true follower
(*umma*)[1], and will receive lessons from my tomb at every dawn."

He (Abu 'l-Ḥasan) said, "I have also seen him in a dream and
have heard this from the spirit of the Shaykh."

Every dawn he would set his face towards the grave and stand
(there) in attention till the forenoon,

And either the apparition of the Shaykh would come to him,
or without anything spoken his difficulty would be solved,

Till one day he came auspiciously (to visit the grave): the 1930
graves were covered with new-fallen snow.

He saw the snows, wreath on wreath like flags, mound (piled)
on mound; and his soul was grieved.

From the shrine of the (spiritually) living Shaykh came to
him a cry, "Hark, I call thee that thou mayst run to me.

Hey, come quickly in this direction, towards my voice: if the
world is (full of) snow, (yet) do not turn thy face away from me."

From that day his (spiritual) state became excellent, and he
saw (experienced) those wondrous things which at first he was
(only) hearing (knowing by hearsay).

How the slave wrote another letter to the king when he
received no reply to the first letter.

That evil-thinking one wrote another letter, full of vitupera- 1935
tion and clamour and loud complaint.

He said, "I wrote a letter to the king: oh, I wonder if it
arrived there and found its way (to him)."

The fair-cheeked (king) read that second one also, and as be-
fore he gave him no reply and kept silence.

The king was withholding all favour from him[2]: he (the slave)
repeated the letter five times.

"After all," said the chamberlain, "he is your (Majesty's)
slave: if you write a reply to him, 'tis fitting.

What diminution of your sovereignty will occur if you cast 1940
looks (of favour) on your slave and servant?"

He (the king) said, "This is easy; but he is a fool: a foolish
man is foul and rejected of God.

Though I pardon his sin and fault, his disease will infect me
also.

---

[1] *I.e.* his relation to me will be that of the *umma* (religious community) to
the prophet whom they follow.
[2] *Khushk áwurdan,* "to show silent aversion."

From (contact with) an itchy person a whole hundred become itchy, especially (in the case of) this loathsome reprobate itch.

May the itch, lack of intelligence, not befall (even) the infidel His (the fool's) ill-starredness keeps the cloud rainless.

1945 On account of his ill-starredness the cloud sheds no moisture: by his owlishness the city is made a desert.

Because of the itch of those foolish ones the Flood of Noah devastated a whole world (of people) in disgrace.

The Prophet said, 'Whosoever is foolish, he is our enemy and a ghoul who waylays (the traveller).

Whosoever is intelligent, he is (dear to us as) our soul: his breeze and wind is our sweet basil.'

(If) intelligence revile me, I am well-pleased, because it possesses something that has emanated from my emanative activity.

1950 Its revilement is not without use, its hospitality is not without a table;

(But) if the fool put sweetmeat on my lip, I am in a fever from (tasting) his sweetmeat."

If you are goodly and enlightened, know this for sure, (that) kissing the arse of an ass hath no (delicious) savour.

He (the unsavoury fool) uselessly makes your moustache fetid; your dress is blackened by his kettle without (there being) a table (of food).

Intelligence is the table, not bread and roast-meat: the light of intelligence, O son, is the nutriment for the soul.

1955 Man hath no food but the light: the soul does not obtain nourishment from aught but that.

Little by little cut (yourself) off from these (material) foods— for these are the nutriment of an ass, not that of a free (noble) man—

So that you may become capable of (absorbing) the original nutriment, and may eat habitually the dainty morsels of the light.

'Tis (from) the reflexion of that light that this bread has become bread; 'tis (from) the overflowing of that (rational) soul that this (animal) soul has become soul.

When you eat once of the light-food, you will pour earth over the (material) bread and oven.

1960 Intelligence consists of two intelligences; the former is the acquired one which you learn, like a boy at school,

From book and teacher and reflexion and (committing to) memory, and from concepts, and from excellent and virgin (hitherto unstudied) sciences.

(By this means) your intelligence becomes superior to (that of) others; but through preserving (retaining in your mind) that (knowledge) you are heavily burdened.

You, (occupied) in wandering and going about (in search of knowledge), are a preserving (recording) tablet; the preserved tablet is he that has passed beyond this.

The other intelligence is the gift of God: its fountain is in the midst of the soul.

When the water of (God-given) knowledge gushes from the 1965 breast, it does not become fetid or old or yellow (impure);

And if its way of issue (to outside) be stopped, what harm? for it gushes continually from the house (of the heart).

The acquired intelligence is like the conduits which run into a house from the streets:

(If) its (the house's) water-way is blocked, it is without any supply (of water). Seek the fountain from within yourself!

Story that some one was consulting another, who said,
"Consult some one else, for I am your enemy."

A certain person was consulting some one, that he might be delivered from perplexity and from a quandary.

"O man of good name," he replied, "seek another, not me, 1970 and explain to him the matter for consultation.

I am an enemy to you: do not attach yourself to me; one is never successful (never wins success) from the counsel of an enemy.

Go, seek one who is a friend to you: undoubtedly a friend seeks (what is) good for his friend.

I am an enemy: it is inevitable that from egoism I should go crookedly (play false) and show enmity towards you.

'Tis not a (just) condition to demand of a wolf (that he should perform) the task of a watchman (shepherd): to demand (anything) from the wrong place is a negation of the demand.

Without any doubt I am an enemy to you: how should I show 1975 you the way? I am a highwayman.

Whoever is sitting with friends is amidst a flower-garden (though he be) in a bath-furnace.

Whoever in the world sits with an enemy, he is in a bath-furnace (though he be) in a flower-garden.

Vex not your friend by egoism, lest your friend become your adversary and enemy.

Do good unto the people for your God's sake or for the peace of your own soul,

That you may always see (them) friendly in your sight, and 1980 that ugly ideas arising from hatred may not come into your heart.

Since you have behaved with enmity (towards me), abstain (from consulting me): consult a friend who arouses (your) affection."

He replied, "I know you, O Bu 'l-Hasan, to be one who has long deemed me an enemy;

But you are a reasonable and spiritual man: your reason will not allow you to go crookedly (play false)."

The (carnal) nature desires to take revenge on its adversary: the reason is an iron chain upon the flesh.

1985　It comes and prevents it (the flesh) and restrains it: the reason is like a police-inspector for it in its good and evil (actions).

The reason that is allied to Faith is like a just police-inspector: it is the guardian and magistrate of the city of the heart.

It is mentally alert like a cat: the thief remains in the hole, like a mouse.

Wherever the mouse gets the upper hand, no cat is there, or (at least) there is (only) the (unreal) form of a cat.

What cat (is to be compared with the reason)? The Faith-regarding reason which is in the body is the lion that overthrows the lions.

1990　Its roar is the magistrate (controller) of the tearing (carnivorous) animals; its shout is the preventer of the browsing (herbivorous) animals.

(If) the city is full of thieves and clothes-robbers, let there be a police-inspector if you will, or let there be none[1].

How the Prophet, on whom be peace, appointed a youth of Hudhayl to be commander of an expeditionary force in which there were elders and veteran warriors.

The Prophet was sending a force to fight against the unbelievers and repel insolence.

He chose a youth of Hudhayl and appointed him commander of the army and leader of the cavalry.

The foundation of an army is unquestionably the chief in command: a people without a chief are a body without a head.

1995　That you are (spiritually) dead and decrepit—all this is because you have abandoned the chief.

On account of laziness and avarice and egoism you are drawing your head back (behaving in a headstrong manner) and making yourself the head.

(You are) like the beast that flees from the burden: it takes its head (goes its own way) into the mountains.

Its master is running after it, crying, "O giddy-headed one, on every side there is a wolf in quest of an ass.

If thou disappear now from mine eye, the mighty wolf will approach thee from every direction.

2000　He will chew thy bones like sugar, so that thou wilt never see life again.

---

[1] *I.e.* his presence or absence makes no difference.

(Or) do not suppose that (immediate destruction); at any rate thou wilt be left without fodder: fire is (finally) extinguished by lack of faggots.

Beware! Do not flee from my control and from the heaviness of the burden, for I am thy (rational) soul."

You also are a beast (of burden), for your carnal soul predominates: the predominant (quality) determines (a thing's nature)[1], O worshipper of self.

The Almighty did not call you an ass, He called you a horse: the Arabs say to the Arab horse "*ta'ál*" ("come").

Muṣṭafá (Mohammed) was God's stable-overseer for the beasts, (which are) the iniquitous carnal soul.

Moved by[2] lovingkindness, He (God) said, "Say, '*ta'álaw* (come ye)[3], to the end that I may train you[4]: I am the trainer.'"

(The Prophet said), "Since I have trained the carnal souls, I have suffered many kicks from these beasts.

Wherever there is one fond of training, he hath no means of avoiding kicks.

Of necessity the most affliction falls on the prophets, for 'tis an affliction to give training to the raw (ignorant).

Ye are stumbling along: at my word (in obedience to my command) go at a jog-trot, that ye may become gentle and be suitable for the king to ride.

The Lord said, 'Say, Come ye, say, Come ye, O beasts that have shied away from discipline.

If they come not, O Prophet, be not grieved: be not full of hatred on account of those twain[5] without steadfastness.'"

The ears of some are deaf to these (cries of) *ta'álaw*: every beast hath a different stable.

Some are put to flight by this call: the stall of every horse is separate.

Some are chagrined by this story[6], for every bird hath a separate cage.

Even the angels too were not peers: for this reason they formed diverse ranks in Heaven.

Children, though they are at one (the same) school, surpass each other in (their) lessons.

Sense-perceptions are possessed by Easterner and Westerner, (but) the function of sight belongs to the ocular sense (alone).

Though a hundred thousand ears be arrayed in rank, they all are in need of the clear eye.

[1] Literally, "the judgement (respecting what a thing is) belongs to the predominant (quality of that thing)."

[2] Literally, "from the pull of."

[3] *Qur'án*, III, 57.

[4] *I.e.* God ordered the Prophet to bid the carnal souls come that he (the Prophet) might train them.

[5] The Jews and Christians. Cf. *Qur'án*, III, 57.

[6] Cf. *Qur'án*, III, 55.

2020　Again, the ranks of ears have a (special) function in respect of hearing the (words of the) Spirit and the Traditions (of the Prophet) and the Revelation.

A hundred thousand eyes do not possess that avenue (faculty): no eye is acquainted with hearing.

Similarly, enumerate each sense, one by one: each one is removed from (incapable of doing) the work of another.

The five external and the five internal senses are (arrayed) in ten ranks in the standing posture of *the* (angels) *ranked* (for worship of God).

Any one who (disobediently) draws back from the rank of (the true) religion will go into the rank that is behind.

2025　Do not make little of the (Divine) Word *ta'álaw* (*come ye*): this Word is an exceedingly great elixir.

If a copper (a base person) turn away in repugnance from your saying (this Word), by no means withhold the elixir from him.

If his magician-like soul has bound (cast a spell upon) him at the present time, (yet) your saying will profit him in his latter end.

O slave (of God), *say, Come ye, say, Come ye*: take heed, for verily *God inviteth unto the (Abode of) Peace*.

Then come back, sire, from egoism and headship: seek a leader, do not desire leadership.

How an objector objected to the Prophet's—on whom be peace— appointing the man of Hudhayl to be commander.

2030　When the Prophet appointed a leader from (the tribe of) Hudhayl for the army whose troops were Divinely aided,

An insolent fellow, through envy, could not endure (to keep silence): he raised objection and opposition[1].

Behold humankind, how dark (unenlightened) they are, and how they are perishing in (desire for) a perishable piece of goods.

On account of pride they all are in separation (from God), dead to the spirit, living in deception[2].

'Tis wonderful that the spirit is in prison, and then (all that time) the key of the prison is in its hand!

2035　That youth (the spirit) is plunged in dung from head to foot, (whilst) the flowing river is (almost) touching his skirt!

(He is) always moving restlessly from side to side beside the place of repose and the couch where he might recline[3]!

The (Divine) light is hidden, and search is the evidence (of its existence), for the heart (spirit) does not seek shelter in vain.

If this world's prison had no refuge, neither would there be any feeling of aversion nor would the heart seek release.

---

[1] Literally, "We do not assent."
[2] Literally, "jugglery" or "trickery."
[3] Literally, "the support for his back."

Thy aversion is dragging thee along, like a custodian, saying,
"O man astray, seek the path of righteousness."

The path is there, but it is hidden in a secret place: its dis- 2040
covery is in pawn to (involves) seeking in vain (before it can be
found).

Separation is secretly in quest of union: in this seeker do thou
discern the face of the sought.

The dead (trees and plants) of the orchard spring up from the
root, saying, "Perceive the Giver of life!"

How should the eyes of these prisoners (of the world) be
always (fixed) on (what lies) beyond, if there were no bringer of
the good news (of deliverance)?

How should there be a hundred thousand befouled ones
seeking water, if there were no water in the river?

(If) there is no rest for thy side upon the earth, (yet) know that 2045
there is a coverlet and mattress at home.

Without (there being) a resting-place there would not be the
restless (seeker); without (there being) that which takes away
the headache of intoxication, there would not be this headache.

He (the objector) said, "Nay, nay, O Messenger of God, do
not appoint any but an old Shaykh to be chief of the army.

O Messenger of God, (even) if the youth is lion-born (heroic),
may none but an old man be head of the army!

Thou too hast said, and thy word is (a true) witness, 'The
leader must be old, must be old.'

O Messenger of God, look on this army, (in which) there are 2050
so many elders and (persons) superior to him."

Do not regard the yellow leaves of this tree, (but) pick its ripe
apples.

How, in sooth, are its yellow leaves void (of worth)? This is
the sign of maturity and perfection.

The yellow leaf of the (elder's) beard and his white hair bring
tidings of joy on account of his mature intelligence.

The newly-arrived green-coloured leaves signify that this
fruit is unripe.

The provision of leaflessness (spiritual poverty) is the sign of 2055
being a gnostic; the yellowness of gold is the (cause of the)
money-changer's ruddiness of face (cheerful countenance).

If he that (still!) is rosy-cheeked has fresh down (on his face),
(yet) he has just begun to learn writing in the school of know-
ledge.

The letters of his handwriting are very crooked (misshapen):
he is a cripple in respect of intelligence, though his body moves
with agility.

Although an old man's feet are deprived of rapid movement,
his intelligence has gotten two wings and has sped to the
zenith.

If you wish for an example (of this), look at Jaʿfar[1]: God gave him wings instead of hands and feet.

2060   Cease from (speaking of) gold (pallor), for this topic is recondite: this heart of mine has become agitated like quicksilver.

From within me a hundred sweet-breathing silent ones put their hands on their lips, signifying, "It is enough."

Silence is the sea, and speech is like the river. The sea is seeking thee: do not seek the river.

Do not turn thy head away from the indications given by the sea: conclude (the subject)—and God best knoweth the right course.

That irreverent (objector) made no pause in[2] the words (which he poured forth) in this fashion from those cold (insipid) lips (of his) in the presence of the Prophet.

2065   Words were assisting (did not fail) him, (but) he was ignorant that hearsay (traditional knowledge) is mere babble in the presence of sight (immediate vision).

Indeed, these matters of hearsay are (only) a substitute for sight: they are not for him who is present, (but) for him who is absent.

Whoever has been caused to attain unto sight, before him these matters of hearsay are idle[3].

When you have sat down beside your beloved, after this banish the *dallálas* (the old women who act as go-betweens).

When any one has passed beyond childhood and has become a man, the letter and the *dallála* become irksome to him.

2070   He reads letters, (but only) for the purpose of teaching (others); he utters words, (but only) for the purpose of making (others) understand.

'Tis wrong to speak by hearsay in the presence of those who see (who are endowed with vision), for it is a proof of our heedlessness and deficiency.

In the presence of the seer silence is to your advantage: on this account came (from God) the allocution, *Be ye silent.*

If he (the seer) bid you speak, speak gladly, but say little and do not draw out (your words) to length;

And if he bid you draw them out to length, speak with the same modesty (as before) and comply with his command,

2075   Even as I (am complying) now, in this goodly enchantment (this enchanting poem), with[4] (the command of) Ẓiyáʾu ʾl-Ḥaqq (the Radiance of God) Ḥusámuʾddín.

---

[1] Jaʿfar ibn Abí Ṭálib, the cousin of the Prophet, fell in battle against the Greeks in A.D. 629. It is said that when the enemy cut off his hands and feet, God gave him wings in order that he might fly to Paradise; whence he is known as al-Ṭayyár (the Flier).

[2] Literally, "made continuous."

[3] Literally, "deprived of their function," "serving no useful end."

[4] Reading ڀ for ڀ (misprint).

When I am cutting short (my discourse) concerning (the Way of) righteousness, he draws me on to speak by a hundred kinds (of contrivance).

O Husámu'ddín, Radiance of the Almighty, inasmuch as thou art seeing, why dost thou seek speech (from me)?

Perchance this demand (on thy part) may arise from (thy) love for the Desired One, (as the poet said), "Give me wine to drink and tell me that it is (wine)[1]."

At this moment His cup is at thy mouth, (but thy) ear says, "Where is the ear's portion?"

(O ear), thy portion is the heat (of love): lo, thou art heated 2080 and intoxicated. It replied, "My greed is greater than this."

How Muṣṭafá, on whom be peace, answered the objector.

When that Arab carried disputation beyond bounds in the presence of sweet-tempered Muṣṭafá,

That king of *Wa 'l-Najm*[2] and that sultan of *'Abas*[3] bit his lip (in anger) and said to the silly prater, "Enough[4]!"

He was putting his hand on his (the objector's) mouth to prevent him, (as though to say), "How long wilt thou speak in the presence of one who knows the occult?"

Thou hast brought dry ordure to one endowed with vision, saying, "Buy this instead of a musk-bag."

O thou of stinking brain and stinking marrow, thou placest 2085 camel's dung beneath thy nose and sayest, "Oh, delicious!"

O squinting crazy fool, thou hast exclaimed in delight, "Oh, oh," that thy bad wares may find a ready sale,

And that thou mayst deceive that pure organ of (spiritual) smell, that which pastures in the celestial rose-garden.

Though his (the saint's) forbearance has feigned to be stupid, one must know one's self a little.

If to-night the mouth of the cooking-pot is left open, yet the cat must have discretion.

If that glorious one (the saint) has feigned to be asleep, he is 2090 (really) very much awake: do not carry off his turban.

How long, O contumacious man devoid of (spiritual) excellence, wilt thou utter these Devil's enchantments in the presence of God's elect one?

This company (of the elect) have a hundred thousand forbearances, every one of which is (immovable) as a hundred mountains.

---

[1] Part of an Arabic verse by Abú Nuwás.
[2] *Qur'án*, Súra LIII.   [3] *Qur'án*, Súra LXXX.
[4] Cf. Book I, *v.* 3527, where the translation should read: Muṣṭafá (Mohammed) bit his lip (in anger) at him (Zayd), as though to say, "Enough."

Their forbearance makes a fool of the wary and causes the keen-witted man with a hundred eyes to lose his way.

Their forbearance, like fine choice wine, mounts by nice degrees up to the brain.

2095 Behold the man drunken with that marvellous (earthly) wine: the drunken man has begun to move crookedly like the queen (in chess).

From (the effect of) that quickly-catching wine the (vigorous) youth is falling in the middle of the road, like an aged man.

Especially (consider the effect of) this (spiritual) wine which is from the jar of *Balá*[1]—not the wine whereof the intoxication lasts (only) one night;

(But) that (wine) from which, (by drinking it) at dessert and in migration (from place to place), the Men of the Cave (the Seven Sleepers) lost their reason for three hundred and nine years.

The women of Egypt drank one cup of that (wine) and cut their hands to pieces[2].

2100 The magicians (of Pharaoh) too had the intoxication of Moses: they deemed the gallows to be their beloved[3].

Ja'far-i Ṭayyár was drunken with that wine: therefore, being beside himself, he was pawning (sacrificing) his feet and hands (for God's sake)[4].

Story of Báyazíd's—may God sanctify his spirit—saying, "Glory to me! How grand is my estate!" and the objection raised by his disciples, and how he gave them an answer to this, not by the way of speech but by the way of vision (immediate experience).

That venerable dervish, Báyazíd, came to his disciples, saying, "Lo, I am God."

That master of the (mystic) sciences said plainly in drunken fashion, "Hark, there is no god but I, so worship me."

When that ecstasy had passed, they said to him at dawn, "Thou saidest such and such, and this is impiety."

2105 He said, "This time, if I make a scandal, come on at once and dash knives into me.

God transcends the body, and I am with the body: ye must kill me when I say a thing like this."

When that (spiritual) freeman gave the injunction, each disciple made ready a knife.

Again he (Báyazíd) became intoxicated by that potent flagon: those injunctions vanished from his mind.

The Dessert came: his reason became distraught. The Dawn came: his candle became helpless.

---

[1] *Balá*, "Yea," refers to the Primal Covenant on the Day of *Alast* (*Qur'án*, VII, 171).
[2] *Qur'án*, XII, 31.   [3] *Qur'án*, VII, 117–122.
[4] See note on *v.* 2059 *supra*.

Reason is like the prefect: when the sultan arrives, the help- 2110
less prefect creeps into a corner.

Reason is the shadow of God: God is the sun: what power
hath the shadow to resist His sun?

When a genie prevails over (gains possession of) a man, the
attributes of humanity disappear from the man.

Whatsoever he says, that genie will (really) have said it: the
one who belongs to this side will have spoken from (the control
of) the one who belongs to yonder side.

Since a genie hath this influence and rule, how (much more
powerful) indeed must be the Creator of that genie!

His (the possessed man's) "he" (personality) is gone: he has 2115
in sooth become the genie: the Turk, without (receiving) Divine
inspiration, has become a speaker of Arabic[1].

When he comes to himself, he does not know a word (of
Arabic). Inasmuch as a genie hath this essence and quality,

Then how, pray, should the Lord of genie and man have in-
feriority to the genie?

If a pot-valiant fellow has drunk the blood of a fierce lion, you
will say that the wine did it, not he;

And if he fashion words of old (pure) gold[2], you will say that
the wine has spoken those words.

A wine hath this (power to excite) disturbance and com- 2120
motion: hath not the Light of God that virtue and potency

To make you entirely empty of self, (so that) you should be
laid low and He should make the Word lofty (within you)?

Though the *Qur'án* is (dictated) from the lips of the Prophet
—if any one says God did not speak it, he is an infidel.

When the *humá* of selflessness took wing (and soared),
Báyazíd began (to repeat) those words.

The flood of bewilderment swept away his reason: he spoke
more strongly than he had spoken at first,

(Saying), "Within my mantle there is naught but God: how 2125
long wilt thou seek on the earth and in heaven?"

All the disciples became frenzied and dashed their knives at
his holy body.

Like the heretics of Girdakúh[3], every one was ruthlessly[4]
stabbing his spiritual Director.

Every one who plunged a dagger into the Shaykh was re-
versely making a gash in his own body.

There was no mark (of a wound) on the body of that possessor
of the (mystic) sciences, while those disciples were wounded and
drowned in blood.

---

[1] Cf. Book I, Preface, near the end of the fourth paragraph, and Jámí,
Nafaḥátu 'l-Uns (ed. Nassau Lees), No. 384.
[2] *I.e.* "if he speak with perfect eloquence."   [3] The Assassins.
[4] Literally, "without distress or fatigue."

2130   Whoever aimed a blow at his throat saw his own throat cut, and died miserably;

And whoever inflicted a blow on his breast, his (own) breast was riven, and he became dead for ever;

And he that was acquainted with that (spiritual) emperor of high fortune, (and) his heart (courage) did not consent to strike a heavy blow,

Half-knowledge tied his hand, (so that) he saved his life and only wounded himself.

Day broke, and the disciples were thinned: wails of lamentation arose from their house.

2135   Thousands of men and women came to him (Báyazíd), saying, "O thou in whose single shirt the two worlds are contained,

If this body of thine were a human body, it would have been destroyed, like a human body, by the daggers."

A self-existent one encountered a selfless one in combat: the self-existent one drove a thorn into his own eye (hurt himself).

O you who stab the selfless ones with the sword, you are stabbing your own body with it. Beware!

For the selfless one has passed away (in God) and is safe: he is dwelling in safety for ever.

2140   His form has passed away and he has become a mirror: naught is there but the form (image) of the face of another.

If you spit (at it), you spit at your own face; and if you strike at the mirror, you strike at yourself;

And if you see an ugly face (in that mirror), 'tis you; and if you see Jesus and Mary, 'tis you.

He is neither this nor that: he is simple (pure and free from attributes of self): he has placed your image before you.

When the discourse reached this point, it closed its lips; when the pen reached this point, it broke to pieces.

2145   Close thy lips (O my soul): though eloquence is at thy command, do not breathe a word—and God best knoweth the right way.

O you who are drunken with the wine (of love), you are on the edge of the roof: sit down or (else) descend, and peace be with you!

Every moment when you enjoy (union with the Beloved), deem that delightful moment to be the edge of the roof.

Be trembling for (fear of losing) the delightful moment: conceal it like a treasure, do not divulge it.

Lest calamity suddenly befall (your) plighted love, take heed, go very fearfully into that place of ambush.

2150   The spirit's fear of loss at the moment of enjoyment is (the sign of its) departure (descent) from the hidden roof-edge.

If you do not see the mysterious roof-edge, (yet) the spirit is seeing, for it is shuddering (with fear).

Every sudden chastisement that has come to pass has taken place on the edge of the turret of enjoyment.

Indeed there is no fall except (on) the edge of the roof: (take) warning from (the fate of) the people of Noah and the people of Lot.

*Explaining the cause of the eloquence and loquacity of that imper-
tinent man in the presence of the Prophet, on whom be peace.*

When the ray (reflexion) of the Prophet's boundless in-
toxication struck (the objector), that stupid fellow also became drunken and merry.

Of course, in consequence of (drunken) glee he became lo- 2155
quacious: the intoxicated man neglected (to observe) respect and began to rave.

Not on every occasion does selflessness (intoxication) work mischief, (but) wine makes the unmannerly person more so.

If he (the wine-drinker) be intelligent, he becomes decorous (displays goodly qualities when beside himself); and if he be evil-natured, he becomes worse.

But since the majority are evil and reprobate, wine has been forbidden to all.

*How the Prophet, on whom be peace, explained the cause of his
preferring and choosing the (young) man of Hudhayl as com-
mander and chief of the army over the heads of the elders and
veterans.*

Cases are decided by the general rule (not by the exceptions): since the majority are evil, the sword was taken away from the hand of the highwayman.

The Prophet said, "O thou who lookest on externals, do not 2160
regard him as a youth and unskilled.

Oh, there is many a black beard and the man (its owner) old (in wisdom); oh, there is many a white beard with a heart (black) as pitch.

Often have I tested his understanding: that youth has shown (the ripe experience of) age in (handling) affairs.

O son, the (really) old is the old in understanding: 'tis not whiteness of the hair in the beard and on the head.

How should he (any old man) be older than Iblís? When he lacks understanding, he is good-for-naught.

Suppose he is a child: (what matter) when he hath the (life- 2165
giving) breath of Jesus (and) is purged of vainglory and vain desire?

That whiteness of hair is a proof of maturity to the bandaged eye that hath little penetration.

Since the blind imitator recognises nothing but (an external) proof, he continually seeks the way (to the truth) in the (outward) sign.

For his sake we have said, 'When you wish to plan (anything), choose an elder (to advise you).'

He who has escaped from the purdah of blind imitation sees by the light of God that which (really) is.

2170   Without proof and without exposition the pure Light cleaves its (the object's) skin and enters into the middle (the core).

To one who regards (only) the appearance, what is (the difference between) the adulterated and genuine coin? How should he know what is in the date-basket?

Oh, there is much gold made black with smoke, that it may be saved from (falling into) the hands of every envious thief.

Oh, there is much copper gilded with gold, that he (the counterfeiter) may sell it to (those of) small understanding.

We, who see the inward (reality) of the whole world, see the heart and look not on the outward form."

2175   The cadis who are concerned with the outward form (the letter of the law) give judgement according to outward appearances.

When he (the suspected person) has uttered the profession of the Faith and has shown some (formal sign of) true belief, at once these people (the cadis) pronounce him a true believer.

There is many a hypocrite who has taken refuge in this outward form and has shed the blood of a hundred true believers in secret.

Endeavour to become old in intelligence and religion, that you may become, like the Universal Intelligence, a seer of the inward (reality).

When the beauteous Intelligence unveiled its face (revealed itself) from non-existence, He (God) gave it a robe of honour and a thousand names.

2180   Of those sweet-breathing names the least is this, that it (the Intelligence) is not in need of any one.

If the Intelligence display its face in visible form, day will be dark beside its light;

And if the shape of foolishness become visible, beside it the darkness of night will be radiant,

For it is darker and more murky than night; but the miserable bat is a buyer (seeker) of darkness.

Little by little accustom yourself to the daylight, else you will remain a bat deprived of splendour.

2185   He (the bat-like person) is the lover of every place where there is difficulty and perplexing doubt, and the enemy of every place where there is the lamp of (spiritual) felicity.

His heart seeks the darkness of perplexity in order that his
acquirements may seem greater (than they are),
So that he may preoccupy you with that difficult question and
make you oblivious of his own evil nature.

*The marks of the wholly intelligent and the half-intelligent and
the whole man and the half-man and the deluded worthless
wretch doomed to perdition.*

The intelligent man is he who hath the lamp: he is the guide
and leader of the caravan.
That leader is one who goes after his own light: that selfless
traveller is the follower of himself.
He is the one that puts faith in himself; and do ye too put 2190
faith in the light on which his soul has browsed.
The other, who is the half-intelligent, deems an (entirely) in-
telligent person to be his eye,
And has clutched him as the blind man clutches the guide,
so that through him he has become seeing and active and
illustrious.
But (as for) the ass who had not a single barley-corn's weight
of intelligence, who possessed no intelligence himself and for-
sook the intelligent (guide),
(Who) knows neither much nor little of the way (and yet) dis-
dains to go behind the guide,
He is journeying in a long wilderness, now limping in despair 2195
and now (advancing) at a run.
He hath neither a candle, that he should make it his leader,
nor half a candle, that he should beg a light.
He hath neither (perfect) intelligence, that he should breathe
the breath of the living, nor hath he a half-intelligence, that he
should make himself dead.
He (the half-intelligent one) becomes wholly dead in (de-
votion to) the man of (perfect) intelligence, that he may ascend
from his own low place to the (lofty) roof.
(If) you have not perfect intelligence, make yourself dead
under the protection of an intelligent man whose words are
living.
He (the man devoid of intelligence) is not living, that he 2200
should breathe in accord with (a) Jesus, nor is he dead, that
he should become a channel for the (life-giving) breath of (a)
Jesus[1].
His blind spirit is stepping in every direction: it will not
escape in the end, but it is leaping up.

[1] *I.e.* "he is not dead (through self-abandonment), so that he should be
brought to (spiritual) life by the influence of a saint."

*Story of the lake and the fishermen and the three fishes, one in-
telligent and one half-intelligent and the third deluded, foolish,
heedless and good-for-naught; and the end of all three.*

This, O obstinate man, is the story of the lake in which there
were three great fishes.

You will have read it in *Kalíla*, but that is (only) the husk of
the story, while this is the spiritual kernel.

Some fishermen passed beside the lake and saw that concealed
(prey).

2205 Then they hastened to bring the net: the fishes noticed and
became aware (of their intention).

The intelligent one resolved to journey, resolved to make the
difficult unwelcome journey.

He said, "I will not consult these (others), for assuredly they
will make me weak (deficient) in power (to fulfil my purpose).

Love of their native place and abode holds sway over their
souls: their indolence and ignorance will strike on (affect) me."

For consultation, some goodly and (spiritually) living person
is required, that he may make thee living; and where is that
living one (to be found)?

2210 O traveller, take counsel with a traveller, for a woman's
counsel will keep thy foot lame.

Pass on from the (literal) expression, "love of country"; do
not stop (at its outward sense), for thy (real) country is Yonder,
O soul: 'tis not on this side[1].

If thou desire thy country, cross to the other bank of the
stream: do not misread this true Ḥadíth[2].

*The inner meaning of the recitation of the ablutionary
prayers by one who performs the ritual ablution[3].*

In the ritual ablution, a separate form of prayer for each
member of the body has been handed down in Tradition.

When you snuff up water into your nose, beg of the self-
sufficient Lord the scent of Paradise,

2215 In order that that scent may lead you towards Paradise: the
scent of the rose is the guide to the rose-trees.

When you perform the act of abstersion, the (proper) form of
prayer and words is this: "O Lord, cleanse me from this (de-
filement).

My hand has reached this place and washed it, (but) my hand
is weak (unable) to wash my spirit.

O Thou by whom the spirit of the unworthy is made worthy,
the hand of Thy bounty is reaching the spirits.

[1] Or, "thy real country is Yonder: the spirit is not on this side."
[2] The Prophet said, "Love of one's country is part of the Faith."
[3] The connexion of this with the preceding verses is explained in *v.* 2230.

This (which) I, vile (as I am), have done was my limit (the utmost within my power): do Thou make clean that (which lies) beyond the limit, O gracious One.

O God, I have washed my skin clean of ordure: do Thou wash this beloved (spirit) clean of worldly taints." 2220

A certain person used to say at the time of abstersion, "O God, let me smell the sweet odour of Paradise" instead of "O God, make me one of those who repent much, and make me one of those who purify themselves," which is the (proper) form of prayer in abstersion; and he (also) used to recite the formula proper to abstersion at the time of rinsing his nose. A venerable man heard (him) and could not endure it.

A certain one said at the time of abstersion, "(O God), unite me with the scent of Paradise!"

(Thereupon) a person said, "You have used a good formula, but you have missed the (proper) hole for the prayer.

Since this prayer was the formula applicable to the nose, why have you applied the nose-formula to the arse?

One free (from sensuality) gets the odour of Paradise from his nose: how should the odour of Paradise come from the rump?"

O thou who hast brought humility into the presence of fools, 2225 and O thou who hast brought pride into the presence of (spiritual) kings,

The pride shown to the base is goodly and fitting. Take heed, do not behave in the reverse manner: the reverse thereof is (the cause of) thy bondage.

The rose grew for the sake of the nostrils: sweet scent is the stipend of the nose, O churl.

The scent of the rose is for organs of smell, O bold man: this hole below is not the place for that scent.

How should the scent of Paradise come to thee from this place? If thou requirest the (sweet) scent, seek it from its (proper) place.

Likewise, "love of country" is right, (but) first, O master, 2230 know (what really is) thy country.

That sagacious fish said, "I will journey, I will withdraw my heart from their advice and counsel."

'Tis no time for counsel. Hark, journey! Like 'Alí, sigh (the secret) into the well[1].

Very seldom is there found a fit confidant for that sigh: go by night and let thy movement be hidden, like (that of) the night-patrol.

[1] It is related that 'Alí whispered into a well the esoteric doctrine which had been communicated to him by the Prophet with a warning that he must not divulge it to any one.

Set out from this lake towards the sea: seek the sea and take leave of this whirlpool.

2235   That wary (fish) made its breast a foot (swam away) and was going from its perilous abode to the sea of light,

Like the deer of which a dog is in pursuit and which keeps running so long as there is a single nerve in its body.

Hare's sleep (heedlessness) with the dog in pursuit is a sin: how indeed is sleep (dwelling) in the eye of him who hath fear?

That fish departed and took the way to the sea: it took the far way and the vast expanse.

It suffered many afflictions, and in the end it went after all towards safety and welfare.

2240   It cast itself into the deep Sea whose bound no eye can reach.

So when the fishermen brought their net (to the lake), the half-intelligent (fish) was bitterly grieved thereat[1],

And said, "Alas, I have lost the opportunity: how did not I accompany that guide?

He went off suddenly, but seeing that he went I ought to have gone after him in hot haste."

'Tis wrong to regret the past: what is gone will not come back: to remember it is of no avail.

Story of the captive bird which gave the (following) injunctions: do not feel sorrow for what is past, think about taking precaution for the present (need), and do not spend time in repenting.

2245   A certain man caught a bird by guile and trap: the bird said to him, "O noble sire,

Thou hast eaten many oxen and sheep, thou hast sacrificed many camels;

Thou hast never in the world been sated by them, neither wilt thou be sated by my limbs.

Let me go, that I may bestow on thee three counsels, that thou mayst perceive whether I am wise or foolish.

(I will give thee) the first of those counsels on thy hand, the second of them on thy plastered roof,

2250   And the third counsel I will give thee on a tree. (Let me go), for thou wilt become fortunate through these three counsels.

(As for) that saying which is (to be said) on thy hand, 'tis this: 'do not believe an absurdity (when thou hearest it) from any one.'"

When it (the bird) had uttered the first grave counsel on his palm, it became free and went (to perch) on the wall (of his house),

And said, "The second is, 'do not grieve over (what is) past: when it has passed from thee, do not feel regret for it.'"

---

[1] Literally, "its palate became bitter."

After that, it said to him, "In my body is concealed a solitary (large and precious) pearl, ten dirhems in weight.

By thy soul's truth (as sure as thou livest), that jewel was thy 2255 fortune and the luck of thy children.

Thou hast missed the pearl, for it was not thy appointed lot (to gain it)—a pearl the like of which is not in existence."

Even as a woman big with child keeps wailing at the time of parturition, so the Khwája began to cry out clamorously.

The bird said to him, "Did not I admonish thee, saying, 'Let there be no grief in thee for what passed yesterday'?

Since it is past and gone, why art thou grieving? Either thou didst not understand my counsel or thou art deaf.

And (as regards) the second counsel I gave thee, (namely), 2260 'Do not from misguidedness put any belief in an absurd statement,'

O lion[1], I myself do not weigh ten dirhems: how should the weight of ten dirhems be within me?"

The Khwája came back to himself (recovered his wits) and said, "Hark, disclose the third (piece of) excellent counsel."

"Yes," said the bird, "thou hast made good use of those (former counsels), that I should tell (thee) the third counsel in vain!"

To give counsel to a sleepy ignoramus is to scatter seed in nitrous soil.

The rent of folly and ignorance does not admit of being 2265 patched up: do not give the seed of wisdom to him (the fool), O counsellor.

How the half-intelligent fish devised a means (of escape) and feigned to be dead.

The second fish said in the hour of tribulation, when he was left sundered from the shadow (protection) of the intelligent one,

"He hath gone towards the sea and is freed from sorrow: such a good comrade hath been lost to me!

But I will not think of that and will attend to myself: at this (present) time I will feign to be dead.

Then I will turn my belly upwards and my back downwards and will move on the water.

I will move upon it as weeds move, not by swimming as a 2270 person (swimmer) does.

I will become dead, I will commit myself to the water: to die before death is to be safe from torment."

To die before death is to be safe, O youth: even so hath Muṣṭafá (Mohammed) commanded us.

[1] *I.e.* "O gallant man."

He said, "Die, all of you, ere death come; else ye will die with (the certainty of suffering) sore afflictions (hereafter)."

He (the fish) died in that manner and threw his belly upwards: the water was carrying him, now alow, now aloft.

2275   Every one of those pursuers (the fishermen) bore great vexation (in his heart), saying, "Alas, the best fish is dead."

He (the fish) was made glad by their saying "Alas": (he said to himself), "This trick of mine has come off, I am delivered from the sword."

Then a worthy fisherman seized him and spat on him and flung him on the ground.

He (the half-intelligent fish), rolling over and over, went secretly into the water; the (entirely) foolish one remained (where he was), moving to and fro in agitation.

That simpleton kept leaping about, right and left, in order that he might save his skin[1] by his own efforts.

2280   They cast the net, and he (at last) remained in the net: foolishness ensconced him in that fire (of perdition).

On the top of the fire, on the surface of a frying-pan, he became the bedfellow of Folly.

(There) he was seething from the heat of the flames: Reason was saying to him, "*Did not a warner come to thee?*"

He, from the rack of torture and tribulation, was replying like the souls of the unbelievers: *they said, "Yea."*

Then again he was saying, "If this time I escape from this neck-breaking affliction,

2285   I will not make my home except in a sea: I will not make a lake my dwelling-place.

I will seek the boundless sea and become safe: I will go in safety and welfare for ever."

Explaining that the promise made by the fool at the moment of seizure (punishment) and contrition is faithless, for though they should be sent back, they would surely return to that which they were forbidden to do, and verily they are liars. The false dawn keeps not faith.

Reason was saying to him, "Folly is with thee: with Folly (as thy companion), the promise will be broken.

The keeping of promises appertains to reason: thou hast not reason: begone, O thou whose value is that of an ass!

Reason remembers its covenant: understanding rends the veil of forgetfulness.

2290   Since thou hast not reason, forgetfulness is thy ruler: it is thy enemy and the bringer-to-naught of thy devising."

---

[1] Literally, "cloak" or "mantle."

From deficiency of reason the wretched moth does not remember the flame and the burning and the (crackling) sound (when its wings are scorched).

When its wings are burnt, it repents; (but) cupidity and forgetfulness dash it (again) into the flame.

Grasp and apprehension and retentiveness and keeping in mind belong to Reason, for Reason has raised those (faculties).

When the pearl is not there, how should its lustre exist? When there is none to remind (admonish the fool), how should he turn back (from folly)?

Moreover, this wish (to escape from the consequences of his folly) arises from his want of reason, for he does not see what is the nature of that folly. 2295

That contrition was the result of pain, not of Reason which is bright as a treasure.

When the pain departed, that contrition became naught: that repentance and contrition hath not the worth (even) of dust.

That contrition burgeoned[1] from (was produced by) the darkness of pain; hence (as the proverb says) day wipes out the words of night[2].

When the darkness of pain is gone and he (the fool) has become happy, its result and product also goes from his heart.

He is making vows of repentance, whilst the Pír, Reason, is crying, "*Though they should be sent back, they would surely return.*" 2300

Explaining that imagination (wahm) is the counterfeit of Reason and in opposition to it, and that though it resembles Reason it is not Reason; and the story of the replies given to each other by Moses, on whom be peace, who was the possessor of Reason, and Pharaoh, who was the possessor of imagination.

Reason is the contrary of sensuality: O brave man, do not call (by the name of) Reason that which is attached to sensuality.

That which is a beggar of sensuality—call it imagination: imagination is the counterfeit of the sterling gold of the rational faculties.

Without a touchstone, imagination and reason are not clearly distinguished: quickly bring both to the touchstone.

The *Qur'án* and the (spiritual) state of the Prophets are this touchstone: they, like a touchstone, say to the counterfeit coin, "Come,

That by contact with me thou mayst see thyself (and know) that thou art not worthy of my higher and lower (degrees of spirituality)." 2305

[1] Literally, "formed fruit."
[2] *I.e.* vows made in the hour of pain are broken as soon as the pain is removed.

If a saw make Reason (to be severed into) two halves, it (Reason) will be smiling like gold in the fire.

Imagination belongs to Pharaoh, the world-incendiary; Reason to Moses, the spirit-enkindler.

Moses went on the way of non-existence (self-negation): Pharaoh said to him, "Tell (me), who art thou?"

He said, "I am Reason, the messenger of the Almighty: I am the proof of God, I am the protection against error."

2310   "Nay," said he, "hush, cease from (this ecstatic) outcry: tell (me) thy ancient lineage and name."

"My lineage," he said, "(is derived) from His dust-pit; my original name is 'the meanest of His slaves.'

I am the slave-born (slave) of that unique Lord—born of the (womb and) loins of slaves female and male.

My original lineage (is derived) from earth and water and clay: God gave unto water and clay a soul and heart.

To earth also will return this earthen body of mine; to earth thou likewise wilt return, O terrible one.

2315   Our origin and the origin of all the proud is from a piece of earth, and (there are) a hundred signs thereof;

For thy body receives support (sustenance) from the earth, and from earthly nutriment thy neck is wrapped in folds (of flesh).

When the spirit departs, it (the body) will again become earth in the dreaded and horrible grave.

Both thou and we and all who resemble thee will become earth, and thy power will remain no more."

He (Pharaoh) said, "Thou hast a name other than this lineage: truly that name is more proper for thee—

2320   'Slave of Pharaoh and slave of his slaves,' (a slave) whose body and soul were first nurtured by him (Pharaoh)[1],

A hostile, insolent and unrighteous slave, who fled from this country on account of an ill-omened deed.

Thou art a murderer and treacherous and ungrateful: from just these qualities, forsooth, form a judgement (as to the rest).

(Thou art) in exile, despised and poor and threadbare, since thou didst not acknowledge gratitude and obligation to me."

He (Moses) said, "Far be it that any other person should be a partner in Lordship with that King.

2325   (He is) One: He hath no associate in Kingship; His slaves have no master but Him.

His creatures have no other owner: does any one claim partnership with Him except one that is doomed to perish?

He hath made the design, He is my Designer; if another lay claim (to it), he is a seeker of iniquity.

[1] Literally, "who, through him (Pharaoh), first nurtured his body and soul."

Thou canst not fashion my eyebrow: how canst thou know my soul?

Nay, 'tis thou who art the traitor and the insolent one, for thou claimest duality with God.

If I inadvertently killed a ruffian[1], I killed (him) neither for self's sake nor in sport. 2330

I struck (him) a blow with my fist, and he suddenly fell: one who really had no soul gave up a soul.

I killed a cur: thou the children of him who was sent (by God)—hundreds of thousands of innocent and harmless babes—

Hast killed, and their blood is on thy neck: consider what shall come upon thee because of this blood-drinking of thine.

Thou hast killed the progeny of Jacob—those sought after in hope of slaying me.

In despite of thee God Himself chose me out: that (plot) which thy soul was concocting was overthrown." 2335

He (Pharaoh) said, "Let these things be without any doubt (grant that all this is true): is it (the gratitude) due to me and to the bread and salt (which thou hast eaten)

That thou shouldst treat me with contumely in the presence of the assembled people and make the bright day dark to my heart?"

He (Moses) said, "The contumely of the Resurrection is more grievous, (which thou wilt suffer) if thou do not pay regard to me in good and evil.

Thou canst not bear the bite of a flea: how wilt thou taste (endure) the bite of a snake?

In appearance I am ruining thy work, but (in reality) I am making a thorn into a rose-garden. 2340

Explaining that cultivation consists in devastation and composure in distraction and wholeness in brokenness and success in failure and existence in non-existence; and thus (with) the rest of the contraries and pairs.

A certain man came and was cleaving the soil: a fool cried out and could not control himself,

Saying, 'Wherefore are you ruining this soil and cleaving and scattering it?'

'O fool,' said he, 'begone, do not interfere with me[2]: recognise (the difference of) cultivation from devastation.

How should this (soil) become a rose-garden or cornfield till this soil becomes ugly and ruined?

How should it become orchards and crops and leaves and fruit till its arrangement is turned upside down?' 2345

---

[1] See *Qur'án*, XXVIII, 14.
[2] Literally, "do not advance against me."

Till you pierce the purulent ulcer with a lancet, how will it become well and how will you become healthy?

Till he (the physician) cleanse your (corrupt) humours with medicine, how will the indisposition be removed? How will a cure be effected?

When a tailor cuts (the cloth for) a garment piece by piece, will any one strike that expert tailor,

Saying, 'Why have you torn this choice satin? What can I do with a torn (garment)?'

2350 Whenever they (the builders) put an old building in good repair, do not they first ruin the old one?

Likewise the carpenter, the iron-smith and the butcher—with them (too) there is destruction before restorations.

The pounding of myrobalan and bastard myrobalan—by reason of that destruction they become the means of restoring the body (to health).

Until you crush wheat in the mill, how will our table be garnished with it?

(The obligation of gratitude for) that bread and salt (of thine) demanded that I should deliver thee, O fish, from the net.

2355 If thou accept the counsel of Moses, thou wilt escape from such an evil infinite net.

Inasmuch as thou hast made thyself the slave of sensuality, thou hast made a petty worm[1] into a dragon.

I have brought a dragon for (thy) dragon, that I may correct (thy dragon's) breath by (my dragon's) breath,

So that the breath of that one may be defeated by the breath of this one, and that my serpent may destroy that dragon (of thine).

If thou submittest, thou art freed from two serpents; otherwise, it (thy-dragon) will bring thy spirit to utter perdition."

2360 He (Pharaoh) said, "In truth, thou art an exceedingly cunning sorcerer, for by craft thou hast introduced duality (disunion) here.

Thou hast made the unanimous people into two factions: sorcery makes fissures in rock and mountain."

He (Moses) said, "I am submerged in the message of God: who (ever) saw sorcery together with the name of God?

The substance of sorcery is forgetfulness (of God) and unbelief: the spirit of Moses is the flaming torch of the (true) religion.

How do I resemble sorcerers, O impudent one?—for the Messiah (Jesus) is becoming jealous of my (life-giving) breath.

2365 How do I resemble sorcerers, O polluted one?—for the (Revealed) Books are receiving light from my spirit.

[1] *I.e.* the carnal soul.

Since thou art soaring on the wings of sensuality, inevitably thou bearest (in thy heart) that (ill) thought against me."

Every one whose actions are those of wild beasts hath ill thoughts against the noble.

Since thou art a part of the world, howsoever thou art thou deemest all to be of the same description as thyself, misguided man.

If thou whirl round and thy head whirl round, thy (organ of) sight sees the house whirling round;

And if thou embark in a ship moving on the sea, thou deemest 2370 the sea-shore to be running (along).

If thou art narrow (oppressed) at heart from (being engaged in) combat, thou deemest the whole atmosphere of the world to be narrow;

And if thou art happy as thy friends would desire, this world seems to thee like a garden of roses.

How many a one has gone as far as Syria and 'Iráq and has seen nothing but unbelief and hypocrisy;

And how many a one has gone as far as India and Hirá (Herát) and seen nothing but selling and buying;

And how many a one has gone as far as Turkistán and China 2375 and seen nothing but deceit and hidden guile!

Since he has no object of perception save colour and perfume (external phenomena), let him seek (through) all the climes, (he will see nothing spiritual).

(If) a cow come suddenly into Baghdád and pass from this side (of the city) to that (farther) side,

Of all (its) pleasures and joys and delights she will see nothing but the rind of a water-melon.

(If) straw or hay has fallen on the road, (it is) suitable to his (such a one's) bovine or asinine disposition.

(Hanging) dry on the nail of (his bestial) nature, like strips of 2380 meat (exposed to the sun), his spirit, bound with (the cords of) secondary causes, does not grow;

But the spacious realm where means and causes are torn to shreds (transcended) is *the earth of God*, O most honourable sire.

It is ever changing, like a (fleeting) picture: the spirit beholds in clairvoyance a world (appearing) anew and anew.

(Everything), though it be Paradise and the rivers of Eden, becomes ugly when it is congealed (fixed permanently) in one aspect.

Explaining that every percipient sense of man has different objects of perception too, of which the other senses are ignorant, as (for example) every skilled craftsman is unfamiliar with the work of those skilled in other crafts; and its (another sense's) ignorance of that which is not its business does not prove that those objects of perception are non-existent. Although it virtually denies them, yet here in this place we only mean by its 'denial' its ignorance.

Thy perception is the measure of thy vision of the world: thy impure senses are the veil (which prevents thee from having sight) of the pure (holy men).

2385   Wash thy senses for a while with the water of clairvoyance: know that the garment-washing of the Ṣúfís is like this.

When thou hast become purified, the spirit of the pure ones will tear off the veil and attach itself to thee.

If the whole world be (filled with) light and (radiant) forms, (only) the eye would be aware of that loveliness.

(Suppose) thou hast shut the eye and art bringing forward the ear that thou mayst show unto it the locks and face of an adorable beauty,

The ear will say, "I do not attend to the (visible) form: if the form utter a cry, I will hearken.

2390   I am skilled, but (only) in my own art: my art is (the perception of) a (spoken) word or sound, no more."

(And if thou say), "Hey, nose, come and see this beauteous one," the nose is not fit for this purpose.

"If there be any musk or rose-water, I will smell it: this is my art and science and knowledge.

How should I see the face of that silver-shanked one? Take heed, do not lay (on me) as a task that which cannot be done."

Again, the crooked (perverted) sense hath naught but crooked (perverse) perception, (so) go crookedly into His presence or go straight, as thou wilt (it matters not).

2395   Know for sure that the eye of him who sees double is remote from seeing the Unity, O Khwája who aidest (the true Religion)[1].

Thou who art a Pharaoh art wholly deceit and hypocrisy: (hence) thou knowest no difference between me and thyself[2].

Do not regard (judge of) me from thyself, O false-playing man, that thou mayst not see the single as double.

Regard (judge of) me from me (with my eyes) for one moment, that thou mayst behold a spacious region beyond (phenomenal) existence,

And mayst be delivered from straitness and dishonour and renown (good and evil repute) and behold love within love, and peace (be with thee)!

[1] This may refer to Mu'ínu'ddín, the Parwána of Rúm, who is said to have been one of the poet's disciples.
[2] Here the speaker is the "Moses" of whom the Moslem saint is a type.

Then, when thou hast been delivered from the body, thou [2400] wilt know that ear and nose can become eye.

That sweet-tongued (spiritual) king[1] has said with truth that every hair of gnostics becomes an eye.

Certainly the eye had no eye (vision) at first: it was an embryo of flesh in the womb.

Deem not the fat (the white of the eye) to be the cause of sight, O son; otherwise none would see (visible) forms in dream.

The genie and the demon see the like, and there is no fat in the sight-organ of either.

In fact there was (originally) no relationship between light [2405] and the fat (of the eye): the loving Creator gave them relationship.

Adam is of earth, (but) how does he resemble earth? The genie is of fire without any participation (of the other elements);

(But) the genie is not similar (in form) to fire, though when thou considerest (thou wilt acknowledge that) it is his origin.

The bird is (originally) of wind (air)[2], (but) how does it resemble wind? God gave relationship to the unrelated.

The relation of these derivatives to the originals is ineffable, although He connected them.

Since man is born of dust, where is the relation between this [2410] son and his father?

If there is a relation hidden from the understanding, it is ineffable, and how should the understanding follow its track?

If He did not give the wind vision without eye, how was it making a distinction among the people of 'Ád[3]?

How was it knowing the true believer from the enemy? How was it knowing the wine from the gourd-shaped goblet?

If the fire of Nimrod hath no eye, how is a taking pains (to show respect) towards Abraham (explicable)?

If the Nile had not possessed that light and sight, wherefore [2415] should it have picked out the Egyptians from the Israelites[4]?

If mountain and rock had not been endowed with sight, then how should it (the mountain) have become a friend (accompanist) to David?

If this earth had not possessed a spiritual eye, wherefore should it have swallowed Qárún in such a fashion?

If the Moaning (Pillar) had not possessed the eye of the heart (*oculus cordis*), how should it have seen the separation (from it) of that august one (the Prophet)[5]?

If the gravel had not been possessed of an eye, how should it have given testimony in the closed fist (of Abú Jahl)[6]?

---

[1] Probably Saná'í of Ghazna.
[2] See p. 261, note 1.
[3] See Book I, v. 854 *sqq.*
[4] See below, vv. 2829 and 3494 *sqq*
[5] See Book I, v. 2113 *sqq.*
[6] See Book I, v. 2154 *sqq.*

2420 O intellect, unfold thy wings and pinions: read the Súra (which begins with the words), (*when the earth*) *shall be caused to quake with a mighty quaking*[1].

At the Resurrection how should this earth give testimonies concerning good and evil without having seen?

For *she will relate her* experiences and *informations*: the earth will reveal her secrets to us.

"This sending of me (as a prophet) to thee, O prince[2], is a clear evidence that the Sender was aware

That such a medicine as this is suitable to such a desperate malady, for the purpose of success (in curing it).

2425 Heretofore thou hadst seen visions (warning thee) that God would choose me out (to go to thee),

(And that) I, having taken the rod and the Light in my hand, would break thy insolent horn.

On this account the Lord of the Judgement was showing unto thee terrible visions of diverse sorts,

Suitable to thy evil conscience and thy inordinate disobedience, that thou might'st know that He knows what is proper for thee;

That thou might'st know that He is wise and omniscient and the healer of irremediable maladies.

2430 Through false interpretations thou wert made blind and deaf to those (visions), saying, 'This is caused by heavy slumber';

And the physician and the astrologer in flashes (of intelligence) saw the (true) explanation thereof, but concealed it from (motives) of cupidity.

He (the physician) said, 'Far be it from thy empire and kingship that anxiety should enter into thy consciousness.

When the (human) constitution is indisposed by food that disagrees with it or by (rich) viands, it sees visions in sleep.'

(He said this) because he perceived that thou art not one that desires good counsel, and that thou art violent and blood-drinking and not of lowly nature.

2435 Kings shed blood for righteousness' sake, but their mercy is greater than their severity.

The king must have the nature of the Lord: His mercy hath precedence over His wrath.

Wrath must not prevail (in the king), like (as it does in) the Devil, (so that) he sheds blood unnecessarily for the purpose of guile;

Nor, again, (should) an effeminate mildness (prevail in him), for in consequence of that his wife and handmaids will become harlots.

Thou hadst made thy breast a house for the Devil, thou hadst made hatred a *qibla* (object on which thy mind was bent).

[1] *Qur'án*, XCIX, I.   [2] Moses addresses Pharaoh.

Many are the hearts[1] which thy sharp horn has wounded: lo, 2440
my rod has broken thy froward horn.

How the people of this world attack the people of that (other) world
and charge (against them) as far as the frontier, namely, genera-
tion and propagation, which is the boundary of the Unseen, and
how they (the people of this world) are unaware of the ambush
(prepared for them); for the infidel makes his assault (only) when
the holy warrior does not go to war.

The army of the corporeal ones attacked in the direction of
the fortress and stronghold of the spiritual ones,

In order that they might occupy the frontier-pass of the Un-
seen, so that no pure spirit[2] should come (into the world) from
that quarter.

When the holy warriors do not attack in warfare, the infidels
on the contrary deliver an attack.

When the holy warriors of the Unseen in their forbearance
refrained from delivering an attack on thee, man of evil practice,

Thou madest an attack towards the frontier-passes of the 2445
Unseen, in order that the men of the Unseen should not come
in this direction.

Thou didst lay a (violent) hand upon the loins and wombs,
that thou might'st wickedly occupy (close) the thoroughfare (of
sexual intercourse)[3].

How should'st thou occupy (close) the highway which the
Almighty hath opened for the purpose of procreation?

Thou didst block the passes, O contumacious one, (but) in
despite of thee a captain issued forth.

Lo, I am the captain: I will break thy power. Lo, in His name
I will break thy name and fame.

Come now, close the passes tightly! Laugh at thy moustache 2450
(be the dupe of thy vainglory) a (little) while!

The Divine decree will tear out thy moustache piecemeal,
that thou mayst know that the Decree makes precaution
blind.

Is thy moustache fiercer than that of (the people of) 'Ád, at
whose breath (all) the lands used to tremble?

Art thou more contentious in aspect or (the tribe of) Thamúd,
the like of whom never came into existence?

Though I tell (thee) a hundred of these (proofs), thou art
deaf: thou hearest and pretendest not to have heard.

I repent of the words which I raised up: (now), without 2455
words, I have mixed for thee a medicine

---

[1] Literally, "livers."
[2] Literally, "one whose shirt-bosom is clean."
[3] See Book III, *v.* 872 *sqq.*

Which I will place upon thy raw sore, that it may be assuaged,
or that thy sore and thy beard may be burnt (destroyed entirely)
unto everlasting,

To the end that thou mayst know that He is omniscient, O
enemy: He gives to everything that which befits it.

When hast thou done wrong and when hast thou wrought
evil but thou hast seen (suffered) the effect befitting it?

When hast thou once sent a good deed to Heaven but the like
thereof has followed after[1]?

2460   If thou wilt be observant and vigilant, thou wilt see at every
moment the response to thy action.

When thou art observant and dost grasp the cord (of appre-
hension), thou needest not the coming of the Resurrection (to
reveal the ultimate effects).

He that truly knows (the meaning of) an indication does not
need to have it plainly declared to him.

This tribulation befalls thee from (thy) stupidity in not
understanding the subtle hints and indications.

When thy heart has been blackened and darkened by wicked-
ness, understand! One ought not to become besotted here;

2465   Otherwise, in sooth, that darkness will become an arrow (of
woe), and the penalty of (thy) besottedness will overtake thee.

And if the arrow come not, 'tis from (God's) bounty; not be-
cause of (His) not seeing the defilement (of thy sin).

Hark, be observant if thou wouldst have a (pure) heart, for
something is born to thee in consequence of every action.

And if thou hast an aspiration greater than this, (and if) the
enterprise goes beyond (the spiritual rank of) the observant,

[*Explaining that the earthen body of man, like iron of fine sub-
stance, is capable of becoming a mirror, so that therein even in
this world Paradise and Hell and the Resurrection et cetera are
shown by immediate vision, not in the mode of phantasy.*]

Then, though thou art dark-bodied like iron, make a practice
of polishing, polishing, polishing,

2470   That thy heart may become a mirror full of images, (with) a
lovely silver-breasted (form reflected) therein on every side.

Although the iron was dark and devoid of light, polishing
cleared away the darkness from it.

The iron saw (suffered) the polishing and made its face fair,
so that images could be seen therein.

---

[1] The Turkish commentator, who reads ندیدی instead of نیآمد,
translates: "When hast thou sent a breath (breathed a prayer) to Heaven
but thou hast seen in consequence a (Divine) benefit like unto it?" The
position of نیکیی, however, is against this.

If the earthen body is gross and dark, polish it—for it is receptive to the polishing instrument—

In order that the forms of the Unseen may appear in it, and that the reflexion of houri and angel may dart into it.

God hath given thee the polishing instrument, Reason, to the 2475 end that thereby the leaf (surface) of the heart may be made resplendent.

Thou, O prayerless man, hast put the polisher (Reason) in bonds and hast loosed the two hands of sensuality.

If bonds be put on sensuality, the hand of the polisher (Reason) will be untied.

A piece of iron that became a mirror of the Unseen—all the forms (of the Unseen) would be shot into it.

(But) thou madest (thy heart) dark and didst let the rust into thy nature: this is (the inner meaning of) *they work evil on the earth.*

So hast thou done till now: now do it not. Thou hast made the 2480 water turbid: do not make it more (so).

Do not stir it up (befoul it): let this water become clear, and (then) behold the moon and stars circling therein.

For man is like the water of the river: when it becomes turbid, thou canst not see its bottom.

The bottom of the river is full of jewels and full of pearls: take heed, do not make (the water) turbid, for it is (originally) pure and free (from pollution).

The spirit of man resembles air: when it (air) is mixed with dust, it veils the sky,

And prevents (the eye) from seeing the sun; (but) when its 2485 dust is gone, it becomes pure and undefiled.

Notwithstanding thy complete darkness, God was showing visions unto thee, that thou might'st wend the way of deliverance.

How Moses, on whom be peace, declared (by inspiration) from the Unseen the secret thoughts and visions of Pharaoh, in order that he might truly believe in the omniscience of God or (at least) hold that opinion.

From the dark iron (of thy nature) He, by His power, was showing forth the visions that should come to pass in the end,

In order that thou might'st lessen (refrain from) that injustice and wickedness: thou wert seeing those (visions) and becoming more wicked.

He was showing unto thee hideous forms in dream: thou wert shrinking back from them, and (in reality) they were thy (own) form;

2490   Like the Ethiopian (negro) who saw in the mirror that his face was ugly, et in speculum cacavit,

Saying, 'How ugly thou art! Thou art deserving only of this.' (The mirror replies), 'My ugliness belongs to thee, O vile blind one.

Thou art putting this filth on thy ugly face: it is not on me, for I have splendour.'

At one time thou wert seeing (in vision) thy raiment burnt; at another time thy mouth and eyes stitched up;

Now a (rapacious) animal seeking thy blood; now thy head in the teeth of a wild beast;

2495   Now (in thy dream thou wert) upside down in the midst of a latrine; now sunk in a fierce blood-dyed torrent;

Now from this pure heaven came to thee a voice crying, 'Thou art damned, thou art damned, damned';

Now from the mountains came to thee a voice, (saying) plainly, 'Begone! thou art one of *the people of the left hand*'[1];

Now from every inanimate thing was coming to thee a voice (which cried), 'Pharaoh is fallen into Hell for evermore';

(And thou sawest) worse things than these, which from shame I will not tell, lest thy perverted nature become hot (with anger).

2500   I have told thee a little, O thou who wilt not accept (my warning): from a little thou mayst know that I am acquainted (with the whole).

Thou wert making thyself blind and dead, that thou might'st not bethink thee of the dreams and visions.

How long wilt thou flee? Lo, it is come to thee in despite of thy guile-meditating perception[2].

Explaining that the door of repentance is open.

Hark, do not act (so) henceforth, (but) take precaution, for through (God's) bounty the door of repentance is open.

From the quarter of the West a door of repentance is open to mankind till the Resurrection.

2505   Till the sun lifts up its head (rises) from the West, that door is open: do not avert thy face from it.

By the mercy (of God) Paradise hath eight doors: one of those eight is the door of repentance, O son.

All the others are sometimes open, sometimes shut; and never is the door of repentance but open.

Come, seize the opportunity: the door is open: carry thy baggage thither at once in despite of the envious (Devil).

---

[1] *Qur'án*, LVI, 40 *sqq.*
[2] *I.e.* "The doom shadowed forth in the portents which thou wouldst not heed is about to appear to thee." Another possible rendering is, "Lo, (the result of) the blindness of thy guile-meditating perception is (now) come before thee."

How Moses, on whom be peace, said to Pharaoh, "Accept one counsel from me and take four excellent qualities as recompense."

Come, accept from me one thing and bring (it into practice), and then take from me four as recompense for that."

He replied, "O Moses, what is that one thing? Explain to 2510 me a little about that one thing."

"That one thing," said he, "is that thou shouldst say publicly that there is no god but the Maker,

The Creator of the heavenly spheres and of the stars on high and of man and devil and genie and bird,

The Creator of sea and plain and mountain and desert: His sovereignty is without limit and He is without like."

He (Pharaoh) said, "O Moses, what are those four things that thou wilt give me in recompense? Declare (what they are) and bring (them before me),

That perchance, by the favour of that goodly promise, the 2515 crucifixion (torment) of my unbelief may be assuaged.

Perchance the lock of my hundred maunds' weight of unbelief may be opened by those fair and desirable promises.

Perchance, by the effect of the river of honey, this poison of hatred may be turned into honey in my body;

Or by the reflexion of the river of that pure milk, (my) captive intelligence may be nourished for a moment;

Or perchance, by the reflexion of those rivers of wine, I may be intoxicated and obtain a scent of the delight of (obedience to) the (Divine) command;

Or perchance, by the favour of those rivers of water, my 2520 barren devastated body may gain refreshment—

Some verdure may appear on my barren soil, my thorn-brake may become the Garden of (everlasting) abode;

Perchance, by the reflexion of Paradise and the four rivers, my spirit, through God's befriending (it), may become a seeker of the Friend,

In the same fashion as from the reflexion of Hell I have become fire and am steeped in the wrath of God.

At one moment, from the reflexion of the snake of Hell I have become (engaged in) dropping poison, like a snake, on those who shall dwell in Paradise;

At another time, from the reflexion of the boiling of the hot 2525 water (of Hell), the water of my oppression has made the people (like) rotten bones.

From the reflexion of the *zamharír* (intense cold of Hell) I am (as) the *zamharír*; or from the reflexion of the *sa'ír* (flames of Hell) I am as the *sa'ír*.

I am now the Hell of the poor and oppressed: woe to him whom I suddenly find subject (to me)!"

How Moses, on whom be peace, explained those four excellent qualities (which should be bestowed) as a reward for Pharaoh's coming into the Faith.

Moses said, "The first of those four will be constant health for thy body:

These maladies that are described in (books of) Medicine will be far from thy body, O estimable one.

2530 Secondly, thou wilt have a long life, for death will be cautious of (attacking) thy life;

And after a life uniform (in happiness) this will not be (the sequel, namely) that thou wilt go forth from the world against thy will;

Nay, but (thou wilt go) desiring death as the sucking babe (desires milk), not on account of the pain that holds thee captive.

Thou wilt be seeking death, but not from painful infirmity; nay, thou wilt see the treasure in the ruin of the house (of the body).

Therefore with thine own hand thou wilt take a pick-axe and smite upon the house without any care;

2535 For thou wilt deem the house to be the barrier to the treasure, and this single grain to be the obstacle to a hundred corn-stacks.

This grain, then, thou wilt cast into the fire and adopt the (only) profession[1] that is worthy of a man."

O thou who because of (addiction to) a single leaf hast been left without (enjoyment of) a (whole) orchard, thou art like the worm which (desire for) a leaf has driven away from (deprived of) the vineyard.

When Grace awakened this worm, this worm devoured the dragon of ignorance.

The worm became a vineyard full of fruit and trees: even so is the blessed man transformed.

Exposition of " I was a hidden treasure, and I desired to be known."

2540 Demolish the house, for a hundred thousand houses may be made from the cornelian of this Yemen.

The treasure lies beneath the house, and there is no help (for it): do not be afraid of destroying the house and do not stand still,

For from one treasure in hand it is possible to build a thousand houses without suffering toil and pain.

In the end this house will fall of itself into ruin and the treasure beneath it will certainly be uncovered;

But it (the treasure) will not be thine, since the spirit receives that (Divine) gift as wages for destroying (the house).

---

[1] *I.e.* practice of the Faith as taught by the prophets and saints.

When it has not done that work, its wages are naught: *there* 2545
*is nothing for Man (hereafter) but (the recompense for) that which
he wrought (here).*

After that, thou wilt gnaw thy hand (in remorse), saying,
"Alas, a moon like this was (concealed) under the cloud.

I did not do the good which they told (me to do): the treasure
and the house are gone, and my hand is empty."

Thou hast rented and hired a house: it is not thy property by
any act of sale or purchase.

The period of this hiring is till death, in order that thou mayst
work in it (the house) during this period.

Thou art sewing patches in the shop, (while) under this shop 2550
of thine two mines (of treasure) are buried.

This shop is held on hire: be quick, take the pick-axe and
break up its foundation,

That of a sudden thou mayst lay the axe on the mine and be
delivered from the shop and from patch-sewing.

What is patch-sewing? The drinking of water and the eating
of bread: thou art applying these patches to the heavy cloak.

This cloak, thy body, is always being torn, and thou art
patching it by this eating and drinking of thine.

O thou who art of the progeny of the fortunate King[1], come 2555
to thyself, be ashamed of this patch-sewing.

Tear a patch (piece) from off this shop-floor[2], in order that
two mines (of treasure) may lift up their head (emerge into view)
before thee,

Ere this lease of the hired house come to an end without thy
having gained any profit from it.

Then the owner of the shop will turn thee out and will de-
molish this shop for the sake of the (hidden) mine,

(While) thou at one moment wilt beat thy head in remorse, and
at another tear thy foolish beard,

Saying, "Alas, this shop was mine, (but) I was blind and got 2560
no profit from this place of abode.

Alas, the wind swept our existence away: (the text) *O sorrow
for the servants of God*[3] is come (true) unto everlasting.

[*How Man is deluded by the sagacity and imaginations of his
(carnal) nature and does not seek knowledge of the Unseen, which
is the knowledge possessed by the prophets.*]

I saw (beautiful) pictures and paintings in the house: I was
without self-control in (my) love of the house.

I was unaware of any hidden treasure; otherwise, the axe
would have been (as) the pomander in my hand[4].

---

[1] Adam, whom God created in His own image.
[2] *I.e.* the basis of bodily existence.   [3] *Qur'án*, xxxvi, 29, slightly altered.
[4] *I.e.* "I should have taken delight in holding and wielding the axe (of
self-mortification)."

Ah, if I had given the axe its due, I should now have given a quittance to (should have been quit of) grief.

2565　I was casting my eye on the picture and falling idly in love (with it), like children."

That fortunate Sage[1], then, has said well, "Thou art a child: the house is full of pictures and paintings."

In the *Iláhí-náma* he gave many an injunction, saying, "Raise the dust from (utterly demolish) thine own household."

(Pharaoh said), "Enough, O Moses! Tell (me) the third promise, for my heart has become lost (distraught) from the agitation caused by (eagerness to hear) it."

Moses said, "This third (promise) is a twofold empire—(an empire) appertaining to the two worlds (temporal and spiritual), free from adversary and enemy;

2570　Greater than the empire of which thou art now in possession; for that was (whilst thou wert) at war (with God), and this (will be whilst thou art) at peace (with Him).

He who bestows on thee, (whilst thou art) at war, such an empire as this—consider how (bounteously) He will lay the table for thee (when thou art) at peace.

That (Divine) bounty which gave thee those (goodly) things in thy unrighteousness—consider what will be (its) care (for thee) in thy faithfulness."

"O Moses," said he, "what is the fourth (promise)? Quickly declare (it): my patience is gone and my desire has waxed great."

He said, "The fourth is that thou wilt remain (ever) young, (with) hair (black) like pitch and cheeks (pink) like the *arghawán* (flower of the Judas-tree).

2575　To us (prophets) colour and perfume are very worthless, but thou art low, (so) we have made our words low.

Boasting of colour and perfume and dwelling-place is a joy and deception (only) to children.

[*Explanation of the Tradition, "Speak ye unto men according to the measure of their understandings, not according to the measure of your understandings, so that God and His messenger may not be given the lie."*]

Since my business happens to be with a child, I must accordingly speak the language[2] suited to children,

Saying, 'Go to school, that I may buy a bird for thee or bring (home) raisins and walnuts and pistachio nuts.'

Thou knowest only the youth of the body: take this youthfulness: take the barley, O ass!

2580　No wrinkle will fall upon thy face: thy fortunate youthfulness will remain fresh.

---

[1] Saná'í.　　　　　　[2] Literally, "loose the tongue."

Neither will the witheredness of old age come over thy countenance, nor will thy cypress-like figure be (bent) double;

Nor will the strength of youth vanish from thee, nor in thy teeth will there be decay or pain;

Nec libido et fututio et coitus maritalis adeo deficient ut feminis taedium sit propter languorem tuum.

The glory of youth will be opened to thee in such wise as the good tidings brought by 'Ukkásha opened (to him) the door (of Paradise).

[*The saying of the Prophet, on whom be peace, " Whosoever shall bring me the glad news of the expiration of (the month) Ṣafar, I will give him the glad news of (his being destined to enter) Paradise.*"]

The decease of Aḥmad (Mohammed), (the prophet) of the 2585 last (epoch of) time, will indisputably occur in (the month of) the First Rabí'.

When his heart shall gain knowledge of this moment of decease, he will become intellectually in love with that moment,

And when (the month) Ṣafar comes, he will rejoice on account of Ṣafar, saying, 'After this month I will make the journey.'"

From this longing for (the Divine) guidance he (Mohammed) was crying, every night till daybreak, "O most High Companion on the Way!"

He said, "Any person who gives me the good news, when Ṣafar steps forth from this world,

That Ṣafar is past and that the month of Rabí' is come—for 2590 him I will be a bearer of good news and an intercessor."

'Ukkásha said, "Ṣafar is past and gone." He (Mohammed) said, "O mighty lion (valiant hero), Paradise is thine."

Some one else came, saying, "Ṣafar is past." He (Mohammed) said, "'Ukkásha has borne away the fruit (has gained the reward) for the good news."

Men, therefore, rejoice in the world's departing (from them), while these children rejoice in its abiding (with them).

Inasmuch as the blind bird did not see the sweet water, the briny water seems to it (like) Kawthar.

Thus was Moses enumerating the (gifts of) grace, saying, 2595 "The pure (liquor) of thy fortune will not be turned into dregs."

He (Pharaoh) said, "Thou hast done well and spoken well, but (give me time) that I may take counsel with (my) good friend."

How Pharaoh took counsel with Ésiya (Ásiya) as to believing in Moses, on whom be peace.

He related these words (of Moses) to Ésiya. She said, "Offer up thy soul to this[1], O black-hearted one,

---

[1] Literally, "strew thy soul (as an offering) upon this."

At the back of[1] this speech (of Moses) are many (Divine) favours: enjoy (them) quickly, O virtuous king!

The hour of sowing is come: bravo, (what) a profitable sowing!" She said this and wept and became hot (in urging him).

2600   She sprang up from her place and said, "Blessed art thou! A sun has become a tiara for thee, O poor bald man.

A cap in sooth covers the defect of the baldpate, especially when the cap is the sun and moon.

In that very chamber where thou heardest this (speech), how didst not thou say 'Yes' and (utter) a hundred expressions of praise?

If these words (of Moses) had entered into the ear of the sun, it (the sun) would have come down headlong in hope of this.

Dost thou understand at all what the promise is and what the gift is? God is showing solicitude for Iblís.

2605   When that gracious One called thee back so kindly, oh, 'tis a wonder how thy heart remained unmoved[2],

(And how) thy heart[3] was not burst, so that, by means of that (burst) heart[3] of thine, there might accrue to thee the portion (of felicity) in the two worlds.

The heart[3] that is burst for the sake of God's portion eats fruit from (enjoys felicity in) the two worlds, as the martyrs (do).

True, (this) heedlessness and this blindness is (a manifestation of) Divine Wisdom, in order that he (the heedless man) may endure; but why (be heedless) to such an extent as this?

True, heedlessness is (a manifestation of) Divine Wisdom and Bounty, in order that (his) stock-in-trade may not suddenly fly out of (his) hand;

2610   But not (heedlessness) so great that it becomes an incurable sore and a poison to the spirit and intellect of one who is sick.

Who, really, can find bazaars like this where with a single rose thou art buying (whole) roseries;

(Where) a hundred groves come (are offered) to thee in exchange for one seed, a hundred mines in exchange for one groat?

Kána lilláh is the giving of that groat, in order that *kána 'lláh lahú* may come into (thy) hand[4];

For this weak unstable *hú* (personality) was brought into being by the steadfast (permanent) *hú* of the Lord.

2615   When the *hú* that passes away has surrendered itself to Him, it becomes everlasting and never dies.

---

[1] *I.e.* "hidden beneath."
[2] Literally, "thy gall-bladder remained in its place."
[3] Literally, "gall-bladder."
[4] The Prophet is reported to have said, *Man kána lilláhi kána 'lláhu lahú,* "Whoso belongs (devotes himself) to God, God shall belong to him."

('Tis) like a drop of water (which is) afraid of wind (air) and earth; for by means of these twain it is made to pass away (and perish.

When it has leaped (thrown itself) into the sea, which was its source, it is delivered from the heat of the sun and from wind and earth.

Its outward form has disappeared in the sea, but its essence is inviolate and permanent and goodly.

Hark, O (thou who art like a) drop, give thyself up without repenting, that in recompense for the drop thou mayst gain the Ocean.

Hark, O drop, bestow on thyself this honour, and in the hand 2620 of the Sea become safe from destruction.

Whom indeed should fortune like this befall[1]? A Sea has become the suitor for a drop.

In God's name, in God's name, sell and buy at once! Give a drop, and take (in return) the Sea which is full of pearls.

In God's name, in God's name, do not make any postponement, for these words (of Moses) come from the Sea of Grace.

(All other) grace is lost (vanishes away) in (comparison with) this grace, that one of the lowest is going up to the Seventh Heaven.

Hark, for a marvellous falcon has fallen to thee: no seeker will 2625 find it in (his) search."

He (Pharaoh) said, "I will tell Hámán, O veiled (modest) one: the counsel of the vizier is necessary to the king."

She said, "Do not tell Hámán this secret: what should a blind decrepit old woman know about a falcon?"

Story of the king's falcon and the decrepit old woman[2].

(If) you give a white falcon to a decrepit old woman, she will clip its talons for the sake of (its supposed) welfare.

The blind old woman will blindly clip the talons which are the source of its usefulness in the chase[3],

Saying, "Where has thy mother been, that thy talons are so[4] 2630 long, O prince?"

She clipped its talons and beak and wings: the filthy old hag does this at the time of (at the time when she is moved by) affection.

When she gives it tutmáj[5], it will not eat; (then) she is enraged and tears up her feelings of affection,

---

[1] Literally, "come to hand."
[2] See Book II, v. 323 foll.
[3] Literally, "the foundation of the work (for which it is designed) and of the hunting (in which it is employed)."
[4] Literally, "in this fashion."
[5] A stew made of meat and pastry.

Saying, "I have cooked such (fine) *tutmáj* for thee, and thou art showing pride and insolence.

Thou deservest to be in that trouble and affliction: how should happiness and prosperity be suitable for thee?"

2635 She gives it the *tutmáj* broth, saying, "Take this, if thou dost not wish to eat of the pastry."

The falcon's nature does not accept (rejects) *tutmáj* broth: the old woman frowns, and her anger is prolonged.

In her rage the woman pours down the burning hot soup on its head: the crown of its head is made bald.

On account of the burning pain the tears pour down from its eye: it remembers the kindness of the heart-delighting king.

(Tears pour) from those two charming coquettish eyes, which possess a hundred perfections (derived) from the countenance of the king.

2640 Its eye that *turned not aside* (*má zágh*) has become full of wounds inflicted by the crow (*zágh*): the good eye is (smitten) with pain and anguish by the evil eye.

(It hath) an eye with the (vast) range of the sea, (an eye) from the (immense) range whereof both the worlds appear (no bigger than) a thread of hair.

If thousands of spheres should enter into its eye, they would vanish like a fountain before the ocean.

The eye that has passed beyond these objects of sense-perception and won kisses from vision of the Unseen—

Verily, I do not find a single ear to which I should tell a mystery[1] concerning that beauteous eye.

2645 (If) the lauded and august water were to trickle (from that eye), Gabriel would (eagerly) carry off its drops,

That he might rub them on his wings and beak, if that person of goodly practice[2] give him permission.

The falcon says, "If the anger of the old crone has blazed forth, (yet) it has not consumed my glory and splendour and self-denial and knowledge.

The falcon, (which is) my spirit, will still weave a hundred forms: the blow falls on the she-camel, not on Ṣáliḥ[3].

At a single awful breath that Ṣáliḥ heaves, the back (womb) of the mountain will bring to birth a hundred such she-camels."

2650 (My) heart is saying, "Be silent and observe discretion; otherwise, the (Divine) jealousy will end the warp and woof (of thy existence)."

His jealousy hath a hundred hidden clemencies; else in one moment it would consume a hundred worlds.

---

[1] Literally, "a subtle point."
[2] *I.e.* the Perfect Man (prophet or saint) who is the owner of the illumined eye.   [3] See Book I, v. 2516.

Kingly pride seized the place of (left no room for) admonition in him (Pharaoh), so that he wrenched his heart away from the bonds of admonition,

Saying, "I will take counsel with Hámán, for he is the support of the kingdom and the pivot of power."

The Lord's veracious witness[1] was the counsellor of Muṣṭafá (Mohammed); Bú Lahab became the counsellor of Bú Jahl.

The homogeneity rooted in his nature[2] drew him (towards 2655 Hámán) so (strongly) that those admonishments (of Ásiya) became irksome to him.

Congener flies to congener with a hundred wings and rives (all) bounds asunder in the fancy (desire) for him (who is congenial).

Story of the woman whose child crawled to the top of the water-spout and was in danger of falling; (whereupon) she besought help of 'Alí Murtaḍá, may God ennoble his person.

A woman came to Murtaḍá ('Alí) and said, "A child belonging to me has gone up on to the water-spout.

If I call it, it will not come to my hands; and if I leave it, I am afraid it will fall to the ground.

It is not intelligent, that it should apprehend, like us, if I say, 'Come to me (and escape) from the danger.'

Moreover, it does not understand signs made by the hand; or 2660 if it should understand, it will not hearken: this too is bad (useless).

Many times have I shown to it the milk and the teat, (but) it always turns its eyes and face away from me.

For God's sake—(since) ye, O noble ones, are those who give succour in this world and that (other) world—

Quickly apply the remedy, for my heart is trembling lest I be torn painfully from the fruit of my heart."

He ('Alí) said, "Take another child up to the roof, in order that the boy may see his congener,

And come nimbly from the water-spout to his congener: con- 2665 gener is ever in love with congener."

The woman did so, and when her child saw its congener, it turned its face towards it with delight

And came from the ridge of the water-spout to the roof: know that a congener attracts every congener.

The child came crawling along to the (other) child: it was saved from falling to (the ground) below.

The prophets are of humankind for this reason, that they (humankind), through the homogeneity (of the prophets with them), may be saved from the water-spout.

---

[1] Abú Bakr.
[2] Literally, "the root (innate disposition) of homogeneity."

2670 Therefore he (the Prophet) called himself *a man like you*, that ye might come to your congener and might not become lost;

For homogeneity is a wondrous attractor: wheresoever there is a seeker, his congener is attracting him.

Jesus and Idrís ascended to heaven, since they were homogeneous with the angels.

Again, Hárút and Márút were homogeneous with the body: hence they descended from on high.

The infidels have become homogeneous with Satan: their spirits have become disciples of the devils.

2675 They have learned a hundred thousand evil dispositions; they have sewn up the eyes of intellect and heart.

Their least ugly disposition is envy—that envy which smote the neck of (destroyed) Iblís.

From those curs[1] they have learned hatred and envy, for he (Satan) does not wish the kingdom everlasting (to be granted) to (God's) creatures.

When he sees, on left or right, any one perfect, colic comes to him and pain arises (in him) from envy,

Because every miserable wretch whose stack has been burnt is unwilling that any one's candle should be lighted.

2680 Hark, bring to hand (acquire) some (degree of) perfection, in order that thou too mayst not be aggrieved by the perfection of others.

Beg of God the removal of this envy, that God may deliver thee from the body,

And bestow on thee an inward occupation, from which thou wilt not become disengaged (so as to turn thy attention) outwards.

God gives to a draught of wine such (potency) that one intoxicated with it escapes from the two worlds.

He hath endowed[2] *hashísh* with the property that, for a time, it delivers him (who eats it) from self-consciousness.

2685 God makes sleep to be (constituted) in such a manner that it erases (all) thought of the two worlds.

He made Majnún, through love for a (dog's) skin[3], to be such that he would not know an enemy from a friend.

He hath a hundred thousand wines of this sort which He sets (in authority) over thy (intellectual) perceptions.

For the carnal soul there are the wines of damnation, which carry that ill-starred one out of the (right) way.

For the intellect there are the wines of felicity, so that it gains the abode whence is no departure.

---

[1] *I.e.* the devils.
[2] Literally, "hath put in the hand of *hashísh* the property."
[3] *I.e.* Laylá's dog. See Book III, *v.* 567 *sqq.*

Through its intoxication it uproots the tent of the sky and 2690
takes the way (leading) onward from that (earthly) direction.

Hark, be not deceived, O heart, by every intoxication: Jesus
is intoxicated with God, the ass is intoxicated with barley.

Seek wine like this from these jars: the intoxication (produced)
by it is not (to be obtained) from the bobtailed[1];

For every object of love is like a full jar, one (full of) dregs,
and another pure as pearls.

O connoisseur of wine, beware, taste with precaution, that
thou mayst find a wine free from adulteration.

Both (jars) will intoxicate thee, but this (blessed) intoxication, 2695
drawing (thee along), will lead thee to the Lord of the Judge-
ment,

So that thou wilt be delivered from thought and anxiety and
expedients, (whilst) this intellect (moves) unshackled at the
camel's ambling pace.

Since the prophets are homogeneous with spirit and angel,
they drew angels from heaven.

Wind (air) is the congener and friend of fire, for the tendency
of both is upward.

When you stop the mouth of an empty pot and put it in a
tank or river,

It will not sink till the Resurrection, for its heart (interior) is 2700
void and there is (nothing but) wind (air) in it.

Since the desire of the wind (confined) in it is (to move) up-
ward, it draws upward also the vessel containing it.

Again, the spirits that are homogeneous with the prophets are
moving gradually, like shadows, towards them,

Because its (such a spirit's) intelligence is predominant; and
beyond doubt the intelligence is homogeneous in nature with
the angel;

While in the enemy (of God) the carnal soul's concupiscence
is predominant: the carnal soul is homogeneous with the lowest
(of the low) and goes to it.

The Egyptian was a congener of the reprobate Pharaoh; the 2705
Israelite was a congener of Moses, the Kalím[2].

Hámán was more congenial (than any one else) to Pharaoh:
he (Pharaoh) chose him out and brought him to the high-seat in
the palace.

Inevitably he (Hámán) dragged him (Pharaoh) from the high-
seat to the lowest depth, for those two unclean ones are homo-
geneous with Hell.

Both, like Hell, are burning and contrary to light: both, like
Hell, are exceedingly averse to the light of the heart;

---

[1] *I.e.* "seek the wine of felicity from the blessed saints in whom it is
stored; not from those devoid of blessedness."
[2] *I.e.* "him to whom God spoke."

For Hell says, "O true believer, pass by quickly, since thy light hath taken away (extinguished) the Fire.

2710   Pass, O true believer, for thy light, when it sweeps by[1], quenches my fire."

The man destined for Hell, also, is recoiling from the light, because he hath the nature of Hell, O worshipful one.

Hell flees from the true believer just as the true believer flees with (all) his soul from Hell,

Because his light is not homogeneous with the Fire: the seeker of the light is in reality the contrary of the Fire.

It is related in the *Ḥadíth* that when the true believer prays to God[2] for protection from Hell,

2715   Hell also begs earnestly[3] for protection from him, saying, "O God, keep me far from such-and-such a one!"

'Tis the attracting power of homogeneity (that indicates one's real nature): consider now with whom thou art congenial in respect of infidelity or true religion.

If thou art inclined towards Hámán, thou hast the nature of Hámán; and if thou art inclined towards Moses, thou art a glorifier of God.

And if thou art inclined and impelled towards both, thou art carnal soul and reason, both mingled together.

Both (these) are at war: take heed, take heed, and strive that the spiritual realities may prevail over the (sensuous) forms.

2720   In the world of war 'tis joy enough that thou shouldst always see defeat (inflicted) on the enemy.

Finally that quarrelsome-looking (contumacious) man (Pharaoh) in his hardness (of heart) told Hámán, for the purpose of consultation.

He told (him) the promises of the one (Moses) with whom God spoke, and made that misguided person his confidant.

How Pharaoh took counsel with his vizier, Hámán,
as to believing in Moses, on whom be peace.

He told Hámán when he saw him alone: Hámán sprang up and rent the bosom of his shirt.

That accursed one uttered loud cries and sobs and beat his turban and cap on the ground,

2725   Saying, "How durst he say those vain words so impudently in the face of the king?

Thou hast made the whole world subject (to thy sway); thou, (attended) by fortune, hast made thy estate (brilliant) as gold.

From all parts of the East and West sultans, without (raising) opposition, bring tribute to thee.

---

[1] Literally, "trails its skirt."
[2] Literally, "begs God in prayer."
[3] Literally, "with (all) its soul."

Kings are rubbing their lips joyfully on the dust of thy threshold, O mighty emperor.

When the enemy's horse sees our horse, it turns its face and flees without flogging[1].

Hitherto thou hast been worshipped and adored by the (whole) 2730 world: (now) thou wilt become the meanest of slaves.

To go into a thousand fires is better than this, that a lord should become the servant of a slave.

Nay, kill me first, O king of China, that mine eye may not behold this (servility) in the king.

O emperor, behead me first, that mine eye may not behold this ignominy.

Truly never has there been—and never may there be!—such a thing as this, that the earth should become the sky, and the sky become the earth;

(That) our slaves should become our fellow-servants, (and 2735 that) our timorous ones should become those who (cruelly) wound our hearts;

(That our) enemies (should be) bright-eyed and (our) friends blind: then (in that case) the rose-garden has become for us (like) the bottom of the tomb."

Showing the falsity of Hámán's speech— the curse (of God) be upon him!

He did not know friend from enemy: he was playing backgammon (all) wrong, like a blind man.

Thy enemy is none but thyself, O accursed one: do not despitefully call the innocent (thy) enemies.

In thy sight this evil state (in which thou art) is *dawlat* (worldly fortune), whereof the beginning is *dawádaw* (running to and fro) and the end *lat* (blows).

If by degrees[2] thou do not run away from this worldly 2740 fortune, autumn will come o'er this spring of thine.

East and West have seen many like thee, whose heads have been severed from their bodies.

After all, how should East and West, which are not permanent, make any one enduring?

Thou takest pride in the fact that men, from fear and bondage, have become thy flatterers for a few days.

When men bow in adoration to any one, they are (really) cramming poison into his soul.

When his adorer turns away from him, he knows that that 2745 (adoration) was poisonous and destructive to him.

---

[1] Literally, "without the stick," *i.e.* it needs no inducement to make haste.
[2] Literally, "creeping, creeping."

Oh, blest is he whose carnal soul was abased! Alas for him who became like a mountain from arrogance!

Know that this pride is a killing poison: that fool was intoxicated by the poisonous wine.

When an unhappy wretch drinks the poisonous wine, he nods his head in delight for one moment.

After one moment the poison falls on his spirit: the poison exercises (complete) sway[1] over his spirit.

2750 If you have not firm belief in its being poisonous (and do not know) what (a deadly) poison it is, look at the people of 'Ád.

When one king gains the upper hand (prevails) over another king, he kills him or confines him in a dungeon;

But if he find a fallen wounded man, the king will make a plaster for him and bestow gifts on him.

If that pride is not poison, then why did he kill the (vanquished) king without (his having committed any) crime or offence?

And how did he treat this other (helpless) man (so) kindly without (his having performed any) service? From these two actions you may recognise (the poisonous nature of) pride.

2755 No highwayman ever attacked a beggar: does a wolf ever bite a dead wolf?

Khiẓr made a breach in the boat[2] in order that the boat might be saved from the wicked.

Since the broken (contrite) one will be saved, be thou broken (contrite). Safety lies in poverty: enter into poverty.

The mountain that possessed some cash in its mine was riven to pieces by the strokes of the pick-axe.

The sword is for him who has a (high and proud) neck; no blow falls on the shadow that is thrown (flat upon the ground).

2760 Eminence is naphtha and fire, O misguided one: O brother, how (why) art thou going into the fire?

How should anything that is level with the earth become a target for arrows? Consider!

(But if) it raise its head from the earth, then, like targets, it will suffer blows irremediable.

This egoism is the ladder of (climbed by) the creatures (of God): they must fall from this ladder in the end.

The higher any one goes, the more foolish he is, for his bones will be worse broken.

2765 This is (constitutes) the derivatives (of the subject), and its fundamental principles are that to exalt one's self is (to claim) copartnership with God.

Unless thou hast died and become living through Him, thou art an enemy seeking to reign in copartnership (with Him).

---

[1] Literally, "giving and taking."   [2] Qur'án, XVIII, 70.

When thou hast become living through Him, that (which thou hast become) is in sooth He: it is absolute Unity; how is it co-partnership?

Seek the explanation of this in the mirror of (devotional) works, for thou wilt not gain the understanding of it from speech and discourse.

If I tell that which I have within, many hearts will immediately be turned into blood.

I will refrain; indeed, for the intelligent this (which has been 2770 said) is enough: I have shouted twice, if any one is in the village[1].

To sum up, Hámán by means of those evil words waylaid Pharaoh in such a (terrible) way as this.

The morsel, felicity, had reached his (Pharaoh's) mouth, (when) he (Hámán) suddenly cut his throat.

He gave Pharaoh's stack to the wind (destroyed him): may no king have such a minister!

How Moses, on whom be peace, despaired of Pharaoh's accepting the true faith, because the words of Hámán made an impression on Pharaoh's heart.

Moses said, "We have shown kindness and generosity, (but) verily it was not the portion allotted to thy dominion[2].

The dominion that is not righteous—regard it as having 2775 neither hand nor sleeve[3].

The dominion that is stolen (usurped) is without heart and without soul and without eye.

The dominion which the vulgar have given to thee they will take back from thee as a debt.

Give up to God the dominion held on loan, that He may bestow on thee the dominion to which all consent."

How the Amírs of the Arabs wrangled with Muṣṭafá (Mohammed), on whom be peace, saying, "Share the kingdom with us, in order that there may be no contention"; and how Muṣṭafá, on whom be peace, answered and said, "I am commanded (by God) in respect of this Amírate"; and the arguments on both sides.

The Amírs of the Arabs assembled and began to wrangle in the Prophet's presence,

Saying, "Thou art an Amír; every one of us is an Amír like- 2780 wise: distribute this kingdom and take thy share.

---

[1] *I.e.* "I have given sufficient instruction if there is any one capable of receiving it."

[2] *I.e.* "thou wert not destined to accept my kindness and thereby gain the kingdom everlasting."

[3] *I.e.* it has no real power, either inwardly or outwardly. For "hand" and "sleeve" see Book II, v. 3253.

Each (of us) is seeking equity in regard to his share: do thou wash thy hands of our share."

He replied, "God hath given the Amírate to me: He hath given me the chief authority and the absolute command,

Saying, 'This is the epoch and cycle of Ahmad (Mohammed): hark, accept his command! *Have fear (of God)!*'"

The party (of Amírs) said to him, "We too are (made) rulers by that (Divine) destiny, and God hath given the Amírate to us."

2785 He said, "(Yes), but to me God gave it as a possession, and to you (only) as a loan for the sake of (furnishing you with) provisions for the road.

My Amírate is lasting till the Resurrection; the Amírate held on loan will be shattered."

The (opposing) party said, "O Amír, do not say too much (about this): what is thy argument for seeking more (than thy share)?"

Forthwith, by the bitter command (of God), a cloud arose; (then) came the torrent: the countryside was filled (with the flood).

The exceedingly frightful torrent set its face towards the town: the townsfolk (were) making loud lamentation, all (were) terrified.

2790 The Prophet said, "Now the time is come for the test, in order that opinion may become ocular vision."

Each Amír flung his lance (into the flood), that in the test it might become a barrier against the torrent.

Then Muṣṭafá (Mohammed) cast his wand upon it—that sovereign wand that reduced (his foes) to helplessness.

The rapid water of the boiling tameless torrent swept away the lances like a bit of straw.

All the lances disappeared, while that wand stood on the surface of the water like a sentry.

2795 From anxious regard for that wand the mighty torrent turned its face away, and the flood-water departed.

When they beheld that great matter wrought by him, those Amírs, (overcome) by dread, confessed—

Save three persons, whose rancour was prevailing: they, from disbelief, called him a magician and soothsayer.

The kingship that has been tied on (artificially) is weak like that; the kingship that has grown up (naturally) is august like this.

If thou didst not see the lances together with the wand, (yet) consider the names of them (the Amírs) and consider the name of him (Mohammed), O noble one!

2800 Their names the rapid torrent of death has borne away; his name and his puissant fortune are not dead.

For him the drum is always beaten five times (daily): on this wise every day till the Day of Resurrection.

"If thou hast intelligence, (thou wilt see that) I have done kindnesses; and if thou art an ass, I have brought the rod for the ass[1].

I will turn thee out of this stable in such wise that I will make thy ears and head bloody with (blows of) the rod.

In this stable asses and men are getting no quarter from thy oppression.

Lo, I have brought the rod, for correction's sake, for every ass 2805 that is not approved.

It will become a dragon in subduing thee, for thou hast become a dragon in (thy) deeds and disposition.

Thou art a mountain-dragon without mercy; but look at the dragon of Heaven!

This rod comes as a taste (sample) from Hell, saying, 'Ho! take refuge in the Light;

Else thou wilt be left helpless in my teeth: there will be no escape for thee through my passes.'

This was a rod; it is now a dragon, to the end that thou mayst 2810 not say, 'Where is God's Hell?'"

Explaining that one who knows the power of God will not ask, "Where are Paradise and Hell?"

God makes Hell to be wheresoever He will: He makes the zenith to be a snare and trap for the bird.

Likewise from thy teeth arise pangs of pain, to the end that thou mayst say, "'Tis Hell and the dragon."

Or He makes the water of thy mouth to be (sweet as) honey, that thou mayst say, "'Tis Paradise and the robes (of Paradise)."

He makes sugar to grow from the roots of the teeth, that thou mayst know the power of the ordinance of the (Divine) decree.

Do not, then, bite the innocent with thy teeth: bethink thee 2815 of the stroke that is not to be guarded against.

God makes the Nile to be blood for the Egyptians; He makes the Israelites safe from calamity,

That thou mayst know that with God there is discrimination between the sober (traveller) on the Way and the intoxicated.

The Nile has learned from God to discriminate, for it opened (the door) for these (Israelites) and shut fast (the door) against those (Egyptians).

His grace makes the Nile intelligent; His wrath makes Cain foolish.

He, from kindness, created intelligence in lifeless things; He, 2820 because of His wrath, cut off intelligence from the intelligent one.

[1] This and the following verses are addressed by Moses to Pharaoh.

By (His) grace an intelligence appeared in lifeless matter, and through (His) chastisement knowledge fled from the intelligent.

There, by (His) command the rain-like intelligence poured down; here, intelligence saw God's anger and took to flight.

Clouds and sun and moon and lofty stars, all come and go according to arrangement.

None comes but at its appointed hour, so that it neither lags behind the time nor (arrives) before.

2825 How hast not thou understood this from the prophets? They brought knowledge into stone and rod,

That thou, (judging) by analogy, might'st undoubtingly deem the other lifeless things to be like rod and stone (in this respect).

The obedience (to God) of stone and rod is made manifest and gives information concerning the other lifeless things,

That (they say), "We are cognisant of God and obedient (to Him): we all are (bearing witness to His wisdom) not by chance and in vain.

As (for example) the water of the Nile: thou knowest that at the time of drowning it made a distinction between the two peoples;

2830 (And) as the earth: thou knowest it to be possessed of knowledge, at the time of (its) sinking, in regard to Qárún whom He subdued and swept away;

(And) as the moon, which heard the (Divine) command and hastened (to obey) and then became two halves in the sky and split;

(And) as the trees and stones which everywhere overtly made the salaam to Muṣṭafá (Mohammed).

Reply to the materialist who disbelieves in the Deity and says that the world is eternal.

Yesterday some one was saying, "The world is originated in time: this heaven is passing away, and God is its inheritor."

A philosopher said, "How do you know (its) temporal origin? How should the rain know the temporality of the cloud?

2835 You are not even a mote of the (celestial) revolution: how should you know the temporality of the sun?

The little worm that is buried in filth—how should it know the end and beginning of the earth?

You have heard this by rote from your father: through foolishness you have become involved in this (belief).

What is the demonstrative argument for its temporality? Tell (me) or else keep silence and do not seek (indulge in) excessive talk."

He said, "One day I saw two parties searching in this deep sea,

(Engaged) in disputation and controversy and desperate 2840
battle: a crowd gathered round those two persons.

I went towards the crowded multitude and took notice of
their (the disputants') affair.

One was saying, 'The sky will pass away: without any doubt,
this edifice hath a builder.'

The other said, 'It is eternal and timeless[1]: it hath no builder,
or else it is (itself) the builder.'

He (his adversary) said, 'You have denied the Creator, the
Producer of day and night and the Giver of sustenance.'

He (the philosopher) said, 'Without clear evidence, I will not 2845
listen to that which an ignoramus has accepted by rote.

Come, bring the proof and evidence, for never in the world
will I hearken to this without proof.'

'The proof,' he replied, 'is within my soul: my evidence is
hidden within my soul.

You, from weakness of eye, are not seeing the new moon: (if)
I am seeing it, do not you be angry with me.'

There was much debate, and the people became perplexed as
to the beginning and end of this well-ordered celestial sphere.

He (the pious man) said, 'Friend, within me is a (decisive) 2850
proof: I have a (manifest) sign indicating the temporal origin of
the sky.

I possess the certainty: for him that hath certain knowledge
the token thereof is that he will go into the fire.

Like the inmost feelings of love in lovers, that proof, (you
must) know, does not come (to utterance) on the tongue.

The inmost meaning of my words is not apparent, except (in)
the pallor and haggardness of my face.

Tears and blood roll on my cheeks and become the proof of
His (the Beloved's) comeliness and beauty.'

He (the philosopher) replied, 'I do not deem these things to 2855
be such a proof as would be a manifest sign to the vulgar.'

He (the other) said, 'When a base and a genuine coin
boast, saying (to each other), "Thou art base; I am good and
valuable,"

Fire is the final test: (the test is) that these two rivals should
be dropped into the fire.

(Then) the vulgar and the elect will become acquainted with
their (real) state and will advance from opinion and doubt to
certain knowledge.

Water and fire, O (dear) soul, are the test for the pure and the
base coin that is hidden.

Let me and thee, both of us, go into the fire and become a 2860
lasting proof for the perplexed.

---

[1] Literally, "without 'when?'" *i.e.* the question "When did it come into
existence?" is inadmissible.

Let me and thee, both of us, fall into the sea, for thou and I are a sign unto this multitude.'

Even so they did and entered the fire: both cast themselves upon the heat of the fire.

The God-proclaiming man who engaged in controversy was saved, while that bastard (impostor) was burnt in the fire.

Hear from the muezzin this announcement, to the confusion of the foolish transgressors,

2865   That this name (Mohammed) has not been burnt (destroyed) by Death, since its bearer was a prince and most noble.

In the course of time hundreds of thousands of the veils of the unbelievers have been rent by this laying down of stakes.

When they (the devout men and the philosopher) made the wager, the truth prevailed as regards immortality and evidentiary miracles and the answer (given to unbelievers).

I perceived that he who spoke (in support) of the priority (of non-existence) and of the temporal origin of the celestial sphere was victorious and in the right."

The unbeliever's argument is always shamefaced: where is a single sign that indicates the truth of that unbelief?

2870   Where in this world is (to be found) a single minaret in praise (honour) of the unbelievers, so that it should be a sign (of their veracity)?

Where is (to be found) a single pulpit where a preacher commemorates the life of an unbeliever?

The face of gold and silver coins, from (bearing) their (the prophets') names, is giving a token of this truth till the Resurrection.

The dies of the kings are ever being changed: behold the die of Aḥmad (Mohammed) till the end of the world[1].

Show (me) the name of a single unbeliever on the design (stamped) on the face of any piece of silver or gold!

2875   Even (supposing that you) do not admit (arguments), behold this Miracle, (manifest) like the sun, hundred-tongued, whereof the name is *Ummu 'l-Kitáb*[2].

None dares either steal (take away) a single letter thereof or add to the plain Word.

Become a friend to the conqueror, that thou mayst conquer: beware, do not become a friend to the vanquished, O misguided man!

The unbeliever's argument is just this, that he says, "I see no place of abode except this external (world)."

He never reflects that, wherever there is anything external, that (object) gives information of hidden wise purposes.

---

[1] Literally, "till the final and permanent place of abode."
[2] The *Qur'án*.

The usefulness of every external object is, indeed, internal: 2880
it is latent, like the beneficial quality in medicines.

Commentary on the Verse, "And We did not create the heavens
and the earth and what is between them save with real
ground": (*i.e.*) "*I did not create them for the sake of just this
which ye see; nay, but for the sake of the essential meaning and
everlasting providence which ye see not.*"

Does any painter paint a beautiful picture[1] for the sake of the
picture itself, without hope of conferring benefit?

Nay, (he paints it) for the sake of guests and young people
who by diverting themselves (with it) may be relieved from
cares.

From his picture (arises) the joy of children and the re-
membering of departed friends by their friends.

Does any potter make a pot in haste for the sake of the pot
itself and not in hope of the water?

Does any bowl-maker make a finished bowl for the sake of 2885
the bowl itself and not for the sake of the food?

Does any calligrapher write artistically for the sake of the
writing itself and not for the sake of the reading?

The external form is for the sake of the unseen form; and that
took shape for the sake of another unseen (form).

Count up these corollaries to the third, fourth, or tenth in
proportion to (your) insight.

As (for example) the moves in chess, O son: behold the result
of each move in the next one.

They made this (move) for the sake of that concealed move, 2890
and that for the next, and that (again) for such and such.

Even so (proceed), having perceived reasons within reasons,
one after the other, in order that you may arrive at victory and
checkmate.

The first is for the sake of the second, like mounting on the
steps of a ladder;

And deem the second to be for the sake of the third, (and so
on) to the end, in order that you may arrive, step by step, at the
roof.

The desire to eat is for the sake of the semen: that semen is
for the sake of procreation and the light (which glows in the eyes
of parents).

The man of dull sight sees naught but this: his intelligence is 2895
without motion, like the plants of the earth.

Whether the plant is summoned (to move) or not summoned,
its foot remains stuck fast in the mud.

[1] Literally, "the beauty of the picture."

If its head move with the motion of the wind, go, be not deceived by its moving its head.

Its head says, "We obey, O zephyr!" Its foot says, "We refuse to obey: let us alone!"

Since he (the man of dull sight) does not know how to move (on the Way to God), he advances like the vulgar, stepping (forward) on trust, like a blind man.

2900   Consider what comes of acting on trust in warfare: (it is vain) like the trust of dice-players.

But those insights that are not frozen (dense and dull) are nothing if not piercing and veil-rending.

He (such a one) sees with his own eye at the present moment that which will come to pass in ten years.

Similarly, every one sees the unseen and the future, (both) good and evil, according to the measure of his insight.

When the barrier in front and the barrier behind are removed, the eye penetrates and reads the tablet of the Unseen.

2905   When he (such a one) looks back to the origin of existence, the past circumstances and beginning of existence display themselves (to him)—

(Namely), the disputation of the terrestrial angels with the (Divine) Majesty as to making our Father (Adam) the Vicegerent.

When he casts his eye forward he sees plainly that which shall be (all that shall come to pass) till the (Last) Congregation.

Therefore he sees back to the root of the root (the primal origin), and he sees forward clairvoyantly to the Day of Decision.

Every one, according to the measure of his spiritual enlightenment, sees the things unseen in proportion to the polishing (of the heart's mirror).

2910   The more he polishes, the more he sees and the more visible does the form (of things unseen) become to him.

If you say that that (spiritual) purity is (bestowed by) the grace of God, this success in polishing (the heart) is also (derived) from that (Divine) bounty.

That (devotional) work and prayer is in proportion to the (worshipper's) aspiration: *Man hath nothing but what he hath striven after*.

God alone is the giver of aspiration: no base churl aspires to be a king.

God's assignment of a particular lot to any one does not hinder (him from exercising) consent and will and choice;

2915   But when He brings some trouble on an ill-fated man, he (that man) ungratefully packs off in flight[1];

----
[1] Literally, "causes his baggage to flee."

(Whereas), when God brings some trouble on a good-fortuned (blessed) man, he always (approaches and) abides[1] nearer (to God).

In battle the pusillanimous from fear for their lives have chosen the means (resource) of flight,

(While) the courageous, also from fear for their lives, have charged towards the ranks of the enemy.

Rustams (heroes) are borne onward by (their) fear and pain; from fear, too, the man of infirm spirit dies within himself.

Tribulation and fear for one's life are like a touchstone: there- 2920 by the brave man is distinguished from every coward.

How God made a revelation to Moses, on whom be peace, saying, "O Moses, I who am the exalted Creator love thee."

God spoke to Moses by inspiration of the heart, saying, "O chosen one, I love thee."

He (Moses) said, "O Bountiful One, (tell me) what disposition (in me) is the cause of that, in order that I may augment it."

He (God) said, "Thou art like a child in the presence of its mother: when she chastises it, it still lays hold of her.

It does not even know that there is any one in the world except her: it is both afflicted with headache (sorrow) by her and intoxicated (with joy) by her.

If its mother give it a slap, still it comes to its mother and 2925 clings to her.

It does not seek help from any one but her: she is all its evil and its good.

Thy heart, likewise, in good or evil (plight) never turns from Me to other quarters.

In thy sight all besides Me are as stones and clods, whether (they be) boys or youths or old men."

Just as *Thee we worship*[2] in yearning entreaty, (so) in tribulation *we ask help*[2] of none but Thee.

This *Thee we worship* is (used) idiomatically for the purpose 2930 of (expressing) appropriation[3], and that (appropriation) is for the purpose of negating hypocrisy.

Of Thee we ask help also is for the purpose of appropriation: he (who recites these words) appropriates and restricts the asking of help,

Meaning, "We perform worship to Thee alone; we have hope of help from Thee alone."

---

[1] Literally, "lays down his baggage."
[2] *Qur'án*, I, 4.
[3] The emphatic form *iyyáka* (Thee) denotes that the worship is appropri-_ated to God exclusively.

*How a king was enraged with his boon-companion, and an inter-
cessor interceded on behalf of the object of (the king's) anger and
begged the king (to pardon the offender); and how (when) the
king accepted his intercession, the boon-companion resented the
action of the intercessor and asked, "Why did you intercede?"*

A king was enraged with a boon-companion and was about to
reduce him to smoke and dust[1].

The king drew his sword from the scabbard that he might in-
flict upon him the punishment for that disobedience.

2935 No one had the courage to utter a word nor any intercessor
to venture on intercession,

Except one amongst the courtiers named 'Imádu 'l-Mulk,
(who was) privileged in respect of intercession, like Muṣṭafá
(Mohammed).

He sprang up and at once prostrated himself: the king im-
mediately put away from his hand the sword of vengeance,

And said, "If he is the (very) Devil, I forgive him; and if he
has done a satanic deed, I cover it up.

Since thou[2] hast intervened, I am satisfied, (even) if the
culprit has committed a hundred acts of harm.

2940 I can break (annul) a hundred thousand angers, seeing that
thou hast such excellence and such worth;

(But) nowise can I break (annul) thy supplication, because thy
supplication is assuredly my supplication.

(Even) if he had thrown earth and heaven into confusion, this
man would not have escaped from (my) vengeance;

And if (the whole world) atom by atom had become a sup-
pliant (for his release), he would not have saved his head from
the sword at this moment.

We confer no obligation on thee (by this), O noble one; but
(on the contrary) 'tis (only) to explain thy honour (the honour
in which I hold thee), O boon-companion.

2945 Thou didst not make this (intercession), for assuredly I made
it, O thou whose qualities are buried in my qualities.

In this (matter) thou art the one employed to do the work, not
the (prime) doer (of it), inasmuch as thou art borne by me and
art not (thyself) the bearer.

Thou hast become (the instrument of my action, according to
the text) *Thou didst not throw when thou threwest:* like the foam,
thou hast abandoned thyself in the wave.

Thou hast become '*not*'; (now) take up thy abode beside
'*except*[3].' This is wonderful, that thou art both a prisoner and
a prince.

[1] Literally, "raise smoke and dust from him."
[2] Literally, "thy foot."
[3] Referring to the Moslem profession of faith, "There is *not* any god
except Allah."

Thou didst not give what thou gavest: the king gave it. He alone is. God best knoweth the right course."

And the boon-companion who had been delivered from the 2950 stroke of calamity was offended with this intercessor and drew back from (his former) fealty.

He cut off all (relations of) friendship with that sincere man, and turned his face to the wall in order that he might not give (him) the salaam.

He became estranged from his intercessor; in astonishment at this the people began to talk,

Saying, "(If) he is not mad, how did he cut off friendly relations with the person who redeemed his life?

He (the intercessor) redeemed (saved) him from beheading at that moment: he (the culprit) ought to have become the dust of his (the intercessor's) shoe.

He has gone the reverse way and has taken (the course of) re- 2955 nouncing (his friend): he has taken to cherishing enmity against a beloved like this."

Then a certain mentor reproached him, saying, "Why are you acting so unjustly towards a loyal friend?

That elect beloved redeemed your life and saved you from beheading at that moment.

If he had done evil (towards you), you ought not to have turned away (from him; but) that praiseworthy friend was especially your benefactor."

He replied, "Life is freely given for the king's sake: why should he come as an intercessor between (us)?

At that moment mine was (the state described by the words) 2960 —'I am with God in a state wherein no chosen prophet is my peer[1].'

I desire no mercy but the blows of the king; I desire no refuge except that king.

I have naughted all besides the king for the reason that I have devoted myself to the king.

The king, if he behead me in his wrath, will bestow on me sixty other lives.

'Tis my business to hazard (and lose) my head and to be selfless; 'tis the business of my sovereign king to give (me) a (new) head."

Honour to the head that is severed by the King's hand! Shame 2965 on the head that betakes itself to another!

The night which the King in his wrath covered with pitch (pitchy darkness) holds in disdain a thousand days of festival.

Verily, the circumambulation performed by him who beholds the King is above wrath and grace and infidelity and religion.

---

[1] This is a well-known *Ḥadīth* of the Prophet.

Not one word (capable of) expressing it has (ever) come into the world, for it is hidden, hidden, hidden,

Inasmuch as these glorious names and words were manifested from the reel (uttered from the mouth) of Adam.

2970 *He (God) taught (him) the names* was an Imám (an infallible authority) for Adam; but (the teaching was) not in the garb of (letters such as) *'ayn* and *lám*.

When he put on his head the cap of water and clay, those spiritual names became black-faced,

For they assumed the veil of letters and breath, (only) in order that the essential reality might (gradually) be made manifest to the water and clay.

Although from one point of view speech is a revealer, yet from ten points of view it is a curtain and concealer.

How Khalíl (Abraham) answered Gabriel, on both of whom be peace, when he asked him, "Hast thou any need?"—"As regards need of thee, no!"

"I am the Khalíl (Abraham) of the present time[1], and he is the Gabriel: I do not want him as a guide (to deliver me) in calamity.

2975 He did not learn respectfulness (as he might) from noble Gabriel, who asked the Friend of God (Abraham) what was his wish,

Saying, 'Hast thou a wish?—that I may help (thee to obtain it); otherwise, I will flee and make a speedy departure.'

Abraham said, 'No; begone out of the way! After direct vision the intermediary is (only) an inconvenience.'

On account of this present life the (Divine) messenger is a link for the true believers, because he is the intermediary (between them and God).

If every heart were hearing the hidden (Divine) revelation, how should there be in the world any words and sounds (to make it known)?

2980 Though he (the intercessor) is lost in God and headless (devoid of self-existence), yet my case is more delicate than that.

His act is the act of the king, but to my infirmity the good (which he did) appears to be evil."

That which is the very essence of grace to the vulgar becomes wrath to the noble favourites (of God).

Much tribulation and pain must the vulgar endure in order that they may be able to perceive the difference;

For, O (my) companion in the Cave[2], these intermediary words are, in the sight of one united (with God), thorns, thorns, thorns.

---

[1] *I.e.* "in the present case."
[2] *I.e.* "my sincere friend." The title was given to Abú Bakr, who passed three nights with the Prophet in a cave south of Mecca, when the Quraysh were pursuing him.

Much tribulation and pain and waiting were needed in order 2985
that that pure spirit might be delivered from the (intermediary)
words:

But some (persons) have become more deaf (than others) to
this echo; some, again, have become purified and have mounted
higher.

This tribulation is like the water of the Nile: it is water to the
blessed and blood to the damned.

The more one descries the end, the more blessed is he: the
greater one sees the crop (to be), the more zealously he sows,

Because he knows that this world of sowing is for the sake of
the (Last) Congregation and (for the sake of) gathering in (the
harvest).

No contract (of sale) was (ever made) for the sake of itself; 2990
nay, but for the sake of (being in) the position of (making) gain
and profit.

There is no disbeliever, if you look (carefully), whose disbelief
is for the sake of the disbelief itself;

Nay, but (it is) for the purpose of subduing his adversary in
envy (of him), or seeking superiority and self-display.

And that superiority too is for the sake of some other desire:
the forms give no relish without the essential meanings.

You ask "Why art thou doing this?" because the forms are (as)
the oil, and the essential meaning is (as) the light.

Otherwise, wherefore is this saying "why"?—since (hypo- 2995
thetically) the form is for the sake of the form itself.

This saying "why" is a question concerning the use (reason):
it is bad to say "why" for any cause but this.

Wherefore, O trusty one, should you desire (to know) the use
(reason)?—since (hypothetically) the use of this (form) is only
this (form itself).

Hence it is not (in accordance with) wisdom that the forms of
heaven and (those of) the people of the earth should be (created)
for this only.

If there is no Wise (Creator), what is (the reason of) this
orderly arrangement (the cosmos)? And if there is a Wise
(Creator), how is His action devoid (of meaning)?

No one makes pictures and colouring in a bath-house except 3000
for (some) purpose (either) right or wrong.

*How Moses, on whom be peace, besought the Lord, saying, " Thou
didst create creatures and destroy them," and how the answer
came.*

Moses said, "O Lord of the Reckoning, Thou didst create
the form: how didst Thou destroy it again?

Thou hast made the form, male and female, that gives unto
the spirit increase (of joy), and then Thou dost ruin it: why?"

God said, "I know that this question of thine is not from disbelief and heedlessness and idle fancy;

Else I should have corrected and chastised thee: I should have afflicted thee on account of this question.

3005 But (I know that) thou wishest to discover in My actions the wisdom and hidden meaning of (phenomenal) duration,

That thou mayst acquaint the vulgar therewith and by this means make every raw (ignorant) person to become cooked.

Thou hast become a questioner on purpose to disclose[1] (this matter) to the vulgar, albeit thou art acquainted with it;

For this questioning is the half of knowledge, and this ability (to ask questions) does not belong to every outsider."

Both question and answer arise from knowledge, just as the thorn and the rose from earth and water.

3010 Both perdition and salvation arise from knowledge, just as bitter and sweet (fruit) from moisture.

This hatred and love arise from acquaintance, and from wholesome food (arise both) sickness and (bodily) powers.

That Kalím (Moses) became (like) an ignorant enquirer in order that he might make the ignorant acquainted with this mystery.

Let us too feign ourselves to be ignorant thereof and elicit the answer to it (to the question) as (if we were) strangers (seeking information).

(Similarly) the ass-sellers became rivals to one another in order that they might open the way to[2] the contract (of sale).

3015 Then God spake unto him, saying, "O thou who possessest the most excellent (understanding), since thou hast asked (the question), come, hear the answer.

O Moses, sow some seed in the earth, that thou thyself mayst render justice to this (question)."

When Moses had sown and the seed-corn was complete (in growth) and its ears had gained beauty and symmetry,

He took the sickle and was cutting that (crop); then a voice from the Unseen reached his ear,

Crying, "Why dost thou sow and tend some seed-corn and (now) art cutting it when it has attained to perfection?"

3020 He replied, "O Lord, I destroy and lay it low because straw is here and (also) grain.

The grain is not suitable (to be stored) in the straw-barn; the straw likewise is bad (for putting) in the corn-barn.

'Tis not wisdom to mix these twain: it (wisdom) makes necessary the separation (of them) in winnowing."

He (God) said, "From whom didst thou gain this knowledge, so that by means of the knowledge thou didst construct a threshing-floor?"

---

[1] Literally, "thou hast purposely become a questioner in disclosing."
[2] Literally, "become the key to the lock of."

He replied, "Thou, O God, gavest me discernment." He (God) said, "Then how should I not have discernment?"

Amongst the created beings are pure spirits; there are (also) 3025 spirits dark and muddy.

These shells are not in one grade: in one (of them) is the pearl and in another the (worthless) bead.

It is necessary to make manifest (the difference between) this good and evil, just as (it is necessary) to make manifest (distinguish) the wheat from the straw.

(The creation of) these creatures of the world is for the purpose of manifestation, to the·end that the treasure of (Divine) providences may not remain hidden.

He (God) said, "I was a hidden treasure": hearken! Do not let thy (spiritual) substance be lost: become manifest!

Explaining that the animal spirit and the particular (discursive) reason and the imagination and the fancy may be compared to buttermilk, while the spirit, which is everlasting, is hidden in this buttermilk, like the butter.

Thy true substance is concealed in falsehood, like the taste of 3030 butter in the taste of buttermilk.

Thy falsehood is this perishable body; thy truth is that lordly spirit.

(During many) years this buttermilk, (which is) the body, is visible and manifest, (while) the butter, (which is) the spirit, is perishing and naughted within it,

Till God send a messenger (prophet), a (chosen) servant, a shaker of the buttermilk in the churn,

That he may shake (it) with method and skill, to the end that I may know that (my true) ego was hidden;

Or (till) the speech of a (chosen) servant[1], which is part of (the 3035 speech of) him (the prophet), enter into the ear of him who is seeking inspiration.

The true believer's ear is retaining our inspiration[2]: such an ear is closely linked to the caller (the perfect saint)—

Just as (for example) the infant's ear is filled with its mother's words, (and then) it (the infant) begins to speak articulately;

And if the infant have not a right (rightly-hearing) ear, it does not hear its mother's words and becomes a mute.

Every one born deaf has always been dumb: (only) that one who heard (speech) from his mother became a speaker.

Know that the deaf ear and the dumb man are the result of a 3040 certain defect; for it (the deaf ear) is not capable of (hearing) words and being taught.

---

[1] *I.e.* a saint.
[2] *I.e.* the inspiration imparted by us who are divinely inspired.

The (only) one that possessed speech without being taught is God, whose attributes are separated (exempt) from infirmities,

Or one like Adam whom God instructed without the screen (mediation) of mother and nurse and necessaries,

Or the Messiah (Christ) who, through being taught by the Loving (God), at his birth came speaking into the world,

For the purpose of repelling the suspicion as to his birth (and proving) that he was not born of fornication and wickedness.

3045   A (great) shaking was required in the effort that the buttermilk might render back that butter from its (inmost) heart.

The butter in the buttermilk is (invisible) like non-existence; the buttermilk has raised its banner (has become manifest) in existence.

That which seems to you to be (really) existent is (mere) skin, while that which seems to have perished—that (in reality) is the root.

The buttermilk has not (yet) taken (the form of) butter and is old: lay it (in store) and do not squander it till you pick out (the butter from it).

Hark, turn it knowingly from hand to hand (side to side), that it may reveal that which it has hidden;

3050   For this perishable (body) is a proof of the everlasting (spirit): the maundering of the intoxicated is a proof of (the existence of) the Cupbearer.

Another parable on the same subject.

The gambols of the lion on the banner are indicative of winds concealed (from view)[1].

If there were not the movement of those winds, how would the dead lion leap into the air?

By that (means) you know whether the wind is the east-wind or the west-wind: this (movement of the lion) is the explanation of that occult matter.

This body is like the lion on the banner: thought is causing it to move continually.

3055   The thought that comes from the east is (as) the (refreshing) east-wind, and that which (comes) from the west is (as) the west-wind fraught with pestilence.

The east of this wind of thought is different[2]; the west of this wind of thought is from Yonder side.

The moon is inanimate, and its east is inanimate: the heart's east is the soul of the soul of Soul.

The east of that Sun[3] which illumines the inward part—the sun of day is (only) the husk and reflexion thereof;

---

[1] See Book I, v. 603 sqq.   [2] I.e. different from the physical east.
[3] I.e. the spirit or rational soul.

For when the body is dead (and) without the (vital) flame, neither day nor night appears to it;

But though it (the flame) be not (there), (yet) when this 3060 (spiritual Sun) is (present) in perfection, it (the Sun) maintains itself intact without night and day,

Just as the eye, without moon and sun, sees moon and sun in dream.

Since our sleep is the brother of death, O such and such, know (the difference of) that brother from this brother.

And if they tell thee that that is the branch (derivative) of this, do not hear (believe) it, O follower of authority, without (having) certain knowledge.

During sleep thy spirit is beholding the representation of a state (of things) which thou wilt not behold, whilst thou art awake, in twenty years,

And thou art running, for (whole) lifetimes, to the sagacious 3065 (spiritual) kings in quest of the interpretation thereof,

Saying, "Tell (me), what is the interpretation of that dream?" To call such a mystery a "branch" is currishness.

This is the sleep of the vulgar; but truly the sleep of the elect is the root of (their) privilege and election.

There must needs be the elephant, in order that, when he sleeps supinely[1], he may dream of the land of Hindustán.

The ass does not dream of Hindustán at all: the ass has never journeyed from Hindustán to a foreign country.

There is need of the elephant-like and very robust spirit, that 3070 in sleep it may be able to go speedily to Hindustán.

Because of desire the elephant remembers Hindustán; then by night that remembrance of his takes form.

(The worship commanded in the text) *Remember ye Allah* is not a (devotional) work (that is within the reach) of every rascal; (the command) *Return thou* is not (a fetter) on the foot of every reprobate[2].

But still do not thou despair, be an elephant; and if thou art not an elephant, be in quest of transmutation.

Behold the alchemists of Heaven; hear at every moment the sound (of the words that come) from the (spiritual) makers of the philosophers' stone.

They are designers in the celestial atmosphere; they are 3075 workers for me and thee.

If thou dost not see the musky-bosomed people, behold this touch (laid upon thee), O night-blind (purblind) one.

At every moment the touch is (laid) upon thy apprehension: behold the plants ever springing up anew from thy earth!

---

[1] The elephant sleeps in a standing posture; and probably this is the reason why two of the later MSS read شبان, "by night," instead of ستان, "supine."

[2] *I.e.* it is not a means of drawing him towards God.

Of this (sort) was Ibráhím son of Adham, who beheld in sleep, without veil, the unfolding of the spiritual Hindustán.

(Therefore), of necessity, he burst the (worldly) chains asunder and dashed his kingdom to pieces and disappeared[1].

3080 The sign of beholding Hindustán is that he (who beholds it) starts up from sleep and becomes mad.

He will scatter dust upon (worldly) plans and will burst the links of the chains (that bind him),

Even as the Prophet said of the (Divine) light, that the sign thereof in (men's) breasts

Is that he (who hath the light) withdraws from the abode of delusion[2] and also turns back from the abode of joy[3].

For the exposition of this *hadíth* of Muṣṭafá (Mohammed), hearken to a tale, O sincere friend.

Story of the prince to whom the true kingdom displayed itself, (so that the realities of) "on the Day when a man shall flee from his brother and his mother and his father" became the object of his immediate experience[4]; (and he saw that) the kingdom of this earth-heap of the childish (is like the game) called "castle-taking," (in which) the child that gains the victory mounts upon the earth-heap and says boastfully, "The castle belongs to me," while the other children envy him; for (to play with) earth is the pastime of boys. When the prince was delivered from the bondage of colours, he said, "I say that these coloured pieces of earth (earthly gauds) are just the same vile earth; I do not call them gold and satin and brocade: I have been delivered from this brocade (aksún) and have gone to that which is simple (yaksún)." (God hath said), "And We bestowed wisdom upon him whilst he was yet a boy"; it needeth not the passing of (many) years for (any one to receive) the guidance of God: none speaks of the capacity to receive in (connexion with) the Power of Be, and it is.

3085 A certain king had a young son, adorned with excellence within and without.

He dreamed that suddenly that son died: the pure (pleasure) of the world was changed, for the king, to dregs.

His water-skin (eye) was dried up by the heat of the fire (of anguish), for because of the glow of the fire his tears remained not.

The king became so full of smoke and grief that sighs were finding no way (of entrance) into him.

He was about to die, his body became inert; (but) his life had been left (for completion): the king awoke.

---

[1] See p. 318 *supra*. [2] The present world. [3] Paradise.
[4] Literally, "the ready money of his inward state."

From awaking, there came to him a joy which he had not 3090
experienced in (all) his life;

For (now) from joy likewise he was about to perish: this spirit
and body is mightily shackled with the collar (of death).

This lamp dies from (is extinguished by) the breath of sorrow,
and it also dies from the breath of joy. Here, look you, is a
pleasant jest!

He (Man) is living between these two deaths: this (being)
that resembles one shackled with a collar is an occasion for
laughter.

The king said to himself, "In consequence of the Lord's
causation such a sorrow as that was the cause of joy."

Oh, wonderful (that) the same thing from one aspect (is) death 3095
and from another aspect a quickening with life and a provision!

The same thing is destructive in relation to one circumstance,
while again it is preservative in regard to another.

Bodily joy is perfection in regard to that which is of the pre-
sent world, (but it is) defect and failure in regard to the Day of
the latter end.

The oneiromancer, too, declares laughter in dreams to be (a
presage of) weeping with regrets and griefs,

(While) for weeping in dreams joy and gladness are (presaged)
in the interpretation, O gleeful man.

The king pondered, saying, "This sorrow, indeed, is past, but 3100
my soul has become suspicious (has misgivings and fears) of
(being afflicted by) one of the same kind;

And if such a thorn enter my foot (if such a calamity befall me)
that the rose departs (that my son dies), I must needs have a
keepsake."

Since the causes of mortality are infinite, which road, then,
shall we bar?

A hundred windows and doors facing towards mordant death
are ever creaking as they are opened,

(But) from greed for (worldly) provision the ear of the covetous
does not hear the harsh creaking of those doors of death.

From the side of the body, pains are the noise of the door; 3105
and from the side of enemies, maltreatment is the noise of the
door.

My dear friend[1], read for one moment the table of contents
of (books on) Medicine; look at the flaming fire of diseases!

Through all those tumours (maladies) there is a way (for
death) into this house: at every two steps there is a pit full of
scorpions.

(The king said), "The wind is fierce and my lamp is a docked
(imperfect) one: I will light another lamp from it,

---

[1] Literally, "(O thou who art as dear as) the soul of the head," *i.e.* the soul
that is the rational principle in man.

So that maybe one complete (lamp) will arise from them both, if that one lamp be put out by the wind,"

3110 Like the gnostic who, for the sake of (gaining) freedom from care, has lit the candle of the heart (spirit) from this defective lamp of the body,

In order that, one day when this (bodily lamp) dies of a sudden, he may place before his eye the candle of the spirit.

He (the king) did not understand this; therefore in his heedlessness he applied the perishing candle to another perishable.

How the king brought his son a bride for fear of his race coming to an end.

(The king said to himself), "It is necessary, then, to seek a bride for him, that from this marriage offspring may appear,

(So that) if this falcon (my son) return to the state of mortality his young may become a falcon after (the death of) the falcon,

3115 (And that) if the form of this falcon go from here, his inward meaning may endure in his son.

On account of this, that renowned (spiritual) king, Muṣṭafá (Mohammed), said, 'The son is the marrow of his father.'

For this reason all people, (being moved) by heartfelt love, teach their children (their own) trades,

To the end that these inward meanings may remain in the world when that body of theirs becomes hidden.

God in His wisdom has given them intense desire for the right guidance of every little one capable (of learning).

3120 I too, for the purpose of (ensuring) the continuance of my race, will seek for my son a wife of good principles.

I will seek a girl who is the offspring of a righteous man, not the offspring of a stern-visaged king."

This righteous man is himself a king, he is free, he is not the prisoner of lust and gluttony.

They (the people) have given (those) prisoners the title of "king" by inversion, just as Káfúr (Camphor) is the name of that negro.

The blood-drinking (deadly) wilderness is named mafáza (place of safety); the vulgar call the leper Níkbakht (Fortunatus).

3125 They have described the prisoner of lust and anger and ambition by the name of Mír or Ṣadr-i ajall (most honourable prince).

To those prisoners of Doom (asírán-i ajal) the vulgar in (all) the lands have given the title of "most honourable Amírs" (amírán-i ajall).

They call high-placed (Ṣadr) him whose soul is (placed) low in the vestibule, that is to say, (worldly) power and riches.

When the king chose (matrimonial) relationship with an ascetic, this news came to the ears of (his) ladies.

How the king chose the daughter of a poor ascetic for his son and how the ladies of the harem raised objections and disdained the (proposed) alliance with the dervish.

The prince's mother, from deficiency of understanding, said, "According to reason and tradition equality (of rank) is requisite.

Thou from stinginess and miserliness and shrewdness wishest 3130 to ally our son with a beggar."

He (the king) said, "It is a fault to call the righteous man a beggar, for through the grace of God he is spiritually rich.

He is taking refuge in contentment because of piety, not because of meanness and laziness, like the beggar.

The penury which arises from contentment and piety is distinct from the poverty and penury of the base.

If that one (the beggar) find a single groat, he bows his head (in homage), while this one (the righteous man) in his lofty aspiration recoils from a treasure of gold.

The king who from cupidity is betaking himself to everything 3135 unlawful—the man of noble mind calls him a beggar."

She (the prince's mother) said, "Where are his cities and castles (to furnish) the wedding-outfit, or (where are his means of) scattering gems and pieces of gold?"

He (the king) said, "Begone! Whosoever prefers to care for religion, God cuts off from him all remaining cares."

The king prevailed and gave (in marriage) to him (his son) a maiden of goodly nature, belonging to the family of a righteous man.

Verily, she had none to rival her in loveliness: her face was brighter than the sun at morn.

Such was the maiden's beauty; and her qualities were such 3140 that, on account of their excellence, they are not (to be) contained in (any) description.

Make religion thy prey, that in consequence (as a corollary) there may come (to thee) beauty and riches and power and advantageous fortune.

Know that the next world, in respect of ownership, is (like) files of camels: the present world is its corollary, like the (camels') hair and dung.

(If) thou choose the hair, the camel will not be thine, and if the camel be thine, what value has the hair?

When the marriage (matrimonial alliance) with the family of the uncontentious righteous folk was achieved (successfully arranged) by the king,

By (Divine) destiny a decrepit old witch, who was in love with 3145 the handsome and generous prince—

An old woman of Kábul—bewitched him with a sorcery of which the magic of Babylon (itself) would be envious.

The prince fell in love with the ugly hag, so that he abandoned his bride and the wedding.

A black devil and woman of Kábul suddenly waylaid (seduced) the prince.

That stinking[1] ninety years old hag left to the prince neither wisdom nor understanding.

3150   For a (whole) year the prince was captivated: the sole of the hag's shoe was the place where he bestowed his kisses.

Association with the hag was mowing (consuming) him, till through wasting away (only) half a spirit remained (in him).

Others had the headache (were sorely grieved) on account of his weakness, (while) he, from the intoxicating effect of the sorcery, was unconscious of himself.

This world had become (as) a prison to the king, while this son (of his) was laughing at their tears.

The king became exceedingly desperate in the struggle[2] (to save his son): day and night he was offering sacrifice and giving alms (but without avail),

3155   For whatever remedy the father might apply, (the son's) love for the old hag would always increase.

Then it became clear to him that that (infatuation) was absolutely a (Divine) mystery, and that thenceforth his (only) remedy was supplication.

He was prostrating himself in prayer, saying, "It beseems Thee to command: to whom but God belongeth the command over God's kingdom?

But this poor wretch is burning like aloes-wood: take his hand (help him), O Merciful and Loving One!"

(So did he pray) until, because of the "O Lord! O Lord!" and lamentation of the king, a master-magician came from the road into his presence.

How the king's prayer for the deliverance of his son from the witch of Kábul was granted.

3160   He had heard from afar the news that that boy had been captivated by an old woman,

A crone who in witchery was unrivalled and secure from likeness and duality.

Hand is above hand, O youth, in skill and in strength up to the Essence of God.

The ultimate end of (all) hands is the Hand of God: the ultimate end of (all) torrents is undoubtedly the sea.

From it the clouds take their origin, and in it too the torrent hath an end.

[1] Literally, "cui vulva foetida est."
[2] Literally, "victory and checkmate," a metaphor derived from the game of chess.

The king said to him, "This boy has passed out of control (has 3165 lost his wits)." He (the magician) said, "Look you, I am come as a potent remedy.

None of these sorcerers is equal to the old woman except me, the sagacious one, who have arrived from yonder shore.

Lo, by command of the Creator, I, like the hand of Moses, will utterly destroy her sorcery;

For to me this knowledge hath come from yonder region, not from having been schooled in the sorcery which is held cheap (by the wise).

I am come to undo her sorcery, so that the prince may not remain pale-faced.

Go to the graveyard at the hour of the meal taken before 3170 dawn: beside the wall is a whitened tomb.

Dig up that place in the direction of the qibla[1], that thou mayst behold the power and the working of God."

This story is very long, and you (O reader) are weary: I will relate the cream (of it), I dismiss what is superfluous.

He (the magician) untied those heavy knots[2]: then he gave to the king's son a way (of escape) from the affliction.

The boy came to himself and with a hundred tribulations went running towards the throne of the king.

He made prostration and was beating his chin on the earth: 3175 the boy held in his arms a sword and winding-sheet[3].

The king ordered the city to be decorated, and the citizens and the despairing disappointed bride rejoiced.

The (whole) world revived once more and was filled with radiance: (the people said), "Oh, what a wondrous difference between that day (of sorrow) and to-day[4]!"

The king made such a (lavish) wedding-feast for him that sugared julep was (placed) before the dogs.

The old witch died of vexation and gave up her hideous face and (foul) nature to Málik[5].

The prince was left in amazement: (he said to himself), "How 3180 did she rob me of understanding and insight?"

He beheld a newly wedded bride like the beauteous moon, who was (as a brigand) infesting the road of beauty (and occupying it) against (all) the (other) fair ones[6].

He became senseless and fell on his face: for three days the heart (consciousness) vanished from his body.

Three days and nights he became unconscious of himself, so that the people were (sorely) perturbed by his swoon.

---

[1] *I.e.* towards Mecca.
[2] *I.e.* he broke the spells.
[3] As a token that he acknowledged his sin and was ready to pay the penalty.
[4] Literally, "Oh, wonderful! That day a day and to-day a day!"
[5] The Keeper of Hell.
[6] *I.e.* she eclipsed them all in beauty.

By means of rose-water and (other) remedies he came to himself (again): little by little, good and evil were apprehended by him (once more).

3185   After a year the king said to him jokingly in conversation, "O son, bethink thee of that old friend (of thine),

Bethink thee of that bedfellow and that bed: do not be so faithless and harsh!"

"Go to!" said he; "I have found the abode of joy, I am delivered from the pit of the abode of delusion."

'Tis even so: when the true believer has found the way towards the Light of God, he averts his face from the darkness (of this world).

Explaining that the prince is Man[1], the vicegerent of God, and that his father is Adam, the chosen one, the vicegerent of God, he to whom the angels bowed in worship; and that the old hag of Kábul is the World which separated Man from his Father by sorcery, while the prophets and saints are (like) the physician who applied the remedy.

O brother, know that thou art the prince born anew in the old world.

3190   The witch of Kábul is this World which made men captive to colour and perfume.

Since she hath cast thee into this polluted stream, continually recite and utter (the words), *Say, I take refuge.*

In order that thou mayst be delivered from this witchery and this distress, beg of *the Lord of the daybreak* that thou mayst say "I take refuge."

The Prophet called this world of thine an enchantress because through her spells she lodged mankind in the pit.

Beware! The stinking hag hath hot (potent) spells: her hot breath hath made kings captive.

3195   She is *the witches who blow (on knots)* within (thy) breast: she is the (means of) maintaining the knots of sorcery.

The sorceress, (who is) the World, is a mightily cunning woman: 'tis not in the power of the vulgar to undo her sorcery;

And if (men's) understandings could loose her knot, how should God have sent the prophets?

Hark, seek one whose breath is pure, a looser of knots, one who knows the mystery of *God doeth whatso He willeth.*

She (the World) hath imprisoned thee, like a fish, in her net: the prince remained (there) one year, and thou sixty.

3200   From (being enmeshed in) her net thou art in tribulation sixty years: neither art thou happy nor (dost thou walk) in the way of the Sunna.

---

[1] Literally, "the child of Adam."

Thou art a miserable unrighteous man: neither is thy worldly life good (happy) nor art thou delivered from guilt and sins.

Her (the World's) breathing hath made these knots tight: seek, then, the breathing of the unique Creator,

In order that "*I breathed of My spirit into him*" may deliver thee from this (sorcery) and say (to thee), "Come higher!"

The breathing of sorcery is not consumed save by the breathing of God: this (the former) is the breathing of (Divine) wrath, (while) that (the latter) exhalation is the breathing of (Divine) love.

His mercy is prior to His wrath: (if) thou desirest priority (in 3205 spiritual rank), go, seek that (attribute) which is prior,

That thou mayst attain unto the souls that *are wedded*; for lo, this, O ensorcelled prince, is thy way of escape.

With the existence of the old woman[1], there can be no undoing (of the knots), (whilst thou art) in the net and in the arms of that (paramour) full of blandishments.

Hath not the Lamp of the peoples[2] called this world and that world the two fellow-wives (who are always quarrelling with each other)?

Therefore union with this (world) is separation from that (world): the health of this body is the sickness of the spirit.

Hard is the separation from this transitory abode: know, then, 3210 that the separation from that permanent abode is harder.

Since it is hard for thee to be separated from the form, how hard must it be to be parted from its Maker!

O thou that hast not the patience to do without the vile world, how, O friend, how hast thou the patience to do without God?

Since thou hast not the patience to do without this black water, how hast thou the patience to do without God's (pure) fountain?

Since thou art restless without this (worldly) drink, how art thou (remaining patiently) apart from *the righteous* and from *they shall drink* (of the wine of Paradise)?

If for one moment thou behold the beauty of the Loving One 3215 and cast thy soul and existence into the fire (of love),

After that thou wilt regard this (worldly) drink as a carcase, when thou beholdest the glory and splendour of nighness (unto Him).

Like the prince, thou wilt attain unto thy Beloved; then thou wilt draw out from thy foot the thorn of self.

Strive for selflessness, find thy (true) self as soon as possible—and God best knoweth the right course.

Take heed, never be wedded to self: do not, like an ass, be always falling into water and mud.

---

[1] *I.e.* "So long as the World exists for thee."
[2] *I.e.* the Prophet.

3220 That stumbling arises from shortsightedness; for like a blind man, he (such a one) does not see the ups and downs.

Make the scent of Joseph's shirt thy stay, because his scent makes the eye clear.

The hidden Form and the Light of that Brow have made the eyes of the prophets far-seeing.

The Light of that Countenance will deliver (thee) from the fire: hark, be not content with borrowed light.

This (borrowed) light makes the eye to see that which is transient: it makes body and mind and spirit to be scabby (diseased).

3225 It has the appearance of light, but in reality it is fire: keep thy hands off it, if thou desire the (true) radiance.

The eye and spirit that sees (only) the transient falls on its face continually wherever it goes.

A far-seeing man who lacks knowledge may see far, just as (one has) far sight in dreams.

You are asleep with parched lips on the bank of the river, and (in your dream) are running in search of water towards the mirage.

You see the mirage far away and run (towards it): you become in love with your own sight.

3230 In the dream you boast to your friends, saying, "I am the one whose heart possesses vision, and (I am) the one that rends the veil.

Lo, I see water yonder: hark, make haste that we may go there"—and 'tis (only) the mirage.

At every step you hurry farther away from the water, whilst you keep running on towards the perilous mirage.

Your very setting-out has become the barrier (which prevents you) from (seeing) this that has come close to you.

Oh, many a one sets out to some place from the spot where the object of his quest is (to be found).

3235 The (far) sight and boasting of the sleeper is of no avail; it is naught but a phantasy: hold aloof from it.

Thou art sleepy, but anyhow sleep on the Way[1]: for God's sake, for God's sake, sleep on the Way of God,

That perchance a Traveller (on the Way) may attach himself to thee and tear thee from the phantasies of slumber.

(Even) if the sleeper's thought become (subtle) as a hair, he will not find the way to the Abode by that subtlety.

Whether the sleeper's thought is twofold or threefold, still it is error on error on error.

3240 The waves are beating upon him without restraint, (whilst) he asleep is running in the long wilderness.

The sleeper dreams of the sore pangs of thirst, (whilst) the water is *nearer unto him than the neck-vein.*

[1] *I.e.* "do not abandon the Way and sleep elsewhere."

Story of the ascetic who, notwithstanding his destitution and numerous family, was rejoicing and laughing in a year of drought whilst the people were dying of hunger. They said to him, " What is the occasion for joy? It is an occasion for a hundred mournings." " For me at any rate 'tis not (so)," he replied.

Even as (for example) that ascetic was laughing in a year of drought, while all (his) folk were weeping.

So they said to him, " What is the occasion for laughter, (when) the drought has uprooted (destroyed) the true believers?

The (Divine) mercy hath closed its eyes to us: the plain is burnt by the fierce sun.

Crops and vineyards and vines are standing black: there is no 3245 moisture in the earth, neither up nor down.

The people are dying from this drought and torment by tens and hundreds like fish far from the water.

Thou art taking no pity on the Moslems; (yet) the true believers are kinsmen and one body (of) fat and flesh.

The pain of one part of the body is the pain of all (its parts), whether it be the hour of peace or war."

He (the ascetic) replied, " In your eyes this is a drought, (but) to my eye this earth is like Paradise.

I am beholding in every desert and everywhere ears of corn in 3250 abundance, reaching up to the waist;

(I see) the wilderness full of ears of corn (tossed) in waves by the east-wind, (so that it is) greener than the leek.

By way of trial I am putting my hand thereon: how should I remove my hand and eye?

Ye are friends of Pharaoh, (who is) the body, O base people: hence the Nile seems to you to be blood.

Quickly become friends of Moses, (who is) the intellect, in order that the blood may remain not and ye may behold the river-water.

(If) an injustice is proceeding from (is being done by) thee 3255 towards thy father, that father will become (as) a (biting) cur in thine eyes.

That father is not a cur: 'tis the effect of (thy) injustice that such mercy appears to thy sight (as) a cur.

Since the brethren (of Joseph) had envy and anger, they were regarding Joseph as the wolf.

When thou hast made peace with thy father, anger is gone; that currishness departs, and thy father at once becomes thy friend.

Explaining that the whole world is the form of Universal Reason, (and that) when by trespassing you act unjustly towards Universal Reason, in most cases the aspect of the world increases your vexation, just as when you show ill-feeling to your father the aspect of your father increases your vexation and you cannot (bear to) look on his face, though before that he will have been the light of your eye and the comfort of your soul.

The whole world is the form of Universal Reason, which is the father of whosoever is a follower of the (Divine) Word.

3260 When any one shows excessive ingratitude to Universal Reason, the form of the universe appears to him (as) a cur accordingly.

Make peace with this Father, abandon disobedience, that the water and clay (the world) may appear (to thee as) a carpet of gold.

Then the Resurrection will become thy present state (immediate experience): heaven and earth will be transfigured before thee.

Since I am ever at peace with this Father, this world is like Paradise in my sight.

At every moment (appears) a new form and a new beauty, so that from seeing the new (visions) ennui dies away.

3265 I see the world to be full of bounty—the waters constantly gushing from the springs.

The noise of their water is coming into mine ear: my inner consciousness and intelligence are being intoxicated.

(I see) the boughs dancing like penitents[1], the leaves clapping their hands like minstrels.

The gleam of the mirror is flashing through the (cover of) felt cloth: think how it will be if the mirror (itself) be displayed!

I am not telling one (mystery) out of thousands, because every ear is filled with a doubt.

3270 To Opinion this saying (of mine) is (only) a joyful announcement (concerning the future), (but) Reason says, 'What (occasion for) announcement? It is my cash in hand (actual and present experience).'"

Story of the sons of 'Uzayr, on whom be peace, who were making inquiries about their father from (one who really was) their father. "Yes," he replied, "I have seen him: he is coming." Some (of them) recognised him and became unconscious, (while) others did not recognise him and said, "He has only announced (our father's coming): what is this unconsciousness?"

(The case is) like (that of) the sons of 'Uzayr who came into the thoroughfare, asking news of their father.

---

[1] *I.e.* those who have been newly converted to the mystical life.

They had grown old, while their father had been made young. Then suddenly their father met them.

So they inquired of him, saying, "O wayfarer, we wonder if thou hast news of our 'Uzayr;

For some one told us that to-day that man of (great) authority would arrive from abroad after we had given up hope (of seeing him)."

"Yes," he replied, "he will arrive after me." That one (the son of 'Uzayr) rejoiced when he heard the good tidings, 3275

Crying, "Joy to thee, O bringer of the good news!" But the other (son) recognised (him) and fell (to the ground) unconscious,

Saying, "What occasion is there for good tidings, O scatterbrain, when we have fallen into the mine (the very midst) of sugar?"

To Opinion it is (merely) good tidings, whereas in the sight of Reason it is ready cash (actuality), because the eye of Opinion is veiled by missing (the object sought).

It is pain to the infidels and glad news to the faithful, but in the eye of the seer it is immediate experience.

Inasmuch as the lover is intoxicated at the moment of immediacy, he is necessarily superior to infidelity and faith. 3280

Indeed, both infidelity and faith are his door-keeper (who secures him from intrusion); for he is the kernel, while infidelity and religion are his two rinds.

Infidelity is the dry peel that has averted its face (from the kernel); faith, again, is the peel (inner integument) that has gained a delicious flavour.

The place for the dry peels is the fire, (but) the peel attached to the spiritual kernel is sweet.

The kernel itself is above the grade of "sweet": it is above "sweet" because it is the dispenser of deliciousness.

This discourse hath no end: turn back, that my Moses may cleave the sea asunder[1]. 3285

This (preceding part) of the discourse hath been spoken suitably to the intelligence of the vulgar; the remainder thereof hath been concealed.

The gold, (which is) thy intelligence, is in fragments, O suspected one: how should I set the stamp of the die upon clippings?

Thy intelligence is distributed over a hundred important affairs, over thousands of desires and great matters and small.

Thou must unite the (scattered) parts by means of love, to the end that thou mayst become sweet as Samarcand and Damascus.

---

[1] Literally, "may raise dust from the sea," *i.e.* "that my speech may reveal the mysteries of the Truth."

3290   When thou becomest united, grain by grain, from (after thy dispersion in) perplexity, then it is possible to stamp upon thee the King's die;

And if thou, foolish man, become greater than a *mithqál* (dinar), the King will make of thee a cup of gold.

Then thereon will be both the name and the titles of the King and also his effigy, O thou that cravest to attain,

So that the Beloved will be to thee both bread and water and lamp and minion and dessert and wine.

Unite thyself—union is (a Divine) mercy—that I may be able to speak unto thee that which is;

3295   For speaking is for the purpose of (producing) belief: the spirit of polytheism is quit (devoid) of belief in God.

The spirit that has been distributed over the contents of the (mundane) sphere is shared amongst sixty passions;

Therefore silence is best: it gives peace to it (to that spirit); therefore (I ought to follow the adage) " Silence is the answer to fools."

This I know, but intoxication of the body is opening my mouth without volition on my part,

Just as in sneezing and yawning this mouth becomes open without your willing it.

Commentary on the Tradition, " Verily, I ask pardon of God seventy times every day."

3300   Like the Prophet, I repent seventy times daily of speaking and giving out (mysteries);

But that intoxication becomes a breaker of (vows of) penitence: this intoxication of the body causes oblivion and tears the robe (of penitence).

The (Divine) purpose of making manifest the (things of) long ago (the eternal things) cast an intoxication upon the knower of the mystery,

(So that) with such drum and banner (conspicuousness) the hidden mystery has become water gushing from (the fountain of) "the Pen is dry[1]."

The infinite Mercy is flowing continually: ye are asleep to the perception thereof, O men!

3305   The sleeper's garment drinks water from the river, (while) the sleeper is seeking the mirage in his dream.

He keeps running (to and fro), saying, "Yonder there is hope of water": by this (false) thought he has barred the way against himself.

Because he said "yonder" he became far from here (from the place where the water is): (through resting) in a vain imagination he was banished from a reality.

[1] *I.e.* Divine predestination.

They (the worldly) are far-seeing (for their selfish ends) and very fast asleep spiritually: take some mercy upon them, O travellers on the Way!

I never saw thirst (eager desire) induce sleep: (only) the thirst of the unintelligent induces sleep.

The (true) intelligence, indeed, is that which was fed by God, 3310 not the intelligence that was bestowed by (the planet) Mercury.

Explaining that the particular (discursive) intellect does not see beyond the grave and, as regards all the rest, is subject to the authority of the saints and prophets.

The foresight of this intellect extends (only) to the grave, while that of the spiritual man is till the blast of the trumpet (of Resurrection).

This intellect does not pass beyond a grave and sepulchre, and this (intellectual) foot does not tread the arena of marvels.

Go, become quit of this foot and this intellect: seek the eye appertaining to the invisible (the inward eye) and enjoy (contemplation).

How should one subservient to a preceptor and in pupilage to a book find, like Moses, light from (his own) bosom?

From this (scholastic) study and this intellect comes naught 3315 but vertigo; therefore leave this study and adopt (in its stead) expectation.

Do not seek (spiritual) eminence from disputation: for him who is expectant (of Divine inspiration) listening is better than speaking.

The office of teaching is a sort of sensual desire: every sensual fancy is an idol (source of polytheism) in the Way.

If every busybody had found the track (had attained) to His grace, how should God have sent so many prophets?

The particular intellect is like the lightning and the flash: how is it possible to go to Wakhsh[1] in a flash?

The light of the lightning is not for guidance on the way; nay, 3320 it is a command to the cloud to weep.

The lightning of our intellect is for the sake of weeping, to the end that non-existence may weep in longing for (real) existence.

The child's intellect said, "Attend school"; but it cannot learn by itself.

The sick man's intellect leads him to the physician; but his intellect is not successful in curing him.

Mark, the devils were going heavenward and listening to the secrets on high

And carrying away a little of those secrets, till the shooting 3325 stars quickly drove them from heaven,

[1] Name of a town and district in Khuttal on the Upper Oxus.

Saying, "Begone! A prophet is come there (on the earth): from him will be obtained whatsoever ye crave.

If ye are seeking priceless pearls, *enter the houses by their doors.*

Keep knocking that door-ring and stand at the door: there is no way for you in the direction of the vault of heaven.

Ye need not take this long road: We have bestowed on an earthly one the secrets of the mystery.

3330 Come to him, if ye are not disloyal; be made sugar-cane by him, though ye are (empty) reeds."

That Guide will cause verdure to grow from thy earth: he is not inferior to the hoof of the horse of Gabriel[1].

Thou wilt be made verdure, thou wilt be made fresh anew, if thou become the dust of the horse of a Gabriel—

The life-giving verdure which Sámirí put into the (golden) calf, so that it became endowed with the (vital) essence.

From that verdure it took life and bellowed—such a bellowing as confounded the foe.

3335 If ye come loyally to the possessors of the mystery, ye will be freed from the hood, like a falcon—

The hood that binds eye and ear, whereby the falcon is (made) wretched and abject.

The hood is (placed as) a blind on the eyes of falcons because its (the falcon's) whole desire is for its own kind.

When it has been severed from its kind, it associates with the king: the falconer unveils its eye.

God drove the devils from His place of watch, (He drove) the particular intellect from its autonomy,

3340 Saying, "Do not domineer: thou art not autonomous; nay, thou art the pupil of the heart and predisposed (to learn from it).

Go to the heart, go, for thou art a part of the heart: take heed, for thou art a slave of the just King."

To be His slave is better than being a sovereign, for "*I am better*[2]" is the word of Satan.

Do thou see the distinction and pick out (choose by preference), O prisoner, the slavery of Adam from the pride of Iblís.

He who is the Sun of the Way uttered the saying, "Good (*túbá*) betide every one whose carnal soul is abased!"

3345 Behold the shade of Túbá (the tree in Paradise) and sleep well; lay thy head in the shade and sleep without lifting thy head (haughtily).

The shade of (one) "whose carnal soul is abased" is a pleasant place for reclining: it is a (good) sleeping-place for him that is predisposed to that (spiritual) purity.

---

[1] This refers to the handful of dust from the footprint of Gabriel's horse that, on being cast into the golden calf, caused it to low. See *Qur'án*, xx, 96.

[2] *Qur'án*, vii, 11. "I am better than he (Adam): Thou didst create me of fire and him of clay."

If thou go from this shade towards egoism, thou wilt soon become disobedient (to God) and lose the way.

Explaining (the Verse), "O ye that believe, do not put (yourselves) forward in the presence of God and His Apostle." *Since thou art not the Prophet, be one of the religious community; since thou art not the sovereign, be a subject.*

Go therefore, be silent in submission beneath the shade of the command of the Shaykh and Master;

Otherwise, though thou art predisposed and capable, thou wilt become deformed through boasting of (thy) perfection.

Thou wilt be deprived even of (thy good) predisposition, if 3350 thou rebel against the Master of the mystery who is endowed with knowledge.

Do thou still have patience in cobbling; for if thou be impatient, thou wilt become a rag-stitcher.

If the stitchers of old clothes had patience and forbearance, all of them too would become stitchers of new garments through (acquisition of) knowledge.

Thou strivest much, and at last even thou thyself sayest in weariness that the intellect is a fetter,

Like the philosopher (who) on the day of his death perceived his intellect to be very poor and feeble[1],

And in that hour disinterestedly confessed (the truth), saying, 3355 "(Impelled) by acuteness of mind we galloped in vain.

In delusion we drew (scornfully) away from the holy men, we swam in the sea of phantasy."

In the spiritual Sea swimming is naught (of no avail): here is no resource but the ship (ark) of Noah.

Thus said that king of the prophets[2], "I am the ship in this universal Sea,

Or that person who, in respect of my (inward) clairvoyances, has become a true vicegerent in my stead."

We (saints) are the ship (ark) of Noah in the Sea, in order that 3360 thou mayst not turn thy face away from the ship, O youth.

Go not, like Canaan[3], to every mountain: hear from the *Qur'án* (the warning), "*There is naught that will protect (thee) to-day.*"

This ship, because of the bandage (on thy vision), seems to thee low, (while) the mountain of (intellectual) thought seems very high.

Beware, beware! Do not regard this "low" with contempt: regard the grace of God that is attached (to it).

Do not regard the height of the mountain of thought, for a single wave turns it upside down.

---

[1] Literally, "without gear and provision."
[2] Mohammed. [3] Noah's disobedient son.

3365 If thou art (like) Canaan, thou wilt not believe me though I foster (for thy sake) two hundred times as many counsels.

How should Canaan's ear accept these words? for God's seal and signet is upon it.

How should admonition pass through God's seal? How should the new (admonition) avert the (eternal) pre-ordainment?

But I am telling the news of good fortune in the hope that thou art not (like) Canaan.

Thou wilt make this confession at last. Hark, from the first day do thou behold the last!

3370 Thou canst see the end: do not make blind and old thine eye that sees the end.

Whosoever is blessedly a seer of the end will never stumble in wayfaring.

Unless thou desire this incessant lying down and rising up (this stumbling on the way), sharpen thine eye with the dust on the foot of a holy man.

Make the dust of his foot collyrium for thine eye, that thou mayst strike off the head of the blackguards;

For through this pupilage and this poverty (of spirit), (though) thou be (as) a needle, thou wilt become (a trenchant sword like) Dhu 'l-faqár[1].

3375 Use the dust of every elect one as collyrium: it will both burn the eye and do it good.

The eye of the camel is very luminous[2] because he (the camel) eats thorns for the sake of (increasing) the light of his eye.

Story of the mule's complaining to the camel (and saying), " I often fall on my face when going along, while you seldom do so: why is this?" and the camel's answer to him.

One day a mule saw a camel, since he had been put into a stable with him.

He (the mule) said, "I often fall on my face in hill and road and in market and street.

Particularly (in descending) from the top of the mountain to the bottom I come down on my head every moment from terror.

3380 Thou dost not fall on thy face: why is it? Or maybe in sooth thy pure spirit is destined to felicity.

I come down on my head every instant and strike my knees (on the ground): by that slipping I make muzzle and knees all bloody.

My pack-saddle and trappings become awry (lie in disorder) on my head, and I always get a beating from the muleteer[3];

---

[1] Name of a sword which belonged to the Prophet.
[2] Literally, "light-shedding."
[3] Literally, "the hirer."

Like the unintelligent man who, from corrupt understanding, in (the case of his committing) sin continually breaks (his vow of) penitence.

Through weakness of resolution that breaker of (vows of) penitence becomes the laughing-stock of Iblís in the world.

He constantly comes down on his head, like a lame horse, for his load is heavy and the road is (full of) stones. 3385

He is always getting blows on his head from the Unseen, that man of luckless nature, from breaking (his vows of) penitence.

Then again he repents with infirm resolution: the Devil spits (in scorn) and shatters his penitence.

Weakness on weakness! (Yet) his arrogance is such that he regards with contempt those that attain (to God).

O camel, thou who art a type of the true believer dost not fall on thy face, nor dost thou turn up thy nose (in disdain).

What hast thou that thou art so untouched by bane and free from stumbling and dost not fall on thy face?" 3390

He (the camel) said, "Though every felicity is from God, there are many differences between me and thee.

I have a high head, my eyes are high: lofty vision is a protection against injury.

From the top of the mountain I see the mountain-foot, I see every hollow and level, fold by fold,

Just as that most noble prince (the perfect saint) saw his future destiny till the day of death.

That person of goodly qualities knows at the present time what will happen after twenty years. 3395

That God-fearing man did not see his own destiny only; nay, the destiny of (every) inhabitant of the West and East.

The Light makes its abode in his eye and heart. Wherefore does it make (its abode there)? For love of home.

(He is) like Joseph, who at first dreamed that the sun and moon bowed in worship before him:

After ten years, nay, more, that which Joseph had seen came to pass[1].

That (saying), 'he sees by the Light of God,' is not vain: the Divine Light rives the sky asunder. 3400

In thine eye that Light is not. Go! Thou art in pawn to the animal senses.

From weakness of eye thou seest (only) in front of thy foot: thou art weak and thy guide, too, is weak.

The eye is the guide for hand and foot, for it sees (both) the right and the wrong place.

Another thing is that my eye is clearer; another, that my nature is purer,

---

[1] Literally, "raised its head."

3405 Because I am one of the lawfully begotten, not one of the children of adultery and the people of perdition.

Thou art one of the children of adultery: without doubt the arrow flies crookedly when the bow is bad."

How the mule declared the replies of the camel to be true and acknowledged his (the camel's) superiority to himself and besought his aid and took refuge with him sincerely; and how the camel treated him with kindness and showed him the way and gave help in fatherly and kingly fashion.

The mule said, "Thou hast spoken the truth, O camel." This he said and filled his eye with tears.

He wept awhile and fell at his (the camel's) feet and said, "O chosen of the Lord of men,

What harm will it do if thou, by (favour of) thy blessedness, wilt receive me into thy service?"

3410 He (the camel) said, "Since thou hast made confession in my presence, go (in peace), for thou art saved from the contaminations of Time.

Thou hast given justice (hast made just amends) and art saved from tribulation: thou wast an enemy, thou hast become one of the leal.

The evil disposition was not original (innate) in thy person; for from original evil comes naught but denial.

The borrowed (temporary) evil is such that he (in whom it appears) makes confession and desires to repent;

Like Adam, whose lapse was temporary: of necessity he showed penitence at once.

3415 Since the sin of Iblís was original, for him there was no way to precious penitence.

Go, for thou art delivered from thyself and from the evil disposition and from the (flaming) tongue of the Fire and from the teeth of the wild beasts (of Hell).

Go, for now thou hast grasped felicity, thou hast thrown thyself into everlasting fortune.

Thou hast gained (that which is signified by the words) *Enter in amongst My servants*; thou hast annexed (the implication of) *Enter into My Paradise.*

Thou hast made a way for thyself (to enter) amongst His servants; thou hast gone into Eden by the secret way.

3420 '*Guide us,*' thou saidst, '*in the straight path*': He took thy hand and led thee to the abode of bliss.

Thou wast fire: thou hast become light, O noble one; thou wast an unripe grape: thou hast become a (ripe) grape and raisin.

Thou wast a star: thou hast become the Sun. Rejoice! God best knoweth the right."

O Ẓiyá'u 'l-Ḥaqq (Radiance of God) Ḥusámu'ddín, take thy honey and cast it into the basin of milk,

To the end that that milk may escape from having its savour corrupted and may gain much increase of savour from the Sea of Deliciousness,

(And) may be united with the Sea of *Alast*: when it becomes 3425 the Sea, it is delivered from every corruption;

(If) it find a passage into that Sea of honey, no contamination will have an effect upon it.

Roar like a lion, O Lion of God, in order that that roar may mount to the seventh tier (of Heaven)!

(But) what knowledge (thereof) hath the weary surfeited soul? How should the mouse know the roar of the lion?

(Therefore) write thy (spiritual) experiences with gold-water for the sake of every one of goodly substance whose heart is (deep) as the sea.

This spirit-augmenting discourse is (like) the water of the 3430 Nile: O Lord, let it seem blood to the eye of the Egyptian!

How the Egyptian entreated the Israelite, saying, "Of thine own intention fill a jug from the Nile and put it to my lips, that I may drink. (I beseech thee) by the right of friendship and brotherhood; for the jug which ye Israelites fill from the Nile for yourselves is pure water, while the jug which we Egyptians fill is pure blood."

I heard that an Egyptian, on account of thirst, came into the house of an Israelite.

He said, "I am thy friend and kinsman: to-day I have become in need of thee,

Because Moses wrought sorcery and enchantments, so that he made the water of the Nile to be blood for us.

The Israelites drink pure water from it, (but) to the Egyptians the water has become blood from the spell laid on our eyes.

Look, the Egyptians are dying of thirst in consequence of their 3435 ill-fortune or their evil nature.

Fill one cup with water for thyself, that this old friend may drink of thy water.

When thou fillest that cup for thine own sake, 'twill not be blood, 'twill be water pure and free (from taint).

I too will drink the water as thy parasite; for a parasite, in following (his host), is relieved from anguish."

He (the Israelite) said, "O (thou who art to me as) soul and world, I will do (this) service (for thee); I will pay (thee) regard (in this matter), O (thou who art as) my two bright eyes!

I will do according to thy desire, I will rejoice (to serve thee); 3440 I will be thy slave, I will act (generously) as a freeman."

He filled the cup with water from the Nile, put it to his lips, and drank one half (of the water).

(Then) he tilted the cup towards him who craved the water, saying, "Drink thou too!" That (water) became black blood.

Again he tilted it on this side (towards himself): the blood became water (once more). The Egyptian was enraged and incensed.

He sat down awhile till his anger departed; after that, he said to him, "O mighty sword (of the Faith),

3445 O brother, what is the expedient for (loosing) this knot?" He (the Israelite) said, "(Only) he that is God-fearing drinks this (water)."

The God-fearing man is he that has become quit of (has renounced) the way of Pharaoh and has become like unto Moses.

Become (as) the people of Moses and drink this water; make peace with the Moon and behold the moonbeams.

There are a hundred thousand darknesses in thine eye (which arise) from thy wrath against the servants of God.

Extinguish wrath, open the (spiritual) eye, rejoice, take a lesson from (true) friends, become a teacher (of the Truth).

3450 How wilt thou become my parasite (follower) in scooping up (the water) when thou hast an unbelief (as great) as Mount Qáf?

How should a mountain go into the cavity (eye) of a needle, unless indeed it become a single thread?

By asking forgiveness (of God) make the mountain (like) a straw, and (then) take joyously the cup of the forgiven and drain (it) joyously!

Inasmuch as God hath made it unlawful to the unbelievers, how wilt thou drink of it (whilst thou art endued) with this imposture?

How should the Creator of imposture buy (accept) thy imposture, O fabricator of fiction?

3455 Become (like) the kinsfolk of Moses, for deceit is useless: thy deceit is (like) measuring the empty wind.

Will the water dare to turn aside from the command of the Lord and bestow refreshment on[1] the unbelievers?

Or dost thou suppose that thou art eating bread? Thou art eating snake-venom and (that which causes) wasting away of the spirit.

How should bread restore to health the spirit that averts its heart from the command of the Beloved Spirit?

Or dost thou suppose that when thou readest the words of the *Mathnawí* thou hearest them gratis (without giving aught in return)?

3460 Or that the discourse of wisdom and the hidden mystery comes easily into thy ear and mouth?

[1] Literally, "show aqueousness to."

It comes in, but, like fables, it shows (only) the husk, not the kernel of the berries,

(As) a sweetheart who has drawn a veil over her head and face and has hidden her face from thine eye.

By reason of contumacy the *Sháhnáma* or *Kalíla* seems to thee just like the *Qur'án*.

The difference between truth and falsehood is (visible) at the moment when the collyrium of (Divine) favour opens the eye;

Otherwise, dung and musk are both the same to one whose nose 3465 is obstructed (by disease), since (in him) there is no sense of smell.

His aim is to divert himself from ennui (by reading such books), and neglect the Word of the Almighty,

That by means of that (entertaining) discourse he may quench the fire of distress and anxiety and provide a cure (for his malady).

For the purpose of quenching this amount of fire, pure water and urine are alike in skill (are equally serviceable).

Both this urine and (this) water will quench the fire of distress, just as (it is quenched) during sleep.

But if thou become (really) acquainted with this pure water, 3470 which is the Word of God and spiritual,

All distress will vanish from the soul, and the heart will find its way to the Rose-garden,

Because every one who catches a scent of the mystery of the (Divine) scriptures flies into an orchard with[1] a running brook.

Or dost thou suppose that we see the face of the Saints as it is (in reality)?

Hence the Prophet remained in astonishment, saying, "How are the true believers not seeing my face?

How are the people not seeing the light of my face, which has 3475 borne away the prize from the orient sun?

And if they are seeing (it), wherefore is this perplexity?"— until a revelation came (to him from God), saying, "That face is in concealment.

In relation to thee it is the moon, and in relation to the people it is the cloud, in order that the infidel may not see thy face for nothing.

In relation to thee it is the bait, and in relation to the people it is the trap, in order that the vulgar may not drink of this chosen wine."

God said, "*Thou seest them looking*," (but) they are (like) the pictures in a bath-house: *they do not see*.

The form appears, O worshipper of form, as though its two 3480 dead eyes were looking.

Thou art showing reverence before the eye of the image, saying, "I wonder why it pays no regard to me.

---

[1] Literally, "and into."

Wherefore is this goodly image (so) very irresponsive that it does not say '*alayk* (on thee be peace!) in reply to my salaam?

It does not nod its head and moustache generously in regard for my having made a hundred prostrations before it."

God, though He does not nod the head outwardly, (yet) in regard for that (worship of Him) bestows an inward delight,

3485 Which is worth two hundred noddings of the head: in this fashion, after all, do Intellect and Spirit nod the head.

(If) thou serve Intellect in earnest, the regard of Intellect (for thee) is (shown by this), that it increases (thy) righteousness.

God does not nod the head to thee outwardly, but He makes thee a prince over the princes (of the world).

To thee God gives secretly something (of such power) that the people of the world bow down before thee,

Just as He gave to a stone such virtue that it was honoured by His creatures: that is to say, (it became) gold.

3490 (If) a drop of water gain the favour of God, it becomes a pearl and bears away the palm from gold.

The body is earth; and when God gave it a spark (of His Light) it became adept, like the moon, in taking possession of the world.

Beware! this (worldly empire) is a talisman and a dead image: its eye hath led the foolish astray from the (right) path.

It appears to wink: the foolish have made it their support (have put their trust in it).

How the Egyptian besought blessing and guidance from the Israelite, and how the Israelite prayed for the Egyptian and received a favourable answer to his prayer from the Most Gracious and Merciful (God).

The Egyptian said, "Do thou offer a prayer (for me), since from blackness of heart I have not the mouth (fit for offering an acceptable prayer),

3495 For it may be that the lock of this heart will be opened and that a place will be (granted) to this ugly one at the banquet of the beauteous.

Through thee the deformed may become endowed with beauty, or an Iblís may again become one of the Cherubim;

Or, by the august influence of Mary's hand[1], the withered bough may acquire the fragrance of musk and freshness and fruit."

Thereupon the Israelite fell to worship and said, "O God who knowest the manifest and the hidden,

To whom but Thee should Thy servant lift his hand? Both the prayer and the answer (to prayer) are from Thee.

[1] *I.e.* "through thy spiritual power which resembles that of Mary." Cf. *Qur'án*, XIX, 25.

Thou at first givest the desire for prayer, and Thou at last 3500 givest likewise the recompense for prayers.

Thou art the First and the Last: we between are nothing, a nothing that does not come into (admit of) expression."

He was speaking in this wise, till he fell into ecstasy[1] and his heart became senseless.

(Whilst engaged) in prayer, he came back to his senses (and witnessed the effect of his prayer): *Man shall have nothing but what he hath wrought.*

He was (still) praying when suddenly a loud cry and roar burst from the heart of the Egyptian,

(Who exclaimed), "Come, make haste and submit (the pro- 3505 fession of) the Faith (for my acceptance), that I may quickly cut the old girdle (of unbelief).

They have cast a fire into my heart, they have shown affection with (all) their soul for an Iblís (like me).

Praise be to God! Thy friendship and (my) not being able to do without thee have succoured me[2] at last.

My consortings with thee werè (as) an elixir: may thy foot never disappear from the house of my heart!

Thou wert a bough of the palm-tree of Paradise: when I grasped it, it bore me to Paradise.

That which carried away my body was a torrent: the torrent 3510 bore me to the brink of the Sea of Bounty.

I went towards the torrent in hope of (obtaining) water: I beheld the Sea and took pearls, bushel on bushel."

He (the Israelite) brought the cup to him, saying, "Now take the water!" "Go," he replied; "(all) waters have become despicable in my sight.

I have drunk such a draught from *God hath purchased*[3] that no thirst will come to me till the Congregation (at the Last Judgement).

He who gave water to the rivers and fountains hath opened a fountain within me.

This heart[4], which was hot and water-drinking—to its high 3515 aspiration water has become vile.

He (God), for the sake of His servants, became (symbolised by) the (letter) *káf* of *Káfí* (All-sufficing), (in token of) the truth of the promise of *Káf, Há, Yá, 'Ayn, Sád*[5].

(God saith), 'I am All-sufficing: I will give thee all good, without (the intervention of) a secondary cause, without the mediation of another's aid.

---

[1] Literally, "the bowl fell from the top of the roof."
[2] Literally, "have taken my hand."
[3] *Qur'án*, IX, 112.
[4] Literally, "liver."
[5] These five Arabic letters stand at the beginning of the nineteenth Súra of the *Qur'án*.

I am All-sufficing: I will give thee satiety without bread, I will give thee sovereignty without soldiers and armies.

I will give thee narcissi and wild-roses without the spring, I will give thee instruction without a book and teacher.

3520   I am All-sufficing: I will heal thee without medicine, I will make the grave and the pit a (spacious) playing-field.

To a Moses I give heart (courage) with a single rod, that he may brandish swords against a multitude.

(Such) a light and splendour do I give to the hand of Moses that it is slapping the sun (in triumph).

I make the wooden staff a seven-headed dragon, which the female dragon does not (conceive and) bring to birth from the male.

I do not mingle blood in the water of the Nile: in sooth by My cunning I make the very essence of its water to be blood.

3525   I turn thy joy into sorrow like the (polluted) water of the Nile, so that thou wilt not find the way to rejoicings.

Again, when thou art intent on renewing thy faith and abjurest Pharaoh once more,

Thou wilt see (that) the Moses of Mercy (has) come, thou wilt see the Nile of blood turned by him into water.

When thou keepest safe within (thee) the end of the rope (of faith), the Nile of thy spiritual delight will never be changed into blood.'

I thought I would profess the Faith in order that from this deluge of blood I might drink some water.

3530   How did I know that He would work a transformation in my nature and make me a (spiritual) Nile?

To my own eye, I am a flowing Nile, (but) to the eyes of others I am at rest."

Just as, to the Prophet, this world is plunged in glorification of God, while to us it is heedless (insensible).

To his eye, this world is filled with love and bounty; to the eyes of others it is dead and inert.

To his eye, vale and hill are moving swiftly: he hears subtle discourse from clod and brick.

3535   To the vulgar, all this (world) is a bound and dead (thing): I have not seen a veil (of blindness) more wonderful than this.

To our eye, (all) the graves are alike; to the eyes of the saints, (one is) a garden (in Paradise), and (another is) a pit (in Hell).

The vulgar would say, "Wherefore has the Prophet become sour (of visage) and why has he become pleasure-killing?"

The elect would say, "To your eyes, O peoples, he appears to be sour;

(But) come for once into our eyes, that ye may behold the laughs (of delight described) in (the Súra beginning with the words) *Hal atá (Did not there come?)*[1]."

---

[1] Qur'án, Súra LXXVI.

That appears (to thee) in the form of inversion (illusion) from 3540
the top of the pear-tree: come down, O youth!

The pear-tree is the tree of (phenomenal) existence: whilst
thou art there, the new appears old.

Whilst thou art there, thou wilt see (only) a thorn-brake full
of the scorpions of wrath and full of snakes.

When thou comest down, thou wilt behold, free of cost, a
world filled with rose-cheeked (beauties) and (their) nurses.

*Story of the lewd woman who said to her husband, " Those illusions
appear to thee from the top of the pear-tree, for the top of that
pear-tree causes the human eye to see such things: come down
from the top of the pear-tree, that those illusions may vanish."
And if any one should say that what that man saw was not an
illusion, the answer is that this (story) is a parable, not a (pre-
cise) similitude. In the (story regarded as a) parable this amount
(of resemblance) is sufficient, for if he had not gone to the top of
the pear-tree, he would never have seen those things, whether
illusory or real.*

That woman desired to embrace her paramour in the presence
of her foolish husband.

Therefore the woman said to her husband, "O fortunate one, 3545
I will climb the tree to gather fruit."

As soon as she had climbed the tree, the woman burst into
tears when from the top she looked in the direction of her
husband.

Marito dixit, "O cinaede improbe, quis est ille paedicator qui
super te incumbit?

Tu sub eo velut femina quietus es: O homo tu vero catamitus
evasisti."

"Nay," said the husband: "one would think thy head is
turned (thou hast lost thy wits); at any rate, there is nobody here
on the plain except me."

Uxor rem repetivit. "Eho," inquit, "iste pileatus quis est 3550
super tergo tuo incumbens?"

"Hark, wife," he replied, "come down from the tree, for thy
head is turned and thou hast become very dotish."

When she came down, her husband went up: (then) the
woman drew her paramour into her arms.

Maritus dixit, "O scortum, iste quis est qui velut simia super
te venit?"

"Nay," said the wife, "there is no one here but me. Hark,
thy head is turned: don't talk[1] nonsense."

He repeated the charge against his wife. "This," said the 3555
wife, "is from the pear-tree.

----

[1] Literally, "spin."

From the top of the pear-tree I was seeing just as falsely as you, O cuckold.

Hark, come down, that you may see there is nothing: all this illusion is caused by a pear-tree."

Jesting is teaching[1]: listen to it in earnest, do not thou be in pawn to (taken up with) its appearance of jest.

To jesters every earnest matter is a jest; to the wise (all) jests are earnest.

3560 Lazy folk seek the pear-tree, but 'tis a good (long) way to *that* pear-tree.

Descend from the pear-tree on which at present thou hast become giddy-eyed and giddy-faced.

This (pear-tree) is the primal egoism and self-existence wherein the eye is awry and squinting.

When thou comest down from this pear-tree, thy thoughts and eyes and words will no more be awry.

Thou wilt see that this (pear-tree) has become a tree of fortune, its boughs (reaching) to the Seventh Heaven.

3565 When thou comest down and partest from it, God in His mercy will cause it to be transformed.

On account of this humility shown by thee in coming down, God will bestow on thine eye true vision.

If true vision were easy and facile, how should Muṣṭafá (Mohammed) have desired it from the Lord?

He said, "Show (unto me) each part from above and below such as that part is in Thy sight."

Afterwards go up the pear-tree which has been transformed and made verdant by the (Divine) command, "*Be*."

3570 This tree has (now) become like the tree connected with Moses[2], inasmuch as thou hast transported thy baggage towards (hast been endued with the nature of) Moses.

The fire (of Divine illumination) makes it verdant and flourishing; its boughs cry "*Lo, I am God*."

Beneath its shade all thy needs are fulfilled: such is the Divine alchemy.

That personality and existence is lawful to thee, since thou beholdest therein the attributes of the Almighty.

The crooked tree has become straight, God-revealing: *its root fixed (in the earth) and its branches in the sky.*

The remainder of the story of Moses, on whom be peace.

3575 For there came to him from the peremptory Revelation a message, saying, "Put crookedness aside now, *and be upright*."

This tree of the body is (like) Moses' rod, concerning which the (Divine) command came to him—"Let it fall from thy hand,

---

[1] *I.e.* "idle tales convey instruction."   [2] The Burning Bush.

That thou mayst behold its good and evil; after that, take it up (again) by command of Him."

Before his dropping it, it was naught but wood; whenever he took it up by His command, it became goodly.

At first it was shaking down leaves for the lambs; (afterwards) it reduced to impotence that deluded people.

It became ruler over the party of Pharaoh: it turned their 3580 water into blood and caused them to beat their heads with their hands.

From their sown fields arose famine and death on account of the locusts which devoured the leaves,

Till from Moses, when he considered[1] the ultimate issue, there went up involuntarily a prayer (to God)—

"For what reason is all this disablement (of them) and striving (to convert them), since this multitude will never become righteous?"

The (Divine) command came (to him), saying, "Follow Noah! Refrain from considering the end (of the matter) as it has been disclosed (to thee).

Take no heed of that, since thou art one who calls (the people) 3585 to the (true) Way. The command, '*Deliver the message*,' is there: it is not void (of meaning)."

The least purpose (thereof) is that through this persistence of thine that obstinacy and rebellious pride (of the infidels) may be displayed,

So that God's showing the way (to some) and letting (others) be lost may become evident to all the followers of religious sects.

Inasmuch as the object of existence was the manifestation (of these two Divine attributes), it must be tested by means of exhorting (to obedience) and leading astray.

The Devil persists in (seducing to) error; the Shaykh persists in guiding aright.

When that grievous command (of God) proceeded step by 3590 step (pursued its course), the whole Nile was turned into blood from end to end,

Till (at last) Pharaoh came in person to him (Moses), humbly entreating him, his tall figure bent double,

And said, "O (spiritual) sovereign, do not that which we did: we have not the face to offer words (of excuse).

I will become obedient to thy command with every bit (of my body); I am accustomed to be held in honour: do not deal hardly with me.

Hark, move thy lips in mercy, O trusted one, that it (thy prayer) may shut this fiery mouth (of Divine anger)."

He (Moses) said, "O Lord, he is deceiving me; he is deceiving 3595 Thy deceiver.

---

[1] Literally, "when his consideration fell upon."

Shall I hearken (to him) or shall I too give him deceit (in return), in order that that puller of the branch may recognise the root?[1]

For the root (origin) of every cunning and contrivance is with us[2]: whatsoever is on the earth, its root (origin) is from Heaven."

God said (to Moses), "That cur (Pharaoh) is not worth even that: fling a bone to the cur from a distance.

Hark, shake the rod, so that the sods may give back whatever the locusts have destroyed,

3600 And let the locusts immediately become black, that the people may behold the transformation wrought by God;

For I have no need of means: those means are (only) for the purpose of (serving as) a screen and covering,

To the end that the natural philosopher may attach himself to the drug[3]; and that the astronomer may turn his face to the star;

And that the hypocrite, from greed, may come to market at daybreak for fear of (finding) no demand for his wares,

Without having performed his devotions or washed his face: (whilst) seeking morsels (for himself) he has become a morsel for Hell."

3605 The spirit of the vulgar is devouring and being devoured, like the lamb that feeds on hay.

The lamb is feeding, while the butcher rejoices, saying, "For our sake it feeds on the grass of (its) desire."

In respect of food and drink thou art doing the work of Hell: thou art fattening thyself for its (Hell's) sake.

Do thine own work, feed on the daily bread of Wisdom, that the glorious heart (spirit) may become fat.

Bodily eating and drinking is the obstacle to this (spiritual) eating and drinking: the spirit is like a merchant, while the body is like a highwayman.

3610 (Only) at the time when the highwayman is consumed like firewood is the candle of the spirit resplendent;

For thou art (in reality) that (spiritual) intelligence, and (all) the rest (of thee) is a mask concealing the intelligence. Do not lose thy (real) self, do not strive in vain!

Know that every sensual desire is like wine and beng: it is a veil over the intelligence, and thereby the rational man is stupefied.

The intoxication of the intelligence is not (caused by) wine alone: whatsoever is sensual shuts the (spiritual) eye and ear.

Iblís was far removed from wine-drinking: he was drunken with pride and unbelief.

---

[1] *I.e.* "in order that Pharaoh, whose deceit is only derivative, may recognise the real source of all human action."

[2] *I.e.* with God and His prophets.

[3] *I.e.* "in order that he may attribute the cure of disease to drugs instead of ascribing it to God."

The drunken man is he who sees that which is not: (to 3615 him) what is (really) a piece of copper or iron appears to be gold.

This discourse hath no end. (God said), "O Moses, move thy lips, that the herbage may spring forth."

He (Moses) did so, and immediately the earth became green with hyacinths and costly grains.

That folk fell to (eating) the food, since they had suffered famine and were (almost) dead from ravenous hunger.

For several days they ate their fill of the gift, (both) those who were inspired by that breath (of Moses) and the (other) human beings and the quadrupeds.

When their bellies were filled and they grasped the (Divine) 3620 bounty and the necessity was gone, then they waxed insolent (in disobedience).

The carnal soul is a follower of Pharaoh: beware, do not satisfy it, lest it remember its ancient infidelity.

Without the glowing heat of the fire (of mortification) the carnal soul will never become goodly: hark, do not beat the iron till it has become like live coals.

Without hunger the body makes no movement (towards God): 'tis cold iron thou art beating. Know (this for sure)!

Though it weep and wail most piteously, it will never become a true believer. Take heed!

It is like Pharaoh: in (the time of) famine it lays its head before 3625 Moses, as he (Pharaoh) did, making supplication;

(But) when it has been freed from want, it rebels (once more): when the donkey has cast off his load, he kicks.

So, when its business has gone forward (prosperously), it (the carnal soul) forgets its sighs and lamentations.

The man who lives in a city (many) years, as soon as his eye goes asleep,

Beholds another city full of good and evil, and his own city comes not into his memory at all,

So that (he should say), "I have lived there (so many years); 3630 this new city is not mine: here I am (only) in pawn[1]."

Nay, he thinks that in sooth he has always lived in this very city and has been born and bred in it[2].

What wonder (then) if the spirit does not remember its (ancient) abodes, which have been its dwelling-place and birth-place aforetime,

Since this world, like sleep, is covering it over as clouds cover the stars?—

Especially as it has trodden so many cities, and the dust has not (yet) been swept from its perceptive faculty,

[1] *I.e.* not a permanent resident.
[2] Literally, "that his origin and habit has always been in this very city."

3635   Nor has it made ardent efforts that its heart should become pure and behold the past;

That its heart should put forth its head (peep forth) from the aperture of the mystery and should see the beginning and the end with open eye.

The diverse modes and stages of the nature of Man from the beginning.

First he came into the clime (world) of inorganic things, and from the state of inorganic things he passed into the vegetable state.

(Many) years he lived in the vegetable state and did not remember the inorganic state because of the opposition (between them);

And when he passed from the vegetable into the animal state, the vegetable state was not remembered by him at all,

3640   Save only for the inclination which he has towards that (state), especially in the season of spring and sweet herbs—

Like the inclination of babes towards their mothers: it (the babe) does not know the secret of its desire for being suckled;

(Or) like the excessive inclination of every novice towards the noble spiritual Elder, whose fortune is young (and flourishing).

The particular intelligence of this (disciple) is derived from that Universal Intelligence[1]: the motion of this shadow is derived from that Rose-bough.

His (the disciple's) shadow disappears at last in him (the Master); then he knows the secret of his inclination and search and seeking.

3645   How should the shadow of the other's (the disciple's) bough move, O fortunate one, if this Tree move not?

Again, the Creator, whom thou knowest, was leading him (Man) from the animal (state) towards humanity.

Thus did he advance from clime to clime (from one world of being to another), till he has now become intelligent and wise and mighty.

He hath no remembrance of his former intelligences (souls); from this (human) intelligence also there is a migration to be made by him,

That he may escape from this intelligence full of greed and self-seeking and may behold a hundred thousand intelligences most marvellous.

3650   Though he fell asleep and became oblivious of the past, how should they leave him in that self-forgetfulness?

From that sleep they will bring him back again to wakefulness, that he may mock at his (present) state,

---

[1] *I.e.* the Logos with whom the Master (the Perfect Man) is identified.

Saying, "What was that sorrow I was suffering in my sleep?
How did I forget the states of truth (the real experiences)?

How did not I know that that sorrow and disease is the effect
of sleep and is illusion and phantasy?"

Even so this world, which is the sleeper's dream: the sleeper
fancies that it is really enduring,

Till on a sudden there shall rise the dawn of Death and he 3655
shall be delivered from the darkness of opinion and falsehood.

(Then) laughter at those sorrows of his will take possession of
him when he sees his permanent abode and dwelling-place.

Everything good or evil that thou seest in thy sleep will be
made manifest, one by one, on the Day of the (Last) Congre-
gation.

That which thou didst in this sleep in the (present) world will
become evident to thee at the time of awaking.

Take care not to imagine that this (which thou hast done) is
(only) an evil action committed in this (state of) sleep and that
there is no interpretation (thereof) for thee.

Nay, this laughter (of thine) will be tears and moans on the 3660
Day of interpretation, O oppressor of the captive!

Know that in the hour of thy awakening thy tears and grief
and sorrow and lamentation will turn to joy.

O thou that hast torn the coat of (many) Josephs, thou wilt
arise from this heavy slumber (in the form of) a wolf.

Thy (evil) dispositions, one by one, having become wolves
will tear thy limbs in wrath.

According to (the law of) retaliation, the blood (shed by thee)
will not sleep (remain unavenged) after thy death: do not say,
"I shall die and obtain release."

This immediate retaliation (which is exacted in the present 3665
world) is (only) a makeshift: in comparison with the blow of
that (future) retaliation this is a (mere) play.

God hath called the present world *a play* because this penalty
is a play in comparison with that penalty.

This penalty is a means of allaying war and civil strife: that
one is like a castration, while this one resembles a circumcision.

*Explaining that the people of Hell are hungry and make lamentable
entreaty to God, saying, "Cause our portions to be fat and let
the provender reach us quickly, for we can endure no more."*

This discourse hath no end. (God said), "Hark, O Moses,
let those asses go to the grass,

That they may all be fattened by that goodly fodder. Hark,
(let them in), for We have wrathful wolves.

We surely know the plaintive cry of Our wolves: We make 3670
these asses a means of livelihood for them.

The gracious alchemy breathed from thy lips wished to make these asses human.

Much kindness and favour didst thou show in calling them (to God), (but) 'twas not the fortune and provision allotted to those asses.

Therefore let the quilt of bounty cover them, that the slumber of forgetfulness may overtake them speedily,

So that, when this troop (of asses) shall start up from suchlike slumber, the candle will have been extinguished and the cup-bearer will have gone.

3675 Their rebellious disobedience kept thee in a (great) perplexity: therefore they shall suffer in retribution a (great) sorrow,

To the end that Our justice may step forth and bestow in retribution what is appropriate to every evil-doer;

For the King, whom they were not seeing openly, was (always) with them secretly in their lives."

Inasmuch as the intellect is with thee, overseeing thy body, and though this perception of thine is unable to apprehend it,

(Yet) its perception, O such and such, is not unable to apprehend thy motion and rest when it tries[1],

3680 What wonder if the Creator of that intellect too is with thee? How art thou not conceding (the truth of that)?

He (some one) pays no heed to his intellect and embarks on[2] evil; afterwards his intellect rebukes him.

You forgot your intellect, your intellect did not (forget you), since that act of rebuke is the result of its presence (attention).

If it had not been present (attentive) and had been heedless, how should it have slapped you in rebuke?

And if your carnal soul had not been inattentive to it, how should your madness and heat have acted thus?

3685 Hence you and your intellect are like the astrolabe: by this means you may know the nearness of the Sun of existence.

Your intellect is indescribably near to you: it is neither to the left nor to the right nor behind nor in front.

How (then) should not the King be indescribably near? for intellectual search cannot find the way (to Him).

The motion that you have in your finger is not in front of your finger or behind it or to the left or to the right.

At the time of sleep and death it (the motion) goes from it (the finger); at the time of waking it rejoins it.

3690 By what way doth it come into your finger, (that motion) without which your finger hath no use?

The light of the eye and pupil, by what other way than the six directions doth it come into your eye?

---

[1] Literally, "at the trial."
[2] Literally, "comes into touch with," "cleaves to."

The world of creation is endued with (diverse) quarters and directions, (but) know that the world of the (Divine) Command[1] and Attributes is without (beyond) direction.

Know, O beloved, that the world of the Command is without direction: of necessity the Commander is (even) more without direction.

The intellect was (ever) without direction, and the Knower of the exposition[2] is more intelligent than intellect and more spiritual even than spirit.

No created being is unconnected with Him: that connexion, 3695 O uncle, is indescribable,

Because in the spirit there is no separating and uniting, while (our) thought cannot think except of separating and uniting.

Pursue that which is without separation and union by (aid of) a spiritual guide; but the pursuit will not allay your thirst.

(Yet) pursue incessantly, if you are far from the Source, that the vein of (true) manhood (in you) may bring you to the attainment (of your desire).

How should the intellect find the way to this connexion? This intellect is in bondage to separation and union.

Hence Muṣṭafá (Mohammed) enjoined us, saying, "Do not 3700 seek to investigate the Essence of God."

(As regards) that One whose Essence is an object of thought[3], in reality the (thinker's) speculation is not concerning the Essence.

It is (only) his (false) opinion, because on the way to God there are a hundred thousand veils.

Every one is naturally attached to some veil and judges that it is in sooth the identity ('ayn) of Him.

Therefore the Prophet banished this (false) judgement from him (the thinker), lest he should be conceiving in error a vain imagination.

And (as for) him in whose judgement (conception of God) 3705 there is irreverence, the Lord hath doomed the irreverent to fall headlong.

To fall headlong is that he goes downward and thinks that he is superior,

Because such is the case of the drunken man who does not know heaven from earth.

Go ye and think upon His wonders, become lost (to yourselves) from the majesty and awe (of Him).

When he (who beholds the wonders of God) loses beard and moustache (abandons pride and egoism) from (contemplating) His work, he will know his (proper) station and will be silent concerning the Worker (Maker).

---

[1] *I.e.* the suprasensible world of the Creative Word, *Kun*, "Be!"
[2] God.
[3] Literally, "concerning whose Essence there is an act of thought."

3710 He will only say from his soul, "I cannot (praise Thee duly),"
because the declaration thereof is beyond reckoning and bound.

*How Dhu 'l-Qarnayn[1] went to Mount Qáf and made petition,
saying, "O Mount Qáf, tell me of the majesty of the Attributes
of God"; and how Mount Qáf said that the description of His
majesty is ineffable, since (all) perceptions vanish before it; and
how Dhu 'l-Qarnayn made humble supplication, saying, "Tell
of His works that thou hast in mind and of which it is more easy
for thee to speak."*

Dhu 'l-Qarnayn went towards Mount Qáf: he saw that it was
(made) of pure emerald,
And that it had become a ring surrounding the (whole) world.
He was amazed at that immense creation (work of God).
He said, "Thou art the mountain (indeed): what are the
others? for beside thy magnitude they are (but) playthings."
It replied, "Those (other) mountains are my veins: they are
not like unto me in beauty and glory.

3715 I have a hidden vein in every land: (all) the regions of the
world are fastened to my veins.
When God wills an earthquake in any land, He bids me and
I cause the vein to throb.
Then I make to move mightily the vein with which the
(particular) land is connected.
When He says 'Enough!' my vein rests. I am (apparently) at
rest, but actually I am in rapid motion"—
At rest, like the (medicinal) ointment, and very active
(efficacious); at rest, like the intellect, while the speech (im-
pelled) by it is moving[2].

3720 In the opinion of him whose intelligence does not perceive
this, earthquakes are caused by terrestrial vapours.

*An ant, walking on a piece of paper, saw the pen writing and began
to praise the pen. Another ant, which was more keen-sighted,
said, "Praise the fingers, for I deem this accomplishment to pro-
ceed from them." Another ant, more clear-sighted than either,
said, "I praise the arm, for the fingers are a branch of the arm,"
et cetera.*

A little ant saw a pen (writing) on a paper, and told this
mystery to another ant,
Saying, "That pen made wonderful pictures like sweet basil
and beds of lilies and roses."
The other ant said, "That artist is the finger, and this pen is
actually (no more than) the derivative (instrument) and the sign."

---

[1] Alexander the Great.

[2] Or, taking زو = زود, "while the speech is moving quickly."

A third ant said, "It is the work of the arm, by whose strength the slender finger depicted it."

In this fashion it (the argument) was carried upward till a 3725 chief of the ants, (who) was a little bit sagacious,

Said, "Do not regard this accomplishment as proceeding from the (material) form, which becomes unconscious in sleep and death.

Form is like a garment or a staff: (bodily) figures do not move except by means of intellect and spirit."

He (the wise ant) was unaware that without the controlling influence of God that intellect and heart (mind) would be inert.

If He withdraw His favour from it for a single moment, the acute intellect will commit (many) follies.

When Dhu 'l-Qarnayn found it (Mount Qáf) speaking, he 3730 said, after Mount Qáf had bored the pearls of speech,

"O eloquent one, who art wise and knowest the mystery, expound to me the Attributes of God."

It answered, "Go, for those qualities are too terrible for (oral) exposition to put its hand on them,

Or for the pen to dare inscribe with its point information concerning them on the pages (of books)."

He said, "Relate a lesser tale concerning the wonders of God, O goodly divine."

It said, "Look, the King (God) hath made a plain full of snow- 3735 mountains, for the distance of a three hundred years' journey—

Mountain on mountain, beyond count and number: the snow comes continually to replenish them.

One snow-mountain is being piled on another: the snow brings coldness to the earth.

At every moment snow-mountain is being piled on snow-mountain from the illimitable and vast storehouse.

O king, if there were not a valley (of snow) like this, the glowing heat of Hell would annihilate me."

Know that (in this world) the heedless are (like) snow-moun- 3740 tains, to the end that the veils of the intelligent may not be consumed.

Were it not for the reflexion (effect) of snow-weaving (chilling) ignorance, that Mount Qáf would be consumed by the fire of longing.

The Fire (of Hell) in sooth is (only) an atom of God's wrath; it is (only) a whip to threaten the base.

Notwithstanding such a wrath, which is mighty and surpassing all, observe that the coolness of His clemency is prior to it.

('Tis) a spiritual priority, unqualified and unconditioned. Have you seen the prior and the posterior without duality (have you seen them to be one)?

3745 If you have not seen them (as one), that is because of feeble understanding; for the minds of God's creatures are (but) a single grain of that mine.

Lay the blame on yourself, not on the evidences of the (true) Religion: how should the bird of clay reach the sky of the (true) Religion?

The bird's lofty soaring-place is (only) the air, since its origin is from lust and sensuality.

Therefore be dumbfounded without nay or yea, in order that a litter may come from (the Divine) Mercy to carry you.

Forasmuch as you are too dull to apprehend these wonders (of God), if you say "yea" you will be prevaricating;

3750 And if you say "nay," the "nay" will behead (undo) you: on account of that "nay" (the Divine) Wrath will shut your (spiritual) window.

Be, then, only dumbfounded and distraught, nothing else, that God's aid may come in from before and behind.

When you have become dumbfounded and crazed and naughted, you have said with mute eloquence, "*Lead us.*"

It (the wrath of God) is mighty, mighty; but when you begin to tremble, that mighty (wrath) becomes assuaged and equable,

Because the mighty shape is for (terrifying) the unbeliever; when you have become helpless, it is mercy and kindness.

How Gabriel, on whom be peace, showed himself to Muṣṭafá (Mohammed), God bless and save him, in his own shape; and how, when one of his seven hundred wings became visible, it covered the horizon (on all sides), and the sun with all its radiance was veiled over.

3755 Muṣṭafá said in the presence of Gabriel, "Even as thy shape (really) is, O friend,

Show it to me sensibly and visibly, that I may behold thee as spectators (who fix their eyes on an object of interest)."

He replied, "Thou canst not (bear this) and hast not the power to endure it; the sense (of sight) is weak and frail: 'twould be grievous for thee (to behold me)."

"Show thyself," said he, "that this body may perceive to what an extent the senses are frail and resourceless."

Man's bodily senses are infirm, but he hath a potent nature within.

3760 This body resembles flint and steel, but in quality (intrinsically) it is a striker of fire.

Flint and steel are the birth-place whence fire is brought into being: (from them) fire is born, domineering over both its parents.

Fire, again, exercises sway over the bodily nature: it is dominant over the body and flaming;

Yet again, there is in the body an Abraham-like flame whereby the tower of fire is subdued.

In consequence (of this) the all-accomplished Prophet said symbolically, "We are the hindmost and the foremost."

The material form of these twain (flint and steel) is vanquished 3765 by a (hammer and) anvil, (but) in quality (intrinsically) they are superior to the mine of iron ores.

Therefore Man is in appearance a derivative of the world, and intrinsically the origin of the world. Observe this!

A gnat will set his outward frame whirling round (in pain and agitation); his inward nature encompasses the Seven Heavens.

When he (the Prophet) persisted (in his request), he (Gabriel) displayed a little the awful majesty by which a mountain would be reduced to dust.

A single royal pinion (of his) covered the east and the west: Muṣṭafá (Mohammed) became senseless from awe.

When Gabriel saw him senseless from fear and dread, he came 3770 and drew him into his arms.

That awe is the portion of aliens, while this fond affection is freely bestowed on friends.

Kings, when seated on the throne, have formidable guardsmen (around them) with swords in their hands,

Staves and lances and scimitars, so that (even) lions would tremble in awe;

The shouts of sergeants with their maces, by the terror of which (men's) souls are enfeebled.

This is for the high and low in the street, to announce to 3775 them (the presence of) an emperor.

This pomp is for the sake of the vulgar, that those people may not put on the tiara of arrogance;

That it may break their egoism and that the self-conceited carnal soul may not work mischief and evil.

The country is preserved from that by the king's having force and authority to inflict punishment.

Therefore those vain desires are extinguished in (men's) souls: awe of the king prevents that disaster.

Again, when he (the king) comes to the private banquet, how 3780 should awe or retaliation be (in place) there?

There clemency on clemency is (shown) and mercies overflowing; you will hear no noise but that of the harp and flute.

In time of war there is the terrible drum and kettle-drum; in the hour of feasting with favourites there is (only) the sound of the harp.

The Board of Audit[1] is for the vulgar, while the fair ones resembling peris are for the cup-companion.

---

[1] ديوانِ مُحاسب can also mean "the devils who call to account."

The coat of mail and the helmet are for the battle, while this silken raiment and music are for the bower.

3785 This topic hath no end, O generous one: conclude it, and God best knoweth the right course.

The (corporeal) senses in Aḥmad (Mohammed), which are mortal[1], are now laid asleep under the soil of Yathrib (Medina),

But that mighty-natured part of him, which is unconquerable[2], dwells, without having suffered corruption, within *the abode of truth* (in Paradise).

The bodily attributes are exposed to corruption; the everlasting spirit is a shining sun,

Incorruptible, for it is not of the east; unchangeable, for it is not of the west.

3790 How was the sun (ever) dumbfounded by a mote? How was the candle (ever) made senseless by a moth?

The body of Aḥmad was liable to that (corruption): know that this corruption belongs (only) to the body,

Such as sickness and sleep and pain; the spirit is untouched by these affections and wholly detached (from them).

Indeed I cannot describe the spirit, and if I describe it, quaking would fall upon this (world of) phenomenal existence and spatiality.

If its fox (the body) was perturbed for a moment, belike the lion-spirit was then asleep.

3795 That lion which is immune from sleep was (apparently) asleep: lo, a complaisant terrible lion!

The lion feigns to be asleep so (well) that those curs think he is quite dead;

Else, who in the world would dare to rob a poor man (even) of a grain of turpeth mineral?

The foam (body) of Aḥmad was torn (powerfully affected) by that sight (of Gabriel), (but) his sea (spirit) surged up (displayed itself in action) for love of the foam.

The moon (the spirit of Aḥmad) is entirely a bounteous light-diffusing hand: if the moon have no hand (with which to bestow light), let it have none!

3800 If Aḥmad should display that glorious pinion (his spiritual nature), Gabriel would remain dumbfounded unto everlasting.

When Aḥmad passed beyond the Lote-tree (on the boundary of Paradise) and his (Gabriel's) place of watch and station and farthest limit,

He said to him (Gabriel), "Hark, fly after me." He (Gabriel) said, "Go, go; I am not thy companion (any farther)."

He answered him, saying, "Come, O destroyer of veils: I have not yet advanced to my zenith."

---

[1] Literally "setting," "subject to decline."
[2] Literally, "cleaving the ranks (of the enemy, like a hero)."

He replied, "O my illustrious friend, if I take one flight beyond this limit, my wings will be consumed."

This tale of the elect losing their senses in (contemplation of) 3805
the most elect is (naught but) amazement on amazement.

Here all (other) unconsciousnesses are (a mere) play. How long will you keep possession of your soul? for it is (a case of) abandoning your soul.

O "Gabriel," though you are noble and revered, you are not the moth nor the candle either.

When the candle calls at the moment of illumination, the soul of the moth does not shrink from burning.

Bury this topsy-turvy discourse: make the lion contrariously the prey of the onager[1].

Stop up thy word-sweating water-skin, do not open the bag 3810 of thy reckless talk.

He whose (intellectual and spiritual) parts have not passed beyond the earth—this is absurd and reckless talk in *his* view.

Do not resist them, O my beloved; deal gently with them, O stranger lodging in their home.

Give (them) what they wish and desire, and satisfy them, O emigrant dwelling in their land.

Till (the hour of) coming to the king and to sweet delight, O man of Rayy be on good terms with the man of Merv[2].

O "Moses," in presence of the Pharaoh of the time you must 3815 speak softly *with mild words*.

If you put water into boiling oil, you will destroy (both) the trivet and the kettle.

Speak softly, but do not speak aught except the truth: do not offer temptation in your mildness of address.

The time of afternoon is come: cut short the discourse, O thou whose expression (of the hidden truth)[3] makes (the people of) the age acquainted (with reality).

Do thou tell the clay-eater that sugar is better: do not show injurious softness, do not give him clay.

Speech would be a spiritual garden to the soul, if it were in- 3820
dependent of letters and sounds.

Oh, there is many a one in whom this donkey's head amidst the sugar-plantation has fixed a thorn![4]

He, (seeing it) from afar, supposed that it (the sugar-plantation)

---

[1] The poet is addressing himself. Probably he means, "Let discretion (the timid onager) prevail over valour (the fierce lion)."
[2] See Book I, *v.* 288.
[3] Literally, "thy squeezing out the juice." In this verse the word '*aṣr* is used in three different meanings.
[4] The "donkey's head" (scarecrow) signifies the anecdotes by which the author seeks to convey spiritual truth; but he points out here that these anecdotes, if taken literally, are an obstacle to the attainment of that truth.

is just that (donkey's head), nothing more; (so) he was retiring, like a ram vanquished in fight.

Know for sure that the (literal) form (of speech) is (like) that donkey's head in the vineyard and highest Paradise of the spiritual reality.

O Ẓiyá'u 'l-Ḥaqq Ḥusámu'ddín, bring this donkey's head into that melon-field,

3825   In order that, when the donkey's head has died to (has passed beyond) the skinning-place, that kitchen[1] may bestow on it another growth (a spiritual regeneration).

Hark, the shaping (of the poem) is from me, and the spirit (of it) from thee; nay, (I spoke) in error: truly both this and that are from thee.

Thou art glorified in Heaven, O conspicuous Sun: be thou also glorified on earth unto everlasting,

That the inhabitant of the earth may become one in heart and one in aim and one in nature with the sublime celestial.

(Then) separation and polytheism and duality will disappear: in real existence there is (only) unity.

3830   When my spirit (fully) recognises thy spirit, they (both) remember their being one in the past,

And on the earth become (as) Moses and Aaron, sweetly mingled like milk and honey.

When it (my spirit) recognises (thy spirit) a little and (then) denies (it), its denial becomes a veil covering (the truth).

Many a one who recognised (part of the truth) averted his face: that Moon was angered by his ingratitude.

Hence the evil spirit became unable to recognise the spirit of the Prophet and turned on its heel.

3835   You have read all this: read (the Súra beginning with the words) *Lam yakun*[2], that you may know the obstinacy of that old infidel.

Ere the (bodily) form of Aḥmad (Mohammed) displayed its glory, the description of him (in the Pentateuch and the Gospel) was a phylactery for every infidel.

"There is some one like this" (they said): "(let us wait) till[3] he shall appear"; and their hearts were throbbing at the imagination of (seeing) his face.

They were prostrating themselves (in prayer), crying, "O Lord of mankind, wilt Thou bring him before our eyes as quickly as may be?"

(This they did) in order that, by *asking (God) to grant them victory* in the name of Ahmad, their enemies might be overthrown.

---

[1] The Turkish Commentator reads *mabṭakha* (melon-garden) for *maṭbakha* (kitchen), but all my MSS. have the latter reading, which agrees better with *maslakha* (skinning-place).
[2] *Qur'án*, XCVIII.   [3] Read ﺗﺎ with G.

Whenever a formidable war arose, Aḥmad's pertinacity in 3840
onset was always their succour;

Wherever there was a chronic sickness, mention (invocation)
of him (Aḥmad) was always their healing medicine.

In (all) their way his form was coming into their hearts and
into their ears and into their mouths.

How should every jackal perceive his (real) form? Nay, (they
perceived only) the derivative of his form, that is to say, the
imaginal idea (of it).

If his (real) form should fall on the face of a wall, heart's blood
would trickle from the heart of the wall;

And his form would be so auspicious for it (would bestow 3845
such blessing on it) that the wall would at once be saved from
having a double face.

Beside the single-facedness (sincerity) of the pure (in spirit),
that double-facedness has become a fault (even) in the wall.

All this veneration and magnification and affection (which they
had shown towards the Prophet) the wind swept away, as soon
as they saw him in (bodily) form.

The false coin saw the fire and immediately became black:
when has there (ever) been a way for the false coin (of hypocrisy)
to enter the (pure) heart?

The false coin was talking boastfully of its desire for the
touchstone, that it might cast the (sincere) disciples into doubt.

A worthless one falls into the snare of its deceit; (for) from 3850
every base fellow the thought pops up,

That if this were not genuine coin, how should it have be-
come eager for the touchstone?

It desires the touchstone, but one of such a kind that its
falseness will not be clearly exposed thereby.

The touchstone that keeps hidden the quality (of that which
is tested) is not a (true) touchstone, nor (is it) the (discrimin-
ating) light of knowledge.

The mirror that keeps hidden the defects of the face to
flatter[1] every cuckold

Is not a (true) mirror; it is hypocritical. Do not seek such a 3855
mirror so long as you can (help).

[1] Literally, "from regard for the feelings of."

APPENDIX

SHOWING the changes required in order to bring the translation of Books I, II and III (vv. 1–2835) into agreement with the text of the Qóniya MS., designated as G, which was transcribed in A.H. 677–A.D. 1278.

BOOK I

Preface, p. 3, l. 1. *Read* which is the roots of the roots of the (Mohammedan) Religion.
Preface, p. 3, l. 23. After *the purified* add (*It is*) *a revelation from the Lord of created beings.*
Preface, p. 3, l. 24. Omit *either* and *or behind.*
Preface, p. 4, l. 2. *After* God *read* and the Imám of right guidance and certainty.
Preface, p. 4, l. 3 from foot. *Read* Glory be to God alone, and God bless our Lord Mohammed and his kin and the people of his house; and *God is our sufficiency, and how goodly a guardian is He!*
1. *Read* Listen to this reed how it complains, telling a tale of separations. 2. *Read* man and woman have moaned in (unison with) my lament. 22. *Read* is purged entirely of covetousness and defect. 35. *This verse follows the Heading.* **Heading.** *How the king fell in love with the sick handmaiden and made plans to restore her health.* 38. *Omit* the soul of. 47. *Read* Each of us is a learned Messiah. 53. *Read* oxymel increased the bile; *and* was producing dryness. 55, **Heading.** Omit *to the king* and read *how the king turned his face.* 57. *Read* praise and prayer. 64. *Read* a skilled physician. 78, **Heading.** *Omitted.* 80. *After* heaven *read* without buying and selling and without speaking and hearing. 82. *Read* the dishes (of food) and the bread from heaven *and* there remained for us the toil. 93, **Heading.** Read *The meeting of the king with the saint who had been shown to him in dream.* 96. *Read* O light of God. 101, **Heading.** *Omitted.* 107. *Read* from yellow or black bile. 119. *Read* so wondrous strange as the Sun, the everlasting spiritual Sun which hath no yesterday. 121. *Read* But the Sun by which the aether was brought into existence hath no peer. 137. *Read* He said, "Tell this openly and nakedly: talk of religion is better overt than covert." 144, **Heading.** Omit *with the hand-maiden.* 159. *Read* masters and town and dwelling. 162. *Read* He reckoned up her friends and town. 177. *Read* the seed *and* its inward secret. 181. *Read* The promise of the noble is a flowing (bountiful) treasure. 186. *Read* Those two Amírs came to Samarcand (and went) to the goldsmith, bearing the good news from the king. 209. *Read* this hunter. 216. *Read of* love and pain. 222, **Heading.** *Omitted.* 222. *Read* that man. 229. *Read* the cup of (spiritual) life. 244. *Read* is happy at that moment. 255. *Read* at the moment when I struck (such a blow). 258. *Read* every sort of hidden (unfamiliar) thing. 260. *Read* cried to the dervish, as rational persons (might have done). 270. *Read* and that one full of sugar. 273. *Read* the Light of the One (God). 290. *Read* and if

(he be called) "hypocrite," he becomes fierce and filled with fire (rage). **300.** *Read* every certainty. **311.** *Read* (is what) the present necessity. **331.** *Transpose this and the following verse.* **341.** *Omit* resembling thee. **344.** *Read* my nose and lips. **361.** *Read* in amazement at that hidden (mysterious) plot. **368.** *Read* they were inquiring. **389.** *After* cage *read* independent, neither ruling nor ruled by any one. **395.** *Read* (inasmuch as) the intellect too is carried off. **401.** *Read* on their leg. **406.** *Transpose* the Cave *and* the Friend. **417.** *Read* and, below, its shadow is speeding. **445.** *Read* garlic in the walnut cake. **460.** *Read* became in bondage to (a prey to) that vizier. **471.** *Read* the power of Him. **487** *Omit* nothing more. **498.** *Read* how will you catch a scent from the garden of Unity? **499.** *Read* Twelve scrolls. **500, Heading.** Read *these differences lie.* **501.** *Read* one-coloured as the zephyr. **536.** *Read* is it not metamorphosis to become earth and clay, O contumacious one? **565.** *Read* admonition and discourse (conveyed) by the tongue and (through the) ear. **582.** *Read* of its own accord its heart will crave bread. **604.** *Read* may that which is unseen never fail! **608.** *Read* who will make inquiry of thee? [کيست for کیت in the text is a misprint]. **620.** *Read* between pupils and masters. **621.** *Read* And if you say that he (the assertor of free-will) takes no heed of (the Divine) compulsion, (and that) God's moon (majesty) hides its face (from him) in the cloud (of his own blindness). **636.** *Read* (But) in the act for which you have no inclination and desire, you make yourself a necessitarian. **660.** *Read* The text of those scrolls was diverse: all were (different) like the letters from *alif* to *yá.* **739.** *This verse precedes the Heading.* **755.** *Read* not these seven heavens (which are) held in high regard. **757.** *Read* from those stars. **763.** *Read* nightingales are in love with the face of the rose. **766.** *Read* this gross colour. **775.** *Read* the black water hidden in the jug; know that the self is the fountain. **776.** *Read* the idol-making self is a fountain (jetting muddy water) on the Water-way (the Way that leads to the Water of Life). **777.** *Read* but the fountain-water is making jets incessantly. **798.** *Read* the power and grace of God. **801.** *Read* except the sweetness of (the true) religion. **812.** *Read* and called (the name of) Mohammed. **813.** *Read* (Divine) favours and knowledge (derived) immediately from God. **816.** *Read* And if God wishes. **827.** *Read* How does such a lofty flame not burn? **829.** *Read* "I am the same, O idolater." **851.** *Read* by the command of God the wind devours (extinguishes) fire. **854, Heading.** *Omitted.* **862.** *Read* The religious are not burned by the fire of lust. **897.** *Read* Moreover, the insolent are pleased. **900.** *Read* were continually harassed. **903.** *Read* Henceforth do not come in quest of any prey, *and omit* beyond thy allowance. **929, Heading.** Omit *again.* **935.** *Read* Then He will give you hints. **941.** *Read* O inconsiderate sluggard. **943.** *Read* (How absurd) to be a necessitarian and sleep amidst highwaymen! **945.** *Read* from whom the understanding flies away. **978.** *Read* for one or two little days. **990.** *Read* and fill it with the wind of Divine majesty. **1002.** *Read* After this manner every prophet in the world used to call the peoples. **1014.** *Read* the ascetic of six hundred thousand years. **1027.** *Read* Attend *for* Listen. **1029.** *Read in the second half of the verse* behold the cunning of the hare and how he overthrew the lion. **1032.** *Read* the leviathan and the sea are. **1065.** *Read* When his understanding has been his teacher at the beginning, after this. **1116.** *Read* while the horse in truth is sweeping him.   **1119.** *Read* but where is this horse?   **1128.** *Read* and thou didst not see the colours.   **1150, Heading.** Omit *and the lion's anger with him.*   **1154.** *Read* elephants *for* oxen *and* lion *for* elephant.   **1156.** *Read* the hare's sleep of heedlessness.   **1160.** *Read* the poison of every knowledge.   **1177.** *Read* made two of me.   **1178.** *After* lion *read* this was what happened to me, and it has been told to thee (just as it happened).   **1186.** *Read* how, I wonder, will the water bear away a mountain?   **1188.** *Read* A Moses kills Pharaoh, with his army and mighty host, by means of the river Nile.   **1202.** *Read* all the birds came to pay him obeisance.   **1213.** *Read* sick and deaf and palsied.   **1228.** *Read* If my claim is (made) with falsehood.   **1242.** *Read* was, in the sight of God, this figure (of thee) who art (now) with me.   **1248.** *Read* If until the Resurrection I reckon up the praise of this Adam whose name I am celebrating, I fall short (of what is due).   **1255.** *Read* (Divine) destiny, then, is a cloud.   **1272.** *Read* a pale complexion has the sound (signification) of patience.   **1273.** *Read* takes *for* took *bis.*   **1283.** *Read* pestilential *for* foul.   **1304, Heading.** Omit *in the water.*   **1311.** *Read* O you who on account of (your) high estate are committing an act of injustice, know that you are digging a well (pit) for yourself.   **1321.** *Read in the second half of the verse* you are weaving a curse upon yourself at that moment.   **1332.** *Read in the second half of the verse* in (your) badness you became forgetful of goodness.   **1338.** *Read in the second half of the verse* Thou hast opened to all the treasure of (Thy) beneficence.   **1348.** *Read* and of that which surrounds the soul—nay, do not ask of those things!   **1351.** *Read* O thou lion that liest alone at the bottom of this well, thy fleshly soul, like the hare, has shed and drunk thy blood.   **1353.** *Read* O my people.   **1358.** *Read* they bowed (in homage) and said to him, "Hark!"   **1368.** After this verse add the **Heading,** *How the hare admonished the beasts, saying, "Do not rejoice in this!"*   **1382.** *Read* and the parts always have the nature of the whole.   **1415, Heading.** Read *under the tree.*   **1427, Heading.** *Omitted.*   **1437.** *Read* nobles and commons.   **1453.** *Read* breathes into its ear. [دهن in the text is a misprint for دمن].   **1457.** *Read* "Shall I do that? He said that (bade me do that)."   **1467.** *Read* the unseen and the future became.   **1480.** *Read* both the action of God and our action.   **1487.** *Read* comprehends all.   **1495.** *Read* make thy friend pleased (with thee).   **1499.** *Read* when did you see the man afflicted with a (morbid) tremor (to be) sorry?   **1500.** *Read* This is the intellectual quest—(but) what (sort of) intellect is that ingenious one? (the object of its quest is) that perchance.   **1504.** *Read* in the case of that (spiritual quest) *for* in searching into that (subject).   **1512.** *Read* we are His cloud shedding rain-drops abundantly.   **1515, Heading.** Read *in this clay of the body.*   **1532.** *Read* connexion with Man.   **1547, Heading.** Read *the merchant to whom the captive parrot.*   **1552.** *Read* The parrot said to him.   **1561.** *Read* if thou art unwilling to do me justice.   **1585.** *Omit* from this (matter).   **1593.** *Read* is like stone and is also like iron.   **1598.** *Read* at one time they are (like) the wound and at another time (like) the plaster.   **1605.** *Read* O bold man *or* O pensioner [مرد جری].

1608. *Read in the first half of the verse* He (the saint) brings red roses from the fire.   **1612.** *Read* the knowledge that goes into the disbelieving man.   **1615, Heading.** Omit *or shall we?*   **1617.** *Read* if thou wishest, do thou cast down.   **1628.** *Read* And enter ye.   **1649.** *Read* returned home (prosperously) to the joy of his friends.   **1651.** *Read* what thou hast seen and said. **1666.** *Read in the second half of the verse* call Zayd (his) murderer on account of (Zayd's having been) the original cause (of his death). **1691.** *Read* thereupon she trembled, fell. **1693.** *Read* sprang up. **1699.** *Read* thou art a great damage (very injurious) to mankind. **1707.** *Read* darkness-consuming light *and* day-enkindling dawn. **1736.** *This verse is omitted.* **1739.** *Read* Heart-ravishers (loved ones) seek with (all their) soul those who have lost their hearts (to them). **1755.** *Read* Him *for* Me *bis.* **1758.** *Read* both (my power of) causing (thee) to understand and (my) tongue (itself) would be consumed. **1767.** *Read* to sit at his door. **1776.** *Read* How shall not I be like night...? **1789.** *Read* do Thou come, O Giver of the Command. **1807.** *Read* O Thou who art the Dawn of the dawn and its Refuge. **1824.** *Read* Whatever they strive (to do), whether man or woman. **1836.** *Read* (evil) eyes and angers. **1845.** *Read* counsels devoid of hypocrisy. **1867.** *Read* The fleshly soul was made a Pharaoh by (receiving) many praises. **1871.** *Read* "Truly a dead man has risen from the grave." **1872.** *Read* they may entrap him. **1876.** *Read* the good-for-nothing Devil is fleeing from you. **1877.** *Read* He who (formerly) clung to your skirt fled from you when you became like this. **1884.** *Read* these winds absorb it. **1885.** *Read* when they absorb it. **1897.** *Read* full of buds and roses and cypresses. **1911.** *Read* mayst display flowers. **1926.** *Read* cast aside this fancy and vain imagining. **1931.** *Read* the soul of every dead one starts up from the body's grave. **1935.** *Read* O ye whom death (in your hearts) hath made naught underneath the skin. **1949.** *Read* Either take it from the hindmost light—there is no difference—or from the candle of the Spirit. **1955.** *Read* gained therefrom extinction; from its everlastingness the dead (soul) put on the mantle (of eternal life). **1962.** *Read* from desire of a morsel *and* Seek ye always (to draw forth) the thorn. **1980.** *Read* from the effect produced by faithfulness. **1981.** *Read* there reason becomes lost, lost, O comrade. **2008.** *Read* is without relations. **2022.** *Read* the secrets of the rose. **2025.** *Read* the flash of the lightning. **2055.** *Read* Against the sayings of the Saints *and omit* (against them). **2056.** *Read* in order that thou mayst escape. **2078.** *Read* what sweet one is there that did not become unsweet. **2088.** *Read* when he had played a long while. **2093.** *Read* Without wing or foot. **2112.** *Read* the (spiritual) apprehension of (possessed by) stone and wood. **2125.** *Read* are cast into doubt by a half-imagination. **2131.** *Read* The lord of *for* One possessed of. **2132.** *Read* (yet) they are under the protection of the clear-sighted people. **2169.** *Read* he saw there no one but that old man. **2184.** *Read* The old man trembled when he heard this, biting his hand and quivering all over. **2190.** *Read* none in the world can know *and omit* except Him. **2199, Heading.** Omit *which is non-existence (of self).* **2212.** *Read* Feelings and words beyond. **2223.** *Read* two goodly angels are always making proclamation. **2230.** *Read* bestowed what belonged to the King upon His enemies. **2240.** *Read* devour it entirely. **2246.** *Read* (He was) a sea (of bounty), and the pearls (in it) came pure (untarnished) from his munificence. **2261.** *Read* we have been beheaded by the sword of want. **2263.** *Read* (when) he goes to sleep at night, I will tear the tattered cloak from his body. **2268.** *Read* except jasper. **2275.** *Read* would be ashamed of his inward (thoughts and feelings). **2288, Heading.** Omit *patience and.* **2303.** *Read* they kill those that are fattest. **2304.** *Read* this tale of gold.

2312. *Read* when one is empty and one full to the brim. **2325.** *Read* this bone. **2330.** *Read* may thy (superior) talent and understanding fall short of. **2331.** *Read* this is wonderful. **2335.** *Read* from greed of getting. **2347.** *Read* how should he strip him? **2356.** *Read* May the fire consume him, because. **2359.** *Read* in order that it may not suffer harm by having its head crushed. **2369.** *Read* O Prince of mankind *for* O King. **2374.** *Read* majesty *for* light. **2384.** *Read* the sound of the harp. **2400.** *Read* By thy soul, this is not *and add* of mine *after* moaning. **2411.** *Read* ass *for* beast. **2428.** *Read* by whose words the (whole) world was intoxicated. **2430.** *Read* between them both *and omit* O King. **2434.** *Read* because they are fierce and very impudent in their behaviour. **2447, Heading.** Read *like poison and antidote.* **2456.** *Omit* sappy. **2457.** *Read* grafted *for* firmly planted. **2471.** *Substitute for this verse* The original source of oil (the oil-producing tree) is made to grow by means of water: how (then) does it (oil) finally become opposed to water? **2481.** *Read* know that Pharaoh's abhorrence (of Moses). **2501.** *Read* A world has been left nailed fast in night, waiting expectantly, depending on the sun and the day. **2505.** *After* this world *read* that Guide was inwardly alone. **2515.** *Read* The spirit is like Ṣáliḥ, and the body. **2517.** *Omitted.* **2519.** *Read* God became secretly united with a body. **2531.** *Read* divulged *for* ratified. **2538.** *Read* When they all gave themselves up to despair. **2541.** *Read* that town. **2542.** *Read* smoke and naphtha. **2544.** *Read* their spirits shedding tears, like hailstones. **2549.** *Read* have ye bestowed. **2558.** *Read* Do not recite incorrectly, O thou who recitest correctly the perspicuous (Qur'án). **2562.** *Read* For the host of (their) ill-omened exactions of vengeance? **2567.** *Read* traditional ideas *for* the standards of tradition *and* they set their feet (trampled) on the head of Reason, this venerable Guide. **2588.** *Read in the second half of the verse* its taste will deal him a blow that pierces his liver. **2600.** *Read* it is a remedy. **2612.** *Omit* Hence *and read* this kingdom and banner. **2636.** *Read* He to whom the Light of God has become a guide is not a slave to effects or causes. **2637.** *Read* Or (if he is a slave to them) Love will throw. **2638.** *Read* He has no need to make (his) love known. **2640.** *Read* Although the inner meaning is visible in this outward form. **2646.** *Read* The wife said, "Dost thou intend to treat me with kindness?" **2653.** *Read* "I am not contained at all in 'high' and 'low'." **2659.** *Read* Every angel was saying *and* on the face of the earth. **2661.** *Read* with this dust. **2687.** *Read* Companionship with kings. **2699.** *Read* that the King who wants naught may take pity on me. **2703.** *Read* When with all thy might thou dost (endeavour to) rise up. **2707.** *Read* If his treasury is full of splendid merchandise, (yet) he will have no water like this: 'tis rare. **2716.** *Read* there is running the Tigris (whose water is) sweet as sugar. **2719.** *Read* a single drop in that pure river. **2722.** *Read in the second half of the verse* it is naught but pure wine and the source of pleasures (to the taste). **2750.** *Read* evidentiary sign *for* mirror. **2758.** *Read* Conception is created: it has been begotten. **2768.** *Read* sorrow and joy which are a lot (received) in the heart (which befall the heart). **2774.** *Read* went to meet him. **2779.** *Read* O ye on whose religion pieces of gold. **2780.** *Read* who have come from the King. **2806.** *Read* he remained (as) the thorn. **2821.** *Read* Regard the king as a reservoir, his retainers as the pipes: the water runs through the pipe into the ponds (receptacles). **2832.** *Read* With the master. **2850.** *Read* for he was inattentive and very blind to the Tigris. **2856.** *Read* by way of the Tigris *for* by water. **2858.** *Read* this bounteous King. **2859.** *Read* coin as that. **2866.** *Read* and thy brokenness has in truth become soundness. **2878.** *After* Arab *read* till he arrived at that (exalted) court and that (high) fortune. **2883.** *Read* that branch (derivative) has been adorned by the pure root (source). **2888.** *Read* for the sake of every idolater. **2891.** *Read* is the gift of Lordship. **2897.** *Read* like the thoughts of lovers. **2903.** *Read* and this wife is the appetitive soul and cupidity. **2911.** *Read* the strength of thy spirit. **2914.** *Read* to *yá* (Y) from *alif* (A). **2917.** *Read* beautiful and splendid. **2923.** *Read* the (fair) colour of that and the rust (foul colour) of this. **2926.** *Read* every star in the sky is part of the Moon. **2937.** *Read* pearls *for* beads. **2942.** *After* potent *read* especially the wine that is from the presence (of God). **2965.** *Read* the shadow (protection) of the chosen favourite of God. **2974.** *Read* through the help of the spiritual influence of the Pírs. **2977.** *Read* they must lay before the guest. **2978.** *Read* before the king *for* before them. **2986.** *Omit* of the beauty. **2998.** *After* said he *read* the pain has become too great: do not strike (further) blows. **2999.** *Read* and then remained in bewilderment. **3000.** *Omit* Then *and read* angrily flung. **3014.** *Read* tie fast the burden of the fetters. **3037.** *Read* If I should not behead *them that think ill of God*, it would be the essence of wrong. **3049.** *Read* the kernel (real understanding) and right consideration. **3056, Heading.** After *any friend that is 'I'* add *Begone!* **3070.** *After* than the dead *read* is compelled (helpless) in the hand of (under the power of) His bringing (it) into existence. **3077, Heading.** *Omitted.* **3081.** *Read* they traverse the road. **3096.** *Read* the moon becomes. **3104.** *Read* "Divide this for eating." **3106.** *Read* And that goat. **3115.** *Read* At that moment the fox uttered a hundred thanksgivings, saying, "(how lucky) that the lion called me up after the wolf." **3129.** *Read* Unless Noah had had a hand (a powerful aid) from God. **3144.** *Read* keep watch, then, over your hearts. **3148.** *Read* When he rubs our coin. **3152.** *Read* to that hand. **3171.** *Read* O youth, he who is empty-handed at the door of friends is like a man without wheat in the mill. **3181.** *Read* And mayst go forth from this womb-like world and mayst go from the earth into a wide expanse. **3182.** *Read* refers to an exceedingly sublime expanse belonging to the prophets. **3190.** *Read* proceed from the prophets. **3212,** note. *Read* has galloped with ten horses. **3220.** *Read* digs a channel for the gardens of the Universal Soul. **3221.** *Read* Who is able to cleanse the channel of his (sensual) self? Man's knowledge is made beneficial (only) by God's knowledge. **3226.** *Read* So that he (the patient) fancies. **3238.** *Read* His (the scribe's) heart was burning, hence he was unable. **3243.** *Read* he *for* the uncle. **3246.** *Read* their chain *and* pride in this and that. **3247.** *Read* cut in pieces *for* cloven. **3249.** *After* wasp *read* at that moment his nature is intent on a means of removing (the pain). **3256.** *Read* from an illumined neighbour. **3265.** *Read* and we have very beauteous cheeks *for* and we are tall. **3278.** *Read* against that wall. **3289.** *Read* that Faith. **3291.** *Read* will arise *for* will it extort. **3298, Heading.** After *they have besieged* add *and how his prayer was granted.* **3312.** *Read* since they are estranged from the august Reason. **3313.** *Read* is fallen low. **3319.** *Read* since they are irrational and reprobate and base. **3325.** *Read* it bestows kindness on the wet grass.

3329. *Read* from the flock of sheep. **3342.** *Read* which fire does with grass. **3344.** *Read* at that time *for* from the latticed window (of Heaven). **3348.** *Read* the infidel soul *for* the soul of arrogance. **3350.** *Read* look not heedlessly upon the doers of black deeds *and omit* who have been made forgetful (of God). **3359.** *Read* 'twill only be from surmise. **3371.** *Read* Surely he has always been ill-disposed towards me *for* He has been my enemy. **3372.** *Omit* and give you health. **3375.** *Read* "Thanks (to God) that I paid my respects to him just now." **3377.** *Read* began seeking abusive terms. **3384.** *Read* Many are they that have gone astray from (true) piety, (because) they set their hearts. **3385.** *Read* there is many a foul thing that you think pure. **3390.** *Read* The Prophet said to a hypocrite. **3402.** *Read* the son of the prophet Noah. **3416.** *Read* execrate egoism and the self-conceited (egoist). **3419.** *Read* They were saying this. **3432.** *Read* without purity of spirit how should he (any one) be fully intelligent? **3438.** *Read* riders and carried. **3451.** *Read* that burden *and* so that you may behold the barn (store-house) of knowledge within (you). **3469.** *Read* When the Chinese and the Greeks presented themselves, the Greeks were more skilled in the knowledge (of the art of painting). **3472.** *Read* then that excellent (king) opened the treasury *and omit* that they might receive that (which they sought). **3474.** *Read* pictures *for* colours. **3479.** *Omit* as he encountered it *and read* of his wits and understanding. **3480.** *Read* drew up *for* removed. **3485.** *Read* is the attribute of the heart, (which) receives the infinite form. **3486.** *Read* The formless infinite form of the Unseen shone forth on Moses from his bosom, (being reflected) from the mirror of his heart. **3487.** *Read* nor in the empyrean nor the earth nor the sea nor the Fish. **3491.** *Read* without any veil. **3497.** *Read* the (mystical) self-effacement of (spiritual) poverty. **3499.** *Instead of this verse read* They who dwell in God's *seat of truth* are higher than the Throne and the Footstool and the Void. **3500.** *Read* O sincere comrade. **3504.** *Read* all religion is one *for* nativity and continued growth are one. **3505.** *Read* Eternity and everlastingness. **3506.** *Read* Produce (a gift) suitable to the understanding of (intelligible to) the minds of this country (the phenomenal world). **3511.** *Read* At the present time there hath been made manifest to this (illumined) class of men (what shall come to pass) *on the Day when.* **3513.** *Read* their state is known from the bodily marks. **3516.** *Read* "It is very comely" *for* "Nay, it is comely." **3524.** *Read* Turk and Hindú shall become manifest (shall be clearly discerned) from among that company. **3526.** *Read* plainly and with ocular vision *and omit* like (multitudes of) people. **3537.** *Read* And those who have been made to run athirst round it I will show clearly at this moment. **3549.** *Read* deceit and (hypocritical) advice. **3554.** *Read* both imposture (*daghal*) and armpit (*baghal*). **3555.** *Read* it (the eye) sees the world. **3556.** *Read* the King's covering. **3565.** *Read* they remain in bondage to particulars. **3595.** *Read* those persons were running up and down *and omit* amidst the cornfields. **3605.** *Read* absorbed in it. **3617.** *Read* the might and majesty belonging to the Unseen are divulged. **3624.** *Read* When he saw the ring on his finger, his perplexity and doubt vanished all at once. **3625.** *Read* Imagination *for* Anxiety. **3629.** *Read* When (if) I cleave the sky manifestly, how should I say. **3630.** *Read* they may spread (the carpet of) endeavour. **3641.** *Read* close thy lips, and the lip is better silent. **3647.** *Read* the radiance and presence of the Sun. **3651.** *Read*

Like the new moon or the moon three days old or the full moon, every angel has (a particular) perfection and light and (spiritual) worth. **3654.** *Read* that angel who resembles him or her. **3655.** *Read* Since the eye of the dim-sighted man could not bear the sunlight, the star became a candle to him, that he might find the way. **3658.** *Instead of this verse read* O base man, how would the star be needed to demonstrate the (existence of) sunlight? **3659.** *Read* I was a man, but *it is revealed to me.* **3665.** *Read* behold how *for* thereon. **3671.** *Read* obliterated in the light of the knowledge of our (Divine) King. **3673.** *Read* When dawn comes. **3693.** *Read* Slumber is dead, (unlawful) food is dead; they are friends (to each other). **3713.** *Read* the fire of your avarice. **3714.** *Read* What are water and vinegar? Deal out bread. **3730.** *Read* that from the reflexion of that vision (of thine) a flame. **3743.** *Read* and the particular reason is (like) the rind. **3757.** *Read* O thou who art (like) the goodliness of a wide expanse after (the oppressive confinement of) evil fate. **3759.** *Read* thou art scattering light. **3768.** *After* amazed *read* the bird of hope and desire begins to fly *and omit* on (the wings of) the idea. **3772.** *Read* Until the scent from the Unseen shall come to your nose, say, will you see anything except your nose? **3773, Heading.** *After the Heading add the following verse:* Then that devoted friend, who had been newly converted to Islám, in his enthusiasm and delight said to 'Alí. **3773.** *Omit* He said. **3774.** *Read* O (dear) soul, the seven planets, (each) in turn, do a (particular) service for a time to every embryo. **3797.** *Read* recollection of Him *for* His wind. **3802.** *Read* Since a motive (other than God) entered (my heart) in the (holy) war, I deemed it right to sheathe the sword. [*In the text of this verse,* vol. 1, p. ٣٦٢, *note, read* ديدم نهان *for* اندر ميان]. **3813.** *Read* at the time of litigation. **3814.** *Read* the law does not assign to them the weight of a straw. **3816.** *Read* dies exceedingly bitter. **3821.** *Read* heedlessness *for* perplexity. **3836.** *Read* inasmuch as sin has become like obedience. **3844, Heading.** *After* the Faithful *add* 'Alí. **3860.** *Read* that God has cancelled. **3865.** *Omit* everlasting. **3871.** *Read* Advantages, then, are. **3889.** *Read* Who indeed would have. **3891.** *Read* Any one on whom that decree might come (fall). **3893, Heading.** Read *the accursed Iblís.* **3893.** *Read* The eye of *for* One day. **3901.** *Read* from those who are sincere. **3909.** *Read* And if Thou utter abuse of the moon and sun. **3910.** *Read* the sky and the empyrean. **3920.** *Read* what is the blind man. **3924, Heading.** Omit *the Prince of the Faithful.* **3925.** *Read* I see the enemy. **3937.** *Read* separation (plurality) *for* revolution. **3944.** *Read* narcissus-pot. **3957.** *Read* (Only) the evil mind which judges by its own ignorance and cupidity will think that of him (impute that motive to him). **3972.** *Read* If ye utter this on your tongues *and* will be left. **3988.** *Read* so many throats and such. **3996.** *Read* such a well-nourished rose.

BOOK II

11. *Read* Close this mouth that you may see plainly: gullet and mouth are the eye-bandage (which makes you blind) to yonder world. **32.** *Read* Lest it cover its face to (conceal itself from) thee at once, thou must. **50.** *Read* In the bazaar where the people of the Last Congregation (on the Day of Judgement) are (purchasers). **58.** *Read* Sometimes He (God) makes the *mushabbih* (who regards Him as immanent in phenomena) a *muwaḥḥid* (an assertor of His transcendence). **60.** *Read* he is doing that

in order to assert. **63.** *Omitted.* **68.** *Read* departure *for* liberation.
84. *Read* you have a feeling of anguish: the eye cannot do without the
light of the window. **158.** *Read* the presence of a friend (of God) is (like)
a book (which is open) before (one). **159.** *Read* ink of letters (letters
written with ink). **165.** *Read* The heart that is the rising-place of the
moonbeams (of Divine light) is for the gnostic (the means of revelation
indicated by the words) *its doors shall be opened.* [*In the text read*
فَتَّحَتْ أَبْوَابِهَاسْت *and cf. Qur'án,* xxxix, 71.] **169.** *Read* the fruit
(produce) *for* the wheat. **178.** *Omitted.* **186.** *Read* are our bodies.
222. *Omit* sort of. **240.** *Omit* Then *and read* rolled frequently on his
side. **241.** *After* morn *read* and at once laid the saddle firmly on the
ass's back. **285.** *Read* Before them (the prophets) we were all alike.
298. *Read* That Friend (of God) said, "*I love not them that set.*"
323. *Read* Religion is not (like) the falcon. **332.** *Read* (Yet) how shouldst
thou take flight from Paradise to Hell. **345.** *Read* loses its play (ceases
to revolve). **360.** *Read* thou art of that cycle *for* thou art far from that.
363. *Read* and those two breasts (of her) are tingling in love for it (her
babe). **376, Heading.** Omit *may God sanctify,* etc. **384.** *Read* living and
joyous. **409.** *Read* "What was this, anyhow?" **419.** *Read* the water
flows on pure (and) undisturbed. **510.** *Read* it would have been shivered
to pieces and its heart would have been filled with blood. **512.** *Read*
acquainted with this. **523.** *The hemistichs are transposed.* **530.** *Read* the
tumult (caused) by longing and ecstasy of spirit. **546.** *Omitted.* **646.**
Read both to his (moral) degeneracy and his insolvency. **654.** *Read*
the insolvency of the Devil. **655.** *Read* or do any trade with him. **674.**
Read "What, then," he rejoined, "have we been doing until now?" **690.**
After non-existence *read* in the world of (phenomenal) existence who is
(to be found) except the idle? **714.** *Read* they take away. **716.** *Read* its
fortune gives to drink. **774.** *The original reading seems to have been* He is
like Moses, and his body is his Pharaoh. **788.** *Read* this difficulty and
doubt. **803.** *Read* And if He take away your shoes. **839.** *Omitted.*
856. *Read* Your thought, (namely), "Do not see awry, look well!" is just
the light and radiance of that Pearl. **868.** *Read* foul smell of the mouth.
881. *Read* If any one saw *and omit* indeed. **898.** *Read* the divers. **911.**
Read That (splendour) which grew from Adam and which the hand of
Seth gathered. **935.** *Read* are (as) rinds. **953.** *Read* the produce (of
the garden) became the substance: take (it and) behold the object.
967. *Read* brought the tools (into existence) and the pillars (which come)
from the forests. **977.** *Read* these accidents. **1000.** *Read* the effect is
the child (born) from it. **1003.** *Read* arrived at this point: he either saw
or did not see a sign from him. **1014.** *Read* in succession (without
intermission, دَمَادِم) *for* moment after moment (دَمَادِم). **1044.** *Read*
have become soft as wool. **1056.** *Read* He is within the snare (of God) and
is laying a snare: by your life, neither that (snare) will escape (destruction)
nor will this (man). **1069.** *Read* why should we listen. **1122.** *Read* else
I would make that blind one see. **1137.** *Read* wrathful and terrible.
1141. *Read* is the place of delight. **1254.** *Read* Your fleshly soul is
fleeing mightily from him. **1259.** *Omitted.* **1266.** *Read* (be) quick,
devote the old man (your old age) generously (to serving God).
1300. *Read* This world, like straws in the hand (control) of the wind,

(which is) the (world) unseen, is a helpless object before the power and sway of the Unseen. **1301.** *Read* It (this control) makes it. **1321–1323.** *Omitted.* **1410.** *Read* This (visible) wolf took pity (on Joseph). **1425.** *Read* from those comers (to the Cave) *for* from those Sleepers. **1427.** *Read* From that marvellous Jungle, where is (dwells) the wise Lion. **1438.** *Read* as (in the case of) the murdered man and the cow of Moses. **1468.** *Read* This is a mistake. **1471.** *Read* in reality he was a slave, and Luqmán was his master. **1497.** *Read* He knew the secret, (but) quietly drove his ass on that road (pursued his way) for the sake. **1500.** *Read* if you hide. **1506.** *Omit* whatsoever you may cogitate and *and after* make *add* O solicitous one. **1506 and 1507.** *Transposed.* **1514.** *Read* "Go, my son," said he, "and call Luqmán." **1545.** *Read* Know that the nature of lightning is that it *taketh away.* **1553.** *Read* the delight of "He causes the (blessed) men to hope for." **1561, Heading.** *Omit* King's. **1582.** *Read according to* Vol. ii, *p.* 302, *note* 3. **1604.** *Read* Her body saw him as a hoopoe. **1610.** *Read* it sees only a groat. **1614.** *Read* Since the earth *and* lay their heads. **1620.** *Omitted.* **1644.** *The order of the following verses is* 1647, 1649, 1645, 1646, 1648, 1650. **1663.** *Read* radiant without the sky. **1668.** *Read* how can he scent it? **1675.** *Read* Zakariyyá (Zacharias) *for* the father of Yaḥyá. **1714.** *Omitted.* **1737.** *Read* these words of yours. **1749.** *Read* a desert. **1759.** *Read* the spirit *for* the inward (spirit). **1766.** *Read* if the martyr be bathed in blood, do not wash him. **1772.** *Read* God spake secretly in the inmost heart of Moses. **1865.** *Read* How art thou in regard to those bilious ones. **1866.** *Read* as the sun of the east does: we are hypocrisy. **1883.** *Read* He gave him so many apples. **1884.** *Read* when you have not suffered injury *for* What have I done to you? **1956.** *Read* Thou hast heard. **1967.** *Omitted.* **1970.** *Read* removed *for* rescued *and possibly* from the battle (with the dragon). **1975.** *Read* though at first it produces dazzlement; yes (it does). **1992.** *Read* this stony heart [رادل سنگ این].

2049. *Read* how didst thou make opposition to my prophethood? **2065.** *Read* earnestness and admonition. **2103.** *Add* in the desert *after* running about. **2109.** *Read* lives in dung. **2121.** *Read* If, then, Iblís too had become. **2124.** *Read* driving away the flies (which were) on him. **2140.** *Read* But he that makes God his support in (keeping) his promise. **2141, Heading.** Read *to visit the (sick) Companion.* **2145.** *This verse is followed by verses* 2152–2155. **2157.** *Read* Thou whom I have made (radiant as) the place of sunrise by (illumining thee with) the Divine Light. **2171.** *Read* I will cause each one to set out in a (different) direction. **2195.** *Read* Many a fool in the world has tacked himself on to 'Alí and the Prophet. **2205.** *Read* We have jumped out. **2270.** *Read* no clear understanding or judgement. **2296.** *Read* and that he might turn away his face from difficulty (unsuccess). **2379.** *Read* squeezing the thief *for* squeezing (him) to the dregs. **2387.** *Read* a drunken man lying. **2413.** *Read* will go to that quarter. **2461.** *Omitted.* **2491.** *Read* his clemency averts the arrow of affliction. **2504.** *Omitted.* **2511.** *Read* O wind, drive the fire into his field. **2525.** *Read* and renouncing heat (sensual appetite). **2536.** *Read* that evil. **2543.** *Read* are bearing witness to His Lordliness, and both are bowing down in worship. **2582.** *Read* visible in (their) escape (from occultation). **2584.** *Read* and putting them, like a woman, in thy bosom. **2587.** *Read* robes of honour and felicity. **2612, Heading.** *Omit and pretence.* **2654.** *Read* You are fire: I cannot help being burned by you. **2672**. *Read* these knots. **2721**. *Read* you are going. **2764**. *This verse precedes the Heading.* **2776**. *Read* A certain man said, "Give (me) that sigh, and may this (ritual) prayer of mine be (bestowed) on thee as a gift!" **2800**. *Read* repentance will befall (me). **2838**. *Read* soul-illumining. **2842**. *Read* Beware, do not go. **2866**. *Read* they returned and laid hold of (demanded the fulfilment of) the past promise. **2867**. *Read* excuse (pretence and dissimulation) *for* treachery. **2868**. *Read* He (the Prophet) said, "Ye are exceedingly bad-hearted and hostile." **2879**. *Read* contrivance and deceit. **2913**. *Read* your camel has disappeared. **2946**. *Instead of this verse read* Contemplate this sky repeatedly, for God hath said, *Then turn thy gaze again (towards it).* **2959**. *Read* menace and intimidation. **2978** *and* **2979**. *Transposed.* **2995**. *Read* the camel of that friend and kinsman. **3026**. *Read* Thou hast mocked, then, at those. **3037**. *Read* Finding fault with one's self is the (right) remedy. **3044**. *Omit* so that *and read* he fell into a pit (of perdition) so that he became. **3046**. *Read* and suddenly fell upon a village. **3049**. *Read in the first half of the verse* Why are ye casting me into the pit of death? **3057**. *Read* the face, *or* the (bountiful) cloud, of (Divine) Mercy. **3081**. *Read* for one moment partake of this food and drink. **3104**. *Read* if they know the retribution (which shall take place) at the Resurrection. **3109**. *Read* and exert themselves in maltreating them that have. **3117**. *Read* to put you under some earth. **3121**. *Read* Your eye *for* Your body. **3131**. *Read* the light of the Sun. **3142**. *Read* thou seest them not, for thou art blind, O miserable wretch. **3179**. *Read* these two. **3201**. *Read* should vanish from thee. **3203**. *Read* bears (one) *for* soars. **3208**. *Read* The (true) king is he that goes into the presence of the King. **3210**, **Heading**. Omit *may God sanctify*, etc. **3211**. *Read* (Whilst) that spiritual king was stitching his mantle, an Amír suddenly came to that spot. **3215**. *Read* (And why) he renounced the sovereignty of the Seven Climes. **3231**. *Read* and this world is as the husk. **3236**. *After* one another *read* all these five have grown (are derived) from a sublime root (source). **3238**. *Read* increases love; love increases. **3244**. *Read* garden *for* verdant meadows. **3245**. *Read in the second half of the verse* so that severally they may go towards that Paradise. **3246**. *Read* without the proper meaning, without tongue, and without metaphor. **3248**. *Read* which is (perceived) from intuition. **3249**. *Read* When every sense has become. **3254**. *Read* the intellect flies (moves) in a more occult manner than the (vital) spirit. **3258**. *Read* because it is of the Unseen. **3279**. *Read* He (God) gives to Man instruments. **3287**. *After* a bird *read* like the angels, it will go towards heaven. **3294**. *Read* through the fissures (channels). **3296**. *Read* water and stream. **3299**. *Read* look at the stream and at this movement of the weeds (in it). **3325**. *Read* Who is the dead? **3351**. *Read* by their jealousy. **3363**. *Read* that hyena. **3385**. *Read* as a soul full of wickedness. **3398**. *Read* the perverted intellect is always squinting (envious). **3424**, **Heading**. After *prayer-carpet* add *How is that?* **3426**. *Read* Although thou knowest that any dirty child makes unclean every place he comes to. **3461**. *Read* devoted *for* accustomed *and* that prevent their access (to it). **3462**. *Read* he in his folly regarded Adam with contempt. **3468**. *Read* he is making himself like a captain over me. **3469**. *Read* headstrong in him *for* strongly implanted *and* the fire (of passion) blaze up in him. **3472**. *Read* in tribulation *for* in the beginning. **3502**. *Read* was real, why did it not become abiding. **3520.** *Read* verily your prayer is gone beforehand (already), O misguided man. **3533.** *Read* an allowance of four loaves. **3565.** *Read* Ja'far-i Ṭarrár *for* Ja'far-i 'Ayyár. **3577.** *Read* from a near friend. **3592.** *Read* How should he mistake it? **3604.** *Omit* at once *and read* bowed in worship, O intelligent one. **3608.** *Read* Because Mary at the time of her delivery was far away both from strangers and kinsfolk. **3625.** *Omit* also *and* O worshipful one *and read* pick out the meaning from the tale. **3632.** *Read* are for the purpose of (showing) the declension and (grammatical) construction. **3639.** Read *the wicked men for the wicked women*. **3651.** *Read* O great sir, in such and such a very tremendous and huge country. **3654.** *Read* There for years he travelled much. **3670.** *Read* O ignorant man *for* thou hast gone astray *and* hence thou art without fruit and produce from the bough of reality. **3693.** *Read* (Even) if your words appear uniform (seem to express agreement), in effect they are the source of contention and anger. **3694.** *Read* effect *for* virtue. **3699.** *Read* the words of the corporealists (materialists). **3726.** *Read* no one (ever) engaged in a battle with himself. **3766.** *Read* fostered thee as a nurse *for* nursed thee. **3772.** *Read* whose house is ill-smelling. **3778.** *Read* this *for* yonder. **3795.** *Instead of this verse read* Then that company remained in need (unsatisfied) till the dervish should finish the (ritual) prayer. **3802.** *Read* opened his eyes towards heaven.

BOOK III

Preface, p. **4**, l. **21.** *Read* the Giver of superiority.

Preface, p. **4**, l. **23.** *Omit* in despite of a party *and read* They (the unbelievers) desire to extinguish the Light of God.

Preface, p. **4**, penult. Omit *And praise be to God*, etc.

17. *Read* Bestowal of mouthfuls comes (to pass) from every one to some one. **19.** *Read* guile and deceit. **169.** *Read* Prayers, then, are rejected. **295.** *Read* and (now), through greed, thou art going *and omit* like a bear. **366.** *Read* why art thou troubling me? **420.** *Read* break with the dervish (who is) the treasurer (of the Divine bounty). **435.** *Read* They (the ducks) say to the falcon. **480.** *Read* He hath said, "Shall He be forgetful...?" **644.** *Read* after that. **667.** *Read* to be a gnostic and distraught. **682.** *Read* of trials, O son. **688.** *Read* till the blast of the trumpet. **713.** *Read* O thou who hast quaffed the cup of Naught from a phantom. **797, Heading.** Read *probations*. **935.** *Read* When (the world of) space makes an assault upon (the world of) non-spatiality, it falls headlong. **986.** *Read* smell in the direction of that mystery. **995.** *Read* was searching for a big snake round about the mountains and in the days of snow. **1017.** *Omitted.* **1062.** *Omit* and. **1108.** *Read* with the morning sun. **1123.** *Read* that Way. **1132.** *Read* (yet) thou art not lost. **1183.** *Instead of this verse read* He said to them in (their) dream, "O my sons, it is not possible (to speak) openly: do not utter this (request)." **1199.** *Omitted.* **1216.** *Read* turned away (and came) to Egypt. **1311.** *Read* these waves are the Flood. **1425.** *Read* for (at one moment) he is (made) greater. **1426.** *Read* In respect of gaining (the 'state') *for* In similitude. **1434.** *Read* plunged in love of the Glorious (God). **1444.** *Read* a cock *for* chanticleer. **1458.** *Read* cause the cloud to rain in the direction of every land. **1470.** *Read* a hundred (melodious) voices. **1487.** *Read* the

bold cow jumped. **1501** *and* **1502.** *Transposed.* **1615.** *Read* Since col-
lectedness (spiritual quiet) was coming. **1675.** *Read* the strength of the
pull and (the might of) Destiny. **1683.** *Read* a Shaykh, (one) of the
Abdál (exalted saints). **1706.** *Read* who hast come. **1725.** *The order of
the following verses is* 1729–1737, 1727, 1728, 1726, 1738. **1746, Heading.**
Read *How the mule related (his story) to the camel.* **1777.** *Add* O sire
after in thy heart. **1790.** *Read* O thou whose hopes are false *for* O
hopeless one. **1813.** *Read* and the revelation of any (Divine) aid. **1834.**
Read Even in your waking state you will dream dreams, and the gates
of Heaven withal will open (to you). **1876.** *Read* I am content if His
fire kill me. **1878, Heading.** Omit *pray and.* **1895.** *Read* and on whose
table is every sort. **1907.** *Read* Without tasking himself. **1910.** *Read*
from fear of pain. **1959.** *Read* sets out to go. **2019.** *Read* that ye may
be made happy by these trees. **2086.** *Read* O (thou who art a) clear-
sighted Imám (precentor), the leader in the ritual prayer must always
be clear-sighted. **2115.** *Read* that praise. **2201.** *Read* To think ill of the
world. He (the prudent man). **2298.** *Read* them *for* these (persons).
2315, Heading. Omit *the prophet.* **2336.** *Read* or reproach or (anything
else whether) more or less. **2345.** *Read* rebel in tribulation. **2363.** *Read*
(if) this be what Love demands, 'tis well. *Omit* Say, (is it not so)?
2407. *Read* (If) thou regardest as the (only) light this (light of the sun)
which the animals too have seen, what, then, is. **2436.** *Read* the
adversary of every oppressed person. **2474.** *Read* his grandfather.
2625. *Read* it comes not into sight, for it is a way without locality.
2699. *Read* So that it will bring forth new leaves from the old (bough).
2708. *Read* our fee comes many a time from God. **2815.** *Read* a sun
is (enveloped) in a veil (of darkness) through the eclipse (occultation) of
him (the perfect saint).